COMBAT
CODES

Blenheim I K7147/D of No. 110 Sqn beautifully illustrates the method of identification used by bomber squadrons before the introduction of unit code letters in September 1938 – the squadron number being applied on the fuselage. Many units also carried their badges within the grenadeshaped frame, usually worn on the fin. (Gp Capt W. S. G. Maydwell)

This formation of Blenheim IVs of No. 59 Sqn seen in 1940 displays several variations in the application of the code. TR-H and TR-F have shorter, thicker, letters than the other two aircraft, although all have the T overlapping the wing roots. (Graham Salt)

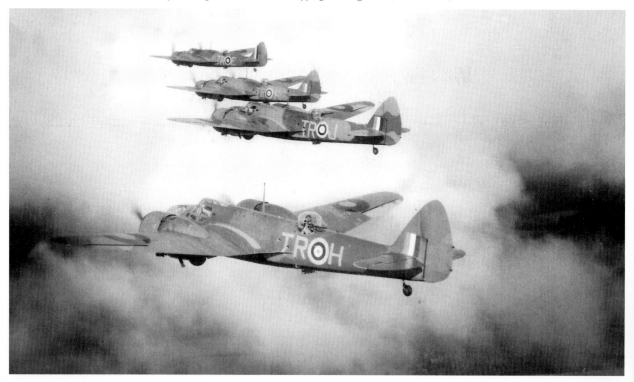

COMBAT CODES

A Full Explanation And Listing Of British, Commonwealth and
Allied Air Force Unit Codes Since 1938

Vic Flintham and Andrew Thomas

Pen & Sword
AVIATION

To the late
Reverend John D. R. Rawlings
An enthusiast's enthusiast

First published in Great Britain in 2003
by Airlife Publishing Ltd

Published in this format in 2008 by
Pen & Sword Aviation
An imprint of
Pen & Sword Books Ltd
47 Church Street
Barnsley
South Yorkshire
S70 2AS

ISBN 978 1 84415 691 7

Printed and bound in England
By CPI UK

Pen & Sword Books Ltd incorporates the Imprints of Pen & Sword Aviation,
Pen & Sword Maritime, Pen & Sword Military, Wharncliffe Local History, Pen & Sword Select,
Pen & Sword Military Classics and Leo Cooper.

For a complete list of Pen & Sword titles please contact
PEN & SWORD BOOKS LIMITED
47 Church Street, Barnsley,
South Yorkshire, S70 2AS, England
E-mail: enquiries@pen-and-sword.co.uk
Website: www.pen-and-sword.co.uk

Acknowledgements

In addition to the five individuals mentioned in the preface, many others have contributed material and support. Not least is Peter Green who over many years of friendship has been generous in the extreme in supporting others with his vast reservoir of knowledge and photographs – we have not hesitated to draw on his advice. Another significant contributor, especially in the provision of photographs, is Sqn Ldr Chris ('Joe') Ashworth. Their correspondence and visits have always been much valued, as has that of Jim Oughton who has been of particular help with Liberator units.

More recently, Air Commodore Graham Pitchfork MBE has been an enthusiastic supporter, casting an eagle eye for material in his capacity as the Archivist of the Aircrew Association. To the latter group we owe a special debt as members, all former aviators, have responded to appeals and obscure queries. Chris Shores, the author of the superb series of air campaign histories, has unearthed much new material as has his co-worker on several projects, Brian Cull, valued friends both. Another friend, Chris Thomas, has also made our joint researches a pleasure as well as productive. The contributions of Norman Franks and Dick Ward of Modeldecal were also helpful. Also, the advice of long standing friend Wg Cdr Jeff Jefford MBE, has always been highly valued.

Overseas, we received outstanding support in respect of the Commonwealth Air Forces from Neil Mackenzie, David Wilson and Sqn Ldr John Bennett RAAF, in Australia. Charles Darby's input from New Zealand was invaluable, as was that of Ken Smy and Michael Schoeman from South Africa, while Larry Milberry in Canada opened many doors, and the information provided by John Griffin was also of enormous help. The contributions of P V S Jagan Mohan and Sqn Ldr Rana Chhina in India too were valuable. Assistance and information on the RNorAF was kindly provided by Lt Col Helge Sandnes RNorAF, Cato Guhnfeld and Nils Mathrud. Cdre H J E van der Kop MLD and Andre van Haute were most helpful regarding the Dutch and Belgian units respectively. Likewise, Wojtek Matusiak assisted with information on the Polish units, as did Zdenek Hurt who provided similar assistance regarding the Czech aspects.

Chaz Bowyer readily shared his large information archive during the early researches, while the assistance of Sqn Ldr Norman Robertson was much appreciated. Roger Hayward proved the oracle of all things Beaufort and more. More recently Roger Freeman, doyen of the 8th AF writers, has turned up much material; we are specially indebted to him for his help in producing much of the colour photograph section and for proof-reading the USAAF appendix. Thanks too to Harry Holmes for help with USAAF material and particularly to Ken Wakefield who late in the day helped with US Army photographs and codes.

Various official bodies, associations and societies helped considerably too. Over many years Graham Day at the MoD Air Historical Branch has always answered even the most obscure queries and organised access to the albums and diaries of long disbanded units which proved invaluable and from which so much new information and photographs came. Likewise, Reg Mack and Rick Barker, both formerly of the Aviation Records Dept at the RAF Museum, provided much new material for publication from that superb archive and readily assented to its use. The staffs of the Imperial War Museum in London, the RNZAF Museum in Christchurch, the Australian War Memorial, Canberra, the SAAF Museum, Pretoria and the Public Record Office, Kew too were always supportive.

Special thanks are due to Mrs Jean Buckberry, the former Head Librarian of the College Library, RAF College Cranwell, for her enthusiasm and for the ready access to that excellent facility. Air Britain has been mentioned elsewhere, and thanks are due to their 'codes' specialist, Ron Durand. Some existing squadrons and numerous squadron associations in the UK and Commonwealth countries too have assisted and for their contributions we are grateful.

The Editors and staff of several magazines have forwarded letters to correspondents and published appeals which have been most helpful. Particular thanks go to Alan W Hall who some years ago published several articles in Aviation News on Pre-War RAF Codes which subsequently drew many useful comments and responses. Thanks too are due to Ken Delve, Director of Aviation at Key Publishing, and formerly editor of FlyPast and to his successor Ken Ellis – enthusiasts both. In France Phil Listemann of Aero Journal has also been a most useful and helpful contact. More recently another friend, Tony Holmes of Osprey Publishing, has shared material and proved the conduit to other new contacts.

The contributions of other friends and enthusiasts has produced much of the new information and photographs and their awareness of the seemingly never-ending search has been much appreciated. They include: the late Dr John Allin, Peter Arnold for access to his superb Spitfire archive, the late Dr Arthur Banks, L J Batchelor, Gerry Beauchamp, Peter Berry, Dave Birch, Tim Bishop, Roy Bonser, Martin Bowman, Keith Braybrooke, Alec Brew, Steve Brooking, Robin Brooks, Robin A Brown, Russell Brown, Dugald Cameron, Alan Carlaw, Bill Chorley, S M Coates, E A Cromie of the Ulster Aviation Society, Dick Cronin, Jerzy Cynk, John Evans, Jonathon Falconer, A P Fergusson, J D Fergusson, Martyn Ford-Jones, Neville Franklin, Sqn Ldr Chris Goss, Brian Goulding, James Goulding, Dr David Gunby, John Hamlin, Terry Hancock, Andrew Hendrie, Mike Hodgeson, Mike Hooks, Ted Hooton, Stuart Howe, David Howley, Leslie Hunt, Paul Jackson, Phillip Jarratt, George Jenks, David Legg of the Catalina Society, G S Leslie, Roger Lindsay, Peter Lloyd, Peter London, Alec Lumsden, R S G Mackay, Dave Marchant, Maurice Marsh, Ken Merrick, Eric Morgan, Don Neate, Roy Nesbit, Pat Otter, Neil Owen, Michael Payne, the late Arthur Pearcy, Brian Pickering, Dr Alfred Price, Neil Robinson of Scale Aircraft Modelling, Graham Salt, Dilip Sarkar, Andy Saunders, Stewart Scott, Jerry Scutts, Ian Simpson, David J Smith, the late Gordon Swanborough, Eric Taylor, Gp Capt WJ Taylor, the late Acknowledgements 00.qxd 14/01/2003 09:24 Page v Owen Thetford, the late Geoff Thomas, Dave Vincent, Sqn Ldr D W

'Joe' Warne, David Watkins, Alan Watson, Clive Williams, Ray Williams.

Others, mainly ex-Servicemen or their families, have been courteous and supportive during our research. Sadly a number have passed away in the intervening years, but we record out thanks to all of the following: Wg Cdr R I Adams, Eric Adamson, Ron Aris, Tom Armstrong, Reg Ashmead, G Austen, Wg Cdr Stanley Baggott DFC, Bill Baird, Gp Capt G B M Bell, Eric Bevington-Smith, V F Bingham, Peter Brewster, Wg Cdr G H Briggs DFC, DFM, B Blunt, Air Marshal Sir Ivor Broom KCB CBE DSO DFC AFC, Stan Bryant, Flt Lt J E Buchan DFM, J E Bury, F C Butt, D M Campbell, Sqn Ldr A F Carlisle, G E Carter CD, G S W Challen DFM, Sqn Ldr A M Charlesworth, Wg Cdr H J Cobb DSO DFC, AFC, Sqn Ldr R A Collis DFC, David Collyer, Sqn Ldr D A S Colvin, the late Wg Cdr Peter Cook DMM Rhod AF, Rupert Cooling, AVM C W Coulthard CB AFC, Sqn Ldr Tom Cushing, J D Davies, the late Wg Cdr E C Deansley DFC, Wg Cdr B O Dias OBE DFC, D M Dixon, Gp Capt TAF Elsdon OBE DFC, J E H Fail, Bill Fleming, Wg Cdr R B Fleming DFC AFC, Geoff Flowerday, J W Gardner, Sqn Ldr J W Gee DFC, Sqn Ldr D Giles DFC, John Goodwin, A R Gordon, Gp Capt R C Haine OBE DFC, A J B Harding, Wg Cdr O L Hardy DFC AFC, 'Bluey' Haregreaves, Gp Capt H W Harrison, Alan Hartley, late Sqn Ldr C Haw DFC DFM Order of Lenin, Brian Hicks, R E Hilliard, Gp Capt G J C Hogan DFC AFC, late Gp Capt F WM Jensen CBE DFC AFC, Jack te Kloot, P N G Knowles, Gp Capt E P Landon DFC, LA Leetham, G A B Lord, Ron Lowe, 'Jock' Manson, A J Mallandaine, R W H May, D P F McCaig, TM McCammon, WH McGiffin OBE TD, R S McGill, Gp Capt W G Moseby DSO DFC, Mrs S G Overton, Lou Peeters, late Gp Capt J Pelly-Fry DSO, Peter Rackliff, Sqn Ldr J V Rees, Alan Richardson, Sqn Ldr PH P Roberts, late Sqn Ldr Roddy Robertson, Wg Cdr J Rose CMG MBE DFC, Wilfred Shearman, Sqn Ldr S W Sills DFM, late E W Sockett, John Stretton, Wg Cdr A G Todd DFC, Wg Cdr E F P Wheller, Wg Cdr N Williamson DFC, Gp Capt J B Wray DFC.

Most of the photographs used in this book have been supplied by the aforementioned. However, despite considerable efforts to trace original sources, in some cases through the passage of time this has proved nearly impossible. Unless the original source is evident, we have credited images to the immediate source. Uncredited photographs are from the authors' collections. If any credits have been misapplied we readily apologise, but trust that their inclusion adds to the authenticity of this book.

Preface

That this book came to be written is the result of a shared interest and an unmet demand. For many years both authors have been writing and researching various aspects of military aviation history. For his part AST has specialised in RAF and Commonwealth unit histories and similar subjects that included details of RAF and related unit codes, together with supporting photographic evidence. VF has concentrated on the post-WW2 use of air power with particular emphasis on the aircraft employed and their operational use in combat. Both are committed to getting high quality data analysed and presented in a way which meets the needs of a wide audience. For both authors the need to identify the unit to which a particular aircraft belonged was vital, hence a necessity for a knowledge of RAF and Allied unit code letters and markings. With this common requirement and as friends for almost three decades, it was natural that they would collaborate on this project.

The foundations for the book were laid by five great British observers and recorders to whom the authors are indebted. Between them they have researched the subject in great detail and have identified much of the material upon which the present work is based. They also had in common a desire to advance knowledge before personal financial gain and all were long-serving members of Air-Britain, membership of which is commended to all serious aviation researchers. Their collected writings have formed the basis of all reliable British aviation libraries; their own publications relevant to this book are noted in the bibliography in Appendix K. They are:

Mike Bowyer, who is the doyen of 'spotters' (for which read recorders), and who shared in the authorship of the first code book with John Rawlings.
Mike has also written numerous books on aircraft as well as wartime and post-war markings. Jim Halley, who has masterminded the Air-Britain monographs on RAF serials and who in 1988 wrote the authoritative *Squadrons of the Royal Air Force*. The late Rev John D R Rawlings, who set new standards of research with his 1969 *Fighter Squadrons of the RAF* and who subsequently co-authored the first book to address the subject of RAF unit codes. Bruce Robertson, who in 1956 published a book on camouflage and markings which was ground-breaking to the extent that his description of roundel types is now firmly established as 'official'. Ray Sturtivant, who published the first list of codes in *Air Pictorial* in 1955 and who has subsequently written countless books including the classic *Squadrons of the Fleet Air Arm* and *RAF Training and Support Units*. Additionally, he provided much useful support in the final stages by checking the voluminous drafts and adding many details, especially of dates and examples.

Notwithstanding the initial work of the above, as more material became available in recent years it became apparent that some kind of new 'codes' book was needed, not least that the original Squadron Codes book was now virtually unobtainable to a new generation of ever more demanding enthusiasts and researchers. Thus after several false starts, we finally came together to produce the current work. As is explained elsewhere, with no official lists of unit codes apparently surviving, it cannot be claimed to be definitive, but the authors are satisfied that it is as much as current information allows, and certainly not too far below 100%. Throughout, where confirmation of use is missing this is indicated and much of the newer information is based on reliable documentary sources or photographs. The subject is, inevitably, a jigsaw, with material or photographs remaining unknown until a small piece of information surfaces, often years later. An example is a photograph of an 'SX' coded Blenheim IVf which surfaced several years ago. The date and location were known, but nothing seemed to fit until during the research for this book a small snippet of information about Spitfires also coded 'SX' was found, which also referred to a Blenheim fighter. Thus was found the unit of the Blenheim in the photo and the code of a small and little known unit – No. 1 Coastal Artillery Co-operation Unit. Generally, unless there was some other supporting (though not necessarily conclusive) evidence, reported sightings have been omitted. While undoubtedly many will have been accurately reported, too many have not been and have led to confusion. By way of example the possible allocation of 'YR' to the Hurricanes of No. 208 Sqn in the desert may be cited. The quoted aircraft was Z4967, which did indeed serve with No 208, and was noted with a code of 'YR-G'. Nos 208's aircraft are, however, well recorded as carrying 'RG' and this is clearly a mis-recording of 'RG-Y'. In the course of many years of research the authors have amassed a large number of relevant photographs, many kindly lent by those acknowledged elsewhere. With a limit on the number of illustrations which could be included here, possibly the hardest part has not been what to include, but what to leave out. The final selection is therefore a pragmatic choice where the authors have tried to illustrate as many codes on as many of the aircraft types mentioned as well as offering a reasonable reproduction quality. It is increasingly difficult these days to provide unpublished photographs, particularly illustrating code letters, but it is hoped that those selected will at least not be too well known and will offer a degree of freshness. The authors offer special thanks to Sebastian Cox, the Head of the RAF Air Historical Branch, for kindly agreeing to write the Foreword. Above all others, though, thanks are due to their spouses, Mary Thomas and Christine Flintham, for their love and support over the years, and especially their forbearance through the final months of work. The format and layout is one which has been designed to be easy and usable to readers. Above all, it is hoped that this book should sit on the 'ready to hand' section of the reference bookshelf. If it does so, and is regularly referred to, then the aim will have been achieved.

Vic Flintham, Dassels, Herts
Andrew Thomas, Heckington, Lincs
February 2007

Foreword

It is more than twenty years since Michael J. F. Bowyer and John D. R. Rawlings made the first attempt to produce a comprehensive guide to the labyrinthine complexities of squadron code letters. The current authors have built on the solid foundations of that earlier work to produce a much revised and expanded guide. Any work of this nature must draw on the knowledge and efforts of a great many individuals, each imparting their own small piece to the overall jigsaw, but to fit all those pieces into a coherent picture requires skill and dedication applied over many years. There are few more knowledgeable individuals than Vic Flintham and Andy Thomas, both of whom are well known for their unstinting efforts to record different aspects of our aeronautical history. With a subject which was originally shrouded in secrecy and the cloaking veil of 'security', it is often only through such long-term dedication that we can create a proper picture. The understandable fear at the time that any compromise of the codes could lead to unnecessary loss or disaster meant that much of the original documentation was destroyed once it had been superseded, making the historians' task that much more difficult.

Such fears also extended to wartime photographs, where the censor would not permit the details of individual pilots or squadrons to be published, and where, as the authors indicate, any mistaken publication of such details would lead to a change in the unit's codes. As a result many wartime pictures were inadequately captioned, and in the Air Historical Branch it has been the practice for many years for the photographic archivists to use works of reference such as this to help us to pin down the elusive units featured in these 'anonymous' photographs. This book will undoubtedly come to be regarded as a prime reference source for any serious student of the RAF in the last century. It will obviously prove of great value to model makers and enthusiasts, as well as the serious historian, but will also find a wider audience amongst artists, picture, film and TV researchers and librarians.

All of us owe a debt of gratitude to the authors for the sustained years of enthusiasm and dedication which go into a work such as this, and for the clarity and thoughtfulness with which they have set it all down.

Sebastian Cox
Head of Air Historical Branch (RAF)

The only 'code' known to have been worn by a V-bomber was on Vulcan B.2 XH539 of the A&AEE which carried the initials of its pilot Flt Lt Tim Mason. It was seen thus marked at Edwards AFB in the US in 1968; the AFSC badge is seen just ahead of the letters. (MinTech)

Content

This P-38J Lightning (44-23515) was lent to the Base Commander 54 Base, Air Cdre Sharp, at Coningsby and given RAF markings and painted PRU blue overall. It was used for target marking duties in late 1944. The significance of the initials DPA is unclear, but they are thought to relate to an Air Ministry Directorate rather than an individual. (J. Rabbetts)

Piper L-4H 4329248/YC wears full French markings, but conforms to the US and British method of identification for AOP and Liaison units in Italy where it was seen in July 1944. It served with la section aérienne d'observation d'artillerie du II/64 RA. (ECPA)

CHAPTER 1

How to Use this Book

This book has been written for a wide audience. Not only is it aimed at enthusiasts, aviation historians and modellers, but also at general historians, researchers, genealogists, editors and librarians. This wide readership has dictated the approach and thus the layout of material in what the authors hope is a logical and easy to follow format.

The experienced aviation researcher or enthusiast wanting to check a code will probably go straight to chapter 3 or one of the later chapters if he or she knows the period and service in question. Those with less background knowledge in military aviation are advised to read this chapter in detail and then find their code in chapter 3 and follow the trail from there to the indicated chapter or appendix. The notes below explain briefly the background to codes (there is a full explanation in chapter 2), other forms of markings, types of units and finally examples of how to track usage from codes.

The Boundaries of the Book

In principle, the contents of this book are confined to RAF and Allied unit codes from just before the Second World War to its end; to American codes from 1942 to 1945 in Europe; to RAF codes post-war; and to codes used by some reconstituted Allied air forces which continued using the system and in part to maintain the traditions of wartime squadrons. A master list of all known codes within these boundaries is set out in chapter 3.

Two-letter unit codes for aircraft were initiated by the RAF in 1938 as war loomed (see chapter 4). Prior to that, Royal Flying Corps (RFC), Royal Naval Air Service (RNAS) and RAF units used a variety of emblems to indicate the parent unit of an aircraft. Many bomber and reconnaissance units actually used the squadron number as the unit identifier. Background notes to the use of these markings are provided in chapter 2. The emblems were well publicised and thus the successor two-letter codes were intended to hide the identity of the unit. The official orders listing the codes were classified 'top secret' and few have survived. The codes were almost totally changed in 1939 (see chapter 5).

The use of these codes had been extended to some Commonwealth air forces by the beginning of the war (see chapters 6–10), and they were adopted by Allied squadrons operating within the RAF and manned by personnel from the occupied countries. When the United States Army Air Force (USAAF) entered the air war in Europe in 1942 the scheme was extended to include its units. The USAAF also used modified forms of unit codes in the Mediterranean theatre of operations (MTO) and a further refinement was the use of broadly similar codes by light aircraft of the US Army. USAAF

and Army codes merit a book in their own right but are summarised at appendices A and B.

Throughout the war, and subsequently, the Fleet Air Arm has used its own coding system. Although quite different from that of the RAF, in some cases, especially where aircraft types may have served with both services, the presentation of the codes may appear similar and thus give rise to confusion. Therefore, an outline of the Royal Navy system with identified codes and units is given at appendix C.

After the war, the RAF continued to use two-letter codes into the early 1950s (see chapter 11). The Royal Canadian Air Force (RCAF) and several European air forces also continued with the practice for some years as it was a robust, simple and proven method of unit and aircraft identification. In addition it may in some cases have maintained a unit tradition (also covered in chapter 11).

In early 1944 Transport Command introduced the use of callsigns as externally marked codes and these are described in chapter 12. From shortly after VE Day Flying Training, Technical Training and Reserve Commands also applied three-letter unit codes (see chapter 13). From the early 1950s, for various short periods, single-letter codes differentiating units on a single station only were used in 2nd TAF Germany (see chapter 14), Coastal Command (see chapter 15) and Flying Training Command (see chapter 16).

From the 1970s the RAF restarted the use of single-letter codes for some operational units and these are described in chapter 17. Additionally, throughout most of the period covered by this book certain middle- to senior-rank officers have been permitted to apply their initials to aircraft; these are listed in chapter 18.

From 1946 the USAAF dropped the two-letter codes but for twenty years or so used 'buzz numbers', including two letters, to identify low-fliers. From the mid-1960s the USAF used twoletter unit and then base identifiers. Neither of these systems falls within the scope of the present volume.

What Are Unit Codes?

Military units of all sorts use identifiers in the form of names and/or numbers and symbols. These are typically intended to encourage *esprit de corps* in peacetime and to serve as a means of reassembling or rallying a formation during or after combat. As described in the next chapter Royal Flying Corps units used geometric designs as identifiers and the post-First World War RAF continued with various forms of heraldic and/or geometric devices. However, these were widely known and offered no security in the event of conflict.

Thus were introduced two-letter squadron codes for

application to aircraft flown by operational units. They were designed to be used in conjunction with an individual aircraft identity character in a way which meant that every aircraft had a very visible and unique identity. The term 'codes' is, however, somewhat of a misnomer since they were allocated to units on no discernible basis. From 1943, as two-letter combinations began to run out, the letters C and I were used for the first time and numbers were also combined, but still in a two-character format.

The codes were supposed to be presented across the national identity roundel in the form 'AB⊙C' where AB is the squadron marking and C is the individual aircraft letter. This is the most common form of presentation. However, there were variations of presentation such as C⊙AB (typically on the right-hand side of the fuselage) or even A⊙BC, ⊙AB-C or ABC.

Other Forms of Marking

Aircraft in British and Commonwealth service carry several forms of identifier. The first and most basic is the constructor's (or construction) number (c/n) which is applied by the manufacturer to a company system. This is usually a sequential number preceded by a company or type prefix. The number is marked on a plate, usually to be found within the cockpit area. This number is unique to the aircraft.

British military aircraft have in addition a serial number which uniquely identifies the aircraft within the services. The system started in 1911 and has continued in use. After using simple numbers up to 9999 the scheme extended to four numbers preceded by a letter starting with A. By 1938, the start of the period covered by the present book, no serials before the J prefix remained in use. K, L, N, P, R, T, V, W, X and Z were all applied by about the end of 1940.

It should be noted that O, Q, U and Y were not used to avoid confusion with other letters, while N duplicated a naval series from 1916 to 1925. All the bearers of the original N serials were obsolete by the time it was applied second time around. M was used for (maintenance) instructional airframes, the letter usually being placed as a suffix after a unique number which replaced the original serial. By way of example, Hawker Audax K1996 on being relegated for ground instructional purposes was allocated a maintenance M serial, 1141M. Prefix S had been applied to naval aircraft from 1925 to 1930, many of which were still in service at the outbreak of war. One peculiarity were two-letter, four-number serials, usually beginning J, K or S, with R being the second letter, as worn on KR2793 which was a Vickers Valentia in use with No. 216 Squadron in 1939. This format, used before the war, signified a rebuilt aircraft, where the original serial was retained but with the R inserted.

Not all serials were used – some were deliberately omitted for security reasons (blackout serials), while others related to cancelled orders and were thus not taken up. When the singleletter, four-number combinations were exhausted, two-letter three-number combinations were used, ignoring the letters C, I, O, Q, U and Y. Further, no serials beginning G were officially used. By the end of the war serials had reached about VN*** (at the time of writing they have reached ZZ*** and

thus a new system is imminent). Usually serials do not change in service, but some rebuilt types may be given completely new serials. Similarly, an aircraft originally on the civil register and then acquired by the military would have had at least two identities.

Serials were displayed on the rear fuselage (or in earlier times on the fin and/or rudder), usually in 8 in (20 cm) high characters, except on Fleet Air Arm aircraft where the serials were only 4 in (10 cm) high. From 1946 bombers had 24 in (60 cm) fuselage serials. Before and after the Second World War serials were also displayed under the lower wing. Occasionally serials were hyphenated, typically those produced by de Havilland, for example Tiger Moth N-9395 at one time coded '71' of 10 EFTS. De Havilland was also idiosyncratic with the presentation of Vampire serials, for example TG/380. Ground instructional airframes in the M series often retain the original serial with the new number marked, in the form 4897M.

There were one or two other markings to be seen on wartime aircraft. Where a serial was given a suffix G in the form NT301/G (a Mosquito NF.30) the G indicated that the airframe incorporated secret components and must be guarded at all times on the ground. The second peculiarity was the term 'SNAKE' applied to aircraft destined for ferry to the Far East. The term indicated that the much-needed aircraft was not to be diverted from delivery while in transit through the Middle East.

Other rarer forms of identifier were Air Ministry serials applied in 1945–6 to captured aircraft in the form AIR MIN 11 (Ta 152H) and air race numbers on the wing and fuselage and/or fin, an example being Spitfire F.22 code RAN of 607 Squadron marked '4' for the Cooper Trophy race of 1948.

Units

The basic RAF, FAA and Commonwealth operational unit is the squadron, comprising anything between three and thirty-six aircraft (but usually between twelve and twenty). From time to time squadrons would be formed into wings of two or more squadrons, but the wing would be a relatively short-lived organization, lacking continuity and tradition. Squadron numbers were allocated as follows:

1–199	Regular RAF squadrons, many being originally RFC units prior to April 1918
200–299	Regular RAF squadrons, mainly former RNAS units prior to April 1918. Thus the lower numbered in this series have longer histories than higher-numbered squadrons in the former series.
300–309, 315–318	Polish squadrons based in the UK under Polish Air Force control
310–313	RAF squadrons formed of Czechoslovak personnel
320–322	RAF squadrons formed of Dutch personnel
326–329, 340–347	RAF squadrons formed of Free

	French personnel
330–334	RAF squadrons formed of Norwegian personnel
335–336	RAF squadrons formed of Greek personnel
349–350	RAF squadrons formed of Belgian personnel
351–352	RAF squadrons formed of Yugoslav personnel
353–361	Regular RAF units mainly in India
400–443	RCAF squadrons UK, MedME or FE based
450–467	RAAF squadrons UK, MedME or FE based
485–490	RNZAF squadrons UK, FE or Africa based
500–504	Special Reserve RAF squadrons formed in the mid- to late 1920s
510–599	Regular RAF squadrons, often performing second-line tasks
600–616	Auxiliary Air Force squadrons formed between 1925 and 1938 on a territorial basis
617–650	Regular RAF squadrons, often performing second-line tasks
651–666	Regular RAF air observation post squadrons formed of Royal Artillery aircrew
667–695 & 1435	Regular RAF squadrons. No. 1435 was originally a Malta-based flight which when expanded to squadron size retained the same number
700–799	FAA second-line squadrons
800–899	FAA front-line squadrons (including 860, formed of Dutch naval personnel during the Second World War)
1700–1853	FAA front-line and reserve squadrons.

Smaller operational units were flights, usually comprising between two and twelve aircraft. In the first instance many of these were numbered in the 400 series, but to avoid confusion with the Commonwealth squadrons, they were later renumbered in the 1400 series. Further general flight numbers were in the ranges 1500–1699 and 1300–64, while 1900–70 were used after the war by air observation squadrons. The range 1700–1899 was not used to avoid confusion with the FAAsquadrons in that range. Finally, the numbers 1330–36, 1380–85 and 1651–99 were used by conversion units.

For training purposes wartime basic or elementary flying training schools operated locally and, as mentioned, did not have unit codes (but usually had individual aircraft codes in addition to serials). After the war, many flying training schools did use unit codes. Flying training schools were numbered

sequentially from 1 to 23 and 31 to 41 in Canada.

During the war pilots progressed to front-line squadrons via operational training units (OTUs) which were numbered from 1 to 152 (with many gaps). From 1945 onwards they were disbanded or redesignated as advanced flying schools numbered 201–15 or operational conversion units (OCUs) numbered 226–42. Most applied codes in the contemporary format and during the war many OTU staff or students flew on operational sorties, particularly in the Bomber or Coastal Command units.

The remaining flying units applying codes were generally of four types: the specialised training units, typically those for navigators or radio operators; specialised development units, whose role was to test and implement new tactics; experimental units, whose function was to test new equipment; and, a miscellany of units set up for brief periods and for very specific short-term needs like letter delivery, pest control or publicity purposes.

Identifying Units

Those readers very familiar with the subject will probabl know which chapter or appendix to make for without the need to use the main index (chapter 3). For those less experienced, perhaps with nothing more than a photograph showing a code, chapter 3 lists all known code combinations in numero-alpha sequence. If the subject looks as though it was wartime, any codes matching those shown and noted as being in chapter 5 are the most likely starting place. Go then to chapter 5 and every type flown by each unit using the target code will be listed, usually with examples. Knowing the type helps to narrow the search so the authors have ensured that there is at least one photograph of all significant – and many unusual – types to have worn codes. The photographic index is at Appendix I.

If the answer is still not clear, the reader might do well to

Spitfire LFVb in typical mid to late war markings and displaying the code HA, which would suggest either Nos 126 or 218 Sqns RAF or No. 129 Sqn RCAF. The latter flew Hurricanes, while 218 was a bomber unit. No. 126 Sqn did fly the Spitfire V, but in Malta, and the photo does not appear to depict an aircraft with Middle East-type markings. The answer, however, lies in the wrong presentation of the AF code of the Air Fighting Development Unit with the individual identifier H. Of note is the serial presentation (believed to be EN449) high up on the sky fuselage band. (Peter Arnold Collection)

read this chapter carefully and also chapter 2, which between them explain the use and application of codes and some of the problems in presentation and identification. Where there are options, clues such as other markings, camouflage schemes and backgrounds might help with identifying the air arm and/or location. One further aid in seeking the unit identity of RAF aircraft is the serial number if it is visible on a photograph. The Air- Britain series of monographs on serial batches lists the recorded service use of each example and it is strongly recommended that you refer to it. But what of the handful of occasions when the code does not fit with the details in the listings? The first check might be in chapter 13, where all known personal 'codes' are listed (also incorporated into the main index at chapter 3).

If the unit rather than the code is known, a number of appendices (A–D) list the more significant and extensive groupings by unit rather than code. For more confined categories, the codebased lists in the chapters are short enough to enable fast scanning to identify the unit sought.

If there is still no answer, the type of aircraft may well give a clue as to why and at least to what type of unit it belonged. Training aircraft, for example, were not generally coded within the common two-character scheme. Many flew very locally to their home bases and so there was no need for unit identifiers; most carried just individual markings, usually in the form of numbers. Post-war training aircraft continued this system although many training and reserve units carried three-letter codes with a fourth individual letter. These are listed in chapter 11.

Finally, for readers with photographic or other evidence of codes which are not listed in this book feel free to e-mail the authors at vf@vflintham.demon.co.uk. It is just possible that the photograph you have shows a hitherto unknown code – they keep on turning up!

Careful detective work has confirmed this Blenheim IVF as belonging to No. 1 Coastal Artillery Co-operation Flight – a hitherto unrecorded application. R3840 SX-D is seen at Odiham around September 1941.
(Alan Holt via P. H. T. Green Collection)

Similar types, same unit, same place, same date – different presentations! The middle photograph shows Anson XI NL231 XE-D, below is Anson C.19 VP513 XE-C, both of the Central Bomber Establishment seen at RAF Marham, 20 September 1947. Note also the variation in lettering style.
(via J. D. Oughton)

The use of the unit codes XC by No. 26 Sqn resulted in this clever adaptation of the war code it was actually coded XC-O. The squadron badge is displayed on the fin. (Ron Brittain)

This photo is yet another example of the care needed in trying to identify the unit from the code. Which RAF units operated the Boston or the Havoc I Turbinlite with code T8? At first glance it could be an unknown allocation, but in fact the aircraft were flown by No. 771 NAS of the Fleet Air Arm. Probably the most ready clue is the typical FAA code presentation. The Boston III is W8282 and the Turbinlite Havoc either W8338 or Z2270. (Gregor Lamb)

Another example of things not being what they seem. Spitfire Vb of the Lee-on-Solent Spotting Pool and coded 4 actually belongs to the US Navy's VCS-7 which also used the code 6. VCS-7 exchanged its Seagulls for borrowed RAF Spitfires for just a few weeks around D-Day to spot naval gunfire in Normandy. (Author's Collection)

This one still defeats us! Spitfires Mk IIs possibly at RAF Digby in early 1944 display the code AO of an unknown unit. This is probably a specialist flight or unit and the aircraft coded AO-? appears to be serialed P8562. The most likely conclusion is that the unit could be the AFDU, but confirmation one way or the other is lacking. (B. Buss via R. Durand)

Spitfire Vc BR294/GL-E, illustrates another anomaly when one examines the national markings. They are British, but the use of orthochromatic film has resulted in a transposition of the roundel colours, with the outer yellow band showing dark. The aircraft belongs to No. 185 Sqn and is seen after an agricultural landing at Hal Far, Malta, on 2 July 1942. (Sqn Ldr P. H. P. Roberts)

CHAPTER 2

An Introduction to Unit Markings and Codes

A Matter of National Identity

From the very earliest days of military aviation the requirement for identifying aircraft for various purposes was established. First, and perhaps most important, came the need to establish the nationality of an aircraft to prevent it being fired upon by friendly forces and, conversely, to identify an enemy machine.

The imaginative French Air Service had seen this need as early as 26 July 1912 and represented their national tricolour in the form of a cockade, or roundel, which remains in use to this day. However, for the British and German air services, it took the hard experience of the early battles of the First World War for them to realise the need for some form of identification.

German aircraft began using the 'black cross pate' during autumn 1914 when the war was still one of manoeuvre and the first recorded report was made in Belgium by the commander of an RNAS armoured car, a Lt Osmond, who noted the marking on the 28 September. By this time several pilots of the Royal Flying Corps (RFC) had reported being fired upon by their own troops while others who had force-landed had been treated with hostility and suspicion by the local populace, the pilots having no immediate means of identifying themselves as British. As a result, and on their own initiative, some pilots began painting a Union Flag beneath the wings of their aircraft – as a matter of self-preservation! The Admiralty made the marking mandatory on Royal Naval Air Service (RNAS) aircraft from 28 October 1914, though by then experience from the field had shown that from any distance the red cross of St George appeared too similar to the German black cross.

Thus on 11 December 1914 the RFC's field headquarters ordered that a marking similar to the French cockade or roundel should be used, but with the colours reversed, while the RNAS ordered that a red ring with a white centre be used on its aircraft. Soon afterwards, the RNAS too adopted the same roundel as the RFC and this has remained the basis for the recognised marking for British military aircraft ever since.

Units Distinguished

Having evolved a method of identifying their nationality, as the size of the RFC and RNAS on the Western Front grew, so did the need to identify aircraft of the same unit in the air. Some units had used unofficial embellishments for a time but on 23 April 1916 RFC Headquarters introduced a method of unit identity that comprised simple geometric devices and bars marked on the fuselage. These were retained in some form through the war, though from 22 March 1918 they were dropped from all except aircraft of the scout squadrons. The rallying of aircraft during an air battle also became important and so the aircraft of flight or section leaders were identified by streamers attached to rudders or interplane struts. Additionally, individual aircraft were often identified by an aircraft letter or number. In many cases this was repeated above, and occasionally beneath, the wing, thus allowing ready identification in the air and on the ground. These various methods largely remained for the remainder of the First World War.

During the years after the First World War, the newly formed RAF quickly established traditions, including unit crests or badges. These were based on heraldic principles and the earliest invariably incorporated as the central feature of their design a symbol, usually with some more or less obvious significance. No. 41 Squadron, for example, used a red double-armed cross, adapted from the arms of St Omer, where it had been based in 1918.

After the First World War the need to identify individual aircraft remained and so large individual letters or numbers continued in use for most types. An Air Ministry Order (AMO) dated 18 December 1924 gave air officers commanding (AOCs) the discretion to identify aircraft of individual flights within a squadron by the use of colour – red, yellow and blue for 'A', 'B' and 'C' flights respectively. Thus aircraft letters and parts of the airframe, such as wheel hubs, were coloured – as, usually, were the fins on the aircraft of the flight commander.

From around mid-1924 the few home-based fighter squadrons began to decorate their aircraft with colourful markings, some of which remain in use to this day, but on these machines individual aircraft letters (if used) tended to be small and for use on the ground. Bombers and others by

The type and form of unit markings used by the RFC and RAF during the First World War can be seen on RE8 A3660/2, which wears the two inward-sloping bars of No. 34 Sqn. (J. M. Bruce/G. S. Leslie Collection)

The colourful markings so typical of the inter-war period are exemplified by the broad black and yellow stripes on these Gauntlet IIs of No. 213 Sqn. (via Philip Jarrett)

They also wear the Squadron's hornet emblem within a standardised fighter spearhead frame. (ACM Sir Humphrey Edwards-Jones)

One of the first recorded uses of unit codes at the time of the Munich crisis of late September 1938 were the Demons of No. 23 Sqn at Wittering. K5698/MS-G shows the newly applied codes and the camouflage which has obliterated the serial, resulting in the rough chalking of the last two digits on the rudder. (MoD)

contrast usually restricted themselves to the squadron number in the flight colour and, perhaps, some form of unit badge, and these markings remained the norm through to the late 1930s. In this period the most general form of unit identification painted on aircraft was the key element from the squadron badge incorporated in a frame, the nature of which described the function of the unit: spearhead, fighter; grenade, bomber; six point star, reconnaissance. RAF squadron badges were widely publicised, for example through the medium of cigarette cards, and offered no security in their widespread application on aircraft. The use of the squadron number marked in large numerals on the aircraft in the late 1930s spared the potential enemy any effort at all!

Towards the end of the inter-war period, as modern monoplanes entered service in camouflage schemes, markings became limited to the unit number and/or an aircraft letter and unit badge, usually worn on the fin. Notwithstanding the general instructions, there was considerable variety in the style and form of markings, especially within differing roles.

Unit Identity Codes

The most significant change of the inter-war years, and thus the raison d'être for this book, was the introduction of unit identification letters, more commonly referred to as squadron or unit codes. This is in fact a misnomer in that the two-letter

unit allocation followed no apparent recognisable pattern and so were not 'codes' in the literal sense, though the only document (AMO A154/39) to list the entire allocation does refer to them as 'code letters'.

When at the time of the Munich crisis in September 1938 the RAF mobilised, orders were issued for camouflage to be applied to aircraft and for markings to be toned down. This was usually achieved by over-painting the white segment of the roundel and the removal of squadron markings and numbers. In place of the latter markings there was a requirement for the unit identification letters to be used.

The first use of these 'code' letters was on or about 25 September 1938; however, many units did not apply them immediately and in reality it was not until the late spring of 1939 that the task was completed. Even then some units did not, it appears, apply them. At this time codes were applicable to aircraft of operational units only, and those likely to become involved in operations. Thus, overseas, Middle East-based squadrons applied them, often on uncamouflaged aircraft, while units based in India, other than possibly those with a reinforcement role, did not. When codes were applied it was usual for them to be worn to one side of the fuselage roundel, with the individual aircraft letter on the other.

Because of the need for secrecy in the identification of the allocation of codes to units, little documentation has survived and there remain gaps or room for supposition. Indeed where an allocation to a unit is known, evidence of its actual use may be lacking. The only known list of unit codes for the period is contained in the unclassified Air Ministry Order A154/39 dated 27 April 1939. Relevant parts of this significant document are reproduced below:

ORGANISATION AND ADMINISTRATION OF UNITS

A154 – Identification Markings on Aircraft of Operational Units and Marking of Unit Equipment (27.4.39)

1. It has been decided to adopt a standard system of identification marking on aircraft of operational

squadrons throughout the service, at home and abroad, and on those items of equipment which are liable to be taken into the air.

2. The system is to be adopted forthwith.

3. No marking other than those described hereunder are to be permitted on operational units.

4. Aircraft identification markings.
   a The identification markings to be carried on aircraft are as follows: [Author's note: The positions of roundels and serial numbers are described at this point, but only the notes on unit identification letters are reproduced here]

Type of Marking	Detail	Location
Alphabetic letters to indicate squadron and identity of individual aircraft	(i) Two letters to indicate number of squadron	Either forward or aft of the national marking on both sides of the fuselage
	(ii) One letter to indicate individual aircraft	On the other side of the aircraft national marking on both sides of the fuselage

5. The code letters allotted to squadrons are shown at the appendix to this order. They are to be painted in grey paint (Stores Ref. 33B/157). The letters are to be 48 in. high and are to be made up of strokes 6 in. in width. Smaller letters are to be used only when the space available on the fuselage makes such a course unavoidable.

6. Squadron badges may be carried if desired on aircraft but they must be removable at short notice without leaving any trace.

Appendix
Squadron	Code Letters
No 1 Squadron	NA
No 2	KO
No 3	etc.........

This fascinating document then details the allocated code letters for all existing and planned units as well as all unused squadron numbers from 1 to 350, from 500 to 520 and from 600 to 650.

Hastily camouflaged Gladiator I K7981/RN-D of No. 72 Sqn had its serial chalked on the rudder and its roundels overpainted. It met with this accident on 22 February 1939 and became a maintenance airframe. (D. M. Dixon)

Coincident with No. 72 Sqn receiving Spitfire Is in April 1939 was the publication of a list of unit codes which gave No. 72's as SD, which were applied to their new aircraft on arrival. (No. 72 Sqn Records)

As can be seen, having introduced a uniform system of identifying a unit's aircraft, the publication of this list and the approval to identify these code letters with well-publicised unit markings meant that security was not, at this time, the consideration. It was probably an act of pragmatism, as most units had after Munich returned to their pre-war station. However, at the commencement of war in September 1939, an entirely new sequence of code letters came into force for operational aircraft as laid down in Secret Document SD 110. This was the only time that the entire sequence was changed.

As many units immediately changed station, it was no longer a simple matter to identify the unit codes with particular squadrons and thus gain an accurate order of battle for the RAF, an important factor as the number of squadrons increased. Furthermore, although SD 110 was periodically reissued or amended, because of the sensitivity of the information preceding issues were destroyed and none seem to have survived.

It is a matter of surmise, but the authors believe that two SD 110 lists existed in 1938, one for implementation on mobilisation as happened at the Munich period and another for action on the outbreak of hostilities. There is ample evidence to support what is admittedly a theory in that several units in late 1938 and early 1939 were using one set of code letters that were then changed following the issue of AMO A154/39 as shown above. However, in September 1939 on the outbreak of war, these units reverted to their original codes. The supposition is that several units applied codes from the wrong list and that this was only corrected following the issue of AMO A154/39. Documentary proof is found in the No. 64 Sqn records, which on 27 September 1938 state: 'Instructions received from HQ Fighter Command that all aircraft are to be camouflaged and marked in accordance with SD110(1).' The (1) suffix strongly suggests that there was more than one list extant.

An example is No. 72 Squadron which in late 1938 applied the code letters RN to its Gladiator Is, as recorded on K7981/RN-D which crashed in February 1939 and was photographed at the site on the date. No. 72's re-equipment with Spitfires coincided with the issue of AMO A154/39 which listed the squadron's codes as SD, where it would be evident that the squadron had been using the incorrect letters. The codes on its new monoplanes were thus changed, as on K9942/SD-V which interestingly still exists as a proud exhibit at the RAF Museum, Hendon. Contemporary photographs also show No. 72's Spitfires wearing the squadron's 'Swift' badge within a white spearhead on the fin, as specified in the AMO.

On the outbreak of war in September 1939 No. 72 Sqn was given the codes RN once more and these were painted on to its Spitfire Is like P9444/RN-A seen in early 1940. This has led to the presumption of there being two lists as described in the text. (via M. W. Payne)

Sqn	Originally applied code	Spring 1939 code	September 1939 code
4	TV	FY*	TV
6	ZD	XE?*	JV
16	KJ	EE*	UG
33	SO	TN*	NW
63	*ON*	*NE*	*ON*
72	RN	SD*	RN
78	ED	YY*	EY
80	OD	GK*	YK
151	TV	GG*	DZ
166	*AS*	*GB?*	*AS*
220	HU*	PK?	NR
228	TO*	BH	DQ
602	*LO*	*ZT*	*LO*

* Code allocated in AMO A154/39

With the wholesale change of codes on the outbreak of war the squadron reverted to its original code RN, which continued in use until the end of the war. No. 4 Squadron's Lysanders underwent a similar process, going from TV in September 1938 to FY in April 1939 before reverting to TV again the following September. That a second, secret, list must have been held by units pending an implementation/mobilisation order is supported by the example of the Fairey Battles of the Harwell-based Nos 105 and 226 Squadrons. They had been alerted to prepare to move to France and had applied their 'wartime' codes, GB and MQ respectively, as early as August 1939. More specific dates for mobilisation are derived from a report that the North Weald-based Blenheims of No. 604 Squadron were seen wearing code NG from 24 August 1939 and a photograph of one of No. 42 Squadron's ancient Vildebeeste wearing AW on the 29th.

To add further to the confusion surrounding the use of codes in the period up to October 1939, several units which did change codes in the spring of 1939 adopted a third combination in September at the outbreak of war! Those units known to have changed codes during the pre-war period are listed below, with those which reverted to their originally applied codes shown in italics.

Among the known uses of wartime codes from late August 1939 were the obsolescent Vildebeeste IVs of No. 42 Sqn, the date, 29.8.39, obligingly being etched onto the negative by the station photographer. (RAF Bircham Newton Records)

Even more puzzling is the situation with several of the squadrons which were formed in November/December 1939 as part of the rapid expansion of Fighter Command. Three of these, Nos 92, 145 and 266 Squadrons, used the codes allocated in AMO A154/39, until mid-1940 in No. 92's case and 1941 for the others. Even more intriguingly, No. 247 Squadron, which was not formed at Plymouth until July 1940, also used its A154/39 code HP on Gladiators and Hurricanes until mid-1941. This must have caused some confusion, for nearby at Exeter the previous month the Gunnery Research Unit had been formed which, quite correctly, wore HP on its various second-line types.

Undoubtedly the most remarkable hangover from this pre-war Air Ministry Order, however, was No. 510 Squadron which was one of the many units listed and allocated a code but which had not been formed at the time. When it was formed its miscellany of communications types was uncoded. However, when it acquired a Mohawk in late 1943, this was coded RG – which was the allocated code for the unit in 1939. A coincidence possibly, but an intriguing fact nonetheless.

Notwithstanding the apparently random system, the codes of two units did not change in September 1939. No. 2 Squadron retained KO until early 1941 while No. 213 used AK from the time it received Hurricanes in January 1939 until it relinquished its Tempests on re-equipping with Vampires in January 1950 – a remarkable continuity.

An Integrated System

With their new codes and squadrons dispersed to war stations, the need for security in their identity then became evident. For while locals would know of a unit at a nearby airfield and probably its identity, and would see its codes, a move further afield would, for a time, disguise a squadron's identity, especially as there were no accessible published lists and a censored press. Indeed when a member of the press on a visit to Martlesham Heath in late 1940 inadvertently published some (now wellknown) photographs of DT-coded

Only two units carried their pre-war codes into the Second World War, and only No. 213 Sqn retained them through until codes were finally dropped. Hurricane I L1770/AK-A shows the pre-war use. (D. M. Dixon)

Hurricanes and captioned them as belonging to No. 257 Squadron, they were recoded FM in early 1941.

The initial allocation of unit codes soon expanded to include OTUs and support units such as anti-aircraft co-operation units (AACUs), while later some numbered flights and station flights were also allocated codes, though not all were actually used. Flying training units, however, lay outside this system and were generally identified by fleet numbers on their aircraft, rather than a recognisable unit code.

Initially, when a squadron was posted overseas, it retained the original codes while abroad and these were not duplicated at home. However, by the middle of the war, and to make more letter combinations available new codes were allocated on arrival overseas. Conversely, units moving back to, or reforming in, the UK were usually allocated new combinations. Overseas, unit codes were not always displayed, depending on local rules. Presumably for security reasons at the time of Operation *Torch*, many North African and, earlier in 1942, Malta-based fighter units were allocated a single letter code, but most had reverted to more conventional codes by the invasion of Sicily in July 1943.

The system adopted by the RAF became widely used, with the air forces of the Commonwealth eventually using a very similar system, though for their home-based units they allocated their own combinations. Where home-based Commonwealth squadrons served alongside the RAF – for example Royal Australian Air Force (RAAF) units in Malaya and the South African Air Force (SAAF) in North Africa – their allocations came from the local command. So did the codes for the many 'Article XV' 400-series-numbered Commonwealth squadrons which were generally formed in the UK and which were fully integrated into the RAF command organisation.

The initial home-based Royal Canadian Air Force (RCAF)

Hurricane IIc BP629/AK-K retains No. 213's codes during service in North Africa in early 1943. (F. Leeson)

allocation made on 1 August 1939, however, was undoubtedly based on AMO A154/39. Why is uncertain, but when codes were introduced on Canada-based RCAF squadrons in August 1940, in every case they replicated those in the A154/39 listing, even where there was no equivalent RAF unit formed at the time; an example was RE on No. 118 Squadron RCAF. Presumably to differentiate them from RAF units, the codes on Canada-based RCAF units were underlined, and appeared thus: FG-A.

All home-based RCAF unit codes were changed in May 1942 and this time these combinations bore no relationship to similarly numbered RAF units. Further widespread adoption of the RAF code system came with deployment of the United States Army Air Force (USAAF) to the UK, and their early units generally used combinations not previously used by the RAF. However, as the USAAF's 8th and 9th Air Forces grew and the numbers of RAF, Commonwealth and Free European squadrons expanded there was a need for further combinations. In spite of the expansion of the system to OTUs and other units, up until 1943 the letters I and C had not been used, nor had numbers. Thus from late that year I and C were available for use and alphanumeric combinations began to be allocated, particularly to the USAAF.

Additionally, many of the heavy bomber squadrons of Bomber Command had an establishment of more than twenty four and so some individual aircraft were given letters with a bar above. In February 1943 this practice was officially stopped when third (C) flights were added and given a different combination: No. 90 Squadron continued to use WP but its new C Flight used XY, for example.

For the RAF, a major change came about in late 1942 (described in chapter 5), when it was announced that '… the use of squadron code letters within Coastal Command will be dispensed with, with effect from 1 November 1942. It will be noted however that the third letter for individual aircraft identification may be kept.'

This instruction remained in force until around August 1943 when Coastal Command instituted a form of numerical code for operational squadrons, based on individual stations. The system continued in use until the summer of 1944 when it was replaced and all its units issued with a new set of codes. The numerical code system, designed for security and based around individual stations, appears to have been used intermittently and probably caused as much confusion for the RAF as the enemy!

Although not unit codes as such, other letter combinations were often seen and could be assumed to be squadron codes. They belonged, however, to wing leaders or other senior officers who from 1941 had been permitted to use their initials on their personal aircraft in place of the unit code, and have since usually been referred to as personal codes. Such codes were usually painted either side of the fuselage roundels in the normal manner; often just two letters were used, but sometimes as many as four! Although applied mainly to fighters or fighterbombers, there is at least one example of a Stirling bearing the initials of a station commander.

Overseas, the use of two-letter codes continued, and with the establishment under Allied command of the ex-Vichy French units in the Mediterranean theatre, some of these

No. 213 Sqn received Mustang IVs in early 1945 which were uncamouflaged but initially kept the unusual code presentation; after the war the code appeared more conventionally either side of the roundel. (No. 213 Sqn Records)

units were also allocated unit codes, usually alphanumeric. Thus, as can be seen, the basic RAF unit code system was used across the world by almost all Commonwealth air forces and by Allied units in the UK and elsewhere. It had proved a robust and relatively simple way to identify a unit's aircraft as well as offering – at least in the short term – a modicum of security.

Post-war Applications

After the end of the war two-character unit codes remained in use with the RAF and a number of Commonwealth and Allied air forces, though not with any kind of integrated system. Some of the latter, as they became re-established in their homelands, perpetuated the 300 series RAF squadron numbers, keeping their wartime codes for identification. As they expanded and formed new squadrons, new combinations were allocated, though in some cases the individual aircraft letter was replaced by a number, as adopted by the Royal Netherlands Air Force.

Interestingly, although the post-war French air force reverted to a groupe/escadre (wing) organisation, the successors to some of the wartime Free French units retained the use of their wartime codes for several years until a complete reorganisation of the French coding system. The RCAF also developed a unique system of unit codes after the war and these continued in use to the late 1950s, but in the RAAF and Royal New Zealand Air Force (RNZAF) codes had virtually disappeared by the end of the 1940s. Probably the last Commonwealth use of unit codes were the maritime PV-1 Venturas of the SAAF, which continued wearing their codes until 1960.

Within the RAF, aircraft in operational commands continued to use two-character codes but when the squadrons of the Auxiliary (later Royal Auxiliary) Air Force (RAuxAF) were re-established in 1946 they became part of Reserve Command. For operational and training units of this formation, as well as eventually, those of Flying Training and Technical Training Commands, three-letter unit codes were adopted. The first letter denoted the command, for example R for Reserve, the next two the unit, for example AV for No. 615 Squadron thus giving the code of RAV which appeared on one side of the fuselage roundel with the aircraft letter on the other. Sometimes, however, particularly in training units, the letters could appear equally on either side of the roundel. These codes were a means of identifying aircraft and units, and as they were not intended for security they ran sequentially.

The codes for Flying Training Command had F as the first letter, while Technical Training Command used T. The unit letters for this latter Command appear in fact to have been

When re-equipped from the Spitfire to the Mustang III in Italy in mid-1944, the codes were placed forward of the roundel spaced ahead of the aircraft letter. (No. 213 Sqn Records)

The final type to wear No. 213 Sqn's long-used codes was the Tempest F.6 which was camouflaged for service in Palestine and the Middle East. The AK codes were retained until the Tempests were replaced by Vampires in late 1949. (No. 213 Sqn Records)

Whitley II K7244/LT-G of No. 7 Sqn wears its pre-war codes, which were also used by the RCAF early in the war, though the latter underlined their letters. (via Author's Collection)

taken from the letters of the station, as they were not sequential. For example, No. 4 Radio School at Swanton Morley used TSM while No. 1 School of Photography at Wellesbourne Mountford used TWM. Almost all known combinations could be worked into this method.

When the RAuxAF squadrons were transferred from Reserve to Fighter Command in 1949 they reverted to the two-character codes. Some, like No. 602 Squadron, reused their old wartime codes (LO) while others like No. 614 were allocated new combinations (7A).

Within the RAF, the end of the long-used two-character codes began when some of the overseas Tempest squadrons began re-equipping with Vampires, which remained uncoded. At home, in the summer of 1950, squadrons of Fighter Command began to return to their long-cherished colourful squadron markings. In April the following year Bomber Command ordered the removal of unit codes from its aircraft, which were then identified by coloured spinners on Lincolns and, later, the addition of squadron badges.

In that year too the German-based squadrons of the 2nd Tactical Air Force also stopped using codes and replaced them with a single-letter identification system which was based around the station on which the squadron was based. Then from 1953 to 1954 squadron markings began reappearing and gradually the single-letter codes ceased to be used. The Squadrons of Coastal Command also dropped the use of two-letter codes in 1951 and adopted a station-based single-letter code system which lasted until 1956–7. Aircraft of some units, however, continued to wear two-letter codes, notably the Chipmunks of the Metropolitan Communications Squadron

Although of poor quality, this view of Vampire FB.5 WA365 of No. 605 (County of Warwick) Sqn was taken soon after the Fighter Command instruction superseding codes with colourful markings. It shows the squadron's new red-outlined pale blue bars flanking the roundel, but still retains its code letters NR-C on the nose, a most unusual occurrence. (via R. L. Ward)

When the RCAF introduced unit codes at the beginning of the Second World War the letters exactly replicated the April 1939 RAF list, thus Shark III 550/LT-M of No. 7 Sqn seen at Prince Rupert in mid-1941 had the same codes as No. 7 Sqn RAF before the war. (via J. D. Oughton)

and the Vampires and Hunters of the Chivenor-based No. 229 OCU. Resplendent in the colourful nose markings of No. 234 (Shadow) Squadron but carrying the codes ES-77 on the tail, Hunter F Mk 4 XF941, when photographed at RAF Benson in September 1960, was probably the last recorded use of a two-letter unit code on an RAF aircraft.

By the early 1960s codes had also pretty much disappeared from use by the Belgian and Dutch air forces. Squadron codes were still occasionally seen, however, as the Royal Norwegian Air Force continued their use until 1970. The wartime codes applied to the RAF's Norwegian squadrons thus still appeared on such unlikely types as the F-5A Freedom Fighter, F-104G Starfighter, HU-16B Albatross and P-3B Orion, the last examples of a system which had been first employed in 1938.

Management Tools

Unit identification codes began to reappear in the RAF from 1969 when the Wessex helicopters of No. 72 Squadron at RAF Odiham were seen wearing a letter A ahead of their aircraft letter. Later, its sister unit No. 18 Squadron was seen wearing B. Although not designed for security or identification in the air a system again evolved, but this time essentially as a management tool. With several squadrons on a station there might be two or more aircraft with the same letter, so it was easier for the identification of individual aircraft on the ground to refer to aircraft with their unit and aircraft letter. Thus, at Odiham, Alpha Charlie was Wessex C of No. 72 Squadron.

That the system was based on a particular force or aircraft type became evident when the Pumas of the newly formed No. 33 Squadron appeared wearing C; when they were received in October 1971 No. 230's machines were coded D. Gradually, through the 1970s and early 1980s this system became more and more widespread, mainly within the tactical aircraft forces. As ever there were notable exceptions, for when the Canberras of the various Wyton-based units were coded, the Devon light transports of the permanently based detachment of No. 207 Squadron were included and coded D. The Canberras used A, B, C and E for No. 39 Squadron, No. 231 OCU, and Nos 100 and 360 Squadrons respectively.

Usually, the unit letter appeared before the aircraft letter, with the former beginning with A. However, when the Buccaneers at Lossiemouth received codes in the early 1980s they wore F, S and C as the unit identifiers for Nos 12 and 208 Squadrons and No. 237 OCU respectively. The unit codes were also worn after the aircraft letter as on XV864/KF of No. 12 Squadron. Why the unusual letters? It is more than tempting to suggest that the unit badge had something to do with it – No. 12's being a Fox, No. 208's a Sphinx and No. 237 OCU's a Cutlass!

The Future

The single letter system remains in use to this day with certain units. From 1997 some aircraft were coded with an 'operation' code not related to any specific unit or a home station. Among those were Harrier GR Mk 7s 'W' (for Operation *Warden*) and Tornado GR Mk 1s with 'J' (for Operation *Jural*). From 2002 new codes were being applied to the Torando air defence fleet on an individual aircraft basis, regardless of unit. Examples were ZE758/YI of No 5 Sqn and ZE160/TX from No 25 Sqn. However, from 2006, the Tornado and Harrier fleets are being coded with a three digit number relating to their construction squence. Transport and other support units use either single letters or the last two or three numbers of their serials.

In 1943 No 617 Sqn was formed for the specific purpose of making specialised attacks on three German dams. Its Lancasters were coded 'AJ' and in 1992 617 Sqn with the Torndao GR Mk 1 once more applied these letters to its aircraft. In a link with the past the individual aircraft letters replicated those of Lancasters which had mounted the epic raid nearly 50 years earlier. The Typhoon fleet is, at the time of writing, applying single letters, but surpisingly No 3 Sqn has reverted to its wartime code of QO. There is also an increasing move towards the application of wartime codes within special commemorative markings.

One of the last known uses of the 'conventional' two-letter unit code was on this Hunter F.4 of No. 229 OCU in the markings of No. 234 Sqn, which was photographed at RAF Benson in September 1960. (J. D. R. Rawlings)

CHAPTER 3

Main Index Of Known RAF And Allied Codes

Code	Unit	See Chapter or Appendix	Code	Unit	See Chapter or Appendix
0	340 BS, 97 BG	A	2I	443	5
1	2(C)OTU	5	2K	1668 HCU	5
1	53	5	2L	302 TCS, 441 TCG	A
1	58	5	2L	9 MU	5
1	59	5	2M	520	5
1	143	5	2N	81 FS, 50 FG	A
1	144	5	2N	SF Foulsham	5
1	172	5	2O	84 GCF	5
1	201	5	2P	644	5
1	206	5	2Q	88 GCF	5
1	228	5	2R	50 TCS, 314 TCG	A
1	235	5	2S	834 BS, 486 BG	A
1	236	5	2U	785 BS, 466 BG	A
1	407	5	2V	18 GCF	11
1	341 BS, 97 BG	A	2V	547	5
1	Dartmouth Pool RCAF	7	2W	3 SGR	5
1B	84 GCF	5	2W	33 PS, 363 RG	A
13	86th Inf Div	B	2W	SGR	11
2	86	5	2X	85 OTU	5
2	224	5	2X	?	11
2	235	5	2Y	345	5
2	236	5	2Y	345/GC 2/2	11
2	220	5	2Z	510 FS, 405 FG	A
2	280	5	2	235	5
2	304	5	3	248	5
2	404	5	3	254	5
2	407	5	3	333	5
2	422	5	3	423	5
2	455	5	3	489	5
2	461	5	3	547	5
2	502	5	3	612	5
2	342 BS, 97 BG	A	3	20 (R)	17
2	Dartmouth Pool RCAF	7	3	233 OCU	17
21	8th Arm Div	B	32	119/228 FA Gps	B
23	Arty HQ, 1st Army	B	33	9th Inf Div	B
24	Arty HQ, 3rd Army	B	34	1st Inf Div	B
25	2nd Inf Div	B	36	4th Inf Div	B
26	VII Corps Arty	B	37	76th Inf Div	B
28	XII Corps Arty	B	38	8th Inf Div	B
29	XV Corps Arty	B	39	V Corps Arty	B
2A	669 BS, 416 BG	A	3A	53 TCS, 61 TCG	A
2A	SF St Eval	11	3B	23 MU	5
2A	SF St Eval	5	3B	93 TCS, 439 TCG	A
2B	272 MU	5	3C	1 LFS	5
2C	838 BS, 487 BG	A	3D	48 MU	11
2D	24	5	3D	82 TCS, 436 TCG	A
2G	836 BS, 487 BG	A	3E	100 GCF	5
2H	SF Brawdy	5	3F	313 TCS, 349 TCG	A

Code	Unit	See Chapter or Appendix	Code	Unit	See Chapter or Appendix
3F	BAFO CW	5	4Q	59 OTU	5
3G	111 OTU	5	4Q	CCFATU	5
3H	80 OTU	5	4R	325 RNethAF	11
3I	14 TCS, 61 TCG	A	4R	844 BS, 489 BG	A
3J	13 MU	11	4S	CSE	11
3J	99 TCS, 441 TCG	A	4T	585 BS, 394 BG	A
3K	1695 BDTF	5	4T	SF Portreath	5
3L	391 BS, 34 BG	A	4U	30 MU	5
3L	FCCRS	11	4U	89 TCS, 438 TCG	A
3M	48 GCF	11	4V	302 FTU	5
3M	679	5	4W	406 FS, 371 FG	A
3O	601 BS, 398 BG	A	4W	SF Snaith	5
3O	SF Wratting Common	5	4X	1692 Flt	5
3P	324 RNethAF	11	4X	230	11
3P	515	5	4Z	1699 Flt	5
3Q	852 BS, 491 BG	A	4Z	791 BS, 467 BG	A
3R	1 BAF	11	4Z	BCCF	11
3R	832 BS, 486 BG	A	5	20 (R)	17
3S	3 GCF	5	5	5 METS	5
3T	22 FS, 36 FG	A	51	69th Inf Div	B
3T	SF Acaster Malbis	5	52	3rd Arm Div	B
3U	GC 1/4	11	53	4th Arm Div	B
3V	1 GCF	11	54	5th Arm Div	B
3W	322	5	55	6th Arm Div	B
3W	322 RNethAF	11	56	7th Arm Div	B
3X	38 MU	5	57	82nd AB Div	B
3X	87 TCS, 438 TCG	A	58	101st AB Div	B
3Y	577	5	59	18th FA Gp	B
4	206	5	5A	329	5
4	VCS 7	C	5A	329/ GC 1/2	11
4*	414 BS, 97 BG	A	5B	84 GSU	5
40	16th Arm Div	B	5C	671 BS, 416 BG	A
43	29th Inf Div	B	5D	31	11
44	30th Inf Div	B	5D	644 BS, 410 BG	A
45	35th Inf Div	B	5D	SF Gibraltar	5
46	79th Inf Div	B	5E	385 FS, 364 FG	A
47	83rd Inf Div	B	5F	147	5
48	90th Inf Div	B	5F	5 ERS	A
49	2nd Arm Div	B	5G	299	5
4A	310 TCS, 315 TCG	A	5G	299 RNethAF	11
4B	2 GCF	5	5H	668 BS, 416 BG	A
4B	5 GCF	5	5H	SF Chivenor	5
4C	36 TCS, 316 TCG	A	5I	643 BS, 409 BG	A
4D	74	11	5I	SF Benson	11
4D	74	5	5J	126	5
4E	1687 BDTF	5	5K	39 MU	11
4F	837 BS, 487 BG	A	5K	86 TCS, 437 TCG	A
4H	142	5	5L	187	5
4J	3(C)OTU	5	5M	15 RS, 10 PG	A
4J	305 TCS, 442 TCG	A	5M	15 RS, 67 RG	A
4J	5 MU	5	5N	38 GCF	5
4K	506 FS, 404 FG	A	5O	521	5
4K	SF West Malling	11	5Q	504 FS, 339 FG	A
4L	574 BS, 391 BG	A	5R	33	11
4L	SF Melton Mowbray	5	5R	33	5
4M	34	11	5S	691	11
4M	695	11	5S	691	5
4M	695	5	5T	233	5
4N	394 FS, 367 FG	A	5V	439	5
4N	833 BS, 486 BG	A	5W	587 BS, 394 BG	A
4P	513 FS, 406 FG	A	5X	48 TCS, 313 TCG	A

Code	Unit	See Chapter or Appendix	Code	Unit	See Chapter or Appendix
5Y	384 FS, 364 FG	A	7E	327	5
5Z	856 BS, 492 BG	A	7E	327 RNethAF	11
6*	756 BS, 459 BG	A	7E	327/ GC 1/3	11
62	III Corps Arty	B	7F	485 FS, 370 FG	A
63	Arty HQ, 9th Army	B	7G	641 BS, 409 BG	A
65	94th Inf Div	B	7G	SF Northolt	5
67	9th Arm Div	B	7H	306 TCS, 442 TCG	A
68	XIII Corps Arty	B	7H	84 GCF	5
69	XII Corps Arty	B	7I	497 BS, 344 BG	A
6A	700 RNethAF	11	7I	SF Acklington	5
6A	789 BS, 467 BG	A	7J	508 FS, 404 FG	A
6B	599 BS, 397 BG	A	7J	7 BAF	11
6B	SF Tempsford	5	7K	ASRTU	5
6C	14 LS	A	7L	59 OTU	5
6C	14 LS	B	7N	SFU	5
6C	PRDU	11	7N	SFU/CSE	11
6D	20	11	7O	?	5
6D	631	11	7Q	850 BS, 490 BG	A
6D	631	5	7R	524	5
6E	44 TCS, 316 TCG	A	7S	83 GSU	5
6F	1669 HCU	5	7T	196	5
6G	223	5	7U	23 FS, 36 FG	A
6H	1688 BDTF	5	7U	SF Bardney	5
6H	96	5	7V	752 BS, 458 BG	A
6J	34	11	7W	848 BS, 490 BG	A
6K	730 BS, 452 BG	A	7X	645 BS, 410 BG	A
6L	787 BS, 466 BG	A	7X	SF Aldergrove	5
6M	1 PTS	5	7Y	429 FS, 474 FG	A
6M	494 FS, 48 FG	A	7Z	105 OTU	5
6N	505 FS, 339 FG	A	7Z	1381 (T)CU	11
6O	582	5	7Z	1381 (T)CU	5
6Q	647 BS, 410 BG	A	8*	758 BS, 459 BG	A
6Q	SF Pembroke Dock	5	86	78th Inf Div	B
6R	41 OTU	5	87	84th Inf Div	B
6S	190	5	89	99th Inf Div	B
6T	608	11	8A	298	5
6T	608	5	8A	298 RNethAF	11
6U	415	5	8C	100 TCS, 441 TCG	A
6V	53 FS, 36 FG	A	8C	12 MU	5
6V	SF Cottesmore	5	8D	220	11
6X	854 BS, 491 BG	A	8E	295	5
6Y	171	5	8F	105 (T)OTU	5
6Z	19 MU	5	8H	8 GCF	5
6Z	96 TCS, 440 TCG	A	8I	18 BS, 34 BG	A
7*	757 BS, 459 BG	A	8I	2 APS	5
70	? 42nd Inf Div	B	8I	APS Acklington	11
72	2nd French Arm Div	B	8J	326	5
73	17th AB Div	B	8J	326/ GC 2/7	11
74	26th Inf Div	B	8J	435	5
75	4th Inf Div	B	8K	571	5
76	?	B	8L	393 FS, 367 FG	A
78	10th Arm Div	B	8L	92	11
79	280th FABn	B	8M	266	5
7A	614	11	8M	862 BS, 493 BG	A
7B	5	11	8N	405 FS, 371 FG	A
7B	595	11	8O	BAFO CW	5
7B	595	5	8O	9th AF Recon Sqn	A
7C	296	5	8P	525	5
7D	57 MU	5	8Q	291	5
7D	731 BS, 452 BG	A	8Q	34	11
7D	80 TCS, 436 TCG	A	8Q	695	11

Code	Unit	See Chapter or Appendix	Code	Unit	See Chapter or Appendix
8R	153 LS	A	A	201	15
8R	153 LS	B	A	202	15
8R	846 BS, 489 BG	A	A	217	15
8S	31 BAF	11	A	229 OCU (65(R))	17
8S	328 RNethAF	11	A	233 OCU	17
8T	298	5	A	234	14
8T	314 RNethAF	11	A	256	14
8U	646 BS, 410 BG	A	A	266	14
8U	SF Ballykelly	5	A	3	14
8V	31 PS, 10 PG	A	A	3	17
8V	61 OTU	5	A	5	17
8W	612	11	A	8	5
8W	612	5	A	9	17
8X	31 BG/ GB 1/22	11	A	17	17
8Y	15 MU	5	A	39/1 PRU	17
8Y	98 TCS, 440 TCG	A	A	42	15
8Z	295	5	A	43	17
9*	759 BS, 459 BG	A	A	56(R)	17
92	?	B	A	68	14
93	103rd Inf Div	B	A	72	17
94	106th Inf Div	B	A	81	5
97	14th Arm Div	B	A	93	14
9A	858 BS, 492 BG	A	A	94	14
9B	436 FS, 479 FG	A	A	126	5
9C	82 OTU	5	A	541	14
9D	401 FS, 370 FG	A	A	879	C
9E	312 TCS, 349 TCG	A	A	4 FTS	16
9E	BAFO Comms Flt	5	A	5 RFU	5
9F	597 BS, 397 BG	A	A	131 OTU	5
9F	SF Stradishall	5	A	5th Army Arty HQ	B
9G	441	5	A	32 BS, 301 BG	A
9H	857 BS, 492 BG	A	A	95 FS, 82 FG	A
9I	326	5	A	RAFC	16
9I	326 RNethAF	11	A0	783	C
9J	227	5	A1	737	C
9K	1 TTU	11	A1	754	C
9M	1690 B(D)TF	5	A1	767	C
9N	127	5	A1	769	C
9O	44 MU	5	A1	827	C
9O	85 TCS, 437 TCG	A	A1	828	C
9P	85 OTU	5	A2	514	5
9Q	404 FS, 371 FG	A	A2	737	C
9R	229	5	A2	741	C
9S	14 LS	A	A2	810	C
9S	MAEE	5	A2	812	C
9T	SFU	5	A3	1653 CU	5
9U	644	5	A3	230 OCU	11
9V	GC 2/5	11	A3	741	C
9W	296	5	A3	753	C
9X	1689 Flt	11	A3	814	C
9X	1689 Flt	5	A3	818	C
9X	95 TCS, 440 TCG	A	A4	115	5
9Y	132 OCU	5	A4	195	5
9Y	20 MU	5	A4	719	C
9Z	728 BS, 452 BG	A	A4	740	C
A	1 RAAF	6	A4	751	C
A	112	14	A4	753	C
A	118	14	A4	794	C
A	120	15	A4	795	C
A	14	17	A4	820	C
A	19	17	A5	3 LFS	5

Code	Unit	See Chapter or Appendix
A5	740	C
A5	753	C
A5	754	C
A5	794	C
A5	818	C
A5	821	C
A6	1833	C
A6	257	11
A6	389 FS, 366 FG	A
A6	753	C
A6	783	C
A6	800	C
A7	1830	C
A7	395 FS, 368 FG	A
A7	753	C
A7	801	C
A7	803	C
A8	391 FS, 366 FG	A
A8	791	C
A8	803	C
A9	160 RS, 363 RG	A
A9	380 FS, 363 FG	A
A9	710	C
A9	791	C
A9	SF	C
A9	SF Woodbridge	5
AA	1st Arm Div Arty HQ	B
AA	400 RCAF	11
AA	75	11
AA	75	5
AA	personal code	18
AA4	751	C
AA5	740	C
AA5	751	C
AAC	personal code	18
AAY	personal code	18
AB	1557 RATF	5
AB	1st Arm Div 27th FA Bn	B
AB	401 RCAF	11
AB	423	5
AC	?	5
AC	138	11
AC	1st Arm Div 68th FA Bn	B
AC	402 RCAF	11
AC	736	C
ACB	personal code	18
ACS	personal code	18
AD	?	5
AD	113	5
AD	1st Arm Div 91st FA Bn	B
AD	251	5
AD	403 RCAF	11
AD	60	4
AD	personal code	18
ADJL	personal code	18
ADS	personal code	18
AE	130 RCAF	7
AE	1409 Flt	5
AE	402	5
AE	59	5
AF	404 RCAF	11
AF	6 RCAF	7
AF	607	5
AF	AFDU	5
AF	GC 3/6	11
AF	personal code	18
AFO	personal code	18
AG	?	5
AG	122 RCAF	7
AG	330 BS, 93 BG	A
AG	334	5
AG	4 IAF	8
AG	405 RCAF	11
AG	personal code	18
AGM	personal code	18
AGP	personal code	18
AH	332	5
AH	332 RNorAF	11
AH	406 RCAF	11
AH4	735	C
AH7	735	C
AH8	707	C
AH8	SF	C
AHD	personal code	18
AI	20 OTU	5
AI	Fictitious	F
AI16	personal code	18
AJ	356 FS, 354 FG	A
AJ	407 RCAF	11
AJ	617	17
AJ	617	5
AJ	SF North Luffenham	5
AJ	personal code	18
AK	? 334 RNorAF	11
AK	1657 CU	5
AK	213	11
AK	213	4
AK	213	5
AK	408 RCAF	11
AKG	personal code	18
AL	429	5
AL	429	5
AL	? 52	5
AL	79	4
AL	personal code	18
ALW	personal code	18
AM	14 OTU	5
AM	410 RCAF	11
AM	77 RAAF	6
AMT	personal code	18
AN	13	4
AN	13 RCAF	7
AN	160 RCAF	7
AN	411 RCAF	11
AN	417	5
AN	553 BS, 386 BG	A
AN	SF Gt Dunmow	5
AO	211	4
AO	223	5
AO	412 RCAF	11
AO	AFDU?	5
AP	? TCS, ? TCG	A

Code	Unit	See Chapter or Appendix	Code	Unit	See Chapter or Appendix
AP	130	11	AX	202	5
AP	130	5	AX	421 RCAF	11
AP	186	5	AX	77 OTU	5
AP	413 RCAF	11	AY	110	4
AP	72	11	AY	110 RCAF	7
AP	80	5	AY	17 OTU	5
APS	APS Lubeck	11	AZ	234	5
AQ	14 RCAF	7	AZ	3 OTU RCAF	7
AQ	276	5	AZ	4 GTTF	A
AQ	414 RCAF	11	AZ	627	5
AR	309	5	AZ	717 RNorAF	11
AR	460	5	B	2	14
AR	772 ?	C	B	4	14
AR0	730	C	B	5	14
AR1	705	C	B	11	17
AR2	710	C	B	14	14
AR2	713	C	B	14	17
AR2	747	C	B	17	17
AR3	710	C	B	18	17
AR3	713	C	B	29	17
AR3	747	C	B	67	14
AR4	710	C	B	87	14
AR4	713	C	B	92	17
AR4	747	C	B	111	17
AR5	710	C	B	130	14
AR5	713	C	B	145	14
AR5	747	C	B	203	15
AR6	710	C	B	206	15
AR7	710	C	B	224	15
AR8	772	C	B	230	15
AR8	SF Ronaldsway	C	B	242	5
AR9	772	C	B	269	15
AS	166	4	B	750	C
AS	166	5	B	881	C
AS	416 RCAF	11	B	4 FTS	16
AS	Op Goodwill	11	B	131 OTU	5
AT	417 RCAF	11	B	231 OCU	17
AT	60 OTU	5	B	CTSF	17
AT1	714	C	B	CTSF/39	17
AT2	714	C	B	personal code	18
AT3	717	C	B	RAFC	16
AT4	717	C	B	SAOEU	17
AU	148	11	B	SAOEU	17
AU	418 RCAF	11	B	WCF	17
AU	421	5	B	2 RAAF	6
AU	PTS RNorAF	11	B	96 FS, 82 FG	A
AV	121	5	B	352 BS, 301 BG	A
AV	335 FS, 4 FG	A	B	II Corps Arty HQ	B
AV	Wittering SF	5	B0	784	C
AV	personal code	18	B0	898	C
AVH	personal code	18	B1	814	C
AVRJ	personal code	18	B2	390 FS, 366 FG	A
AW	339 BS, 96 BG	A	B2	768	C
AW	42	5	B2	TTF BAF	11
AW	420 RCAF	11	B3	161 RS, 363 RG	A
AW	504	4	B3	381 FS, 363 FG	A
AW	personal code	18	B3	SF Wyton	11
AX	1 SAAF	11	B4	282	5
AX	1 SAAF	10	B4	282	5
AX	107 RS, 67 RG	A	B4	387 FS, 365 FG	A
AX	14 RNZAF	9	B6	363 FS, 357 FG	A

Code	Unit	See Chapter or Appendix
B6	SF Spilsby	5
B7	374 FS, 361 FG	A
B7	896	C
B7	SF Waddington	5
B8	379 FS, 362 FG	A
B8	701	C
B8	705	C
B8	770	C
B8	782	C
B8	896	C
B8	SF Woodhall Spa	5
B9	?	C
B9	1562 Met Flt	5
B9	544 FS, 357 FTG	A
B9	898	C
BA	125 RCAF	7
BA	277	5
BA	654 BS, 25 BG	A
BA	3rd Inf Div Arty HQ	B
BA	424 RCAF	11
BA	personal code	18
BAE	personal code	18
BB	226 OCU	11
BB	27 OTU	5
BB	3rd Inf Div, 9th FA Bn	B
BB	425 RCAF	11
BB	427 RCAF	11
BC	3rd Inf Div, 10th FA Bn	B
BC	426 RCAF	11
BD	227 OCU	11
BD	3rd Inf Div, 39th FA Bn	B
BD	4 RCAF	7
BD	43 OTU	5
BD	51 OTU	5
BD	personal code	18
BE	237 OCU	11
BE	3rd Inf Div, 41st FA Bn	B
BE	720 RNorAF	11
BE	8 OTU	11
BE	8 OTU	5
BF	14	4
BF	14 RCAF	7
BF	28	5
BF	5 RAAF	6
BF	54 OTU	5
BF	personal code	18
BFR	personal code	18
BG	334 BS, 95 BG	A
BG	660	5
BH	215	4
BH	228	4
BH	300	5
BH	430 RCAF	11
BH	personal code	18
BH1	718	C
BH2	718	C
BH6	718	C
BI	568 BS, 390 BG	A
BJ	271	5
BJ	SF Holme	5
BK	115	4
BK	115	5
BK	115 RCAF	7
BK	35 RAAF	6
BK	546 BS, 384 BG	A
BK	personal code	18
BK	SSCF	11
BL	1656 HCU	5
BL	40	11
BL	40	5
BL	609	4
BL3	765	C
BM	433	5
BN	?	5
BN	1401 Met Flt	5
BN	170	5
BN	240	5
BN	359 BS, 303 BG	A
BN	435 RCAF	11
BO	368 BS, 306 BG	A
BO	436 RCAF	11
BOG	personal code	18
BQ	438 RCAF	11
BQ	451	5
BQ	550	5
BQ	600	5
BR	184	5
BR	434 RCAF	11
BR8	772	C
BR9	772 ?	C
BR9	SF Ayr	C
BS	120	11
BS	148	4
BS	160	11
BS	160	5
BS	1651 CU	5
BS	Trenton SF RCAF	11
BT	113	4
BT	113 RCAF	7
BT	1686 BDTF	5
BT	252	5
BT	30 OTU	5
BT	33 RAAF	6
BT	441 RCAF	11
BT	personal code	18
BTU	BTU	18
BU	214	5
BU	442 RCAF	11
BU	80 RAAF	6
BU	BAD 1	A
BV	102 RAAF	6
BV	126 RCAF	7
BV	444 RCAF	11
BW	335 RNorAF	11
BW	58	4
BWR	personal code	18
BX	?	5
BX	338 BS, 96 BG	A
BX	666	5
BX	86	5
BY	23 OTU	5
BY	58	5

Code	Unit	See Chapter or Appendix	Code	Unit	See Chapter or Appendix
BY	59	11	C6	804	C
BY	59	5	C7	1 FP	5
BY0	790	C	C7	555 FS, 496FTG	A
BY1	780	C	C7	786	C
BY8	794	C	C7	805	C
BZ	107	4	C7	808	C
BZ	127	5	C8	640	5
BZ	82 OTU	5	C8	701	C
BZ	86 OTU	5	C8	705	C
BZ	AAS RCAF	11	C8	733	C
C	3	17	C8	770	C
C	4	17	C8	786	C
C	5	17	C8	804	C
C	17	17	C9	718	C
C	20	17	C9	733	C
C	33	17	C9	GC1/5	11
C	100	17	C9	SF Crail	C
C	654	5	CA	112 (T)Rt RCAF	11
C	899	C	CA	189	5
C	131 OTU	5	CA	3SAAF	10
C	228 OCU (64(R))	17	CA	34thInfDivArtyHQ	B
C	236 OCU	15	CA	Edmonton SF RCAF	1
C	237 OCU	17	CAG	personal code	18
C	2 TAF CS	14	B	125thFABn	B
C	3 RAAF	6	B	31	11
C	RAFC	16	B	CACCF RCAF	11
C	VI Corps Arty HQ	B	B	MCS	11
C	97 FS, 82 FG	A	B	MCS	5
C	353 BS, 301 BG	A	C	123RFRCAF	11
C0	778	C	CC	151st FABn	B
C1	407	5	CC	569BS,390BG	A
C1	711	C	CC	SF Holmsley South	5
C1	785	C	CD	?RCAF	11
C1	786	C	CD	175th FA Bn	B
C2	396 FS, 368 FG	A	CD	Fictitious	F
C2	711	C	CE	1668 HCU/5 LFS	5
C2	785	C	CE	185th FABn	B
C2	786	C	CE	Army FA RNorAF	11
C2	BCIS	5	CEM	personal code	18
C3	?	11	CEO	personal code	18
C3	162 RS, 363 RG	A	CF	?RCAF	11
C3	382 FS, 363 FG	A	CF	625	5
C3	711	C	CFA	personal code	18
C3	785	C	CFB	personal code	18
C3	786	C	CFC	personal code	18
C3	800	C	CFG	personal code	18
C3	815	C	CG	38 FS, 55 FG	A
C4	388 FS, 365 FG	A	CG	personal code	18
C4	711	C	CG	Sea Island SF RCAF	11
C4	785	C	CG	SF Binbrook	5
C4	786	C	CGL	personal code	18
C4	816	C	CGP	personal code	18
C5	364 FS, 357 FG	A	CH	SF Swin derby	5
C5	364 FS, 357 FG	A	CH	103 S&R Fit RCAF	11
C5	711	C	CH	365 FS, 358 FG	A
C5	785	C	CI	576 BS, 392 BG	A
C5	786	C	CI	personal code	18
C5	817	C	CJ	123 RFRCAF	11
C5	SF Tibbenham	5	CJ	203	11
C6	51	5	CJ	203	5
C6	711	C	CJ	71 TCS, 434 TCG	A

Code	Unit	See Chapter or Appendix
CJ	personal code	18
CK	CEPE RCAF	11
CL	SF Little Staughton	5
CL	?RCAF	11
CL	338 FS, 55 FG	A
CM	107 OTU	5
CM	1333(T)CU	11
CM	42 GCF	5
CM	78 TCS, 435 TCG	A
CM	personal code	18
CMM	personal code	18
CN	73 TCS, 434 TCG	A
CO	84 OTU	5
CO	FIU	5
CP	SF Topcliffe	5
CP	367 FS, 358 FG	A
CQ	708 BS, 447 BG	A
CQ	CNS RCAF	11
CR	162	11
CR	162	5
CR	370 FS, 359 FG	A
CR	personal code	18
CRC	personal code	18
CS	13 RAAF	6
CS	513	5
CS	SF Upwood	11
CSV	personal code	18
CT	52 OTU	5
CT	712 BS, 448 BG	A
CU	72 TCS, 434 TCG	A
CV	3 RAAF	6
CV	3 RAAF	5
CV	368 FS, 359 FG	A
CV	RAF test RCAF	11
CV	SF Tuddenham	5
CW	76 TCS, 435 TCG	A
CWL	personal code	18
CX	107 RU RCAF	11
CX	14	11
CX	14	5
CY	343 FS, 55 FG	A
CY	SF Ludford Magna	5
CZ	412 (Jet Fit) RCAF	11
CZ	84 OTU	5
D	11	17
D	31	17
D	207	17
D	230	17
D	131 OTU	5
D	235 OCU	15
D	4FTS	16
D	4 FTS (208(R))	17
D	4 FTS (234(R))	17
D	6 FTS	16
D	7 FTS	16
D	CGS	5
D	LTF	17
D	RAFC	16
D	4 RAAF	6
D	419 BS, 301 BG	A
D1	737	C
D1	784	C
D1	790 B	C
D2	1606 Fit	5
D2	732	C
D2	784	C
D3	397 FS, 368 FG	A
D3	784	C
D4	?	C
D4	620	5
D4	879	C
D5	386 FS, 365 FG	A
D5	784	C
D5	807	C
D6	642 BS, 409 BG	A
D6	809	C
D6	885	C
D6	SF Hethel	5
D7	503 FS, 339 FG	A
D8	22 MU	5
D8	770	C
D8	94 TCS, 439 TCG	A
DA	?	5
DA	1FTS RCAF	11
DA	1322 Fltor ADLS	5
DA	153 RS, 67 RG	A
DA	210	5
DA	273 MU	5
DA	36th Inf Div, Arty HQ	B
DA	Trenton TT Fit RCAF?	11
DAB	personal code	18
DAM	personal code	18
DB	1FTS RCAF	11
DB	11 OTU SAAF	10
DB	131st FABn	B
DB2	2 SAAF	11
DB	2 SAAF	10
DB	3 CU RAAF	6
DB	411	5
DB	personal code	18
DBH	personal code	18
DC	132nd FABn	B
DC	577 BS, 392 BG	A
DC	CFS RCAF	11
DC	personal code	18
DC	SF Oakington	5
DD	133rd FABn	B
DD	15 RAAF	6
DD	22 OTU	5
DD	45	4
DD	CEPE RCAF	11
DE	155th FABn	B
DE	5 RCAF	7
DE	61 OTU	11
DE	61 OTU	5
DEK	personal code	18
DF	?RCAF	11
DF	221	5
DF	324 BS, 91 BG	A
DF	CBE	11
DFS	personal code	18
DG	150	4

Code	Unit	See Chapter or Appendix	Code	Unit	See Chapter or Appendix
DG	155	5	DU	312	11
DG	422	5	DU	312	5
DG	AROS RCAF	11	DU	312RNethAF	11
DGA	personal code	18	DU	341/ GC 3/2	11
DGH	personal code	18	DU	EC 2/2 AdlA	11
DGM	personal code	18	DU	70	4
DGS	personal code	18	D	SF Skeabrae	5
DH	1ANS RCAF	11	DV	129	5
DH	1664 CU	5	DV	237	5
DH	540	11	DV	271	5
DH	personal code	18	DV	77	11
DHL	personal code	18	DV	93	11
DI	570BS,390BG	A	DW	93	5
DI	SF Kemble	5	DW	610	11
DJ	15. C Fit	5	DW	610	5
DJ	2 (M) OTU RCAF	11	DW	personal code	18
DJ	450	5	DX	230	5
DJ	North Bay TF RCAF	11	DX	245	5
DJF	personal code	18	DX	4SAAF	10
DJS	personal code	18	DX	57	11
DJW	personal code	18	DX	57	5
DK	158	5	DY	102	5
DK	32 OTU RCAF	7	DZ	151	5
DK	AAS RCAF	11	DZ	162 RCAF	7
DK	personal code	18	E	6	17
DL	432 RCAF	11	E	7	17
DL	54	4	E	15	17
DL	54	5	E	23	17
DL	91	11	E	360	17
DL	91	5	E	800	C
DL	92	11	E	730TU	5
DL	421 Fit	5	E	7FTS	16
DM	119 RCAF	7	E	5RAAF	6
DM	248	5	E	17th FA Gp, 7th Army	B
DM	36	11	E1	?	C
DMA	personal code	18	E1	767	C
DN	416	E	E1	769	C
DN	416	5	E2	375 FS, 361 FG	A
DO	personal code	18	E2	767	C
DO	Fictitious	F	E2	768	C
DP	140	5	E2	769	C
DP	193	5	E2	SF Warboys	5
DP	30	4	E3	731	C
DP	718RNorAF	11	E3	732 BS, 453 BG	A
DPA	personal code	18	E4	377 FS, 362 FG	A
DQ	1402 Met Fit	11	E4	731 ?	C
DQ	228	5	E4	769	C
DQ	41RAAF	6	E4	813	C
DQ	551 FS, 495FTG	A	E4	SF Wickenby	5
DR	1555 RATF	5	E5	62 TCS, 314 TCG	A
DR	1697 ADLS	5	E5	824	C
DRS	452BS,322BG	A	E6	402 FS, 370 FG	A
DRW	personal code	18	E6	731 ?	C
DS	personal code	18	E7	570	5
DS	511 BS,351 BG	A	E8	702	C
DS	personal code	18	E8	733 BS, 453 BG	A
DT	SF Llanbedr	5	E8	SF	C
DT	192	5	E9	376 FS, 361 FG	A
DT	257	5	E9	SF Westcott	5
DU	personal code	18	EA	145 RCAF	7
DU	22 RAAF	6	EA	45th Inf Div Arty HQ	B

Code	Unit	See Chapter or Appendix	Code	Unit	See Chapter or Appendix
EA	49	11	EP	84GCF	5
EA	49	5	EP	84GCF	11
EB	158th FABn	B	EP	personal code	18
EB	30 BAF	11	EPA	personal code	18
EB	41	4	EPW	personal code	18
EB	41	11	EQ	?	5
EB	41	5	EQ	408	5
EC	160th FABn	B	EQ	57	4
EC	578 BS, 392 BG	A	EQ	Fictitious	F
EC	personal code	18	ER	258	5
EC	PRDU	11	ER	1552 RATF	11
EC	SF Odiham	5	ER	450 BS, 322 BG	A
EC	SF Odiham	11	ERB	personal code	18
ED	171st FABn	B	ES	13 PS, 7 PG	A
ED	21 OTU	5	ES	229 OCU	11
ED	4 OTU RCAF	7	ES	48 FS, 12 FG	A
ED	78	4	ES	48 FS, 14 FG	A
ED	personal code	18	ES	541	5
EDM	personal code	18	ES	82	11
EE	16	4	ES	personal code	18
EE	16	5	ET	2 OTU RCAF	7
EE	189th FABn	B	ET	336 BS, 95 BG	A
EE	31	5	ET	435 RCAF	11
EE	404	5	ET	662	5
EE	565 BS, 389 BG	A	ET	personal code	18
EE	SF Elvington	5	EU	26 OTU	5
EF	102	11	EV	1 CU RAAF	6
EF	15	4	EV	180	5
EF	232	5	EV	13 OTU	5
EF	36 OTU RCAF	7	EW	307	5
EG	16	11	EW	47	4
EG	268	11	EW-?	personal code	18
EG	34	5	EWW	personal code	18
EG	487	5	EX	11	11
EH	31 RAAF	6	EX	117 RCAF	7
EH	55 OTU	5	EX	199	5
EH	personal code	18	EY	233	4
EHT	personal code	18	EY	60 RAAF	6
EI	714 BS, 448 BG	A	EY	78	11
EJ	127	5	EY	78	5
EJ	CCFIS, CCIS	5	EY	80	5
EJ	personal code	18	EZ	1380 TSCU	5
EJC	personal code	18	EZ	81 OTU	5
EK	1656 HCU	5	F	12	17
EK	168	5	F	16	17
EL	?600	5	F	25	17
EL	10 OTU	5	F	41	17
EL	181	5	F	81, 151 Wing	5
EL	SF	C	F	154?	5
ELM	personal code	18	F	185	5
EM	207	11	F	842	C
EM	207	5	F	72 OTU	5
EMD	personal code	18	F	240 OCU	17
EN	121 RCAF	7	F	2FTS	16
EN	18 OTU	5	F	4FTS	16
ENW	personal code	18	F	6FTS	16
EO	15 OTU	5	F	ASWDU	15
EO	404	5	F	6 RAAF	6
EP	104	11	F	36th FA Gp	B
EP	104	5	F1	714	C
EP	351 BS, 100 BG	A	F1	717	C

Code	Unit	See Chapter or Appendix	Code	Unit	See Chapter or Appendix
F1	747	C	FDH	personal code	18
F2	635	5	FDI-O	CFS	13
F2	714	C	FDQ-T	10FIS.8EFTS	13
F2	717	C	FDU-W	Beam Approach School	13
F2	747	C	FDWCFS	CFS	13
F3	438	5	FDY	SFC,SATC	13
F4	492 FS, 48 FG	A	FE	2 OTU RNZAF	9
F4	747?	C	FE	560TU	5
F4	826	C	FE	6 (C)OTU	5
F5	428 FS, 474FG	A	FE	633rd FA Bn	B
F5	829	C	FEA-E	1 GTS	13
F6	670BS,416BG	A	FEG-K	3GTS	13
F8	734BS,453BG	A	FEP	21HGCU	13
F9	711	C	FF	132	5
F9	SF	C	FF	178thFABn	B
FA	13thFABgde	B	FFA-D	10AGS	13
FA	236	5	FFF-G	HAGS	13
FA	281	5	FFI-K	5 ANS, 1 ANS	13
FA	82 RAAF	6	FFM-P	7ANS,2ANS	13
FA	OS RNorAF	11	FFS-V	10 ANS	13
FA	personal code	18	FG	194thFABn	B
FAA-G	19 SFTS, FTS, RAFC	13	FG	283	5
FAH	personal code	18	FG	335	5
FAI-M	20SFTS,2FTS	13	FG	433 RCAF	11
FAN-P	21 SFTS	13	FG	7 RCAF	7
FAS-T	16(P)FTS	13	FG	72	11
FB	17th FA Bn	B	FG	personal code	18
FB	24 OTU	5	FG	-	F
FB	35	11	FGA-B	EAAS, RAFFC	13
FB	CEPE RCAF	11	FGB	personal code	18
FB	personal code	18	FGC	EAAS, RAFFC	13
FB	WCU	11	FGE-G	EANS, CNS, CNCS	13
FBA-E	7 SFTS, 7 FTS	13	FGG	personal code	18
FBG-K	6 SFTS, 6 FTS	13	FH	141stFABn	B
FBP-V	3 SFTS. 3 FTS	13	FH	15 OTU	5
FC	571 BS,390BG	A	FH	53	5
FC	630th FA Bn	B	FH	personal code	18
FC	CEPE RCAF	11	FHA-B	1 EFTS	13
FC	personal code	18	FHE-G	2 EFTS	13
FC	SF Kenley	5	FHI-K	3 EFTS	13
FC	SF Northolt	5	FHM-O	4 EFTS	13
FCA-C	17SFTS,FTS,1 FTS	13	FHP	personal code	18
FCCS	personal code	18	FHQ-S	6 EFTS	13
FCD-G	17SFTS,FTS,1 FTS	13	FHV-X	7 EFTS	13
FCI-M	22 SFTS, 22 FTS	13	FI	173rd FA Bn	B
FCT	EC FS, E FS, RAFC	13	FI	830TU	5
FCT	personal code	18	FI	WTU	5
FCU-Y	EC FS, E FS, RAFC	13	FIC	11 EFTS	13
FD	114	4	FIJ-K	15 EFTS	13
FD	1659HCU	5	FIN-P	16 EFTS	13
FD	294	5	FIR-S	18 EFTS	13
FD	34 RAAF	6	FIV-X	21 EFTS	13
FD	36th FA Bn	B	FJ	11 RAAF	6
FD1	813	C	FJ	164	5
FD3	704	C	FJ	248th FA Bn	B
FD4	811	C	FJ	261	5
FD5	762	C	FJ	37	4
FD6	762	C	FJ	63	11
FD8	720	C	FJA-D	22 EFTS	13
FD9	778	C	FJF-G	24 EFTS	13
FDA-H	21(P)AFU,1(P)RFU	13	FJJ-K	28 EFTS	13

Code	Unit	See Chapter or Appendix
FJN-P	29 EFTS	13
FJR-X	CGS	13
FK	209	4
FK	219	5
FK	631stFABn	B
FKA-B	1511 BAT Fit	13
FKD	1537 BAT Fit	13
FKF	1547 BAT Fit	13
FKN	FTC Comms Fit	13
FKO	21 Gp Comms Fit	13
FKP	23 Gp Comms Fit	13
FKQ	25 Gp Comms Fit	13
FKR	54 Gp Comms Fit	13
FKS	SF Cranwell	13
FL	634th FA Bn	B
FL	704BS,446BG	A
FL	81	5
FLA	Cambridge UAS	13
FLB	Aberdeen UAS	13
FLC	Edinburgh UAS	13
FLD	Glasgow UAS	13
FLE	Queens (Belfast) UAS	13
FLF	St Andrews UAS	13
FLG	Liverpool UAS	13
FLH	Manchester UAS	13
FLI	Leeds UAS	13
FLJ	Durham UAS	13
FLK	Birmingham UAS	13
FLL	Nottingham UAS	13
FLM	Bristol UAS	13
FLN	Swansea UAS	13
FLO	London UAS	13
FLP	Southampton UAS	13
FLQ	Oxford UAS	13
FLR	Perth UAS	13
FLS	Wolverhampton UAS	13
FLT	Derby UAS	13
FLU	Yatesbury UAS	13
FLV	Cambridge UAS	13
FM	257	5
FMA-B	201 AFS	13
FMD	personal code	18
FME	202 AFS	13
FMI-K	203 AFS	13
FMO	204 AFS	13
FMT	personal code	18
FN	133 RCAF	7
FN	331	5
FN	331 RNorAF	11
FN	453	5
FN	932nd FA Bn	B
FN	personal code	18
FO	1665HCU	5
FO	527 BS, 379 BG	A
FO	75	4
FO	933rd FA Bn	B
FO	SF Wick	5
FOG	personal code	18
FP	1683BDTF	5
FP	935th FA Bn	B
FQ	120TU	5

Code	Unit	See Chapter or Appendix
FR	525 BS, 379 BG	A
FR	936th FA Bn	B
FR	SF Mansion	5
FRC	personal code	18
FS	148	5
FS	937th FA Bn	B
FS	personal code	18
FSC	personal code	18
FT	353 FS, 354 FG	A
FT	43	5
FT	938th FA Bn	B
FT	SF Mildenhall	5
FU	453	5
FU	458	5
FU	939th FA Bn	B
FV	130TU	11
FV	130TU	5
FV	205	5
FV	230	4
FV	976 FA Bn	B
FW	556 BS, 387 BG	A
FW	SF Rivenhall	5
FX	234	11
FX	266	11
FX	6RAAF	6
FX	62	5
FX	3 TEU	5
FX	977th FA Bn	B
FY	34 OTU RCAF	7
FY	4	4
FY	4 RCAF	7
FY	611	5
FY	611	11
FY	985th FA Bn	B
FZ	100	5
FZ	23 OTU	5
FZ	65	4
FZ	94	5
FZ	995th FA Bn	B
G	20	17
G	43	17
G	54	17
G	87	5
G	134, 151 Wing	5
G	813	C
G	2FTS	16
G	4FTS	16
G	5 FTS	16
G	JASS	15
G	7 RAAF	6
G	77th FA Gp	B
G1	?	C
G1	718	C
G1	761	C
G2	19 GCF	11
G2	19 GCF	5
G2	22 PS, 7 PG	A
G2	761	C
G3	718	C
G3	761	C
G3	812	C

Code	Unit	See Chapter or Appendix	Code	Unit	See Chapter or Appendix
G4	362 FS, 357 FG	A	GI	622	5
G4	761	C	GI	985th FA Bn	B
G4	SF Skellingthorpe	5	GJ	213	4
G5	190	5	GJ	1 (F) OTU RCAF	11
G5	761	C	GJ	63 or 12 OTU	5
G5	825	C	GJ	68 BS, 44 BG	A
G6	761	C	GJ	SF Duxford	5
G6	802	C	GK	162 RCAF	7
G6	863 BS, 493 BG	A	GK	459	5
G6	MCCS	5	GK	52 OTU	5
G7	BCFEU	5	GK	80	4
G8	378 FS, 362 FG	A	GKG	personal code	18
G8	HQ Flt	C	GL	11 OTU SAAF	10
G8	SF Wing	5	GL	14 OTU	5
G9	430	5	GL	1529 RATF	5
G9	509 FS, 405 FG	A	GL	185	5
G9	712	C	GL	410 BS, 94 BG	A
G9	SF Henstridge	C	GL	5 SAAF	10
GA	? RCAF	11	GL	personal code	18
GA	112	5	GM	1 FTS RCAF	11
GA	16 OTU	5	GM	18 (NEI) RAAF	6
GA	18th FA Bgde HQ	B	GM	42 OTU	5
GA	208	4	GM	personal code	18
GA	21 RAAF	6	GN	10 RAAF	6
GA	75 RAAF	6	GN	10 RAAF	5
GA	8 RCAF	7	GN	249	11
GAM	personal code	18	GN	249	5
GB	? RCAF	11	GN	427 BS, 303 BG	A
GB	105	5	GN	BDU	5
GB	141st FA Bn	B	GN	CBE	11
GB	166	4	GO	328 BS, 93 BG	A
GB	Op Goodwill	11	GO	42 OTU	5
GBJ	personal code	18	GO	94	5
GC	137 Tspt Flt RCAF	11	GO	CFE	11
GC	173rd FA Bn	B	GO	FIS RCAF	11
GC	579 BS, 392 BG	A	GP	1 FTS RCAF	11
GC	personal code	18	GP	1661 HCU	5
GC	SF Pershore	5	GP	personal code	18
GCK	personal code	18	GP0	771	C
GD	932nd FA Bn	B	GP2	727	C
GD	FIS RCAF	11	GP8	771	C
GD	personal code	18	GP9	771	C
GD	SF Horsham St Faith	5	GQ	1 (F) OTU RCAF	11
GDE	personal code	18	GQ	134	5
GE	349	5	GQ	355 FS, 354 FG	A
GE	349 BAF	11	GQ	SF North Killingholme	5
GE	58	5	GR	119 RCAF	7
GE	933rd FA Bn	B	GR	1586 SDF	5
GF	1	10A	GR	24 RAAF	6
GF	3 OTU RNZAF	9	GR	301	11
GF	56 OTU	5	GR	301	5
GF	936th FA Bn	B	GR	92	5
GFA	personal code	18	GR	personal code	18
GG	1 FTS RCAF	11	GRC	personal code	18
GG	151	4	GS	330	5
GG	1667 HCU	5	GS	830TU	5
GG	937th FA Bn	B	GS	CFS RCAF	11
GG	personal code	18	GT	156	5
GH	216	11	GT	personal code	18
GH	938th FA Bn	B	GU	18	4
GHB	personal code	18	GU	2 FTS RCAF	11

Code	Unit	See Chapter or Appendix
GV	35	5
GV	103	4
GV	1652 HCU	5
GV	3 CAC del RCAF	7
GV	AAS RCAF	11
GV	Auxiliary Sqn BAF	11
GVW	personal code	18
GW	340	5
GW	340/ GC 4/2	11
GW	400 RCAF	11
GW	personal code	18
GX	415	5
GX	548BS,385BG	A
GX	SF Bradwell	11
GY	109 (T)OTU	5
GY	1383 TSCU	5
GY	367BS,306BG	A
GZ	12	5
GZ	32	11
GZ	32	5
GZ	611	4
H	1 MRS/SMR	15
H	111	17
H	178th FA Gp	B
H	216	11
H	4 FTS	16
H	8RAAF	6
H	807	C
H1	845	C
H2	49TCS,313TCG	A
H3	111 (C)OTU	5
H3	814	C
H4	1653 CU	5
H5	392 FS, 367FG	A
H5	887	C
H6	735BS,453BG	A
H6	894	C
H7	346	5
H7	346/ GB 2/23	11
H8	42 BAF	11
H8	835BS,486BG	A
H9	586BS,394BG	A
H9	712	C
H9	713	C
H9	SF Shepherd's Grove	5
HA	126	5
HA	129 RCAF	7
HA	218	5
HA	71stFABgdeHQ	B
HA3	762	C
HB	194thFABn	B
HB	229	5
HB	239	5
HB	Fictitious	F
HB	personal code	18
HBW	personal code	18
HC	?HCS	11
HC	512	5
HC	935th FA Bn	B
HCG	personal code	18
HD	38	5

Code	Unit	See Chapter or Appendix
HD	466	5
HD	personal code	18
HE	263	11
HE	263	5
HE	605	4
HE	939th FA Bn	B
HE	976th FA Bn	B
HEW	personal code	18
HF	183	5
HF	40 RAA	6
HF	54	11
HF	977th FA Bn	B
HF	Fictitious	F
HFB	personal code	18
HFO'N	personal code	18
HG	154	5
HG	332	5
HG	428 RCAF	11
HG	995th FA Bn	B
HGG	personal code	18
HH	175	5
HH	2 ANS RCAF	11
HH	273	4
HH	273	5
HH	personal code	18
HI	?	5
HI	66	11
HJ	200TU	5
HJ	9 RCAF	7
HJW	personal code	18
HK	269	5
HK	FLS	5
HK	personal code	18
HL	26	4
HL	307 FS, 31 FG	A
HL	83 FS, 78 FG	A
HL	SF Gransden Lodge	5
HL	personal code	18
HM	11 CURAAF	6
HM	136	5
HM	1677TTF	5
HM	32 OTU RCAF	7
HM	personal code	18
HMS	personal code	18
HMT	personal code	18
HN	20	11
HN	20	5
HN	705BS,446BG	A
HN	93	5
HNT	personal code	18
HO	143	5
HO	418 RCAF	11
HO	487 FS, 352FG	A
HO	56 OTU	5
HP	247	5
HP	567 BS, 389 BG	A
HP	GRU	5
HP	SF Full Sutton	5
HPB	personal code	18
HQ	14 RNZAF	9
HQ	56 OTU	5

Code	Unit	See Chapter or Appendix	Code	Unit	See Chapter or Appendix
HQ	FIS RCAF	11	I9	575	5
HQ	GTS RNZAF	9	I9	SF	C
HR	?	5	IA	366 FS, 358 FG	A
HR	551 BS,385BG	A	IA	SF Syerston	5
HR	NEFSF	5	IA	69 RAA	B
HR	personal code	18	IB	43GCF	5
HS	109	11	IB	77 TCS, 435 TCG	A
HS	109	5	IB	GPTF	5
HS	192	5	IB	69 RAA 1 Bn	B
HS	260	5	IC	623	5
HS	3 FTS RCAF	11	IC	SF S campion	11
HT	154	5	IC	69 RAA 2 Bn	B
HT	601	11	ID	74 TCS, 434 TCG	A
HT	3 FTS RCAF	11	ID	69 RAA 3 Bn	B
HT	Fictitious	F	IE	709 BS, 447 BG	A
HU	1 AGS RCAF	11	IF	840 TU	5
HU	220	4	IG	439 RCAF	11
HU	406	5	IG	713 BS, 448 BG	A
HU	78 RAAF	6	IH	1 PFS	A
HV	27 FS, 1 FG	A	II	?	5
HV	61 FS, 56 FG	A	II	116	5
HV	73	4	II	347 BS, 99 BG	A
HV	8	5	II	590TU	5
HV	SF East Kirkby	5	III	348 BS, 99 BG	A
HW	100	11	IJ	710 BS, 447 BG	A
HW	100	5	IK	BCIS	5
HWA	personal code	18	IL	115	5
HWB	personal code	18	IN	613 BS, 401 BG	A
HX	?RCAF	11	IN	SF Valley	5
HX	226 OCU	11	IO	41 OTU	5
HX	61 OTU	5	IO	715 BS, 448 BG	A
HY	88	4	IP	BCIS	5
HY	WPU RCAF	11	IP	BCIS	11
HZ	44 GCF	5	IQ	150	5
I	346 BS, 99 BG	A	IQ	Fighter School BAF	11
I	CFS	16	IR	711 BS, 447BG	A
I0	716	C	IRC	personal code	18
I1	714	C	IRG	personal code	18
I1	766	C	IS	22 BAF	11
I2	48	5	IS	703 BS, 445 BG	A
I2	714	C	IT	?	5
I2	766	C	IT1-7	767	C
I3	714	C	IV	369 FS, 359 FG	A
I3	717	C	IV	416 BS, 99 BG	A
I3	766	C	IV	SF Upper Heyford	5
I3	GC2/3	11	IW	614 BS, 401 BG	A
I4	567	5	IW	SF Chilbolton	5
I4	717	C	IY	615 BS, 401 BG	A
I5	105 (T) OTU	5	IY	SF Dunsfold	5
I5	1381 TSCU	5	J	27	17
I5	769	C	J	93	5
I6	?	C	J	846	C
I6	30 PS, 10 PG	A	J	RAFC	16
I6	32 MU CF	5	J	Op Jural	17
I6	766	C	J	9 RAAF	6
I6	769	C	J	French Corps	B
I7	493 FS, 48 FG	A	J1	794	C
I7	766	C	J2	435 FS, 479 FG	A
I7	815	C	J2	794	C
I8	440	5	J3	755 BS, 458 BG	A
I8	821	C	J3	794	C

Code	Unit	See Chapter or Appendix	Code	Unit	See Chapter or Appendix
J4	753 BS, 458 BG	A	JJ	174	5
J4	758X	C	JJ	274	5
J4	794	C	JJ	422BS,305BG	A
J4	854	C	JK	10 RCAF	7
J5	3	11	JK	personal code	18
J6	1521 RATF	11	JL	10 OTU	5
J6	406 BS, 482 BG	A	JL	Chatham SR Fit RCAF	11
J	303 TCS, 442 TCG	A	JM	20 OTU	5
J7	8MU	5	JM	32 RAAF	6
J8	24 MU	5	JM	personal code	18
J8	92TCS,439TCG	A	JMC	personal code	18
J9	1668 HCU	5	JMR	personal code	18
J9	714	C	JMT	personal code	18
J9	SF Eglinton	C	JN	150	5
JA	100	5	JN	30	11
JA	1652 CU	5	JN	66 RAAF	6
JA	65 Fighter Wing HQ	A	JN	75	5
JA	6th FA Gp HQ	B	JO	463	5
JA	Saskatoon SF RCAF	11	JO	62	4
JAK	personal code	18	JOC	personal code	18
JAM	personal code	18	JP	120TU	5
JAS	personal code	18	JP	21	4
JB	1380 HSCU	5	JP	personal code	18
JB	4 FTS RCAF	11	JQ	2AACU	5
JB	59th Arm FA Bn	B	JQ	SF Breighton	5
JB	81 OTU	5	JR	161	5
JB	personal code	18	JR	personal code	18
JBII	personal code	18	JRG	personal code	18
JBW	personal code	18	JS	160TU	5
JC	1AFS RCAF	11	JS	60 SAAF	11
JC	69th Arm FA Bn	B	JS	personal code	18
JC	personal code	18	JSC	personal code	18
JCB	personal code	18	JT	256	5
JCF	personal code	18	JT	720 RNorAF	11
JCW	personal code	18	JU	111	11
JD	545 BS, 384 BG	A	JU	111	5
JD	93rd Arm FA Bn	B	JU	2 CU RAAF	6
JD	personal code	18	JU	202	4
JD	SF Grimsetter	5	JU	707BS,446BG	A
JE	107 RAAF	6	JV	3 RNZAF	9
JE	195	5	JV	6	11
JE	26BAF	11	JV	6	5
JE	personal code	18	JV	SF Finningley	11
JEFF	personal code	18	JW	3 OTU RCAF	11
JEJ	personal code	18	JW	326BS,92BG	A
JF	1654 HCU	5	JW	44	4
JF	3	5	JW	CFE/FLS	5
JF	3 OTU RCAF	11	JW	personal code	18
JF	personal code	18	JWB	personal code	18
JFE	personal code	18	JX	?RCAF	11
JG	17 OTU	5	JX	1	11
JG	personal code	18	JX	1	5
JGH	personal code	18	JY	121 RCAF	7
JGT	personal code	18	JZ	15RNZAF	9
JH	203 AFS	11	JZ	57 OTU	5
JH	317	5	JZ	FGS RNZAF	9
JH	74	4	JZ	personal code	18
JH	personal code	18	JZ	534 BS, 381 BG	A
JHD	personal code	18	K	1 FTS	16
JHW	personal code	18	K	10RAAF	6
JI	514	5	K	35th FA Gp	B

Code	Unit	See Chapter or Appendix	Code	Unit	See Chapter or Appendix
K	756	C	KE	MSFU	5
K	899	C	KE	personal code	18
K	CFS	16	KF	1662 CU	5
K1	756	C	KF	5 CU RAAF	6
K1	760	C	KG	1380 T(S)CU	5
K1	766	C	KG	204	5
K1	831	C	KG	3 OTU	5
K2	7GCF	11	KG	81 OTU	5
K2	747	C	KH	403	5
K2	766	C	KH	411 RCAF	11
K3	766	C	KH	Trenton SF RCAF	11
K3	800	C	KI	55 FS, 20 FG	A
K4	511 FS, 405FG	A	KJ	11 OTU	5
K4	737	C	KJ	14 SU RNZAF	9
K5	33BAF	11	KJ	16	4
K5	584 BS, 394 BG	A	KJ	4 SAAF	10
K5	763	C	KK	1477 Flt	5
K5	766	C	KK	15 OTU	5
K5	SF Pocklington	5	KK	333	5
K6	430 FS, 474 FG	A	KK	333 RNorAF	11
K6	804	C	KK	personal code	18
K6	808	C	KL	11 RCAF	7
K7	1840	C	KL	269	4
K7	236 OCU	11	KL	54	5
K7	6 OTU	5	KL	Moose Jaw SF RCAF	11
K7	6 OTU	11	KL	personal code	18
K7	729	C	KM	44	11
K7	744	C	KM	44	5
K8	602 BS, 398 BG	A	KM2	?	C
K8	885	C	KML	personal code	18
K8	SF Katukurunda	C	KN	5 RNZAF	9
K8	SF Wymeswold	5	KN	77	11
K9	494 BS, 344 BG	A	KN	77	5
K9	715	C	KNL	personal code	18
K9	772	C	KO	115	11
K9	SF Inskip	C	KO	115	5
K9	SF Tain	5	KO	2	4
KA	13 GCF	5	KO	2	5
KA	1685 BDTF	5	KO	2 RAAF	6
KA	82 OTU	5	KO	2 RCAF	7
KA	9	4	KP	111 ASR Flt RAAF	6
KA	9 RCAF	7	KP	226	4
KA	HQ 1st DMI Arty Regt	B	KP	409	5
KB	142	4	KQ	13 OTU	5
KB	1661 CU	5	KQ	3 FTS RCAF	11
KB	1st Bn (French)	B	KQ	502	4
KB	personal code	18	KQ	55	5
KBBC	personal code	18	KR	? RCAF	11
KC	137 Tspt Flt RCAF	11	KR	1667 CU	5
KC	238	5	KR	203 AFS	11
KC	2nd Bn (French)	B	KR	226 OCU	11
KC	617	11	KR	61 OTU	11
KC	617	5	KR	61 OTU	5
KC	personal code	18	KR	personal code	18
KD	168 RCAF	7	KS	557 BS, 387 BG	A
KD	226 OCU	11	KS	personal code	18
KD	30 OTU	5	KS	SF Tarrant Rushton	5
KD	3rd Bn (French)	B	KSY	personal code	18
KE	440 RCAF	11	KT	1 Wing BAF	11
KE	4th Bn (French)	B	KT	105 C&RF RCAF	11
KE	BLEU	11	KT	11 BAF	11

Code	Unit	See Chapter or Appendix	Code	Unit	See Chapter or Appendix
KT	1660 HCU ?	5	L8	347	5
KT	32	4	L8	347/ GB 1/25	11
KT	7 RAAF	6	L8	765	C
KU	430/1430 Flt	5	L8	781	C
KU	47	5	L9	190	5
KU	53 OTU	5	L9	716	C
KV	1429 Flt	5	L9	762	C
KV	17 AOP Flt RAAF	6	L9	781	C
KV	Fictitious	F	L9	797	C
KW	267	5	LA	235	5
KW	425	5	LA	2906 OTG	A
KW	615	5	LA	35th FA Gp HQ	B
KW	personal code	18	LA	607	11
KX	311	5	LB	1st Bn 77th FA Regt	B
KX	1448 Flt	5	LB	21 SAAF	11
KX	529	5	LB	28 OTU	5
KX	558 BS, 387 BG	A	LB	32 OTU RCAF	7
KY	242	11	LB	34	4
KY	242	5	LB	84 RAAF	6
KY	366 BS, 305 BG	A	LBP	personal code	18
KZ	287	5	LC	2nd Bn 77th FA Regt	B
L	?	5	LC	77 FS, 20 FG	A
L	11	14	LC	SF Feltwell	5
L	16	14	LD	108	5
L	20	14	LD	117	5
L	45(R)	17	LD	250	5
L	71	14	LD	418 BS, 100 BG	A
L	96	14	LE	242	5
L	98	14	LE	40	11
L	152	5	LE	630	5
L	210	15	LF	37	5
L	228	15	LF	526 BS, 379 BG	A
L	240	15	LF	Comox SF RCAF	11
L	266	14	LF	SF Predannack	5
L	2 FTS	16	LG	13 GCF	5
L	CFS	16	LG	215	5
L	11 RAAF	6	LG	11 OTU	5
L0	701	C	LG	322 BS, 91 BG	A
L0	746	C	LG	personal code	18
L0	781	C	LH	350 FS, 353 FG	A
L1	780	C	LH	SF Mepal	5
L1	798	C	LHB	personal code	18
L2	434 FS, 479 FG	A	LJ	211	4
L2	760	C	LJ	3 GTTF	A
L2	798	C	LJ	112 ASRF	6
L3	512 FS, 406 FG	A	LJ	600	11
L3	765	C	LJ	614	5
L3	798	C	LJ	personal code	18
L3	815	C	LK	51	5
L4	27 MU 5		LK	87	5
L4	798	C	LK	578	5
L4	815	C	LK	AMCCF RCAF	11
L4	826	C	LL	1513 RATF	5
L4	91 TCS, 439 TCG	A	LL	401 BS, 91 BG	A
L5	297	11	LL	personal code	18
L5	297	5	LM	113 RCAF	7
L5	819	C	LM	62 FS, 56 FG	A
L6	1669 HCU	5	LM	71 FS, 1 FG	A
L6	806	C	LM	71 FS, 1 FG	A
L7	271	5	LM	personal code	18
L7	406 BS, 801 BG	A	LM	SF Elsham Wolds	5

Code	Unit	See Chapter or Appendix	Code	Unit	See Chapter or Appendix
LN	350 BS, 100 BG	A	M	22 FTS	16
LN	83 GCF	5	M	3 FTS	16
LN	99	5	M	6 FTS	16
LO	216	5	M	617	17
LO	602	11	M	7 FTS	16
LO	602	4	M	9 AFTS	16
LO	602	5	M	CFS	16
LOB	personal code	18	M	IV Corps Arty HQ	B
LOL	personal code	18	M	personal code	18
LP	237 OCU	11	M$	836	C
LP	283	11	M1	836	C
LP	283	5	M2	33 MU	5
LP	409 RCAF	11	M2	768	C
LP	6 (C)OTU	5	M2	836	C
LP	8 OTU	11	M2	88 TCS, 438 TCG	A
LQ	405	5	M3	5 Grp FU	5
LR	1667 HCU	5	M3	729 BS, 452 BG	A
LR	31 OTU RCAF	7	M3	836	C
LR	56	4	M4	587	5
LS	15	11	M4	836	C
LS	15	5	M5	128	5
LS	61	4	M6	309 TCS, 315 TCG	A
LT	7	4	M6	83 GCF	5
LT	22 OTU	5	M7	91 GCF	5
LT	1681 BDTF	5	M8	4 GCF	5
LT	7 RCAF	7	M8	728	C
LU	101	4	M8	772	C
LU	118 RCAF	7	M9	1653 CU	5
LU	1 CAC det	7	M9	740	C
LU	MSFU	5	M9	SF Machrihanish	C
LV	18 RNZAF	9	MA	114 RCAF	7
LV	201 Flt RAAF	6	MA	161	5
LV	5 CAC det RCAF	7	MA	651	5
LV	57 OTU	5	MB	? RAAF	6
LV	SF C Bordon RCAF	11	MB	220	5
LV	personal code	18	MB	236	5
LVC	personal code	18	MB	52	4
LW	318	5	MB	651	5
LW	607	4	MB	personal code	18
LW	74, 75, 76 SW	5	MC	79 FS, 20 FG	A
LW	personal code	18	MC	SF Fiskerton	5
LX	225	5	MCR	personal code	18
LX	54 OTU	5	MD	133	5
LX	228 OCU	11	MD	336 FS, 4 FG	A
LY	1 PRU	5	MD	458	5
LY	14	5	MD	526	5
LY	149	4	MD	651	5
LY	30 RAAF	6	MD	personal code	18
LY	314 TCS, 349 TCG	A	ME	488	5
LY	PRU	5	MF	108	4
LZ	111 RCAF	7	MF	260	5
LZ	421 Flt	5	MF	280	5
LZ	66	11	MF	59 OTU	5
LZ	66	5	MF	CFE	11
M	1 FTS	16	MF	FLS	5
M	10 AFTS	16	MG	7	5
M	12 RAAF	6	MG	7	11
M	2 FTS	16	MG	GHTF	5
M	205 AFS	16	MH	? RCAF	11
M	206 AFS	16	MH	? RCAF	11
M	215 AFS	16	MH	51	11

Code	Unit	See Chapter or Appendix	Code	Unit	See Chapter or Appendix
MH	51	5	MOYA	51	12
MH	83 RAAF	6	MOYB	99	12
MH	personal code	18	MOYC	511	12
MHD	personal code	18	MOYD	24	12
MHM	personal code	18	MOYD	59	12
MI	812 BS, 482 BG	A	MOYF	242	12
MI	Fictitious	F	MOYG	206	12
MID	personal code	18	MOYU	HQ India CF	12
MJ	1680 (T) Flt	5	MP	76	11
MJ	21 RAAF	6	MP	76	5
MJ	personal code	18	MP	86 RAAF	6
MJL	personal code	18	MP	personal code	18
MK	126	5	MQ	15 BS, 27 BG	A
MK	13 RCAF	7	MQ	226	5
MK	20 OTU	5	MR	245	11
MK	500	5	MR	245	5
MK	67 RAAF	6	MR	3 IAF	8
MK	701 BS, 445 BG	A	MR	4 CAC det RCAF	7
MK	personal code	18	MR	97	4
ML	12 OTU	5	MR	personal code	18
ML	2 FTS RCAF	11	MRA	personal code	18
ML	605	5	MRIF	personal code	18
MLB	personal code	18	MS	17 SAAF	11
MLD	personal code	18	MS	23	4
MLR	personal code	18	MS	273	5
MMS	personal code	18	MS	29 BAF	11
MN	350	5	MS	535 BS, 381 BG	A
MN	350 BAF	11	MS	HCF	11
MN	408 RCAF	11	MS	personal code	18
MOAY	31	12	MS	SF Church Fenton	11
MOAZ	Colerne CF	12	MT	105	4
MODA	1 P&GTS	12	MT	122	5
MODA	24	12	MT	22 SAAF	11
MODB	53	12	MU	338 RNorAF	11
MODC	24	12	MU	60	5
MODC	27	12	MV	119 (NEI) RAAF	6
MODC	62	12	MV	53 OTU	5
MODD	233	12	MV	600	4
MODF	30	12	MW	101 (C Flt)	5
MOFA	18	12	MW	217	5
MOFB	77	12	MWSR	personal code	18
MOFC	62	12	MX	120 RCAF	7
MOFG	46	12	MX	1653 CU	5
MOFG	114	12	MX	307 FS, 78 FG	A
MOFM	114	12	MX	82 FS, 78 FG	A
MOGC	242 OCU	12	MX	SF Glatton	5
MOGF	?	12	MY	11 RCAF	7
MOHA	297	12	MY	278	5
MOHC	113	12	MZ	? RCAF	11
MOHC	295	12	MZ	413 BS, 96 BG	A
MOHD	47	12	MZ	83 OTU	5
MOJZ	36	12	N	1 FTS	16
MOKD	24	12	N	13 RAAF	6
MOND	SF Benson	12	N	194th FA Gp HQ	B
MONY	MCS	12	N	2 BANS	16
MORC	240 OCU	12	N	2 FTS	16
MORG	30	12	N	202 AFS	16
MOSC	30	12	N	215 AFS	16
MOVF	622	12	N	22 FTS	16
MOWA	40	12	N	27	17
MOWB	59	12	N	3 FTS	16

Code	Unit	See Chapter or Appendix	Code	Unit	See Chapter or Appendix
N	6 FTS	16	NK	31 GRS RCAF	7
N	7 FTS	16	NL	341	5
N	821	C	NL	341/ GC 3/2	11
N	CFS	16	NLA	personal code	18
N	RAFC	16	NM	? RCAF	11
N1	812	C	NM	230	5
N2	383 FS, 364 FG	A	NM	268	5
N3	47 TCS, 313 TCG	A	NM	34 TCS, 315 TCG	A
N3	496 BS, 344 BG	A	NM	76	4
N4	744	C	NN	310	11
N5	111 RS, 69 RG	A	NN	310	5
N5	1850	C	NN	8 RAAF	6
N6	744	C	NO	? RCAF	11
N6	810	C	NO	116 RCAF	7
N7	603 BS, 398 BG	A	NO	320	5
N7	744	C	NO	85	4
N7	SF Lyneham	5	NP	158	5
N8	600 BS, 398 BG	A	NP	personal code	18
N8	723	C	NQ	24	5
N8	SF Waterbeach	5	NQ	423 RCAF	11
N9	SF Blackbushe	5	NQ	43	4
NA	1	4	NR	113 ASR Flt RAAF	6
NA	1 RAAF	6	NR	220	5
NA	1 RCAF	7	NR	605	11
NA	146	5	NS	201	11
NA	428	5	NS	201	5
NA	91st Inf Div Arty HQ	B	NS	52 OTU	5
NB	1 (I)SFTS	5	NS	Fictitious	F
NB	1 IAF	8	NT	203	5
NB	346th FA Bn	B	NT	29 OTU	5
NB	67 BS, 44 BG	A	NU	1382 (T)CU	11
NC	4	5	NU	1382 (T)CU	5
NC	347th FA Bn	B	NU	240 OCU	11
ND	10 BAF	11	NV	144	4
ND	11 SAAF	10	NV	23 RAAF	6
ND	1666 HCU	5	NV	325 BS, 92 BG	A
ND	236	5	NV	79	5
ND	348th FA Bn	B	NV	3	10A
NE	143	5	NV	BLEU	11
NE	63	4	NW	286	5
NE	916th FA Bn	B	NW	3 RAAF	6
NF	138	11	NW	33	5
NF	138	5	NW	personal code	18
NF	16 AOP Flt RAAF	6	NX	131	5
NF	488	5	NX	200 Flt RAAF	6
NG	604	11	NX	CFE	5
NG	604	5	NY	1665 HCU	5
NG	860 BS, 493 BG	A	NZ	304	5
NH	? RCAF	11	O	1 FTS	16
NH	119	5	O	2 FTS	16
NH	12 RAAF	6	O	202 AFS	16
NH	274	5	O	203 AFS	16
NH	530	5	O	205 AFS	16
NH	38	4	O	22 FTS	16
NH	415	5	O	3 FTS	16
NI	451	5	O	6 FTS	16
NJ	207	4	O	7 FTS	16
NJ	73 RAAF	6	O	708	C
NJ	MSFU	5	O	8 AFTS	16
NK	100	5	O	806B	C
NK	118	5	O	9 AFTS	16

Code	Unit	See Chapter or Appendix	Code	Unit	See Chapter or Appendix
O	CFS	16	ODV	10	12
O0	772 ?	C	ODW	52	12
O1	735	C	ODX	1680 Flt	12
O2	1702	C	ODY	1333 (T)CU	12
O3	BCDU	5	ODZ	BOAC	12
O4	1792	C	OE	168	5
O4	735	C	OE	268	5
O4	774	C	OE	335 BS, 95 BG	A
O5	805	C	OE	36	5
O5	892	C	OE	661	5
O5	BSDU	5	OE	98	4
O6	298	5	OF	97	11
O6	816	C	OF	97	5
Ø6	885	C	OFA	10	12
O7	514 FS, 406 FG	A	OFA	437	12
O7	707	C	OFB	206	12
Ø7	888	C	OFB	271	12
O8	575 BS, 391 BG	A	OFB	62	12
O8	707	C	OFD	575	12
O8	772	C	OFG	46	12
O8	804	C	OFH	216	12
O8	SF Merryfield	5	OFM	435	12
O9	SFCS	5	OFN	575	12
O9	772	C	OFR	238	12
O9	SF Burscough	C	OFT	187	12
Ø9	893	C	OFU	233	12
OA	22	5	OFV	271	12
OA	342	5	OFV	78	12
OA	1322 Flt	5	OFZ	BOAC	12
OA	342/ GB 1/20	11	OG	1665 HCU	5
OB	45	11	OG	172	5
OB	45	5	OGW	personal code	18
OB	53 OTU	5	OH	120	5
OB	697th FA Bn	B	OHC	1665 HCU	12
OB	92 RAAF	6	OHD	301	12
OC	? RCAF	11	OHL	113	12
OC	359 FS, 356 FG	A	OI	1665 HTCU	11
OC	698th FA Bn	B	OI	2	11
OC	SF Sandtoft	5	OI	2	5
OD	28 SAAF	11	OJ	149	11
OD	4 OTU RNZAF	9	OJ	149	5
OD	56 OTU	5	OJ	4 FTS RCAF	11
OD	6 (C)OTU	5	OK	3 SGR	5
OD	80	4	OK	450	5
ODA	24	12	OK	personal code	18
ODC	238	12	OKD	24	12
ODD	437	12	OKZ	BOAC	12
ODD-E	62	12	OL	83	11
ODF	147	12	OL	83	5
ODJ	78	12	OL	RNFS	5
ODK	241 OCU	12	OLB	246	12
ODK	512	12	OLM	206	12
ODK	575	12	OLP	426	12
ODM	436	12	OLW	86	12
ODN	271	12	OLX	220	12
ODO	437	12	OLZ	BOAC	12
ODP	525	12	OM	107	11
ODR	48	12	OM	107	5
ODS	575	12	OM	11	11
ODT	53	12	OM	37 RAAF	6
ODU	31	12	ON	124	5

Code	Unit	See Chapter or Appendix	Code	Unit	See Chapter or Appendix
ON	56	11	OZ	210	11
ON	63	4	OZ	24 SAAF	11
ON	63	5	OZ	24 SAAF	10
ON	Downsview SF RCAF	11	OZ	412 RCAF	11
OO	13	5	OZ	82	4
OO	1663 HCU	5	OZZ	BOAC	12
OO	personal code	18	P	1 FTS	16
OP	11 OTU	5	P	10 AFTS	16
OP	11 SU RNZAF	9	P	14 RAAF	6
OP	3	4	P	2 FTS	16
OP	3 RCAF	7	P	207 AFS	16
OP	32 OTU RCAF	7	P	22 FTS	16
OP	42 Flt/Sq SAAF	11	P	3 FTS	16
OQ	5	11	P	4 FTS (19(R))	17
OQ	5	5	P	6 FTS	16
OQ	172	5	P	7 FTS	16
OQ	1385 HTCU	11	P	757	C
OQ	52 OTU	5	P	856	C
OQ	FLS	5	P	9 AFTS	16
OQ	533 BS, 381 BG	A	P	CFS	16
OQZ	BOAC	12	P	CFS	17
OR	323 BS, 91 BG	A	P0	790	C
OR	BBU	5	P0	SF	C
ORJ	51	12	P1	762	C
ORK	242	12	P1	794	C
ORL	46	12	P1	849	C
ORP	196	12	P2	572 BS, 391 BG	A
ORS	299	12	P2	762	C
ORT	1588 HD Flt	12	P2	790 ?	C
OS	279	5	P2	794	C
OS	3 RAAF	6	P2	SF Marston Moor	5
OS	357 FS, 355 FG	A	P3	1701 ?	C
OS	528	5	P3	692	5
OS	SF Sturgate	5	P3	784	C
OSD	232	12	P3	790 ?	C
OSK	233	12	P4	153	5
OT	? RCAF	11	P5	297	5
OT	5 RNZAF	9	P5	763	C
OT	58	11	P5	887	C
OT	540	5	P6	489	5
OU	JATC Rivers RCAF	11	P6	801	C
OV	197	5	P6	894	C
OV	8 BAF	11	P7	748	C
OW	426	5	P7	760	C
OX	22 OTU	5	P7	801	C
OX	40	4	P7	87 GCF	5
OX	43 RAAF	6	P7	880	C
OXG	163	12	P8	784	C
OY	11 RCAF	7	P8	790B	C
OY	13 OTU	11	P8	794	C
OY	13 OTU	5	P8	801	C
OY	48	5	P9	58 OTU	5
OYA	51	12	P9	720	C
OYB	246	12	P9	ASWDU	11
OYC	511	12	P9	SF Dale	C
OYD	24	12	PA	3 TEU	5
OYF	242	12	PA	30 RNZAF	9
OYR	59	12	PA	5 RNZAF	9
OYZ	BOAC	12	PA	55 OTU	5
OZ	179	11	PA	655	5
OZ	179	5	PA	8 RNZAF	9

Code	Unit	See Chapter or Appendix	Code	Unit	See Chapter or Appendix
PB	10	4	PP	203	4
PB	10 RCAF	7	PP	25 OTU	5
PB	1684 BDTF	5	PP	311	11
PB	26 OTU	5	PP	311	5
PB	655	5	PP	311 RNethAF	11
PB	personal code	18	PP	71 RAAF	6
PB1	personal code	18	PP	personal code	18
PC	655	5	PPH	personal code	18
PC	813 BS, 482 BG	A	PQ	117 RCAF	7
PD	303	5	PQ	2 TEU	5
PD	655	5	PQ	58 OTU	5
PD	87	4	PQ	206	5
PDW	personal code	18	PR	403 RCAF	11
PE	1662 HCU	5	PR	609	11
PE	328 FS, 352 FG	A	PR	609	5
PF	227 OCU	11	PR	Fictitious	F
PF	43 OTU	11	PS	264	11
PF	43 OTU	5	PS	264	5
PF	443 RCAF	11	PS	personal code	18
PF	51 OTU	5	PST	personal code	18
PF	LAS	11	PT	1 SFTS (I)	5
PFS	personal code	18	PT	27	5
PG	608	4	PT	420	5
PG	619	5	PT	personal code	18
PH	12	11	PU	1 PRU RAAF	6
PH	12	5	PU	187	11
PH	27 SAAF	11	PU	187	5
PH	CFE	5	PU	360 BS, 303 BG	A
PH	personal code	18	PU	53	11
PHB	personal code	18	PV	275	5
PI	360 FS, 356 FG	A	PV	424 RCAF	11
PI	SF Silverstone	5	PW	111 CF RCAF	11
PJ	130	5	PW	224	4
PJ	59	4	PW	57 OTU	5
PJS	personal code	18	PW	personal code	18
PK	220	4	PWB	personal code	18
PK	315	5	PX	? 214	5
PK	38 RAAF	6	PX	295	5
PL	144	5	PX	336 RNoAF	11
PL	535 BS, 381 BG	A	PX	CEPE RCAF	11
PLB	personal code	18	PY	1527 RATF	5
PM	103	5	PY	407 BS, 92 BG	A
PM	personal code	18	PY	84	5
PMB	personal code	18	PY	2	10A
PMcLB	personal code	18	PZ	456	5
PMO	personal code	18	PZ	486 FS, 352 FG	A
PN	14 RAAF	6	PZ	53	5
PN	1552 RATF	5	Q	2 FTS	16
PN	164 or 426? RCAF	11	Q	205 AFS	16
PN	252	5	Q	3 FTS	16
PN	30	5	Q	6 FTS	16
PN	41	4	Q	7 FTS	16
PN	449 BS, 322 BG	A	Q	853	C
PN	personal code	18	Q	93 FS	A
PO	104	4	Q	CFS	16
PO	4 CAC det RCAF	7	Q1	781	C
PO	46	5	Q2	?	C
PO	467	5	Q2	790 BS, 467 BG	A
PO	personal code	18	Q3	613	11
PO-B	personal code	18	Q4	854	C
PP	2 FTS RCAF	11	Q4	861 BS, 493 BG	A

Code	Unit	See Chapter or Appendix	Code	Unit	See Chapter or Appendix
Q5	31 BG/ GB 1/19	11	QQ	1651 HCU	5
Q6	1384 HTCU	5	QQ	83	4
Q6	4 BS, 34 BG	A	QR	61	11
Q7	29 MU	5	QR	61	5
Q7	90 TCS, 438 TCG	A	QS	1 R&C RAAF	6
Q8	23 TCS, 349 TCG	A	QS	620	5
Q8	BAFO CW	5	QT	121 KU RCAF	11
Q9	61 TCS, 314 TCG	A	QT	142	5
Q9	SF Belfast	C	QT	401 RCAF	11
QA	297	5	QT	57	11
QA	654	5	QU	49 FS, 12 FG	A
QB	424	5	QU	49 FS, 14 FG	A
QB	654	5	QU	RAFNICF	11
QC	168	5	QV	19	11
QC	654	5	QV	19	5
QD	304	5	QW	1516 RATF	5
QD	42	4	QW	412 BS, 95 BG	A
QD	654	5	QX	224	5
QE	12	4	QX	CCCF	5
QE	12 RCAF	7	QX	50	4
QE	331 BS, 94 BG	A	QY	1666 HCU	5
QE	4 RAAF	6	QY	254	5
QE	CFE	5	QY	452 RAAF	6
QE	CFE	11	QZ	103 RU RCAF	11
QF	1323 Flt	5	QZ	4 OTU	5
QF	98	4	R	2 FTS	16
QF	PFNTU	5	R	205 AFS	16
QG	53 OTU	5	R	21 RAAF	6
QG	6 CAC det RCAF	7	R	22 FTS	16
QH	100 RAAF	6	R	3 FTS	16
QH	302	5	R	CFS	16
QI	361 FS, 356 FG	A	R0	SF	C
QI	SF Swanton Morley	5	R1	814	C
QJ	? RCAF	11	R1	FP ?	C
QJ	337 BS, 96 BG	A	R2	7 BS, 34 BG	A
QJ	420 RCAF	11	R2	710	C
QJ	616	5	R2	713	C
QJ	92	5	R2	747	C
QJ	BAFO CW	5	R2	812	C
QK	? 3 APS	5	R2	PAU	5
QK	506 BS, 44 BG	A	R3	410 FS, 373 FG	A
QK	87 RAAF	6	R3	710	C
QK	APS Sylt	11	R3	713	C
QL	22 RS, 69 RG	A	R3	747	C
QL	413	5	R3	772	C
QL	76 Wing	5	R4	18 APC	5
QM	254	5	R4	710	C
QM	42	11	R4	713	C
QM	532	5	R4	747	C
QN	? RCAF	11	R4	773	C
QN	214	11	R4	803 BS, RCM	A
QN	28 OTU	5	R5	1839	C
QN	5 RCAF	7	R5	710	C
QO	167	11	R5	713	C
QO	3	5	R5	747	C
QO	3	17	R5	771	C
QO	432	5	R5	839 BS, 487 BG	A
QP	2 FS, 52 FG	A	R6	1844	C
QP	334 FS, 4 FG	A	R6	1851	C
QP	406 RCAF	11	R6	710	C
QP	SF Kirmington	5	R6	713	C

Code	Unit	See Chapter or Appendix	Code	Unit	See Chapter or Appendix
R6	747	C	RCM	1 RFS	13
R7	AEU	5	RCN	4 RFS	13
R7	710	C	RCO	6 RFS	13
R7	713	C	RCP	7 RFS	13
R7	747	C	RCQ	8 RFS	13
R7	776	C	RCR	11 RFS	13
R7	GR 2/33	11	RCS	16 RFS	13
R8	274 MU	5	RCT	18 RFS	13
R8	776	C	RCU	22 RFS	13
R8	797	C	RCV	24 RFS	13
R9	639	5	RCW	25 RFS	13
R9	SF Stretton	C	RCW	personal code	18
RA	100	4	RCX	2 RFS	13
RA	128 RCAF	7	RCY	5 RFS	13
RA	27 BAF	11	RCZ	9 RFS	13
RA	410	5	RD	32 OTU RCAF	7
RA	personal code	18	RD	423 BS, 306 BG	A
RA	S of AC RCAF	7	RD	67	5
RAA	500 Sqn	13	RD	personal code	18
RAB	501 Sqn	13	RDE	personal code	18
RAB	personal code	18	RduV	personal code	18
RAC	502 Sqn	13	RDY	personal code	18
RAD	504 Sqn	13	RE	118 RCAF	7
RAG	600 Sqn	13	RE	229	5
RAH	601 Sqn	13	RE	329 BS, 93 BG	A
RAI	602 Sqn	13	RE	36 RAAF	6
RAJ	603 Sqn	13	RE	CFE	5
RAK	604 Sqn	13	RE	CFE	11
RAL	605 Sqn	13	REB	personal code	18
RAN	607 Sqn	13	RF	1510 RATF	11
RAO	608 Sqn	13	RF	204	4
RAP	609 Sqn	13	RF	303	5
RAQ	610 Sqn	13	RF	personal code	18
RAR	611 Sqn	13	RFB	personal code	18
RAS	612 Sqn	13	RG	1472 AACF	5
RAT	613 Sqn	13	RG	208	11
RAU	614 Sqn	13	RG	208	5
RAV	615 Sqn	13	RG	510	5
RAW	616 Sqn	13	RG	552 BS, 386 BG	A
RB	10 RAAF	6	RG	Moose Jaw SF RCAF	11
RB	10 RAAF	5	RG	TCMF	5
RB	20 RAAF	6	RGD	personal code	18
RB	35 SAAF	11	RH	88	5
RB	66	4	RH	personal code	18
RB	personal code	18	RHC	personal code	18
RBH	personal code	18	RHG	personal code	18
RBL	personal code	18	RHH	personal code	18
RC	5 LFS	5	RHR	personal code	18
RC	personal code	18	RI	334 RNoAF	11
RCA	RCCF 13		RIKE	personal code	18
RCB	12 RFS	13	RJ	454 BS, 323 BG	A
RCD	15 RFS	13	RJ	46	4
RCE	61 Gp CF	13	RJ	personal code	18
RCF	62 Gp CF	13	RJ	SF Thornaby	5
RCG	63 Gp CF	13	RJC	personal code	18
RCH	64 Gp CF	13	RJG	personal code	18
RCH	personal code	18	RK	10 OTU	5
RCI	66 Gp CF	13	RK	3 SU RNZAF	9
RCJ	17 RFS	13	RK	42 RAAF	6
RCK	3 RFS	13	RL	279	5
RCL	14 RFS	13	RL	38	11

Code	Unit	See Chapter or Appendix	Code	Unit	See Chapter or Appendix
RL	603	4	RUY	Leeds UAS	13
RL	SLAIS	5	RUZ	Southampton UAS	13
RL	Test Unit RCAF	11	RV	1659 HCU	5
RLS	personal code	18	RW	36	5
RM	26	5	RWM	personal code	18
RM	personal code	18	RWO	personal code	18
RMG	personal code	18	RX	25	4
RMH	personal code	18	RX	407 RCAF	11
RN	700 BS, 445 BG	A	RX	456	5
RN	72	4	RY	313	11
RN	72	5	RY	313	5
RO	29	11	RZ	241	5
RO	29	5	S	208	17
RO	SF Chatham RCAF	11	S	809	C
ROA	661/1960 Flt	13	S	851	C
ROB	662	13	S	882	C
ROC	663	13	S	3 FTS	16
ROD	664	13	S	8 AFTS	16
ROG	665	13	S	207 AFS	16
RP	288	5	S	CFS	16
RPB	personal code	18	S	RAFFC	16
RQ	509 BS, 351 BG	A	S	Tornado F.3 OEU	17
RQ	SF Colerne	5	S	22 RAAF	6
RR	?	5	S1	719	C
RR	120 (NEI) RAAF	6	S1	794	C
RR	407	5	S2	32 TCS, 314 TCG	A
RR	566 BS, 389 BG	A	S2	741	C
RR	615	4	S2	9 BAF	11
RR	personal code	18	S3	709	C
RR	SF Filton	5	S3	736	C
RS	120 RCAF	7	S3	741	C
RS	157	5	S3	851 BS, 490 BG	A
RS	229 OCU	11	S4	715	C
RS	30	11	S4	826	C
RS	30	5	S4	845 BS, 489 BG	A
RS	33	5	S5	709	C
RSA	23 RFS	13	S5	741	C
RSB	10 RFS	13	S5	821	C
RST	personal code	18	S5	828	C
RT	112	5	S6	41 GCF	11
RT	114	11	S6	MCCS	11
RT	114	5	S6	709	C
RT	706 BS, 446 BG	A	S6	774	C
RT	8	11	S6	79 TCS, 436 TCG	A
RT	personal code	18	S6	803	C
RU	414	5	S6	815	C
RU	554 BS, 386 BG	A	S6	MCCS	5
RU	Rockcliffe RCAF	11	S7	500	11
RU	SF Hendon	5	S7	748	C
RUA	Aberdeen UAS	13	S7	804	C
RUB	Birmingham UAS	13	S7	815	C
RUC	Cambridge UAS	13	S8	328	5
RUD	Durham UAS	13	S8	328/ GC 1/7	11
RUE	Edinburgh UAS	13	S8	792	C
RUG	Glasgow UAS	13	S9	16 GCF	5
RUL	London UAS	13	S9	34 PS, 10 PG	A
RUM	Manchester UAS	13	S9	SF St Merryn	C
RUN	Nottingham UAS	13	SA	445 RCAF	11
RUO	Oxford UAS	13	SA	456	5
RUQ	Queens (Belfast) UAS	13	SA	486	5
RUS	St Andrews UAS	13	SA	88th Inf Div, Arty HQ	B

Code	Unit	See Chapter or Appendix	Code	Unit	See Chapter or Appendix
SB	? RCAF	11	SR	101	11
SB	337th FA Bn	B	SR	101	5
SB	464	5	SS	1552 RATF	5
SB	personal code	18	SS	451 BS, 322 BG	A
SBG	personal code	18	SS	personal code	18
SC	338th FA Bn	B	ST	? RCAF	11
SC	612 BS, 401 BG	A	ST	25 SAAF	11
SC	personal code	18	ST	228 OCU	11
SC	SF Prestwick	5	ST	54 OTU	5
SCW	personal code	18	ST9	SF Stretton	C
SD	339th FA Bn	B	SU	544 BS, 384 BG	A
SD	501	11	SU	SU/87 PR Flt RAAF	6
SD	501	5	SU	Summerside SF RCAF	11
SD	504	5	SV	1663 HCU	5
SD	72	4	SV	2 AOS RCAF	11
SD	Fictitious	F	SV	218	4
SD	personal code	18	SV	4 BAF	11
SE	431	5	SV	402 RCAF	11
SE	913th FA Bn	B	SV	76 RAAF	6
SE	95	5	SW	1678 HCU	5
SEP	personal code	18	SW	253	5
SF	13 RAAF	6	SW	33 RS, 67 RG	A
SF	137	5	SW	43	11
SF	personal code	18	SW	personal code	18
SFS	personal code	18	SX	1 CACU	5
SG	3 OTU	5	SX	352 FS, 353 FG	A
SG	550 BS, 385 BG	A	SX	SF Methwold	5
SG	Lincolnshire FS SF	5	SY	139	4
SG	SGCF RNZAF	9	SY	613	5
SH	216	5	SZ	147 RCAF	7
SH	240	4	SZ	316	5
SH	64	11	T	15(R)	17
SH	64	5	T	26	14
SH	75 TCS, 435 TCG	A	T	36	15
SH	85 RAAF	6	T	56	17
SI	339 RNorAF	11	T	79	14
SI	814 BS, 482 BG	A	T	93	14
SJ	1 RNZAF	9	T	112	14
SJ	21 OTU	11	T	204	15
SJ	21 OTU	5	T	220	15
SJ	25 RAAF	6	T	249	5
SJ	70	5	T	256	14
SK	165	11	T	757	C
SK	165	5	T	853	C
SK	93 RAAF	6	T	2 FTS	16
SL	13 OTU	11	T	205 AFS	16
SL	13 OTU	5	T	23 RAAF	6
SL	442 RCAF	11	T	3 FTS	16
SM	305	5	T	4 FTS (74(R))	17
SM	personal code	18	T0	767	C
SN	230 OCU	11	T2	46 MU	5
SN	243	5	T2	83 TCS, 437 TCG	A
SO	145	5	T3	45 TCS, 316 TCG	A
SO	33	4	T3	717 RNorAF	11
SO	547 BS, 384 BG	A	T3	758 ?	C
SO	South-East FS SF	5	T4	767	C
SP	110 RCAF	5	T4	847 BS, 489 BG	A
SP	400	5	T5	10 FS, 50 FG	A
SP	404 RCAF	11	T5	SF Abingdon	5
SP	SF Doncaster	5	T6	573 BS, 391 BG	A
SQ	500	4	T6	769	C

Code	Unit	See Chapter or Appendix	Code	Unit	See Chapter or Appendix
T6	SF Melbourne	5	THO	Hornchurch SF	13
T7	1834	C	TIH	1 FPU	13
T7	650	5	TJ	202	5
T8	1836	C	TJ	272	5
T8	722	C	TJ	52 OTU	5
T8	771	C	TJ	7 SAAF	10
T8	853 BS, 491 BG	A	TJJ	personal code	18
T9	722	C	TK	149	5
T9	784 BS, 466 BG	A	TL	35	11
T9	SF Twatt	C	TL	35	5
TA	12 LASU RAAF	6	TLO	SF Locking	13
TA	15(R)	17	TM	111	4
TA	2 SAAF	10	TM	111 RCAF	7
TA	235 OCU	11	TM	245	5
TA	313 RNethAF	11	TM	504	11
TA	4 (C)OTU	11	TM	504	5
TA	4 (C)OTU	5	TM	personal code	18
TA	85th Inf Div, Arty HQ	B	TMA	4 RS	13
TAL	Aldermaston CF	13	TMD	4 RS	13
TB	153	5	TME	4 RS	13
TB	315 RNethAF	11	TML	4 RS	13
TB	328th FA Bn	B	TN	161 RCAF	7
TB	51	11	TN	30 OTU	5
TB	77 Sqn	5	TN	33	4
TB	personal code	18	TN	personal code	18
TBB	personal code	18	TO	203 AFS	11
TBR	Staff College Flt	13	TO	226 OCU	11
TC	170	5	TO	228	4
TC	316 RNethAF	11	TO	61 OTU	11
TC	personal code	18	TO	61 OTU	5
TC	329th FA Bn	B	TOC	2 ITS	13
TCA	1 RS	13	TP	198	5
TCE	Carew Cheriton SF	13	TP	306 RNethAF	11
TCN	Cranwell SF	13	TP	73	5
TCO	Cosford SF	13	TP	personal code	18
TCR	1 RS	13	TQ	102	4
TCW	Carew Cheriton SF	13	TQ	104 KU Flt RCAF	11
TD	126	5	TQ	2 CAC det RCAF	7
TD	320	5	TQ	202	5
TD	403rd FA Bn	B	TQ	559 BS, 387 BG	A
TD	453	5	TQ	SF Bramcote	5
TD	82 OTU	5	TR	59	5
TDE	EARS Debden	13	TR	personal code	18
TE	1401 Flt	5	TRB	personal code	18
TE	521	5	TRH	personal code	18
TE	53	4	TS	333 BS, 94 BG	A
TE	910th FA Bn	B	TS	548	5
TE	personal code	18	TS	657	11
TF	127 RCAF	7	TSA	SF St Athan	13
TF	200	5	TSI	RAF (Belgian) TS	13
TF	29 OTU	5	TSM	4 RS	13
TF	422 RCAF	11	TSN	RAF (Belgian) TS	13
TFA	1 SP	13	TSO	27 GCF	13
TG	GC 3/3	11	TSW	personal code	18
TH	20	11	TT	CFE	5
TH	418	5	TT	1658 HCU	5
TH	personal code	18	TT	personal code	18
THA	Halton SF	13	TTE	22 GCF	13
THE	Parachute Test Flt	13	TU	510 BS, 351 BG	A
THI	A&AEE	13	TU	Fictitious	F
THL	24 GCF	13	TU	SF Dyce	5

Code	Unit	See Chapter or Appendix	Code	Unit	See Chapter or Appendix
TUL	personal code	18	UC	602nd Glider FA Bn	B
TV	151?	4	UD	419 RCAF	11
TV	1660 HCU	5	UD	452	5
TV	4	4	UD	460th Para FA Bn	B
TV	4	5	UE	?	5
TV	personal code	18	UE	228	5
TW	141	11	UE	463rd Para FA Bn	B
TW	141	5	UF	24 OTU	5
TW	90	4	UF	522nd FA Bn	B
TW	personal code	18	UF	601	5
TWM	1 SP	13	UG	16	5
TWY	TTCCF	13	UG	1654 HCU	5
TX	11 OTU	5	UH	1682 BDTF	5
TX	22 RNZAF	9	UH	2 RNZAF	9
TX	9 LASU RAAF	6	UH	202 AFS	11
TY	24 OTU	5	UH	21 OTU	11
TZ	310	5	UH	21 OTU	5
TZ	AMC RCAF	11	UK	CFE	11
T-	767	C	UL	576	5
U	2 FTS	16	UL	608	5
U	22 FTS	16	UM	1 FTS RCAF	11
U	24 RAAF	6	UM	152	11
U	8 AFTS	16	UM	152	5
U	881	C	UM	626	5
U1	758	C	UN	? RCAF	11
U1	780	C	UN	63 FS, 56 FG	A
U1	827	C	UN	94 FS, 1 FG	A
U2	SF Talbenny	5	UN	94 FS, 1 FG	A
U2	598 BS, 397 BG	A	UN	SF Faldingworth	5
U2	758	C	UO	19 OTU	5
U2	780	C	UO	266	5
U2	798	C	UP	4	11
U3	758	C	UP	605	5
U3	780	C	UP	79 RAAF	6
U3	815	C	UQ	1508 RATF	5
U3	818	C	UQ	211	5
U3	RWE	5	UR	13 OTU	5
U4	667	5	UR	2 BAF	11
U4	811	C	US	1 RAAF	6
U4	816	C	US	2 IAF	8
U5	1846	C	US	56	11
U5	51 MU	5	US	56	5
U5	81 TCS, 436 TCG	A	UT	17	11
U5	822	C	UT	461	5
U6	1846	C	UT	51	4
U6	327	5	UU	203 AFS	11
U6	327/ GC 1/3	11	UU	226 OCU	11
U6	436	5	UU	61 OTU	11
U6	801	C	UU	61 OTU	5
U7	1846	C	UV	115 RCAF	7
U7	ADLSS	5	UV	17	4
U8	786 BS, 466 BG	A	UV	460	5
U9	411 FS, 373 FG	A	UV	8 RAAF	6
UA	269	5	UW	3 TEU	5
UA	43 TCS, 315 TCG	A	UW	4 TEU	5
UB	?	5	UW	55 OTU	5
UB	10 LASU RAAF	6	UW	7 RNZAF	9
UB	164	5	UX	1476 Flt	5
UB	455	5	UX	214	4
UB	601st FA Bn	B	UX	327 BS, 92 BG	A
UB	63	11	UX	82	5

Code	Unit	See Chapter or Appendix	Code	Unit	See Chapter or Appendix
UX	99 RAAF	6	VI	169	5
UX	CFE	5	VJ	10 BATF	5
UX	CFE/DFLS	11	VK	238	5
UY	1 OTU RCAF	7	VK	358 BS, 303 BG	A
UY	10 OTU	5	VK	85 GCF	5
UY	21 RNZAF	9	VL	12 SAAF	11
UY	26 SU RNZAF	9	VL	12 SAAF	10
UZ	306	5	VL	167	5
V	1435	5	VL	322	5
V	25 RAAF	6	VL	personal code	18
V	personal code	18	VM	1561 Met Flt	5
V10	1852	C	VM	231	5
V11	1835	C	VM	4 CU RAAF	6
V11	1849	C	VM	552 FS, 495 FTG	A
V11	1853	C	VN	405 RCAF	11
V16	1850	C	VN	50	11
V2	? CSE	5	VN	50	5
V2	855 BS, 491 BG	A	VO	98	11
V4	1846	C	VO	98	5
V4	304 TCS, 442 TCG	A	VP	SF Exeter	5
V4	6 MU	5	VQ	18 OTU	5
V4	812	C	VQ	201	4
V5	412 FS, 373 FG	A	VR	102 KU Flt RCAF	11
V6	615	11	VR	22	4
V6	RWE	5	VR	419	5
V7	1845	C	VS	31	11
V7	1851	C	VS	510	5
V7	738	C	VS	MCS	11
V7	CSE	11	VSB	personal code	18
V7	RWE	11	VT	? RCAF	11
V8	1850	C	VT	1556 RATF	5
V8	570	5	VT	216	4
V8	738 ?	C	VT	25 BAF	11
V9	1848	C	VT	30	5
V9	502	11	VT	453 BS, 323 BG	A
V9	502	5	VU	246	5
V9	776 ?	C	VU	36	4
VA	125	5	VV	235	5
VA	264	11	VV	SF Sumburgh	5
VA	657	5	VW	118 RCAF	7
VA	84	5	VW	SF Chedburgh	5
VA	personal code	18	VX	109 RS, 67 RG	A
VB	14 OTU	5	VX	206	5
VB	334	5	VY	85	11
VB	657	5	VY	85	5
VC	1 FTS RCAF	11	VY	personal code	18
VC	657	5	VZ	412	5
VC	414	5	W	1/3/4	17
VD	123 RCAF	7	W	2 FTS	17
VD	657	5	W	205 AFS	16
VD	CGS	5	W	206 AFS	16
VE	532 BS, 381 BG	A	W	234	14
VE	SF Kirton-in-Lindsey	5	W	4 FTS	16
VF	336 FS, 4 FG	A	W	5 FTS	16
VF	5 FS, 52 FG	A	W	CFS	16
VF	99	4	W0	734	C
VF	SF Lindholme	5	W0	750	C
VF	SF Lindholme	11	W0	752	C
VG	210	4	W1	750	C
VG	285	5	W1	857	C
VH	444 RCAF	11	W2	749	C

Code	Unit	See Chapter or Appendix
W2	80	11
W2	80	5
W3	311 FS, 50 FG	A
W3	752	C
W3	SF Hemswell	11
W4	753	C
W4	760 ?	C
W4	GPU	5
W4	GR 1/33	11
W5	640 BS, 409 BG	A
W5	754	C
W5	793	C
W5	SF Castle Camps	5
W6	18 MU	5
W6	755	C
W6	793	C
W6	97 TCS, 440 TCG	A
W7	37 TCS, 316 TCG	A
W7	760	C
W7	793	C
W7	857	C
W8	760	C
W8	789	C
W8	793	C
W8	849 BS, 490 BG	A
W9	24 MU	5
W9	751	C
W9	760	C
W9	789	C
W9	3 CCRS	A
WA	? 5 OTU	5
WA	SF Manorbier	5
WA	524 BS, 379 BG	A
WA	HQ RACL	B
WAD	personal code	18
WAS	personal code	18
WATN	personal code	18
WB	BCIS	11
WB	BCIS	5
WB	RACL 1st Bn	B
WC	309	5
WC	personal code	18
WC	RACL 2nd Bn	B
WCW	personal code	18
WD	206	4
WD	SF Leeming	5
WD	335 FS, 4 FG	A
WD	4 FS, 52 FG	A
WD	4 FS, 52 FG	E
WD	personal code	18
WE	23 OTU	5
WE	59	5
WES	personal code	18
WF	238	11
WF	364 BS, 305 BG	A
WF	525	5
WFD	personal code	18
WG	128	5
WG	26 OTU	5
WH	330	5
WH	330 RNorAF	11

Code	Unit	See Chapter or Appendix
WH	APS Acklington	11
WHC	personal code	18
WI	69	11
WJ	17 OTU	5
WK	1316 Flt	5
WK	135	5
WKL	personal code	18
WL	434	5
WL	612	5
WL	personal code	18
WM	68	5
WN	172	5
WN	527	5
WO	13 OTU	5
WP	220	5
WP	243	5
WP	89	5
WP	90	11
WP	90	5
WPB	personal code	18
WQ	12 GCF	5
WQ	209	11
WQ	209	5
WQ	604	4
WQ	66 BS, 44 BG	A
WR	248	5
WR	354 FS, 355 FG	A
WR	40 SAAF	10
WRM	personal code	18
WS	9	11
WS	9	5
WT	35	4
WT	142	4
WT	456 BS, 323 BG	A
WT	personal code	18
WTC	personal code	18
WU	225	5
WV	18	11
WV	18	5
WV	702 BS, 445 BG	A
WW	369 BS, 306 BG	A
WX	302	5
WX	653 BS, 25 BG	A
WY	28 OTU	5
WY	541	11
WZ	19	4
WZ	309 FS, 31 FG	A
WZ	84 FS, 78 FG	A
WZ	SF Gravely	5
X	229	5
X	261	5
X	2 FTS	16
X	5 FTS	16
X	6 FTS	16
X	22 FTS	16
X	203 AFS	16
X	8 AFTS	16
X	CFS	16
X0	778	C
X2	596 BS, 397 BG	A
X2	SF Stoney Cross	5

Code	Unit	See Chapter or Appendix	Code	Unit	See Chapter or Appendix
X3	111 OTU	5	XQ	86	5
X3	755	C	XR	2 GCF	5
X4	859 BS, 492 BG	A	XR	334 FS, 4 FG	A
X5	59 TCS, 61 TCG	A	XR	349 BS, 100 BG	A
X5	758	C	XR	71	5
X6	290	5	XS	106	4
X6	757	C	XS	2 FTS RCAF	11
X7	788 BS, 467 BG	A	XS	MSFU	5
X8	6 GCF	5	XT	1657 CU	5
X9	299	5	XT	603	11
X9	517	5	XT	603	5
XA	489	5	XU	49	4
XA	549 BS, 385 BG	A	XU	7	5
XA	HQ 67 RAA	B	XV	2	5
XA	SF Essex sector	5	XV	2 OTU RCAF	11
XB	224	11	XW	18 OTU	5
XB	224	5	XX	34 RS, 69 RG	A
XB	457	5	XX	6 RCAF	7
XB	2 TEU	5	XX	6 RNZAF	9
XB	58 OTU	5	XX	MOTU RNZAF	9
XB	457 RAAF	6	XX	personal code	18
XB	67 RAA 1st Bn	B	XY	1 CAC det RCAF	7
XC	26	11	XY	186	5
XC	26	5	XY	90	5
XC	67 RAA 2nd Bn	B	XY	203 AFS	11
XD	13 OTU	5	XZ	39	5
XD	139	11	Y	1 FTS	16
XD	139	5	Y	206 AFS	16
XD	67 RAA 3rd Bn	B	Y	22 FTS	16
XE	123	5	Y	835	C
XE	6	4	Y	Comm Flt RAAF	6
XE	6 RCAF	7	Y0	790	C
XE	CBE	11	Y0	SF	C
XE	67 RAA 4th Bn	B	Y1	759	C
XF	19 OTU	5	Y1	837	C
XG	16 OTU	5	Y2	442	5
XH	218	5	Y2	700	C
XH	296	5	Y2	759	C
XJ	13 OTU	5	Y3	202	11
XJ	6 CU RAAF	6	Y3	518	11
XJ	719 RNorAF	11	Y3	518	5
XK	272	5	Y3	759	C
XK	365 BS, 305 BG	A	Y4	759	C
XK	406 RCAF	11	Y4	763	C
XK	46	11	Y5	495 BS, 344 BG	A
XK	46	5	Y5	759	C
XL	1335 CU	11	Y5	SF Dallachy	5
XL	20 OTU	5	Y6	759	C
XL	226 OCU	11	Y7	701 RNethAF	11
XM	182	5	Y7	759	C
XM	332 BS, 94 BG	A	Y7	760	C
XM	652	11	Y7	86 OTU	5
XN	22 OTU	5	Y8	1831	C
XO	112	4	Y8	507 FS, 404 FG	A
XO	112 RCAF	7	Y8	765	C
XO	16 RNZAF	9	Y8	794	C
XO	24 BAF	11	Y9	15 TCS, 61 TCG	A
XO	57 OTU	5	Y9	323 RNethAF	11
XP	135 RCAF	7	Y9	764	C
XP	174	5	Y9	SF	C
XQ	64	4	YA	14 RCAF	7

Code	Unit	See Chapter or Appendix
YA	555 BS, 386 BG	A
YA	SF Netheravon	5
YA	HQ 64 RAA	B
YB	17	5
YB	29	4
YB	508 BS, 351 BG	A
YB	7 CU RAAF	6
YB	SF Bentwaters	5
YB	64 RAA 1st Bn	B
YC	10 RS, 69 RG	A
YC	27 OTU	5
YC	75 RNZAF	9
YC	64 RAA 2nd Bn	B
YD	255	5
YD	64 RAA 3rd Bn	B
YE	289	5
YE	personal code	18
YF	280	5
YF	358 FS, 355 FG	A
YF	SF Scampton	5
YG	156 C Flt	5
YG	502	5
YH	1 GRS RCAF	7
YH	11	4
YH	11	5
YH	21	11
YH	21	5
YI	423	5
YJ	351 FS, 353 FG	A
YJ	SF Methering'm	5
YK	274	5
YK	80	5
YL	27 OTU	5
YL	3 BAF	11
YM	1528 RATF	5
YM	409 BS, 93 BG	A
YN	601	4
YN	652 BS, 25 BG	A
YO	1 RCAF	5
YO	401	5
YO	564 BS, 389 BG	A
YO	8 RCAF	7
YO	SF Down Ampney	5
YP	23	11
YP	23	5
YQ	217	4
YQ	616	11
YQ	616	5
YQ	9 RAAF	6
YR	? 208	5
YR	20 OTU	5
YS	271	5
YS	77	11
YT	? RCAF	11
YT	65	11
YT	65	5
YU	455 BS, 323 BG	A
YU	SF Lossiemouth	5
YV	48 GCF	5
YW	1660 HCU	5
YW	230 OCU	11

Code	Unit	See Chapter or Appendix
YX	54 OTU	5
YX	614	5
YY	1332 CU	5
YY	1332 HTCU	11
YY	241 OCU	11
YY	78	4
YZ	1651 HCU	5
YZ	2 CAC det RCAF	7
YZ	4 RNZAF	9
YZ	617	5
Y_	736B	C
Y_	787	C
Z	5 FTS	16
Z	835	C
Z	Survey Flt RAAF	6
Z0	790	C
Z1	163	5
Z1	790	C
Z2	437	5
Z4	10 MU	5
Z4	301 TCS, 441 TCG	A
Z5	462	5
Z5	754 BS, 458 BG	A
Z6	23 BAF	11
Z7	29 TCS, 313 TCG	A
Z8	45 MU	5
Z8	771	C
Z8	790	C
Z8	84 TCS, 437 TCG	A
Z9	519	5
ZA	10	11
ZA	10	5
ZA	31	4
ZA	8 CU RAAF	6
ZA	MCS	11
ZA	HQ 63 RAA	B
ZB	1658 HCU	5
ZB	63 RAA 1st Bn	B
ZC	367 BAF	11
ZC	63 RAA 2nd Bn	B
ZD	116 RCAF	7
ZD	222	11
ZD	222	5
ZD	6	4
ZD	63 RAA 3rd Bn	B
ZE	293	5
ZE	52	5
ZE	CFE; NFLS	11
ZE	JATC Flt? RCAF	11
ZF	308	5
ZF	549	5
ZG	10 OTU	5
ZG	20 RNZAF	9
ZG	5 SU RNZAF	9
ZH	266	5
ZH	501	4
ZJ	96	5
ZK	24	4
ZK	24	5
ZK	25	11
ZK	25	5

Code	Unit	See Chapter or Appendix
ZK	337 RNorAF	11
ZL	427	5
ZL	77	4
ZM	12 RS, 67 RG	A
ZM	149 RCAF	7
ZM	185	4
ZM	201	5
ZN	106	5
ZO	196	5
ZP	1473 Flt	5
ZP	15 SAAF	10
ZP	457 RAAF	6
ZP	74	5
ZQ	BCIS	11
ZQ	BBU	11
ZQ	FIU/FIDU	5
ZR	132 RCAF	7
ZR	1333 CU	5
ZR	2 OTU	5
ZR	107 (T)OTU	5
ZR	613	4
ZR	613	5
ZS	1336 CU	5
ZS	153 LS, 67 RG	A
ZS	233	5
ZT	20 OTU	5
ZT	258	5
ZT	602	4
ZT	97 C Flt	5
ZU	1664 HCU	5
ZU	334 RNethAF	11
ZV	19 OTU	5
ZW	1359 Flt	5

Code	Unit	See Chapter or Appendix
ZW	140	5
ZW	48	4
ZW	personal code	18
ZX	1(B)OTU RNZAF	9
ZX	10 RNZAF	9
ZX	145	5
ZX	3 TEU	5
ZX	4 TEU	5
ZX	55 OTU	5
ZX	702 RNethAF	11
ZY	247	11
ZY	247	5
ZZ	220	5
ZZ	58 OTU	5
ZZ	2 TEU	5
ZZ	personal code	18
ZZ4	personal code	18
ZZII	personal code	18
ZZIII	personal code	18

CHAPTER 4

RAF Pre-war (1938-9)

When the RAF mobilised because of the Munich crisis in September 1938, among other measures camouflage was applied to aircraft, markings were toned down and unit markings removed. The latter were generally replaced by a two-letter combination identifying the unit and the squadron code; the background is fully described in chapter 2. The codes were first seen on or about 25 September 1938. Their application was initially patchy, but gradually over succeeding months, especially after new equipment arrived, they became more widely used, such that by mid-1939 the aircraft of most home-based squadrons carried codes.

Codes were also carried by overseas-based aircraft, though in India it is believed only by those with a reinforcement role such as the Valentias of No. 31 Squadron. On the outbreak of war in September 1939, an entirely new sequence of code letters came into force for operational aircraft, the only time that the entire sequence was changed.

As suggested in chapter 2, it is likely that two code lists existed in 1938, one for implementation on mobilisation as happened at the Munich period and another for action on the outbreak of hostilities. This would account for the change of code by some units in the spring of 1939 only for them to revert to their apparently original code when war began. Conversely, other than Nos 2 and 213 Squadrons, which retained the same letters throughout the war and beyond, some other units continued wearing their pre-war codes into the war for a time, and may not have changed until re-equipment during late 1939 or early 1940.

Code	Unit	Type	Dates (noted or to 9.39)	Example	Theatre	Remarks
AD	60	Blenheim I	c 6.39-2.40	L8526/AD-N	India	Used to c 3.40
AK	213	Hurricane I	1.39-50	L1914/AK-M	UK	Used until 1950
AL	79	Gauntlet II	10.39-11.39	K7880/AL-B	UK	
AL	79	Hurricane I	11.38	L1716/AL-D	UK	
AN	13	Lysander II	1.39	L4761/AN-B	UK	*on Hectors late 38?*
AO	211	Hind	c 10.38-4.39	K6833/AO-N	ME	Not on Blenheim
AS	166	Whitley I	6.39	K7184/AS-A	UK	used to c 4.40
AW	504	Hurricane I	3.39	L1956/AW-*	UK	
AW	504	Battle II	c 6.39	N2097/AW-*	UK	used as a trainer
AY	110	Blenheim I	c 11.38-6.39	L1304/AY-Y	UK	
AY	110	Blenheim IV	6.39	N6207/AY-N	UK	
BF	14	Wellesley I	c 6.39	L2654/BF-F	MedME	
BH	215	Harrow II	late 38-6.39	K7032/BH-K	UK	
BH	215	Wellington I	7.39	L4388/BH-B	UK	
BH	228	Sunderland I	6.39	N6135/BH-V	MedME	replaced TO
BK	115	Wellington I	3.39	L4221/BK-U	UK	? use on Harrows. Used to c 4.40
BL	609	Battle I	c 1.39-9.39	N2098 or 9/BL-Y	UK	
BL	*609*	*Spitfire I*	*8.39*	*L1083/BL-**	*UK*	
BS	148	Wellington I	3.39	L4304/BS-ZN		? use on Heyfords
BT	113	Hind	4.39-6.39	K****/BT-T	MedME	
BT	*113*	*Blenheim I*	*?*	*?*	*MedME*	
BW	58	Whitley II, III	c 11.38	K9006/BW-E	UK	
BZ	107	Blenheim I	c 9.38-5.39	L1298/BZ-A	UK	
BZ	*107*	*Blenheim IV*	*5.39*		*UK*	
DD	45	Wellesley I	c 4.39-6.39	L2659/DD-R	UK	*possibly also on Blenheim*
DG	*150*	*Battle I*	*c 3.39*	*K9483/DG-O*	*UK*	*? use probable*
DL	54	Gladiator I	c 9.38-3.39	K****/DL-S	UK	
DL	54	Spitfire I	3.39	K9883/DL-T	UK	
DP	30	Blenheim I	c 6.39	K7096/DP-A	Iraq	
DU	70	Valentia I	c 10.38	K1311/DU-L	UK	
EB	41	Spitfire I	1.39-3.39	*****/EB-F	UK	Early use of wartime code
ED	78	Whitley I	9.38-4.39	K7156/ED-A	UK	replaced by YY
EE	16	Lysander I	4.39	L4795/EE-M	UK	replaced KJ
EF	15	Battle II	c 11.38	K9233/EF-J	UK	

Code	Unit	Type	Dates (noted or to 9.39)	Example	Theatre	Remarks
EQ	57	Blenheim I	*c* 11.38	L8597/EQ-T	UK	
EW	47	Wellesley I	*c* 6.39	L2650/EW-B	MedME	
EY	233	Anson I	*c* 11.38	K6298/EY-V	UK	
FD	114	Blenheim I	10.38-4.39	L1206/FD-H	UK	
FD	114	Blenheim IV	4.39	N6155/FD-F	UK	
FJ	37	Harrow II	*c* 1.39-5.59	K6959/FJ-B	UK	
FJ	*37*	*Wellington I*	*5.39*		*UK*	
FK	*209*	*Stranraer I*			*UK*	
FO	75	Harrow I	10.38-7.39	K6954/FO-E	UK	
FO	75	Wellington I	7.39	L4371/FO-Q	UK	
FV	230	Sunderland I	*c* 3.39-9.39	L2164/FV-Z	FE	
FY	4	Lysander II	4.39	L4746/FY-L	UK	replaced TV
FZ	65	Gladiator I	10.39-3.39	K7941/FZ-U	UK	
FZ	65	Spitfire I	3.39	K9956/FZ-P	UK	
GA	208	Lysander I	*c* 4.39	L4711/GA-B	MedME	
GB	*166*	*Whitley I*			*UK*	*? use*
GG	151	Hurricane I	*c* 12.38	L1724/GG-M	UK	replaced TV?
GJ	213	Hurricane I	1.39-4.39	L1772/GJ-*	UK	
GK	80	Gladiator I	*c* 4.39	K****/GK-Z	UK	replaced OD
GU	18	Blenheim I	5.39	L1165/GU-M	UK	
GV	103	Battle I	*c* 3.39	K9263/GV-B	UK	
GZ	*611*	*Spitfire I*	*c* *5.39*	*L1036/GZ-N*	*UK*	*? use probable*
HE	605	Gladiator II	1.39-*c* 10.39	N5586/HE-K	UK	
HE	605	Hurricane I	8.39	N2349/HE-V	UK	
HH	273	Vildebeeste III	8.39	K****/HH-B	FE	Used into WW2
HL	26	Lysander II	*c* 2.39	L4774/HL-*	UK	*Possibly on Hectors*
HU	220	Anson I	*c* 10.38-6.39	K6207/HU-M	UK	*? replaced by PK*
HV	73	Hurricane I	*c* 9.38	L1578/HV-A	UK	
HY	88	Battle II	*c* 3.39	K9674/HY-F	UK	
JH	*74*	*Gauntlet II*	*c* *10.38-2.39*		*UK*	
JH	74	Spitfire I	2.39	K9875/JH-N	UK	
JO	62	Blenheim I	*c* 10.38	K7174/JO-L	UK	
JP	21	Blenheim I	*c* 3.39	L1279/JP-L	UK	
JU	*202*	*London II*			*MedME*	
JW	44	Blenheim I	10.38-2.39	L1267/JW-Q	UK	
JW	44	Hampden I	2.39	L4085/JW-A	UK	
KA	9	Wellington I	*c* 2.39	L4276/KA-M	UK	
KB	142	Battle I	3.39	K9321/KB-M	UK	
KJ	16	Lysander I	10.38-3.39	L6855/KJ-Q	UK	replaced by EE
KL	269	Anson I	*c* 10.38	K6259/KL-G	UK	
KO	2	Lysander II	*c* 10.38	L6852/KO-H	UK	Used until 1941
KP	226	Battle I	10.38-8.39	K7624/KP-B	UK	MQ from 8.39
KQ	502	Anson I	*c* 1.39	N50**/KQ E	UK	
KT	32	Gauntlet II	9.38-10.38	K5330/KT-P	UK	
KT	32	Hurricane I	10.38	L1659/KT-G	UK	
LB	34	Blenheim I	*c* 4.39	L1252/LB-H	UK, FE	
LJ	211	Blenheim I	*c* 5.9-9.39	L1490/LJ-R	ME	
LO	602	Gauntlet II	1.39-5.39	K7879/LO-K	UK	replaced by ZT
LR	56	Hurricane I	9.38	L1593/LR-C	UK	
LS	*61*	*Blenheim I*	*?*	*?*	*UK*	
LS	61	Hampden I	2.39	L4114/LS-P	UK	
LT	7	Whitley II	10.38-5.39	K7253/LT-L	UK	
LT	*7*	*Anson I*	*c* *3.39*		*UK*	
LT	*7*	*Hampden I*	*c* *4.39*		*UK*	
LU	101	Blenheim I	*c* 10.38-4.39	L4888/LU-V	UK	
LU	101	Blenheim IV	4.39	L****/LU-N	UK	
LW	607	Demon	*c* 9.38-12.38	K****/LW-T	UK	
LW	607	Gladiator I	*c* 12.38	L7939/LW-J	UK	
LY	149	Heyford I, II	*c* 10.38-3.39	K****/LY-A	UK	
LY	149	Wellington I	1.39	L4259/LY-R	UK	
MB	52	Battle I	3.39	K7606/MB-N	UK	
MF	108	Blenheim I	*c* 10.38	L1275/MF-M	UK	
MR	*97*	*Whitley II*			*UK*	

Code	Unit	Type	Dates (noted or to 9.39)	Example	Theatre	Remarks
MS	23	Demon	9.38-12.38	K5698/MS-G	UK	
MS	23	Blenheim If	12.38	L1466/MS-N	UK	
MT	105	Battle I	c 10.38	K7685/MT-*	UK	*Codes soon dropped*
MV	600	Demon	10.38-1.40	K****/MV-E	UK	
MV	600	Blenheim If	1.39	L6682/MV-R	UK	
NA	1	Hurricane I	10.38	L1694/NA-F	UK	
NE	63	Battle I	10.38-3.39	K9423/NE-G	UK	replaced ON
NH	38	Wellington I	11.38	L4242/NH-S	UK	
NJ	207	Battle II	c 11.38	K9200/NJ-Z	UK	
NM	76	Wellesley I	c 11.8-4.39	K7748/NM-H	UK	
NM	*76*	*Hampden I*	*3.39*		*UK*	
NM	*76*	*Anson I*	*3.39*		*UK*	
NO	85	Hurricane I	9.38	L1635/NO-B	UK	
NQ	43	Hurricane I	11.38	L1726/NQ-D	UK	
NV	144	Blenheim I	10.38-3.39	K7081/NV-K	UK	
NV	144	Hampden I	3.39	L4141/NV-P	UK	
OD	80	Gladiator I	9.38-4.39	K7903/OD-B	MedME	replaced by GK
OE	*98*	*Battle II*	*?*	*?*	*UK*	
ON	63	Battle I	3.39	L4958/ON-R	UK	replaced by NE
OP	3	Gladiator I	c 11.38-5.39	K7958/OP-Q	UK	
OP	3	Hurricane I	5.39	L1937/OP-T	UK	
OX	40	Battle II	c 10.38	K9308/OX-S	UK	
OZ	82	Blenheim I	c 10.38	L1333/OZ-S	UK	
PB	10	Whitley II/IV	c 10.38	K9020/PB-L	UK	
PD	87	Hurricane I	9.38	L1646/PD-X	UK	
PG	608	Demon	10.38-3.39	K****/PG-P	UK	
PG	608	Anson I	3.39	N5359/PG-N	UK	Used into early WW2
PJ	59	Hector	9.38-5.39	K9691/PJ-M	UK	
PJ	59	Blenheim IV	5.39	L8791/PJ-Y	UK	
PK	220	Anson I	c 7.39	K6182/PK-A	UK	
PN	41	Spitfire I	1.39	K98**/PN-M	UK	
PO	104	Blenheim I	c 6.39	L****/PO-*	UK	
PP	203	Singapore III	late 38	K4584/PP-C	MedME	
PW	*224*	*Anson I*			*UK*	
PW	224	Hudson I	5.39	N7212/PW-*	UK	
QD	*42*	*Vildebeeste IV*			*UK*	
QE	12	Battle II	9.38	K9377/QE-F	UK	
QF	98	Battle II		K9638/QF-*	UK	*Mistakenly used for OE?*
QQ	83	Hampden I	3.39	L4094/QQ-K	UK	
QX	50	Hampden I	12.38	L4076/QX-D	UK	
RA	100	Vildebeeste III	c 6.39	K6384/RA-T	FE	
RB	66	Spitfire I	11.38	K9812/RB-T	UK	
RF	204	London II	c 10.38-6.39	K5911/RF-G	UK	
RF	204	Sunderland I	6.39	L5802/RF-F	UK	
RJ	46	Gauntlet II	c 10.38-3.39	K****/RJ-Q	UK	
RJ	46	Hurricane I	3.39	L1797/RJ-N	UK	
RL	603	Gladiator I	3.39	K7924/RL-*	UK	
RN	72	Gladiator I	10.38-4.39	K7981/RN-D	UK	replaced by SD
RR	615	Gauntlet II	11.38-5.39	K7854/RR-K	UK	
RR	615	Gladiator II	5.39	N5581/RR-C	UK	
RX	25	Gladiator	10.38-1.39	K****/RX-L	UK	
RX	25	Blenheim If	12.38	L6679/RX-L	UK	
SD	72	Spitfire I	4.39	K9934/SD-K	UK	replaced RN
SH	240	London II	c 7.39	K6929/SH-A	UK	? use on Singapores
SO	33	Gladiator I	9.38-3.39	K8055/SO-H	MedME	replaced by TN
SQ	500	Anson I	3.39	N5225/SQ-M	UK	*? use on Hinds*
SV	218	Battle I	9.38	K9273/SV-R	UK	
SY	139	Blenheim I	10.38-8.39	K7064/SY-H	UK	
SY	139	Blenheim IV	8.39	N6225/SY-M	UK	
TE	53	Blenheim IV	1.39	L4851/TE-D	UK	*? use on Hectors*
TM	111	Hurricane I	10.38	L1821/TM-L	UK	
TN	33	Gladiator I	3.39	L7619/TN-*	UK	replaced SO
TO	228	Stranraer I	c 10.38-4.39	K7296/TO-V	UK	

Code	Unit	Type	Dates (noted or to 9.39)	Example	Theatre	Remarks
TO	228	Sunderland I	11.38-6.39	N9020/TO-W	UK, MedME	replaced by BH
TQ	102	Whitley III	*c* 10.38	K8950/TQ-H	UK	
TV	4	Lysander II	*c* 10.38-3.39	L4746/TV-L	UK	replaced by FY
TV	151?	Gauntlet II	9.38-12.38	K****/TV-E	UK	replaced by GG
TW	90	Blenheim I	10.38	L1283/TW-H	UK	
TW	90	Blenheim IV	3.39	L4879/TW-B	UK	
UT	51	Whitley III	*c* 3.39	K8980/UT-E	UK	
UV	17	Gauntlet II	10.38-6.39	K7822/UV-R	UK	
UV	17	Hurricane I	6.39	L1609/UV-D	UK	
UX	214	Harrow II	*c* 11.38-5.39	K6985/UX-E	UK	
UX	214	Wellington I	5.39	L4345/UX-L	UK	
VF	99	Wellington I	*c* 3.39	L4297/VF-*	UK	
VG	210	Sunderland I	*c* 3.39	L5799/VG-D	UK	
VQ	201	London II	*c* 10.38	L7042/VQ-W	UK	
VR	22	Vildebeeste III	*c* 3.39	K4596/VR-H	UK	
VT	216	Valentia I	*c* 10.38	K3612/VT-D	MedME	
VU	36	Vildebeeste III	*c* 3.39	K4161/VU-G	FE	
WD	206	Anson I	*c* 3.39	K6179/WD-A	UK	
WQ	604	Demon	9.38-1.39	K****/WQ-D	UK	
WQ	604	Blenheim If	1.39	L4908/WQ-Q	UK	
WT	35	Battle II	*c* 3.39	K9471/WT-M	UK	*? use on Ansons*
WZ	19	Spitfire I	*c* 9.38	K9790/WZ-N	UK	
XE	*6*	*Hardy*	*?*	*?*	*MedME*	*? replaced ZD*
XO	112	Gladiator I	6.39	K7954/XO-L	MedME	
XQ	64	Blenheim If	12.38	L1472/XQ-L	UK	*? use on Demons*
XS	106	Hampden I	5.39	L4182/XS-*	UK	*? use on Battles*
XS	106	Anson I	5.39	N5165/XS-K	UK	
XU	49	Hampden I	3.39	L4045/XU-Q	UK	
YB	29	Demon	9.38-12.38	K****/YB-*	UK	
YB	29	Blenheim If	12.38	L1453/YB-K	UK	
YH	11	Blenheim I	8.39	L1820/YH-N	FE	WW2 code applied early
YN	*601*	*Gauntlet II*	*c 9.38-1.39*	*K7888/YN-J*	*UK*	
YN	601	Blenheim If	L8680/YN-A	UK		
YQ	217	Anson I	*c* 10.38	K8813/YQ-V	UK	
YY	78	Whitley I	*c* 10.38	K7201/YY-G	UK	Replaced ED
ZA	31	Valentia I	*c* 6.39	KR2340/ZA-P	UK	
ZD	6	Hardy	*c* 10.38-?	K5916/ZD-T	UK	*? replaced by XE*
ZH	501	Hurricane I	?	L1866/ZH-*	UK	
ZK	*24*	*?*			*UK*	*? use pre-war. Used in WW2*
ZL	77	Whitley III	*c* 11.38	K8977/ZL-P	UK	*? use on Wellesleys*
ZM	185	Hampden I	6.39	L4194/ZM-B	UK	*? use on Ansons & Battles*
ZR	*613*	*?*	*?*	*?*	*UK*	
ZT	602	Spitfire I	5.39	L1019/ZT-G	UK	replaced LO
ZW	*48*	*Anson I*	*?*	*?*	*UK*	

Typical of the equipment of Bomber Command during the late 1930s is the Handley Page Harrow. This Mk II, K7014/BH-L of No. 215 Sqn wears the toned down markings of the Munich period, but is readily identifiable by the squadron's porcupine badge on the nose! (W. Huntley)

Unit codes were also introduced overseas by 1939 as evidenced in this view of Blenheim I K7096/DP-A of the Iraq-based No. 30 Sqn. The first unit overseas to receive the Blenheim, this squadron later used them as long-range fighters. (via John Hamlin)

Based in Egypt and the Sudan were several squadrons with Wellesley Is, including No. 45 at Helwan where L2656/DD-R undergoes maintenance outside one of the large hangars in early 1939. (via Ian Simpson)

With its serial number overpainted and markings toned down, Gladiator I FZ-O of No. 65 Sqn has a sombre appearance at Hornchurch in Essex in early 1939 shortly before they were given up for Spitfires. (W. Huntley)

Flt Lt George Pinkerton poses in front of Gauntlet II K7879/LO-K of No. 602 (City of Glasgow) Sqn of the Auxiliary Air Force at Abbotsinch in May 1939. This is one of the few photographs to come to light of coded Gauntlets. (via Dugald Cameron)

The lumbering Handley Page Heyford remained in service with several squadrons into 1939. Though they have never been previously thought to have worn unit codes, this sadly unidentified Mk II coded LY-A, of No. 49 Sqn, seen in the spring of 1939, proves otherwise and may well be seen being dismantled for disposal. (Yorkshire Air Museum)

Apprentices at the Technical School at Locking work on Blenheim I L1165/GU-M renumbered as 1455M, which retains the pre-war codes of its service with No. 18 Sqn. Immediately behind is an unidentified Demon coded YB which had served with No. 29 Sqn at the time of the Munich crisis and which was replaced by the Blenheim If in December 1938. (P. H. T. Green Collection)

This superb view of a Battle I shows K9423/NE-G of No. 63 Sqn wearing the code letters adopted in accordance with the Air Ministry Order 27 April 1939. They replaced ON which appear to have been reused by this unit from September 1939. (Gp Capt W. S. G. Maydwell)

Unlike the aircraft of some units, the army co-operation Hectors of the Odiham based No. 59 Sqn were camouflaged and marked in a standard manner as evidenced by K9890/PJ-B in early 1939 shortly before being replaced by the Blenheim IV. (No. 59 Sqn Records)

Units based in Singapore before the war also adopted unit codes as shown by Vildebeest III K4599/VU-J of No. 36 Sqn as it conducts torpedo training over the Johore Strait. The codes and red/blue roundels contrast with the coloured wheel spats and fin badge. (RAFM)

Stranraer I K7296/TO-V of No. 228 Sqn rides peacefully at anchor at Calshot water in early 1939, looking quite at home among the tall ships. This unit was in the process of receiving Sunderlands at the time, also coded TO, though the code changed soon after moving to Egypt. (Author's Collection)

The Hawker Hardys of No. 6 Sqn in Palestine retained their full prewar colour scheme until the outbreak of war, merely following the instructions to apply unit codes as is well shown in this view of K5916/ZD-T at Lydda. (Gp Capt J. Pelly-Fry)

CHAPTER 5

RAF Wartime

Single-character

At several periods during the Second World War some operational theatres ceased the use of the conventional two-letter unit code and substituted a single letter. The system, probably introduced for security purposes, was applied on operational squadrons mainly in Malta during 1942–3 and on some Spitfire units in North Africa during and after the Operation Torch landings in Algeria from November 1942. In both cases the singleletter codes were eventually replaced by the normal two-letter variety, generally by mid-1943. With the exceptions of Nos 229 and 249 Squadrons, the periods of use of single-letter codes on Malta are not certain, particularly as, in the desperate conditions during the siege, aircraft were often transferred from one unit to another. The allocation of some codes to several units is based on photographic evidence, is assumed by the authors, and is indicated as such.

As ever there were exceptions, and research has shown that a single-letter unit identifier was used on the Hurricanes of No. 126 Squadron on Malta in the summer of 1941, and were retained for several months. Likewise the unique

squadron, No. 1435 – the only one to have a four-digit number as it had originally been a Malta-based flight that was expanded – continued to use its single-letter code for its entire existence.

Elsewhere, a single-letter code was also used by the aircraft of Aden-based No. 8 Squadron, being introduced in 1943 to differentiate them from other Aden-based aircraft. The Hurricanes of the No. 151 Wing expedition to northern Russia in late 1941 also used a form of single-letter code, but for somewhat different reasons. To accommodate the Soviet-style Cyrillic script identity numbers which were placed aft of the roundel, the normal individual letter was placed forward of the roundel in place of the second letter of the unit code. Thus the FL and GQ codes of Nos 81 and 134 Squadrons became F and G for the expedition.

Finally, single-letter codes were introduced on aircraft of some of the individual flights within several operational or refresher training units in the UK and Mediterranean area by 1944, probably after the system had been superseded in operational formations.

Code	Unit	Type	Dates	Example	Theatre	Remarks
5	5 METS	Beaufighter	*c* 43-44	****/5-F	MedME	
5	5 METS	Beaufort	*c* 43-44	****/5-Z	MedME	
5	5 METS	Gordon	*c* 43-44	****/5-Q	MedME	
5	5 METS	Hurricane	*c* 43-44	****/5-V	MedME	
5	5 METS	Wellington	*c* 43-44	****/5-A	MedME	
6	600	Beaufighter VI	*c* 43-44	MM***/6-M	MedME	
6	600	Mosquito XIX	1.45-8.45	TA133/6-X	MedME	
A	126?	Spitfire Vc	*c* mid-late	42 E****/A-M	Malta	
A	81	Spitfire Vc	*c* 11.43-*c* 5.43	EP650/A-R	MedME	
A	8	Blenheim V	*c* 43	BA490/A-2	Aden	
A	8	Wellington XIII	12.43-5.45	JA271/A-E	Aden	
A	EACF	Hudson VI	7.44-5.46	FK500/A-A	Africa	
A	57 OTU	Spitfire I	*c* 3.41	*****/A-C	UK	
A	131 OTU	Catalina Ib; IV	*c* 44-45	JK251/AM	UK	Catalina Flt
A	5 RFU	Spitfire IX	*c* 44-45	MA707/A-3	MedME	
A	5 RFU	Kittyhawk I	*c* 44-45	AK578/A-K	MedME	
B	242	Spitfire Vc	*c* 11.42-*c* 5.43	ER2**/B-E	MedME	
B	131 OTU	Catalina Ib; IV	*c* 44-45	JX383/BL	UK	
C	131 OTU	Sunderland III	*c* 44-45	W6066/CL	UK	Sunderland Flt
C	MedME CS	Baltimore V	*c* 44-45	FW373/C-C	MedME	
C	654	Auster AOP IV	*c* 44	MT281/C-11	MedME	
D	CGS	Spitfire Vb	*c* 44-45	AB210/D-K	UK	
E	73 OTU	Tomahawk IIb	*c* 43	AK431/E-D	MedME	
F	81	Hurricane IIb	9.41-11.41	Z4006/FV-54	Russia	

Code	Unit	Type	Dates	Example	Theatre	Remarks
F	185?	Spitfire Vc	c 8.42-c late 42		Malta	
F	154?	Spitfire Vc	c 11.42-c 5.43	***42/F-H	MedME	
F	72 OTU	Spitfire Vc	c 43-44	ER934/F-A	MedME	
G	134	Hurricane IIb	9.41-11.41	Z5159/GV-33	Russia	
G	87	Spitfire Vc	c 11.42-c 7.43		MedME	
G	87	Spitfire IX	c 6-7.43	EN455/G-R	MedME	
J	93	Spitfire Vc	c 11.42-c 5.43	ER979/J-J	MedME	
L	152	Spitfire Vc	c 11.42-c 5.43	JG871/L-E	MedME	
T	249	Spitfire Vb	c 5.42-c 7.43	EP131/T-O	Malta	
T	249	Spitfire Vc	c 5.42-c 7.43	BR568/T-M	Malta	
T	249	Spitfire IX	c 6.43-c 7.43	EN256/T-B	Malta	
V	1435	Spitfire Vb; c	c 8.42-9.44	EP436/V-S	Malta/MedME	
V	1435	Spitfire IX	3.43-4.45	MH660/V-Y	Malta/MedME	
X	126	Hurricane I	mid 41-10.41	Z3033/X-N	Malta	
X	229	Spitfire Vc	c 8.42-c 7.43	EP641/X-J	Malta	
X	229	Spitfire IX	1.43-3.44	EN519/X-V	Malta	

Two-character

Code	Unit	Type	Dates	Example	Theatre	Remarks
2A	SF St Eval	Oxford	45	ED268/2A-C	UK	
2A	SF St Eval	Martinet	45	EM439/2A-J	UK	
2B	272 MU		45		UK	use not known
2D	24		45			use not known
2H	SF Brawdy		45		UK	use not known
2I	443	Spitfire IX	3.44-3.45	MK366/2I-V	UK, Eur	
2I	443	Spitfire XVI	1.45-3.46	TD191/2I-P	Eur	
2I	443	Spitfire XIV	1.46-3.46	TZ198/2I-M	Eur	
2K	1668 HCU	Lancaster III	1.45-3.46	LM170/2K-X	UK	
2K	1668 HCU	Beaufighter VIf	3.45-3.46	V8615/2T-K	UK	
2L	9 MU		45		UK	use not known
2M	520	Halifax V	2.44-6.45	LL520/2M-H	MedME	
2M	520	Hurricane IIc	6.44-4.46	PZ830/2M-D	MedME	
2M	520	Martinet I	9.44-12.45	NR291/2M-T	MedME	
2M	520	Halifax II		DG344/2M-G	MedME	
2M	520	Halifax III	4.45-4.46	NA223/2M-O	MedME	
2N	SF Foulsham	Spitfire IX	45	MH439/2N-N	UK	not confirmed
2O	84 GCF	Hurricane IV	c 45	PG488/2O-C	Eur	
2P	644	Halifax III	8.44-11.45	NA672/2P-L	UK	
2P	644	Halifax V	10.44-45	LL381/2P-Q	UK	
2P	644	Halifax VII	3.45-9.46	NA348/2P-J	UK	
2Q	88 GCF	Anson XII	5.45-12.45	PH645/2Q-J	Eur	
2V	547	Liberator V	11.43-44	BZ821/2V-Q	UK	
2V	547	Liberator VI	6.44-6.45	EW299/2V-H	UK	
2V	547	Liberator VIII	3.45-6.45	KK327/2V-M	UK	
2W	3 SGR	Anson I	c 45-3.46	EG413/2W-H	UK	
2X	85 OTU	Master II	6.44-6.45	DK927/2X-Y	UK	
2X	85 OTU	Martinet I	6.44-6.45	JN508/2X-Y	UK	
2Y	345	Spitfire Vb	3.44-9.44	AA943/2Y-T	UK	
2Y	345	Spitfire IX	9.44-4.45	PT913/2Y-Y	UK, Eur	
2Y	345	Spitfire XVI	4.45-11.45	TD338/2Y-P	Eur	
3B	23 MU		45		UK	use not known
3C	1 LFS	Lancaster	11.43-11.44	R5500/3C-K	UK	
3E	100 GCF		45		UK	use not known
3F	BAFO CW		45		Eur	use not known

Code	Unit	Type	Dates	Example	Theatre	Remarks
3G	111 OTU	Halifax VI	c 12.45	NA253/3G-*	UK	
3H	80 OTU	Spitfire IX	4.45-3.46	BS395/3H-Y	UK	
3K	1695 BDTF	Hurricane IIc	2.44-7.45	LF575/3K-S	UK	
3K	1695 BDTF	Hurricane IV	2.44-7.45	KZ714/3K-D	UK	
3K	1695 BDTF	Spitfire Vb	2.44-7.45	AR278/3K-H	UK	
3K	1695 BDTF	Martinet I	2.44-7.45	MS869/3K-V	UK	
3M	679	Martinet I	12.43-6.45	HN958/3M-Q	UK	
3M	679	Hurricane IIc	12.43-6.45	KZ661/3M-V	UK	
3O	*SF Wratting Common*			45	UK	*use not known*
3P	515	Mosquito VI	3.44-6.45	NS957/3P-V	UK	
3S	3GCF	Anson XII	45-46	PH788/3S-R	UK	
3S	3GCF	Master II	3.45-7.46	AZ702/3S	UK	
3S	3GCF	Proctor III	45-50	LZ567/3S-A	UK	
3T	*SF Acaster Malbis*				UK	*use not known*
3W	322	Spitfire XIV	6.44-8.44	****/3W-*	UK	
3W	322	Spitfire IXb	8.44-11.44	MJ964/3W-V	UK	
3W	322	Spitfire XVIe	11.44-10.45	TB747/3W-D	UK	to RNethAF
3X	*38 MU*				UK	*use not known*
3Y	577	Oxford I	12.43-6.46	V3151/3Y-N	UK	
3Y	577	Beaufighter X	11.44-7.45	RD713/3Y-R	UK	
3Y	577	Spitfire Vb	6.45-7.45	BM569/3Y-F	UK	
3Y	577	Spitfire XVI	6.45-6.46	SM511/3Y-J	UK	
3Y	577	Anson I	45-46	NL245/3Y-Y	UK	
4B	*2 GCF*		45		UK	*use not known*
4B	*5 GCF*	*Anson, Oxford*	45-12.45		UK	*use not known*
4D	74	Spitfire IX	5.44-3.45	PT858/4D-P	UK	
4D	74	Spitfire XVI	3.45-5.45	TB6774/4D-V	UK	
4E	1687 BDTF	Spitfire Vb	7.44-10.46	AB487/4E-S	UK	
4E	1687 BDTF	Hurricane IIc	11.44-10.46	LF561/4E-U	UK	
4E	1687 BDTF	Martinet I	11.44-10.46	MS624/4E-M	UK	
4H	142	Mosquito XXV	10.44-9.45	KB449/4H-V	UK	
4H	?	Lancaster III	c 45	*****/4H-Z	UK	Reverse painting of H4 of 1653 CU?
4J	*5 MU*		45	*****/4J-H	UK	*use not known*
4J	*3(C)OTU*	Wellington XIII	mid 43-44		UK	
4L	*SF Melton Mowbray*			45	UK	*use not known*
4M	695	Henley III	12.43-6.44	L3354/4M-P	UK	
4M	695	Hurricane IIc	12.43-9.45	PZ751/4M-W	UK	
4M	695	Martinet I	12.43-5.45	HN958/4M-C	UK	
4M	695	Vengeance IV	11.44-5.47	HB545/4M-A	UK	
4Q	59 OTU	Typhoon Ib	3.45-6.45	SW531/4Q-A	UK	1 Sqn
4Q	59 OTU	Martinet	3.45-6.45	JN666/4Q-C	UK	1 Sqn
4Q	CCFATU	Vengeance IV	9.45-2.46	HB364/4Q	UK	
4Q	CCFATU	Martinet I	9.45-2.46	EM650/4Q-J	UK	
4Q	CCFATU	Spitfire XVI	9.45-2.46	TE256/4Q-V	UK	
4Q	CCFATU	Queen Martinet	9.45-2.46	RH168/4Q-G	UK	
4T	*SF Portreath*		45		UK	*use not known*
4U	*30 MU*		45		UK	*use not known*
4V	*302 FTU*		45		UK	*use not known*
4X	1692 Flt	Mosquito VI	7.43-6.45	LR301/4X-5	UK	
4X	1692 Flt	Anson I	7.43-6.45	DG718/4X-27	UK	
4Z	1699 Flt	Fortress IIF	10.44-6.45	SR376/4Z-W	UK	
4Z	1699 Flt	Liberator VI	10.44-4.45	TS538/4Z-B	UK	
5A	329	Spitfire Vb	2.44-3.44	MH595/5A-B	UK; Eur	
5A	329	Spitfire IX	2.44-11.45	NH601/5A-K	UK; Eur	
5A	329	Spitfire XVI	2.45-4.45	TB388/5A-H	UK; Eur	

The Spitfire squadrons participating in the invasion of North Africa in late 1942 wore a single letter as a unit code for a time. No. 93 Sqn used J which is seen on Spitfire Vc J-J, ER979 at Souk el Khemis with its pilot in early 1943. It was shot down on 17 April. (Peter Arnold Collection)

By late 1944, when this photograph was taken, some second-line units in the Mediterranean area were identified by a single-letter code. One such unit was No. 5 Refresher Flying Unit at Perugia where these Spitfire IXs, including MA545/A-12, sit in the snow. (Graham Salt)

These bubble-canopied Spitfire XVIs in full French markings belong to No. 345 Sqn which had fought through the north-west Europe campaign. The nearest aircraft is believed to be TD388/2Y-P; the introduction of numbers with letter into the code sequence greatly increased the available combinations. (Col L. Robveille)

Seen during a target towing sortie for the destroyer HMCS Iroquois on 4 January 1945, Defiant TT III T3919/5S-W of No. 691 Sqn also shows the unit codes to advantage. Most of the unit's various types also wore the code. (A. Cole)

Albemarle I coded 9W-N of No. 296 Sqn wears full black and white AEAF identification stripes when seen in the late summer of 1944. Used for support and delivery of Airborne Forces, it was later replaced by the Stirling IV. (via J. D. R. Rawlings)

Lancaster I HK551/A4-E displays the codes allocated to C Flight of No. 115 Sqn. By the middle of the war many bomber squadrons were so large that a separate code was allocated to the third flight. An aircraft with No. 115's KO code is in the background. (A. T. Douglas)

Meteorological reconnaissance squadrons normally flew several types at the same time, usually long-range aircraft. No. 251 Sqn flew from Iceland mainly using AD coded Hudson IIIas like V8988/AD-Z and Fortress IIas like FK197/AD-E seen in mid-1945. (G. Flowerday)

At the end of the war many squadrons switched to transport duties using converted bombers or maritime aircraft. One such was No. 59 Sqn which flew Liberator C.VIs like KL687/AE-R from which all camouflage paint had been stripped. (via M. J. F. Bowyer)

Cameras are loaded into a Polish manned Lysander III, V7437/AR-V of No. 309 Sqn in 1941 and which proclaims its nationality with the national red and white checked marking aft of the roundel. (via P. Skulski)

Possibly as a security measure, on re-equipping with Catalinas in April 1941, Gibraltar-based No. 202 Sqn adopted the codes AX which were also worn on the few Sunderlands it also flew such as Mk III DV962/AXQ. (via N. Mackenzie)

Code	Unit	Type	Dates	Example	Theatre	Remarks
5B	84 GSU	Tempest V	12.44-11.45	EJ871/5B-L	UK	
5D	SF Gibraltar		45		MedME	use not known
5F	147	Halifax VII	45-9.46	PN300/5F-*	UK	probable
5G	299	Stirling IV	1.44-2.46	LJ891/5G-D	UK	
5H	SF Chivenor	Beaufighter	45		UK	use not confirmed
5J	126	Spitfire IXb	5.44-12.44	MH438/5J-X	MedME	
5J	126	Mustang III	12.44-8.45	KH564/5J-H	MedME	
5J	126	Mustang IV	8.45-3.46	KH729/5J-E	MedME	
5J	126	Spitfire XVI	2.46-3.46	TE397/5J-X	MedME	
5L	187		45		UK	use not known
5N	38 GCF	Proctor III	c 45-49	LZ792/5N-S	UK	
5N	38 GCF	Oxford II	44-46	PH299/5N-D	UK	
5O	521	Halifax III	1.46-3.46	RG363/5O-C	UK	
5O	521	Hurricane IIc	6.44-4.46	PZ818/5O-K	UK	
5O	521	Fortress II	12.44-2.46	FA696/5O-B	UK	
5O	521	Fortress IIa	12.44-2.46	FL452/5O-U	UK	
5R	33	Spitfire IXe	4.44-12.44	BS239/5R-E	UK, Eur	
5R	33	Typhoon Ib	44-12.44	EK495/5R-L	UK, Eur	
5R	33	Tempest V	12.44-11.45	SN315/5R-Y	Eur	
5S	691	Defiant III	12.43-4.45	N1728/5S-G	UK	
5S	691	Oxford II	12.43-2.49	LW868/5S-B	UK	
5S	691	Hurricane IIc	3.44-8.45	LF638/5S-P	UK	
5S	691	Vengeance IV	4.45-5.47	FD193/5S-G	UK	
5S	691	Martinet	8.45-2.49	JN513/5S-S	UK	
5T	233	Dakota III	3.44-12.45	KG403/5T-UQ	UK	
5T	233	Dakota IV	3.44-12.45	KJ844/5T-T	UK	
5V	439	Hurricane IV	1.44-4.44	LD570/5V-Z	UK	
5V	439	Typhoon Ib	1.44-8.45	SW423/5V-J	UK	
5W	SF Snaith		45		UK	use not known
6B	SF Tempsford		45		UK	use not known
6D	631	Henley TT III	12.43-2.45	L***/6D-T	UK	
6D	631	Spitfire Vb	6.45-7.45	AB186/6D-J	UK	
6D	631	Martinet	9.44-2.49	HN884/6D-K	UK	
6F	1669 HCU	Halifax V	8.44-11.44	EB248/6F-O	UK	
6F	1669 HCU	Lancaster III	8.44-3.45	PB215/6F-M	UK	
6G	223	Liberator IV	8.44-7.45	TS526/6G-T	MedME	
6G	223	Liberator VI		KL594/6G-V	MedME	
6G	223	Fortress II	4.45-7.45	SR283/6G-X	MedME	
6G	223	Fortress III	4.45-7.45	KL836/6G-Z	MedME	
6H	1688 BDTF	Martinet I	2.44-9.46	HP352/6H-S	UK	
6H	1688 BDTF	Hurricane IIc	3.44-11.44	LF579/6H-P	UK	
6H	1688 BDTF	Spitfire Vb	3.44-9.46	BM134/6H-D	UK	
6H	1688 BDTF	Tiger Moth	3.44	T7351/6H-K	UK	
6H	96	Halifax III	12.44-3.45	MZ464/6H-Q	UK	
6O	582	Lancaster I	4.44-9.45	ME623/6O-C	UK	
6O	582	Lancaster III	4.44-9.45	PB141/6O-F	UK	
6Q	SF Pembroke Dock				UK	use not known
6R	41 OTU				UK	use not known
6S	190	Halifax III	5.45-1.46	NA406/6S-N	UK	
6T	608	Mosquito XX	8.44-4.45	KB265/6T-F	UK	
6T	608	Mosquito 25	10.44-4.45	KB413/6T-V	UK	
6T	608	Mosquito XVI	1.45-8.45	RV359/6T-X	UK	
6U	415	Halifax III	7.44-5.45	NA185/6U-A	UK	
6U	415	Halifax VII	3.45-5.45	RG447/6U-S	UK	
6V	SF Cottesmore				UK	use not known
6Y	171	Stirling III	9.44-1.45	LJ559/6Y-J	UK	

Code	Unit	Type	Dates	Example	Theatre	Remarks
6Y	171	Halifax III	9.44-7.45	NA110/6Y-Z	UK	
6Z	*19 MU*		*45*		*UK*	*use not known*
7B	595	Martinet	12.43-2.49	EM697/7B-Z	UK	
7B	595	Spitfire Vb	11.44-46	BM628/7B-M	UK	
7B	595	Oxford II	44-2.49	NM808/7B-S	UK	
7B	595	Spitfire IX	7.45-4.48	PT753/7B-G	UK	
7C	296	Halifax III	10.44-2.46	NA657/7C-C	UK	
7D	*57 MU*		*45*		*UK*	*use not known*
7E	*327*	*Spitfire IX*	*10.43-11.45*		*MedME*	*use not known*
7G	*SF Northolt*		*45*		*UK*	*use not known*
7H	*84 GCF*		*45*			*use not known*
7I	*SF Acklington*		*45*		*UK*	*use not known*
7K	*S&RTU*	*Sea Otter I, Walrus*	*7.45-4.49*		*UK*	*reported*
7L	59 OTU	Typhoon Ib	3.45-6.45	SW562/7L-D	UK	3 Sqn
7M	*1 PTS*		*45*		*UK*	*use not known*
7N	SFU	Anson I	7.44-9.46	LV291/7N-K	UK	
7N	SFU	Beaufighter X	7.45-9.46	KW337/7N-S	UK	
7N	SFU	Wellington XIV	7.45-9.46	NC887/7N-O	UK	
7N	SFU	Stirling IV	7.45-9.46 UK			
7O	*?*	*Anson*	*46*		*UK*	*reported*
7R	524	Wellington XIII	4.44-12.44	MF320/7R-C	UK	
7R	524	Wellington XIV	12.44-5.45	NB854/7R-K	UK	
7S	83 GSU	Typhoon Ib	3.44-8.45	MN135/7S-Q	UK	
7S	83 GSU	Spitfire IX	3.44-8.45	NH175/7S-O	UK	
7S	83 GSU	Mustang III	3.44-8.45	FB***/7S-*	UK	
7S	83 GSU	Tempest V	9.44-8.45	EJ760/7S-H	UK	
7S	83 GSU	Spitfire XIV	10.44-7.45	RM685/7S-F	UK	
7T	196	Stirling IV	2.44-3.46	LJ948/7T-C	UK	
7T	196	Stirling V	1.46-3.46	PJ912/7T-L	UK	
7U	*SF Bardney*		*45*		*UK*	*use not known*
7X	*SF Aldergrove*		*45*		*UK*	*use not known*
7Z	105 OTU	Wellington X	6.44-8.45	HE242/7Z-Q	UK	to 1381 (T)CU
7Z	1381 (T)CU	Wellington X	8.45-12.49	HE242/7Z-Q	UK	ex 105 OTU
7Z	1381 (T)CU	Dakota III	8.45-2.48	FD944/7Z-R	UK	
8A	298	Halifax V	11.43-10.44	LL224/8A-A	UK	
8A	298	Halifax III	10.44-8.45	NA119/8A-T	UK	
8A	298	Halifax VII	5.45-12.46	PN259/8A-G	UK	
8C	*12 MU*		*45*		*UK*	*use not known*
8E	295	Stirling IV	7.44-1.46	LJ652/8E-X	UK	
8F	105 (T)OTU	Wellington X	6.44-8.45	MF521/8F-R	UK	
8F	105 (T)OTU	Dakota IV	6.45-8.45	KJ875/8F-GE	UK	to 1381 CU
8F	1381 CU	Dakota III	8.45-	KJ825/8F-GE	UK	ex 105 OCU
8H	*8 GCF*		*45*		*UK*	*use not known*
8I	2 APS	Martinet	12.45-2.46	HP327/8I-16	UK	
8I	2 APS	Harvard IIb	12.45-2.46	KF342/8I-S	UK	
8I	2 APS	Mosquito VI	12.45-2.46	TA555/8I-B	UK	
8I	2 APS	Master II	12.45-2.46	DM128/8I-F	UK	
8I	2 APS	Spitfire XVI	12.45-2.46	TE178/8I-M	UK	
8I	2 APS	Mustang IV	12.45-2.46	KM218/8I-K	UK	to APS Acklington
8J	*435*	*Dakota*	*45*		*UK*	*use not known*
8J	326	Spitfire IX	12.43-11.45	ML301/8J-L	MedME	
8K	571	Mosquito XVI	4.44-9.45	ML963/8K-K	UK	
8M	*266*		*45*		*UK*	*use not known*
8O	*BAFO CW*		*45*		*Eur*	*use not known*
8P	*525*		*45*		*UK*	*use not known*

Code	Unit	Type	Dates	Example	Theatre	Remarks
8Q	291	Tiger Moth II	12.43-6.45		UK	
8Q	291	Martinet TT.I	12.43-6.45	HN862/8Q-F	UK	
8Q	291	Vengeance IV	11.44-6.45	HB519/8Q-C	UK	
8Q	291	Hurricane IIc	3.44-6.45	PZ751/8Q-W	UK	
8T	298	Halifax III	10.44-8.45	NA677/8T-C	UK	
8T	298	Halifax VII	5.45-12.46	PN259/8T-G	UK,	FE B Flt
8U	SF Ballykelly	Spitfire XVI	c 45	RW388/8U-U	UK	
8V	*61 OTU*	*Warwick*		*****/8V-K*	*UK*	*reported*
8W	612	Wellington XIV	6.43-7.45	NB977/8W-M	UK	
8Y	*15 MU*		*45*		*UK*	*use not known*
8Z	295	Albemarle II	10.43-7.44	V1740/8Z-A	UK	
8Z	295	Stirling IV	7.44-2.46	LK439/8Z-S	UK	
9C	82 OTU	Wellington III, X	c 44-45	*****/9C-K	UK	
9E	*BAFO Comms Flt*		*45*		*Eur*	*use not known*
9F	SF Stradishall	Oxford I	45-46	PG968/9F-*	UK	
9G	441	Spitfire IX	3.44-6.45	MK465/9G-F	UK	
9G	441	Mustang III	5.45-8.45	HB876/9G-L	UK	
9I	326	Spitfire IX			Eur	
9J	227	Lancaster I	10.44-9.45	RF131/9J-B	UK	
9J	227	Lancaster III	10.44-9.45	LM678/9J-O	UK	
9M	1690 B(D)TF	Hurricane IV	2.44-10.45	LF374/9M-A	UK	
9N	127	Spitfire IX	4.44-1.45		UK	
9N	127	Spitfire XVI	11.44-4.45	RR257/9N-Y	Eur	
9O	*44 MU*		*45*		*UK*	*use not known*
9P	85 OTU	Wellington X	6.44-6.45	HE813/9P-O	UK	C Flt
9R	229	Spitfire IX	4.44-12.44	MH939/9R-R	UK	
9R	229	Spitfire XVI	12.44-1.45	SM390/9R-H	UK	
9S	MAEE	S-45 Seaford	45-3.46	MZ271/9S-B	UK	
9S	MAEE	A-37 Shrimp	45-3.46	TK580/9S-J	UK	
9T	SFU	Wellington XIV	45-1.46	NC885/9T-Z	UK	
9T	SFU	Oxford I	45-1.46	PH345/9T-S	UK	
9T	SFU	Stirling IV	45	*****/9T-M	UK	
9U	644	Halifax V	3.44-12.44	LL402/9U-F	UK	
9U	644	Halifax IIIa	8.44-11.45	NA349/9U-Q	UK	
9U	644	Halifax VII	3.45-9.46	NA314/9U-R	UK, MedME	
9W	296	Albemarle I	1.43-11.44	V1699/9W-H	UK	
9W	296	Halifax V	9.44-3.45	LL441/9W-N	UK	
9W	296	Halifax III	1.45-1.46	NA613/9W-J	UK	
9X	1689 Flt	Anson X	2.44-5.45	NK751/9X-K	UK	
9X	1689 Flt	Proctor III	2.44-5.45	HM400/9X-F	UK	
9X	1689 Flt	Spitfire XVI	2.44-5.45	TE184/9X	UK	
9X	1689 Flt	Argus II	2.44-5.45	HB600/9X	UK	
9X	1689 Flt	Oxford I	2.44-5.45	RR333/9X-P	UK	
9Y	132 OTU	Beaufort II	8.43-5.46	ML658/9Y-N	UK	
9Y	132 OTU	Beaufighter VI	44-8.44	JL549/9Y-FM	UK	
9Y	132 OTU	Mosquito VI	4.44-2.45	RF797/9Y-BT	UK	
9Y	132 OTU	Mosquito III	6.44-5.46	LR517/9Y-BG	UK	
9Y	132 OTU	Beaufighter X	8.44-5.46	RD437/9Y-Q	UK	
9Y	132 OTU	Oxford I	44-5.46	P6801/9Y-A	UK	
A1	1 AACU	Henley III	41-42	L3317/A1-B	UK	A Flt
A2	514	Lancaster II	12.43-6.44	DS787/A2-D	UK	C Flt
A2	514	Lancaster III	6.44-8.45	PA186/A2-G	UK	C Flt
A3	1653 CU	Stirling	11.43-11.44	N3702/A3-J	UK	
A3	1653 CU	Lancaster I, III	11.44-11.46	ND877/A3-A	UK	
A4	115 C Flt	Lancaster II	11.43-5.44	DS827/A4-D	UK	Displayed as A4
A4	115 C Flt	Lancaster III	11.43-8.44	ND758/A4-A	UK	Displayed as A4

Code	Unit	Type	Dates	Example	Theatre	Remarks
A4	195	Lancaster III	10.44-8.45	HK587/A4-D	UK	A, B Flts
A5	3 LFS	Lancaster I	12.43-1.45	L7532/A5-P	UK	
A9	*SF Woodbridge*	*Oxford*			*UK*	*use not known*
AA	75	Wellington Ia	4.40-9.40	P9206/AA-A	UK	
AA	75	Wellington Ic	4.40-1.42	L7848/AA-V	UK	
AA	75	Wellington III	1.42-10.42	BJ832/AA-Z	UK	
AA	75	Stirling I	12.42-8.43	BF399/AA-O	UK	
AA	75	Stirling III	2.43-4.44	EF408/AA-P	UK	
AA	75	Lancaster I, III	4.44-10.45	ND756/AA-M	UK	
AB	423	Sunderland III	5.42-9.42	W6053/AB-E	UK	
AB	1557 RATF	Oxford	late 45-46	AP484/AB-C	UK	ex 1557 BATF
AC	?	Spitfire IX	c 1944-5	PT492/AC-J	MedME	Personal code or CA (3 SAAF) mis-painted
AD	113	Blenheim IV	3.40-12.42	T2177/AD-V	MedME, FE	
AD	113	Hurricane IIc	9.43-4.45	KX924/AD-*	FE	
AD	113	Thunderbolt I	4.45-5.45	HD173/AD-N	FE	
AD	113	Thunderbolt II	6.45-10.45	KJ343/AD-P	FE	
AD	*? 251*	*Halifax*	*9.44*	******/AD-P*	*UK*	*Coastal Cmnd*
AD	251	Warwick ASR I	8-10.45	HG174/AD-R	Eur	
AD	251	Anson I	8.44-10.45	LT199/AD-D	Eur	
AD	251	Hudson III	8.44-8.45	V8988/AD-Z	Eur	
AD	251	Fortress II	3.45-10.45	FK197/AD-E	Eur	
AD	251	Fortress III	c 4.45-10.45	HB792/AD-D	Eur	
AE	402	Hurricane I	3.41-5.41	P3021/AE-X	UK	ex 112 Sqn RCAF
AE	402	Hurricane IIb	5.41-3.42	BE417/AE-K	UK	
AE	402	Spitfire Vb	3.42-7.44	BL812/AE-N	UK	
AE	402	Spitfire IX	5.42-8.44	BS428/AE-U	UK	
AE	402	Spitfire XIVe	8.44-6.45	RN119/AE-J	UK	
AE	1409 Flt	Mosquito PR XVI	45-46	ML897/AE-D	UK	
AF	607	Gladiator I	9.39-5.40		UK, Eur	
AF	607	Hurricane I	3.40-6.41	P2874/AF-F	UK	
AF	607	Hurricane IIa, IIb	6.41-3.42		UK	
AF	607	Hurricane IIb, IIc	6.42-9.43	BD833/AF-Z	FE	
AF	607	Spitfire Vc	9.43-3.44		FE	
AF	607	Spitfire VIII	7.44-6.45	MT954/AF-L	FE	
AF	AFDU	Boston III	7.43-4.44	W8286/AF-Z	UK	
AF	AFDU	Defiant	c 42	V1121/AF-P	UK	
AF	AFDU	Spitfire	c 42	X4815/AF-S	UK	
AF	AFDU	Spitfire Vb	42-43	BL820/AF-T	UK	
AG		Stirling	42	*****/AG-K	UK	
AG	?	Dakota	6.44	KG317/AG-6	UK	
AG	334	Mosquito FB VI	5-11.45	RF873/AG-F	Eur	
AH	332	Spitfire I	1.42	X4238/AH-L	UK	
AH	332	Spitfire Va, Vb	4.42-11.42	BL430/AH-S	UK	
AH	332	Spitfire IX	11.42-4.45	BS429/AH-R	UK	to RNorAF
AI	20 OTU	Wellington X	43-7.45	NA833/AI-A	UK	C Flt
AJ	617	Lancaster III	3.43-6.43	ED932/AJ-G	UK	
AJ	617	Mosquito VI	6.44-?	NT205/AJ-C	UK	target marker
AJ	SF North Luffenham	Oxford	46	*****/AJ-A	UK	
AK	1657 CU	Stirling I	10.42-9.44	R9192/AK-B	UK	
AK	1657 CU	Stirling III	4.43-12.44	LK446/AK-D	UK	
AK	1657 CU	Stirling IV	5.44-12.44	EF309/AK-V	UK	
AK	213	Hurricane I	1.39-3.42	P2882/AK-R	UK	
AK	213	Hurricane IIb	41-42	BM966/AK-T	MedME	
AK	213	Hurricane IIc	1.42-5.44	BP123/AK-S	MedME	

Code	Unit	Type	Dates	Example	Theatre	Remarks
AK	213	Spitfire Vc	2.44-5.44	JK277/AK-*	MedME	
AK	213	Spitfire IX	2.44-6.44	MH676/AK-K	MedME	
AK	213	Mustang III	5.44-3.45	FB337/AK-A	MedME	
AK	213	Mustang IV	2.45-2.47	KM326/AK-D	MedME	
AL	429	Wellington III	11.42-4.43	BJ755/AL-Q	UK	
AL	429	Wellington IX	1.43-8.43	HE414/AL-H	UK	
AL	429	Halifax II	8.43-1.44	JD374/AL-M	UK	
AL	429	Halifax V	10.43-3.44	LL171/AL-U	UK	
AL	429	Halifax III	3.44-5.45	MZ318/AL-F	UK	
AL	429	Lancaster I, III	3.45-3.46	PA225/AL-G	UK	
AL	52?	Battle II	*c* 5.40	K94**/AL-G	UK	
AL	429	Wellington X	11.42-4.43	BJ755/AL-Q	UK	
AM	14 OTU	Wellington Ic	9.42-43	Z8963/AM-G	UK	C Flt
AM	14 OTU	Wellington X	1.44-6.45	LN862/AM-Q	UK	C Flt
AM	14 OTU	Hurricane IIc	8.44-6.45	MW341/AM-A	UK	C Flt
AM	14 OTU	Martinet	4.43-9.44	HP522/AM-B	UK	C Flt
AM	14 OTU	Hampden I		P1209/AM-43	UK	C Flt
AN	417	Spitfire IIa	11.41-2.42	P8570/AN-R	UK	
AN	417	Spitfire Vb	2.42-3.42	AB797/AN-Z	UK	
AN	417	Hurricane IIc	9.42-1.43	BP590/AN-R	MedME	
AN	417	Spitfire Vc	11.42-9.43	ER531/AN-M	MedME	
AN	417	Spitfire VIII	7.43-4.45	JF526/AN-F	MedME	
AN	417	Spitfire IX	3.44-6.45	MJ730/AN-T	MedME	
AN	SF Gt Dunmow	Oxford	45-46	PH117/AN-P	UK	
AO	223	Wellesley I	9.39-4.41	L2556/AO-B	Africa	
AO	AFDU?	Spitfire II	*c* 43	P8562?/AO-*	UK	
AP	186	Hurricane IV	8.43-11.43	KZ577/AP-D	UK	
AP	186	Typhoon Ib	11.43-2.44	JR250/AP-*	UK	
AP	186	Spitfire Vb	2.44-4.44	W3305/AP-*	UK	
AP	186	Lancaster III	10.44-7.45	PB483/AP-X	UK	
AP	130	Spitfire XIV	8.44-5.45	RM699/AP-S	UK, Eur	
AP	130	Spitfire IXb	5.45-10.46	TA804/AP-K	UK	
AP	80	Gladiator	*c* 8.40-?	K8009/AP-*	MedME	? adopted when Hurricanes tx to 274 Sqn
AQ	276	Lysander IIIA	10.41-5.42	V9463/AQ-H	UK	
AQ	276	Walrus I	10.41-11.45	W3026/AQ-N	UK	
AQ	276	Spitfire IIc	11.42-6.44	P8131/AQ-C	UK	
AQ	276	Spitfire Vb	4.43-6.45	EN841/AQ-O	UK	
AQ	276	Anson	3.43-6.45	NK325/AQ-T	UK	
AQ	276	Defiant	5.42-5.43	N3372/AQ-T	UK	
AQ	276	Warwick ASR.1	4.44-10.44	BV531/AQ-P	UK	
AR	460	Lancaster III	5.43-10.45	JB613/AR-A	UK	
AR	309	Lysander III	11.40-10.42	V9484/AR-M	UK	
AS	166	Whitley I	9.39-4.40	K7184/AS-A	UK	
AS	166	Wellington III	1.43-4.43	X3334/AS-W	UK	
AS	166	Wellington X	2.43-9.43	HF589/AS-M	UK	
AS	166	Lancaster I, III	9.43-11.45	LM521/AS-F	UK	
AT	60 OTU	Blenheim V	43-45	AZ897/AT-18	UK	
AT	60 OTU	Mosquito II	5.43-3.45	DZ722/AT-14	UK	yellow
AT	60 OTU	Mosquito III	5.43-3.45	HJ978/AT-*	UK	to 13 OTU
AT	13 OTU	Mosquito III	3.45-45	*****/AT-D	UK	ex 60 OTU
AU	421	Spitfire Vb	5.42-5.43	BL658/AU-Y	UK	
AU	421	Spitfire IX	5.43-12.44	NH183/AU-K	UK	
AU	421	Spitfire XVI	12.44-7.45	*****/AU-Y	Eur	
AV	121	Hurricane IIb	5.41-11.41	Z3669/AV-D	UK	
AV	121	Spitfire IIa	10.41-11.41	P8136/AV-S	UK	

Code	Unit	Type	Dates	Example	Theatre	Remarks
AV	121	Spitfire Vb	11.41-9.42	BM590/AV-R	UK	to 335 FS 4 FG USAAF qv
AV	Wittering	SF Spitfire F.21	1945-6	LA299/AV-H	UK	
AW	42	Vildebeeste III	9.39-4.40	K6397/AW-*	UK	
AW	42	Vildebeeste IV	9.39-4.40	K6411/AW-D	UK	
AW	42	Beaufort I, II, IIA	4.40-7.42		UK	
AW	42	Beaufort IA, II	6.42-10.42	DE110/AW-B	MedME	
AW	42	Beaufort I	4.40-12.42	L9890/AW-L	UK	
AW	42	Beaufort II	3.42-4.43	AW364/AW-W	FE	
AW	42	Blenheim V	2.43-10.43	BA103/AW-H	FE	
AW	42	Hurricane IIc	10.43-1.45	LD294/AW-X	FE	
AW	42	Hurricane IV	11.44-6.45	LD101/AW-D	FE	
AW	42	Thunderbolt II	7.45-12.45	KJ302/AW-P	FE	
AW	*664*		*45*			*use not known*
AX	202	Catalina Ib	5.41-late 42	AH562/AX-J	MedME	
AX	202	Sunderland II	3.42-*c* 8.42	W6002/AX-R	MedME	
AX	202	Sunderland III	3.42-9.42	DV958/AX-T	MedME	
AX	*77 OTU*	*Wellington*			*MedME*	
AY	17 OTU	Anson I	4.40-43	AX478/AY-N	UK	B Flt
AY	17 OTU	Martinet	43-11.46	JN422/AY-N	UK	B Flt
AY	17 OTU	Hurricane II, IV	8.44-5.45	PG442/AY-W	UK	B Flt
AY	17 OTU	Spitfire XVI	44.45	TB674/AY-A	UK	B Flt
AY	17 OTU	Wellington X	6.43-11.46	LP847/AY-G	UK	B Flt
AZ	234	Spitfire I	3.40-10.40	P9363/AZ-N	UK	
AZ	234	Spitfire IIa	9.40-11.41	P7269/AZ-P	UK	
AZ	234	Spitfire Vb	11.41-9.44	AR378/AZ-W	UK	
AZ	234	Spitfire Vc	11.42-4.43	EE681/AZ-C	UK	
AZ	234	Mustang III	9.44-8.45	FB215/AZ-Y	UK	
AZ	234	Mustang IV	3.45-8.45	KM305/AZ-X	UK	
AZ	627	Mosquito IV	11.43-9.45	DZ597/AZ-A	UK	
AZ	627	Mosquito XVI	6.44-9.45	PF444/AZ-N	UK	
AZ	627	Mosquito XX	7.44-9.45	KB215/AZ-H	UK	
AZ	627	Mosquito XXV	10.44-9.45	KB625/AZ-L	UK	
B4	282	Warwick ASR I	2.44-mid 45	HF978/B4-H		
B4	*282*	*Anson, Walrus*	*1.43-44*		*UK*	*reported*
B6	*SF Spilsby*				*UK*	*use not known*
B7	*SF Waddington*				*UK*	*use not known*
B8	*SF Woodhall Spa*				*UK*	*use not known*
B9	1562 Met Flt	Spitfire XI	12.45-2.46		UK	
BA	277	Lysander III	12.41-2.45	V9545/BA-C		
BA	277	Walrus	12.41-2.45	HD917/BA-U		
BA	277	Defiant I	5.42-5.43	V1121/BA-O		
BA	277	Spitfire IIc	12.42-5.44	R6719/BA-T		
BA	277	Spitfire Vb	5.44-2.45	AD366/BA-Z		
BB	27 OTU	Wellington III	11.41-9.44	BK606/BB-P	UK	
BB	27 OTU	Wellington X	6.43-6.45	NA909/BB-H	UK	
BB	27 OTU	Master II	44-6.45	*****/BB-X	UK	
BC	*511*		*45*			*use not known*
BD	51 OTU	Blenheim If	3.41-10.42	*****/BD-V	UK	
BD	51 OTU	Blenheim IVf	8.41-10.42		UK	
BD	51 OTU	Blenheim V	5.42-1.43		UK	
BD	43 OTU	Auster III	9.43-2.46	NX454/BD-E	UK	
BD	43 OTU	Auster V	10.44-5.47	TJ672/BD-B	UK	
BD	43 OTU	Reliant	44-46	FK913/BD-S	UK	
BE	*8 (C) OTU*	*Spitfire XI*	*45-10.46*		*UK*	*use not known*
BF	28	Audax	9.39-1.42	K4853/BF-J	FE	
BF	28	Lysander II	9.41-12.42	P9139/BF-A	FE	

Code	Unit	Type	Dates	Example	Theatre	Remarks
BF	54 OTU	Blenheim IVf	5.41-2.43	R2778/BF-X	UK	C Sqn
BF	54 OTU	Blenheim If	11.41-3.43	L6734/BF-H	UK	C Sqn
BF	54 OTU	Beaufighter	6.42-5.45	T3159/BF-Z	UK	C Sqn
BG	660	Auster V	10.45	MT115/BG-G	Eur	
BH	300	Battle I	7.40-10.40	N2241/BH-G	UK	
BH	300	Wellington Ic	10.40-41	X3175/BH-L	UK	
BH	300	Wellington IV	8.41-1.43	Z1252/BH-F	UK	
BH	300	Wellington III	1.43-4.43	BJ972/BH-S	UK	
BH	300	Wellington X	3.43-4.44	HF598/BH-E	UK	
BH	300	Lancaster I, III	4.44-10.46	PA233/BH-J	UK	
BI	*SF Holme*				*UK*	*use not known*
BJ	271	Albatross	10.40-4.42	AX904/BJ-W	UK	
BJ	271	Harrow	5.40-5.45	K6993/BJ-L	UK	
BJ	271	Hudson III	1.42-4.42	T9424/BJ-*	UK	
BK	115	Wellington I	9.39-4.40	N2878/BK-H	UK	continued use of pre-war code
BL	*40*	*Battle II*	*9.39-12.39*			*reported*
BL	40	Blenheim IV	12.39-11.40	R3612/BL-V	UK	
BL	40	Wellington Ic	11.40-2.42	X9630/BL-J	UK	
BL	40	Wellington Ic	5.42-6.43	HE108/BL-K	MedME	
BL	40	Wellington III	5.42-8.43	DF680/BL-A	MedME	
BL	40	Wellington X	5.43-5.45	HE766/BL-J	MedME	
BL	40	Liberator IV	3.45-1.46	KK311/BL-A	MedME	
BL	1656 HCU	Manchester Ia	10.42-3.43	L7434/BL-Y	UK	
BL	1656 HCU	Lancaster I, III	10.42-11.43	ME583/BL-O	UK	
BL	1656 HCU	Halifax II	10.42-12.44	HR927/BL-*	UK	
BL	1656 HCU	Hurricane IIc	*c* 3.45	PG537/BL-W	UK	
BL	1656 HCU	Spitfire Vb	12.44-3.45	AB467/BL-B	UK	
BM	433	Halifax III	9.43-1.45	MZ417/BM-Q	UK	
BM	433	Lancaster	1.45-10.45	NG496/BM-N	UK	
BN	*240*	*Lerwick I*	*9.39-11.39*			*? use on type*
BN	240	London II	9.39-6.40	K5255/BN-H	UK	
BN	240	Stranraer	6.40-4.41	K7293/BN-Z	UK	
BN	240	Catalina	3.41-6.42	AM269/BN-K	UK	
BN	170	Mustang I	6.42-12.42		UK	
BN	1401 Met Flt	Spitfire IX	9.45-6.46	TA825/BN-S	Eur	
BN	*?*	*Spitfire Vc*	*JK446/BN-B*		*MedME*	*reported*
BP	457	Spitfire I, IIa	6.41-9.41	X4817/BP-C	UK	
BP	457	Spitfire V	6.41-6.42	BL351/BP-H	UK	
BQ	600	Blenheim If	9.39-2.41	L8679/BQ-O	UK	
BQ	600	Blenheim IVf	11.39-4.40	L4905/BQ-M	UK	
BQ	600	Beaufighter If	9.40-11.42	R2256/BQ-F	UK	
BQ	600	Beaufighter IIf	4.41-4.42	R2***/BQ-H	UK	
BQ	600	Beaufighter VIf	2.42-*c* 10.42	ND172/BQ-B	UK	
BQ	600	Mosquito XIX	12.44-8.45	TA123/BQ-H	MedME	
BQ	451	Spitfire Vc	2.43-3.44	LZ949/BQ-B	MedME	
BQ	451	Spitfire IX	12.43-8.44	MT676/BQ-M	MedME	
BQ	550	Lancaster I, III	11.43-10.45	PA995/BQ-V	UK	
BR	184	Hurricane IIb	12.42-12.43	HW716/BR-*	UK	
BR	184	Hurricane IV	6.43-3.44	KZ703/BR-H	UK	
BR	184	Typhoon Ib	12.43-9.45	MN301/BR-Y	UK, Eur	
BS	1651 CU	Stirling I	1.42-2.44	N6048/BS-P	UK	
BS	1651 CU	Stirling III	7.43-11.44	EH904/BS-R	UK	
BS	1651 CU	Lancaster III	11.44-7.45	HK655/BS-F	UK	
BS	160	Liberator V	11.45-9.46	KL533/BS-G	FE, UK	poss UK only
BT	252	Beaufighter Ic	12.41-5.42	T4767/BT-T	MedME	

Code	Unit	Type	Dates	Example	Theatre	Remarks
BT	252	Beaufighter VI	9.42-4.43	X8025/BT-F	MedME	
BT	30 OTU	Wellington III	6.42-6.45	BK347/BT-Z	UK	
BT	30 OTU	Wellington X	10.43-6.45	MF503/BT-N	UK	
BT	1686 BDTF	Tomahawk	6.42-late 43	AH769/BT-G	UK	
BU	214	Wellington Ic	9.39-4.42	N2778/BU-R	UK	
BU	214	Wellington II	6.41-4.42	W5442/BU-V	UK	
BU	214	Stirling I	4.42-1.44	R9197/BU-V	UK	
BU	214	Stirling III	4.42-1.44	BK717/BU-U	UK	
BU	214	Fortress III	11.44-7.45	HB763/BU-T	UK	
BX	86	Blenheim IV	12.40-11.41	V5462/BX-E	UK	
BX	86	Beaufort I	5.40-2.42	AW253/BX-A	UK	
BX	86	Beaufort II, IIA	12.41-8.42	AW253/BX-A	UK, MedME	
BX	666	Auster				allocated not used
BX	?	Halifax	42-43	*****/BX-T	UK	reported
BY	23 OTU	Wellington III	6.42-3.44	X3366/BY-Q	UK	
BY	58	Halifax II	12.42-5.45	JP328/BY-H	UK	
BY	59	Liberator VIII	9.45-6.46	KL650/BY-D	UK	
BZ	82 OTU	Wellington III	6.43-12.44	BJ890/BZ-T	UK	D Flt
BZ	86 OTU	Wellington X	6.44-10.44	LN935/BZ-V	UK	formed from 82 OTU
C1	407	Wellington XIV	c 11.44-6.45	HF302/C1-J	UK	
C2	BCIS	Oxford 45			UK	not confirmed
C5	SF Tibbenham	Proctor I		45 P6252/C5	UK	not allocated
C6	51	Halifax III	1.44-8.45	LW677/C6-B	UK	C Flt
C7	1 FP	Anson, Oxford	12.45-46		UK	unconfirmed
C8	640	Halifax III	1.44-5.45	NA222/C8-O	UK	
C8	640	Halifax VI	4.45-5.45	R8604/C8-Z	UK	
CA	189	Lancaster I, III	10.44-11.45	PA182/CA-W	UK	
CB	MCS	Dominie I	4.44-7.48	HG705/CB-U	UK	
CC	SF Holmsley South				UK	use not known
CE	1668 HCU	Manchester I	8.43-11.43	L7307/CE-*	UK	to 5 LFS
CE	5 LFS	Lancaster I	11.43-3.45	W4328/CE-T	UK	ex 1668 HCU
CF	625	Lancaster III	10.43-10.45	PD206/CF-B2	UK	
CG	SF Binbrook		45		UK	use not known
CH	SF Swinderby		45		UK	use not known
CJ	203	Liberator VI	10.44-3.46	KL559/CJ-C	FE, UK	poss UK only
CL	SF Little Staughton		45		UK	use not known
CM	107 OTU	Wellington III	3.44-7.45	MF504/CM-N	UK	
CM	107 OTU	Dakota III	5.44-3.45	TS434/CM-O	UK	to 1333 TSCU
CM	1333 TSCU	Dakota III	5.44-3.45	TS434/CM-O	UK	ex 107 OTU
CM	42 GCF				UK	not used
CO	84 OTU	Wellington X	c 43-5	LN234/CO-A	UK	
CO	FIU?	Mosquito FB VI	c late 44	HR176/CO-X	UK	
CP	SF Topcliffe				UK	use not known
CR	162	Mosquito XX	2.45-	KB191/CR-L	UK	
CR	162	Mosquito XXV	12.44-7.46	KB415/CR-C	UK	
CR	162	Oxford	12.44-7.46		UK	
CS	513	Stirling III	9.43-11.43	V3528/CR-C	UK	use not confirmed
CS	SF Upwood					use not confirmed
CT	52 OTU	Spitfire V			UK	use not confirmed
CV	3 RAAF	Kittyhawk I-IV	12.41-11.44	FS407/CV-Z	MedME	
CV	3 RAAF	Mustang III	11.44-4.45	FB299/CV-Y	MedME	
CV	SF Tuddenham		46		UK	use not known
CX	14	Mosquito VI	6.45-3.46	PZ439/CX-C		
CX	14	Wellington XIV	11.44-6.45	NB909/CX-K	UK	
CY	SF Ludford Magna				UK	use not known
CZ	84 OTU	Martinet I	43-44	MS852/CZ-B	UK	

Air Sea rescue units used several types including modified fighters like this Spitfire Vb BL591/BA-U of No. 276 Sqn at Shoreham, which wears the AEAF stripes adopted at the time of D-Day. A Sea Otter, also probably coded, is behind. (Author's Collection)

Among transport aircraft pressed into RAF service early in the Second World War was the elegant de Havilland DH 91 Albatross. Two served with No. 271 Sqn and wore full unit markings, including codes, AX904/BJ-W shown. It was named Franklin after the great explorer. (Real Photos)

Photographed at Stranraer on 5 April 1941 soon after delivery, Catalina I AM269/BN-K has already been given the No. 240 Sqn code letters, which varied in size and position in the early Catalina units. (MoD)

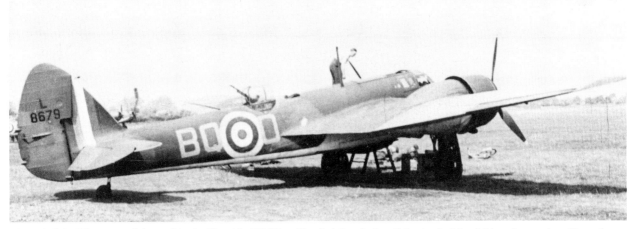

These Blenheim If long-range fighters of the Auxiliary No. 600 (City of London) Sqn display all the standard day fighter colours and markings when seen in the summer of 1940; L8679/BQ-O is nearest. (Author's Collection)

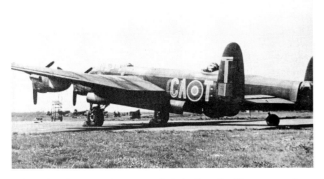

Fulbeck-based No. 189 Sqn was a relatively short-lived Lancaster unit formed in October 1944. Its codes thus included the letter C, which had initially not been used because of possible confusion with other letters; ME374/CA-T is shown. (via Ian Simpson)

During the round of squadron renumbering at the end of the war, many of the 'new' units reused their old code letters rather than those of the unit which had been renumbered. One such was No. 14 Sqn which used CX previously worn on its Wellingtons and which replaced the NE code of No. 143 Sqn from which it had been renumbered. Illustrated is Mosquito VI PZ439/CX-C. (Wg Cdr E. Praill)

Code	Unit	Type	Dates	Example	Theatre	Remarks
D2	1606 Flt	Martinet	11.42-4.45	HN954/D2-F	UK	
D4	620	Stirling IV	3.44-7.45	LJ566/D4-Y	UK	
D4	620	Halifax VII	5.45-7.46	PP375/D4-X	UK, MedME	
D6	*SF Hethel*		*45*		*UK*	*use not known*
D8	*22 MU*		*45*		*UK*	*use not known*
DA	*1322 Flt or ADLS*	*Anson X*	*c 44-45*	*NK707/DA-M*	*UK*	*reported*
DA	210	Sunderland I	9.39-4.41	L5798/DA-A	UK	
DA	210	Catalina I	4.41-3.44	W8420/DA-O	UK	
DA	210	Catalina IIa	8.42-12.43	VA729/DA-P	UK	
DA	*273 MU*					*use not known*
DA	? 84 GCS	Anson	45-46	NK707/DA-M	UK	
DB	411	Spitfire II	7.41-10.41	P7923/DB-R	UK	
DB	411	Spitfire Vb	10.41-10.43	AA836/DB-S	UK	
DB	411	Spitfire IX	10.43-5.45	MK434/DB-R	UK	
DB	411	Spitfire XVI	6.45-3.46	RM928/DB-N	UK	
DC	*SF Oakington*				*UK*	*use not known*
DD	22 OTU	Wellington Ic	8.41-c 43	X9791/DD-D	UK	A Flt
DD	22 OTU	Wellington III	12.42-1.45	DF563/DD-B	UK	A Flt
DD	22 OTU	Wellington X	12.42-8.45	LN546/DD-S	UK	A Flt
DE	61 OTU	Spitfire XIV	10.45-9.46	SM922/DE-*	UK	
DF	221	Wellington Ic	12.40-6.42	T2979/DF-L	UK	
DF	221	Wellington VIII	1.42-4.43	W5615/DF-C	UK	
DG	422	Lerwick I	4.42-11.42	L7260/DG-P	UK	unconfirmed
DG	422	Catalina Ib, IIIa	6.42-11.42	FP103/DG-A	UK	unconfirmed
DG	422	Sunderland III	11.42-43	ML884/DG-Z	UK	
DG	155	Spitfire VIII	1.44-12.45	MD220/DG-V	FE	
DH	1664 CU	Halifax II	5.43-11.44	DG280/DH-M	UK	
DH	1664 CU	Halifax III	5.43-4.45	LK661/DH-N	UK	
DH	1664 CU	Lancaster I, III	11.43-12.44	*****/DH-W	UK	
DH	1664 CU	Halifax V	5.44-11.44	LL137/DH-S	UK	
DI	*SF Kemble*				*UK*	*use not known*
DJ	15	Stirling III	7.43-12.43	EF391/DJ-M	UK	C Flt
DJ	15	Lancaster	12.43-44	NG445/DJ-E	UK	C Flt
DJ	450	Kittyhawk I	12.41-4.42	AK912/DJ-J	MedME	
DK	158	Stirling V	6.45-12.45	PJ889/DK-B	UK	
DL	54	Spitfire Vc	9.42-4.44	MA863/DL-K	SWPA	Australia based
DL	54	Spitfire VIII	4.44-9.45	A58-498/DL-D	SWPA	
DL	91	Spitfire IIa	1.41-5.41	P7970/DL M	UK	
DL	91	Spitfire Vb, Vc	3.41-4.43	AR387/DL-O	UK	
DL	91	Spitfire XII	4.43-3.44	EN625/DL-K	UK	
DL	91	Spitfire XIV	3.44-8.44	RB174/DL-T	UK	
DL	91	Spitfire IX	8.44-4.45	MK732/DL-C	UK	
DL	91	Spitfire F.21	4.45-10.46	LA279/DL-U	UK	
DL	421 Flt	Hurricane IIc	1.41-2.41	Z2312/DL-H	UK	
DL	421 Flt	Spitfire IIa	1.41-2.41	P7307/DL-J	UK	
DM	248	Beaufighter X	6.43-1.44	JM348/DM-Q	UK	
DM	248	Mosquito XVIII	1.44-2.45	MM424/DM-H	UK	
DM	248	Mosquito VI	12.43-9.46	RS610/DM-Y	UK	
DN	416	Spitfire II	11.41-4.42	P8275/DN-*	UK	
DN	416	Spitfire Vb	3.42-1.44	EW950/DN-Y	UK	
DN	416	Spitfire IX	3.43-12.44	BS411/DN-U	UK, Eur	
DN	416	Spitfire XVI	12.44-9.45	SM191/DN-T	Eur	
DN	416	Spitfire XIV	9.45-3.46	N****/DN-D	Eur	
DP	140	Spitfire PR.IV	41-42	P9328/DP-*	UK	
DP	1416 Flt	Spitfire I	3.41-9.41	P9328/DP-*	UK	
DP	1416 Flt	Blenheim IV	8.41-9.41	V5656/DP-*	UK	

Code	Unit	Type	Dates	Example	Theatre	Remarks
DP	140	Spitfire PR.IV	41-42	P9328/DP-*	UK	
DP	193	Typhoon Ib	12.42-8.45	RB227/DP-P	UK, Eur	
DQ	228	Sunderland I	9.39-8.42	P9600/DQ-T	MedME UK	
DQ	228	Sunderland II	3.42-11.43	W3989/DQ-L	MedME UK	
DQ	228	Sunderland III	3.42-2.45	W4016/DQ-S	UK	
DR	1697 ADLS	Hurricane II	5.44-12.44	PG597/DR-Q	UK	
DR	1697 ADLS	Hurricane IV	5.44-45	PG597/DR-Q	UK	
DR	1555 RATF	Oxford	2.46-8.47	NJ285/DR-D	UK	
DS	*SF Llanbedr*				UK	*use not known*
DT	192	Wellington Ic	1.43-2.43	N2772/DT-E	UK	
DT	192	Wellington III	1.43-5.43	HE380/DT-J	UK	
DT	192	Wellington X	1.43-3.45	HE498/DT-S	UK	
DT	192	Mosquito IV	1.43-4.45	DZ376/DT-M	UK	
DT	192	Halifax V	7.43-11.43	DK246/DT-R	UK	
DT	192	Anson I	2.44-8.45	NK718/DT-K2	UK	
DT	192	Halifax III	3.44-8.45	MZ795/DT-V	UK	
DT	192	Mosquito XVI	9.44-8.45	NS797/DT-N	UK	
DT	257	Hurricane I	6.40-2.41	V7137/DT-G	UK	
DU	312	Hurricane I	8.40-5.41	V6921/DU-R	UK	
DU	312	Hurricane IIa, b	5.41-12.41	Z3437/DU-K	UK	
DU	312	Spitfire Vb	12.41-2.44	AA911/DU-D	UK	
DU	SF Skeabrae	Spitfire VII	*c* 12.43- *c* 3.44	MD114/DU-G	UK	
DU	312	Spitfire IX	1.44-2.46	MH474/DU-F	UK	
DV	129	Spitfire Vb	8.41-6.43	EE602/DV-V	UK	
DV	129	Spitfire IXc	6.43-4.44	RR185/DV-Q	UK	
DV	129	Spitfire IX	5.45-9.46	NH317/DV-N	UK	
DV	129	Mustang III	4.44-5.45	FX862/DV-K	UK	
DV	237	Spitfire IX	3.44-12.45	MJ849/DV-X	MedME	
DV	237	Mustang IV	12.45		MedME	to 93 Sqn
DV	93	Mustang IV	1.46-12.46	KI727/DV-J	MedME	ex 237 Sqn
DV	271	Dakota III, IV	*c* 44-46	KN403/DV-Y	UK	
DW	610	Spitfire I	9.39-2.41	L1000/DW-M	UK	
DW	610	Spitfire Vb	7.41-3.44	BL302/DW-R	UK	
DW	610	Spitfire XIV	12.43-3.45	RB167/DW-E	UK, Eur	
DX	245	Hurricane I	3.40-8.41	P3762/DX-E	UK	
DX	245	Hurricane IIb	8.41-1.43	Z3470/DX-?	UK	
DX	57	Blenheim IV	3.40-late 40	L9248/DX-	Eur, UK	
DX	57	Wellington Ic	11.40-2.42	Z8794/DX-H	UK	
DX	57	Wellington II	7.41-2.42	W5434/DX-Y	UK	
DX	57	Wellington III	12.41-10.42	X3658/DX-P	UK	
DX	57	Manchester I	*c* 9.42		UK	Conversion Flt
DX	57	Lancaster I	9.42-5.46	NG398/DX-N	UK	
DX	230	Sunderland I	3.42-12.42	L5806/DX-Q	MedME	
DY	102	Whitley III	9.39-11.39	K9015/DY-B	UK	
DY	102	Whitley V	11.39-2.42	N1380/DY-R	UK	
DY	102	Halifax II	12.41-5.44	LW241/DY-Y	UK	
DY	102	Halifax III	4.44-9.45	LW179/DY-E	UK	
DY	102	Halifax VI	7.45-9.45	RG502/DY-Q	UK	
DZ	151	Hurricane I	9.39-2.42	V6931/DZ-D	UK	
DZ	151	Hurricane II	6.41-2.42	Z3467/DZ-Y	UK	
DZ	151	Defiant I	12.40-7.42	N3328/DZ-Z	UK	
DZ	151	Defiant II	4.42-7.42	AA436/DZ-V	UK	
DZ	151	Mosquito II	4.42-8.43	W4097/DZ-N	UK	
DZ	151	Mosquito XII	5.43-5.44	HK183/DZ-W	UK	
DZ	151	Mosquito VI	8.43-10.43	HR350/DZ-P	UK	
DZ	151	Mosquito XIII	11.43-1-.44	MM448/DZ-E	UK	

Code	Unit	Type	Dates	Example	Theatre	Remarks
DZ	151	Mosquito 30	10.44-10.46	NT536/DZ-F	UK	
E1	1 AACU	Henley III	41-42	L3354/E1-D	UK	E Flt
E2	*SF Warboys*				*UK*	*use not known*
E4	*SF Wickenby*				*UK*	*use not known*
E7	570	Albemarle	11.43-8.44	V1814/E7-M	UK	
E7	570	Stirling IV	7.44-1.46	LJ991/E7-W	UK	
E9	*SF Westcott*				*UK*	*use not known*
EA	49	Hampden I	9-39-4.42	AE354/EA-S	UK	
EA	49	Manchester I	6.41-7.42	L7453/EA-T	UK	
EA	49	Lancaster I, III	7.42-8.45	DV238/EA-O	UK	
EB	41	Spitfire I	1.39-4.41	X4178/EB-K	UK	
EB	41	Spitfire IIa	10-40-8.41	P7666/EB-Z	UK	
EB	41	Spitfire Vb	8.41-3.43	AD504/EB-W	UK	
EB	41	Spitfire XII	2.43-9.44	MB798/EB-U	UK	
EB	41	Spitfire XIV	9.44-9.45	RM913/EB-P	UK, Eur	
EC	SF Odiham	Proctor III	*c* 45	LZ559/EC-L	UK	
ED	21 OTU	Wellington Ic	1.41-11.42	R1090/ED-K	UK	A Flt
ED	21 OTU	Wellington X	9.44-2.47	LP438/ED-O	UK	A Flt
EE	404	Blenheim IVf	4.41-1.43	N3525/EE-H	UK	
EE	404	Beaufighter IIf	9.42-3.43	V8131/EE-T	UK	
EE	404	Beaufighter XI	5.41-1.43	JM111/EE-T	UK	
EE	404	Beaufighter X	9.43-9.44	NE355/EE-H	UK	
EE	16	Lysander II	9.39-mid 40	L4795/EE-M	UK	
EE	31	Valentia	9.39-9.41	K4634/EE-J	FE	
EE	*SF Elvington*				*UK*	*use not known*
EF	232	Hurricane I	7.40-8.41	Z7075.EF-L	UK	
EF	232	Spitfire Vb	4.42-2.44	BL520/EF-D	UK, MedME	
EF	232	Spitfire IX	5.43-10.44	MK137/EF-G	MedME	
EG	487	Ventura II	8.42-9.43	AJ209/EG-V	UK	
EG	487	Mosquito VI	8.43-9.45	NS840/EG-X	UK, Eur	
EG	34	Blenheim If	9.39-11.41	L1480/EG-M	FE	
EG	34	Blenheim IV	6.41-42	*****/EG-A	FE	
EG	34	Hurricane IIc	8.43-3.45	LB957/EG-N	FE	small unit code
EG	34	Thunderbolt II	3.45-10.45	KL841/EG-U	FE	small unit code
EG	355	Liberator VI	9.44	EV902/EG-S	FE	
EH	55 OTU	Hurricane I	11.40-1.44	W9135/EH-R	UK	A, E Flts
EH	55 OTU	Hurricane IIa	6.43-1.44	Z2686/EH-*	UK	A, E Flts
EH	55 OTU	Hurricane X	12.44-45	AC238/EH-R	UK	A, E Flts
EH	55 OTU	Typhoon Ib	12.44-6.45	EK413/EH-V	UK	A, E Flts
EH	3 TEU	Typhoon Ib	3.44-12.44	EK413/EH-V	UK	
EH	3 TEU	Mustang III	3.44-12.44	FX892/EH-*	UK	
EH	4 TEU	Hurricane I	1.44-3.44	W9185/EH-L	UK	
EJ	CCFIS, CCIS	Master II	2.45-10.45	AZ587/EJ-K	UK	
EJ	127	Hurricane IIb	6.42-3.44	BP289/EJ-X	MedME	
EJ	127	Hurricane IIc	8.43-3.44	KX102/EJ-U	MedME	
EK	168	Tomahawk IIb	6.42-8.42	AK118/EK-A	UK	
EK	1656 HCU	Lancaster I, III	10.42-11.45	NN814/EK-O	UK	D Flt
EL	*10 OTU*		*45*		*UK*	*use not known*
EL	181	Typhoon Ib	9.42-9.45	R8833/EL-D	UK, Eur	
EL	*? 600*	*Auster III*	*8.43-4.44*	*MZ223/EL*	*UK*	*poss personal*
EM	207	Manchester I	11.40-3.42	L7488/EM-Q	UK	
EM	207	Hampden I	4.41-8.41	AE297/EM-H	UK	
EM	207	Lancaster I	1.42-8.49	PD217/EM-Z	UK	
EN	18 OTU	Wellington III	43-12.44	BJ672/EN-R	UK	
EO	15 OTU	Wellington Ic	4.40-43	X9683/EO-F	UK	
EO	404	Beaufighter X	9.44-4.45	NV427/EO-L	UK	

Code	Unit	Type	Dates	Example	Theatre	Remarks
EO	404	Mosquito VI	3.45-5.45	RF875/EO-R	UK	
EP	104	Blenheim IV	9.39-4.40	L8795/EP-B	UK	
EP	104	Wellington II	4.41-7.43	W5437/EP-Q	UK, MedME	
EP	104	Wellington X	7.43-3.45	LN665/EP-J	MedME	
EP	104	Liberator VI	2.45-11.45	KL373/EP-U	MedME	
EP	84 GCF	Anson X	44-47	NK456/EP	Eur	no individual letters
EP	84 GCF	Anson XII	45-12.47	PH765/EP	Eur	
EP	84 GCF	Anson XIX	2.46-47	TX165/EP	Eur	
EP	84 GCF	Messenger I	45-12.47	RH375/EP	Eur	
EP	84 GCF	Proctor III	45	DX228/EP	Eur	
EP	84 GCF	Auster V	45-46	TJ568/EP	Eur	
EP	84 GCF	Oxford	45-46	T1200/EP	Eur	
EP	84 GCF	Spitfire XI	9.45-12.47	PL830/EP	Eur	
EP	84 GCF	Savoia SM82	*c* 5.45-46	VN158/EP	Eur	
EQ	408	Hampden I	6.41-10.42	P5392/EQ-W	UK	
EQ	408	Manchester I	5.42-6.42	L7401/EQ-A	UK	
EQ	408	Halifax II	12.42-10.43	HR858/EQ-V	UK	
EQ	408	Lancaster II	10.43-7.44	LL675/EQ-M	UK	
EQ	408	Halifax III	7.44-2.45	NR124/EQ-S	UK	
EQ	408	Halifax VII	2.45-5.45	NP712/EQ-R	UK	
EQ	408	Lancaster X	5.45-9.45	KB919/EQ-J	UK	
EQ	*?*	*Liberator VI*	*2.45*	******/EQ-L*	*UK*	*100 Group*
ER	258	Hurricane I, II	*c* 8.41	V6813/ER-V	UK	
ES	541	Spitfire XIX	5.44-4.45	PS887/ES-B	UK	
ET	*662*	*Auster V*	*9.44-12.45*		*Eur*	*reported*
EU	26 OTU	Wellington Ic	1.42-8.43	DV885/EU-A	UK	E Flt
EU	26 OTU	Martinet	3.43-8.44	HP436/EU-W	UK	E Flt
EU	26 OTU	Hurricane IIc	*c* 43-44	LF766/EU-F	UK	E Flt
EV	180	Mitchell II	9.42-9.45	FL678/EV-J	UK	
EV	180	Mitchell III	10.44-9.45	KJ705/EV-T	UK	
EV	180	Mosquito XVI	9.45-5.46	PF488/EV-C	Eur	
EV	13 OTU	Mosquito III	45	PZ235/EV-B	UK	
EW	307	Defiant I	9.40-8.41	N3437/EW-K	UK	
EW	307	Beaufighter IIf	8.41-5.42	T3048/EW-U	UK	
EW	307	Beaufighter VIf	5.42-1.43	X8005/EW-R	UK	
EW	307	Mosquito II	12.42-1.45	DZ260/EW-B	UK	
EW	307	Mosquito VI	8.43-11.43	HR141/EW-P	UK	
EW	307	Mosquito XII	12.42-1.45	HK165/EW-A	UK	
EW	307	Mosquito XXX	10.44-11.46	RK951/EW-N	UK	
EW	307	Oxford I	1.46-12.46	EB810/EW	UK	
EX	199	Wellington III	11.42-5.43	X3812/EX-Q	UK	
EX	199	Wellington X	3.43-7.43	LN406/EX-G	UK	
EX	199	Stirling III	7.43-3.45	EF450/EX-N	UK	
EX	199	Halifax III	2.45-7.45	NA275/EX-W	UK	
EY	80	Hurricane IIc	1.42-4.43	BE492/EY-Y	MedME	
EY	80	Spitfire Vc	4.43-4.44	JG938/EY-B	MedME	
EY	80	Spitfire IX	7.43-11.43	JL228/EY-3	MedME	
EY	78	Whitley V	9.39-3.42	T4209/EY-Q	UK	
EY	78	Halifax II	2.42-1.44	W1015/EY-V	UK	
EY	78	Halifax III	1.44-8.45	MZ361/EY-D	UK	
EY	78	Halifax VI	4.45-7.45	RG652/EY-E	UK	
EZ	81 OTU	Whitley V	9.42-5.45	Z6676/EZ-S	UK	
EZ	81 OTU	Wellington X	11.44-8.45	NA962/EZ-H	UK	to 1380 TSCU
EZ	1380 TSCU	Wellington X	8.45-1.46	LP912/EZ-A	UK	ex 81 OTU
F1	1 AACU	Henley III	41-42	L8380/F1-D	UK	F Flt
F2	635	Lancaster III	3.44-9.45	PB627/F2-B	UK	

Code	Unit	Type	Dates	Example	Theatre	Remarks
F2	635	Lancaster VI	7.44-8.45	ND418/F2-Q	UK	
F3	438	Hurricane IV	11.43-5.44	LD973/F3-O	UK	
F3	438	Typhoon Ib	3.44-8.45	MN398/F3-A	UK, Eur	
FA	236	Blenheim If	12.39-7.40	L1257/FA-F	UK	
FA	236	Blenheim IV	7.40-3.42	L6797/FA-Q	UK	
FA	236	Beaufighter I	10.41-2.42	T4724/FA-A	UK	
FA	281	Defiant I	4.42-7.43	T3951/FA-H	UK	
FA	281	Anson I	4.43-11.43	EG467/FA-F	UK	
FA	281	Warwick I	11.43-10.45	BV404/FA-A4	UK	
FB	24 OTU	Whitley V	3.42-4.44	AD674/FB-D	UK	A Flt
FB	24 OTU	Wellington X	4.44-7.45	LP355/FB-S	UK	A Flt
FC	SF Northolt	Hurricane IIa	5.41-3.42	Z2487/FC-T	UK	Fighter Command Tactics Officer
FC	SF Northolt	Spitfire II	*c* 9.42-11.42	*****/FC-T	UK	FCTO
FC	SF Northolt	Spitfire II	*c* 9.42-11.42	*****/FC-O	UK	FCTO
FC	*SF Kenley*					*use not known*
FD	294	Walrus	9.43-4.46	W2789/FD-	MedME	
FD	1659 HCU	Oxford II	11.44-9.45	AS471/FD-Z	UK	
FD	1659 HCU	Halifax V	10.42-9.44	LL505/FD-*	UK	
FD	1659 HCU	Halifax III	9.44-9.45	HX268/FD-V	UK	
FD	1659 HCU	Lancaster III	11.44-9.45	LM753/FD-B	UK	
FE	56 OTU	Hurricane I	12.40-4.43	N2471/FE-E	UK	C, D Flts
FE	56 OTU	Typhoon Ib	12.44-2.46	MN956/FE-P	UK	
FE	6 (C)OTU	Hudson III	41-42	*****/FE-D	UK	
FF	132	Spitfire I	7.41-11.41	R7250/FF-L	UK	
FF	132	Spitfire II	9.41-4.42	P8671/FF-*	UK	
FF	132	Spitfire Vc	3.42-9.43	BM129/FF-S	UK	
FF	132	Spitfire IXb	9.43-1.44	MH486/FF-H	UK	
FF	132	Spitfire IXe	7.44-12.44	NH305/FF-R	UK, Eur	
FF	132	Spitfire VIII	2.45-5.45	LV661/FF-*	FE	
FF	132	Spitfire XIV	5.45-4.46	RN143/FF-A	FE	
FG	335	Hurricane I	10.41-9.42	Z4027/FG-S	MedME	
FG	282	Walrus II	2.45-45	Z1758/FG-P	MedME	
FG	282	Sea Otter II	3.45-8.45	JM975/FG-X	MedME	
FH	15 OTU	Wellington Ic	4.40-3.44	L7853/FH-W	UK	
FH	15 OTU	Martinet I	8.42-3.44	JN297/FH-7	UK	
FH	53	Liberator V	5.43-5.45	BZ720/FH-N	UK	
FH	53	Liberator VI	6.44-6.46	EW302/FH-G	UK	
FH	53	Liberator VIII	2.45-6.46	KH388/FH-B	UK	
FI	WTU	Warwick I	6.43-10.43	BV305/FI-F	UK	yellow codes
FI	83 OTU	Hurricane IIc	6.44-10.44	LF380/FI-D	UK	Gunnery Flt
FJ	164	Spitfire Va	4.42-9.42	P7505/FJ-J	UK	
FJ	164	Spitfire Vb	9.42-1.43	AR294/FJ-V	UK	
FJ	164	Hurricane IId	2.43-43	KX413/FJ-H	UK	
FJ	164	Hurricane IIc	6.43-10.43	KX561/FJ-G	UK	
FJ	164	Hurricane IV	5.43-3.44	KX561/FJ-G	UK	
FJ	164	Auster I	*c* 9.45	LB375/FJ	UK	
FJ	164	Typhoon Ib	1.44-6.45	JP367/FJ-J	UK	
FJ	164	Spitfire IX	6.45-8.46	TB548/FJ-B	UK	
FJ	164	Spitfire XVI	7.46-8.46	TE342/FJ-*	UK	to 63 Sqn
FJ	261	Hurricane IIc	10.43-6.44	HW803/FJ-B	FE	
FJ	261	Thunderbolt I	6.44-10.44	FL849/FJ-G	FE	
FJ	261	Thunderbolt II	8.44-9.45	KJ335/FJ-W	FE	
FK	219	Blenheim If	10.39-12.40	L6709/FK-P	UK	
FK	219	Beaufighter If	10.40-5.43	R2204/FK-J	UK	
FK	219	Beaufighter VI	5.43-1.44	V8738/FK-L	MedME	

Code	Unit	Type	Dates	Example	Theatre	Remarks
FK	219	Mosquito III	1.44-9.46	TV970/FK-V	UK	
FK	219	Mosquito XVII	2.44-12.44	HK315/FK-N	UK	
FK	219	Mosquito XXX	6.44-9.46	MV522/FK-F	UK	
FK	*?*	*Spitfire IX*	*c 44-c45*	*M****/FK-T*	*MedME*	*219 Sqn or personal code?*
FL	81	Spitfire Vb	4.42-10.42	AR398/FL-T	UK	
FL	81	Spitfire Vb, Vc	10.42-11.43	JK322/FL-4	MedME	
FL	81	Spitfire IX	5.42-11.43	EN203/FL-O	MedME	
FL	81	Spitfire VII	11.43-6.45	JF698/FL-J	FE	
FL	81	Thunderbolt II	6.45-6.46	HD145/FL-D	FE	
FM	257	Hurricane IIa	5.41-9.42	Z5050/FM-T	UK	
FM	257	Hurricane IIc	1.42-9.42		UK	
FM	257	Typhoon Ib	6.42-3.45	MN598/FM-P	UK, Eur	
FN	453	Spitfire Va	6.42-8.42	*****/FN-A	UK	ex 331 Sqn aircraft; changed to FU
FN	331	Hurricane IIb	8.41-11.41	BD734/FN-D	UK	
FN	331	Spitfire IIa	11.41-4.42	P8190/FN-F	UK	
FN	331	Spitfire Vb	3.42-10.42	AR291/FN-A	UK	
FN	331	Spitfire IX	10.42-11.45	PV210/FN-R	UK, Eur	to RNoAF
FO	1665 HCU	Stirling	43-44		UK	
FO	*SF Wick*				UK	*use not known*
FP	1683 BDTF	Tomahawk IIa	43-44	AH899/FP-F	UK	
FQ	12 OTU	Wellington III	41-43	Z1732/FQ-H	UK	
FQ	12 OTU	Wellington X	11.42-6.45	NC681/FQ-W	UK	
FR	*SF Manston*				UK	*use not known*
FS	148	Wellington I	9.39-4.40	L4303/FS	UK	No a/c letter carried
FS	148	Lysander IIIa	2.44-6.45	T1750/FS-B	MedME	
FS	148	Halifax II	3.43-11.44	JN896/FS-L	MedME	
FS	148	Stirling IV	11.44-12.44	LK181/FS-F	MedME	
FS	148	Liberator VI	3.45-1.46	KL545/FS-Z	MedME	
FT	43	Hurricane I	9.39-4.41	L1727/FT-R	UK	
FT	43	Hurricane IIa	4.41-4.42	Z2772/FT-N	UK	
FT	43	Hurricane IIb	4.41-9.42	BD715/FT-M	UK	
FT	43	Hurricane IIc	12.41-3.43	HV817/FT-C	UK MedME	
FT	43	Spitfire Vc	2.43-1.44	JG936/FT-C	MedME	
FT	43	Spitfire IX	8.43-5.47	MH711/FT-E	MedME	
FT	43	Spitfire VIII	8.44-11.44	MT680/FT-E	MedME	
FT	*SF Mildenhall*				*UK*	*use not known*
FU	453	Spitfire Vb	6.42-1.44	BL593/FU-A	UK	
FU	453	Spitfire IXb	3.43-6.43	EN522/FU-F	UK	
FU	453	Spitfire IXe	1.44-2.45	PL204/FU-T	UK, Eur	
FU	453	Spitfire XVI	11.44-1.46	SM243/FU-J	Eur	
FU	453	Auster I	3.45-9.45	LB378/FU	Eur	
FU	453	Spitfire XII	9.45-1.46	TZ111/FU-R	Eur	
FU	458	Wellington IV	9.41-3.42	Z1182/FU-G	UK	
FV	13 OTU	Blenheim IV	11.40-4.44	V5688/FV-H	UK	A Flt
FV	13 OTU	Mitchell II	5.43-6.45	FW114/FV-D	UK	A Flt
FV	13 OTU	Mosquito VI	11.43-5.47	TA538/FV-K	UK	A Flt
FV	13 OTU	Mosquito II	45-46	DD625/FV-R	UK	A Flt
FV	205	Singapore III	c 4.40-10.41	K6916/FV-J	FE	
FV	205	Catalina I	3.41-3.42	Z2153/FV-K	FE	
FW	*SF Rivenhall*				UK	*use not known*
FX	62	Blenheim I	39-1.42	L1107/FX-L	FE	
FX	3 TEU	Beaufighter	c 7.44	*****/FX-M	UK	
FY	611	Spitfire I	5.39-3.41	L1034/FY-N	UK	
FY	611	Spitfire II	8.40-2.42	W3816/FY-K	UK	
FY	611	Spitfire Vb	6.41-7.44	BM594/FY-X	UK	

These Stirling IVs of No. 620 Sqn, with LK304/D4-W nearest and D4-S beyond, wear the alphanumeric codes introduced in the mid-war years to increase available combinations. Airborne Forces squadrons were large and were usually allocated two codes – No. 620's other being QS. (via M. J. F. Bowyer)

A poor but very rare photograph shows an early reconnaissance Spitfire PR V (Type G), P9328 of No. 140 Sqn at the Benson satellite of Mount Farm wearing the little used DP codes. Individual aircraft letters were not worn. (No. 140 Sqn Records)

Spitfire HF.VII MD114/DU-G carries the colours and markings adopted for high-altitude fighter operations when being used by the Station Flight at Skeabrae in Orkney. The 'DU' codes for the Flight's Spitfire VIIs were the same as No. 312 (Czech) Sqn. This aircraft first flew in December 1943 long after the Czech unit had left. (The Orkney Library, Kirkwall)

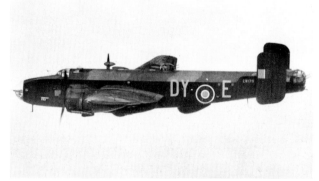

The full standard Bomber Command colour scheme and markings from 1942 are shown to advantage in the excellent view of Halifax III LW179/DY-E of Yorkshire-based No. 102 Sqn in late 1944. It was lost in a raid on Magdeburg on 16 January 1945. (Author's Collection)

Mosquito FB VI RF838/EO-A of No. 404 Sqn RCAF taxies for another mission from Banff in April 1945 and shows the white-outlined codes added to enhance their visibility. No. 404's code changed after the shortlived numerical codes were dropped by Coastal Command. (No. 404 Sqn Records)

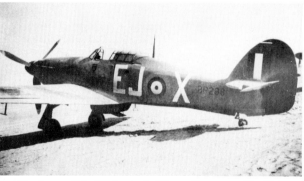

The Hurricanes of No. 127 Sqn in the Western Desert were identified by the codes EJ, as shown in this rare view of Mk IIb BP289/EJ-X in mid-1942. (T. R. Bennett)

These Mitchell IIs of No. 180 Sqn wear the unit's EV letters on the fuselage forward of the roundels, but because of the waist gun positions the aircraft letter was positioned on the nose. FL218/EV-W named Nulli Secundus leads FL185/EV-R and four others in July 1943. (via J. D. Oughton)

This MU in Egypt is the setting for a very rare view of a Hurricane of the Greek-manned No. 335 Sqn around July 1943. The white-outlined codes are believed to be red while the roundels and fin flashes were possibly modified to reflect the Greek colours, blue/white/blue; Mk IIb Z4007/FG-S is shown. (102 MU Records)

The Spitfire Vbs of No. 331 (Norwegian) Sqn stop off at Catterick for a refuel while in transit between Skeabrae and North Weald on 4 May 1942. They wear the national flag under the cockpit, but otherwise wear the standard fighter colour scheme. (Cato Guhnfeldt Collection)

Most of the RAF's Italian-based Liberator bomber squadrons wore unit codes, but generally carried the aircraft letter on the fin. Liberator B.VI KL545/FS-Z of No. 148 Sqn had its serial added underwing by the time it was photographed in January 1946. (No. 148 Sqn Records)

Code	Unit	Type	Dates	Example	Theatre	Remarks
FY	611	Spitfire IX	7.42-7.44	EN562/FY-B	UK	
FY	611	Mustang IV	1.45-8.45	KM132/FY-S	UK	
FZ	94	Kittyhawk I	3.42-4.42	AK739/FZ-R	MedME	
FZ	94	Hurricane I	5.42-8.42	*****/FZ-P	MedME	
FZ	100	Lancaster III	1.43-44	EE140/FZ-C	UK	C Flt
FZ	23 OTU	Wellington III	6.42-3.44	BJ818/FZ-H	UK	
FZ	23 OTU	Oxford I	*c* 43	*****/FZ-W	UK	
G2	19 GCF	Dominie	45	X7338/G2-A	UK	
G2	19 GCF	Anson X	45-46	NK332/G2-C	UK	
G2	19 GCF	Oxford	45-50	V3190/G2-D	UK	
G4	*SF Skellingthorpe*				UK	*use not known*
G5	190	Stirling IV	1.44-7.45	LJ934/G5-Y	UK	
G5	190	Halifax III	5.45-1.46	MZ976/G5-V	UK	
G5	190	Halifax VII	5.45-1.46	PN287/G5-R	UK	
G6	MCCS	Anson X	45	NK768/G6-O	UK	
G7	BCFEU	Lancaster I	3.45-12.45	PD329/G7-Y	UK	
G7	BCFEU	Mosquito B XXV	*c* 45	KB433/G7-Z	UK	
G7	BCFEU	Mosquito B XX	*c* 45	KB362/G7-N	UK	
G8	*SF Wing*				UK	*use not known*
G9	430	Spitfire XIV	11.44-8.45	RM857/G9-E	Eur	
GA	16 OTU	Anson I	4.40-3.47	N9825/GA-L	UK	A Flt
GA	16 OTU	Oxford I	42-46	AS146/GA-V	UK	A Flt
GA	16 OTU	Wellington Ic	42-44	Z1171/GA-B	UK	A Flt
GA	16 OTU	Lysander III	8.41-2.43	T1435/GA-Y	UK	A Flt
GA	16 OTU	Master II	43	AZ574/GA-A	UK	A Flt
GA	16 OTU	Mosquito VI	44-2.47	RS643/GA-O	UK	A Flt
GA	16 OTU	Mosquito III	12.44-2.47	RR289/GA-L	UK	A Flt
GA	16 OTU	Mosquito XVI	12.44-2.47	PF488/GA-T	UK	A Flt
GA	16 OTU	Mosquito XX	12.44-9.45	KB352/GA-K	UK	A Flt
GA	16 OTU	Mosquito XXV	12.44-9.45	KB501/GA-C	UK	A Flt
GA	112	Tomahawk IIb	7.41-12.41	AK402/GA-F	MedME	
GA	112	Kittyhawk Ia	12.41-10.42	AK700/GA-B	MedME	
GA	112	Kittyhawk III	10.42-4.44	FR115/GA-W	MedME	
GA	112	Kittyhawk IV	3.44-6.44	FT949/GA-H	MedME	
GA	112	Mustang III	6.44-5.45	KH579/GA-L	MedME	
GA	112	Mustang IV	2.45-12.46	KM107/GA-M	MedME	
GB	105	Battle I, II	9.39-6.40	K7578/GB-F	UK	
GB	105	Blenheim IV	6.40-5.42	V6014/GB J	UK	
GB	105	Mosquito IV	11.41-3.44	DZ518/GB-A	UK	
GB	105	Mosquito IX	7.43-8.45	ML913/GB-A	UK	
GB	105	Mosquito XVI	3.44-2.46	PF407/GB-V	UK	
GC	*SF Pershore*				UK	*use not known*
GD	SF Horsham St Faith	Oxford	45-47	T1386/GD-*	UK	
GD	SF Horsham St Faith	Mustang IVa		KH754/GD-*	UK	
GE	58	Whitley III	9.39-3.40	K8964/GE-R	UK	
GE	58	Whitley V	3.40-5.42	N1470/GE-J	UK	
GE	58	Whitley VII	5.42-12.42	BD568/GE-W	UK	
GE	349	Tomahawk I	1.43-4.43	AH775/GE-N	Africa	
GE	349	Spitfire Vb	6.43-2.44	BL334/GE-F	UK	
GE	349	Spitfire Vc	10.43-2.44	AR490/GE-A	UK	
GE	349	Spitfire IX	2.44-2.45	MK130/GE-P	UK, Eur	
GE	349	Spitfire XVI	5.45-10.46	TE274/GE-K	Eur	to BAF
GF	56 OTU	Hurricane I	12.40-4.43	*****/GF-T	UK	A, B Flts
GF	56 OTU	Tempest V	12.44-2.46	EJ846/GF-E	UK	A, B Flts

Code	Unit	Type	Dates	Example	Theatre	Remarks
GG	1667 HCU	Halifax V	7.43-1.45	EB190/GG-H	UK	
GG	1667 HCU	Lancaster I	6.43-11.45	HK734/GG-K	UK	
GG	1667 HCU	Lancaster III	6.43-11.45	JB306/GG-E	UK	
GI	622	Stirling III	8.43-12.43	EJ113/GI-Q	UK	
GI	622	Lancaster I, III	12.43-8.45	LL782/GI-H	UK	
GJ	63 or 12 OTU	Battle I	40	P2272/GJ-*	UK	
GJ	*SF Duxford*				*UK*	*use not known*
GK	52 OTU	Spitfire IIa	3.41-42	P7962/GK-K	UK	E Flt
GK	*162*		*45*		*UK*	*use not known*
GK	459	Hudson III	2.42-43	V8992/GK-B	MedME	
GL	185	Hereford I	9.39-4.40	L6030/GL-G	UK	
GL	185	Hampden I	9.39-4.40	L4201/GL-T	UK	
GL	185	Anson I	9.39-4.40	N9832/GL-G	UK	
GL	185	Hurricane I	11.41-6.42	V4092/GL-*	UK	to 14 OTU
GL	14 OTU	Anson I	4.40-10.43	R3399/GL-X	UK	ex 185 Sqn
GL	14 OTU	Hampden I	4.40-12.42	P1276/GL-M1	UK	
GL	14 OTU	Hereford	4.40-5.41	L6070/GL-A2	UK	
GL	14 OTU	Wellington Ic	7.42-4.44	AD594/GL-U	UK	
GL	185	Hurricane IIb	4.41-3.42	Z2402/GL-P	MedME	
GL	185	Spitfire Vc	2.42-9.44	BR166/GL-A	MedME	
GL	185	Spitfire VIII	8.44-10.44	JF342/GL-3	MedME	
GL	185	Spitfire IX	12.43-8.45	MA452/GL-A	MedME	
GL	1529 RATF	Oxford	12.44-1.46	PH356/GL-D	UK	
GM	42 OTU	Blenheim IV	7.41-42	Z5764/GM-C	UK	
GN	10 RAAF	Sunderland I	9.39-1.40	N9050/GN-D	UK	
GN	249	Hurricane I	6.40-8.41	V6728/GN-Z	UK	
GN	249	Hurricane IIb	2.41-3.42	BD789/GN-G	UK MedME	
GN	249	Spitfire Vb	2.42-9.44	EP828/GN-Z	MedME	
GN	249	Spitfire Vc	2.42-9.44	ES306/GN-T	MedME	
GN	249	Spitfire IX	6.43-6.45	PT681/GN-A	MedME	
GN	249	Mustang III	9.44-6.45	KH543/GN-F	MedME	
GN	249	Mustang IV	6.45-8.45	KH682/GN-B	MedME	
GN	BDU	Lancaster III	7.42-11.45	PB986/GN-X	UK	
GO	94	Gladiator I, II	9.39-6.41	L7616/GO-D	MedME	
GO	94	Kittyhawk I	4.42-5.42	AL133/GO-Y	MedME	
GO	94	Hurricane IIc	5.42-4.44	HW738/GO-G	MedME	
GO	94	Spitfire Vc	3.44-2.45	JK435/GO-D	MedME	
GO	94	Spitfire IX	2.44-4.45	MH703/GO-B	MedME	
GO	AFDU	Spitfire XIV	8.44-12.44	MV253/GO-E	UK	to CFE
GO	*42 OTU*	*Whitley V*	*5.43-4.45*	*Z9487/GO-H*	*UK*	*not confirmed*
GP	1661 HCU	Manchester Ia	11.42-43	R5839/GP-G	UK	
GP	1661 HCU	Lancaster I	1.43-1.44	W4113/GP-J	UK	
GP	1661 HCU	Halifax II	1.43-12.43	L9613/GP-A	UK	
GP	1661 HCU	Stirling III	11.43-12.44	LK616/GP-G	UK	
GP	1661 HCU	Oxford	44-8.45	V3574/GP-Y	UK	
GQ	134	Spitfire Vb	12.41-4.42	AD298/GQ-G	UK	
GQ	134	Hurricane IIc	12.43-8.44	LB885/GQ-V	FE	
GQ	134	Thunderbolt I	9.44-6.45	FL804/GQ-F	FE	
GQ	134	Thunderbolt II	9.44-6.45	KJ275/GQ-T	FE	
GQ	*SF North Killingholme*				*UK*	*use not known*
GR	92	Blenheim If	11.39-5.40	L6776/GR-D	UK	
GR	92	Spitfire I	3.40-6.41	P9367/GR-A	UK	
GR	301	Battle I	7.40-11.40	P6567/GR-E	UK	
GR	301	Wellington Ic	10.40-9.42	X9666/GR-N	UK	
GR	301	Wellington IV	8.41-4.43	Z1257/GR-J	UK	

Code	Unit	Type	Dates	Example	Theatre	Remarks
GR	1586 SD Flt	Halifax V	11.43-11.44	JD319/GR-A	MedME	to 301 Sqn
GR	1586 SD Flt	Liberator III	11.43-11.44	BZ800/GR-D	MedME	to 301 Sqn
GR	301	Halifax II	11.44-3.45	JP231/GR-A	MedME	ex 1586 SD Flt
GR	301	Halifax V	11.44-3.45	LL118/GR-C	MedME	ex 1586 SD Flt
GR	301	Liberator V, VI	11.44-3.45	KG994/GR-R	MedME	ex 1586 SD Flt
GR	301	Warwick III	5.45-1.46	HG275/GR-S	UK	
GR	301	Halifax VIII	1.46-12.46	PP225/GR-W	UK	
GS	330	Northrop N-3PB	6.41-1.43	18/GS-T	Eur	
GS	83 OTU	Wellington III	7.43-10.44	BK151/GS-A	UK	
GS	83 OTU	Wellington X	7.43-10.44	LN542/GS-O	UK	
GS	83 OTU	Martinet I	7.43-10.44	MS570/GS-Y	UK	
GT	156	Wellington Ic	2.42-6.42	N2841/GT-C	UK	
GT	156	Wellington III	3.42-1.43	X3710/GT-W	UK	
GT	156	Lancaster VII	7.45-8.45	NX688/GT-B	UK	
GT	156	Lancaster III	1.43-9.45	JA909/GT-B	UK	
GV	35	Halifax III	1.42-10.42	W1234/GV-I	UK	C Flt
GV	1652 HCU	Halifax I	1.42-4.43	L9607/GV-F	UK	C&D Flts
GV	1652 HCU	Halifax II	1.42-11.44	DT721/GV-G	UK	C&D Flts
GV	1652 HCU	Halifax V	43-11.44	LL227/GV-R	UK	C&D Flts
GV	1652 HCU	Halifax III	44-6.45	MZ557/GV-J	UK	C&D Flts
GW	340	Spitfire IIa	11.41-3.42	P7829/GW-C	UK	
GW	340	Spitfire Vb	3.42-2.44	EN904/GW-A	UK	
GW	340	Spitfire IXb	10.42-2.45	PL427/GW-W	UK, Eur	
GW	340	Spitfire XVI	2.45-11.45	TB285/GW-P	Eur	
GX	415	Beaufort I	9.41-3.42	N1102/GX-R	UK	
GX	415	Blenheim IV	12.41-6.42	L9479/GX-Y	UK	
GX	415	Hampden I	1.42-3.44	AT232/GX-A	UK	
GX	*SF Broadwell*		*45*		*UK*	*use not known*
GY	109 (T)OTU	Dakota III	8.44-8.45	KG662/GY-R	UK	to 1383 TSCU
GY	1383 TSCU	Dakota III	8.45-8.46	KG660/GY-P	UK	ex 109 (T)OTU
GZ	32	Hurricane I	9.39-7.41	P3522/GZ-V	UK	
GZ	32	Hurricane IIb	7.41-11.42	Z5351/GZ-*	UK	
GZ	32	Hurricane IIc	11.41-5.43	HL859/GZ-F	UK	
GZ	32	Spitfire Vc	4.43-9.45	MA698/GZ-C	UK, MedME	
GZ	32	Spitfire VIII	12.43-7.44	*****/GZ-N	MedME	
GZ	32	Spitfire IX	6.43-7.44	EN115/GZ-T	MedME	
GZ	12	Lancaster	9.43-8.46	DV158/GZ-A	UK	C Flt
H1	1 AACU	Henley III	41 42	L3381/H1-E	UK	
H3	*111 (C)OTU*				*Bahamas*	*use not known*
H4	1653 CU	Stirling III	11.43-11.44	BK763/H4-T	UK	A Flt
H4	1653 CU	Lancaster III	11.44-11.46	PB421/H4-J	UK	A Flt
H7	346	Halifax V	5.44-6.44	LL227/H7-K	UK	
H7	346	Halifax III	6.44-4.45	NA121/H7-D	UK	
H7	346	Halifax VI	3.45-11.45	RG592/H7-P	UK	to FAF
H9	*SF Shepherd's Grove*				*UK*	*use not known*
HA	218	Battle I	9.39-6.40	K9353/HA-J	UK	
HA	218	Blenheim IV	7.40-11.40	R3666/HA-J	UK	
HA	218	Wellington Ic	11.40-2.42	R1448/HA-L	UK	
HA	218	Wellington II	3.41-12.41	W5448/HA-Z	UK	
HA	218	Stirling I	1.42-4.43	N6129/HA-X	UK	
HA	218	Stirling III	8.43-3.44	EF504/HA-P	UK	
HA	218	Lancaster III	8.44-8.45	SW269/HA-R	UK	
HA	126	Hurricane I	6.41-3.42	P3731/HA-J	MedME	
HA	126	Spitfire V	3.42-5.42	E****/HA-M	MedME	
HB	239	Gladiator I	9.40-1.42	N2304/HB-G	UK	
HB	239	Lysander II	9.40-1.42	L4786/HB-U	UK	

Code	Unit	Type	Dates	Example	Theatre	Remarks
HB	239	Tomahawk IIa	6.41-5.42	AH793/HB-Z	UK	
HB	239	Hurricane IIc	1.42-5.42	BP397/HB-J	UK	
HB	239	Mustang I	5.42-9.43	AM238/HB-V	UK	
HB	239	Mosquito III	12.43-10.44	DZ297/HB-*	UK	
HB	239	Mosquito VI	9.44-2.45	PZ226/HB-B	UK	
HB	239	Mosquito 30	1.45-7.45	NT362/HB-S	UK	
HB	239	Anson I	44	LT588/HB-Q	UK	
HB	229	Hurricane IIc	9.41-4.42	Z4967/HB-D	MedME	
HB	229	Spitfire Vb	c mid 42	EP136/HB-H	MedME	
HB	229	Spitfire Vc	c mid 42	JK725/HB-B	MedME	
HB	229	Spitfire IX	5.44-12.44	MA423/HB-A	MedME	
HC	512	Dakota III	6.43-3.46	KG625/HC-AF	UK, Eur, MedME	
HC	512	Dakota IV	4.45-3.46	KN641/HC-BW	UK, Eur, MedME	
HC	512	Anson X	44-45	NK528/HC-D	UK	
HD	38	Wellington Ia	9.39-1.42	N2756/HD-U	UK	
HD	38	Wellington Ic	9.39-1.42	R3213/HD-H	UK	
HD	466	Wellington X	11.42-9.43	HE152/HD-L	UK	
HD	466	Halifax II	9.43-11.43	DT559/HD-L	UK	
HD	466	Halifax III	11.43-5.45	HX235/HD-D	UK	
HD	466	Halifax VI	5.45-10.45	RG565/HD-K	UK	
HE	263	Gladiator I	10.39-6.40	K7942/HE-H	UK, Eur	
HE	263	Gladiator II	10.39-6.40	N5633/HE-K	UK, Eur	
HE	263	Hurricane I	6.40-11.40	N2349/HE-V	UK	
HE	263	Whirlwind I	6.40-12.43	P7011/HE-H	UK	
HE	263	Typhoon Ib	12.43-8.45	MN823/HE-J	UK, Eur	
HF	183	Typhoon Ib	11.42-6.45	JR260/HF-J	UK, Eur	
HF	183	Tempest II	8.45-11.45	MW755/HF-W	UK	
HG	332	Spitfire Va	1.42-2.42		UK	
HG	154	Spitfire VII	11.44-2.45	MD185/HG-U	UK	
HG	154	Mustang IV	2.45-3.45	KH765/HG-R	UK	
HH	273	Vildebeeste IV	9.39-c 41	K****/HH-B	FE	continued use of pre-war code
HH	175	Hurricane IIb	3.42-4.43	BE482/HH-T	UK	
HH	175	Typhoon Ib	4.43-9.45	EK455/HH-H	UK	
HI	63 OTU	Beaufighter IIf	6.43-3.44	T3146/HI-U	UK	
HI	63 OTU	Beaufort IA	c 4.44	JM554?/HI-G	UK	
HJ	20 OTU	Wellington I	40-41	L4305/HJ-D	UK	
HJ	20 OTU	Wellington XIV	c 43	NB999/HJ-A	UK	
HK	FLS	Spitfire Vb	1.44-12.44	AR399/HK-Q	UK	
HK	FLS	Spitfire IX	1.44-12.44	BS227/HK-J	UK	
HK	FLS	Hurricane X	1.44-12.44	AG111/HK-G	UK	
HK	269	Warwick I	10.44-3.46	BV519/HK-A	UK, Eur	
HK	269	Spitfire Vb	2.44-3.46	BL939/HK-M	UK, Eur	
HL	SF Gransden Lodge				UK	use not known
HM	136	Hurricane IIb	1.41-11.41	BD729/HM-A	UK, FE	
HM	136	Hurricane IIc	42-10.43	HW620/HM-E	FE	
HM	136	Spitfire Vc	10.43-3.44	MH637/HM-P	FE	
HM	136	Spitfire VIII	1.44-10.45	MT567/HM-B	FE	
HM	136	Spitfire XIV	11.45-5.46	RN193/HM-A	FE	
HM	1677 TTF	Martinet I	3.44-1.46	HP326/HM-A	UK	
HN	93	Havoc I	12.40-12.41	AX916/HN-L	UK	
HN	93	Spitfire Vb	6.42-11.42	BM514/HN-B	UK	
HN	93	Spitfire Vc	11.42-8.43	BR487/HN-V	MedME	
HN	93	Spitfire IX	7.43-9.45	MA636/HN-N	MedME	
HN	20	Audax	9.39-12.41	K4859/HN-B	FE	
HN	20	Lysander II	12.41-5.43	N1270/HN-A	FE	

Code	Unit	Type	Dates	Example	Theatre	Remarks
HN	20	Hurricane IId	3.43-9.45	KX229/HN-H	FE	
HN	20	Spitfire VIII	9.45-4.46	MV329.HN-X	FE	
HO	143	Beaufighter I	6.41-12.41	T3350/HO-N	UK	
HO	143	Blenheim IVf	12.41-9.42	L9478/HO-P	UK	
HO	143	Beaufighter IIf	9.42-3.43	V8204/HO-Z	UK	
HO	143	Beaufighter XIc	3.43-4.44	JL880/HO-C	UK	
HO	143	Beaufighter X	4.43-10.44	LX973/HO-R	UK	
HO	*56 OTU*	*Hurricane*	*c 42*	*****/HO-R*	*UK*	*? 56 OTU HQ recorded in error*
HP	GRU	Wallace I TT	*c* 40-42	K4344/HP-K	UK	
HP	GRU	Beaufighter I	*c* 41	T3911/HP-K	UK	
HP	GRU	Henley III	41-42	L3247/HP-*	UK	
HP	GRU	Defiant I	*c* 42	N1549/HP-M	UK	
HP	GRU	Spitfire Vb	*c* 42	AR406/HP-A	UK	
HP	GRU	Puss Moth	9.42-10.43	ES917/HP-L	UK	
HP	GRU	Battle TT	*c* 43-44	L5776/HP-J	UK	
HP	GRU	Wellington X	*c* 43	LN151/HP-O	UK	
HP	GRU	Tempest V	*c* 44-45	EJ529/HP-D	UK	
HP	247	Gladiator II	8.40-2.41	N5682/HP-K	UK	
HP	247	Hurricane I	12.40-6.41	W8270/HP-V	UK	
HP	247	Hurricane IIa	6.41-1.42	Z2682/HP-R	UK	
HP	247	Hurricane IIb	6.41-1.42	Z3662/HP-E	UK	
HP	*SF Full Sutton*				*UK*	*use not known*
HQ	56 OTU	Typhoon Ib	12.44-9.45	JP746/HQ-P	UK	X Sqn
HQ	56 OTU	Tempest V	12.44-2.46	EJ804/HQ-M	UK	X Sqn
HR	?	Wellington Ic	*c* 41-42	R1660/HR-O	UK	
HR	*NEFSF*				*UK*	*use not known*
HS	109	Anson I	12.40-8.42	R9812/HS-G	UK	
HS	109	Wellington Ic	1.41-8.42	T2968/HS-H	UK	
HS	109	Mosquito IV	8.42-6.44	DK331/HS-D	UK	
HS	109	Mosquito IX	4.43-9.45	LR511/HS-Q	UK	
HS	109	Mosquito XVI	12.43-9.45	PF408/HS-B	UK	
HS	260	Kittyhawk Ia	2.42-10.42	ET1016/HS-D	MedME	
HS	260	Kittyhawk IIa	6.42-5.43	FL233/HS-O	MedME	
HS	260	Kittyhawk III	12.42-4.44	FR507/HS-D	MedME	
HS	260	Mustang III	4.44-8.45	HB971/HS-E	MedME	
HS	260	Mustang IV	6.45-8.45	*****/HS-P	MedME	
HS	192	Whitley V	*c* 44	P5047/HS N	UK	C Flt
HT	154	Spitfire IIa	11.41-3.42		UK	
HT	154	Spitfire Va	2.42-10.42	P8700/HT-X	UK	
HT	154	Spitfire Vb	11.42-4.43	BM588/HT-F	MedME	
HT	154	Spitfire Vc	11.42-4.44	ER676/HT-E	MedME	
HT	154	Spitfire IX	7.43-9.44	MA580/HT-S	MedME	
HU	406	Beaufighter IIf	6.41-6.42	R23**/HU-M	UK	
HU	406	Beaufighter VIf	6.42-8.44	ND221/HU-P	UK	
HU	406	Mosquito XII	6.43-8.44	HK180/HU-A	UK	
HU	406	Mosquito XXX	7.44-8.45	NT477/HU-H	UK	
HV	8	Vincent	9.39-*c* 12.41	K4706/HV-N	MedME	
HV	8	Blenheim I	9.39-*c* 12.41	L6655/HV-Y	MedME	
HV	SF East Kirkby	Lancaster I	45	LM517/HV-C	UK	
HW	100	Lancaster I, III	1.43-5.46	EE180/HW-D	UK	
HX	61 OTU	Spitfire I	6.41-12.43	X4648/HX-O	UK	
HX	61 OTU	Spitfire Vb	9.44-7.45	EN917/HX-R	UK	
HX	61 OTU	Spitfire IX	45-46	EN917/HX-R	UK	
HX	61 OTU	Master III		W8562/HX-5	UK	
HX	61 OTU	Spitfire XVI	1.46-2.47	TE196/HX-F	UK	

Code	Unit	Type	Dates	Example	Theatre	Remarks
HZ	*44 GCF*	*45-8.46*			*UK*	*use not known*
I2	48	Dakota IV	3.44-1.46	KG337/I2-UC	UK	
I4	567	Martinet I	12.43-7.45	JN293/I4-C	UK	
I4	567	Hurricane IV	12.43-6.45	LF577/I4-Z	UK	
I4	567	Oxford	12.43-6.46	V4262/I4-N	UK	
I4	567	Barracuda II	12.43-2.45	P9941/I4-V	UK	
I4	567	Spitfire XVI	7.45-6.46	SM278/I4-M	UK	
I4	567	Vengeance IV	4.45-6.46	HB364/I4-Q	UK	
I4	567	Tiger Moth	*c* 44-45	N6540/I4-W	UK	
I5	*105 (T)OTU*				*UK*	*use not known; to 1381 TSCU*
I5	1381 TSCU	Wellington X	8.45-11.46	MF703/I5-X	UK	ex 105 (T)OTU
I6	*32 MU CF*				*UK*	*use not known*
I8	440	Typhoon Ib	2.44-8.45	MN637/I8-Y	UK, Eur	
I9	575	Dakota III, IV	2.44-8.46	FZ593/I9-V	UK, MedME	
I9	575	Anson I	1.44-5.45	NK674/I9-M	UK	
I9	575	Anson X	1.44-5.45	NK534/I9-J	UK	
IA	*SF Syerston*				*UK*	*use not known*
IB	GPTF	Dakota III	1.45-11.45	TS433/IB-D	UK	
IB	43 GCF	Anson XII	45-49	PH661/IB-*	UK	
IC	623	Stirling III	8.43-12.43	EF199/IC-L	UK	
IF	84 OTU	Wellington X	9.43-6.45	LN175/IF-F	UK	B, D Flts
IF	84 OTU	Anson	9.43-6.45	EG373/IF-P	UK	B, D Flts
II	59 OTU	Typhoon Ib	3.45-6.45	MN804/II-E	UK	2 Sqn
II	116	Lysander III	2.41-1.43	T1430/II-O	UK	
II	116	Hurricane I	11.41-5.45	V7112/II-F	UK	
II	?	Halifax III	44	*****/II-A	UK	
IK	BCIS	Halifax III	12.44-46	MZ873/IK-W	UK	
IL	115	Lancaster III	11.44-8.45	NG205/IL-D	UK	C Flt
IM	*90*				*UK*	*use not known*
IN	*SF Valley*				*UK*	*use not known*
IO	*41 OTU*				*UK*	*use not known*
IP	BCIS	Lancaster III	12.44-6.47	NG343/IP-U	UK	
IP	150	Spitfire V	12.44-6.47		UK	
IQ	150	Lancaster III	11.44-12.45	JB613/IQ-Y	UK	
IT	?	*Mosquito IV*	*3.44*		*UK*	*yellow codes*
IV	SF Upper Heyford	Anson	*c* 45	NK954/IV-E	UK	
IV	SF Upper Heyford	Oxford	*c* 5.44	NM798/IV	UK	
IW	*SF Chilbolton*				*UK*	*use not known*
IY	*SF Dunsfold*				*UK*	*use not known*
J1	1 AACU	Henley III	41-42	L3356/J1-E	UK	
J6	*1521 RATF*		*45*		*UK*	*use not known*
J7	*8 MU*		*45*		*UK*	*use not known*
J8	*24 MU*		*45*		*UK*	*use not known*
J9	1668 HCU	Lancaster III	8.43-12.45	HK741/J9-M	UK	
JA	100	Lancaster III	*c* 44-45	R5702/JA-V	UK	C Flt
JA	1652 CU	Halifax II	1.42-11.44	DT786/JA-A	UK	A&B Flts
JA	1652 CU	Halifax V	1.42-11.44	LL237/JA-W	UK	A&B Flts
JB	81 OTU	Whitley V	7.42-5.45	N1480/JB-V	UK	
JB	81 OTU	Anson I	10.42-8.45	MG589/JB-W	UK	
JB	81 OTU	Oxford II	5.43-8.45	PH121/JB-*	UK	
JB	81 OTU	Spitfire Vb	3.45-8.45	EP411/JB-A	UK	to 1380 TSCU
JB	1380 HSCU	Anson I	8.45-1.46	EG608/JB-V	UK	ex 81 OTU
JB	*11 GCF*		*45*		*UK*	*use not known*
JD	*SF Grimsetter*				*UK*	*use not known*
JE	195	Typhoon Ib	11.42-4.44	JP407/JE-L	UK	

Code	Unit	Type	Dates	Example	Theatre	Remarks
JE	195	Tiger Moth II	*c* 43	DE209/JE-Z	UK	Sqn hack
JE	195	Lancaster I	10.44-8.45	JB475/JE-G	UK	C Flt
JF	3	Tempest V	5.44-8.45	NV767/JF-T	UK, Eur	
JF	1654 HCU	Stirling III	2.44-12.44	EE899/JF-B	UK	
JF	1654 HCU	Lancaster III	12.44-9.45	HK681/JF-R	UK	
JG	17 OTU	Blenheim I	4.40-4.43	*****/JG-17	UK	D Flt
JG	17 OTU	Blenheim IV	4.40-4.43	P4839/JG-E	UK	D Flt
JG	17 OTU	Wellington X	6.43-3.47	NA795/JG-A	UK	D Flt
JG	17 OTU	Spitfire Vb	4.43-*c* 46	BL415/JG-H	UK	D Flt
JH	317	Hurricane I	2.41-7.41	V7339/JH-X	UK	
JH	317	Hurricane II	7.41-12.41	Z3568/JH-X	UK	
JH	317	Magister	10.41-	T9808/JH-K	UK	
JH	317	Spitfire Vb	10.41-9.43	AA762/JH-W	UK	
JH	317	Spitfire IX	8.42-5.45	MJ551/JH-A	UK	
JH	317	Spitfire XVI	5.45-12.46	TD128/JH-M	UK	
JI	514	Lancaster II	9.43-9.44	DT785/JI-D	UK	
JI	514	Lancaster I, III	6.44-8.45	LM719/JI-B	UK	
JJ	274	Spitfire IXc	5.44-8.44	MH603/JJ-K	UK	
JJ	274	Tempest V	8.44-9.45	EJ783/JJ-N	Eur	to 174 Sqn
JJ	174	Tempest V	9.45-3.46	NV772/JJ-E	Eur	ex 274 Sqn
JL	10 OTU	Whitley V	8.42-7.43	BD282/JL-L	UK	
JM	20 OTU	Wellington Ic	5.40-7.45	N2859/JM-N	UK	A Flt
JM	20 OTU	Wellington X	*c* 43-7.45	LP752/JM-L	UK	A Flt
JN	150	Battle I	9.39-10.40	L5540/JN-C	UK	
JN	150	Wellington Ic	10.40-6.42	T2622/JN-D	UK	
JN	150	Wellington III	4.42-8.43	X3448/JN-N	UK, MedME	
JN	150	Liberator II	11.41-4-42	AL506/JN-X	UK	Bomber Cmnd trials
JN	150	Wellington X	6.43-10.44	LP207/JN-J	MedME	
JN	75	Stirling I	10.42-8.43	R9283/JN-K	UK	C Flt
JN	75	Lancaster III	3.44-10.45	HK600/JN-K	UK	C Flt
JO	463	Lancaster I, III	11.43-9.45	ED949/JO-A	UK	
JP	12 OTU	Wellington III	42-*c* 43	X3338/JP-P	UK	B Flt
JP	12 OTU	Wellington X	*c* 43-6.45	LP648/JP-O	UK	B Flt
JQ	2 AACU	Roc	40-41	L3146/JQ-*	UK	
JQ	2 AACU	Henley	40-41	L3419/JQ-Z	UK	
JQ	2 AACU	Battle	40-2.43	L5644/JQ-U	UK	
JQ	2 AACU	Hector	40-41	K8150/JQ-L	UK	
JQ	2 AACU	Gladiator II	41-? 43	N2308/JQ-M	UK	
JQ	*SF Breighton*		*45*		*UK*	*use not known*
JR	161	Lysander IIIa	4.44-6.45	T1770/JR-A	UK	
JR	161	Halifax V	4.44-6.45	DG245/JR-W	UK	
JS	16 OTU	Hampden I	4.40-5.42	AD538/JS-V1	UK	C Flt
JS	16 OTU	Wellington Ic	42-44	T2606/JS-Y	UK	C Flt
JS	16 OTU	Wellington III	9.42-1.45	HE431/JS-P	UK	C Flt
JS	16 OTU	Mosquito XX	12.44-9.45	KB351/JS-T	UK	C Flt
JS	16 OTU	Mosquito XVI	12.44-3.47	PF482/JS	UK	C Flt
JS	16 OTU	Anson I	-3.47	NK888/JS-*	UK	C Flt
JT	256	Defiant I	11.40-5.42	N3445/JT-F	UK	
JT	256	Hurricane I	3.41-5.42	V7010/JT-C	UK	
JT	256	Beaufighter If	5.42-1.43	X7845/JT-G	UK	
JT	256	Beaufighter VI	6.42-5.43	V8501/JT-R	UK	
JT	256	Mosquito XII	5.43-9.45	HK124/JT-T	UK, MedME	
JT	256	Mosquito XIII	2.44-9.45	MM583/JT-D	MedME	
JT	256	Spitfire IX	5.44-8.44	EN135/JT-B	MedME	
JT	256	Mosquito VI	4.45-10.45	RF680/JT-S	MedME	
JT	256	Mosquito XIX	9.45-9.46	TA150/JT-O	MedME	

Code	Unit	Type	Dates	Example	Theatre	Remarks
JU	111	Hurricane I	9.39-5.41	L1823/JU-K	UK	
JU	111	Spitfire I, IIa	5.41-9.41	P7625/JU-*	UK	
JU	111	Spitfire Vb	8.41-10.42	EP166/JU-N	UK	
JU	111	Spitfire Vc	11.42-1.44	JK329/JU-S	MedME	
JU	111	Spitfire IX	6.43-5.47	PL168/JT-A	MedME	
JU	111	Spitfire VIII	7.43-12.43	JG925/JU-Q	MedME	
JV	6	Hardy	9.39-4.40	K****/JV-V	MedME	
JV	6	Lysander I	2.40-6.42	L6857/JV-P	MedME	
JV	6	Lysander II	2.40-6.42	L6878/JV-D	MedME	
JV	6	Hurricane I	2.41-1.42	Z4350/JV-*	MedME	
JV	6	Hurricane IIc	12.41-4.42	BP182/JV-X	MedME	
JV	6	Hurricane IId	4.42-12.42	HV669/JV-E	MedME	
JV	6	Hurricane IV	7.43-1.47	KZ609/JT-S	MedME	
JV	6	Spitfire IX	12.45-12.46	PT470/JT-C	MedME	
JW	CFE/FLS	Spitfire IX	1.43-12.44	MK176/JW-V	UK	
JW	CFE/FLS	Beaufighter X	c 43	*****/JW-D	UK	
JX	1	Hurricane I	9.39-2.41	P3395/JX-B	Eur, UK	
JX	1	Hurricane IIa	2.41-6.41	Z3455/JX-T	UK	
JX	1	Hurricane IIb	3.41-9.42	Z3826/JX-O	UK	
JX	1	Hurricane IIc	7.41-9.42	BE215/JX-I	UK	
JX	1	Typhoon Ib	7.42-4.44	EJ974/JX-T	UK	
JX	1	Spitfire IXb	4.44-5.45	MK997/JX-F	UK	
JZ	57 OTU	Spitfire I	c 41-42	AR213/JZ-E	UK	
JZ	57 OTU	Spitfire IIa	12.40-6.45	P7296/JZ-22	UK	
JZ	57 OTU	Spitfire Vb	41-6.45	AD765/JZ-X	UK	
K1	1 AACU	Henley III	41-42	L3331/K1-C	UK	
K5	*SF Pocklington*		*45*		*UK*	*use not known*
K7	6(C)OTU	Hurricane IIc	c 44-45	*****/K7-HB	UK	
K7	6(C)OTU	Oxford I	45-7.47	N4737/K7-DC	UK	TT Flt
K8	*SF Wymeswold*		*45*		*UK*	*use not known*
K9	*SF Tain*		*45*		*UK*	*use not known*
KA	1685 BDTF	Tomahawk I	6.43-4.44	AH861/KA-K	UK	
KA	1685 BDTF	Hurricane IIc	4.44-8.44	MW368/KA-H	UK	
KA	1685 BDTF	Martinet I	6.43-11.44	MS920/KA-E	UK	
KA	82 OTU	Wellington III	6.43-44	BJ675/KA-L	UK	
KA	82 OTU	Martinet I	6.43-12.44	MS570/KA-B	UK	
KA	*13 GCF*	*Martinet I*	*6.45-5.46*	*MS928/KA-E*	*UK*	*ex 1685 BDTF or 82 OTU aircraft?*
KB	1661 CU	Lancaster I, III	12.44-8.45	ED944/KB-Y	UK	
KB	1661 CU	Mosquito XIII	12.44-8.45	MM617/KB-A	UK	
KC	617	Lancaster III	5.43-6.45	LM492/KC-Q	UK	
KC	617	Lancaster VII	6.45-9.46	NX783/KB-G	UK	
KC	238	Hurricane IIb	5.42-9.43	BP166/KC-J	MedME	
KC	238	Spitfire Vc	1.43-4.44	EP953/KC-G	MedME	
KC	238	Spitfire IX	9.43-10.44	MK486/KC-M	MedME	
KC	238	Spitfire VIII	6.44-10.44	LV729/KC-B	MedME	
KD	30 OTU	Wellington III	7.42-6.45	BK546/KD-O	UK	D Flt
KD	30 OTU	Wellington X	12.43-6.45	LN180/KD-X	UK	D Flt
KD	30 OTU	Moth Minor	8.42-10.43	W7975/KD-Z	UK	D Flt
KE	MSFU	Sea Hurricane Ia	5.41-9.43	L1889/KE-E	UK	
KF	1662 CU	Lancaster I	1.43-11.43	W4241/KF-Q	UK	A Flt
KF	1662 CU	Halifax V	11.43-4.45	LL502/KF-G2	UK	A Flt
KG	204	Sunderland I	9.39-late 41	L5800/KG-J	UK, Eur, Africa	
KG	204	Sunderland III	9.42	DD833/KG-M	UK, Eur, Africa	
KG	81 OTU	Whitley V	7.42-5.45	LA767/KG-Q	UK	
KG	81 OTU	Wellington X	12.44-8.45	NC986/KG-X	UK	

Spitfire F.21 LA215/GO-G was fitted with a contra-rotating propeller and was tested by the Central Fighter Establishment at Tangmere during 1945. This style of marking was to last into the early post-war years. (Norman L. R. Franks)

Possibly the most distinctive marking worn by an RAF unit during the Second World War was the shark's teeth worn by No. 112 Sqn's aircraft from 1941. None the less, the squadron also continued to use its code letters GA, and both identification features are seen on this Mustang IV at the end of the war. (No. 112 Sqn Records)

This Hampden torpedo bomber of No. 415 Sqn RCAF is AT236/GX-R and is seen off the Scottish coast in the spring of 1942. When it was retasked into two different roles later in the war, the Squadron's code changed each time. (via Roger Hayward)

The Hereford was a Hampden variant fitted with the in-line Napier Dagger engine. They served briefly with No. 185 Sqn in the spring of 1940 whose GL code continued in use when it became part of No. 14 OTU in April 1940; L6070/GL-A2 was one on charge. (via Harry Moyle)

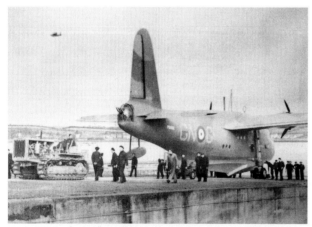

No. 10 Sqn RAAF was re-equipping with Sunderland Is in the UK when war was declared. More generally identified with the RB code, it is little known that initially the squadron was allocated GN as seen here on P9602/GN-G in December 1940. The code changed in early 1940, possibly because it was the same as No. 249 Sqn. (via N. Mackenzie)

In the spring of 1942 the codes of many Western Desert fighter squadrons were changed. One was No. 94 Sqn which in May reverted to GO (here on a Kittyhawk I), which it had earlier worn on Gladiators, but which had changed to FZ for a time. (Wg Cdr J. F. Edwards)

By the time No. 154 Sqn was re-equipped with Mustangs in February 1945 for long-range escort duties, camouflage was largely dispensed with. On returning from the Mediterranean the previous summer, its codes were changed from HT to HG, well shown here on Mk IV KH765/HG-R. (E. Andrews)

The Halifax C.VIII transports saw only limited use with two Polish squadrons, Nos 301 and 304, at Chedburgh. They carried the Polish check marking on the nose, as seen on PP324/GR-V. (via J. D. Oughton)

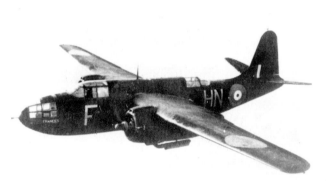

This Havoc I BT461 wears the identity code for No. 93 Sqn, which was formed for operations with aerial mines for night defence tasks. The name Frances is a personal touch on an otherwise standard night scheme on HN-F in 1941. (W. Huntley)

Among the 1930s-vintage biplanes in use during the early years of the Second World War were the HP-coded Wallace IIs of the Gunnery Research Unit like K4344/HP-K at Exeter. The code was also worn by No. 247's Gladiators and Hurricanes based nearby, but to avoid confusion it adopted ZY in 1941. (Westlands)

At the same time as No. 93 Sqn in the UK used HN, in India the code was also allocated to No. 20 Sqn which used it on various types from 1940, including Spitfire FR.XIVs which arrived in late 1945; NH924/HN-F is shown. (J. Howarth)

Many of the newly formed Canadian squadrons in the UK from 1943 included numerals in their codes. One was No. 440 Sqn, which flew Typhoons like MP149/I8-P, seen in October 1944. It had previously flown P-40s in Alaska as No. 111 Sqn, which were coded in the RCAF's 'home' combinations. (Canadian Forces)

The Dakota transports of Nos 48 and 575 Squadrons had a different form of presentation, in which the letter was much larger than the numeral. This is well illustrated on KJ864/I9-V of No. 575 soon after the war. During the war the code was red, thinly outlined in white. (R. C. Sturtivant)

A total of five Liberator IIs was issued to No. 150 Sqn of Bomber Command in November 1941 for use as night bombers, but plans changed and they were withdrawn in January 1942 and passed to No. 108 Sqn in Egypt. While with No. 150, however, they did wear the unit's codes as seen on AL506/JN-X after its arrival in Egypt. (W. Griffiths)

Patrolling from Ballyhalbert in December 1942 is Beaufighter VIf X8443/JT-B of No. 256 Sqn, which used this code from its formation on Defiants and retained it following its move to the Mediterranean. (B. J. Wild)

Lysander IIs of No. 6 Sqn including L6878/JV-D and L6887/JV-E, patrol over the Suez Canal Zone in February 1940. This famous squadron adopted this code in September 1939 and retained the combination for almost ten years. (via R. L. Ward)

The RAF's senior squadron, No. 1, used JX as an identity throughout the war, ending on Spitfire F.21s like LA267/JX-L at its traditional home at Tangmere in the summer of 1945. The code was retained by the squadron until 1950. (L. Haynes)

The Tomahawk IIbs of No 1685 Bomber Defence Training Flight at Ossington used the code KA and were used to train bomber crews in fighter evasion tactics. The codes of many of these flights have rarely been illustrated; AH861/KA-K is shown. (via Air Cdre G. R. Pitchfork)

The Norwegian-manned No. 333 Sqn had two flights for coastal operations off their homeland. One flew Mosquito fighter bombers and one Catalina flying boats, but both types were identified by the code letters KK as seen on Catalina IV JV933/KK-C of A Flight at Woodhaven. (Cato Guhnfeldt Collection)

The first true helicopter in RAF service was the Hoverfly I, a couple being used by No. 529 Sqn in the summer of 1945 for calibration work. One was KK993/KX-R which shows the unusual presentation of the letters. (via Eric Myall)

A few autogyros were used by the RAF during the Second World War including several impressed civilian Cierva C.30As. One was DR623/KX-N (formerly G-ACWH) of No. 529 Sqn which used it for radar calibration duties. (Norman Hill)

The Cairo-based communications unit, No. 267 Sqn, used a wide miscellany of types, most of which wore its allocated code KW seen here on a Proctor, and which also adorn a Hawker Audax behind. (P. H. T. Green Collection)

Code	Unit	Type	Dates	Example	Theatre	Remarks
KG	1380 T(S)CU	Wellington X	8.45-1.46	NC809/KG-P	UK	
KH	403	Tomahawk IIa	3.41-7.41	AH882/KH-R	UK	
KH	403	Spitfire I	5.41-7.41	R6611/KH-T	UK	
KH	403	Spitfire IIa	7.41-9.41	P7552/KH-Q	UK	
KH	403	Spitfire Vb	9.41-1.43	AB865/KH-T	UK	
KH	403	Spitfire IX	1.43-12.44	MJ355/KH-H	UK	
KH	403	Spitfire XVI	12.44-6.45	TB752/KH-Z	UK	
KI	*SF Coningsby*		*45*		*UK*	*use not known*
KJ	11 OTU	Wellington I	4.40-*c* 44	L4381/KJ-A	UK	
KJ	11 OTU	Wellington X	*c* 43-9.45	LP430/KJ-H	UK	
KJ	11 OTU	Defiant I	8.42-*c* 44	L7011/KJ-A	UK	
KJ	11 OTU	Martinet I	8.42-9.45	JN587/KJ-B	UK	
KJ	11 OTU	Hurricane IIc	8.44-9.45	LF757/KJ-L	UK	
KJ	11 OTU	Master II	8.44-9.45	AZ382/KJ-E	UK	
KJ	11 OTU	Oxford II	*c* 44-9.45	NM971/KJ-V	UK	
KJ	11 OTU	Hurricane	45	LF772/KJ-B	UK	
KK	15 OTU	Wellington Ic	4.40-3.44	T2945/KK-L	UK	
KK	15 OTU	Wellington X	*c* 43-3.44	NA952/KK-Z	UK	
KK	333	Mosquito III	44-45	LR560/KK-C	UK	
KK	333	Mosquito VI	5.44-5.45	HR116/KK-F	UK	
KK	333	Catalina Ib	5.44-2.45	W8424/KK-B	UK	
KK	333	Catalina IVa	5.44-11.45	JV933/KK-C	UK, Eur	to RNorAF
KL	54	Spitfire I	3.39-2.41	K9883/KL-T	UK	
KL	54	Spitfire IIa	2.41-5.41	P7618/KL-Z	UK	
KL	54	Spitfire Va	5.41-8.41	R7279/KL-S	UK	
KM	44	Hampden I	2.39-12.41	AE257/KM-X	UK	
KM	44	Manchester I	2.42-10.42	L7430/KM-N	UK	conversion flt
KM	44	Lancaster I	12.41-9.47	R5556/KM-C	UK	
KN	77	Whitley III	9.39-10.39	K8977/KN-P	UK	
KN	77	Whitley V	9.39-10.42	BD195/KN-M	UK	
KN	77	Whitley VII	6.42-10.42	Z6968/KN-A	UK	
KN	77	Halifax II	10.42-5.44	JB804/KN-Q	UK	
KN	77	Halifax V	10.43-6.44	LL126/KN-W	UK	
KN	77	Halifax III	5.44-3.45	MZ715/KN-Z	UK	
KN	77	Halifax VI	3.45-8.45	RG536/KN-Y	UK	
KN	77	Dakota IV	7.45-11.46	KP232/KN-K	FE	
KO	2	Lysander II	9.39-9.40	N1203/KO-M	UK	
KO	2	Lysander III	9.40-7.42	T1532/KO-D	UK	
KO	2	Defiant I	*c* 6.40	N1572/KO-I	UK	
KO	2	Tomahawk I	8.41-4.42	AK247/KO-H	UK	
KO	115	Wellington Ia	11.39-8.40	N2988/KO-Q	UK	
KO	115	Wellington Ic	4.40-3.42	P9299/KO-O	UK	
KO	115	Wellington II	40	W5449/KO-Q	UK	
KO	115	Wellington III	11.41-3.43	BK362/KO-P	UK	
KO	115	Lancaster II	3.43-5.44	DS626/KO-J	UK	
KO	115	Lancaster III	3.44-1.50	ND720/KO-D	UK	
KP	409	Defiant I	7.41-10.41	T3937/KP-S	UK	
KP	409	Beaufighter IIf	8.41-6.42	T3145/KP-K	UK	
KP	409	Beaufighter VIf	6.42-5.44	MM865/KP-D	UK	
KP	409	Mosquito XIII	3.44-7.45	MM560/KP-F	UK, Eur	
KQ	13 OTU	Blenheim IV	4.40-6.43	V6083/KQ-S	UK	
KQ	13 OTU	Oxford II	43-2.47	V374`/KQ-C	UK	
KQ	13 OTU	Mitchell II	5.43-6.45	FW119/KQ-A	UK	
KQ	13 OTU	Mosquito III	6.43-5.47	HJ990/KQ-M	UK	
KQ	13 OTU	Mosquito II	45-46	DZ706/KQ-*	UK	
KQ	13 OTU	Mosquito VI	45-2.47	RS624/KQ-V	UK	

Code	Unit	Type	Dates	Example	Theatre	Remarks
KQ	55	Blenheim I	c 9.39-12.40	*****/KQ-M	MedME	
KQ	55	Blenheim IV	c 6.40-1.41	T2383/KQ-*	MedME	
KR	1667 CU				UK	use not known
KR	61 OTU	Spitfire I	6.41-12.43	*****/KR-C	UK	
KR	61 OTU	Spitfire IIa		*****/KR-H	UK	
KR	61 OTU	Spitfire Vb	9.44-7.45	*****/KR-W	UK	
KR	61 OTU	Mustang III	12.44-9.46	SR415/KR-D	UK	
KS	SF Tarrant Rushton		45		UK	use not known
KT	1660 HCU ?	Stirling IV	8.44-2.45	LK603/KT-K	UK	not confirmed
KU	47	Vincent	9.39-7.40	K6364/KU-*	Africa	to 430 Flt
KU	47	Wellesley I	6.39-3.43	L2652/KU-O	Africa	
KU	47	Mosquito VI	10.44-3.46	TE650/KU-Y	FE	
KU	430/1430 Flt	Vincent I	c 10.44-6.41	K4685/KU-6	Africa	ex D Flt 47 Sqn
KU	53 OTU	Spitfire I	2.41-c 43	AR255/KU-F	UK	
KU	53 OTU	Lysander III	8.41-43	T****/KU-X	UK	
KU	53 OTU	Master III	6.42-4.44	DL559/KU-D	UK	
KU	53 OTU	Spitfire Vb	c 43-45	**965/KU-E	UK	
KU	53 OTU	Martinet	44-5.45	JN647/KU-U	UK	
KV	1429 Flt	Wellington Ic	1.42-2.43	DV884/KV-X	UK	
KW	615	Gladiator I	9.39-5.40	N2304/KW-R	UK	
KW	615	Hurricane I	4.40-7.41	R4194/KW-R	UK	
KW	615	Hurricane IIa	2.41-4.41	Z2703/KW-M	UK	
KW	615	Hurricane IIc	6.42-10.43		FE	
KW	615	Spitfire Vc	9.43-6.44	MA292/KW-D	FE	
KW	615	Spitfire VIII	6.44-6.45	MD234/KW-R	FE	
KW	615	Thunderbolt II	5.45-9.45	KL856/KW-D	FE	
KW	425	Wellington III	7.42-5.43	Z1729/KW-T	UK	
KW	425	Wellington X	3.43-10.43	HE903/KW-W	MedME	
KW	425	Halifax III	12.43-5.45	LW715/KW-Q	UK	
KW	425	Lancaster X	5.45-9.45	KB926/KW-F	UK	
KW	267	Hudson VI	8.40-10.43	FK504/KW-S	MedME	
KW	267	Proctor	8.40-42	P****/KW	MedME	no indiv letter
KW	267	Audax	8.40-42	K****/KW	MedME	no indiv letter
KX	311	Wellington Ic	8.40-7.43	P9230/KX-B	UK	
KX	1448 Flt	Cierva C-30A	2.42-6.43	AP507/KX-H	UK	Became 529 Sqn
KX	529	Rota I	6.43-10.45	K4233/KX-F	UK	
KX	529	Hornet Moth	6.43-10.43	W5754/KX-W	UK	
KX	529	Hoverfly I	4.45-10.45	KK998/KX-R	UK	
KY	242	Stirling V	2.45-1.46	PK152/KY-A	UK	
KZ	287	Defiant I	2.42-10.43	N1581/KZ-Q	UK	
KZ	287	Oxford I	4.42-6.46	HN164/KZ-D	UK	
KZ	287	Martinet I	9.43-6.46	MS528/KZ-B	UK	
KZ	287	Beaufighter IIf	11.44-7.46	V8159/KZ-F	UK	
KZ	287	Tempest V	11.44-6.46	JV764/KZ-R	UK	
KZ	287	Spitfire XVIe	10.45-6.46	TB625/KZ-A	UK	
L4	27 MU		45		UK	use not known
L5	297	Albemarle I	7.43-10.44	P1400/L5-K	UK	
L5	297	Halifax III	10.44-3.46	LK988/L5-H	UK	
L6	1669 HCU	Halifax V	8.44-11.44	DT786/L6-P	UK	
L6	1669 HCU	Lancaster I, III	11.44-3.45	NE179/L6-B	UK	
L7	271	Dakota	1.44-12.45		UK	
L8	347	Halifax V	6.44-7.44	LK999/L8-D	UK	
L8	347	Halifax III	7.44-4.45	NA681/L8-G	UK	
L8	347	Halifax VI	3.45-11.45	RG669/L8-G	UK	to GB 1/25 FAF
L9	190	Stirling IV	1.44-5.45	LJ818/L9-X	UK	
L9	190	Halifax III	5.45-12.45	LW385/L9-H	UK	

Code	Unit	Type	Dates	Example	Theatre	Remarks
L9	190	Halifax VII	5.45-1.46	PN286/L9-B	UK	
LA	235	Blenheim IVf	2.40-12.41	T1807/LA-E	UK	
LA	235	Beaufighter Ic	12.41-1.43	T4731/LA-V	UK	
LA	235	Beaufighter IIc	5.42-7.44	EL404/LA-Y	UK	
LA	235	Beaufighter X	7.43-7.44	LX860/LA-C	UK	
LA	235	Mosquito VI	6.44-7.45	HR114/LA-R	UK	
LB	28 OTU	Wellington Ic	5.42-10.44	DV846/LB-X	UK	
LB	28 OTU	Wellington II	5.42-10.44	BK153/LB-B	UK	
LB	28 OTU	Wellington X	12.42-10.44	MF537/LB-B	UK	
LC	*SF Feltwell*				*UK*	*use not known*
LD	108	Blenheim I	9.39-4.40	L1214/LD-M	UK	
LD	108	Blenheim IV	10.39-4.40	L1269/LD-U	UK	
LD	108	Anson I	9.39-4.40	N5173/LD-S	UK	
LD	117	Hudson IIIa	42-43	FK370/LD-H	MedME	
LD	117	Hudson VI	7.42-9.43	EW970/LD-Q	MedME	
LD	250	Tomahawk IIb	4.41-4.42	AK498/LD-C	MedME	
LD	250	Kittyhawk II	4.42-10.42	AL116/LD-V	MedME	
LD	250	Kittyhawk III	10.42-1.44	FL904/LD-C	MedME	
LD	250	Kittyhawk IV	1.44-8.45	FX616/LD-S	MedME	
LD	250	Mustang III	8.45-1.47	KH520/LD-Y	MedME	
LE	242	Hurricane I	1.40-2.41	V6675/LE-V	UK	
LE	242	Hurricane IIb	2.41-2.42	Z2632/LE-A	UK, FE	
LE	242	Spitfire Vc	4.42-4.44	Z2632/LE-A	UK, MedME	
LE	242	Spitfire IX	6.43-10.44	JL230/LE-B	MedME	
LE	630	Lancaster III	11.43-7.45	JA872/LE-N	UK	
LF	37	Wellington Ia	9.39-11.40	L7779/LF-P	UK	
LF	37	Wellington Ic	10.40-3.43	T2837/LF-F	UK	
LF	37	Wellington X	8.42-12.44	LP646/LF-P	MedME	
LF	37	Liberator VI	10.44-3.46	KH285/LF-H	MedME	
LF	*SF Predannack*				*UK*	*use not known*
LG	215	Wellington I, Ia	7.39-4.40	N2912/LG-G	UK	
LG	11 OTU	Wellington Ic	4.40-*c* 41	N2892/LG-B3	UK	
LG	*13 GCF*	*Spitfire V*	*45*		*UK*	*use not known*
LH	*SF Mepal*				*UK*	*use not known*
LJ	614	Lysander II	10.40-1.42	R9024/LJ-P	UK	
LJ	614	Lysander III	10.40-1.42	R9124/LJ-P	UK	
LJ	614	Blenheim IV	7.41-9.42	V5534/LJ-K	UK	
LK	87	Hurricane I	9.39-6.41	L1790/LK-K	UK	
LK	87	Hurricane IIa	6.41-11.42	Z3775/LK-B	UK	
LK	87	Hurricane IIc	11.42-1.44	HL865/LK-R	MedME	
LK	87	Spitfire Vc	4.43-8.44	JG866/LK-J	MedME	
LK	87	Spitfire IX	6.43-12.46	NH346/LK-M	MedME	
LK	51	Halifax II	43-1.44	JN883/LK-A	UK	
LK	578	Halifax III	1.44-3.45	MZ527/LK-D	UK	
LL	1513 RATF	Oxford	9.45-12.46	NM250/LL-B	UK	
LM	*SF Elsham Wolds*		*45*		*UK*	*use not known*
LN	99	Wellington I	9.39-10.42	T2501/LN-F	UK	
LN	99	Wellington II	41-10.42	W5458/LN-Z	UK	
LN	*83 GCF*				*Eur*	*use not known*
LO	602	Spitfire I	9.39-6.41	X4722/LO-E	UK	
LO	602	Spitfire IIa	5.41-7.41	P8396/LO-A	UK	
LO	602	Spitfire Vb	7.41-3.44	AR438/LO-W	UK	
LO	602	Spitfire IX	10.43-11.44	MJ147/LO-B	UK, Eur	
LO	602	Spitfire XVI	11.44-5.45	SM350/LO-A	Eur	
LO	216	Hudson VI	7.42-4.43	EW947/LO-N	MedME	
LP	283	Warwick I	3.44-3.46	BV292/LP-Z	MedME	

Code	Unit	Type	Dates	Example	Theatre	Remarks
LP	*6 (C) OTU*	*Mosquito III*	*46*		*UK*	*use not known*
LQ	405	Wellington II	4.41-6.42	W5421/LQ-T	UK	
LQ	405	Halifax II	4.42-9.43	W1112/LQ-E	UK	
LQ	405	Lancaster III	8.43-5.45	PA970/LQ-Y	UK	
LQ	405	Lancaster X	5.45-6.45	KB968/LQ-P	UK	
LR	1667 HCU	Lancaster III	11.44-10.45	PD444/LR-J	UK	
LS	15	Battle I	9.39-12.39	P2177/LS-X	UK	
LS	15	Blenheim IV	12.39-11.40	R3777/LS-W	UK	
LS	15	Wellington Ic	11.40-5.41	T2806/LS-N	UK	
LS	15	Stirling I	4.41-1.43	N3656/LS-H	UK	
LS	15	Stirling III	1.43-12.43	EF333/LS-X	UK	
LS	15	Lancaster III	12.43-3.47	HK619/LS-V	UK	
LT	22 OTU	Wellington Ic	4.41-12.42	DV934/LT-C	UK	B Flt
LT	22 OTU	Wellington III	12.42-7.45	DF578/LT-C	UK	B Flt
LT	22 OTU	Wellington X	12.42-7.45	HE498/LT-X	UK	
LT	22 OTU	Martinet	*c* 44	HP447/LT-R	UK	
LT	1681 BDTF	Hurricane IIc	6.43-8.44	LF118/LT-O	UK	
LU	MSFU	Sea Hurricane I	5.41-9.43	V6802/LU-B	UK	
LV	57 OTU	Spitfire I	12.40-12.43	AR212/LV-N	UK	B Flt
LV	57 OTU	Spitfire II	12.40-6.45	P8700/LV-E	UK	B Flt
LV	57 OTU	Spitfire Vb	*c* 44-6.45	EF541/LV-R	UK	B Flt
LW	74, 75, 76 SW	Blenheim IV	2.41-11.46	N3598/LW-K	UK	
LW	74, 75, 76 SW	Hornet Moth	2.41-11.46	W5773/LW	UK	
LW	318	Hurricane IIc	*c* 9.43-2.44	BP443/LW-A	MedME	
LW	318	Spitfire IXe	11.44-8.46	PL763/LW-D	MedME	
LX	225	Lysander II	10.39-7.42	N1256/LX-M	UK	
LX	54 OTU	Beaufighter II	2.42-7.45	V8906/LX-L	UK	
LX	54 OTU	Lysander II	10.42-6.43	L6858/LX-L	UK	
LX	54 OTU	Beaufighter VI	9.43-7.45	ND234/LX-E	UK	
LX	54 OTU	Mosquito III	2.45-5.47	RR282/LX-H	UK	
LX	54 OTU	Mosquito VI	4.46-5.47	RS674/LX-N	UK	
LY	14	Wellesley I	*c* 9.39-12.40	L****/LY-L	MedME	
LY	14	Blenheim IV	9.40-*c* 5.41	T1954/LY-O	MedME	
LY	PRU	Spitfire I(PR)	6.40-11.40	R6903/LY	UK	
LY	1 PRU	Spitfire I(PR)	11.40-10.42	X4386/LY	UK	
LY	1 PRU	Anson I	11.40-10.42	W2361/LY	UK	
LY	1 PRU	Blenheim IV	11.40-10.42	P4899/LY-O	UK	
LY	1 PRU	Hudson II	11.40-10.42	P5139/LY	UK	
LY	1 PRU	Wellington I	11.40-10.42	R2700/LY-P	UK	E Flt
LY	1 PRU	Spitfire IV	2.41-10.42	AB313/LY	UK	
LY	1 PRU	Mosquito I	7.41-10.42	W4059/LY-T	UK	
LY	1 PRU	Mosquito IV	41-10.42	DK310/LY-G	UK	
LZ	66	Spitfire IIa	11.40-2.42	P7735/LZ-M	UK	
LZ	66	Spitfire Vb	2.42-11.43	EE661/LZ-R	UK	
LZ	66	Spitfire IX	11.43-11.44	PT529/LZ-F	UK	
LZ	66	Spitfire XVIe	11.44-4.45	RR245/LZ-S	UK	
LZ	421 Flt	Hurricane I	10.40-2.41	Z2318/LZ-E	UK	Displayed as L-Z
LZ	421 Flt	Spitfire IIa	*c* 12.40-2.41	P7382/LZ-K	UK	Displayed as L-Z
M1	1 AACU	Henley III	41-42	L3399/M1-H	UK	
M1	1 AACU	Defiant TTI	4.42-11.42	DR914/M1-G	UK	
M1	1 AACU	Wallace II	42	K6050/M1-I	UK	
M2	*33 MU*		*45*		*UK*	*use not known*
M3	5 Grp FU	Lancaster I	45	PD329/M3	UK	
M4	587	Martinet I	12.43-12.44	HP216/M4-16	UK	
M4	587	Oxford	12.43-12.44	HN132/M4	UK	
M4	587	Harvard IIb	12.43-12.44	FS767/M4-R	UK	

Code	Unit	Type	Dates	Example	Theatre	Remarks
M4	587	Vengeance IV	10.44-6.46	HB424/M4-M	UK	
M4	587	Hurricane IIc	12.43-6.45	*****/M4-X	UK	
M4	587	Spitfire XVI	7.45-6.46	TB304/M4-V	UK	
M5	128	Mosquito XX	9.44-11.44	KB221/M5-B	UK	
M5	128	Mosquito 25	9.44-11.44	KB449/M5-V	UK	
M5	128	Mosquito XVI	11.44-4.46	PF411/M5-B	Eur	
M6	83 GCF	Anson XIX	45-5.46	PH697/M6-*	Eur	
M7	91 GCF	Tutor	45-46	K3367/M7-*	UK	
M8	4 GCF	Oxford	45-46	P6978/M8-*	UK	
M9	*1653 CU*		*45*		*UK*	*use not known*
MA	161	Lysander IIIa	2.42-4.44	V7907/MA-G	UK	
MA	161	Wellington	42	P2521/MA-V	UK	
MA	161	Whitley V	2.42-12.42	Z9224/MA-P	UK	
MA	161	Havoc I	2.42-12.43	BJ477/MA-R	UK	
MA	161	Halifax II	11.42-10.44	DG286/MA-X	UK	
MA	161	Halifax V	11.42-10.44	LK738/MA-T	UK	
MA	161	Oxford	11.42-3.45	V3677/MA-Q	UK	
MA	161	Hudson III	10.43-6.45	T9439/MA-R	UK	
MA	161	Albemarle	10.42-4.43	P1390/MA-L	UK	
MA	161	Stirling I	*c* 9.44	R9277/MA-I	UK	
MA	161	Stirling IV	9.44-6.45	LK119/MA-Y	UK	
MA	651	Auster IV	5.44-10.45		UK	HQ Flt
MB	236	Beaufighter X	6.43-5.45	RD142/MB-D	UK	
MB	220	Fortress I	*c* 10.41-3.42	AN518/MB-B	MedME	ME det only
MB	651	Auster IV	5.44-10.45		UK	A Flt
MC	651	Auster IV	5.44-10.45	MT306/MC	UK	B Flt
MC	*SF Fiskerton*				*UK*	*use not known*
MD	133	Hurricane IIb	8.41-12.41	Z4999/MD-A	UK	
MD	133	Spitfire IIa	10.41-1.42	P8191/MD-G	UK	
MD	133	Spitfire Vb	1.42-9.42	EN951/MD-U	UK	
MD	133	Spitfire IX	7.42-9.42	BS296/MD-S	UK	to 336 FS 4 FG USAAF qv
MD	458	Wellington Ic	10.42-11.42	BB457/MD-U	MedME	
MD	458	Wellington VIII	11.42-2.44	HX519/MD-F	MedME	
MD	526	Blenheim IV	6.43-5.45	T2001/MD-B	UK	
MD	526	Hornet Moth	6.43-5.45	W5788/MD-R	UK	
MD	526	Oxford I	6.43-5.45	X7200/MD-N	UK	
MD	526	Dominie I	8.43-5.45	T2001/MD-B	UK	
MD	651	Auster IV	5.44-10.45		UK	C Flt
ME	488	Beaufighter VI	6.42-9.43	X8027/ME-W	UK	
ME	488	Mosquito XII	8.43-5.44	HK197/ME-F	UK	
ME	488	Mosquito XIII	10.43-9.44	MM513/ME-D	UK	
ME	488	Mosquito III	*c* 44	LR562/ME-N	UK	
ME	488	Mosquito 30	9.44-4.45	NT372/ME-B	UK	
MF	280	Warwick I	8.43-6.46	HG188/MF-H	UK	
MF	260	Hurricane I	10.41-4.42	Z4266/MF-E	MedME	
MF	260	Kittyhawk Ia	4.42-5.42	AK669/MF-T	MedME	
MF	59 OTU	Hurricane I	12.40-1.44	V7173/MF-X34	UK	
MF	59 OTU	Master III	8.41-7.43	W8650/MF-X	UK	Z Flt
MF	59 OTU	Battle TT	12.41-*c* 42	V1204/MF-XL	UK	Z Flt
MF	59 OTU	Hurricane X	2.42-1.44	AG162/MF-8	UK	
MF	FLS	Typhoon Ib	1.44-12.44	MN208/MF-19	UK	
MF	FLS	Tempest V	1.44-12.44	SN108/MF-N	UK	
MG	7	Hampden I	9.39-4.40	L4160/MG-M	UK	
MG	7	Stirling I	8.40-7.43	N3462/MG-E	UK	
MG	7	Stirling III	3.43-7.43	EF361/MG-B2	UK	
MG	7	Lancaster III	7.43-1.50	PB623/MG-L	UK	

Code	Unit	Type	Dates	Example	Theatre	Remarks
MG	7	Lancaster VI	12.43-11.44	MG675/MG-O	UK	trials only
MH	51	Whitley II	9.39-12.39	K7228/MH-U	UK	
MH	51	Whitley III	9.39-12.39	K8979/MH-B	UK	
MH	51	Whitley IV	11.39-5.40	K9043/MH-G	UK	
MH	51	Whitley V	5.40-11.42	Z9274/MH-O	UK	
MH	51	Halifax III	11.42-1.44	LW287/MH-C	UK	
MH	51	Halifax II	11.42-1.44	LW287/MH-C	UK	
MH	51	Stirling V	6.45-4.46	PJ883/MH-A	UK	
MJ	1680 (T) Flt	Dominie	5.43-2.46	HG723/MJ-N	UK	
MJ	1680 (T) Flt	Dakota	5.43-2.46	FZ670/MJ-O	UK	
MK	500	Anson I	9.39-4.41	N7233/MK-O	UK	
MK	500	Blenheim IV	4.41-11.41	Z6161/MK-T	UK	
MK	500	Hudson III	11.41-4.44	V9094/MK-W	UK	
MK	20 OTU	Anson I	c 7.44-3.45	LT959/MK-F	UK	
MK	126	Spitfire Vc	8.42-8.43	BR471/MK-P	MedME	
ML	*? 257*	*Hurricane I*	*c 6.40*	*L2101/ML-K*	*UK*	*reported*
ML	12 OTU	Wellington III	42-6.45	BK136/ML-R	UK	
ML	12 OTU	Martinet I	43-6.45	JN428/ML-Y	UK	
ML	12 OTU	Oxford I	42-45	*****/ML-Z	UK	
ML	12 OTU	Hurricane IIc	7.44-6.45	*****/ML-H	UK	
MN	350	Spitfire IIa	11.41-4.42	P8727/MN-A	UK	
MN	350	Spitfire Vb	2.42-7.44	BL496/MN-O	UK	
MN	350	Spitfire Vc	3.44-7.44	EE613/MN-E	UK	
MN	350	Spitfire IX	12.43-8.44	MH413/MN-P	UK	
MN	350	Spitfire XIV	8.44-10.46	NH698/MN-C	UK, Eur	
MN	350	Spitfire XVI	8.46-10.46	TD325/MN-M	Eur	to BAF
MP	76	Halifax I	5.41-2.42	L9565/MP-B	UK	
MP	76	Halifax II	10.41-4.43	DT492/MP-H	UK	
MP	76	Halifax V	4.43-2.44	LK902/MP-H	UK	
MP	76	Halifax III	2.44-4.45	NR200/MP-M	UK	
MP	76	Halifax VI	3.45-8.45	TW796/MP-Y	UK	
MP	76	Dakota	5.45-9.46	KN559/MP-S	FE	
MQ	226	Battle I	9.39-5.41	K9182/MQ-J	UK	
MQ	226	Blenheim IV	2.41-11.41	Z7358/MQ-U	UK	
MQ	226	Boston III	11.41-5.43	AL677/MQ-P	UK	
MQ	226	Mitchell II	5.43-9.45	FV900/MQ-F	UK, Eur	
MQ	226	Mitchell III	1.45-9.45	KJ561/MQ-Y	Eur	
MR	245	Hurricane IIb	8.41-1.43	BE496/MR-M	UK	
MR	245	Typhoon Ib	1.43-8.45	JR311/MR-G	UK, Eur	
MS	273	Spitfire VIII	3.44-1.46	LV731/MS-O	FE	
MS	273	Spitfire XIV	11.45-1.46	RN218/MS-F	FE	
MS	*SF Church Fenton*		*45*		*UK*	*use not known*
MT	122	Spitfire I	5.41-10.41	P9500/MT-P	UK	
MT	122	Spitfire II	11.41-2.42	P8252/MT-	UK	
MT	122	Spitfire Vb	2.42-10.42	BM252/MT-E	UK	
MT	122	Spitfire IX	8.43-2.44	BS546/MT-J	UK	
MT	122	Mustang III	1.44-5.45	FB226/MT-K	UK, Eur	
MT	122	Mustang IV	4.45-7.45	KH642/MT-M	Eur	
MT	*126*	*Spitfire Vc*	*42-43*		*MedME*	*reported*
MU	60	Blenheim I	9.39-2.42	L8609/MU-X	FE	
MU	60	Blenheim IV	3.42-8.43	T2291/MU-A	FE	
MU	60	Hurricane IIc	8.43-7.45	LD346/MU-T	FE	
MU	60	Thunderbolt II	7.45-11.46	KL187/MU-M	FE	
MU	GHTF	Lancaster I, III	12.44-6.45	LM473/MU-	FE	
MV	53 OTU	Spitfire I	2.41-6.45	X4344/MV-N	UK	
MV	53 OTU	Spitfire Vb	2.41-6.45	BM572/MV-E	UK	

Code	Unit	Type	Dates	Example	Theatre	Remarks
MW	217	Anson I	9.39-12.40	L9154/MW-S	UK	
MW	217	Tiger Moth II	11.39-6.40	N6839/MW-4	UK	No.6 Coastal Patrol Flight
MW	217	Beaufort I	5.40-5.42	L9807/MW-A	UK	
MW	217	Beaufort II	10.41-5.42	AW212/MW-T	UK	
MW	*101*	*Lancaster III*	*45*		*UK*	*C Flt; use not known*
MX	1653 CU	Liberator II	1.42-10.42	AL***/MX-M	UK	
MX	*SF Glatton*		*45*		*UK*	*use not known*
MY	278	Tiger Moth	*c* 44	R5059/MY-C	UK	
MY	278	Walrus	10.41-10.45	L2307/MY-G	UK	
MY	278	Defiant I	5.42-12.42	T4036/MY-*	UK	
MY	278	Anson I	2.43-7.44	EF985/MY-F	UK	
MY	278	Sea Otter II	5.45-10.45	JM957/MV-M	UK	
MY	278	Warwick I	44-45	HF962/MY-	UK	
MY	278	Spitfire IIc	4.44-2.45	R6965/MY-P	UK	
MY	278	Spitfire Vb	4.44-2.45	AD562/MY-V	UK	
MZ	83 OTU	Wellington III	7.43-10.44	X3793/MZ-G	UK	
MZ	*299*		*45*		*UK*	*use not known*
N7	*SF Lyneham*		*45*		*UK*	*use not known*
N8	*SF Waterbeach*		*45*		*UK*	*use not known*
N9	*SF Blackbushe*		*45*		*UK*	*use not known*
NA	428	Wellington III	11.42-4.43	Z1719/NA-P	UK	
NA	428	Wellington X	4.43-7.43	HE864/NA-D	UK	
NA	428	Halifax V	6.43-1.44	DK237/NA-L	UK	
NA	428	Halifax II	11.43-6.44	JN955/NA-L	UK	
NA	428	Lancaster X	6.44-9.45	KB763/NA-S	UK	
NA	146	Mohawk IV	3.42-4.42	BS788/NA-*	FE	
NA	146	Hurricane II	5.42-6.44	BG685/NA-N	FE	
NA	146	Thunderbolt I	6.44-3.45	HD152/NA-X	FE	
NA	146	Thunderbolt II	9.44-6.45	KL168/NA-S	FE	
NB	1 (I)SFTS	Hart (India)	11.40-7.41	K2130/NB-E	FE	ex 27 Sqn
NB	1 (I)SFTS	Wapiti IIa	11.40-7.41	K1309/NB-*	FE	
NC	4	Mosquito VI	-8.45	SZ980/NC-K	Eur	
ND	236	Blenheim IVf	6.40-3.42	V5432/ND-A	UK	
ND	236	Beaufighter I	3.42-7.42	T4827/ND-N	UK	
ND	236	Beaufighter VIc	6.42-8.43	JL451/ND-K	UK	
ND	1666 HCU	Halifax II	6.43-12.44	DT689/ND-K	UK	
ND	1666 HCU	Lancaster III	11.44-8.45	PB578/ND-R	UK	
ND	1666 HCU	Lancaster X	11.44-8.45	KB720/ND-E	UK	
NE	143	Beaufighter X	2.44-10.44	NE663/NE-G	UK	
NE	143	Mosquito VI	10.44-5.45	PZ413/NE-Y	UK	
NF	138	Whitley V	8.41-10.42	Z9287/NF-K	UK	
NF	138	Lysander IIIA	8.41-11.42	T1508/NF-*	UK	
NF	138	Halifax II	10.42-8.44	W1209/NF-A	UK	
NF	138	Halifax V	3.43-8.44	DG252/NF-B	UK	
NF	138	Oxford	43-45	V3837/NF-Y	UK	
NF	138	Stirling IV	5.44-3.45	LJ913/NF-N	UK	
NF	138	Lancaster I, III	3.45-5.46	NN781/NF-L	UK	
NF	488	Buffalo I	10.41-1.42	W8138/NF-O	FE	
NG	604	Blenheim If	9.39-5.41	L6609/NG-O	UK	
NG	604	Beaufighter I	9.40-4.43	R2101/NG-R	UK	
NG	604	Beaufighter VI	4.43-4.44	V8556/NG-R	UK	
NG	604	Mosquito XII	2.44-9.44	HK183/NG-L	UK	
NG	604	Mosquito XIII	4.44-4.45	MM449/NG-R	UK	
NH	274	Hurricane IIe	10.41-42	DG631/NH-C	MedME	
NH	415	Wellington XIII	9.43-7.44	HZ653/NH-L	UK	
NH	415	Albacore I	11.43-7.44	BF600/NH-P1	UK	to 119 Sqn

Code	Unit	Type	Dates	Example	Theatre	Remarks
NH	415	Halifax III	7.44-44	NA587/NH-Q	UK	
NH	119	Albacore I	7.44-2.45	BF588/NH-M	UK	ex 415 Sqn
NH	119	Swordfish III	1.45-5.45	NF374/NH-M	UK	
NH	*530*	*Havoc, Boston*	*9.42-1.43*		*UK*	*reported*
NI	451	Spitfire IXc	12.44-1.45	MJ833/NI-Z	UK	
NI	451	Spitfire XVI	12.44-6.45	SM465/NI-X	UK	
NI	451	Spitfire XIV	9.45-1.46	TZ130/NI-B	Eur	
NJ	MSFU	Hurricane	5.41-9.43	V6756/NJ-L	UK	
NK	100	Vildebeeste III	c 2.40-2.42	K****/NK-H	FE	
NK	100	Beaufort V	11.41-2.42	T9552/NK-*	FE	
NK	118	Spitfire I	2.41-4.41	N3127/NK-K	UK	
NK	118	Spitfire IIa	3.41-9.41	P7913/NK-H	UK	
NK	118	Spitfire IIb	7.41-9.41	P8662/NK-S	UK	
NK	118	Spitfire Vb	9.41-7.44	AA744/NK-N	UK	
NK	118	Spitfire IX	1.44-3.44	ML348/NK-L	UK	
NK	118	Mustang III	1.45-3.46	KH476/NK-B	UK	
NL	341	Spitfire Vb	1.43-2.44		UK	
NL	341	Spitfire IXb	2.44-3.45	PT472/NL-Z	UK, Eur	
NL	341	Spitfire XVI	3.45-11.45	TB519/NL-L	Eur	to GC 3/2 FAF
NM	230	Sunderland I	9.39-mid 42	L2164/NM-U	MedME	
NM	230	Sunderland III	11.42-43	W6010/NM-V	MedME	
NM	268	Lysander II	8.40-4.42	R1997/NM-L	UK	
NM	268	Tomahawk IIa	5.41-4.42	AH998/NM-V	UK	
NM	268	Mustang I	3.42-4.45	AH775/NM-P	UK	
NN	310	Hurricane I	6.40-3.41	P8809/NN-T	UK	
NN	310	Hurricane IIa	3.41-12.41		UK	
NN	310	Spitfire II	10.41-12.41		UK	
NN	310	Spitfire Vb	11.41-8.44	BL265/NN-L	UK	
NN	310	Spitfire IX	1.44-2.46	BS126/NN-Z	UK, Eur	
NO	*320*	*Anson I*	*6.40-10.41*	*N5202/NO-E*	*UK*	*reported*
NO	320	Hudson I, III	10.40-9.42	T9339/NO-C	UK	
NO	320	Hudson VI	9.42-3.43	FK402/NO-R	UK	
NO	320	Mitchell II	3.43-8.45	FR143/NO-A	UK, Eur	
NO	320	Mitchell III	2.45-8.45	HD358/NO-J	Eur	
NP	158	Wellington II	2.42-6.42	Z8595/NP-Q	UK	
NP	158	Halifax II	6.42-1.44	W1157/NP-A	UK	
NP	158	Halifax III	1.44-6.45	HX331/NP-L	UK	
NP	158	Halifax VI	4.45-7.45	PP167/NP-S	UK	
NQ	24	Wellington I	43-c 44	N2990/NQ-D	UK	
NQ	24	Dakota IV	4.43-46	KP258/NQ-L	UK	
NR	220	Anson I	9.39-11.39	K6209/NR-O	UK	
NR	220	Hudson I	9.39-4.42	N7295/NR-F	UK	
NR	220	Hudson III	2.40-10.41	V9066/NR-O	UK	
NR	220	Hudson V	7.41-4.42	AM815/NR-D	UK	
NR	220	Fortress I	12.41-8.42	AN527/NR-A	UK	
NR	220	Fortress IIa	7.42-7.44	FL459/NR-J	UK	
NS	201	Sunderland III	7.44-6.45	MP760/NS-S	UK	
NS	201	Sunderland V	2.45-c 51	VB881/NS-A	UK	
NS	52 OTU	Spitfire IIb	10.41-1.44	P8348/NS-Y	UK	
NS	52 OTU	Martinet I	10.41-1.44	MS618/NS	UK	
NT	203	Singapore III	9.39-3.40	K6912/NT-D	MedME	
NT	203	Blenheim IVf	5.40-11.42	L9237/NT-J	MedME	
NT	29 OTU	Wellington III	9.42-6.45	BK444/NT-A	UK	B Flt
NT	29 OTU	Wellington X	5.43-6.45	LP434/NT-R	UK	B Flt
NT	29 OTU	Anson I	4.42-5.45	N5064/NT-B	UK	B Flt
NU	1382 (T)CU	Dakota III	8.45-46	KG380/NU-L	UK	

Count the aircraft! This scene of devastation at Dyce on 30 December 1941 shows the Beaufighter Ics of No. 235 Sqn, a coastal fighter unit. T4725/LA-J hit LA-O and a Hudson (both hidden) and T3295/LA-S ran into the lot! But, at least it helped fix the date many years later. (No. 235 Sqn Records)

From the summer of 1944 some coastal strike units placed their unit codes and aircraft letter, separated by a hyphen, on the fuselage above the wings, possibly to avoid being obscured by the AEAF stripes. This is shown to advantage by Mosquito FB VI HR113/LA-V of No. 235 Sqn later in the year. (G. A. B. Lord)

Before the formation of OTUs in April 1940, Bomber Command training was conducted by designated 'Group Pool' squadrons, which usually flew a mix of bombers and trainers. One such was Bicester-based No. 108 Sqn which used LD-coded Ansons like N5172/LD- and Blenheim Is like L1271/LD-B seen in this very rare view. (Peter Lloyd)*

The Merlin-engined Wellington II was used by a number of squadrons from late 1940. A few went to No. 99 Sqn at Waterbeach, though it was never fully equipped; W5458/LN-Z is seen there in 1941 displaying the standard contemporary colour scheme, though with the unofficial nose art! (Sqn Ldr J. W. Gee)

The Hudson was much used in the transport role during the desert campaign by the few units tasked with such duties. One was No. 216 Sqn which in late 1942 flew Hudson VI EW970/LO-Q into a forward desert strip in support of a fighter squadron whose 'hack' was a captured Ju 87D Stuka! (MoD)

The secretive No. 161 Sqn supported Special Operations Executive activities in occupied Europe and flew a variety of aircraft including this Wellington Ic P2521/MA-V used in the summer of 1942, which was modified for 'wireless ops'. (M. Whinney)

When the Fortress I-equipped No. 90 Sqn was disbanded in the UK, its Egyptian-based detachment became No. 220 Sqn (Middle East Detachment), though the main unit was also UK based. The Fortress Is of this detachment received the unit code MB as shown on AN518/MB-B at Shallufa; the UK unit retained its NR code, however. (via G. J. Thomas)

Several squadrons retained Tiger-engined Whitleys into the war. Among them was No. 51 Sqn at Linton on Ouse where Mk IIIs K8979/MH-B and K8978/MH-P display their newly applied wartime codes in September 1939. (No. 51 Sqn Records)

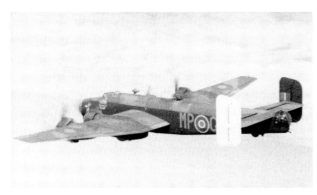

When Bomber Command 'heavies' began mounting daylight raids late in the war, many had coloured identification features applied to the tail surfaces as is well illustrated by Halifax III MP-G of No. 76 Sqn in 1945. (Gp Capt J. Pelly-Fry)

The mighty Thunderbolt became the RAF's standard fighter bomber towards the end of the war in Burma and continued in service for a short time after the war. They carried SEAC markings and codes were usually in white as displayed by Thunderbolt II KL266/MU-S of No. 60 Sqn during a patrol over Java following the Japanese surrender. (via J. D. Oughton)

Code	Unit	Type	Dates	Example	Theatre	Remarks
NU	1382 (T)CU	Dakota IV	8.45-1.48	KJ778/NU-Q	UK	to 240 OCU
NV	79	Hurricane I	9.39-6.41	L1698/NV-R	UK	
NV	79	Hurricane IIb	6.41-3.42	Z2674/NV-M	UK	
NV	79	Hurricane IIc	6.42-7.44	LB880/NV-L	FE	
NV	79	Thunderbolt II	6.44-12.45	KJ202/NV-N	FE	
NW	33	Gladiator II	9.39-9.40	L7614/NW-Q	MedME	code to 3 Sqn RAAF
NW	33	Hurricane I	9.40-*c* 5.41	V7419/NW-V	MedME	
NW	3 RAAF	Gladiator II	9.40-1.41	L9044/NW-2	MedME	retained on 33 Sqn code on tx
NW	286	Defiant TT	11.41-7.44	AA628/NW-V	UK	
NW	286	Hurricane I	11.41-6.43	P2865/NW-X	UK	
NW	286	Oxford I	11.41-5.45	HN138/NW-F	UK	
NX	131	Spitfire I	6.41-9.41	X4175/NX-X	UK	
NX	131	Spitfire IIa	9.41-12.41	P7698/NX-P	UK	
NX	131	Spitfire Vb	12.41-9.43	AD411/NX-B	UK	
NX	131	Spitfire Vc	12.42-9.43	EE746/NX-	UK	
NX	131	Spitfire IX	9.43-3.44	MA848/NX-U	UK	
NX	131	Spitfire VII	3.44-11.44	MD111/NX-Q	UK	
NX	CFE	Master II	2.45-10.46	DL224/NX-D	UK	
NX	CFE	Martinet I	*c* 45	HP487/NX-M	UK	
NY	1665 HCU	Stirling I	7.43-3.44	EF384/NY-G	UK	D Flt
NY	1665 HCU	Stirling III	2.44-12.44	W7529/NY-G	UK	D Flt
NY	1665 HCU	Stirling IV	1.44-11.45	LJ622/NY-X	UK	D Flt
NY	1665 HCU	Hurricane IIc	*c* 44-45	PG609/NY-U	UK	
NY	1665 HCU	Oxford II	6.44	*****/NY-A	UK	
NZ	304	Battle I	8.40-11.40	P6723/NZ-Y	UK	
NZ	304	Wellington Ic	11.40-4.43	Z1112/NZ-M	UK	
NZ	304	Wellington III	6.43-7.43	X3793/NZ-G	UK	
O3	*BCDU*				*UK*	*use not known*
O5	BSDU	Mosquito VI	4.44-7.45	DZ178/O5-	UK	
O6	298	Halifax III	10.44-8.45	NA282/O6-S	UK	
O6	298	Halifax VII	5.45-12.46	NA310/O6-X	FE	
O8	SF Merryfield	Anson I	45-46	AX648/O8-5	UK	
O9	*SFCS*		*45*		*UK*	*use not known*
OA	22	Vildebeeste III	9.39-2.40	K4157/OA-Y	UK	
OA	22	Beaufort I, II	11.39-6.44	L9790/OA-G	UK, FE	
OA	342	Boston IIIa	4.43-4.45	BZ301/OA-S	UK	
OA	342	Boston IV	8.44-4.45	BZ538/OA-B	UK	
OA	342	Mitchell II	3.45-12.45	FW181/OA-W	UK	
OA	342	Mitchell III	5.45-12.45	KJ729/OA-S	UK	
OA	1322 Flt	Anson	*c* .44	*****/OA-U7P	UK	
OB	45	Blenheim I	9.39-3.41	L8612/OB-W	MedME	
OB	45	Blenheim IV	3.41-8.42	Z9888/OB-A	MedME	
OB	45	Vengeance Ia	12.42-5.44	AN711/OB-Q	FE	
OB	45	Mosquito VI	2.44-5.46	TE640/OB-F	FE	
OB	53 OTU	Spitfire Ia	3.41-5.43	*****/OB-P	UK	
OB	53 OTU	Master I	2.42-43	T8766/OB-X	UK	
OB	53 OTU	Spitfire IIa	42-43	*****/OB-X	UK	
OC	*SF Sandtoft*		*45*		*UK*	*use not known*
OD	6 (C)OTU	Hudson I	7.41-10.42	N7338/OD-N	UK	
OD	6 (C)OTU	Hudson III	7.41-10.42	V9029/OD-J	UK	
OD	56 OTU	Typhoon Ib	12.44-2.46	JP790/OD-F	UK	Brunton satt
OD	56 OTU	Tempest V	12.44-2.46	NV735/OD-6	UK	Brunton satt
OE	36	Vildebeeste III	9.39-3.42	K4161/OE-G	UK	
OE	268	Tomahawk IIb	5.41-8.42	AH756/OE-V	UK	a/c to 168 Sqn
OE	168	Tomahawk IIb	7.42-11.42	AK118/OE-A	UK	a/c from 268 Sqn

Code	Unit	Type	Dates	Example	Theatre	Remarks
OE	661	Auster III, IV	8.44-10.45		UK, Eur	
OF	97	Whitley II	9.39-4.40	K7229/OF-A	UK	
OF	97	Manchester I	2.41-2.42	L7453/OF-X	UK	
OF	97	Lancaster I	1.42-7.46	R5605/G/OF-X	UK	
OF	97	Lancaster III	1.42-7.46	JA846/OF-N	UK	
OG	172	Wellington XIV	8.43-6.45	HF130/OG-W	UK	
OG	1665 HCU	Stirling I	7.43-7.44	BK652/OG-M	UK	C Flt
OG	1665 HCU	Stirling III	1.44-12.44	LJ456/OG-R	UK	C Flt
OG	1665 HCU	Stirling IV	4.44-11.45	EF435/OG-M	UK	C Flt
OG	1665 HCU	Halifax III	9.44-11.45	LW208/OG-P	UK	C Flt
OG	1665 HCU	Halifax V	10.44-12.45	LL340/OG-C	UK	C Flt
OG	1665 HCU	Halifax VIII	2.45-11.45	PP368/OG-F	UK	C Flt
OG	1665 HCU	Anson XII	c 6.45-11.45	PH643/OG-W	UK	C Flt
OG	1665 HCU	Halifax VII	7.46-12.46	NA313/OG-T	UK	C Flt
OH	120	Liberator I	6.41-2.43	AM913/OH-X	UK MedME	
OH	120	Liberator II	12.41-12.42	AL542/OH-O	UK	
OH	120	Liberator VIII	12.44-6.45	KH177/OH-D	UK	
OI	2	Spitfire XIV	11.44-1.51	TZ164/OI-A	Eur	
OJ	149	Wellington I	9.39-12.41	X9817/OJ-N	UK	
OJ	149	Wellington II	3.41-12.41	W5399/OJ-Q	UK	
OJ	149	Stirling I	11.41-6.43	R9142/OJ-B	UK	
OJ	149	Stirling III	2.43-9.44	EF192/OJ-S	UK	
OJ	149	Lancaster III	8.44-11.49	PA166/OJ-G	UK	
OK	450	Kittyhawk I	12.41-9.42	AK717/OK-V	MedME	
OK	450	Kittyhawk III	9.42-11.43	FR781/OK-K	MedME	
OK	450	Kittyhawk IV	11.43-8.45	FX450/OK-N	MedME	
OK	450	Mustang III	11.44-8.45	FB244/OK-F	MedME	
OK	3 SGR	Anson I	8.45-3.46	EG226/OK-C	UK	
OL	83	Hampden I	9.39-1.42	P2125/OL-L	UK	
OL	83	Manchester I	6.41-5.42	L7465/OL-H	UK	
OL	83	Lancaster I	5.42-7.46	R5630/OL-T	UK	
OL	83	Lancaster III	5.42-7.46	JA967/OL-S	UK	
OL	RNFS	Hurricane I	c 8.41-12.41	Z4932/OL-B	MedME	803/806 NASs
OM	107	Blenheim IV	9.39-1.42	R3816/OM-J	UK	
OM	107	Boston III	4.42-4.43	Z2179/OM-V	UK	
OM	107	Boston IIIa	1.42-2.44	BZ371/OM-S	UK	
OM	107	Mosquito VI	2.44-9.48	R3816/OM-J	UK, Eur	
ON	63	Battle II	9.39-4.40	L4958/ON-R	UK	
ON	124	Spitfire I, II	5.41-11.41		UK	
ON	124	Spitfire Vb	11.41-7.42	BL330/ON-T	UK	
ON	124	Spitfire VI	7.42-3.43	BR579/ON-H	UK	
ON	124	Spitfire VII	3.43-7.44	MB808/ON-C	UK	
ON	124	Tiger Moth II	43-44	EM879/ON	UK	
ON	124	Spitfire IX	7.44-7.45	PL249/ON-Q	UK	
ON	124	Meteor F.3	7.45-4.46	EE389/ON-Y	UK	to 56 Sqn
OO	13	Lysander II	9.39-5.41	L4767/OO-Z	UK	
OO	13	Gladiator I	8.40	*****/OO-S	UK	
OO	13	Lysander III	5.41-9.41	T1429/OO-C	UK	
OO	13	Blenheim IV	7.41-9.42	V5467/OO-B	UK	
OO	1663 HCU	Halifax II	3.43-11.44	R9374/OO-R	UK	D Flt
OO	1663 HCU	Halifax V	2.44-10.45	EB154/OO-R	UK	D Flt
OO	1663 HCU	Halifax III	10.44-5.45	LK793/OO-K	UK	D Flt
OP	11 OTU	Wellington I	4.40-9.45	L4227/OP-R	UK	C Flt
OP	11 OTU	Wellington X	c 43-9.45	LP978/OP-K	UK	C Flt
OQ	5	Hart (India)	6.40-2.41	K2084/OQ-O	FE	
OQ	5	Mohawk IV	12.41-6.43	BJ441/OQ-J	FE	

Code	Unit	Type	Dates	Example	Theatre	Remarks
OQ	5	Thunderbolt I	9.44-2.46	FL809/OQ-Z	FE	
OQ	172	Wellington XIV	7.43-44	NB837/OQ-V	UK	
OQ	52 OTU	Spitfire Vb	9.41-9.43	BM376/OQ-S	UK	D Flt; to FLS
OQ	FLS	Spitfire IX	8.43-12.44	BS347/OQ-Q	UK	ex 52 OTU
OR	BBU	Lancaster III	5.44-*c* 45	PB619/OR-*	UK	
OS	3 RAAF	Lysander II	*c* 10.40-2.41	P****/OS-I	MedME	
OS	3 RAAF	Hurricane I	2.41-6.41	P3967/OS-B	MedME	
OS	279	Hudson III	11.41-11.44	V9158/OS-T	UK	
OS	*SF Sturgate*		*45*		*UK*	*use not known*
OS	528	Blenheim IV	6.43-9.44	Z6079/OS-U	UK	
OT	540	Mosquito XXXIV	12.44-10.46	PF650/OT-X	UK	to 58 Sqn
OU	485	Spitfire I	3.41-6.41	X4678/OU-C	UK	
OU	485	Spitfire Vb	8.41-7.43	AB918/OU-Y	UK	
OU	485	Spitfire IXb	7.43-8.45	MK172/OU-C	UK	
OU	485	Spitfire XVI	5.45-8.45	TB631/OU-V	UK	
OV	197	Typhoon Ia	11.42-1.43	R7681/OV-Z	UK, Eur	
OV	197	Typhoon Ib	12.42-8.45	JR338/OV-S	UK, Eur	
OW	426	Wellington III	10.42-6.43	X5199/OW-E	UK	
OW	426	Wellington X	3.43-8.43	HE904/OW-C	UK	
OW	426	Lancaster II	6.43-5.44	DS759/OW-K	UK	
OW	426	Halifax III	4.44-1.45	MZ750/OW-S	UK	
OW	426	Halifax VII	6.44-5.45	LW207/OW-W	UK	
OW	426	Liberator VI	7.45-12.45	KL670/OW-G	UK	
OX	22 OTU	Wellington III	12.42-7.45	X3658/OX-P	UK	
OX	22 OTU	Wellington X	12.42-7.45	HF745/OX-U	UK	
OY	48	Anson I	9.39-12.41	K8771/OY-Q	UK	
OY	48	Beaufort I	*c* 5.40-10.40	L9860/OY-F	UK	
OY	48	Hudson IIIa	7.41-10.42	FH378/OY-M	UK	
OY	48	Hudson III	10.41-6.42	V9015/OY-Y	UK	
OY	48	Hudson V	1.42-7.43	AM546/OY-G	UK	
OY	48	Hudson VI	11.42-3.43	FK417/OY-T	UK	
OY	13 OTU	Mosquito VI	3.45-5.47	HJ741/OY-G	UK	
OZ	179	Wellington XIV	44-11.44	HF154/OZ-X	UK	
OZ	179	Warwick V	11.44-5.46	PN828/OZ-V	UK	
OZ	179	Lancaster III	2.46-9.46	RE115/OZ-T	UK	
P2	*SF Marston Moor*		*45*		*UK*	*use not known*
P3	692	Mosquito IV	1.44-6.44	DZ650/P3-L	UK	
P3	692	Mosquito XVI	3.44-9.45	MM183/P3-A	UK	
P4	153	Lancaster III	10.44-9.45	NN803/P4-O	UK	
P5	297	Albemarle I	7.43-10.44	P1471/P5-N	UK	
P5	297	Albemarle V	2.44-12.44	V1823/P5-S	UK	
P5	297	Halifax V	10.44-1.45	LL277/P5-B	UK	
P5	297	Halifax III	2.45-3.46	NA117/P5-J	UK	
P6	489	Beaufighter X	11.43-8.45	NV175/P6-D1	UK	
P6	*SF Banff*		*45*		*UK*	*use not known*
P7	87 GCF	Oxford	45	HM868/P7-02	UK	
P9	58 OTU	Spitfire Vb	3.45-7.45	BL363/P9-23	UK	
P9	58 OTU	Spitfire IX	3.45-7.45	ML211/P9-57	UK	
PA	655	Auster IV	6.44-8.45	MT412/PA-2	MedME	HQ Flt
PA	55 OTU	Hurricane I	11.40-1.44	V7165/PA-27	UK	
PA	55 OTU	Typhoon Ib	12.44-6.45	JR185/PA-H	UK	
PA	55 OTU	Master III	12.44-6.45	W8647/PA-M	UK	
PA	3 TEU	Hurricane IIa	3.44-12.44	Z2966/PA-N	UK	2 Sqn
PA	3 TEU	Hurricane IIb	3.44-12.44	Z3596/PA-D	UK	2 Sqn
PA	3 TEU	Hurricane IV	3.44-12.44	LE834/PA-N	UK	2 Sqn
PA	3 TEU	Typhoon Ib	3.44-12.44	MN400/PA-A	UK	2 Sqn

Code	Unit	Type	Dates	Example	Theatre	Remarks
PA	3 TEU	Rapide	3.44-12.44	W6425/PA-Z	UK	
PB	655	Auster IV	6.44-8.45	TJ396/PB-M	MedME	A Flt
PB	26 OTU	Wellington III	2.43-10.44	X3403/PB-V	UK	
PB	26 OTU	Wellington X	6.43-3.46	LP282/PB-D	UK	
PB	26 OTU	Tomahawk IIa	c 43-3.46	AH885/PB-F	UK	
PB	1684 BDTF	Tomahawk IIa	6.43-3.44	AH899/PB-F	UK	
PC	655	Auster IV	6.44-8.45		MedME	B Flt
PD	303	Mustang IV	4.45-12.46	KM112/PD-D	UK	
PD	655	Auster IV	6.44-8.45		MedME	C Flt
PE	1662 HCU	Halifax II	2.44-4.45	R9498/PE-F2	UK	
PE	1662 HCU	Lancaster I	1.43-11.43	W4154/PE-A	UK	
PF	51 OTU	Blenheim If	7.41-c 43	*****/PF-T	UK	
PF	51 OTU	Blenheim V	5.42-1.43	BA138/PF-B	UK	
PF	43 OTU	Auster IV	11.45-5.47	MT162/PF-J	UK	
PG	619	Lancaster III	4.43-7.45	LM737/PG-A	UK	
PH	12	Battle I	9.39-11.40	L5227/PH-J	UK	
PH	12	Wellington II	10.40-11.42	Z8328/PH-R	UK	
PH	12	Wellington III	8.42-11.42	BJ653/PH-H	UK	
PH	12	Lancaster I	11.42-8.46	W4366/PH-R	UK	
PH	12	Lancaster III	11.42-8.46	PB243/PH-D	UK	
PH	CFE	Tempest V	c 45	NV961/PH-B	UK	
PI	*SF Silverstone*		*45*		*UK*	*use not known*
PJ	130	Spitfire IIa	6.41-10.41	P7374/PJ-N	UK	
PJ	130	Spitfire Va	10.41-2.42	W3314/PJ-F	UK	
PJ	130	Spitfire Vb	10.41-2.44	BL356/PJ-Q	UK	
PJ	130	Spitfire Vc	7.42-2.44	AR614/PJ-E	UK	
PK	315	Hurricane I	2.41-7.41	V6969/PK-U	UK	
PK	315	Spitfire IIa, b	7.41-9.41	P8528/PK-J	UK	
PK	315	Spitfire Vc	8.41-3.44	EP285/PK-B	UK	
PK	315	Spitfire IX	11.42-6.43	EN172/PK-K	UK	
PK	315	Mustang III	3.44-12.46	SR417/PK-W	UK	
PL	144	Hampden I	9.39-1.43	P2080/PL-M	UK	
PL	144	Beaufighter VI	1.43-5.43	JL654/PL-H	UK	
PL	144	Beaufighter X	5.43-5.45	LZ220/PL-M	UK	
PM	103	Battle I	9.39-10.40	L5010/PM-C	UK	
PM	103	Wellington Ic	10.40-8.42	R1234/PM-A	UK	
PM	103	Halifax II	7.42-11.42	W1212/PM-P	UK	
PM	103	Lancaster I, III	11.42-11.45	LM132/PM-I	UK	
PN	*252*	*Blenheim I, IV*	*c 12.40-4.41*		*UK*	*use not known*
PN	252	Beaufighter I	12.40-5.41	T4665/PN-D	UK, MedME	
PN	30	Hurricane I	c 12.41-2.42	Z4839/PN-W	MedME	
PN	1552 RATF	Oxford	9.45-10.46	DF276/PN-A	UK	
PO	46	Hurricane I	9.39-6.41	V7360/PO-B	UK	
PO	467	Lancaster I	11.42-9.45	R5860/PO-B	UK	
PO	467	Lancaster III	11.42-9.45	ED606/PO-X	UK	
PP	311	Liberator V	5.43-3.45	BZ789/PP-B	UK	
PP	311	Liberator VI	3.45-2.46	EV943/PP-F	UK, Eur	
PP	25 OTU	Wellington Ic	5.41-1.43	T2715/PP-E	UK	
PP	25 OTU	Courier	7.42-11.42	W7942/PP-R	UK	
PQ	58 OTU	Spitfire II	1.41-10.43	P****/PQ-Y	UK	
PQ	2 TEU	Spitfire II	10.43-6.44	P****/PQ-9	UK	
PQ	206	Liberator VI	4.44-4.45	BZ984/PQ-S	UK	
PQ	206	Liberator VIII	4.45-4.46	KK250/PQ-T	UK	
PR	609	Spitfire I	9.39-5.41	R6915/PR-U	UK	
PR	609 BAC	Drone	10.40-11.40	PR-?	UK	Sqn hack
PR	609	Spitfire IIa	2.41-5.41	P8235/PR-G	UK	

Code	Unit	Type	Dates	Example	Theatre	Remarks
PR	609	Spitfire Vb	5.41-5.42	W3238/PR-B	UK	
PR	609	Typhoon Ib	4.42-9.45	R7708/PR-V	UK	
PS	264	Defiant I	12.39-9.41	L7029/PS-Z	UK	
PS	264	Defiant II	9.41-7.42	AA410/PS-T	UK	
PS	264	Mosquito II	5.42-3.44	DD636/PS-D	UK	
PS	264	Mosquito XIII	1.44-8.45	MM455/PS-Q	UK	
PT	420	Hampden I	12.41-8.42	AE258/PT-W	UK	
PT	420	Manchester I	5.42-7.42	L7386/PT-X	UK	conversion flight
PT	420	Wellington III	8.42-4.43	DF637/PT-F	UK	
PT	420	Wellington X	2.43-10.43	HE673/PT-D	UK	
PT	420	Halifax III	12.43-5.45	NP251/PT-Y	UK	
PT	420	Lancaster X	4.45-9.45	KB923/PT-N	UK	
PT	27	Blenheim If	11.40-1.42	L6667/PT-D	FE	
PT	1 SFTS (I)	Wapiti IIa	11.40-41	J9754/PT-F	FE	Poss 27 Sqn
PT	1 SFTS (I)	Hart (India)	11.40-41	K2113/PT-B	FE	Poss 27 Sqn
PU	187	Dakota IV	3.45-11.46	KN665/PU-H	UK	to 53 Sqn
PV	275	Lysander IIIa	10.41-8.43	V9749/PV-N	UK	
PV	275	Walrus I	12.41-2.45	L2207/PV-Z	UK	
PV	275	Walrus II	12.41-2.45	HD925/PV-S	UK	
PV	275	Defiant I	5.42-6.43	T3920/PV-*	UK	
PV	275	Spitfire Vb	1.43-2.45	*****/PV-G	UK	
PV	275	Anson I	3.43-8.44	EG525/PV-N	UK	
PW	57 OTU	Spitfire I	12.40-12.43	X4486/PW-L	UK	
PW	57 OTU	Spitfire II	12.40-4.44	*****/PW-Q	UK	
PW	57 OTU	Spitfire Vb	41-6.45	AR424/PW-R	UK	
PX	? 214	Stirling III	c 11.43-1.44		UK	C Flt
PX	295	Whitley V	8.42-11.43	EB298/PX-K	UK	
PX	295	Halifax V	2.43-11.43	DK130/PX-E	UK	
PY	84	Mosquito VI	2.45-11.46	TA497/PY-X	FE	
PY	1527 RATF	Oxford I	45-46	DF396/PY	UK	
PZ	53	Blenheim IV	9.39-7.41	Z5765/PZ-A	UK	
PZ	53	Hudson V	7.41-7.42	AM727/PZ-D	UK	
PZ	53	Hudson III	7.42-2.43	V9232/PZ-A	UK	
PZ	456	Defiant I	6.41-11.41	N3430/PZ-V	UK	
Q1	1 AACU	Henley III	41-42	L3421/Q1-D	UK	
Q6	1384 HTCU	Oxford I	11.45-6.46	NM803/Q6-M	UK	
Q7	*29 MU*		*45*		*UK*	*use not known*
Q8	*BAFO CW*		*45*		*Eur*	*use not known*
QA	297	Whitley V	2.42-2.44	Z9189/QA-P	UK	
QA	654	Auster IV	6.44-6.47		MedME	HQ Flt
QA	*10 OTU*	*Whitley V*	*8.42-7.43*		*UK*	*reported*
QB	424	Wellington III	10.42-4.43	X3426/QB-D	UK	
QB	424	Wellington X	2.43-10.43	HE222/QB-E	UK	
QB	424	Halifax III	12.43-2.45	MZ802/QB-G	UK	
QB	424	Lancaster I, III	1.45-10.45	NG456/QB-D	UK	
QB	654	Auster IV	6.44-6.47		MedME	A Flt
QC	168	Typhoon Ib	9.44-2.45	JR244/QC-S	Eur	
QC	654	Auster IV	6.44-6.47		MedME	B Flt
QD	304	Wellington XIII	7.43-9.43	HZ645/QD-F	UK	
QD	304	Wellington XIV	9.43-7.45	NC888/QD-D	UK	
QD	304	Warwick III	7.45-5.46	HG332/QD-U	UK	
QD	304	Halifax VIII	5.46-12.46	PP270/QD-G	UK	
QD	654	Auster V	12.44-6.47	M****/QD-10	MedME	C Flt
QE	CFE	Mosquito VI	c 45	HR210/QE-T	UK	
QF	PFNTU	Stirling III	4.43-9.43	EF404/QF-M	UK	
QF	PFNTU	Lancaster III	4.43-6.45	ED317/QF-T	UK	

Code	Unit	Type	Dates	Example	Theatre	Remarks
QF	PFNTU	Halifax II	4.43-44	BB367/QF-	UK	
QF	PFNTU	Mosquito XX	c 9.44-6.45	KB351/QF-A2	UK	
QF	PFNTU	Oxford I	c 9.44-6.45	P6798/QF-C3	UK	
QF	1323 Flt	Lancaster III	11.44-9.45	NE142/QF-H	UK	
QG	53 OTU	Spitfire Vb	6.41-5.45	AA739/QG-K	UK	D Flt
QH	302	Spitfire XVI	2.45-12.46	TB278/QH-P	Eur	
QI	*SF Swanton Morley*		*45*		*UK*	*use not known*
QJ	616	Gauntlet II	9.39	K7846/QJ-K	UK	
QJ	616	Spitfire I	10.39-2.41	X4328/QJ-P	UK	
QJ	616	Spitfire IIa	2.41-10.41	P7753/QJ-X	UK	
QJ	92	Spitfire Vb	7.41-2.42	R6919/QJ-L	UK	
QJ	92	Spitfire Vc	8.42-9.43		MedME	
QJ	92	Spitfire IX	3.43-6.43		MedME	
QJ	92	Spitfire VIII	7.43-12.46	JF413/QJ-V	MedME	
QJ	*BAFO CW*		*45*		*Eur*	*use not known*
QK	3 APS	Spitfire IX	8.45-3.46	MJ734/QK-F	UK	
QK	3 APS	Tempest V	8.45-3.46	SN227/QK-	UK	
QL	413	Catalina I	7.41-3.42	W8421/QL-D	UK, FE	
QL	76 Wing	Blenheim IV	2.41-1.42	T2219/QL-N	UK	
QM	254	Beaufighter X	10.43-10.46	RD467/QM-J	UK	
QM	254	Mosquito XVIII	4.45-5.45	PZ254/QM-D	UK	
QM	532	Havoc I	9.42-1.43	AL774/QM-E	UK	
QN	28 OTU	Wellington X	5.42-10.44	LP613/QN-O	UK	
QN	28 OTU	Spitfire IX	11.42-10.44	TB275/QN-F	UK	
QN	28 OTU	Martinet	4.43-10.44	*****/QN-M	UK	
QO	3	Hurricane I	9.39-4.41	L1937/QO-T	UK	
QO	3	Hurricane IIb	4.41-11.41	Z2891/QO-R	UK	
QO	3	Hurricane IIc	4.41-5.43	BD867/QO-Y	UK	
QO	3	Typhoon Ib	2.43-4.44	DN623/QO-H	UK	
QO	3	Tempest V	2.44-5.44	JN733/QO-A	UK	
QO	432	Wellington X	5.43-10.43	HE348/QO-P	UK	
QO	432	Lancaster II	10.43-2.44	DS834/QO-O	UK	
QO	432	Halifax III	2.44-7.44	LW596/QO-D	UK	
QO	432	Halifax VII	6.44-5.45	NP689/QO-M	UK	
QP	*SF Kirmington*				*UK*	*use not known*
QQ	1651 HCU	Stirling I	1.42-2.44	R9243/QQ-K	UK	
QQ	1651 HCU	Stirling III	7.43-11.44	LK488/QQ-E	UK	
QR	61	Hampden I	9.39-10.41	P4379/QR-P	UK	
QR	61	Manchester I	7.41-6.42	L7389/QR-J	UK	
QR	61	Lancaster I, III	6.42-5.46	LM359/QR-B	UK	
QR	61	Lancaster II	10.42-3.43	DS604/QR-W	UK	
QS	620	Stirling III	8.43-2.44	EF203/QS-G	UK	
QS	620	Stirling IV	2.44-7.45	LJ970/QS-S	UK	
QS	620	Halifax VII	5.45-9.46	PP365/QS-H	UK	
QT	142	Battle I	9.39-1.41	K9204/QT-G	UK	
QT	142	Wellington II	11.40-10.41	W5387/QT-V	UK	
QT	142	Wellington IV	10.41-10.42	Z1210/QT-M	UK	
QT	142	Wellington III	9.42-10.43	BK298/QT-O	MedME	
QT	142	Wellington X	8.43-10.44	HE815/QT-Z	MedME	
QT	57	Lancaster I, III	c 44		UK	C Flt
QV	19	Spitfire I	9.39-9.40	X4474/QV-I	UK	
QV	19	Spitfire IIa	9.40-10.41	P7423/QV-Y	UK	
QV	19	Spitfire V	10.41-8.43	AD185/QV-E	UK	
QV	19	Spitfire IX	8.43-2.44	MH616/QV-P	UK	
QV	19	Mustang III	2.44-4.45	FB201/QV-D	UK	
QV	19	Mustang IV	4.45-9.45	KH847/QV-U	UK	

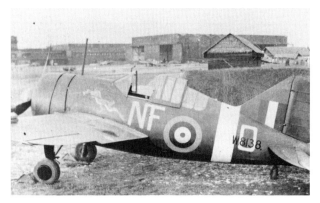

The squadron service of the portly Buffalo was restricted to the Far East, where they fought in vain against Japanese attacks on Malaya and Singapore. The shortest-lived unit was No. 488 Sqn RNZAF whose W8138/NF-O is seen at Kallang shortly before the invasion, wearing a spectacular green dragon personal marking. (D. P. Woodhall)

The antiquated Swordfish saw limited RAF service during the Second World War. The only unit fully equipped was No. 119 Sqn, which used them for nocturnal attacks on German mini-submarines in 1945. This fully armed all black Mk III is NF410/NH-F in the spring of 1945. (Wg Cdr N. Wilkinson)

The first squadron manned by exiled Dutch personnel was No. 320. Its aircraft, like this Hudson III, V8983/NO-F in early 1942, wore standard RAF markings and colours, but with the addition of the Dutch inverted orange triangle emblem. (Cdre H. J. E. van der Kop)

Among the biplanes with which the RAF entered the Second World War were the stately Singapore IIIs of No. 203 Sqn. On the outbreak of war the flying boats were camouflaged and moved to Aden for Red Sea patrols, where K6912/NT-D is seen in about December 1939. (via J. J. Halley)

The height and general size of the Stirling is evident in this view of Mk III ...../NY-C of No. 1665 HCU during the mid-war years. Operational and conversion training units conformed to the standard marking practices and their aircraft were indistinguishable from operational aircraft. (D. Morris)

Beaufort I torpedo bombers of No. 22 Sqn prepare for a sortie from Thorney Island in early 1940. The nearest aircraft are L4461/OA-U and L4459/OA-Z; the squadron retained this code until moving to Ceylon. (RAF Thorney Island Records)

Few photographs of Vengeance dive bombers wearing unit codes have so far come to light; one of the few that has shows Mk I OB-V in the EZ serial range of No. 45 Sqn at Kumbhirgram, India, in October 1943. It also wears a personal 'Saint' marking under the cockpit. (via C. G. Jefford)

Three Stirling IIIs of No. 149 Sqn practise low-level formation flying over the Suffolk countryside on 14 July 1944, by which time the type was nearing the end of its career in the bomber role. (D. Mitchell via Jonathon Falconer)

Many India-based squadrons retained their biplanes well into the war. One was No. 5 Sqn at Lahore where in 1940 Hart (India) K2084/OQD displays full wartime code and markings and its un-camouflaged scheme. (via R. C. B. Ashworth)

Among a number of squadrons to use the Tomahawk in the UK for army co-operation duties was No. 168 whose AH775/OE-N posed for the camera in the late summer of 1942 after it had acquired type C1 roundels. Some of these aircraft, like those in No. 168 Sqn, have rarely been illustrated. (Sir Peter Bristow)

No. 107 Sqn was one of the RAF's first Boston light bomber Squadrons and flew them in the day bombing role. Because of the position of the roundel, Bostons carried the aircraft letter on the nose, though the code was aft of the wing as displayed by AL280 in early 1942. (Gp Capt J. Pelly-Fry)

One Lancaster variant which saw relatively brief service was the Hercules-engined Mk II. One of the operational units equipped with them was No. 426 Sqn RCAF, to which DS713/OW-J belonged when photographed in August 1943. (E. C. G. Jones)

The Warwick GR.V saw brief service in the maritime reconnaissance role toward the end of the war with No. 179 Sqn. Most of its aircraft wore the extant camouflage scheme, but one exception was LM796/OZ-H which was silver-doped overall. The code was retained by No. 210 Sqn when No. 179 was renumbered. (Author's Collection)

One of the highest-numbered squadrons to be formed was No. 692 in the light bombing role at Graveley late in the war. Its Mosquito B.IVs were identified by the combination P3 visible in red on the black fuselage of DZ637/P3-C in 1944. (via Chaz Bowyer)

Torpedo-armed Beaufighter TF.X coded P6-S of No. 489 Sqn RNZAF shows the unusual position of the codes adopted by some Coastal Command squadrons. It is seen on 30 July 1944 over the North Sea escorted by Mustang III FB123/PK-W of No. 315 Sqn. (Sqn Ldr M. Cwynar)

The Wickenby-based Lancasters of No. 12 Sqn had a unique way of displaying the unit codes, as is readily apparent in this view of B.III LM321/PH-H taken in 1943. In contravention of regulations, it also wears a prominent personal nose marking. (No. 12 Sqn Records)

The Battles of No. 103 Sqn formed part of the Advanced Air Striking Force in France in early 1940. In this instance, the unusual position of the roundel is of note, though the code letters are in the correct position! K9264/PM-L seen here was lost on 10 May. (No. 103 Sqn Records)

Hurricane I V7538/PK-O of the Polish-manned No. 315 Sqn is readied for its next sortie from Speke in 1941. The unit code is somewhat larger than normal and the usual Polish emblem is visible in front of the cockpit. (via J. D. R. Rawlings)

No. 264 Sqn was the first to be equipped with Defiants, which were identified by the code PS. By the time this photograph was taken in 1941 it had switched to night-fighter duties, with the dull colour scheme in marked contrast to the prominent code; N1773/PS-H is shown. (via N. L. R. Franks)

No. 1 SFTS(I) evolved from elements of No. 27 Sqn and there is uncertainty over the ownership of this Wapiti IIa, J-9754/PT-F, as the PT combination had been positively identified with No. 27 Sqn. The aircraft of No. 1 SFTS(I) also used the combination NB. (Author's Collection)

Whitley Vs provided the initial equipment for several squadrons formed to deliver and support Airborne Forces. Among them was No. 297 whose Whitley V BD496/QA-E loads another stick of paratroops at Thruxton for a training drop in 1943. (HQ 38 Group Records)

The Warwick C.III transport saw only limited service, but one of the squadrons so equipped was the Polish No. 304 which was based at Chedburgh in Suffolk where HG***/QD-P is at dispersal shortly before the unit's disbandment. (via J. D. R. Rawlings)

In the Mediterranean theatre several fighter squadrons used coloured code letters to enhance their aircraft. One was the RAF's top-scoring squadron, No. 92, which used white-outlined red unit codes, though the individual letter remained white as may be seen in this lovely view of Spitfire VIII MT648/QJ-Q in 1944. (Peter Arnold Collection)

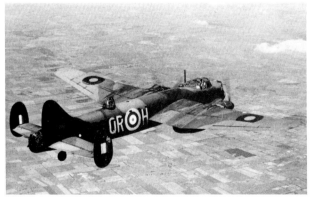

Unfortunately the serial is obscured in this superb view of Manchester I QR-H of No. 61 Sqn, which is seen soon after the squadron received them in mid-1941. The basic bomber colour scheme is shown to advantage and remained little changed throughout the war. (John Stretton)

No. 19 Sqn was one of the units to use the long-range Spitfire II; the ungainly tank may be seen under the port wing of P8077/QV-I at Fowlmere during the summer of 1941. This squadron continued to use this code well into the post-war years. (No. 19 Sqn via P. H. T. Green)

Code	Unit	Type	Dates	Example	Theatre	Remarks
QW	1516 RATF	Oxford I	45-4.46		UK	
QX	224	Hudson I	9.39-7.41	N7315/QX-Y	UK	
QX	224	Hudson V	5.41-7.42	AM563/QX-X	UK	
QX	224	Liberator V	3.43-10.46	FL910/QX-H	UK	
QX	CCCF	Anson I	4.45-5.46	EG223/QX-D	UK	
QX	CCCF	Dominie	4.45-5.46	NR687/QX-F	UK	
QX	CCCF	Oxford I	4.45-5.46	PH420/QX-A	UK	
QY	254	Blenheim IVf	3.40-7.42	T2128/QY-J	UK	
QY	1666 HCU	Halifax II	6.43-12.44	DT667/QY-G	UK	
QY	1666 HCU	Halifax V	*c* 44-12.44	LL519/QY-M	UK	
QY	1666 HCU	Lancaster III	11.44-8.45	PD404/QY-D	UK	
QY	1666 HCU	Spitfire Vb	*c* 3.45	AB403/QY-	UK	
QY	1666 HCU	Hurricane IIc	*c* 3.45	LF400/QY-	UK	
QZ	*4 OTU*		*45*		*UK*	*use not known*
R1	1 AACU	Henley III	41-42	L3313/R1-A	UK	
R2	PAU	Queen Bee	12.40-3.46	LF801/R2-M	UK	
R2	PAU	Proctor IV	*c* 44-3.46	RM170/R2-V	UK	
R4	18 APC	Master II	*c* 2.45-7.45	DL417/R4-E	UK	
R4	18 APC	Martinet I	*c* 2.45-7.45	JN293/R4-11	UK	to 1 APS
R4	1 APS	Master II	7.45-5.46	DL417/R4-E	UK	ex 18 APC
R4	1 APS	Martinet I	7.45-5.46	JN293/R4-11	UK	
R7	*AEU*		*45*		*UK*	*use not known*
R8	*274 MU*		*45*		*UK*	*use not known*
R9	639	Henley III	12.43-4.45	L3327/R9-R	UK	
R9	639	Hurricane IV	*c* 45	KZ655/R9-E	UK	
RA	410	Defiant I	6.41-6.42	V1123/RA-R	UK	
RA	410	Mosquito II	11.42-12.43	DZ757/RA-Q	UK	
RA	410	Mosquito XIII	12.43-8.44	HK462/RA-E	UK	
RA	410	Mosquito XXX	4.44-6.45	MM755/RA-W	UK	
RB	10 RAAF	Sunderland I	9.39-7.42	P9600/RB-E	UK	
RB	10 RAAF	Sunderland II	6.41-11.42	W3993/RB-W	UK	
RB	10 RAAF	Sunderland III	1.42-6.45	DD952/RB-J	UK	
RB	10 RAAF	Sunderland V	7.44-6.45	RN300/RB-Q	UK	
RC	5 LFS	Lancaster III	11.43-4.45	ED593/RC-C	UK	
RD	67	Buffalo I	3.41-2.42	W8220/RD-U	FE	
RD	67	Spitfire VIII	2.44-8.45	MB966/RD-R	FE	
RE	229	Blenheim If	10.39-3.40	K7181/RE-P	UK	
RE	229	Hurricane I	3.40-5.41	P3039/RE-D	UK	
RE	CFE	Tempest V	2.45-47	SN262/RE-M	UK	
RF	303	Hurricane I	8.40-11.41	P3120/RF-D	UK	
RF	303	Spitfire I	1.41-10.41	X4857/RF-F	UK	
RF	303	Spitfire IIa	2.41-7.41	P8073/RF-Z	UK	
RF	303	Spitfire Vb	10.41-6.44	AD247/RF-P	UK	
RF	303	Spitfire IXc	6.43-4.45	MH777/RF-N	UK	
RF	303	Mustang IV	4.45-12.46	KH669/RF-P	UK	
RG	208	Lysander II	9.39-5.42	L4717/RG-F	MedME	
RG	208	Tomahawk IIb	3.42-9.42	A****/RG-*	MedME	
RG	208	Hurricane I, II	11.40-12.43	Z4967/RG-Y	MedME	
RG	208	Spitfire Vc	12.43-7.44	EE861/RG-G	MedME	
RG	208	Spitfire VIII	7.44-10.44	JF572/RG-Y	MedME	
RG	208	Spitfire IX	3.44-6.47	PV117/RG-E	MedME	
RG	510	Mohawk III	late 43-3.44	AR633/RG-E	UK	
RG	1472 AACF	Battle I	6.42-1.43		UK	
RG	1472 AACF	Tomahawk I, II	6.42-43		UK	
RG	TCMF	Spitfire V	*c* 45	X4587/RG-B	UK	no official reference to unit

Code	Unit	Type	Dates	Example	Theatre	Remarks
RH	88	Battle II	9.39-9.41	K9244/RH-L	UK	
RH	88	Blenheim IV	2.41-12.41	Z7427/RH-K	UK	
RH	88	Boston III	9.41-5.43	AL775/RH-D	UK	
RH	88	Boston IIIa	5.43-4.45	BZ322/RH-K	UK	
RH	88	Boston IV	6.44-4.45	BZ449/RH-P	UK	
RJ	*SF Thornaby*		*45*		*UK*	*use not known*
RK	10 OTU	Whitley V	4.40-9.44	BD432/RK-T	UK	A, B Flts
RK	10 OTU	Wellington X	5.44-9.46	NC601/RK-L	UK	A, B Flts
RL	279	Warwick I	11.44-9.45	HG212/RL-G	UK	
RL	279	Hurricane IV	4.45-6.45	KZ383/RL-N	UK	
RL	279	Lancaster III	9.45-3.46	SW295/RL-C	UK	
RL	SLAIS	Hurricane IIc	12.42-1.44	KZ371/RL-S	UK	
RL	SLAIS	Hurricane IV	12.42-1.44	KX878/RL-U	UK	
RM	26	Lysander II, III	9.39-5.42	T1429/RM-H	UK	
RM	26	Tomahawk I	2.41-11.42	AH791/RM-E	UK	
RM	26	Tomahawk IIa	2.41-4.42	AH893/RM-Q	UK	
RM	26	Mustang I	1.42-11.42	AG367/RM-Z	UK	
RN	72	Spitfire I	*c* 40-4.41	X4488/RN-C	UK	
RN	72	Spitfire IIa	4.41-7.41	P7895/RN-N	UK	
RN	72	Spitfire Vb	7.41-7.42	AA945/RN-C	UK	
RN	72	Spitfire Vc	7.42-1.44	JK368/RN-J	UK	
RN	72	Spitfire IX	7.42-12.46	MA444/RN-B	UK	
RO	29	Blenheim If	9.39-2.41	K7135/RO-L	UK	
RO	29	Hurricane I	9.40-12.40	L2090/RO-P	UK	
RO	29	Beaufighter I	9.40-6.43	T4646/RO-G	UK	
RO	29	Beaufighter VI	3.43-5.43	EL164/RO-	UK	
RO	29	Mosquito XII	5.43-4.44	HK129/RO-G	UK	
RO	29	Mosquito XIII	10.43-2.45	MM463/RO-J	UK	
RO	29	Mosquito 30	2.45-8.46	MT490/RO-O	UK	
RP	288	Hurricane IV	11.41-12.44	KZ576/RP-P	UK	
RP	288	Oxford I	3.42-5.45	HN694/RP-H	UK	
RP	288	Spitfire Vb	3.44-6.46	BM271/RP-C	UK	
RP	288	Spitfire XVI	3.44-6.46	SL669/RP-K	UK	
RP	288	Vengeance II	5.45-6.46	HB517/RP-O	UK	
RQ	*SF Colerne*		*45*		*UK*	*use not known*
RR	407	Hudson I	6.41-7.41	T9357/RR-F	UK	
RR	407	Hudson III	11.41-5.42	V9095/RR-G	UK	
RR	407	Hudson V	6.41-4.43	AM556/RR-E	UK	
RR	*?*	*Warwick III*	*45*	*HG298/RR-M*	*UK*	*reported*
RR	*SF Filton*		*45*		*UK*	*use not known*
RS	33	Hurricane IIc	2.42-6.42	BP184/RS-X	MedME	
RS	33	Spitfire Vc	1.43-6.43	ER371/RS-J	MedME	
RS	30	Hurricane I	5.41-8.42	Z4230/RS-C	MedME	
RS	30	Hurricane IIb	6.41-8.42	BG827/RS-W	MedME, FE	
RS	30	Hurricane IIc	8.42-7.44	LB718/RS-X	FE	
RS	30	Thunderbolt I	7.44-1.45	HD269/RS-S	FE	
RS	30	Thunderbolt II	9.44-5.46	KL308/RS-C	FE	
RS	157	Mosquito II	1.42-7.44	W4079/RS-F	UK	
RS	157	Mosquito VI	7.43-4.44	TA482/RS-F	UK	
RS	157	Mosquito XIX	5.44-4.45	MM652/RS-S	UK	
RS	157	Mosquito 30	2.45-8.45	NT382/RS-T	UK	
RT	112	Gladiator I	9.39-7.41	K6134/RT-S	MedME	
RT	114	Blenheim IV	9.39-9.42	T2224/RT-X	UK	
RT	114	Boston V	1.45-5.46	BZ650/RT-Z	MedME	
RT	114	Mosquito VI	11.45-9.46	TE659/RT-B	MedME	to 8 Sqn
RU	414	Lysander IIIa	8.41-6.42	V9445/RU-X	UK	

Code	Unit	Type	Dates	Example	Theatre	Remarks
RU	414	Tomahawk IIb	8.41-7.42	AK195/RU-V	UK	
RU	414	Mustang I	6.42-11.42	AG655/RU-X	UK	
RU	*SF Hendon*		*45*		*UK*	*use not known*
RV	1659 HCU	Halifax IIIa	10.42-11.44	MZ505/RV-J	UK	
RV	1659 HCU	Lancaster I, III	11.44-9.45	PB146/RV-K	UK	
RW	36	Wellington XIV	9.43-6.45	HF310/RW-E	MedME, UK	
RX	456	Beaufighter IIf	*c* 8.42-1.43	T3370/RX-Z	UK	
RX	456	Beaufighter VIf	7.42-3.43	X8138/RX-Z	UK	
RX	456	Mosquito II	1.43-2.44	DD739/RX-X	UK	
RX	456	Mosquito XVII	2.44-2.45	HK321/RX-X	UK	
RX	456	Mosquito 30	12.44-6.45	NT241/RX-W	UK	
RY	313	Spitfire I	3.41-8.41	P9513/RY-X	UK	
RY	313	Spitfire Vb	10.41-10.44	EP644/RY-S	UK	
RY	313	Spitfire IX	9.43-2.46	NH422/RY-Y	UK, Eur	
RZ	241	Lysander II	9.40-3.42	V9707/RZ-P	UK	
RZ	241	Tomahawk II	7.41-4.42	AK138/RZ-L	UK	
RZ	241	Mustang I	3.42-11.42	AM177/RZ-V	UK	
RZ	241	Hurricane IIc	11.42-12.43	KW971/RZ-C	MedME	
RZ	241	Spitfire IX	12.43-6.45	MA425/RZ-R	MedME	
S6	41 GCF	Proctor III	44-45	HM396/S6-J	UK	
S6	41 GCF	Proctor IV	5.44-4.46	NP163/S6-E	UK	
S6	41 GCF	Miles M.28	5.44-4.46	PW937/S6-P	UK	
S6	41 GCF	Anson XIX	45-4.46	VM316/S6-A	UK	
S8	328	Spitfire IX	12.43-11.45		MedME	
S9	16 GCF	Proctor III	45-3.46	LZ565/S9-C	UK	
S9	16 GCF	Dominie	45-3.46	NF896/S9-A	UK	
S9	16 GCF	Oxford I	*c* 45	*****/S9-X	UK	
SA	456	Defiant I	6.41-11.41		UK	
SA	456	Beaufighter II	9.41-*c* 8.43	T3028/SA-V	UK	
SA	486	Hurricane IIb	3.42-8.42	Z5309/SA-K	UK	
SA	486	Typhoon Ib	7.42-4.44	JP901/SA-N	UK	
SA	486	Tempest V	1.44-9.45	JN792/SA-H	UK	
SB	464	Ventura II	9.42-9.43	AE939/SB-G	UK	
SB	464	Mosquito VI	8.43-9.45	MM482/SB-A	UK	
SC	*SF Prestwick*		*45*		*UK*	*use not known*
SD	501	Hurricane I	9.39-5.41	L2124/SD-H	UK	
SD	501	Spitfire I	4.41-6.41	X4381/SD-J	UK	
SD	501	Spitfire Vb	9.41-7.44	AB402/SD-K	UK	
SD	501	Spitfire Vc	9.41-7.44	BR166/SD-A	UK	
SD	501	Spitfire IX	6.43-7.44	MB855/SD-S	UK	
SD	501	Tempest V	7.44-4.45	EJ702/SD-Q	UK	
SD	504	Spitfire Vb	11.42-12.42		UK	aircraft switched from 501 Sqn
SE	95	Sunderland I	5.41-late 41	L5802/SE-F	UK, Africa	
SE	431	Wellington X	12.42-7.43	HE184/SE-M	UK	
SE	431	Halifax V	7.43-4.44	LK639/SE-E	UK	
SE	431	Halifax III	3.44-10.44	LK837/SE-H	UK	
SE	431	Lancaster X	10.44-9.45	KB802/SE-V	UK	
SF	137	Whirlwind I	9.41-6.43	P6993/SF-A	UK	
SF	137	Hurricane IV	6.43-1.44	KZ576/SF-	UK	
SF	137	Typhoon Ib	1.44-8.45	MN431/SF-D	UK, Eur	
SG	*Lincolnshire FS SF*		*45*		*UK*	*use not known*
SG	3 (C) OTU	Whitley V	10.41-9.42	P5065/SG-D	UK	
SH	216	Valentia I	9.39-10.41	K2798/SH-U	MedME	
SH	216	Bombay I	10.39-6.43	L5857/SH-C	MedME	
SH	64	Blenheim If	9.39-4.40	L1474/SH-N	UK	

Code	Unit	Type	Dates	Example	Theatre	Remarks
SH	64	Spitfire I	4.40-2.41	N3122/SH-M	UK	
SH	64	Spitfire IIa	2.41-11.41	P7747/SH-K	UK	
SH	64	Spitfire Vb	11.41-7.44	AA907/SH-S	UK	
SH	64	Spitfire IX	7.42-11.44	BR600/SH-V	UK	
SH	64	Mustang III	11.44-5.46	FZ169/SH-C	UK	
SH	64	Mustang IV	8.45-6.46	KM256/SH-W	UK	
SJ	70	Valentia I	9.39-10.40	K4630/SJ-X	MedME	
SJ	70	Wellington Ic	9.40-early 41	R****/SJ-O	MedME	
SJ	21 OTU	Wellington Ic	1.41-*c* 42	R1082/SJ-L	UK	
SJ	21 OTU	Wellington III	2.43-3.45	*****/SJ-C	UK	
SJ	21 OTU	Wellington X	8.43-3.47	LN893/SJ-W	UK	
SK	165	Spitfire Va	4.42-6	R7229/SK-J	UK	
SK	165	Spitfire Vb	5.42-10.43	EP172/SK-W	UK	
SK	165	Spitfire Vc	7.43-10.43	AR503/SK-Q	UK	
SK	165	Spitfire IX	10.43-2.45	MK426/SK-D	UK	
SK	165	Mustang III	2.45-6.45	HB959/SK-M	UK	
SL	13 OTU	Anson I	4.40-*c* 46	K6165/SL-H	UK	
SL	13 OTU	Blenheim IV	*c* 42	V6027/SL-W	UK	
SL	13 OTU	Tempest II	*c* 45-5.47	MW759/SL-X	UK	
SL	13 OTU	Mosquito VI	11.43-5.47	TA476/SL-A	UK	
SM	305	Wellington Ic	11.40-7.41	R1016/SM-A	UK	
SM	305	Wellington II	7.41-8.42	Z8339/SM-N	UK	
SM	305	Wellington IV	8.42-5.43	R1530/SM-A	UK	
SM	305	Wellington X	5.43-9.43	HF491/SM-	UK	
SM	305	Mitchell II	9.43-12.43	FV937/SM-	UK	
SM	305	Mosquito III	12.43-6.45	LR536/SM	UK, Eur	
SM	305	Mosquito VI	12.43-11.46	NS823/SM-H	UK, Eur	
SN	243	Spitfire Vb	6.42-9.42	AD316/SN-H	UK	
SN	243	Spitfire Vc	1.43-3.44	ER807/SN-E	MedME	
SN	243	Spitfire IX	6.43-9.44	JL375/SN-Z	UK	
SO	145	Blenheim If	11.39-4.40	K7159/SO-N	UK	
SO	145	Hurricane I	3.40-2.41	N2601/SO-H	UK	
SO	145	Spitfire IIa	2.41-2.42	P7605/SO-N	UK	
SO	145	Spitfire Va	7.41-2.42	X4854/SO-A	UK	
SO	South-East FS SF	Oxford I	*c* 45-46	V3895/SO-B	UK	
SO	South-East FS SF	Spitfire XVIe	*c* 12.45	TB532/SO-A	UK	
SP	110 RCAF	Lysander III	*c* 8.40	T1434/SP-N	UK	to 400 Sqn
SP	400	Lysander III	3.41-6.42	T1434/SP-N	UK	ex 110 RCAF
SP	400	Tomahawk I	4.41-7.42	AH806/SP-W	UK	
SP	400	Mustang I	4.42-11.42	AP258/SP-B	UK	
SP	*SF Doncaster*		*45*		*UK*	*use not known*
SR	101	Blenheim IV	9.39-5.41	V5493/SR-G	UK	
SR	101	Wellington Ic	4.41-2.42	R1699/SR-D	UK	
SR	101	Wellington III	2.42-10.42	BJ590/SR-H	UK	
SR	101	Stirling I	*c* 9.42	W7440/SR-X	UK	conversion flt
SR	101	Lancaster I, III	10.42-8.46	NG128/SR-B	UK	
SS	1552 RATF	Oxford I	9.45-10.46	HN130/SS-R	UK	
ST	54 OTU	Beaufighter IIf	5.42-5.45	T3410/ST-F	UK	
ST	54 OTU	Beaufort I	3.43-2.45	LR977/ST-B	UK	
ST	54 OTU	Beaufighter VIf	9.43-7.45	KW101/ST-C	UK	
ST	54 OTU	Martinet I	12.43-5.47	MS779/ST-3	UK	
ST	54 OTU	Spitfire IX	*c* 44-45	MK968/ST-Y	UK	
ST	54 OTU	Anson I	9.44-5.47	MG669/ST-K	UK	
ST	54 OTU	Hurricane IIc	1.45-1.46	PG595/ST-O	UK	
ST	54 OTU	Wellington XVIII	2.45-5.47	ND114/ST-B	UK	
ST	54 OTU	Auster I	*c* 8.45	LB294/ST-W	UK	to 228 OCU

Code	Unit	Type	Dates	Example	Theatre	Remarks
SU	*SF Turnhouse*		*45*		*UK*	*use not known*
SV	1663 HCU	Halifax V	5.43-10.44	DG407/SV-P	UK	
SV	1663 HCU	Halifax IIIa	10.44-5.45	MZ294/SV-Z	UK	
SW	253	Hurricane I	2.40-8.41	L1982/SW-B	UK	
SW	253	Hurricane IId	7.41-9.42	Z3971/SW-S	UK	
SW	253	Hurricane IIc	1.42-9.43		UK, MedME	
SW	253	Spitfire Vc	8.43-11.44	JK868/SW-K	MedME	
SW	253	Spitfire VIII	11.44-5.45	JF899/SW-K	MedME, Eur	
SW	253	Spitfire IX	11.44-5.47	PT655/SW-W	MedME, Eur	
SW	1678 HCU	Lancaster II	3.43-6.44	DS623/SW-T	UK	
SX	1 CACU	Blenheim IVf	9.41-42	R3840/SX-D	UK	
SX	1 CACU	Spitfire II	9.41-10.43	P8333/SX-N	UK	
SX	*SF Methwold*		*45*		*UK*	*use not known*
SY	613	Tomahawk IIa	3.41-4.42	AH931/SY-P	UK	
SY	613	Mustang I	4.42-10.43	AM209/SY-Q	UK	
SY	613	Mosquito VI	11.43-8.45	LR366/SY-L	UK	
SZ	316	Hurricane I	2.41-8.41	W9233/SZ-H	UK	
SZ	316	Spitfire Vb	10.41-4.44	AD562/SZ-S	UK	
SZ	316	Spitfire IX	3.43-9.43	BS463/SZ-G	UK	
SZ	316	Mustang III	4.44-11.46	FB376/SZ-Q	UK	
T2	*46 MU*		*45*		*UK*	*use not known*
T5	*SF Abingdon*		*45*		*UK*	*use not known*
T6	*SF Melbourne*		*45*		*UK*	*use not known*
T7	650	Martinet I	12.43-6.45	HP175/T7-M	UK	
TA	4 (C)OTU	Singapore	3.41-10.42	K4578/TA-	UK	
TA	4 (C)OTU	Stranraer	3.41-10.42	K7300/TA-Y	UK	
TA	4 (C)OTU	London II	6.41-10.42	L7043/TA-K	UK	
TA	4 (C)OTU	Lerwick I	6.41-2.42	L7268/TA-Q	UK	
TA	4 (C)OTU	Catalina I	6.41-10.43	AH568/TA-H	UK	
TA	4 (C)OTU	Sunderland I	11.41-5.43	P9606/TA-E	UK	
TA	4 (C)OTU	Sunderland II	43-44	W3997/TA-R	UK	
TA	4 (C)OTU	Sunderland III	2.43-12.45	W3980/TA-S	UK	
TA	4 (C)OTU	Sunderland V	*c* 10.44-7.47	RN302/TA-H	UK	
TA	4 (C)OTU	Lysander II	*c* 5.43-12.44	V9858/TA-B	UK	
TB	153	Defiant I	10.41-5.42	N3425/TB-*	UK	
TB	153	Beaufighter If	1.42-12.42	X7774/TB-V	UK	
TB	153	Beaufighter VIf	8.42-12.42	V8895/TB-F	UK	
TB	*77 Sqn*	*Halifax*	*43-44*		*UK*	*C Flt reported*
TC	170	Lancaster III	10.44-11.45	RF199/TC-J2	UK	
TD	453	Buffalo	8.41-2.42	AN210/TD-J	FE	
TD	126	Spitfire Vb	12.43-4.44	JG745/TD-U	MedME	
TD	126	Spitfire IX	8.43-12.43		MedME	
TD	82 OTU	Wellington III, X	6.43-12.44		UK	
TD	*320*	*Fokker T-VIIIW*	*6.40-9.40*		*UK*	*reported*
TE	1401 Flt/521	Gladiator II	2.41-4.45	N5902/TE-L	UK	
TE	1401 Flt/521	Spitfire Va	8.42-3.43	R6817/TE-E	UK	
TF	200	Hudson III, IV	5.41-9.43	AE615/TF-X	UK	
TF	29 OTU	Wellington X	5.43-6.45	LP647/TF-Y	UK	C Flt
TH	418	Boston III	11.41-9.43	AL475/TH-T	UK	
TH	418	Mosquito II	3.43-9.43	DZ747/TH-A	UK	
TH	418	Mosquito VI	5.43-9.45	NT115/TH-J	UK	
TJ	272	Beaufighter Ic	11.42-6.43	T4882/TJ-Z	MedME	
TJ	202	Catalina IV	1.44-6.45	JX225/TJ-M	UK	
TJ	52 OTU	Spitfire IX	4.43-10.43	MH530/TJ-J	UK	
TK	149	Stirling III	2.43-9.44	BF520/TK-T	UK	C Flt
TK	149	Lancaster I	8.44-45	PP686/TK-J	UK	C Flt

Code	Unit	Type	Dates	Example	Theatre	Remarks
TL	35	Halifax I	11.40-2.42	L9579/TL-P	UK	
TL	35	Halifax II	1.42-3.44	JP123/TL-F	UK	
TL	35	Halifax III	12.43-3.44	LV818/TL-L	UK	
TL	35	Lancaster III	3.44-10.49	RF183/TL-H	UK	
TM	504	Hurricane I	3.39-11.41	P3774/TM-V	UK	
TM	504	Spitfire II	10.41-10.42	P7926/TM-	UK	
TM	504	Spitfire Vb	1.42-1.44	EE624/TM-R	UK	
TM	504	Spitfire IX	1.44-4.45	PL256/TM-L	UK	
TM	504	Meteor III	4.45-8.45	EE286/TM-Q	UK	to 245 Sqn
TM	245	Meteor III	8.45-9.45	EE2**/TM-R	UK	ex 504 Sqn
TN	30 OTU	Wellington X	10.43-6.45	LN171/TN-U	UK	
TO	61 OTU	Spitfire I	6.41-12.43	*****/TO-B	UK	
TO	61 OTU	Spitfire II	10.42-2.44		UK	
TO	61 OTU	Master II	6.41-7.47	DK881/TO-N	UK	
TO	61 OTU	Martinet I	12.44-7.47	JN297/TO-T	UK	
TO	61 OTU	Harvard IIb	5.45-7.47	FX442/TO-M	UK	to 203 AFS
TP	73	Hurricane I	9.39-11.40	N2358/TP-Z	Eur, UK	
TP	73	Hurricane I	11.40-1.42	V7544/TP-S	MedME	
TP	198	Typhoon Ib	12.42-9.45	MN234/TP-K	UK, Eur	
TP	198	Hurricane I	c 7.43	P3265/TP-*	UK	Sqn hack
TQ	202	London II	9.39-6.41	K5264/TQ-L	UK	
TQ	202	Swordfish I	9.40-6.41	K8354/TQ-D	UK	
TQ	202	Catalina Ib	4.41-1.45	AJ160/TQ-S	UK	
TQ	202	Sunderland I	12.41-9.42	W4024/TQ-N	UK	
TQ	202	Sunderland II	3.42-9.42	DV962/TQ-Q	UK	
TQ	*SF Bramcote*				*UK*	*use not known*
TR	59	Blenheim IV	9.39-9.41	L8793/TR-M	Eur, UK	
TR	59	Hudson V	7.41-8.42	AM789/TR-C	UK	
TR	59	Liberator III	8.42-12.42	FL933/TR-S	Eur, UK	
TS	548	Spitfire VIII	4.44-10.45	A58-413/TS-L	Australia	
TT	1658 HCU	Halifax II	10.42-4.45	W7927/TT-R	UK	D Flt
TT	1658 HCU	Oxford II	10.42-4.45	AB758/TT-L	UK	D Flt
TT	1658 HCU	Halifax III	9.44-4.45	LK864/TT-W	UK	D Flt
TT	CFE	Martinet I	c 4.45	*****/TT-6	UK	
TU	*SF Dyce*		*45*		*UK*	*use not known*
TV	4	Lysander II	9.39-9.40	L4741/TV-N	UK	
TV	4	Lysander III	9.40-6.42	V9587/TV-X	UK	
TV	4	Mustang I	4.42-1.44	AG596/TV-X	UK	
TV	1660 HCU	Stirling III	12.43-1.45	LJ624/TV-C	UK	
TV	1660 HCU	Manchester I	10.42-10.43	R5768/TV-A	UK	
TV	1660 HCU	Lancaster I	10.42-12.43	LL795/TV-Q	UK	
TV	1660 HCU	Lancaster III	1.45-11.46	PB489/TV-S	UK	
TV	1660 HCU	Spitfire Vb	1.45-11.46	BL729/TV-L	UK	
TW	141	Defiant I	4.40-8.41	L7036/TW-H	UK	
TW	141	Beaufighter I	6.41-6.43	V8253/TW-T	UK	
TW	141	Beaufighter VI	5.43-2.44	V8673/TW-K	UK	
TW	141	Mosquito II	10.43-8.44	DD790/TW-L	UK	
TW	141	Mosquito VI	7.44-3.45	PZ165/TW-S	UK	
TW	141	Mosquito 30	3.45-9.45	NT507/TW-F	UK	
TX	11 OTU	Anson I	4.40-c 42	N5173/TX-F	UK	Oakley det
TX	11 OTU	Wellington Ic	4.40-44	Z1108/TX-K	UK	Oakley det
TX	11 OTU	Wellington X	44-9.45	LP707/TX-V	UK	Oakley det
TY	24 OTU	Whitley V	3.42-6.44	AD697/TY-J	UK	B Flt
TY	24 OTU	Anson I	3.42-8.44	AX260/TY-V	UK	B Flt
TY	24 OTU	Wellington III	4.44-7.45	X3939/TY-L	UK	B Flt
TY	24 OTU	Wellington X	4.44-7.45	LN161/TY-F	UK	B Flt

Code	Unit	Type	Dates	Example	Theatre	Remarks
TZ	*310*		*45*		*UK*	*use not known*
U2	*SF Talbenny*		*45*		*UK*	*use not known*
U3	RWE	Fortress III	7.45-9.46	KJ105/U3-C	UK	
U3	RWE	Halifax III	7.45-9.46	MZ491/U3-V	UK	
U4	667	Defiant I, III	12.43-1.45	AA296/U4-J	UK	
U4	667	Oxford I	6.44-12.45	EB722/U4-X	UK	
U4	667	Vengeance IV	10.44-12.45	HB529/U4-E	UK	
U4	667	Spitfire XVI	7.45-12.45	TE283/U4-7	UK	
U5	51 MU	Anson I	45-46	NK957/U5-S	UK	
U6	327	Spitfire IX	*c* 6.45	MJ415/U6-S	Eur	
U6	*436*		*45*		*FE*	*use not known*
U7	ADLSS	Anson X	12.44-4.46	MG865/U7-H	UK	
UA	269	Anson I	9.39-9.40	N5317/UA-R	UK	
UA	269	Hudson I	3.40-3.41	N7303/UA-B	UK	
UA	269	Hudson III	3.41-7.45	T9045/UA-D	UK	
UB	455	Hampden TB I	7.41-12.43	P1287/UB-B	UK	
UB	455	Beaufighter X	12.43-5.45	RD329/UB-X	UK	
UB	164	Spitfire XVI	7.46-8.46		UK	to 63 Sqn
UB	?	Boston III		W8389/UB-X	MedME	
UD	452	Spitfire I	4.41-5.41	P9562/UD-N	UK	
UD	452	Spitfire Vb	8.41-6.42	BL906/UD-E	UK	
UE	228	Sunderland III	3.42-2.45	ML763/UE-J	UK	
UE	228	Sunderland V	2.45-6.45	RN283/UE-M	UK	
UE	*?*	*Hurricane I*	*c* 42-43	*P3026/UE-U*	*UK*	*possibly 59 or 63 OTU or 4 TEU*
UF	601	Blenheim If	9.39-3.40	K7178/UF-K	UK	
UF	601	Hurricane I	3.40-3.41	P3886/UF-K	UK	
UF	601	Hurricane IIb	3.41-1.42	AZ670/UF-J	UK	
UF	601	Airacobra I	8.41-3.42	AH589/UF-L	UK	
UF	601	Spitfire Vc	3.42-1.44	ER220/UF-V	MedME	
UF	601	Spitfire VIII	6.43-6.44	JF483/UF-I	MedME	
UF	601	Spitfire IX	6.44-5.45	MK551/UF-T	MedME	
UF	24 OTU	Whitley V	3.42-4.44	BD366/UF-T	UK	C Flt
UF	24 OTU	Martinet I	43-7.45	JN297/UF-C	UK	C Flt
UF	24 OTU	Oxford I	11.43-8.44	T1073/UF-	UK	C Flt
UF	24 OTU	Hurricane IIc	8.44-7.45	LF751/UF-V	UK	C Flt
UF	24 OTU	Defiant	44-7.45	N3315/UF-V	UK	C Flt
UF	24 OTU	Wellington X	4.44-7.45	NC651/UF-H	UK	C Flt
UF	24 OTU	Wellington III	5.44-7.45	Z1726/UF-A	UK	C Flt
UG	16	Lysander II	9.39-10.40	L4807/UG-J	UK	
UG	16	Lysander III	10.40-6.41	R9018/UG-	UK	
UG	16	Lysander IIIa	5.41-5.43	V9546/UG-	UK	
UG	16	Gladiator II	3.40-9.40	N2304/UG-D	UK	
UG	16	Mustang I	4.42-11.43	AG431/UG-D	UK	
UG	1654 HCU	Manchester Ia	5.42-7.43	L7228/UG-J	UK	A Flt
UG	1654 HCU	Lancaster I	5.42-9.45	W4926/UG-F	UK	A Flt
UG	1654 HCU	Halifax V	9.43-1.44	DG317/UG-J	UK	A Flt
UG	1654 HCU	Stirling III	9.43-11.44	EH923/UG-K	UK	A Flt
UH	1682 BDTF	Hurricane IIc	2.44-8.44	LF743/UH-F	UK	
UH	1682 BDTF	Spitfire XVIe	2.44-8.44	SL756/UH-F	UK	
UH	21 OTU	Anson I	8.41-44	AX295/UH-S	UK	
UH	21 OTU	Hurricane IIc	8.44-3.45	LF763/UH-S	UK	
UH	21 OTU	Oxford I	45-3.47	NM786/UH-J	UK	
UH	21 OTU	Martinet I	45-3.47	JN301/UH-X	UK	
UH	21 OTU	Spitfire XVIe	45-2.47	TE347/UH-G	UK	to 202 AFS
UJ	27 OTU	Wellington X	8.43-6.45	JA341/UJ-T	UK	C Flt

These Lysander IIs L4808/KJ-H and L4805/KJ-B of No. 16 Sqn were photographed in May 1939 and display typical pre-war markings. (Philip Jarrett Collection)

Halifax B.II series I W7676/TL-P of No. 35 Sqn in the summer of 1942 was lost soon after this photograph was taken. (via Neville Franklin)

Hurricane I L1940/OP-R of No. 3 Sqn displays its pre-war OP codes at Biggin Hill in May 1939. (Philip Jarrett Collection)

This Royal Navy Boston III coded T8K belonged to No. 771 Naval Air Sqn based at Twatt in the Orkneys around 1943. (Gregor Lamb)

Spitfire Vc ER622/WR-D of No. 40 Sqn SAAF displays its red and white coloured codes over Tunisia while a colleague formates in early 1943. (SAAF)

Anson I K8782/YQ-G of No. 217 Sqn, seen here in May 1939, not only displays its unit codes but also the unit badge on a six-pointed star on the fin. (Philip Jarrett Collection)

Wellington III Z1572/VR-Q of No. 419 Sqn RCAF, seen in 1942, survived squadron service and was later used for training. (Canadian Forces)

The only RCAF fighter squadron in North Africa was No. 417, whose Spitfire Vcs are seen running-up in April 1943; BR195/AN-T is nearest. (Canadian Forces)

Probably the most distinctively identifiable fighter squadron of the war was No. 12 with its prominent 'shark's teeth' which looked so effective on these Kittyhawk IIIs at Zuara in May 1943. (HQ Strike Command)

Sunderland III ML828/RB-C seen at Mount Batten in 1943 belonged to No. 10 Sqn RAAF. (P. Hulton via P. H. T. Green Collection)

Bombing-up at Colerne in May 1943 is Typhoon Ib EK139/HH-N of No. 175 Sqn. P. H. T. Green Collection)

Typhoon Ib JR371/TP-R of No. 198 Sqn taxies past a gun position at Manston in January 1944. (P. H. T. Green Collection)

Wellington X HE575/Y7-J of No. 86 OTU, seen in mid-1944, became a ground instructional aircraft the following October.

(USAF Academy, Colorado Springs)

Debden-based P-51D Mustang 447218/VF-S wears the codes of the 336th FS but was the aircraft of Col E. V. Stewart. (via Roger Freeman)

Stirling IV LK554/X9-M of No. 299 Sqn joined the unit from No. 620 Sqn on 14 June 1945 and served until March 1946.

(USAF Academy, Colorado Springs)

Spitfire Vb AB981/MY-T served with No. 278 Sqn in the air-sea rescue role in early 1945. (W. S. Rance)

The RAF's first jet fighters were the Meteors of No. 616 (South Yorkshire) Sqn, whose aircraft in May 1945 included Mk III EE278/YQ-Q. (RAFM)

The Hornet F.3s of No. 19 Sqn flew in several colour schemes, two of which are worn by PX293/QV-A and PX332/QV-D. (P. H. T. Green Collection)

This Sikorsky H-5, 9604/OU-604 was part of the RCAF Joint Air Training Centre at Rivers in the 1950s. (DND via Larry Milberry)

Canadair Sabre Mk 4 19584/VH-584 belonged to No. 444 Sqn RCAF at St Hubert in August 1953. (L. de Sansoucy via Larry Milberry)

Meteor F.8s, including EG-3/OV-A, of No. 8 Sqn RBelgAF in the mid 1950s before camouflage was applied. (André van Haute)

Among the last users of unit codes were the SAAF PV-1 Venturas like 6504/MS-W of No. 17 Sqn in the late 1950s. (via Ivan Spring)

Lancaster 10PR FM207/MN-207 was used by No. 408 Sqn RCAF to map much of northern Canada during the 1950s. (Canadian Forces)

CF-100 Mk 5 18768/HG-768 of No. 428 Sqn RCAF at a snowy Val d'Or, Quebec in February 1959. (T. Tarling via Larry Milberry)

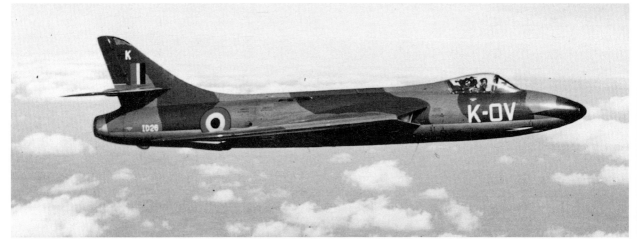

Belgian AF Hunters like F.4 ID-26/OV-K of No. 8 Sqn in the late 1950s wore their code letters on the nose under the cockpit. (André van Haute)

Buccaneer S.2B XX893/DC of No. 237 OCU displays the short-lived codes worn by the Lossiemouth Wing during the mid 1980s. Uniquely, this wing placed the unit letter after the aircraft letter. No. 237's letter C related to its cutlass badge! (Air Cdre G. R. Pitchfork)

The last use of the traditional squadron code was by the RNorAF, SA-16B Albatross 510060/KK-B of No. 333 Sqn retaining them up to the late 1960s. (R. C. B. Ashworth)

Even after camouflaging in desert colours at the time of the Gulf War in 1990–1, codes continued to be worn as on this Tornado GR.1 of No. 15 Sqn. (British Aerospace)

Jaguar GR.1 XZ256/B-P of No. 17 Sqn shows the single-letter codes which the RAF began using generally in the 1970s. (MoD)

C was the code for No. 100 Sqn at Wyton in 1991 and was worn on its Canberras like TT.18 WJ682/C-U and the Hawks that replaced them including XX247/C-M. (British Aerospace)

Harrier GR.7 ZD408/W-K wears the W code used by the Harrier detachment at Incirlik in Turkey for Operation Warden in the early 1990s.

(British Aerospace)

The Tornado F.3s of No. 56 Sqn like ZE253/A-C retained the code after it was renumbered from No. 65 Sqn in 1992. (British Aerospace)

The C code of Puma HC.1 ZA940/C-Y of No. 33 Sqn is from the Support Helicopter Force (SHF) allocation, which included other helicopter types. (MoD/DPR)

Code	Unit	Type	Dates	Example	Theatre	Remarks
UL	608	Anson I	9.39-3.41	N5201/UL-H	UK	
UL	608	Botha I	6.40-11.40	L6171/UL-A	UK	
UL	608	Blenheim IVf	3.41-7.41	Z6043/UL-H	UK	
UL	608	Hudson V	7.41-7.44	AM642/UL-R	UK	
UL	576	Lancaster I	11.43-9.45	PA318/UL-E	UK	
UL	576	Lancaster III	11.43-9.45	PB265/UL-V2	UK	
UM	152	Gladiator II	10.39-2.40	N6450/UM-M	UK	
UM	152	Spitfire I	12.39-4.41	R6801/UM-B	UK	
UM	152	Spitfire IIa	7.40-6.42	P8394/UM-J	UK	
UM	152	Spitfire Vc	4.43-6.43	LZ807/UM-V	MedME	
UM	152	Spitfire Vb	4.42-10.42	BM556/UM-	UK	
UM	152	Spitfire IX	8.43-11.43	N6450/UM-M	MedME	
UM	152	Spitfire VIII	11.43-7.46	MT948/UM-N	FE	
UM	152	Spitfire XIV	1.46-7.46	RM908/UM-G	FE	
UM	626	Lancaster I	11.43-10.45	RA543/UM-A2	UK	
UN	*SF Faldingworth*		*45*		*UK*	*use not known*
UO	266	Spitfire I	1.40-4.41	N3178/UO-K	UK	
UO	266	Spitfire IIa	9.40-9.41	P8167/UO-N	UK	
UO	266	Spitfire Vb	9.41-5.42	W3834/UO-P	UK	
UO	266	Typhoon Ib	2.42-3.42	R7641/UO-A	UK	
UO	19 OTU	Whitley V	5.40-10.44	P4938/UO-CA	UK	A, B Flts
UO	19 OTU	Wellington X	8.44-6.45	NC740/UO-D	UK	A, B Flts
UP	605	Hurricane I	9.39-12.40	P3308/UP-A	UK	
UP	605	Hurricane IIb	12.41-3.42	BG753/UP-V	UK, MedME	
UP	605	Havoc II	7.42-10.42	W8389/UP-X	UK	
UP	605	Boston III	7.42-3.43	AL871/UP-D	UK	
UP	605	Mosquito II	2.43-7.43	DZ760/UP-K	UK	
UP	605	Mosquito VI	5.43-8.45	HJ790/UP-R	UK	to 4 Sqn
UQ	211	Blenheim I	9.39-9.41	L6670/UQ-R	MedME	
UQ	211	Blenheim IV	5.41-2.42	N6178/UQ-V	MedME	
UQ	1508 RATF	Oxford	45	V4237/UQ-	UK	
UR	13 OTU	Mitchell III	4.45-9.45	KJ602/UR-U	UK	
US	56	Hurricane I	9.39-2.41	P3702/US-W	UK	
US	56	Hurricane IIa	2.41-9.41	Z2636/US-U	UK	
US	56	Hurricane IIb	9.41-3.42	Z3442/US-M	UK	
US	56	Typhoon Ia	9.41-12.42	R7558/US-X	UK	
US	56	Typhoon Ib	3.42-5.44	JR503/US-K	UK	
US	56	Spitfire IX	4.44-6.44	ML189/US-H	UK	
US	56	Tempest V	6.44-3.46	EJ742/US-T	UK, Eur	
UT	461	Sunderland II	4.42-5.43	W4004/UT-Z	UK	
UT	461	Sunderland III	8.42-5.45	ML831/UT-H	UK	
UT	461	Sunderland V	3.45-6.45	PP113/UT-D	UK	
UU	61 OTU	Spitfire Vb	10.42-10.45	AB136/UU-F	UK	
UU	61 OTU	Mustang III	12.44-9.46	HB942/UU-G	UK	
UU	61 OTU	Spitfire XVIII	*c* 9.45	TP315/UU-Z	UK	to 203 AFS
UU	61 OTU	Spitfire XIV	10.45-9.46	SM896/UU-B	UK	to 203 AFS
UU	61 OTU	Spitfire XVI	1.46-7.47	RW387/UU-R	UK	to 203 AFS
UV	460	Wellington IV	11.41-8.42	Z1290/UV-T	UK	
UV	460	Halifax II	8.42-10.42	DT481/UV-B	UK	
UV	460	Lancaster I	10.42-5.43	ED421/UV-U	UK	
UW	55 OTU	Hurricane I, II	*c* 41-1.44	V6874/UW-E	UK	to 4 TEU
UW	4 TEU	Hurricane I	1.44-3.44	W9229/UW-*	UK	ex 55 OTU
UW	4 TEU	Hurricane X	1.44-3.44	AG162/UW-X	UK	to 3 TEU
UW	3 TEU A Flt, 1 Sqn	Typhoon Ib	3.44-12.44	MN513/UW-N	UK	ex 4 TEU; to 55 OTU
UW	55 OTU	Typhoon Ib	12.44-6.45		UK	ex 3 TEU
UX	82	Blenheim IV	9.39-3.42	V5515/UX-N	UK	

The Henley was a pre-war design. It was restricted to the target towing role with AACUs but relatively few served with numbered squadrons. One that did was L3327/R9-R which was with No. 639 Sqn at Cleve when photographed off the Devon coast on 7 September 1944. (No. 53 Sqn Records)

Although of relatively poor quality, this view taken at Castle Camps in 1942 shows W4087/RS-B, one of the first all-black night fighter Mosquito NF.IIs of No. 157 Sqn, the first to be equipped. The sooty black finish has already taken on a weathered appearance. (via Stuart Howe)

One of the many RCAF squadrons formed for service in the UK was No. 414 which in 1941 was initially equipped with Lysander IIIs like V9281/RU-M for the army co-operation role. (R. Priddle)

Later in 1941 the Lysanders were replaced in No. 414 Sqn with Tomahawk IIbs like AK185/RU-V and AK276/RU-F, with which it trained to an operational state. These in turn were replaced by Mustangs, but late in 1942 army co-operation squadrons ceased to wear unit codes. (Canadian Forces)

The clipped wings of Spitfire IX RK85/RG-J of No. 208 Sqn are well shown, as is the standard fighter colour scheme when this photo was taken over Italy late in the war during which this unit flew mainly on reconnaissance duties.* (P. H. T. Green Collection)

By July 1945 when this picture was taken many of the RAF's Far-Eastbased Thunderbolt IIs like KL308/RS-C of No. 30 Sqn were in a natural metal finish, with black identity bands, though they retained the two-tone blue SEAC markings. (via G. J. Thomas)

One of the finest fighters of the Second World War was the Tempest V which formed the equipment of No. 486 Sqn RNZAF and which it used to great effect during the last year of the war. One used was JN766/SA-N which displays the standard markings for the time. (via C. H. Thomas)

The RAF's most heavily armed fighter in the early war years was the Whirlwind, which only equipped two squadrons. One was No. 137, identified by the letters SF. One of its aircraft, P7055/SF-S, sits on dispersal in 1942 as behind a section lifts off. (Gp Capt J. B. Wray)

Though designed as a bomber-transport, the Bombay, like L5820/SH-F of No. 216 Sqn at Khartoum in 1940, was mainly used for transport duties in the Middle East. The placement of the unit and aircraft letters aft of the roundel was unusual, though the norm on this type. (Gp Capt J. Pelly-Fry)

RCAF squadrons sent to the UK in 1940 initially kept their Canadian numbers, but to avoid confusion, on 1 March 1941 they were numbered in the 400 series. One was No. 110 (later 400) Sqn which flew Lysander IIIs like T1434/SP-N at Odiham around the time the number changed. (C. Vincent)

The main pre-war bomber-transport in the Middle East was the Valentia and a number survived in service into the war. They equipped No. 70 Sqn until late 1940 and K5605/SJ-U was one of theirs, resplendent in camouflage and toned-down roundels at Helwan in 1940. (A. J. Thorne)

With its serial overpainted, Hurricane I SW-E of No. 253 Sqn taxis past a camouflaged hangar at Northolt during work-up training on 19 April 1940. The absence of fin flashes and yellow outlined fuselage roundels and medium grey codes letters are all as dictated by regulations. (J. B. G. Greenwood)

Another variation on the position of code letters is shown by Mustang I AG509/SY-K of No. 613 (City of Manchester) Sqn as it formates on a colleague in August/September 1942 shortly before the codes were removed. (F. Wells via D. Vincent)

Wearing its newly applied code, London II K6932/TQ-B of No. 202 Sqn sits at anchor in Gibraltar in mid-September 1939. Although outdated, these aircraft would see considerable use patrolling the approaches to the vital Straits until replaced in 1941. (No. 202 Sqn Records)

Awaiting their next meteorological reconnaissance ascent over the North Sea from Bircham Newton on 20 August 1942 are Spitfire Va R6817/TE-E and Gladiator II N5902/TE-L of No. 521 Sqn. The latter is one of the few of its type to wear the type C markings.
(RAF Bircham Newton Records)

Photographs of accidents can be a valuable aid to identifying unknown unit codes. In this instance, this accident to Beaufighter Ic T4882/TJ-Z at Edku in Egypt occurred on 25 March 1942 and helped confirm the code as that of No. 272 Sqn. (R. A. Butt)

HQ Coastal Command decreed that unit codes should be removed from its aircraft in late 1942 and as a consequence, very few photographs of coded early model Liberators have surfaced. One is this previously unpublished view of Liberator III FL930/TR-E of No. 59 Sqn taken around October 1942. (No. 59 Sqn Records)

This extremely rare photograph shows Mustang I AG596/TV-X of No. 4 Sqn during mid-1942 when the squadron was part of Army Co-operation Command. It is interesting to contrast the position of the code with the example from No. 613 Sqn on page 111. (Wg Cdr S. J. Eaton)

One of the Defiant-equipped units to take a mauling during the Battle of Britain was No. 141 Sqn, and as a consequence photographs of its aircraft in day fighter markings are very rare. One that survived the carnage was L7000/TW-P which is seen at Gravesend toward the end of the Battle. (D. Aris)

The unwieldy Blackburn Botha was designed as a torpedo bomber, but saw only very limited operational use with one unit, No. 608 (North Riding) Sqn. The example shown in this poor but very rare photograph, is L7171/UL-A which was taken about the time that it flew its only two operational sorties on 5 and 6 September 1940. (via Roger Hayward)

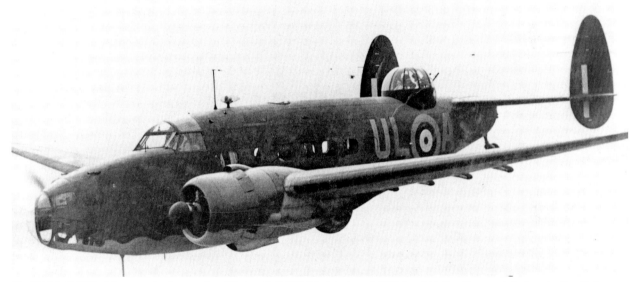

No. 608 (North Riding) Sqn was also the operator of Hudson V AM571/UL-A in August 1941, by which time it was contributing significantly to Coastal Command operations. It is one of the least photographed units, and photographs of the preceding Blenheims have still to come to light. (Flt Lt R. A. Bagnall)

This Mustang III which is in the FD serial range belongs to No. 61 OTU at Rednal and when photographed just before the end of the war displayed another variation in the unit code presentation. Spitfires used by the same unit had them in a standard form. (N. J. French)

A wet Grangemouth airfield on 17 June 1942 is the location of this accident to Hurricane I V6874/UW-E of No. 55 OTU, which is wearing one of several combinations allocated as the aircraft establishment was so large. (HQ No. 81 Group Records)

Code	Unit	Type	Dates	Example	Theatre	Remarks
UX	82	Mosquito VI	7.44-3.46	HR665/UX-C	FE	
UX	CFE	Spitfire IX	9.44-c 46	RK807/UX-Y	UK	
UX	CFE	Spitfire XIV	9.44-c 46	RM704/UX-A	UK	
UX	? 1476 Flt	Anson I	c 43	K6184/UX-P	UK	
UY	10 OTU	Anson I	4.40-10.44	AX297/UY-J	UK	C Flt
UY	10 OTU	Whitley V	c 41-9.44	LA817/UY-S	UK	C Flt
UY	10 OTU	Lysander II	42-c 44	P9088/UY-V	UK	C Flt
UY	10 OTU	Master II	c 42-9.46	EM270/UY-*	UK	C Flt
UY	10 OTU	Defiant I	c 2.43	AA327/UY-*	UK	C Flt
UY	10 OTU	Tomahawk IIb	-43	AK120/UY-*	UK	C Flt
UY	10 OTU	Martinet I	44-9.46	JN255/UY-Y	UK	C Flt
UY	10 OTU	Oxford I	44-9.46	NM787/UY-U	UK	C Flt
UY	10 OTU	Spitfire IX	c 44-9.46	TB344/UY-U	UK	C Flt
UY	10 OTU	Wellington X	6.44-9.46	LP438/UY-R	UK	C Flt
UZ	306	Hurricane I	8.40-4.41	V7118/UZ-V	UK	
UZ	306	Hurricane IIa	4.41-7.41	Z2884/UZ-Z	UK	
UZ	306	Spitfire IIb	7.41-12.41	P8471/UZ-J	UK	
UZ	306	Spitfire Vb	12.41-3.44	EP116/UZ-L	UK	
UZ	306	Spitfire IX	9.42-3.43	BS458/UZ-Z	UK	
UZ	306	Mustang III	3.44-1.47	FB393/UZ-U	UK	
V2	? CSE	Anson XI	NL220/V2-A		UK	not confirmed
V4	6 MU	Dominie	C45-46	NR721/V4	UK	
V7	RWE				UK	use not known
V8	570	Albemarle I	11.43-8.44	V1703/V8-X	UK	
V8	570	Stirling IV	7.44-1.46	LJ667/V8-U	UK	
V9	502	Halifax II	1.45-3.45	JP328/V9-H	UK	
V9	502	Halifax III	2.45-5.45	RG364/V9-D	UK	
VA	657	Auster V	44	NK119/VA	MedME	HQ Flt
VA	84	Blenheim I	9.39-5.41	L1381/VA-G	MedME	
VA	84	Blenheim IV	3.41-6.42	V5579/VA-H	MedME	
VA	125	Defiant I	6.41-4.42	N3459/VA-R	UK	
VA	125	Defiant II	6.41-4.42	AA404/VA-P	UK	
VA	125	Beaufighter IIf	2.42-9.42	T3149/VA-M	UK	
VA	125	Beaufighter VI	9.42-2.44	V8751/VA-G	UK	
VA	125	Mosquito III	42-46	HK355/VA-T	UK	
VA	125	Mosquito XVII	2.44-3.45	HK355/VA-T	UK	
VA	125	Mosquito XXX	2.45-6.46	NT450/VA-B	UK	to 264 Sqn
VB	657	Auster V	44		MedME	A Flt
VB	14 OTU	Wellington Ic	7.42-4.44	L7850/VB-Y	UK	
VB	14 OTU	Anson I	4.40-12.42	R9607/VB-02	UK	
VB	*334*	*Mosquito VI*			*UK*	*use not known*
VC	657	Auster V	44		MedME	B Flt
VC	414	Spitfire FR XIV	c 4.45	NH403?/VC-P	Eur	
VD	657	Auster V	44		MedME	C Flt
VD	CGS	Hampden	12.41-42	P1313/VD-C	UK	Thurleigh det
VD	CGS	Wellington Ic, I	12.41-42		UK	Thurleigh det
VD	CGS	Blenheim IV	12.41-42	V5449/VD-A	UK	Thurleigh det
VE	110	Blenheim IV	9.39-3.42	Z7285/VE-U	UK	
VE	*SF Kirton-in-Lindsey*		*45*		*UK*	*use not known*
VF	SF Lindholme	Oxford I	45-47	T1343/VF-A	UK	
VG	285	Oxford I	3.42-6.45	BG156/VG-V	UK	
VG	285	Defiant I	3.42-1.44	T3923/VG-M	UK	
VG	285	Defiant TT I	3.42-1.44	DR882/VG-J	UK	
VG	285	Martinet	7.43-12.43	RG889/VG-S	UK	
VG	285	Anson I		*****/VG-E	UK	
VI	*169*	*Mustang Ia*	*42*		*UK*	*reported*

Code	Unit	Type	Dates	Example	Theatre	Remarks
VI	169	Beaufighter If	10.43-	X7899/VI-6	UK	
VI	169	Oxford II	10.43-7.44	T1394/VI	UK	
VI	169	Mosquito II	1.44-7.44	DZ310/VI-B	UK	
VI	169	Mosquito VI	6.44-5.45	NS997/VI-C	UK	
VI	169	Mosquito XIX	1.45-8.45	MM644/VI-G	UK	
VJ	10 BAT Flt ?	Anson I	c 6.41	*****/VJ-S	UK	
VK	238	Spitfire I	5.40-6.40	*****/VK-N	UK	
VK	238	Hurricane I	6.40-5.41	P3462/VK-G	UK	
VK	*85 GCF*		*45*		*UK*	*use not known*
VL	167	Spitfire Vb	4.42-6.43	AA976/VL-B	UK	to 322 Sqn
VL	322	Spitfire Vb	6.43-3.44	EP350/VL-F	UK	ex 167 Sqn
VL	322	Spitfire XIV	3.44-6.44	NH699/VL-R	UK	
VL	322	Spitfire IX	8.44-11.44	BS539/VL-B	UK	
VM	231	Lysander II, III	7.40-7.43	P9056/VM-A	UK	
VM	231	Tomahawk I/II	10.41-7.43	*****/VM-Z	UK	
VM	1561 Met Flt	Spitfire XI	12.45-2.46		UK	
VN	50	Hampden I	9.39-5.42	AE370/VN-P	UK	
VN	50	Manchester I	4.42-6.42	R5784/VN-F	UK	
VN	50	Anson I	9.39-4.40	N5193/VN-Y	UK	
VN	50	Lancaster I	5.42-11.46	DV197/VN-T	UK	
VN	50	Lancaster III	5.42-11.46	ME382/VN-A	UK	
VO	98	Battle	9.39-7.41	L5343/VO-S	Eur, UK	
VO	98	Mitchell II	9.42-11.45	FL176/VO-B	UK, Eur	
VO	98	Mitchell III	9.44-11.45	FL176/VO-B	UK, Eur	
VP	SF Exeter	Dominie	c 45-46	NR715/VP-K	UK	
VQ	18 OTU	Lysander III	3.42-10.42	T1586/VQ-Z	UK	
VQ	18 OTU	Wellington X	c 43-12.44	HF420/VQ-P	UK	
VQ	18 OTU	Martinet I	c 44	HP527/VQ-V	UK	
VR	419	Wellington Ic	12.41-11.42	Z1083/VR-O	UK	
VR	419	Wellington III	2.42-11.42	X3711/VR-R	UK	
VR	419	Halifax II	11.42-3.44	JP200/VR-G	UK	
VR	419	Lancaster X	3.44-9.45	KB722/VR-R	UK	
VS	*510*	*?*			*UK*	*poss use before becoming MCS*
VT	30	Blenheim If	9.39-5.41	K7177/VT-N	MedME	
VT	1556 RATF	Oxford	1.46-4.46	NM792/VT-*	UK	
VU	246	York C.1	10.44-10.46	MW165/VU-P	UK	
VV	235	Mosquito VI	6.44-7.45	RS620/VV-G	UK	
VV	*SF Sumburgh*		*45*		*UK*	*use not known*
VW	*SF Chedburgh*		*45*		*UK*	*use not known*
VX	206	Anson I	9.39-6.40	K6179/VX-A	UK	
VX	206	Tiger Moth	11.39-6.40	N6720/VX-*	UK	Coastal Patrol Flt
VX	206	Hudson I	3.40-8.42	P5143/VX-F	UK	
VX	206	Hudson IV	3.40-8.42	AE617/VX-R	UK	
VX	206	Fortress I	8.42-4.44	AN520/VX-X	UK	
VX	206	Fortress II	9.42-3.44	FL440/VX-V	UK	
VY	85	Hurricane I	9.39-7.41	P3854/VY-Q	UK	
VY	85	Havoc I	2.41-9.42	BJ472/VY-R	UK	
VY	85	Havoc II	7.41-9.42	AH514/VY-D	UK	
VY	85	Mosquito III	7.42-5.44	VT612/VY-T	UK	
VY	85	Mosquito II	8.42-4.43	DD732/VY-W	UK	
VY	85	Mosquito XII	2.43-12.44	HK119/VY-S	UK	
VY	85	Mosquito XVII	11.43-9.44	HK282/VY-D	UK	
VY	85	Mosquito XIX	5.44-1.45	MM624/VY-Q	UK	
VY	85	Mosquito XIII	c 6.44	HK379/VY-P	UK	
VY	85	Mosquito XXX	11.44-4.46	MV546/VY-P	UK	

Code	Unit	Type	Dates	Example	Theatre	Remarks
VZ	412	Spitfire IIa	7.41-10.41	P8145/VZ-K	UK	
VZ	412	Spitfire Vb	10.41-11.43	AA868/VZ-F	UK	
VZ	412	Spitfire IX	11.43-5.45	MJ393/VZ-Z	UK	
VZ	412	Spitfire XIV	6.45-3.46	NH905/VZ-N	UK	
W2	80	Spitfire IX	4.44-11.44	MA828/W2-B	UK	
W2	80	Tempest V	8.44-1.48	SN209/W2-E	Eur	
W3	*SF Hemswell*		*45*		*UK*	*use not known*
W4	*GPU*	*Dakota III*	*-12.45*		*UK*	*possible use*
W5	*SF Castle Camps*		*45*		*UK*	*use not known*
W6	*18 MU*		*45*		*UK*	*use not known*
W9	*24 MU*		*45*		*UK*	*use not known*
WA	*? 5 OTU*	*Whitley, Beaufort*	*41*		*UK*	*not confirmed*
WA	*SF Manorbier*		*45*		*UK*	*use not known*
WB	BCIS	Lancaster III	12.44-6.47	PB423/WB-P	UK	
WC	309	Hurricane IIc	4.44-10.44	PG428/WC-W	UK	
WC	309	Mustang III	10.45-1.47	FZ124/WC-X	UK	
WD	*SF*	*Leeming*	*45*		*UK*	*use not known*
WE	59	Liberator V	3.43-3.45	BZ781/WE-A	UK	
WE	59	Liberator VIII	3.45-6.46	KK289/WE-D	UK	
WE	23 OTU	Wellington Ic	4.41-8.42	Z1736/WE-J	UK	
WE	23 OTU	Wellington III	6.42-3.44	Z1736/WE-S	UK	
WF	525	Dakota IV	2.45-12.46	KN285/WF-A	UK	to 238 Sqn
WG	128	Hurricane I	10.41-c 6.42	Z4484/WG-A	Africa	
WG	128	Hurricane IIb	11.41-3.43	BD776/WG-F	Africa	
WG	26 OTU	Wellington Ic	1.42-8.43	DV780/WG-Z	UK	
WG	26 OTU	Wellington III	2.43-10.44	BK130/WG-H	UK	
WG	26 OTU	Wellington X	2.43-3.46	PG347/WG-Y	UK	
WG	26 OTU	Hurricane IIc	8.44-3.46	BE653/WG-M	UK	
WH	330	Sunderland III	2.43-5.45	NJ178/WH-N	UK	
WH	330	Sunderland V	5.45-11.45	ML824/WH-Z	Eur	to RNoAF
WJ	17 OTU	Blenheim I	4.40-4.43	L1059/WJ-A	UK	B, C Flts
WJ	17 OTU	Blenheim IV	4.40-4.43	T2222/WJ-A	UK	B, C Flts
WJ	17 OTU	Anson I	4.40-7.43	AW909/WJ-Z	UK	B, C Flts
WJ	17 OTU	Wellington III	4.43-3.44	Z1598/WJ-B	UK	B, C Flts
WJ	17 OTU	Wellington X	6.43-3.47	NC449/WJ-T	UK	B Flt
WK	135	Hurricane IIa	8.41-11.41	*****/WK-S	UK	
WK	135	Hurricane IIb	1.42-10.43	BG996/WK-E	FE	
WK	135	Thunderbolt I	5.44-6.45	HB975/WK-L	FE	
WK	*1316 Flt*		*45*		*UK*	*use not known*
WL	612	Anson I	9.39-11.41	N9722/WL-E	UK	
WL	612	Whitley V	11.40-12.41	P5070/WL-B	UK	
WL	612	Whitley VII	6.41-6.43	Z9376/WL-M	UK	
WL	612	Wellington VIII	11.42-6.43	HX629/WL-L	UK	
WL	434	Halifax V	6.43-5.44	DK251/WL-F	UK	
WL	434	Halifax III	5.44-12.44	MZ421/WL-A	Eur	
WL	434	Lancaster X	12.44-9.45	KB832/WL-F	UK	
WL	434	Lancaster I	12.44-3.45	PA225/WL-O	UK	
WM	68	Blenheim If	1.41-5.41	Z5722/WM-Z	UK	
WM	68	Beaufighter If	5.41-3.43	X7583/WM-E	UK	
WM	68	Beaufighter VI	1.43-7.44	V8592/WM-L	UK	
WM	68	Mosquito XVII	7.44-2.45	HK250/WM-Z	UK	
WM	68	Mosquito 30	2.45-4.45	NT321/WM-O	UK	
WN	172	Wellington VIII	4.42-3.43	HX379/WN-A	UK	
WN	527	Blenheim IV	6.43-5.45	R3615/WN-Y	UK	
WN	527	Hurricane I	6.43-4.44	P2992/WN-P	UK	
WN	527	Hurricane XII	2.44-4.45	JS290/WN-P	UK	

Code	Unit	Type	Dates	Example	Theatre	Remarks
WN	527	Spitfire Vb	7.44-4.46	AB910/WN-S	UK	
WN	527	Oxford II	9.44-4.46	LX122/WN-P	UK	
WN	527	Wellington X	4.45-4.46	HZ616/WN-M	UK	
WO	13 OTU	Mosquito III	45	DZ722/WO-Z	UK	
WP	90	Blenheim IV	9.39-4.40	L4872/WP-M	UK	
WP	90	Fortress I	5.41-2.42	AN532/WP-J	UK	
WP	90	Stirling I	11.42-5.43	R9306/WP-J	UK	
WP	90	Stirling III	4.43-6.44	BF410/WP-E	UK	
WP	90	Lancaster I, III	5.44-12.47	NN783/WP-E	UK	
WP	89	Beaufighter If	5.42-6.42	X7671/WP-D	MedME	
WP	243	Buffalo II	3.41-2.42	AN196/WP-W	FE	
WP	220	Fortress I	c 12.41	AN518/WP-B	MedME	ME det only
WQ	209	Stranraer I	9.39-4.40	K7302/WQ-B	UK	
WQ	209	Lerwick I	12.39-4.41	L7263/WQ-L	UK	
WQ	209	Catalina I	4.41-3.42	AH530/WQ-T	UK	
WQ	12 GCF	Anson XII	6.45-12.46	PH644/WQ-K	UK	
WQ	12 GCF	Proctor III	6.45-12.46	LZ562/WQ	UK	
WQ	12 GCF	Oxford I	6.45-12.46	NM335/WQ	UK	
WQ	12 GCF	Spitfire IX	45-10.46	PL249/WQ-WA	UK	
WR	248	Blenheim If	10.39-2.40	L1336/WR-E	UK	
WR	248	Blenheim IVf	1.40-7.41	T2131/WR-P	UK	
WR	248	Beaufighter Ic	7.41-7.42	T4774/WR-M	UK	
WR	248	Beaufighter VIc	2.42-6.43	EL264/WR-D	UK	
WR	248	Mosquito XVIII	1.44-2.45	LR363/WR-X	UK	
WR	SF Moreton in-Marsh		45		UK	use not known
WS	9	Wellington Ia	9.39-3.40	N2964/WS-D	UK	
WS	9	Wellington Ic	3.40-9.41	T2619/WS-T	UK	
WS	9	Wellington II	3.40-9.41	W5729/WS-J	UK	
WS	9	Wellington III	9.41-8.42	BJ606/WS-R	UK	
WS	9	Manchester I	9.42-10.42	L7464/WS-D	UK	conversion flt
WS	9	Lancaster I, III	8.42-7.46	JA711/WS-A	UK	
WS	9	Lancaster VII	11.45-4.46	NX678/WS-S	UK	
WU	225	Lysander IIIa	4.42-7.42	V9593/WU-F	UK	
WU	225	Mustang I	5.42-8.42	AG570/WU-G	UK	
WU	225	Spitfire Vc	1.43-1.45	JK112/WU-A	MedME	
WU	225	F-6A Mustang	1.43-6.43	******/WU-B	MedME	USAAF loan
WU	225	Spitfire IX	6.44-1.47	MK300/WU-I	MedME	
WV	18	Blenheim IV	2.40-9.42	R3607/WV-N	UK	
WW	1382 (T)CU		45		UK	use not known
WX	302	Hurricane I	7.40-7.41	P2752/WX-R	UK	
WX	302	Hurricane IIa	3.41-5.41	Z2772/WX-B	UK	
WX	302	Hurricane IIb	7.41-10.41	Z5004/WX-T	UK	
WX	302	Spitfire Vb	10.41-9.43	W3902/WX-A	UK	
WX	302	Spitfire IX	9.43-2.45	MA791/WX-B	UK, Eur	
WX	302	Spitfire XVI	2.45-12.46	TB141/WX-R	Eur	
WY	28 OTU	Master II	5.42-10.44	DM427/WY-Z	UK	
WY	28 OTU	Martinet	43-10.44	HP439/WY-M	UK	
WY	28 OTU	Wellington X	c 43-10.44	LN952/WY-C	UK	
WZ	SF Gravely				UK	use not known
X1	11 FIS	Oxford II	c 44-45	PH231/X1-S	MedME	
X2	SF Stoney Cross		45		UK	use not known
X3	111 (C)OTU	Liberator VI	8.42-5.46	KK321/X3	WI, UK	
X3	111 (C)OTU	Liberator VIII	7.45-5.46	KK297/X3-A	UK	
X3	111 (C)OTU	Martinet I	8.45-1.46	JN483/X3-BB	UK	
X3	111 (C)OTU	Oxford I	8.45-46	PK284/X3-AB	UK	

Although employed on maritime work, in early 1945 Halifax GR.II series Ia JP328/V9-H of No. 502 (Ulster) Sqn had a mainly black colour scheme for its night anti-shipping role in the Skaggerak area. The reason for the contrasting spinner colours between port and starboard is not clear. (via Harry Holmes)

Auster AOP III, NK119/VA was operating with A Flight No. 657 Sqn in support of the 8th Army when seen at Ceprano in the Liri Valley in Italy during June 1944. It was actually on loan from the HQ Flight, hence the VA code. (Aubrey Young)

One of the many squadrons formed for second-line support tasks during the war was No. 285 which, among other types, used this Oxford I HM952/VG-N at Woodvale during 1942–3. (J. Hudson)

By 1943 the Merlin-engined Beaufighter II had been relegated to training units. When V8164/VX was photographed visiting the USAAF 4th FG at Debden at that time it was in the standard colour scheme except for the absence of the individual aircraft letter. (F. Grove)

By the time the Polish No. 309 Sqn switched to the fighter role with the Mustang III, C was being used in unit codes, so it was allocated WC. It also carried the squadron badge under the cockpit, as can be seen on the nearest aircraft, FZ124/WC-X. In the background can be seen the ZW-coded aircraft of Sqn Ldr Z. Wroblewski, the Squadron Leader Flying at Coltishall. (via R. Freeman)

The ASV radar aerials and maritime colours are readily apparent on Whitley VII Z6633/WL-G of No. 612 (County of Aberdeen) Sqn in the spring of 1941, probably at Dyce. When Coastal Command reintroduced codes in 1944, this combination had been reallocated so the code changed to 8W on its Wellingtons. (No. 612 Sqn Records)

When No. 434 Sqn RCAF was formed in England, the WL code previously used by No. 612 Sqn was available and allocated to this heavy bomber unit, as can be seen on Halifax IIIs WL-Y, WL-W and MZ626/WL-T (nearest) as they return from a daylight raid on Sterkrade in late 1944. (Yorkshire Air Museum)

Blenheim IV L4872/WP-M of No. 90 Sqn was used for operational training duties when seen in the spring of 1940, as this unit was designated as a group pool squadron. Soon afterwards the squadron merged to form an OTU, but later pioneered the Fortress into service, also WP-coded. (D. Hornsey)

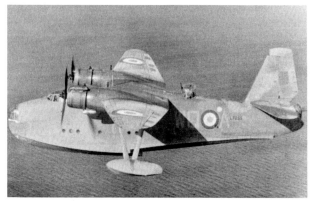

Another of the unsuccessful types introduced to service early in the war was the SARO Lerwick I which served only with No. 209 Sqn before being withdrawn from operational use. This one is L7255/WQ-A and carries the high-visibility roundels adopted for a time as an identity aid to friendly fighters. (via John Evans)

Code	Unit	Type	Dates	Example	Theatre	Remarks
X3	111 (C)OTU	Wellington XIV	8.45-5.46	PG183/X3-CC	UK	
X6	290	Martinet I	12.43-10.45	EM522/X6-D	UK	
X6	290	Spitfire Vb	12.44-10.45	W3641/X6-H	UK	
X8	6 GCF	Oxford	44-8.45	*****/X8-W	UK	
X8	6 GCF	Anson I	44-8.45	AX433/X8-F	UK	
X9	299	Stirling IV	1.44-2.46	PW448/X9-P	UK	
X9	517	Halifax V	11.43-6.46	LL216/X9-A	UK	
X9	517	Halifax III	2.45-6.46	LV839/X9-C	UK	
X9	517	Oxford	*c* 45-46	NM223/X9-Z	UK	
XA	489	Blenheim IV	1.42-3.42	P4835/XA-J	UK	
XA	489	Hampden I	3.42-11.43	AT225/XA-A	UK	
XA	*SF Essex sector*				*UK*	*use not known*
XB	224	Liberator V	3.43-10.46	FL960/XB-O	UK	
XB	224	Liberator VI, VIII	8.44-10.46	KK363/XB-P	UK	
XB	457	Spitfire Vb	8.42-7.43	BR543/XB-T	SWPA	
XB	58 OTU	Spitfire II	1.41-10.43	P****/XB-V	UK	to 2 TEU
XB	2 TEU	Spitfire II	10.43-6.44	P****/XB-Q	UK	ex 58 OTU
XC	26	Spitfire XI	10.45-4.46	PL995/XC-W	UK	
XC	26	Spitfire XIV	6.45-1.47	NH925/XC-N	UK	
XD	139	Blenheim IV	9.39-2.42	L8756/XD-E	UK	
XD	139	Mosquito IV	9.42-7.44	DZ464/XD-C	UK	
XD	139	Mosquito IX	9.43-9.44	ML909/XD-S	UK	
XD	139	Mosquito XVI	2.44-11.48	MM200/XD-E	UK	
XD	139	Mosquito XX	11.43-9.45	KB192/XD-S	UK	
XD	139	Oxford II	44-45	V3787/XD-G	UK	
XD	139	Mosquito XXV	9.44-9.45	KB434/XD-V	UK	
XD	13 OTU	Boston IIIa	5.43-3.45	BZ346/XD-P	UK	
XE	123	Spitfire I	5.41-9.41	R7122/XE-E	UK	
XE	123	Spitfire IIa	9.41-1.42	P8437/XE-K	UK	
XE	123	Spitfire Vb	1.42-4.42		UK	
XE	123	Spitfire Vc	5.43-11.43	ER***/XE-Y	UK	
XE	123	Hurricane IIc	6.44-6.45	JS418/XE-C	FE	
XE	123	Thunderbolt I, II	9.44-6.45	KJ255/XE-J	FE	
XF	19 OTU	Anson I	5.40-6.45	AX431/XF-D	UK	F Flt
XF	19 OTU	Whitley IV	5.40-2.43	X9019/XF-K	UK	F Flt
XF	19 OTU	Lysander III	41-44	P9123/XF-Y	UK	F Flt
XF	19 OTU	Defiant III	10.42-3.43	N1653/XF-*	UK	F Flt
XF	19 OTU	Martinet	6.43-11.44	*****/XF-L	UK	F Flt
XG	16 OTU	Hampden I	4.40-4.42	X2980/XG-A	UK	
XG	16 OTU	Wellington Ic	4.42-1.45	DV509/XG-I	UK	
XG	16 OTU	Wellington III	9.42-1.45	BJ190/XG-F	UK	
XG	16 OTU	Wellington X	43-1.45	NC808/XG-R	UK	
XH	296	Whitley V	6.42-5.43	Z9476/XH-T	UK	
XH	218	Lancaster III	8.44-8.45	ME545/XH-L	UK	C Flt
XJ	13 OTU	Blenheim I	4.40-41	L6620/XJ-D	UK	
XJ	13 OTU	Blenheim IV	4.40-4.44	L6810/XJ-K	UK	
XJ	13 OTU	Mosquito VI	12.43-4.47	PZ475/XJ-V	UK	
XJ	13 OTU	Mosquito III	44-4.47	HJ776/XJ-M	UK	
XJ	13 OTU	Martinet	45	JN416/XJ-*	UK	
XK	272	Blenheim IVf	11.40-4.41	V5754/XK-A	UK	
XK	272	Beaufighter Ic	6.41-*c* 7.41	T3317/XK-*	MedME	
XK	46	Stirling V	2.45-3.46	PJ952/XK-F	UK	
XL	20 OTU	Wellington Ic	5.40-7.45	Z8977/XL-C	UK	D Flt
XL	20 OTU	Wellington III	41-7.45	HE490/XL-A	UK	D Flt
XM	182	Hurricane X	9.42-10.42	AG232/XM-P	UK	
XM	182	Tiger Moth II	*c* 42	*****/XM-I	UK	Sqn Hack

Code	Unit	Type	Dates	Example	Theatre	Remarks
XM	182	Typhoon Ia	9.42-10.42	R7624/XM-D	UK	
XM	182	Typhoon Ib	10.42-9.45	EJ952/XM-S	UK, Eur	
XN	22 OTU	Wellington III	12.42-7.45	DF549/XN-R	UK	C Flt
XN	22 OTU	Wellington X	c 43-7.45	HE610/XN-M	UK	C Flt
XN	22 OTU	Anson I	4.41-7.45	AX256/XN-N	UK	C Flt
XO	57 OTU	Spitfire II	12.40-4.44	*****/XO-A	UK	
XO	57 OTU	Spitfire Vb	41-6.45	BL685/XO-C	UK	
XO	57 OTU	Spitfire I	c 4.42	X4234/XO-F	UK	
XP	174	Hurricane IIb	3.42-4.43	BE684/XP-Y	UK	
XP	174	Typhoon Ib	4.43-4.45	MN683/XP-F	UK, Eur	
XQ	86	Liberator VIII	2.45-5.45	KH291/BX-Y	UK	
XQ	86	Liberator VI	5.45-4.46	KN704/XQ-O	UK	
XR	71	Hurricane I	11.40-5.41	V7608/XR-J	UK	
XR	71	Hurricane IIb	4.41-8.41	Z3174/XR-B	UK	
XR	71	Spitfire IIa	8.41-9.41	P7308/XR-D	UK	
XR	71	Spitfire Vb	9.41-9.42	EN737/XR-K	UK	to 334 FS 4 FG USAAF qv
XR	*2 GCF*		*45*		*UK*	*use not known*
XS	MSFU	Sea Hurricane Ia	5.41-9.43	Z4852/XS-K	NA	
XT	603	Gladiator I	9.39-10.39	K7938/XT-J	UK	
XT	603	Spitfire I	9.39-11.40	L1007/XT-K	UK	
XT	603	Spitfire IIa	10.40-6.41	P7546/XT-E	UK	
XT	603	Spitfire Vb	5.41-4.42	W3111/XT-O	UK	
XT	603	Spitfire XVI	1.45-8.45	SM396/XT-P	UK	
XT	1657 CU	Stirling I	10.42-12.44	N3758/XT-K	UK	
XT	1657 CU	Stirling III	4.43-12.44	EJ120/XT-A	UK	
XU	7	Lancaster III	7.43-45	EE119/XU-G	UK	C Flt
XV	2	Lysander III	9.40-7.42	T1631/XV-H	UK	
XV	2	Tomahawk I, IIa	8.41-4.42	AH916/XV-U	UK	
XV	2	Mustang I, Ia	4.42-5.44	AG620/XV-A	UK	
XW	18 OTU	Anson I	11.40-1.45	N5029/XW-B	UK	
XW	18 OTU	Wellington X	43-1.45	LN529/XW-K	UK	
XW	18 OTU	Defiant III	43-1.45	AA323/XW-C	UK	
XW	18 OTU	Martinet I	43-1.45	HP526/XW-U	UK	
XY	90	Stirling III	2.43-6.44	EF509/XY-X	UK	C Flt
XY	90	Lancaster I	5.44-10.44	LM188/XY-S	UK	C Flt to 186 Sqn
XY	186	Lancaster I	10.44-7.45	NG146/XY-E	UK	ex C Flt 90 Sqn
XZ	39	Blenheim I	9.39-1.41	L8387/XZ-F	UK	
Y2	442	Spitfire IXb	3.44-9.44	MK194/Y2-H	UK, Eur	
Y2	442	Spitfire IXe	9.44-3.45	PL330/Y2-K	UK, Eur	
Y2	442	Mustang IV	3.45-8.45	KH665/Y2-V	UK	
Y3	518	Halifax V	7.43-8.45	DG304/Y3-B	UK	
Y3	518	Oxford II	11.44-9.46	NM662/Y3-Q	UK	
Y3	518	Halifax III	3.45-7.46	RG390/Y3-A1	UK	
Y3	518	Halifax VI	5.46-10.46	RG843/Y3-O	UK	
Y3	518	Hurricane IIc	c 45	PZ810/Y3-Z	UK	
Y3	518	Anson XII	c 45	PH713/Y3-Y	UK	
Y5	*SF Dallachy*		*45*		*UK*	*use not known*
Y7	86 OTU	Wellington X	6.44-10.44	HE575/Y7-J	UK	
YA	*SF Netheravon*		*45*		*UK*	*use not known*
YB	17	Hurricane I	9.39-2.41	V7311/YB-P	UK, Eur	
YB	17	Hurricane IIa	2.41-4.41	Z2081/YB-S	UK	
YB	17	Hurricane IIb	7.41-11.41	Z2799/YB-P	UK	
YB	17	Hurricane IIa	1.42-5.42	Z4849/YB-*	FE	
YB	17	Hurricane IIb	2.42-8.42	BE171/YB-B	FE	
YB	17	Hurricane IIc	8.42-6.44	HV794/YB-*	FE	
YB	17	Spitfire VIII	3.44-6.45	MT719/YB-J	FE	

Code	Unit	Type	Dates	Example	Theatre	Remarks
YB	17	Spitfire XIVe	6.45-2.48	RN150/YB-W	FE	
YB	*SF Bentwaters*		*45*		*UK*	*use not known*
YC	27 OTU	Oxford	42-45	NM800/YC-S	UK	
YD	255	Defiant I	11.40-9.41	N3312/YD-T	UK	
YD	255	Beaufighter IIf	7.41-5.42	R2460/YD-J	UK	
YD	255	Beaufighter VIf	3.42-2.45	X8002/YD-G	MedME	
YD	255	Mosquito XIX	1.45-4.46	TA408/G/YD-D	MedME	
YE	289	Hurricane IIc	12.41-6.45	LF628/YE-S	UK	
YE	289	Oxford I	3.42-6.45	V3170/YE-G	UK	
YE	289	Spitfire Vc	*c* 43-6.45	ES414/YE-X	UK	
YE	289	Martinet I	5.43-4.45	JN670/YE-12	UK	
YE	289	Vengeance IV	3.45-6.45	FD335/YE-M	UK	
YF	280	Anson I	2.42-10.43	DG922/YF-P	UK	
YF	280	Warwick I	10.43-6.46	BV304/YF-P	UK	
YF	SF Scampton	Tiger Moth II	45-46	BB790/YF-Z	UK	
YF	SF Scampton	Lancaster I	45-46	ED932/YF-C	UK	
YG	502	Anson I	9.39-11.40	N5235/YG-J	UK	
YG	502	Whitley V	10.40-2.42	T4222/YG-H	UK	
YG	502	Whitley VII	2.42-2.43	BD677/YG-C	UK	
YG	502	Halifax II	1.43-3.45	R9486/YG-B	UK	
YG	*156 C Flt*	*Lancaster*			*UK*	*use not known*
YH	11	Blenheim I	9.39-12.40	L8520/YH-N	FE, MedME	
YH	11	Blenheim IV	1.41-9.43	Z7984/YH-C	MedME	
YH	21	Blenheim IV	9.39-7.42	V6254/YH-N	UK	
YH	21	Ventura I	5.42-9.43	AE717/YH-O	UK	
YH	21	Ventura II	9.42-10.43	AE918/YH-X	UK	
YH	21	Mosquito IV	43	DZ632/YH-U	UK	
YH	21	Mosquito VI	9.43-10.47	RS532/YH-E	UK, Eur	
YI	423	Sunderland III	44-5.45	ML782/YI-N	UK	
YJ	*SF Methering'm*		*45*		*UK*	*use not known*
YK	80	Gladiator I	9.39-4.41	K8011/YK-O	MedME	
YK	80	Gladiator II	9.39-4.41	K7973/YK-Y	MedME	
YK	80	Hurricane I	6.40-4.41	P2544/YK-T	MedME	to 274 Sqn
YK	274	Hurricane I	8.40-10.41	P2544/YK-T	MedME	ex 80 Sqn aircraft
YL	27 OTU	Martinet I	*c* 43-6.45	JN295/YL-P	UK	
YL	27 OTU	Oxford I	*c* 43-6.45	NM800/YL-S	UK	
YM	1528 RATF				UK	use not known
YO	1 Sqn RCAF	Hurricane I	6.40-3.41	P3873/YO-H	UK	to 401 Sqn
YO	401	Hurricane I	3.41-5.41	P3080/YO-C	UK	ex 1 Sqn RCAF
YO	401	Hurricane IIb	5.41-9.41	Z3577/YO-J	UK	
YO	401	Spitfire Vb	10.41-10.43	AD355/YO-J	UK	
YO	401	Spitfire IX	6.42-12.42	BS177/YO-H	UK	
YO	401	Spitfire IXb	10.43-5.45	MK195/YO-F	UK	
YO	401	Spitfire XIV	5.45-6.45	RM785/YO-T	UK	
YO	*SF Down Ampney*				*UK*	*use not known*
YP	23	Blenheim If	9.39-4.41	L8617/YP-K	UK	
YP	23	Havoc I	3.41-8.42	BD124/YP-D	UK	
YP	23	Boston III	2.42-8.42	AL459/YP-W	UK	
YP	23	Mosquito II	7.42-9.43	DD798/YP-S	MedME	
YP	23	Mosquito VI	5.43-9.45	HX896/YP-D	MedME, UK	
YQ	616	Spitfire IIa	2.41-7.41	P8367/YQ-V	UK	
YQ	616	Spitfire Vb	7.41-10.42	AA879/YQ-U	UK	
YQ	616	Spitfire VI	4.42-12.43	BS114/YQ-A	UK	
YQ	616	Spitfire VII	9.43-8.44	MB768/YQ-X	UK	
YQ	616	Spitfire IX	9.43-8.44	MJ107/YQ-B	UK	
YQ	616	Meteor I	7.44-2.45	EE227/YQ-Y	UK	

Code	Unit	Type	Dates	Example	Theatre	Remarks
YQ	616	Meteor III	12.44-8.45	EE235/YQ-H	UK	
YR	20 OTU	Wellington Ic	5.40-41	R1089/YR-B	UK	C Flt
YR	20 OTU	Hurricane IIc	c 43-7.45	LF736/YR-M	UK	C Flt
YR	20 OTU	Oxford	c 43-7.45	NM789/YR-S	UK	C Flt
YR	20 OTU	Master	c 43-7.45	**414/YR-C	UK	C Flt
YR	20 OTU	Martinet I	c 44-7.45	MS873/YR-L	UK	C Flt
YR	20 OTU	Wellington X	44-7.45	LR414/YR-Q	UK	C Flt
YS	271	Dominie I	5.42-1.44	X7351/YS-A	UK	
YS	271	Dakota III	1.44-12.45	KG406/YS-DH	UK	
YS	271	Dakota IV	5.45-12.45	KJ881/YS-K	UK	to 77 Sqn
YT	65	Spitfire I	9.39-10.41	K9906/YT-T	UK	
YT	65	Spitfire II	11.40-10.41	P7850/YT-C	UK	
YT	65	Spitfire Vb	10.41-8.43	AB786/YT-W	UK	
YT	65	Spitfire IX	8.43-1.44	MH367/YT-C	UK	
YT	65	Mustang III	12.43-3.45	FZ110/YT-S	UK	
YT	65	Mustang IV	3.45-5.46	KM140/YT-E	UK	
YU	*SF Lossiemouth*		*45*		*UK*	*use not known*
YV	*48 GCF*		*45*		*UK*	*use not known*
YW	1660 HCU	Lancaster I	10.42-11.43	R5845/YW-T	UK	
YW	1660 HCU	Lancaster III	1.45-11.46	PB867/YW-R	UK	
YW	1660 HCU	Spitfire Vc	1.45-11.46	BP864/YW-E	UK	
YW	1660 HCU	Hurricane IIc	1.45-11.46	LF572/YW-B	UK	
YW	1660 HCU	Mosquito XIX	1.46-11.46	TA351/YW-J	UK	to 230 OCU
YX	54 OTU	Blenheim If	11.40-2.43	K7159/YX-N	UK	
YX	54 OTU	Beaufighter VIf	9.43-8.45	ND200/YX-P	UK	
YX	54 OTU	Mosquito II	5.44-7.45	DD737/YX-H	UK	
YX	54 OTU	Mosquito III	5.44-4.47	HJ886/YX-U	UK	
YX	54 OTU	Mosquito VI	2.45-5.47	PZ311/YX-M	UK	
YX	54 OTU	Mosquito XII	2.45-	HK126/YX-U	UK	
YX	54 OTU	Mosquito XXX	5.45-5.47	MM817/YX-A	UK	
YX	614	Lysander II	11.39-c 6.40	N1241/YX-O	UK	
YY	1332 CU	Liberator III	8.44-9.45	BZ857/YY-P	UK	
YY	1332 CU	Stirling III	8.44-4.45	PW261/YY-L	UK	
YY	1332 CU	Liberator VI	45-46	KL645/YY-C	UK	
YY	1332 CU	York I	11.45-1.48	MW266/YY-W	UK	
YY	1332 CU	Halifax VII	11.45-12.46	PN236/YY-C	UK	
YZ	1651 HCU	Stirling I	1.42-44	R9197/YZ-U	UK	
YZ	1651 HCU	Stirling III	1.42-44	BK689/YZ-W	UK	
YZ	617	Lancaster I (Special)	6.45-9.46	PD114/YZ-B	UK	on Mk I Specials only
Z1	163	Mosquito XXV	1.45-5.45	KB510/Z1-B	UK	
Z2	437	Dakota III	9.44-6.46	FZ694/Z2-P	UK, Eur	
Z2	437	Anson XI	11.44-2.45	NK700/Z2-NW	Eur	
Z2	437	Dakota IV	2.445-6.46	KN256/Z2-OL	UK, Eur	
Z4	10 MU	Anson I	45-47	EG297/Z4	UK	
Z5	462	Halifax III	8.44-9.45	MZ792/Z5-P	UK	
Z8	*45 MU*		*45*		*UK*	*use not known*
Z9	519	Hampden I	8.43-10.43	P2118/Z9-D	UK	
Z9	519	Spitfire VI	8.43-1.45	BR307/Z9-X	UK	
Z9	519	Hudson III	9.43-3.45	FK744/Z9-C	UK	
Z9	519	Spitfire VII	8.43-12.45	EN506/Z9-V	UK	
Z9	519	Ventura V	10.43-10.44	FN966/Z9-P	UK	
Z9	519	Fortress IIa	11.44-9.45	FK213/Z9-G	UK	
Z9	519	Halifax III	8.45-5.46	RG355/Z9-A	UK	
Z9	519	Oxford I	4.45-5.46	NM353/Z9-P	UK	
ZA	10	Whitley IV	9.39-5.40	K9034/ZA-S	UK	
ZA	10	Whitley V	3.40-12.41	T4143/ZA-J	UK	

Cruising over a patchwork countryside on 28 August 1944 en route to a patrol, Liberator GR VI EW309/XB-S displays its new squadron code after they had recently been reintroduced with Coastal Command. The code letters are coloured red. (No. 53 Sqn Records)

Late in the war No. 26 Sqn adopted the code XC which it then used for several years while based on the Continent and can be seen on this Spitfire FR.XIV on 9 July 1945. (No. 26 Sqn Records)

The Merchant Ship Fighter Unit was a large organisation and as such was allocated several unit code combinations. One was XS as displayed by Hurricane I Z4852/XS-K at Dartmouth, Nova Scotia, where it was used for CAM ship training. (J. Friedlander via C. H. Thomas)

Photographs of aircraft of No. 123 Sqn have always proved elusive, none more so than its Thunderbolts. This unidentified Mk II taxiing, probably at Nazir in early 1945, shows the XE code well. Interestingly it still wears European-style type C roundels underwing. (via Martin Goodman)

This photograph of Defiant I N3333/YD-B of No. 255 Sqn in full dayfighter camouflage was taken at Cranwell some time in December 1940. No. 255 was formed as a night-fighter unit on 23 November with this aircraft being delivered four days later. It is of interest in that most photographs showing this squadron's Defiants show them in the all-black scheme. (via Air Cdre G. R. Pitchfork)

In September 1939, when most unit codes were changed, the Lysanders of No. 2 Sqn continued to use the letters KO. However, shortly before re-equipping with Tomahawks, they were recoded as may be seen on Lysander III T1631/XV-H at Sawbridgeworth in late 1941. (via R. L. Ward)

Hampden I P1258/ZN-W of No. 106 Sqn is seen during a visit to Cranwell in October 1940. It was allocated this unit code on the outbreak of war and retained it on succeeding types until eventual disbandment. (via T. N. Hancock)

Approaching to land at Shepherd's Grove just after the war is natural-metal-finished Stirling V transport PK144/ZO-P of No. 196 Sqn. During the war this unit had supported various major airborne operations, and was allocated two code combinations because of its size. (C. H. Vass)

An unusual type on the strength of the Fighter Interception Unit of the Central Fighter Establishment was Wellington XIII NB855/ZQ-C which, although in Fighter Command, retained its 'Coastal' colours. It is seen in storage after withdrawal from service. (L. Hayes)

Although primarily Anson-equipped, No. 233 Sqn at Bircham Newton had a long-range fighter flight for a short time in 1939–40, equipped with the Blenheim If, one of which was L8716/ZS-4 which was photographed minus its gun pack on 13 January 1940. This flight used individual aircraft numbers rather than letters. (RAF Bircham Newton Records)

Following the introduction of numerical codes in Coastal Command, No. 206 Sqn's Fortress IIs were identified by the number 1, as can be seen on FK190/1-J during 1943. Note the ASV radar aerials on the fin fillet – a seldom seen feature on this type. (M. Hughes)

Heavily weathered Sunderland III JM678/2-G of No. 461 Sqn RAAF was photographed over the coast near its Pembroke Dock base on 10 January 1944. The co-located No. 228 Sqn's aircraft were coded 1. (via D. Vincent)

Mosquito FB.VI HP904/3-E is from the Norwegian-manned B Flight of No. 333 Sqn from Leuchars. Other units there at this time included No. 455 with Beaufighters which were coded 2. (Cato Guhnfeldt Colletion)

The only known use of the code 4 was by No. 206 Sqn, which was allocated the code on joining the St Eval Wing in 1944. It had arrived after the other units, Nos 53 (1), 224 (2) and 547 (3) Sqns, and was given 4 probably to prevent the aircraft of Nos 224 and 547 Sqns being repainted. (No. 206 Sqn Records)

Code	Unit	Type	Dates	Example	Theatre	Remarks
ZA	10	Halifax II	12.41-3.44	HX190/ZA-E	UK	
ZA	10	Halifax III	12.44-8.45	RG426/ZA-X	UK	
ZA	10	Dakota IV	8.45-12.47	KN555/ZA-V	UK	
ZB	1658 HCU	Halifax II	10.42-4.45	R9454/ZB-T	UK	
ZB	1658 HCU	Halifax III	10.42-4.45	LW193/ZB-B	UK	
ZD	222	Blenheim If	11.39-3.40	L8719/ZD-C	UK	
ZD	222	Spitfire I	3.40-3.41	X4416/ZD-J	UK	
ZD	222	Spitfire IIa	3.41-8.41	P7909/ZD-P	UK	
ZD	222	Spitfire Vb	8.41-5.43	BL619/ZD-S	UK	
ZD	222	Spitfire IX	5.43-12.44	BS314/ZD-A	UK	
ZD	222	Tempest V	12.44-10.45	L8719/ZD-C	UK, Eur	
ZE	293	Warwick I	11.43-4.46	BV315/ZE-H	MedME	
ZE	293	Walrus I, II	4.44-4.46	L2217/ZE-P	MedME	
ZE	*52*	*Battle, Blenheim*	10.42-2.43		*UK,MedME*	*reported*
ZF	308	Hurricane I	10.40-4.41		UK	
ZF	308	Spitfire I	4.41-5.41		UK	
ZF	308	Spitfire IIa	5.41-9.41	P8022/ZF-L	UK	
ZF	308	Spitfire Vb	9.41-11.43	BL763/ZF-U	UK	
ZF	308	Spitfire IX	11.43-3.45	MA299/ZF-U	UK, Eur	
ZF	308	Spitfire XVI	3.45-12.46	TB896/ZF-M	Eur, UK	
ZF	549	Spitfire VIII	4.44-10.45	A58-379/ZF-Z	SWPA	
ZG	10 OTU	Whitley IV	4.40-9.44	K9013/ZG-X	UK	D, E Flts
ZG	10 OTU	Whitley V	4.40-9.44	T4131/ZG-K	UK	D, E Flts
ZG	10 OTU	Wellington X	6.44-9.46	HE580/ZG-V	UK	D, E Flts
ZH	266	Typhoon Ia	1.42-9.42	R7645/ZH-B	UK, Eur	
ZH	266	Typhoon Ib	1.42-7.45	MN353/ZH-J	UK, Eur	
ZH	*266*	*Proctor*	*c* 45	*LZ675/ZH-A*		*? Sqn hack*
ZJ	96	Hurricane I	12.40-8.41	P3172/ZJ-J	UK	
ZJ	96	Defiant I	3.41-7.42	T4052/ZJ-H	UK	
ZJ	96	Defiant II	2.42-6.42	AA583/ZJ-M	UK	
ZJ	96	Beaufighter IIf	5.42-9.42	T3364/ZJ-M	UK	
ZJ	96	Beaufighter VI	9.42-11.43	X8025/ZJ-B	UK	
ZJ	96	Mosquito III	8.43-12.44	HJ854/ZJ-M	UK	
ZJ	96	Mosquito XIII	10.43-12.44	HK379/ZJ-F	UK	
ZK	25	Blenheim If	9.39-1.41	L1200/ZK-H	UK	
ZK	25	Beaufighter If	10.40-1.43	X7587/ZK-O	UK	
ZK	25	Mosquito II	10.42-1.44	DD713/ZK-*	UK	
ZK	25	Mosquito VI	9.43-2.45	PZ200/ZK-H	UK	
ZK	25	Mosquito XVII	12.43-10.44	HK288/ZK-X	UK	
ZK	25	Mosquito XXVI	44.-46	KB280/ZK-Z	UK	
ZK	25	Mosquito XXX	9.44-9.46	NT425/ZK-H	UK	
ZK	25	Gladiator II	*c* 40	N5902/ZK	UK	
ZK	24	Wellington I	41-*c* 43	N2990/ZK-9	UK	
ZK	24	Dakota I	4.43-44	FD772/ZK-Y	UK	
ZK	24	Dakota III	4.43-45	KK133/ZK-A	UK	
ZL	427	Wellington III	11.42-5.43	BK389/ZL-L	UK	
ZL	427	Halifax V	5.43-2.44	EB247/ZL-P	UK	
ZL	427	Halifax III	1.44-3.45	LV922/ZL-B	UK	
ZL	427	Lancaster I	2.45-5.46	PA271/ZL-W	UK	
ZL	427	Lancaster III	2.45-5.46	NX550/ZL-V	UK	
ZM	201	London II	9.39-4.40	L7042/ZM-W	UK	
ZM	201	Sunderland I	4.40-1.42	N6138/ZM-V	UK	
ZM	201	Sunderland II	5.41-3.44	T9077/ZM-Y	UK	
ZM	201	Sunderland III	1.42-7.44	W6010/ZM-V	UK	
ZN	106	Hampden I	9.39-3.42	P1320/ZN-B	UK	
ZN	106	Manchester I	2.42-6.42	L7417/ZN-V	UK	

Code	Unit	Type	Dates	Example	Theatre	Remarks
ZN	106	Lancaster I	5.42-2.46	R5677/ZN-B	UK	
ZN	106	Lancaster III	5.42-2.46	NN726/ZN-D	UK	
ZO	196	Wellington X	12.42-7.43	HE167/ZO-A	UK	
ZO	196	Stirling III	7.43-2.44	BK771/ZO-G	UK	
ZO	196	Stirling IV	2.44-3.46	LK428/ZO-B	UK	
ZO	196	Stirling V	1.46-3.46	PJ887/ZO-H	UK	
ZP	74	Spitfire I	9.39-9.40	P9492/ZP-S	UK	
ZP	74	Spitfire IIa	9.40-1.42	P7370/ZP-A	UK	
ZP	74	Spitfire Vb	5.41-7.41	AD473/ZP-S	UK	
ZP	1473 Flt	Wellington Ic	7.42-12.43	Z1021/ZP-R	UK	
ZP	1473 Flt	Wellington III	9.43-2.44	BK179/ZP-Y	UK	
ZP	1473 Flt	Wellington X	9.43-2.44	HZ130/ZP-X	UK	
ZP	1473 Flt	Anson I	7.42-2.44	W1904/ZP-B	UK	
ZQ	FIU	Hurricane I	10.40-	L1592/ZQ-U	UK	
ZQ	FIU	Havoc I	3.41-3.43	AE461/ZQ-A	UK	
ZQ	FIU/FIDU	Beaufighter If	8.40-6.44	R2125/ZQ-V	UK	
ZQ	FIU/FIDU	Mosquito II	3.42-10.44	HJ702/ZQ-D	UK	
ZQ	FIU/FIDU	Mosquito VI	42-46	HJ702/ZQ-D	UK	
ZQ	FIU/FIDU	Beaufighter VIf	42-45	V8329/ZQ-G	UK	
ZQ	FIU/FIDU	Hurricane IIc	43-45	Z3887/ZQ-M	UK	
ZQ	FIU/FIDU	Oxford	c 43-46	PH487/ZQ-A	UK	
ZQ	FIU/FIDU	Mosquito XVII	4.43-45	DZ659/ZQ-H	UK	
ZQ	FIU/FIDU	Mosquito XII	5.43-10.44	HK208/ZQ-19	UK	
ZQ	FIU/FIDU	Mosquito XIII	12.43-1.45	HK478/ZQ-G	UK	
ZQ	FIU/FIDU	Mosquito XIX	9.44-46	MM682/ZQ-K	UK	
ZQ	FIU/FIDU	Wellington XIII	44-8.45	NB855/ZQ-C	UK	
ZQ	FIU/FIDU	Liberator	45	*****/ZQ-E	UK	
ZQ	FIU/FIDU	Auster III	45-46	NJ896/ZQ	UK	
ZQ	FIU/FIDU	Tempest V	45-46	EJ524/ZQ-A2	UK	
ZQ	FIU/FIDU	Mosquito XXX	45-46	NT301/G		
ZQ-W					UK	
ZQ	FIU/FIDU	Welkin II	5.44-8.44	DX289/ZQ-V	UK	
ZQ	FIU/FIDU	Meteor III	46	EE348/ZQ-J	UK	
ZQ	FIU/FIDU	Tempest II	46	MW385/ZQ-T	UK	
ZR	613	Hector I	11.39-6.40	K8116/ZR-K	UK	
ZR	613	Lysander II, III	4.40-4.42	T1438/ZR-F	UK	
ZR	2 OTU	Blenheim IV	5.41-42	Z5723/ZR-Q6	UK	
ZR	107 (T)OTU	Oxford II	5.44-3.45	W6634/ZR-UK	UK	
ZR	107 (T)OTU	Dakota III	5.44-3.45	KG612/ZR-NK	UK	to 1333 CU
ZR	1333 CU	Dakota III	3.45-47	KG422/ZR-F	UK	ex 107 (T)OTU
ZR	1333 CU	Dakota IV	3.45-47	KN634/ZR-W	UK	
ZS	233	Blenheim I	10.39-1.40	L8716/ZS-4	UK	
ZS	233	Hudson I	9.39-7.42	P5117/ZS-S	UK	
ZS	233	Hudson II	10.40-7.41	T9378/ZS-U	UK	
ZS	233	Hudson III	4.41-7.42	T9447/ZS-A	UK	
ZS	233	Hudson V	7.41-7.44	AM559/ZS-V	UK	
ZS	1336 CU	Dakota III	6.45-3.46	KG447/ZS-V	UK	
ZT	258	Hurricane I, IIa	12.40-10.41	Z3826/ZT-A	UK	
ZT	258	Hurricane IIb	3.42-11.43	BM125/ZT-R	FE	
ZT	258	Hurricane IIc	11.43-8.44	LD365/ZT-A	FE	
ZT	258	Thunderbolt I	9.44-1.45	HB984/ZT-S	FE	
ZT	258	Thunderbolt II	11.44-12.45	KJ366/ZT-X	FE	
ZT	20 OTU	Wellington Ic	5.40-8.43	R3232/ZT-H	UK	E Flt
ZT	20 OTU	Anson I	41	N5017/ZT-M	UK	E Flt
ZT	97 C Flt		45		UK	use not known
ZU	1664 HCU	Halifax II	5.43-11.44	BB201/ZU-E	UK	

Code	Unit	Type	Dates	Example	Theatre	Remarks
ZU	1664 HCU	Halifax V	9.43-11.44	DK248/ZU-C	UK	
ZU	1664 HCU	Halifax IIIa	11.44-4.45	MX587/ZU-G	UK	
ZV	19 OTU	Whitley IV	5.40-9.44	K9049/ZV-T	UK	C, D Flts
ZV	19 OTU	Whitley V	5.40-9.44	Z9200/ZV-G	UK	C, D Flts
ZW	140	Spitfire I	9.41-42	R7139/ZW-C	UK	
ZW	140	Blenheim IV	9.41-8.43	R3825/ZW-L	UK	
ZW	1359 Flt		45		UK	use not known
ZX	145	Spitfire Vb	4.42-8.43	AB502/ZX-B	MedME	
ZX	145	Spitfire VIII	8.43-8.45	JF952/ZX-M	MedME	red outlined white
ZX	145	Spitfire IX	6.43-8.45	MT928/ZX-M	MedME	
ZX	4 TEU	Master III	1.44-3.44	DL781/ZX-D	UK	to 3 TEU
ZX	3 TEU	Typhoon Ib	3.44-12.44	SW627/ZX-X	UK	ex 4 TEU
ZX	3 TEU	Master I	3.44-12.44		UK	
ZX	3 TEU	Master III	3.44-12.44	DL781/ZX-D	UK	
ZX	3 TEU	Martinet	3.44-12.44	JN307/ZX-*	UK	to 55 OTU
ZX	55 OTU	Master II	12.44-6.45	T8566/ZX	UK	ex 3 TEU
ZX	55 OTU	Martinet	12.44-6.45		UK	
ZX	55 OTU	Hurricane II	12.44-6.45	*****/ZX-S	UK	
ZY	247	Hurricane IIc	1.42-2.43	BD634/ZY-V	UK	
ZY	247	Typhoon Ib	1.43-8.45	JP505/ZY-T	UK, Eur	
ZY	247	Tempest II	8.45-5.46	MW396/ZY-T	UK	
ZZ	220	Fortress III	4.44-8.45	HB791/ZZ-U	UK	
ZZ	220	Liberator III	10.44-45	LV344/ZZ-C	UK	
ZZ	220	Liberator V	12.44-5.46	BZ984/ZZ-C	UK	
ZZ	220	Liberator VI	12.44-5.46	KN703/ZZ-K	UK	
ZZ	58 OTU	Spitfire II	1.41-10.43		UK	to 2 TEU
ZZ	2 TEU	Spitfire II	10.43-6.44	P****/ZZ-H	UK	ex 58 OTU

Dispersed around Digby in June 1945 are the Mustang IVs of No. 442 Sqn RCAF. The nearest aircraft is KH668/Y2-T, which wears full dayfighter camouflage, while others can be seen in natural metal finish. (A. J. Mallandaine)

No. 518 Sqn based at Aldergrove gave the Hurricanes of its C Flight a double individual letter as can be seen on this Mk IIc, PZ815/Y3-HI. The photograph was taken just after the war and the squadron badge was added to the nose in a pre-war-style six-pointed mullet. (R. E. Hilliard)

With its sooty black finish and the lighter parts of roundels and code overpainted with a dark wash the finish of Whitley V Z9226/ ZA-K of No. 10 Sqn is typical of the night bombers of the winter of 1940/1. The characteristic nose-down attitude of the Whitley is also evident. (MoD)

Some of the Spitfire VIIIs which served in northern Australia with Nos 548 and 549 Sqns had a natural metal finish by 1945 as is illustrated by A58-379/ZF-Z of the latter unit. Although notionally RAF units, their aircraft were given Australian serial numbers. (B. Wallis)

Coastal Command Numerical Codes
1942 to July 1944

On 16 October 1942 an instruction was promulgated within RAF Coastal Comand headed 'Instructions for marking and camouflaging of aircraft'. It stated, *inter alia*,

> ... the use of squadron code letters within Coastal Command will be dispensed with, with effect from 1 November 1942. It will be noted however that the third letter for individual aircraft identification may be kept. (PRO AIR 15/285)

In reality it appears that from mid-1943 a new system of numerical codes was instituted based on stations and involving operational squadrons. Units operating similar types on the same base were given single-digit unit codes, starting with '1'. This was not deemed likely to lead to confusion since Coastal Command units were widely dispersed and aircraft from one wing were unlikely to need to re-formate with those from another.

It seems that in general the lower the unit number the lower the unit code, unless the wing was joined later by a lowernumbered unit. Apeculiarity of the system is that there are fewer '1' coded units than those coded '2'. It appears likely, therefore, that not all units required to use '1' ever applied it, especially if they were the only unit on a base, or possibly the '1' was deemed by default the senior unit! It is known that some transferring units retained their earlier codes, inevitably causing confusion. It also appears that in several cases the higher-numbered units transferred to a new base, which would then have '2' and '3' coded squadrons but not a '1' coded unit which had remained at the original base. The system was eventually abolished in July 1944, when two-character codes were reintroduced.

Known applications of single-number codes are given below, with those suspected being also shown in italics. The two-character unit codes applied before and after the numerical code usage are shown: it should be noted that these were not necessarily applied to aircraft of the types using the numerical code. It needs to be said that some units – especially the strike squadrons operating Beaufighters – moved frequently as operational requirements dictated, and this is reflected in some overlap of dates.

There is no clear pattern to the coastal strike squadrons with no evidence of the North Coates Wing (Nos 236 and 254) using '1' and '2'. Likewise, for Nos 248 and 489 Squadrons, yet with Nos 404 and 455 clearly using '2', someone must have had '1' – No. 489 being at Leuchars at the same time as Nos 455 (2) and 333 (3). With No. 404 Squadron being '2', which unit at Davidstow Moor used '1'?

An example of the system in practice was the Liberator Wing at St Eval in mid-1944. By April 1944 it comprised three squadrons – Nos 53 (1), 224 (2) and 547 (3), however, later in the month a fourth squadron – No. 206 (previously using '1' coded Fortresses in the Azores) arrived. It was coded '4', the only known use of this number. it is tempting to think that this was done rather than re-code or re-paint all the aircraft of the higher-numbered 224 and 547 Squadrons.

Station	Code	Unit	Type	Dates	Example	Prev/later codes
Ballykelly	1	59	Liberator V	9.43-6.45	FL946/1-M	TR/WE
	2	86	*Liberator V*	9.43-6.45		*BX/XQ*
Chivenor	1	172	Wellington XIV	4.42-9.44	HF113/1-P	WN/OG
	1	407	Wellington XII	4.43-7.43	HF115/1-W	RR/-
	2	304	Wellington XIV	2.44-9.44	HF386/2-W	-/QD
	2	407	Wellington XIV	7.43-1.44	NB839/2-R	RR/-
	3	612	Wellington XIV	3.44-9.44	MP714/3-F	WL/8W
Davidstow Moor	*1*	236	*Beaufighter X*	5.44-8.44		*ND & FA/MB*
	2	404	Beaufighter X	5.44-7.44	LZ409/2-S	EE/EO
Holmsley S	1	58	Halifax II	7.43-12.43	HR744/1-O	GE/BY
	2	502	Halifax II	9.43-12.43	YG/V9	
Lagens (Azores)	1	206	Fortress II	10.43-4.44	FK190/1-J	VX/PQ
	2	220	Fortress II	10.43-6.45	FK189/2-X	/ZZ
Langham	2	455	Beaufighter X	4.44-10.44	NE812/2-M	UB/UB
	3	489	*Beaufighter X*	4.44-10.44		*XA/P6*
Leuchars	1	235	*Beaufighter X*	2.1.43-8.43		*LA/LA*
	2	455	Beaufighter X	2.42-4.44	NE775/2-X	UB/UB
	3	333	Mosquito II	5.43-4.44	DZ744/3-G	-/KK
	3	333	Mosquito VI	9.43-9.44	HP904/3-F	-/KK
Limavady	2	407	Wellington XIV	1.44-4.44	HF134/2-M	RR/-
	3	612	Wellington XIV	1.44-3.44	MP714/3-F	WL/8W
Lough Erne	1	201	Sunderland III	11.43-3.44		ZM/NS
	2	422	Sunderland III	11.43-11.44	EK591/2-U	DG/DG
	3	423	Sunderland III	11.42-8.45	EK513/3-J	AB/YI
Manston	1	143	Beaufighter VIc	5.44-9.44		HO/NE
	2	415	*Albacore I*	?.44-7.44		*NH/6U*
N Coates	*1*	143	*Beaufighter VIc*	2.44-5.44		*HO/NE*

Station	Code	Unit	Type	Dates	Example	Prev/later codes
	2	*236*	*Beaufighter X*	*9.42-5.45*		*ND & FA/MB*
	3	*254*	*Beaufighter X*	*11.42-6.45*		*QY/QM*
Pembroke Dock	1	228	Sunderland III	5.43-6.45	ML770/1-P	DQ/UE
	2	461	Sunderland III	4.43-6.45	EK575/2-C	RB/UT
Portreath	1	143	Beaufighter VIc	Sep 43-Feb 44	JM172/1-J	HO/NE
	2	235	Beaufighter X	8.43-9.44		LA/LA
	3	235	Mosquito VI	6.44-9-44	HR118/3-W	LA/LA
	3	248	Beaufighter X	9.43-6.44		WR/DM & VV
St Davids	1	58	Halifax II	12.43-8.44		GE/BY
	2	502	Halifax II	12.43-9.44	HR686/2-J	YG/V9
St Eval	1	53	Liberator V	1.44-9.44	BZ781/1-A	PZ/FH
	2	224	Liberator V	4.44-9.44	BZ877/2-Q	QX/XB
	3	547	Liberator V	1.44-9.44	BZ882/3-P	-/2V
	4	206	Liberator VI	4.44-7.44	EW882/4-L	VX/PQ
Strubby	*2*	*280*	*Warwick II*	*10.43-9.44*		*YF/MF*
Wick	1	144	Beaufighter X	10.43-5.44		PL/PL
	2	404	Beaufighter X	4.43-5.44	NE669/2-A	EE/EO

Right: The first unit codes used by the RAAF were in a sequential single-letter form, thus No. 21 Sqn used R, as seen on the locally built CAC Wirraway A20-21 over Melbourne in 1940. (RAAF)

Below: Toward the end of the Second World War RAAF C-47B Dakotas wore a civil registration on the fin in addition to their full unit identity markings, as may be seen on A65-121/RE-R of No. 36 Sqn some time in 1945. The civil registration VH-RGI is positioned above the fin flash. (F. W. Lecksill)

C H A P T E R 6

RAAF Wartime

This chapter does not include units in the 400 series operating within RAF control in the UK.

The RAAF Minute Paper 9/1/396 dated 15 June 1939 outlined proposals for the identification of RAAF aircraft, described a method of identifying a unit's aircraft and listed proposed unit codes for those then in existence or which were planned for the future. Unlike the well-known RAF system, the RAAF unit code was a sequential single-letter allocation and aircraft would not carry an individual aircraft letter. Thus, No. 1 Squadron was allocated A, No. 2, B etc.

The RAAF HQ Aircraft General Instruction No. C11 dated 22 September 1939 not only formally described, in the form of a technical order, the aircraft finishes and markings, but listed single- letter squadron code letters as given in the 15 June minute paper. These codes were to be grey on camouflaged aircraft and black on aluminium finishes, and were used by operational Australian- based units until early 1942.

However, those squadrons which were deployed alongside the RAF in Europe (No. 10), Middle East (No. 3) and Malaya (Nos 1, 8 and 21) were allocated RAF two-letter codes, it is presumed from the SD 110 listing. So were the many 400-series squadrons formed from 1941 in these theatres. Like any system, there were exceptions.

The P-39 Airacobras and Wirraways of No. 23 Squadron in 1942 wore individual aircraft letters alongside the squadron code letter, T, thus TY, giving rise to the false assumption that TY was this unit's code. Some squadrons which moved into forward areas during 1942 ceased to use the single-letter unit codes, but did use individual aircraft letters from A to Z. Units involved included No. 2 Squadron (Hudson), No. 11 (Catalina), No. 22 (Boston), No. 30 (Beaufighter) and Nos 75 and 77 (Kittyhawks). To add to the confusion, when No. 75 Squadron began to operate with No. 76 at Milne Bay, New Guinea, from about July 1942, the latter squadron introduced a unique system. The letter I was painted directly in front of the individual letter (IA, IB and so on) to distinguish 76's Kittyhawks from those of No. 75, A29- 96/IU and A29-142/IF being examples.

Code	Unit	Type	Dates	Example	Theatre	Remarks
A	1	Anson	8.39-5.40	A4-47	Australia	to US in Malaya
B	2	Anson	8.39-7.40	A4-26	Aus/SWPA	
B	2	Hudson I, II	6.40-5.42	A16-12	Aus/SWPA	
C	3	Demon	39-6.40	A1-59	Australia	to OS, CV in MedME
D	4	Wirraway II	40-43	A20-176	Aus/SWPA	
E	5	Wirraway II	40-43	A20-286	Aus/SWPA	
F	6	Anson	39-7.40	A4-31	Australia	
F	6	Hudson I, II	40-42	A16-73	Aus/SWPA	
G	7	Hudson II, IV	40-42	A16-84	Australia	
H	8	Hudson I, II	41-2.42			to NN in Malaya
J	9	Seagull V	39-42	A2-19	Aus/SWPA	
J	9	Dolphin		A35-1		
K	10	Sunderland I	12.39-40		UK	to GN, RB
L	11 PBY-5	Catalina				use not known
M	12	Anson	12.39-6.40	A4-	Aus/SWPA	use not known
M	12	Hudson	6.40-42	A16-	Aus/SWPA	use not known
M	12	Wirraway II	40-41	A20-132		
N	13	Anson	39-40	A4-4	Australia	
N	13	Hudson I, II	40-42	A16-68	Aus/SWPA	
P	14	Anson	39-5.40	A4-25	Australia	
P	14	Hudson I, II	40-42	A16-29		
R	21	Anson	39-5.40	A4-1	Australia	
R	21	Wirraway I		A20-21		to GA in Malaya
S	22	Anson	39-5.40	A4-21	Australia	
S	22	Wirraway I/II	40-41	A20-198		
T	23	Wirraway I/II	40-41	A20-29	Australia	

Code	Unit	Type	Dates	Example	Theatre	Remarks
T	23	Hudson	41	A16-3		
T	23	Wirraway II	42-43	A20-92/TG		individual a/c letter added
T	23	P-39D Airacobra	42-43	A53-12/TX		
U	24	Wirraway II	40-42	A20-137	Aus/SWPA	
V	25	Wirraway II	40-42	A20-110	Australia	
Y	Comm Flt	Anson	39-41	A4-43	Australia	
Y	Comm Flt	Cadet	39-41	A6-19	Australia	
Z	Survey Flt	Gannet	40-42	A14-6	Australia	

The single-letter codes listed in General Instruction C11 generally fell into disuse from mid-1942 and were superseded by two letter codes promulgated in AFCO-A3 on 4 January 1943. These were periodically updated as further units were formed and remained in use until around 1948, the squadrons based in Japan being among the last to wear them.

As with the RCAF at the start of WW2, when the 1943 list of RAAF codes was promulgated Nos 1 and 2 sqns RAAF were allocated the same codes as 1 and 2 sqns RAF.

Code	Unit	Type	Dates	Example	Theatre	Remarks
AM	77	Kittyhawk III, IV	3.42-9.45	A29-1055/AM-H	SWPA	
AM	77	Mustang IV	9.45-47	A68-761/AM-W	Japan	
BF	5	Wirraway	1.44-12.44	A20-588/BF-R	SWPA	
BF	5	Boomerang	7.43-8.46	A46-214/BF-T	SWPA	
BK	35	C-47 Dakota	44-6.46	A65-100/BK-P	SWPA	
BT	33	Anson	11.42-43			
BT	33	C-47 Dakota	44-46	A65-32/BT-Q	Aus/SWPA	
BU	80	Kittyhawk IV	9.43-7.46	A29-629/BU-B	SWPA	
BV	102	B-24J Liberator	5.45-3.46	A72-340/BV-G	SWPA	
CS	*13*	*Hudson I*				*no known use*
CS	*13*	*PV-1 Ventura*				*no known use*
CV	3	*Tomahawk II*	*1.42*	******/CV*		*no individual a/c code letters*
CV	3	Kittyhawk I-IV	12.41-11.44	FS407/CV-Z (II)	MedME	
CV	3	Mustang III	11.44-4.45	FB299/CV-Y	MedME	
CV	3	Mustang IV	2.45-7.45	KH755/CV-W	MedME	
DB	*3 CU*	*various*				*no known use*
DD	15	Beaufort VIII	1.44-11.45	A9-500/DD-W	Aus/SWPA	
DQ	41	Short S 23 C Class	1.43-6.43	A18-14/DQ-B	Australia	
DQ	41	Dornier Do 24K	6.43-9.44	A49-3/DQ-C	SWPA	
DU	22	Boston III	43-45	A28-11/DU-M	SWPA	
DU	22 A-20A, C, G	Boston	43-45	A28-34/DU-B	SWPA	
DU	22	Beaufort VIII	12.44-10.45		SWPA	
DU	22	Beaufighter 21	45	A8-50/DU-H	SWPA	
EH	31	Beaufighter Ic, VIc, X, XI	43-45	A19-118/EH-W (VI)	SWPA	
EH	31	Beaufighter 21	44-45	A8-17/EH-X	SWPA	
EV	*1 CU*	*Various*			*Aus*	*no use of code*
EY	*60*	*Wirraway*	*6.43-9.43*			*no use of code*
FA	82	P-39F Airacobra	6.43-9.43	A53-6/FA-A	Australia	
FA	82	Kittyhawk Ia	43-44	A29-133/FA-B	SWPA	
FA	82	Kittyhawk III, IV	44-9.45	A29-844/FA-E	SWPA	
FA	82	Mustang IV	10.45-10.48	A68-759/FA-U	SWPA/Japan	
FD	34	C-47 Dakota	43-6.46	A65-12/FD-H	SWPA	
FJ	11	PBY-5, PBY-5A, PB2B-2	43-2.46	A24-69/FJ-P	SWPA	
FX	6	Hudson III/IV	43	A16-73/FX-F	SWPA	
FX	6	Beaufort VIII/Va	8.43-1.46	A9-396/FX-F	SWPA	

Code	Unit	Type	Dates	Example	Theatre	Remarks
GA	21	Wirraway	6.40-11.41	A20-47/GA-B	Australia/FE	
GA	21	Buffalo	10.41-1.42	AN180/GA-B	FE	
GA	75	Kittyhawk III/IV	44-45	A29-1019/GA-E	SWPA	
GM	18 (NEI)	B-25D Mitchell	3.42-45	N5-168/GM-P	SWPA	
GN	10	Sunderland I	9.39-11.39	P9602/GN-G	UK	
GR	24	P-39F Airacobra	c 8.43	A53-3/GR-T	Australia	
GR	24	Vengeance II	4.43-5.44	A27-226/GR-D	SWPA	
GR	24	B-24J Liberator	6.44-45	A72-42/GR-M	SWPA	
HF	*40 PBM*	*Mariner*				*no known use*
HF	*40*	*Sunderland III*				*no known use*
HM	*11 CU*	*Various*				*no known use*
HU	78	Kittyhawk III/IV	43-45	A29-574/HU-Q	SWPA	
HU	78	Mustang IV	45-46	A68-71/HU-A	Australia	
JE	107 OS2U-3	Kingfisher	43-10.45	A48-9/JE-K	SWPA	
JM	*32*	*Hudson III*	*2.42-43*		*Austraia*	*no known use*
JM	32	Beaufort VIII	3.43-11.45	A9-332/JM-F	SWPA	
JN	66	Anson I	5.43-1.44	W1948/JN-W	Australia	
JU	*2 CU*	*Various*				*no known use*
KF	5 CU	Beaufort VIII	6.44-3.46	A9-651/KF-L	Aus/SWPA	
KF	5 CU	DH 84 Dragon	43-4	A34-82/KF-H	Aus/SWPA	
KF	5 CU	UC-64A Norseman	44-6	A71-10/KF-H	Aus/SWPA	
KF	5 CU	Oxford	43	BF976/KF-W	Aus/SWPA	
KF	5 CU	Anson I	43-5	DJ447/KF-L	Aus/SWPA	
KF	5 CU	Walrus	43-5	Z1804/KF-K	Aus/SWPA	
KF	5 CU	Vengeance IVA	44-5	A27-407/KF-U	Aus/SWPA	
KO	2	Hudson IIIA	1.43-12.43	A16-160/KO-X	SWPA	
KO	2	Beaufort VIII	12.43-9.44	A9-576/KO-Z	SWPA	
KO	2	B-25D Mitchell	5.44-12.45	A47-21/KO-l	SWPA	
KO	2	B-25J Mitchell	6.44-5.46	A47-43/KO-B	SWPA	
KP	*111 ASR Flt*	*PBY-5A Catalina*	*12.44-147*		*SWPA*	*no known use*
KP	*111 ASR Flt*	*Beaufort VIII, IX*	*1.46-5.46*		*SWPA*	*no known use*
KT	7	Beaufort Va, VIII	9.42-12.45	A9-182/KT-X	Aus/SWPA	
KV	*17 AOP Flt*	*Various*			*SWPA*	*no known use*
LB	84	Boomerang	2.43-10.43	A46-50/LB-V	SWPA	
LB	84	Kittyhawk III, IV	10.43-1.45	A29-354/LB-T	SWPA	
LB	84	Mustang IV	1.45-1.46	A68-585/LB-V	SWPA	
LJ	*112 ASR Flt*	*PBY-5A Catalina*	*12.44-1/47*		*SWPA*	*no known use*
LV	201 Flt	B-24J, M Liberator	3.45-3.46	A72-357/LV-D	SWPA	
LY	30	Beaufighter I, VI, X	42-8.46	A19-159/LY-C	SWPA	
LY	30	Beaufighter 21	45	A8-84/LY-R	SWPA	
LY	30	Beaufort VIII	1.45-9.45	A9-488/LY-L	SWPA	
MB	?	Lodestar			Australia	
MH	83	Boomerang	6.43-8.45	A46-122/MH-R	SWPA/Aus	
MJ	21	Vengeance Ia	9.43-c 5.44	A27-60/MJ-A	SWPA	
MJ	21	B-24J Liberator	44-45	A72-56/MJ-W	SWPA	
MJ	*21*	*Beaufort VIII*	*1.46-8.46*		*Australia?*	*no known use*
MK	67	Anson I	43-45	EG504/MK-S	SWPA?	
MP	86	Kittyhawk III, IV	43-45	A29-302/MP-B	SWPA	
MP	86	Mustang IV	1.45-12.45	A68-563/MP-O	SWPA	
MV	*119 (NEI)*	*Lodestar, B-25D Mitchell*	*9.43-12.43*		*SWPA*	*no known use*
NA	1	Beaufort VIII	12.43-6.45	A9-378/NA-P	Australia	
NA	1	Mosquito FB VI	1.45-6.46	A52-526/NA-E	SWPA	
NF	*16 AOP Flt*	*Auster V*			*SWPA*	*no known use*
NH	12	Vengeance II	10.42-8.44	A27-230/NH-S	SWPA	
NH	12	B-24J Liberator	8.45-	A72-401/NH-L	SWPA	

Code	Unit	Type	Dates	Example	Theatre	Remarks
NJ	73	Anson	43-7.44	AX261/NJ-K	Australia	
NN	8	Hudson I	41-*c* 2.42	A16-76/NN-F	Malaya	
NR	113 ASR Flt	PBY-5A, PB2B-2R	1.45-4.46	A24-104/NR-K	Aus/Japan	
NV	23	Wirraway	-7.43	A20-347/NV-E	SWPA	
NV	23	Vengeance IA, II	7.43-5.44	A27-235/NV-A	SWPA	
NV	23	B-24J, M Liberator	6.44-45	A72-100/NV-A	SWPA	
NW	3	Gladiator II	10.40-2.41	L9044/NW-Z	MedME	code is for 33 Sqn RAF
NX	200 Flt	B-24J, M Liberator	2.45-12.45	A72-183/NX-R	Aus/SWPA	
OB	*92*	*Beaufort VIII*	*5.45-9.45*		*Australia*	*no known use*
OB	92	Beaufighter 21			SWPA	
OB	92	Mosquito FB 40	6.45-1.46		Australia	
OM	37	C-47B Dakota	44-45	A65-105/OM-V	SWPA	
OM	37	Lodestar	44-45	A67-10/OM-L	Aus/SWPA	
OS	3	Lysander II	*c* 1.41-3.41	*****/OS-I	MedME	
OS	3	Hurricane I	*c* 2.41-6.41	P3765/OS-J	MedME	
OX	43	PBY-5A Catalina	5.43-4.46	A24-70/OX-M	SWPA	
PK	38	C-47A, B Dakota	44-45	A65-60/PK-K	Aus/SWPA	
PN	14	Beaufort V, Va, VII, VIII	12.42-11.45	A9-177/PN-R	SWPA	
PP	71	Anson	12.42-8.44	AW665/PP-B	SWPA	
PU	*1 PRU*	*Wirraway*				*no known use*
QE	4	Wirraway	*c* 12.41-44	A20-637/QE-J	SWPA	
QE	4	Boomerang	6.43-8.45	A46-195/QE-A	SWPA	
QH	100	Beaufort V/VIII	2.42-5.46	A9-626/QH-X	SWPA	
QK	*87*	*P-38, Wirraway, Mosquito PR XVI*	*45*		*SWPA*	*no known use*
QS	1 R&C	Boomerang	*c* 45	A46-***/SQ-A	Australia	
QY	452	Spitfire V	43-1.44	A58-238/QY-G	Australia	
QY	452	Spitfire VIII	1.44-45	A58-532/QY-W	SWPA	
RB	10	Sunderland I-III	11.39-43	W4004/RB-Z	UK	
RB	10	Sunderland V	44-45	ML839/RB-A	UK	
RB	20	PBY-5A Catalina	43-44	A24-81/RB-L	SWPA	
RB	20	PB2B-2 Catalina	45-46	A24-372/RB-Q	SWPA	
RE	36	DC-2	*c* 43	A30-12/RE-A	Australia	
RE	36	C-47A/B Dakota	43-45	A65-48/RE-W	SWPA	
RK	42	PBY-5A Catalina	6.44-11.45	A24-100/RK-L	SWPA	
RR	*120 NEI*	*Kittyhawk IV*	*12.43-*			*no known use*
SF	13	Hudson III	40-43	A16-199/SF-R	Australia	
SF	13	Beaufort VIII	8.43-5.44	A9-380/SF-H	SWPA	
SF	13	PV-1 Ventura	11.44-1.46	A59-68/SF-U	SWPA	
SH	*85*	*Boomerang*	*4.43-1.45*		*Australia*	*no known use*
SH	85	Spitfire V	9.44-12.45	A58-16/SH-R	Australia	
SJ	25	Vengeance II, IV	7.43-1.45	A27-228/SJ-A	Australia	
SJ	25	B-24L, M Liberator	1.45-3.46	A72-150/SJ-L	Aus/SWPA	
SK	93	Beaufort VIII	7.45-5.46	A9-401/SK-A	SWPA	
SK	93	Beaufighter 21	*c* 4.45	A8-85/SK-F	SWPA	
SV	76	Kittyhawk III, IV	4.42-10.45	A29-357/SV-A	SWPA	
SV	76	Mustang IV	10.45-10.48	A68-723/SV-B	SWPA/Japan	
SU	Survey Unit/ 87 PR Flt	Hudson IV	45-46	A16-130/SU-H	Australia	
SU	Survey Unit/ 87 PR Flt	Anson I	45	MG973/SU-D	Australia	
SU	Survey Unit/ 87 PR Flt	Mosquito FB.40, PR.41	46-48	A52-306/SU-S	Australia	

Code	Unit	Type	Dates	Example	Theatre	Remarks
SU	Survey Unit/ 87 PR Sqn	Mosquito PR.XVI	45-47	A52-603/SU-B	Australia	
TA	12 LASU	Beaufort VIII, IX	11.45-4.46	A9-719/TA-A	SWPA	
TA	12 LASU	Tiger Moth	45	A17-489/TA-L	SWPA	
TX	*9 LASU*	*Various*				*no known use*
UB	*10 LASU*	*Beaufort*				*no known use*
UP	79	Spitfire Vc	4.43-12.44	JG807/UP-P	SWPA	
UP	79	Spitfire VIII	12.44-11.45	A58-505/UP-S	SWPA	
US	1	Hudson I	41-*c* 2.42	A16-5/US-B	Malaya	
UV	8	Beaufort VIII	3.43-1.46	A9-238/UV-E	SWPA	
UX	99	B-24J Liberator	2.45-6.46	A72-311/UX-O	Australia	
VM	4 CU	Vengeance IVA	44-46	A27-410/VM-T	Australia	
XB	457	Spitfire Vc	43	BS201/XB-Q	Australia	
XJ	*6 CU*	*Beaufort, Walrus, Dragon, Vengeance*	*4.45-12.45*		*Australia*	*no known use*
XJ	6 CU	Anson I	4.45-12.45	MG842/XJ-T	Australia	
YB	*7 CU*	*Various*				*no known use*
YQ	9	Walrus	5.42-45	X9514/YQ-A	SWPA	
YQ	9	Seagull V	43-45	A2-4/YQ-P	SWPA	
YQ	9	PBY-5A Catalina			SWPA	
ZA	8 CU	Boomerang	2.44-8.44	A46-94/ZA-O	SWPA	
ZA	8 CU	Beaufort VIII	9.44-3.46	A9-369/ZA-J	SWPA	
ZA	8 CU	Walrus	44-45	HD874/ZA-W	SWPA	
ZA	8 CU	PBY-5A Catalina	44-45	A24-92/ZA-X	SWPA	
ZA	*8 CU*	*Vengeance, Do 24K*	*44*		*SWPA*	*no known use*
ZP	457	Spitfire V	43-4.44	A58-44/ZP-U	Australia	
ZP	457	Spitfire VIII	4.44-45	A58-615/ZP-Y	SWPA	

OS2U-3 Kingfisher floatplane A48-12/JE-N of No. 107 Sqn taxies out at Darwin for another sortie in 1944. Because of the possibility confusion with the red Japanese marking, the RAAF adopted a blue/white roundel in the Pacific and East Indies. (via N. Mackenzie)

Among the miscellany of types used for second line duties with No. 12 Local Air Support Unit (LASU) was Tiger Moth A17-489/TA-L, resplendent in full tactical camouflage and markings! (J. Mercer)

In early 1943 the RAAF introduced random two-letter unit codes as shown on these locally built CAC Boomerangs of No. 5 Sqn on 21 July 1944; the nearer aircraft is CA13 A46-200 while beyond is CA19 A46-212/BF-O. (via F. G. Swanborough)

On the few Airacobras used by No. 23 Sqn during 1942, an aircraft letter was placed next to the unit code letter, which led to the idea that the unit's code was TY. P-39D A53-12/T-Y is seen at Lowood, Queensland. (via F. G. Swanborough)

The RAAF was a major user of the Beaufort against the Japanese. This radar-equipped Mk VIII A9-626/QH-X of No. 100 Sqn leads others in an attack on Wewak, New Guinea on 20 January 1945. It was lost three days later. (via R. Hayward)

CHAPTER 7

RCAF Wartime

This chapter excludes units in the 400 series operating within RAF control in the UK.

On 1 August 1939, two-letter unit code combinations were issued to the then existing units of the RCAF and were first ordered to be applied in August 1940. Interestingly, the allocation is precisely the same as the pre-war RAF allocations of April 1939 for squadrons with the same numbers. To distinguish aircraft of home-based units, the codes and aircraft letters were underlined with a bar thus: AB-C. Units such as No. 1 Squadron RCAF (later No. 401 Squadron) that deployed to the UK were allocated codes from the RAF SD 110 listing.

A second list was issued during 1940 and as further squadrons were formed in Canada they were allocated codes from this list. In May 1942 a revised list was issued with

instructions that they were effective immediately for all operational aircraft. On 16 October 1942 RCAF HQ informed both Eastern and Western Air Commands that, for security reasons, the use of unit codes on home-based operational aircraft was to cease immediately. However, as seen in the tables there were numerous exceptions.

While the RCAF did not employ numerical codes per se, during the summer of 1942 the Hurricanes of the Dartmouth-based Nos 126, 127 and 128 Squadrons went on to centralised maintenance and were thus pooled. Unit codes were replaced by the numeral codes 1 and 2, which presumably related to elements of the central maintenance unit.

RCAF overseas units in the period 1939–45 are covered in the RAF section in Chapter 5.

Code	Unit	Type	Dates	Example	Theatre (N America unless noted)	Remarks
1	Dartmouth Pool	Hurricane XII	7.42-45	5489/1-E		126, 127, 128 Sqns
2	Dartmouth Pool	Hurricane XII	7.42-45	5658/2-D		126, 127, 128 Sqns
AE	130	Kittyhawk I	5.42-10.42			
AE	130	Hurricane XII	9.42-3.44	5452/AE-A		
AF	6	Stranraer	5.42-10.42			
AF	6	Norseman IV	5.42-10.42			
AG	122	Shark II	5.42-10.42	504/AG-D		
AG	122	Lysander II	5.42-10.42	445/AG-K		
AG	122	Goose	5.42-10.42	940/AG-P		
AG	122	Norseman IV	5.42-10.42	2480/AG-R		
AN	13	Norseman IV	8.40-5.42	2480/AN-G		
AN	13	Hudson I	8.40-5.42			
AN	13	Goose	11.40-5.42	917/AN-S		
AN	13	Lockheed 10	5.41-5.42	7648/AN-Y		
AN	13	Delta I & II	5.41-11.41	685/AN-P		
AN	13	Bolingbroke IV	10.41-5.42	9034/AN-J		
AN	13	Stranraer	10.41-5.42			
AN	160	Canso A	5.43-6.43	9813/AN-L		
AQ	14	Anson V (P)	6.44-1.47			
AY	110	Lysander II	12.39-2.40		UK	use not known
AZ	3 OTU	?	42-44	?		
BA	125	Hurricane I, XII	5.42-10.42			use not known
BD	4	Stranraer	5.41-10.41			
BF	14	Harvard I	1.42-5.42			
BF	14	Kittyhawk I	1.42-5.42			
BK	115	Bolingbroke I, IV	8.41-5.42	9059/BK-J		
BT	113	Hudson III	2.42-5.42	BW447/BT-T		
BV	126	Hurricane XII	5.42-10.42	BW850/BV-T		
DE	5	Canso A	5.42-10.42	9737/DE-E		
DK	32 OTU	Hampden				use not known
DK	32 OTU	Catalina I	c 41-42	****/DK-G		use not known
DM	119	Bolingbroke I	8.40-8.41	702/DM-A		

Code	Unit	Type	Dates	Example	Theatre (N America unless noted)	Remarks
DM	119	Bolingbroke IV	8.41-5.42	9043/DM-F		
DZ	162	Canso A	*c* 42	9750/DZ-A		
EA	145	Hudson I	5.42-10.42	762/EA-D		
ED	*4 OTU*					*use not known*
EF	*36 OTU*					*use not known*
EN	121	Goose	5.42-10.42	921/EN-B		
ET	*2 OTU*	*Mitchell*	*7.42-8.42*			*use not known*
EX	*117*	*Stranraer*	*9.41-10.41*			*use not known*
FG	7	Shark III	5.42-9.43	546/FG-H		
FN	133	Hurricane XII	6.42-10.42	5398/FN-L		
FY	4	Stranraer	8.39-5.42	915/FY-B		
FY	4	Shark III	5.40-1.42	548/FY-F		
FY	4	Vedette VI	*c* 8.40	816?/FY-F		
FY	34 OTU	Ventura I	5.42-10.42	AE728/FY-F		RAF unit
GA	8	Bolingbroke IV	5.42-10.42			
GK	162	Canso A	*c* 42			
GR	*119*	*Hudson III*	*5.42-10.42*	*BW616/GR-Y*		*not confirmed*
GV	3 CAC det	Lysander II	40-42	461/GV-L		
HA	129	Hurricane XII	8.42-10.42	BW883/HA-X		
HJ	*9*	*Stranraer*	*5.42-10.42*			*use not known*
HM	32 OTU	Hampden	5.42-2.44	P5429/HM-B		
JK	10	Digby	5.42-10.42	751/JK-K		
JY	121	various comms types	5.42-10.42			*use not known*
KA	9	Stranraer	12.41-5.42	916/KA-A		
KD	*168*	*Dakota I, IV*	*2.44-4.46*			*use not known*
KL	11	Hudson III	5.42-10.42	BW403/KL-S?		
KO	2	Lysander II	11.39-12.39			
LB	*32 OTU*	*Hampden*				*use not known*
LM	113	Hudson III	5.42-10.42			
LR	31 OTU	Hudson VI	*c* 42			
LT	7	Shark II/III	12.41-5.42	550/LT-M		
LU	118 (later 1 CAC det)	Lysander II	9.40-5.42	463/LU-D		B Flt
LV	5 CAC det		5.42-10.42			
LZ	111	Kittyhawk I	5.42-10.42	AL201/LZ-H		
MA	114		8.39-10.39			not used
MK	13	Hudson I	5.42-6.42	775/MK-O		
MK	13	Lockheed 10	5.42-6.42	7648/MK-Y		
MK	13	Goose	5.42-10.42	924/MK-G		
MK	13	Stranraer	5.42-10.42	957/MK-F		
MR	4 CAC det					
MX	120	Delta II	8.40-7.41	676/MX-C		
MX	120	Hudson I	3.41-10.41	776/MX-T		
MX	120	Stranraer	11.41-5.42			
MY	*11*					*use not known*
NA	1	Hurricane I	39-40			To YO in UK
NK	*31 GRS*	*Anson*				*use not known*
NO	116	Catalina I	5.42-10.42	W8431/NO-H		
NO	116	Canso A	5.42-8.43			
OP	*3*	*? Wapiti*	*8.39-9.39*			*use not known*
OP	32 OTU	Beaufort I	5.42-10.42	N1029/OP-E		RAF unit
OP	32 OTU	Hampden I	*c* 42	*****/OP-R		
OY	11	Hudson I	10.39-5.42	785/OY-U		
PB	10	Digby	4.40-5.42	748/PB-V		
PO	4 CAC det					
PQ	117	Canso A	5.42-10.42	9701/PQ-N		
QE	*12*	*various types*	*40-42*			*use not known*
QG	6 CAC det					
QN	5	Stranraer	8.39-9.41	913/QN-B		

Code	Unit	Type	Dates	Example	Theatre (N America unless noted)	Remarks
QN	5	Canso A	10.41-5.42	9737/QN-E		
RA	S of AC		8.41-10.42			use not known
RA	128	Hurricane I	6.42-10.42			use not known
RD	34 OTU	Beaufort I	9.41-5.42	N1006/RD-B		RAF unit
RD	34 OTU	Hampden I				
RE	118	Goblin	12.40-9.41	341/RE-N		To 31 OTU
RE	118	Kittyhawk Ia	11.41-5.42	AK857/RE-H		
RS	120	Stranraer	5.42-10.42			
SZ	147	Bolingbroke IV	5.42-10.42	9066/SZ-K		
TF	127	Hurricane XII	7.42-10.42	BW863/TF-V		
TM	111	Shark II	7.40-1.41	501/TM-E		
TM	111	Lysander II	12.39-1.41	416/TM-A		
TM	111	Kittyhawk I	11.41-5.42	AK683/TM-N		
TN	161	Digby	4.43-5.44	754/TN-G		
TQ	2 CAC det					
UV	115	Bolingbroke IV	5.42-10.42	9140/UV-P		
UY	1 OTU		6.42-1.45			
VD	123	Lysander II	1.42-5.42			ex S of AC
VD	123	Goblin	1.42-2.42			
VD	123	Hurricane X	c 10.42	BW878/VD-M		
VW	118	Kittyhawk I	5.42-10.42	AE803/VW-H		
XE	6	Shark II	8.39-12.41	503/XE-B		
XE	6	Stranraer	11.41-5.42			
XE	6	Norseman IV	c 8.40-12.41	696/XE-Z		
XO	112	Lysander II	3.40-6.40			
XP	135	Hurricane XII	7.42-10.42	5579/XP-EI		
XX	6		39-42			use not known
XY	1 CAC det					
YA	14	Harvard I	5.42-10.42	3238/YA-F		
YA	14	Kittyhawk I	5.42-10.42	1059/YA-K		
YH	1 GRS	Anson I				use not known
YO	8	Delta II	8.40-11.41	672/YO-L		
YO	8	Bolingbroke IV	12.40-5.42	9048/YO-T		
YZ	2 CAC det					
ZD	116	Catalina I	7.41-5.42	Z2138/ZD-D		
ZD	116	Canso A	9.41-5.42	9781/ZD-M		
ZM	149	Beaufort I	10.42-6.43	N1030/ZM-N		
ZR	132	Kittyhawk I	5.42-10.42	AK851/ZR-H		

Above: Stranraer I 916/QN-P of No. 5 Sqn cleaves through the water during a take-off from Dartmouth, Nova Scotia, for a patrol off the east coast in June 1940. Although wearing wartime markings, unlike its RAF brethren it has not been camouflaged. (Canadian Forces)

Left: These two Bolingbroke IVs of No. 115 Sqn RCAF are seen flying over Alaska in late 1942. The BK code visible on 9059/BK-J is another example of the use of the RAF pre-war list, being the same as for No. 115 Sqn RAF. The code has been overpainted on the leading aircraft. (Canadian Forces)

Diverted from UK deliveries, these Kittyhawk Is belong to No. 111 Sqn RCAF and are seen on patrol over the Alaskan wilderness on 10 September 1942. They wear a code from the second RCAF issue of the summer of 1942. They are: AL10*/LZ-V; AK905/LZ-D and AL194/LZ-E. (Canadian Forces)

When the home-based RCAF expanded, so desperate was the need for fighters that the antiquated licence-built Grumman G-23 Goblins were pressed into use for air defence duties with No. 118 Sqn. Camouflaged and wearing full unit markings this formation is led by 341/RE-N with 335/RE-Y and 344/RE-W next. (Canadian Forces)

CHAPTER 8

Indian Air Force Wartime

The sole Indian Air Force (IAF) squadron at the outbreak of the Second World War was serving on the North West Frontier and also provided a coastal defence flight. The unit would have conformed to the use of unit codes as dictated by HQ RAF India, though no orders have been traced regarding the allocation of codes or the precise dates that the application and/or changes took effect. In practice, however, squadrons engaged on the frontier did not wear unit codes until ordered to deploy to their war stations.

Changes promulgated for RAF units are reasonably well known, but lack of precise records for the IAF has resulted in an element of educated conjecture. It is therefore probable that the first codes were applied to aircraft of No. 1 Squadron some time in late 1940 or early 1941. While it is unlikely that No. 2 Squadron used codes initially, it is known that they wore codes on their Audaxes and, as they wore No. 28 Squadron's allocated pre-war code US it is more than probable that they were adopted at the time of the re-equipment, that is September 1941. No. 3 Squadron used codes from the outset of its formation in October 1941 and it is probable that No. 4 Squadron did also from formation in February 1942. Information on this latter unit is particularly scarce and therefore its use and allocation is to some extent speculative.

When the squadrons were re-equipped with Hurricanes from late 1942, mainly in the TacR role, codes were dispensed with and their use never revived. The IAF was honoured with the prefix 'Royal' in March 1945.

Code	Unit	Type	Dates	Example	Theatre
AG*	4	Lysander II	2.42-6.43	*****/AG-W	India
MR	3	Audax	10.41-c 6.42	K5581/MR-O	India
NB	1	Wapiti	-8.41	?	India
NB	1	Hart	-11.41	?	India
NB	1	Audax	c 8.40-11.41	?	India
NB	1	Lysander II	8.41-6.42	N1255/NB-F	India/Burma
US	2	Wapiti	3.41-9.41	?	India
US	2	Audax	9.41-1.42	K4838/US-L	India
US	2	Lysander II	12.41-9.42	N****/US-A	India

Note - * possibly AQ

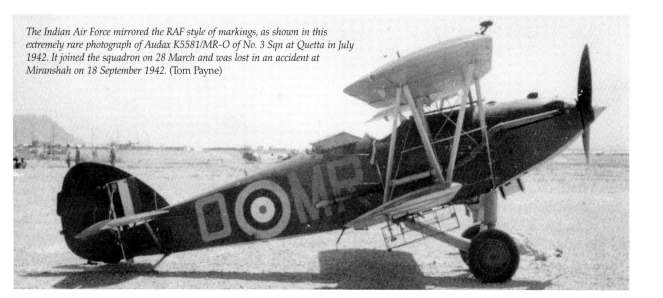

The Indian Air Force mirrored the RAF style of markings, as shown in this extremely rare photograph of Audax K5581/MR-O of No. 3 Sqn at Quetta in July 1942. It joined the squadron on 28 March and was lost in an accident at Miranshah on 18 September 1942. (Tom Payne)

Unit codes were only used by IAF units for a short time. The NB code used by the Lysander IIs of No. 1 Sqn has also been associated with Harts and Wapitis of No. 1 SFTS (I) and the date of the change is unclear. However, they were used by No. 1 Sqn by around late 1940 and were worn through the first Burma campaign as can be seen on L6847/NB-G. (RAF Kai Tak)

The only RNZAF Corsairs to wear any unit identification codes were those retained in New Zealand for operational training with several support units. The F4U-1D Corsair IVs of No. 3 SU used RK but because of the size of the US-style barred roundel, the aircraft letter was worn on the engine cowling. (via C. Darby)

CHAPTER 9

RNZAF Wartime and Post-war

This chapter excludes No. 75 Squadron and units in the 400 series operating within RAF control in the UK.

Like the other Commonwealth squadrons which were formed in the UK or Malaya alongside the RAF, RNZAF squadrons were allocated unit code combinations from the RAF SD 110 listing. New Zealand's total commitment to the Allied war effort in Europe left it dangerously exposed at home but as squadrons formed on either newly acquired US aircraft or obsolescent British biplanes, they were allocated two-letter unit codes, probably (though not confirmed) from a locally issued list.

These codes continued in use on home-based units throughout the Pacific war, though from late 1942 the wearing of codes on operational fighters and bombers deployed forward to the Solomon Islands was discontinued. After the war some of the small number of permanent RNZAF units continued to use squadron codes until the late 1940s.

Code	Unit	Type	Dates	Example	Theatre	Remarks
AX	14	Oxford I	4.49-50	NZ2116/AX	NZ	
FE	4 OTU	Kittyhawk I-IV	42-45	NZ3027/FE-V (Ia)	NZ	
FE	4 OTU	Harvard II	42-45	NZ1044/FE-9	NZ	
GF	3 OTU	PB2B-1	2.44-45	NZ4025/GF-C	Fiji	
HQ	14	Kittyhawk Ia	4.42-44	NZ3036/HQ-Q	NZ	
HQ	14	Harvard II	4.42-42		NZ	
HQ	GTS	Kittyhawk III	43-45	NZ3050/HQ-*	NZ	
HQ	GTS	Harvard IIa	4.42-45	NZ10**/HQ-6	NZ	
HQ	GTS	Hudson III	c 43-44	NZ2058/HQ-W	NZ	
JV	3	Hudson III	41-early 43	NZ2042/JV-G	NZ/SWPA	
JZ	15	P-40E	6.42-4.43	NZ3040/JZ-I	NZ	
JZ	15	P-40N	4.43-44	NZ3128/JZ-B	NZ	
JZ	FGS	Harvard II	43-45?	NZ1039/JZ-C	NZ	
JZ	FLS	F4U-1D Corsair	44-45	NZ5566/JZ-M	NZ	
KJ	14 SU	PV-1 Ventura	44-45	NZ4552/KJ-X	NZ	
KN	5	PBY-5A	46-53	NZ4050/KN-G	NZ/Fiji	
KN	5	Sunderland V	53-c 55	NZ4109/KN-C	NZ/Fiji	
LV	18					*not used*
OD	2 OTU	Kittyhawk III, IV	3.44-45	NZ3136/OD-28 (III)	NZ	
OD	2 OTU	Harvard IIa	44-45	NZ1041/OD-4	NZ	
OP	11 SU	RB-34A Lexington	44-45	NZ4583/OP-K	NZ	
OP	11 SU	PV-1 Ventura	44-45	NZ4624/OP-E	NZ	
OT	5	Singapore III	11.41-11.42	K6918/OT-D	Fiji	
PA	8	Vincent	3.42-5.43	NZ321/PA-H	NZ	
PA	8	Vildebeest III	3.42-5.43	NZ130/PA-B	NZ	
PA	30	Vincent	5.43-11.43	NZ344/PA-H	NZ	
PA	30	Vildebeest	5.43-11.43		NZ	
PA	30	Harvard II	5.43-11.43		NZ	
PA	5	PB2B-1	7.44-45	NZ4033/PA-E	SWPA	
RK	3 SU	F4U-1 Corsair	7.44-?45	NZ5550/RK-S	NZ	
SG	SGCF	DH 89B Dominie	42-43	NZ527/SG	NZ	
SJ	1	Hudson III	9.41-9.43	NZ2078/SJ-W	NZ	
TX	22	Hind	42-43		NZ	
TX	22	Vildebeest III		NZ1../TX-C	NZ	
TX	22	Vincent	10.42-2.43		NZ	

Code	Unit	Type	Dates	Example	Theatre	Remarks
UH	2	Hudson III	12.41-9.43	NZ2014/UH-W	NZ	
UW	7	Vildebeest IV	42-5.43	NZ138/UW-Q	NZ	
UY	21	Hind	9.42-9.43	NZ1524/UY-F	NZ	
UY	21	Harvard II	42	NZ1029/UY-L	NZ	
UY	26 SU	F4U-1 Corsair	44-45	NZ5406/UY-	NZ	
XO	16	P-40E	8.42-44	NZ3029/XO-M	NZ	
XX	6	Hind	?42-9.42	NZ1544/XX-Y	NZ	
XX	6	PBY-5A	5.43-9.45	NZ4011/XX-M	SWPA	
XX	MOCU	Sunderland GR.5	c 55-4.62	NZ4118/XX-A	NZ	
YC	75	Mosquito FB.6	47-50	NZ2328/YC-C	NZ	
YZ	4	*Vincent*				*use not known*
YZ	4	Hudson III	12.41-9.44	NZ20**/YZ-H	Fiji 1942	
ZG	20	Hind	8.42-10.43	NZ15**/ZG-B	NZ	
ZG	5 SU	F4U-1 Corsair	44-45	NZ55**/ZG-1	NZ	
ZX	10	Hudson V	42	NZ2001/ZX-X	NZ	to 1 (B)OTU
ZX	10	Oxford	42	NZ		
ZX	1(B)OTU	Hudson V	42-45	NZ2003/ZX-X	NZ	
ZX	1(B)OTU	PV-1 Ventura	43-6.45	NZ4534/ZX-D	NZ	
XX	6	Sunderland GR.5	4.54-c 55	NZ4114/XX-C	NZ	
ZX	1(B)OTU	Oxford	42	NZ287/ZX-E	NZ	

For service in the south-western Pacific the RNZAF modified its markings to resemble the US type, adding bars to the blue/white roundels. Most aircraft in the operational areas also stopped using unit codes. An exception were the PB2B-1 Catalinas of No. 5 Sqn, as can be seen on NX4033/PA-E and NZ4029/PA-A at Espiritu Santos in March 1945. (RNZAF)

The sudden outbreak of war led to a rapid expansion of the RNZAF, which was forced to form a number of squadrons with obsolescent biplanes for service at home. One was No. 30 Sqn, which flew Vincents, like NZ344/PA-H, seen here in August 1943, which were used until it re-equipped with Avengers which were uncoded. (RNZAF)

Another biplane type pressed into squadron service was the Hind light bomber, which was used by, among others, No. 21 Sqn whose fully camouflaged NZ1524/UY-F is seen flying over Manawatu in early 1943. (via Charles Darby)

Some units of the post-war RNZAF continued to use unit codes, among them a re-formed No. 75 Sqn which flew the Mosquito FB.6 from Ohakea, where NZ2328/YC-C is seen at dispersal. (RNZAF)

CHAPTER 10

SAAF Wartime

Aircraft of the squadrons of the SAAF deployed to operations in the campaign in East Africa did not carry any squadron codes. After they moved north to join the RAF in the desert campaign, codes were allocated to these and the many new squadrons that were subsequently formed. These codes came from the RAF list, possibly a theatre annex to SD 110. Codes were not generally used on units remaining in South Africa,

but the aircraft of 11 OTU replicated the codes allocated to Nos 1 and 2 Squadrons which were serving alongside the RAF in the Mediterranean. Following the end of the war, the deployed squadrons returned to South Africa and the SAAF reconstituted to a peacetime strength. Postwar codes are set out in chapter 11.

Code	Unit	Type	Dates	Example	Theatre	Remarks
AX	1	Hurricane I	4.42-11.42	Z5130/AX-N	MedME	
AX	1	Hurricane IIc	9.42-11.42	HL627/AX-X	MedME	
AX	1	Spitfire Vc	11.42-4.43	ER171/AX-D	MedME	
AX	1	Spitfire VIII	8.43-6.45	JF322/AX-B	MedME	
AX	1	Spitfire IX	c 6.43-10.43	MA532/AX-H	MedME	
AX	11 OTU	Hurricane II	43-45		S Africa	'A' Flt
CA	3	Spitfire IX	2.44-10.45	MJ680/CA-E	MedME	
DB	2	Kittyhawk I, Ia	4.42-6.43	ET871/DB-D	MedME	
DB	2	Kittyhawk III	6.43-7.43		MedME	
DB	2	Spitfire Vc	6.43-3.44	JK674/DB-S	MedME	
DB	2	Spitfire IX	2.44-7.45	MJ416/DB-E	MedME	
DB	11 OTU	Hurricane II	43-45	5283/DB-N	S Africa	'C' Flt
DX	4	Tomahawk II	10.41-6.42	AN249/DX-P	MedME	
GL	5	Tomahawk II	2.42-1.43	AN420/GL-P	MedME	
GL	5	Kittyhawk Ia	43	ET961/GL-Z	MedME	
GL	5	Kittyhawk III, IV	1.43-9.44	FX772/GL-A	MedME	
GL	5	Mustang III	9.44-10.45	KH622/GL-I	MedME	
GL	5	Mustang IV	3.45-10.45	KM110/GL-Z	MedME	
GL	11 OTU	Hurricane II	43-45		S Africa	'B' Flt
KJ	4	Tomahawk IIb	c 11.41-1.42	AK428/KJ-K	MedME	
KJ	4	Kittyhawk I, Ia, III	6.42-7.43	AL189/KJ-N	MedME	
KJ	4	Spitfire V	7.43-5.44	EP682/KJ-E	MedME	
KJ	4	Spitfire IX	5.44-7.45	MA995/KJ-Q	MedME	
ND	11	Kittyhawk IV	10.44-8.45	FX934/ND-K	Med ME	
ND	11	Spitfire IX	8.45-10.45	MJ729/ND-E	Med ME	
OZ	24	Boston III	11.41-c 6.42	Z2228/OZ-N	MedME	
TA	2	Tomahawk II	7.41-5.42	AN311/TA-C	MedME	
TJ	7	Spitfire IX	c 3.44-7.45	JG254/TJ-A	MedME	
VL	12	Boston III	3.42-c 6.42	Z2291/VL-M	Med ME	
WR	40	Hurricane I	1.42-8.42	P2646/WR-B	MedME	
WR	40	Hurricane II	8.42-4.43	**541/WR-X	MedME	
WR	40	Spitfire V	2.43-6.43	EP689/WR-L	MedME	
WR	40	Spitfire IX	6.43-10.45	MK151/WR-F	MedME	
ZP	15	Blenheim V	7.42-7.43	BA311/ZP-BP	MedME	

No 11 OTU at Isipingo in South Africa duplicated the unit codes of several operational units serving in North Africa and the Mediterranean. This Hurricane II, 5307/DB-H, which had nosed over in early 1945 illustrates the point as the Spitfires of No. 2 Sqn SAAF were similarly coded in Italy at this time.
(J. D. R. Rawlings)

The TA codes were only used for a short period by the Tomahawks of No. 2 Sqn SAAF, but the date of this view of TA-C at El Adem is known – 21 November 1941 – since during a sortie over the desert it had collided with an Italian Macchi MC 200. (Gp Capt J. Pelly-Fry)

By 1944, when this line-up of Spitfire IXs of No. 40 Sqn SAAF was seen in Italy, they wore a unit badge on the nose and type C roundels above the wings. The codes were presented in a smaller form than standard and the orange, which replaced the red of the roundels on SAAF aircraft is evident too. (K. Smy)

CHAPTER 11

Royal Egyptian Air Force Wartime

By the time that war with Italy broke out in June 1940 the REAF which had been formed during the 1930s under RAF tutelage, had expanded to become a force of five squadrons. These mainly flew in the army co-operation role but the two fighter squadrons flying Gladiators were integrated into RAF deployments for the defence of the Nile Delta and the Suez Canal, eventually coming under command of 252 (Fighter) Wing of 202 Group. Although generally flying obsolescent equipment, they were a useful reinforcement. Operational REAF squadrons wore unit identification codes from the outbreak of war until around 1942/3.

Code	Unit	Type	Dates	Example	Theatre	Remarks
GF	1 REAF	Lysander I	c 40-c 42?	Y511/GF-U	MedME	
PY	2 REAF	Gladiator I	6.40-c 41	L8028/PY-C	MedME	
NV	3 REAF	Avro 652/Anson I	c 40-43	****/NV-C	MedME	

CHAPTER 12

Post-war British and Allied Use of the Wartime Code System

The two-character system of unit codes continued for some years after the war ended. Indeed the last use of a format devised and introduced into the RAF in 1938 was by the Royal Norwegian Air Force in 1970, which at that time was still using its wartime codes on squadrons which had retained their RAF series numbers.

The reasons for the continued use of the codes was twofold. First, it was a convenient system of unit identifier with which many personnel were familiar. Second, it allowed the maintenance of tradition after the war, with successful squadron numbers and their related codes being retained.

The Canadian system was not strictly a continuation of the wartime unit identifiers, but it was originally based around a similar two-letter unit code with individual aircraft letter identifier, so is described in this chapter for the sake of completeness. With the remaining Services described in this chapter, units retaining their wartime codes are shown in bold type.

generally, but with some exceptions. Some of these were simply the continued use of the wartime code, while others changed. There is thus some inevitable overlap, and some of the codes shown in this section are also shown in chapter 5. However, when there was continuity after the war, wherever possible fresh examples are given.

As with the wartime list in chapter 5, the dates shown are not necessarily those between which the given type was in service with the unit concerned, but only the dates during which it is known, or believed, to have worn the code shown.

In respect of inclusion and exclusion of units in this chapter the authors have been deliberately liberal in their determination. Many wartime units continued in existence for only a few months after the end of the war, frequently into 1946, and these are not included here, being solely confined to chapter 5. Units included in this chapter had a distinct post-war existence.

RAF

The RAF continued to use two-character unit codes on most front-line and some second-line operational units until 1951

Code	Unit	Type	Dates	Example	Theatre	Remarks
2A	SF St Eval	Dominie C.2	46-49		UK	
2A	SF St Eval	Proctor C.3	46-48	Z7214/2A-B	UK	
2A	SF St Eval	Martinet TT.1	46-48	EM439/2A-J	UK	
2A	SF St Eval	Oxford C.2	46-51	X7244/2A-D	UK	
2V	18 GCF	Dominie I	45-46	X7417/2V-D	UK	
2V	18 GCF	Anson C.12	45-51	PH782/2V-C	UK	
2V	18 GCF	Oxford C.2	45-46	T1194/2V-Z	UK	
2V	18 GCF	Anson I	46-49	LS998/2V	UK	
2W	SGR	Anson T.1	3.46-47	EG413/2W-H	UK	
3D	48 MU	Anson C.19	47-51	VM371/3D-*	UK	
3D	48 MU	Anson C.1	47	LS991/3D	UK	
3D	48 MU	Anson C.12	50-51	PH813/3D	UK	
3D	48 MU	Proctor C.3	50-51	DX190/3D-H	UK	
3D	48 MU	Oxford I	50-51	NM663/3D-N	UK	
3J	13 MU	Oxford I	46-1.48	EB969/3J-B	UK	
3J	13 MU	Tiger Moth T.2	46-1.48	T5702/3J-T	UK	
3J	13 MU	Halifax B.6	46-1.48	RG872/3J-F	UK	
3J	13 MU	Dakota C.3	46-1.48	KG311/3J-*	UK	
3L	FCCRS	Spitfire LF.16	12.45-53	TD343/3L-N	UK	
3L	FCCRS	Spitfire FR.18	46-52	TP408/3L-B	UK	
3L	FCCRS	Anson 1	12.45-53	NK995/3L-V	UK	
3L	FCCRS	Oxford	12.45-53	AT480/3L-B	UK	
3M	48 GCF	Proctor C.3	1.46-11.49	DX196/3M-M	UK	
3S	3 GCF	Anson C.19	47-51	VM409/3S-U	UK	

Code	Unit	Type	Dates	Example	Theatre	Remarks
3S 3	GCF	Proctor C.4	50-51	NP228/3S-A	UK	
3V 1	GCF	Anson C.19	45-47	TX205/3V-B	UK	
3V 1	GCF	Proctor C.4	45-51	NP193/3V-D	UK	
4D	74	Meteor F.3	6.45-3.48	EE318/4D-Z	UK	
4D	74	Oxford	c 46	HM790/4D-Y	UK	hack or training
4D	74	Meteor F.4	12.47-10.50	VT106/4D-D	UK	
4D	74	Meteor F.8	10.50-51	VZ577/4D-N	UK	
4D	74	Meteor T.7	50-51	VW430/4D-X	UK	
4K	SF West Malling	Oxford	46-52	T1214/4K	UK	
4K	SF West Malling	Meteor F.4	6.48-1.51	VT185/4K	UK	
4K	SF West Malling	Mosquito T.3	50	VA893/4K	UK	
4M	695	Martinet TT.1	12.46-1.49	PX126/4M-B	UK	
4M	695	Vengeance TT.4	3.45-5.47	HB545/4M-A	UK	
4M	695	Spitfire LF.16	7.45-2.49	TD248/4M-E	UK	
4M	695	Oxford T.2	6.46-2.49	PH458/M4-C	UK	
4M	695	Harvard T.2B	12.46-2.49	KF331/4M-Q	UK	
4M	695	Beaufighter TT.10	12.48-2.49	RD802/4M-D	UK	to 34 Sqn
4M	34	Spitfire LF.16	2.49-8.51	SL666/4M-S	UK	ex 695 Sqn
4M	34	Oxford T.2	2.49-7.51	NJ281/4M-T	UK	
4M	34	Beaufighter TT.10	2.49-7.51	SR911/4M-G	UK	
4M	34	Harvard T.2b	2.49-7.51	KF331/4M-Q	UK	
4S	CSE	Oxford C.2	8.45-9.46	PH348/4S-V	UK	
4S	CSE	Lancaster B.3	3.46-9.46	PA232/4S-D2	UK	
4S	CSE	Mosquito FB.6	3.46-9.46	PZ227/4S-*	UK	
4S	CSE	Mosquito PR.16	-4.47	NS809/4S-N	UK	
4S	CSE	Mosquito NF.30	9.46-51	NT472/4S-O	UK	
4S	CSE	Mosquito NF.36	9.46-c 50	RL266/4S-P	UK	
4S	CSE	Lancaster B.1	9.46-c 50	PA478/4S-B	UK	
4S	CSE	Lancaster B.1(FE)	9.46-c 50	TE858/4S-G	UK	
4S	CSE	Oxford T.1	9.46-c 50	LX122/4S-W	UK	
4S	CSE	Lincoln B.2	49-51	SX947/4S-R	UK	
4X	230	Sunderland GR.5	4.46-51	RN299/4X-P	UK, Eur	
4X	230	Sea Otter ASR.2	47-48	JM805/4X-Q	UK	
4Z	BCCF	Oxford I	45-47	PH765/4Z-C	UK	
4Z	BCCF	Proctor C.3	45-49	LZ680/4Z-S	UK	
4Z	BCCF	Dakota C.3	45-47	KG782/4Z-A	UK	
4Z	BCCF	Anson C.12	45-47	PH823/4Z-G	UK	
4Z	BCCF	Anson C.1	45-47	NK842/4Z-C	UK	
4Z	BCCF	Anson C.19	2.46-51	TX188/4Z-E	UK	

The Martinet continued in service in the target-towing role into the late 1940s. HN884/6D-K of No. 20 Sqn, is resplendent in post-war markings, and is seen completing a shoot over Cardigan Bay in 1949. (Gp Capt K.W.T. Pugh)

Code	Unit	Type	Dates	Example	Theatre	Remarks
5D	31	*Dakota*			FE	*reported only*
5I	SF	Benson Anson C.11	45-46	NL228/5I-G	UK	
5I	SF	Benson Anson C.12	45-46	PH654/5I-D	UK	
5I	SF	Benson Proctor C.2	46-48	BV656/5I-A	UK	
5K	39	MU Tiger Moth T.2	45-50	T7870/5K-B	UK	
5R	33	Tempest F.2	10.46-6.51	PR753/5R-E	Eur, FE	
5R	33	Hornet F.3	4.51-3.55	WB871/5R-P	FE	
5R	33	Mosquito T.3	9.52-2.55	RR308/5R-Z	FE	
5S	691	Oxford 2	12.43-2.49	LW868/5S-B	UK	
5S	691	Vengeance TT.4	4.45-5.47	FD193/5S-G	UK	
5S	691	Martinet TT.1	8.45-2.49	JN513/5S-S	UK	
5S	691	Spitfire F.16E	8.45-2.49	TB759/5S-A	UK	
6C	PRDU	Spitfire PR.19	45-8.47	PS925/6C-X	UK	
6C	PRDU	Hornet PR.2	47-50	PX216/6C-R	UK	
6D	631	Spitfire LF.16	10.45-2.49	TE339/6D-B	UK	
6D	631	Martinet	9.44-2.49	HN884/6D-K	UK	
6D	631, 20	Vampire F.1	-3.49	TG447/6D-V	UK	
6J	34	Martinet	2.49-8.49		UK	
6J	34	Oxford T.2	2.49-7.51	PH467/6J-E	UK	
6J	34	Beaufighter TT.10	2.49-7.51		UK	
6T	608	Harvard T.2B	50-51	FT457/6T-N	UK	
6T	608	Oxford T.1	50-51	NM409/6T-M	UK	
6T	608	Spitfire F.22	-7.50	PK340/6T-3	UK	
6T	608	Meteor T.7	4.50-12.51	WA671/6T-O	UK	
6T	608	Vampire F.3	5.50-51	VT831/6T-P	UK	
7A	614	Harvard T.2B	50-51	FX417/7A-Y	UK	
7A	614	Spitfire F.22	50-7.50	PK501/7A-D	UK	
7A	614	Meteor T.7	50-51	WA687/7A-W	UK	
7A	614	Harvard T.2A	50-51	FX360/7A-X	UK	
7B	595	Spitfire LF.16e	8.45-2.49	TE390/7B-F	UK	
7B	595	Beaufighter TT.10	6.46-2.49	RD577/7B-P	UK	
7B	595	Vampire F.1	12.46-10.48	VF283/7B-O	UK	
7B	595	Martinet	12.43-2.49	EM697/7B-Z	UK	
7B	595	Oxford II	44-2.49	NM808/7B-S	UK	
7B	595	Spitfire IX	7.45-4.48	PT753/7B-G	UK	to 5 Sqn
7B	5	Spitfire F.9	2.49-9.51	ML247/7B-F	UK	ex 595 Sqn
7B	5	Spitfire LF.16e	2.49-9.51	RW388/7B-D	UK	
7B	5	Harvard T.2B	2.49-9.51	KF920/7B-R	UK	
7B	5	Oxford	2.49-9.51	PH318/7B-T	UK	
7B	5	Martinet TT.1	2.49-1.50	NR638/7B-W	UK	
7B	5	Beaufighter TT.10	1.50-9.51	RD812/7B-N	UK	
7K	S&RTU	*Sea Otter I, Walrus*	7.45-4.49		UK	*reported*
7N	SFU/CSE	Anson I	c 48	EF980/7N-L	UK	
7Z	1381 (T)CU	Wellington T.10	8.45-2.48	HE242/7Z-Q	UK	ex 105 OTU
7Z	1381 (T)CU	Dakota C.3	8.45-2.48	KG321/7Z-A	UK	
7Z	1381 (T)CU	Dakota C.4	8.45-2.48	KN631/7Z-N	UK	
8D	220	Liberator C.8	7.45-5.46	KH348/8D-E	UK	
8I	APS Acklington	Martinet TT.1	5.46-3.50	NR299/8I-15	UK	ex 2 APS
8I	APS Acklington	Master T.2	5.46-47	DM211/8I-G	UK	
8I	APS Acklington	Mosquito FB.6	5.46-3.50	TA558/8I-B	UK	
8I	APS Acklington	Mosquito TT.35	-50	TA587/8I-D	UK	
8I	APS Acklington	Harvard T.2b	48-50	KF342/8I-S	UK	
8I	APS Acklington	Mustang 4	5.46-46	KM218/8I-K	UK	
8I	APS Acklington	Mosquito T.3	48-3.50	RR319/8I-A	UK	
8I	APS Acklington	Spitfire LF.16e	48-3.50	TE178/8I-M	UK	
8L	92	Meteor F.8	10.50-c 6.51	WA763/8L-G	UK	

The Harvard T.2B remained a major training type for many years and was also used by a variety of units including No. 2 Armament Practice School at Acklington to whom KF342/8I-S belonged. Yellow overall, it retained type C markings. (Eric Taylor)

After the the war Lancaster bombers like B.VII NX683/BL-G of No. 40 Sqn wore a black and white colour scheme, but with wartime-type markings. This unit was one of several based in the Middle East. UK-based squadrons were similarly coloured. (Dr David Gunby)

Code	Unit	Type	Dates	Example	Theatre	Remarks
8Q	695	Vengeance TT.4	3.45-5.47	HB519/8Q-C	UK	
8Q	695	Tiger Moth T.2	47-2.49		UK	
8Q	695	Martinet I	12.46-1.49		UK	
8Q	34	Beaufighter TT.10	2.49-7.51	RD544/8Q-D	UK	
8Q	34	Spitfire LF.16E	2.49-8.51	TE450/8Q-R	UK	
8Q	34	Harvard T.2B	2.49-7.51	KF405/8Q-6	UK	
8Q	34	Oxford T.2	2.49-7.51	PH418/8Q-L	UK	
8Q	34	Tiger Moth T.2	2.49-7.51	T6809/8Q	UK	
8Q	34	Martinet 1	2.49-7.51	EM575/8Q-N	UK	
8W	612	Spitfire LF.16E	50-7.51	SL718/8W-D	UK	
8W	612	Vampire FB.5	6.51-12.51	VZ325/8W-E	UK	
8W	612	Meteor T.7	6.51-12.51	WH208/8W-V	UK	
8W	612	Harvard T.2B	50-51	FS881/8W-X	UK	
9K	1 TTU	Beaufighter TT.10	8.45-12.47	RD507/9K-E	UK	
9K	1 TTU	Oxford 1	8.45-12.47	PG972/9K-A	UK	
9X	1689 Flt	Anson C.12	46-48	NL247/9X-E	UK	
9X	1689 Flt	Wellington T.10	3.46-51	RP456/9X-S	UK	
9X	1689 Flt	Harvard T.2B	3.46-51	KF710/9X-B	UK	
9X	1689 Flt	Mosquito T.3	3.46-51	VP346/9X-T	UK	
9X	1689 Flt	Lancaster B.1(FE)	3.46-51	RT676/9X	UK	
9X	1689 Flt	Lancaster B.7	3.46-51	NX612/9X	UK	
9X	1689 Flt	Anson C.19	3.46-51	VM318/9X-G	UK	
9X	1689 Flt	Spitfire LF.16	c 46-48	TE184/9X-*	UK	
A3	230 OCU	Lancaster B.1(FE)	3.47-3.49	TW887/A3-T	UK	ex 1653 CU
A3	230 OCU	Mosquito NF.19	4.48-1.49	TA343/A3-H	UK	
A3	230 OCU	Lincoln B.2	3.49-12.51	RE328/A3-A	UK	
A6	257	Meteor F.3	9.46-3.48	EE352/A6-G	UK	
A6	257	Meteor F.4	12.47-8.50	VW266/A6-H	UK	
A6	257	Meteor T.7	49-51	VZ631/A6-A	UK	
A6	257	Meteor F.8	10.50-51	WA819/A6-A	UK	
AA	75	Lincoln B.2	9.45-10.45	RF389/AA-A	UK	
AC	138	Lancaster I	3.45-12.46	PA193/AC-D	UK	Reverted to NF
AJ	617	Oxford C.2	3.46-50	W6578/AJ-A	UK	
AK	213	Mustang 3	5.44-2.47	FB342/AK-X	MedME	
AK	213	Mustang 4	2.45-2.47	KM295/AK-P	MedME	
AK	213	Tempest F.6	1.47-1.50	NX252/AK-J	MedME	
AK	213	Harvard T2B	c 50	EX814/AK-I	MedME	
AP	130	Vampire F.1	10.46-1.47	TG351/AP-V		to 72 Sqn

Code	Unit	Type	Dates	Example	Theatre	Remarks
AP	72	Vampire F.1	1. 47-5.48	VF304/AP-B		ex 130 Sqn
APS	APS Lubeck	Mosquito FB.6	9.47-49	VA890/APS	Eur	
AS	Op Goodwill	Lincoln B.2	summer 46	RF467/AS-B		83/97/100 Sqn a/c prior to South American tour
AU	148	Lancaster B.1	11.46-2.50	TW668/AU-T	UK	
AU	148	Lincoln B.2	1.50-4.51	SX987/AU-Y	UK	
B3	SF Wyton	Oxford 46-47		*****/B3-A	UK	
BB	226 OCU	Hornet F.1		PX238/BB-D	UK	
BB	226 OCU	Vampire F.1	8.46-8.49	TG290/BB-G	UK	
BD	227 OCU	Auster AOP.5	5.47-5.50	TW515/BD-K	UK	
BD	227 OCU	Auster AOP.6	5.47-5.50	VF621/BD-U	UK	
BD	227 OCU	Oxford I	9.49-4.50	V3889/BD-A	UK	
BD	227 OCU	Tiger Moth T.2	5.47-5.50	DE709/BD-X	UK	
BD	227 OCU	Chipmunk T.10	5.47-5.50	WZ882/BD-K	UK	
BE	8 OTU	Spitfire LF.16	46-47	RW395/BE-80	UK	to 237 OCU
BE	237 OCU	Spitfire PR.19	7.47-50	PS908/BE-82	UK	ex 8 OTU
BK	SSCF	Oxford	46-47	NM717/BK-E	UK	
BK	SSCF	Vampire F.1	5.46-6.49	VF303/BK	UK	
BK	SSCF	Auster AOP.5	5.46-1.47	NJ629/BK-D	UK	
BK	SSCF	Meteor F.3	3.47-2.48	EE401/BK-O	UK	
BL	40	Lancaster B.7	1.46-3.47	NX690/BL-A		
BS	160	Liberator GR.VIII	46	KL533/BS-G		to 120 Sqn
BS	120	Liberator GR.VIII	10.46-12.46	KN777/BS-A	UK	ex 160 Sqn
BS	120	Oxford I	11.46-4.49	V3190/BS-X	UK	
BS	120	Lancaster MR.3	12.46-51	RE158/BS-B	UK	
BY	59	York C.1	12.47-10.50	MW143/BY-B	UK	
C3	?	*Meteor F.4*	?	*****/C3-A	UK	
CB	MCS	Dominie 1	4.44-7.48	HG705/CB-U	UK	
CB	MCS	Anson C.12	6.45-2.46	PH841/CB-H	UK	
CB	31, MCS	Anson C.19	3.55-59	VV253/CB-A	UK	
CB	31, MCS	Anson C.21	3.55-9.59	VS578/CB-Z	UK	
CB	31, MCS	Devon C.1	3.55-59	VP952/CB-A	UK	
CB	31, MCS	Chipmunk T.10	3.55-59	WP833/CB-C	UK	

These two Lancaster GR.3s off the Cornish coast near their St Eval base during the summer of 1947 show the differences in code presentation between units on the same station. CJ-A of No. 203 Sqn has much smaller letters in black than the red letters on XB-N of No. 224 Sqn. (via Air Cdre G. R. Pitchfork)

Code	Unit	Type	Dates	Example	Theatre	Remarks
CJ	203	Liberator GR.VI	1.46-10.46	KL565/CJ-B	UK	
CJ	203	Lancaster GR.3	8.46-51	RF311/CJ-G	UK	
CM	1333(T)CU	Dakota	8.45-11.47	KG434/CM-O	UK	ex 107 OTU
CR	162	Oxford	*c* 46	V3528/CR-C	UK	
CS	SF Upwood	Oxford I	46	LX527/CS	UK	
CX	14	Mosquito B.16	4.46-7.48	PF544/CX-F	Eur	
CX	14	Mosquito B.35	4.48-3.51	TH999/CX-A	Eur	
DE	61 OTU	Spitfire XVI	1.46-7.47	SL552/DE-N	UK	
DE	61 OTU	Spitfire XIX	9.46-7.47	PM***/DE-Y	UK	
DE	61 OTU	Spitfire FR.14	48	SM928/DE-A	UK	
DF	CBE	Spitfire LF.16	45-46	SL563/DF-U	UK	
DF	CBE	Spitfire F.22	46	PK658/DF-U	UK	
DF	CBE	Mosquito B.16	12.45-47	PF446/DF-V	UK	
DF	CBE	Mosquito B.17	9.45-	HK327/DF-Y	UK	
DF	CBE	Mosquito T.3	9.45-	LR527/DF-S	UK	
DF	CBE	Mosquito B.35	*c* 12.49	VP184/DF-Y	UK	
DF	CBE	Lancaster B.3	9.45-	PB970/DF-J	UK	
DF	CBE	Lincoln B.2	9.45-12.49	RF520/DF-M	UK	
DF	CBE	Lancaster B.1(FE)	46	PB994/DF-F	UK	
DF	CBE	Meteor F.3	-12.49	EE340/DF-U	UK	
DF	CBE	Meteor F.4	-12.49	VT221/DF-V	UK	
DH	540	Mosquito PR.34	47-8.53	RG234/DH-V	UK	
DH	540	Mosquito T.3	12.47-3.50	VT589/DH-Z	UK	
DL	91	Meteor F.3	10.46-1.47	EE409/DL-F	UK	to 92 Sqn
DL	92	Meteor F.3	2.47-5.48	EE388/DL-C	UK	ex 91 Sqn
DL	92	Meteor F.4	5.48-10.50-	VT286/DL-R	UK	
DM	36	Mosquito FB.6	10.46-10.47	RF877/DM-C	UK	ex 248 Sqn
DQ	1402 Met Flt	Master II	12.45-5.46	DL414/DQ-R	UK	
DV	93	Mustang 4	1.46-12.47	KH727/DV-J	MedME	ex 237 Sqn
DV	77	Dakota	12.46-47	KG358/DV-A	UK	ex 271 Sqn a/c
DW	610	Spitfire F.22	50-7.51	PK511/DW-N	UK	
DW	610	Harvard T.2b	50-51	FT282/DW-Y	UK	
DX	57	Lincoln B.2	8.45-4.51	RF517/DX-X	UK	
DX	57	Washington B.1	5.51-12.51	WF555/DX-H	UK	
EA	49	Lancaster B.1(FE)	8.45-3.50	TW895/EA-P	UK	

One of the few squadrons to use the Chipmunk T.10 trainer was No. 31 when it flew in the communications role from Hendon in the 1950s. For a time they wore the unit's code letters, though the aircraft letter was placed on the engine nacelle as on WZ843/CB-H. (J. D. R. Rawlings)

Although of poor quality, this photograph shows a Spitfire PR.19 of No. 61 OTU in 1946 with the contemporary scheme for high-level PR types, but with an unusual presentation of the codes DE-Y. (via Air Cdre G. R. Pitchfork)

Code	Unit	Type	Dates	Example	Theatre	Remarks
EA	49	Lincoln B.2	11.49-51	RF336/EA-P	UK	
EB	41	Tempest F.5	9.45-4.46	EJ651/EB-E	Eur/UK	
EB	41	Spitfire F.21	4.46-8.47	LA315/EB-O	UK/Eur	
EB	41	Hornet F.1	6.48-8.48	PX277/EB-W	UK	
EB	41	Hornet F.3	7.48-2.51	PX314/EB-F	UK	
EB	41	Mosquito T.3	45-49	VT628/EB-*	UK	
EC	SF Odiham	Harvard T.2b	c 4.47	FS761/EC UK		
EC	PRDU	Meteor PR.3	45-8.47	EE338/EC-Z	UK	
EF	102	Liberator C.V	9.45-2.46	BZ806/EF-K	UK	
EF	102	Liberator C.VI	9.45-2.46	EV880/EF-T	UK	
EG	268	Mosquito FB.6	9.45-3.46		Eur	ex 487 Sqn
EG	268	Spitfire XIV, XIX	c 9.45	*****/EG-J	Eur	Codes ex 487 Sqn
EG	16	Spitfire XIV	9.45-c3.46	*****/EG-R	Eur	Ex 268 Sqn
EG	16	Tempest FB.5	4.46-4.47	SN135/EG-R	Eur	ex 268 Sqn
EG	16	Tempest F.2	4.47-12.48	PR736/EG-M	Eur	
EG	16	Vampire FB.5	12.48-51	VV557/EG-H	Eur	
EJ	CCFIS, CCIS	Buckmaster T.1	10.45-4.46	RP184/EJ-C	UK	
EJ	CCFIS, CCIS	Liberator VI	10.45-4.46	KN738/G/EJ-G	UK	
EJ	CCIS	Beaufort II	10.45-4.46	ML561/EJ-C	UK	
EM	207	Lancaster B.1	4.46-8.49	PD217/EM-Z	UK	
EM	207	Lincoln B.2	7.49-3.50	RE324/EM-C	UK	
EM	207	Washington B.1	7.51-8.51	WF565/EM-B	UK	
EP	104	Lancaster B.7(FE)	11.45-4.47	NX729/EP-P	MedME	
EP	84 GCF	Anson C.12	45-12.47	PH765/EP	Eur	no individual letters
EP	84 GCF	Messenger I	45-12.47	RH375/EP	Eur	
EP	84 GCF	Auster V	45-46	TJ568/EP	Eur	
EP	84 GCF	Oxford	45-46	T1200/EP	Eur	
EP	84 GCF	Spitfire XI	9.45-12.47	PL830/EP	Eur	
ER	1552 RATF	Oxford	12.45-10.46		UK	
ES	82	Spitfire PR.19	10.46-10.47	PM612/ES-C	UK	ex 541 Sqn
ES	229 OCU	Vampire FB.5	12.50-10.56	VX870/ES-L	UK	
ES	229 OCU	Vampire T.11	1.53-11.58	WZ460/ES-20	UK	
ES	229 OCU	Meteor T.7	1.51-3.53	WL345/ES-29	UK	
ES	229 OCU	Hunter F.1	2.54-56	WT699/ES-P	UK	
ES	229 OCU	Hunter F.4	7.55-60	XF961/ES-M	UK	
ES	229 OCU	Hunter T.7	8.58-60	XL569/ES-85	UK	
EX	11	Mosquito B.6	10.48-8.50	SZ984/EX-C	Eur	
EX	11	Vampire FB.5	8.50-12.52	VV634/EX-B	Eur	
EY	78	Dakota C.4	7.45-7.50	KN694/EY-V	MedME	
FB	WCU	Washington B.1	4.50-9.51	WF434/FB-K	UK	to 35 Sqn
FB	35	Washington B.1	9.51-12.51	WF574/FB-S	UK	ex WCU
FG	72	Vampire F.1	2.47-10.48	VF309/FG-W	UK	
FG	72	Vampire F.3	6.48-2.50	VV194/FG-B	UK	
FG	72	Vampire FB.5	11.49-7.52	VZ305/FG-N	UK	
FJ	63	Spitfire LF.16	9.46-12.46	TE402/FJ-A	Eur, UK	ex 164 Sqn
FV	13 OTU	Tempest F.2	45-5.47	MW750/FV-A	UK	
FX	234	Spitfire F.9	7.45-2.46	TD310/FX-C	UK	
FX	234	Meteor F.3	2.46-9.46	EE449/FX-N	UK	to 266 Sqn
FX	266	Meteor F.3	9.46-4.48	EE277/FX-H	UK	ex 234 Sqn
FX	266	Meteor F.4	2.48-2.49	VT104/FX-W	UK	
FY	611	Spitfire F.22	50-6.51	PK650/FY-J	UK	
FY	611	Harvard T2B	50-51	KF640/FY-X	UK	
G2	19 GCF	Proctor C.3	45-46	LZ684/G2-E	UK	
G2	19 GCF	Anson C.19	46-51	TX157/G2-B	UK	
G2	19 GCF	Sea Otter	46-51	JM805/G2-D	UK	
GA	16 OTU	Mosquito VI	44-2.47	RS643/GA-O	UK A Flt	

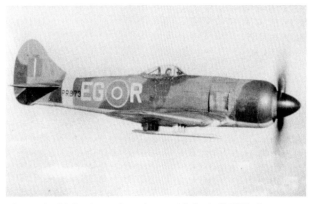

The standard fighter/ground attack type with the 2nd TAF in Germany during the late 1940s was the Tempest F.2, which served with several squadrons including No. 16, whose PR873/EG-R shows off the underwing rocket rails to advantage in 1949. (Ron Brittain)

To beef up Bomber Command's long-range capability during the early 1950s a number of squadrons was issued with ex-USAF Washington B.1s. When No. 35 Sqn was re-formed from the Washington Conversion Unit, it retained its code as may be seen in this poor but rare photograph of WF570/FB-M in late 1951. (P. W. Porter)

Code	Unit	Type	Dates	Example	Theatre	Remarks
GA	16 OTU	Mosquito III	12.44-2.47	RR289/GA-L	UK A Flt	
GA	16 OTU	Mosquito XVI	12.44-2.47	PF488/GA-T	UK A Flt	
GA	16 OTU	Buckmaster I	-2.47	RP180/GA-*	UK A Flt	
GB	Op Goodwill	Lincoln B.2	summer 46	RF468/GB-C	83/97/100 Sqn a/c for South American tour	
GH	216	Dakota C.4	46-1.50	KJ964/GH-P	MedME	
GN	249	Baltimore 5	10.45-4.46	FW367/GN-P	MedME	
GN	249	Mosquito FB.26	3.46-8.46	KA417/GN-C	MedME	
GN	249	Tempest F.6	12.46-3.50	NX200/GN-F	MedME	
GN	CBE	Mosquito B.16	12.45-47	PF401/GN-B	UK	
GN	CBE	Lancaster B.3	46	PB986/GN-X	UK	
GO	CFE	Mosquito FB.6	1.45-1.49	RS554/GO-K	UK	
GO	CFE	Meteor F.3	7.45-1.49	EE281/GO-M	UK	
GO	CFE	Spitfire F.9	46	PV295/GO-C	UK	
GO	CFE	Spitfire F.14	46	MV253/GO-E	UK	
GO	CFE	Spitfire F.21	46	LA235/GO-C	UK	
GO	CFE	Vampire F.1	46-1.49	TG332/GO-I	UK	
GO	CFE	Proctor C.3	c 10.46	LZ792/GO-H	UK	
GO	CFE	Tempest F.2	2.45-48	MW744/GO-S	UK	
GO	CFE	Hornet F.1	48	PX275/GO-F	UK	
GO	CFE	Meteor F.3	48-49	EE281/GO-M	UK	
GR	301	Halifax C.8	1.46-12.46	PP225/GR-W	UK	
GX	SF Broadwell	Anson C.19	48	TX191/GX-A	UK	
GZ	32	Spitfire F.9	9.45-6.47	MA802/GZ-D	MedME	
GZ	32	Spitfire FR.18	4.47-3.49	TP373/GZ-C	MedME	
GZ	32	Vampire F.3	7.48-8.50	VG697/GZ-E	MedME	
H	216	Dakota C.4	3.43-1.50	KK207/H-M	MedME	
HC	HCCS	Proctor C.4	51-52	NP308/HC-H	UK	
HE	263	Meteor F.3	8.45-3.48	EE301/HE-X	UK	
HE	263	Meteor F.4	12.47-51	VT168/HE-E	UK	
HE	263	Meteor T.7	49-51	VW489/HE-Z	UK	
HF	54	Tempest F.2	11.45-10.46	MW774/HF-X	UK	
HF	54	Vampire F.1	10.46-8.48	TG298/HF-F	UK	
HI	66	Meteor F.3	11.46-5.48	EE352/HI-A	UK, Eur	

Code	Unit	Type	Dates	Example	Theatre	Remarks
HI	66	Meteor F.4	5.48-10.49	EE574/HI-H	UK	
HN	20	Spitfire F.14	11.45-5.46	SM933/HN-A	FE	
HN	20	Tempest F.2	5.46-7.47	PR648/HN-K	FE	
HS	109	Mosquito B.16	10.45-12.48	PF484/HS-A	UK	
HS	109	Mosquito B.35	4.48-7.52	VR795/HS-B	UK	
HT	601	Spitfire LF.16e	47-12.49	SL745/HT-G	UK	
HT	601	Harvard T.2B	47-51	FX387/HT-X	UK	
HT	601	Vampire F.3	11.49-51	VT871/HT-N	UK	
HW	100	Lincoln B.2	5.46-4.51	RF472/HW-B	UK	
HX	203 AFS	Spitfire LF.16e	7.47-9.49	TE206/HX-A	UK	
HX	203 AFS	Vampire FB.5	7.47-9.49	VV453/HX-U	UK	
HX	203 AFS	Meteor T.7	5.49-9.49	VW427/HX-X	UK	
HX	203 AFS	Meteor F.4	7.49-9.49	RA440/HX-T	UK	to 226 OCU
HX	226 OCU	Spitfire LF.16e	9.49-3.50	TE184/HX-G	UK	1 (Gunnery) Sqn
HX	226 OCU	Meteor F.4	9.49-6.55	VT314/HX-U	UK	1 (Gunnery) Sqn
HX	226 OCU	Meteor T.7	9.49-6.55	WA602/HX-W	UK	1 (Gunnery) Sqn
HX	226 OCU	Meteor F.8	7.52-6.55	WH317/HX-E	UK	1 (Gunnery) Sqn
HX	226 OCU	Vampire FB.5	9.49-12.50	VV486/HX-L	UK	1 (Gunnery) Sqn
IB	43 GCF	Anson XII	45-49	PH661/IB-*	UK	
IC	SF Scampton	Anson C.19	45-50	VM393/IC-G	UK	
IC	SF Scampton	Oxford C.1	45-51	LB401/IC-A	UK	
IP	BCIS	Spitfire LF.16	45-6.47	TB288/IP-D	UK	
J5	3	Tempest F.5	45-4.48	SN330/J5-H	Eur	
J5	3	Vampire F.1	4.48-5.49	VF279/J5-T	Eur	
J5	3	Vampire FB.5	5.49-50	VV532/J5-A	Eur	
J6	1521 RATF	Oxford	45-46		UK	
JH	203 AFS	Spitfire LF.16e	7.47-9.49	TD206/JH-A	UK	
JN	30	Dakota C.4	11.47-1.51	KN419/JN-O	UK	
JN	30	Valetta C.1	12.50-c 7.52	VW863/JN-G	UK	
JU	111	Spitfire IX	6.43-5.47	PL168/JU-A	MedME	
JV	6	Hurricane IV	7.43-1.47	KZ609/JV-S	MedME	
JV	6	Spitfire F.9	12.45-12.46	NH345/JV-P	MedME	
JV	6	Tempest F.6	12.46-12.49	NX191/JV-H	MedME	
JV	SF Finningley	Oxford		NM799/JV-M	UK	
JX	1	Spitfire F.21	11.44-10.46	LA217/JX-G	UK	
JX	1	Meteor F.3	10.46-9.47	EE458/JX-B	UK	

The Tempest, in its F.6 guise, was also the standard fighter/ground attack type with the RAF in the Middle East, where NX143/GN-H of No. 249 Sqn is seen at Habbaniya in 1947. The white-outlined red code and the resurrection of the pre-war spearhead squadron badge enhance the drab camouflage scheme. (D. H. Newton)

Wearing the standard grey and black bomber colours used through to the early 1950s, these two Lincoln B.2s are seen participating in the flypast at Farnborough in September 1950. The nearest one, coded MGF, belongs to No. 7 Sqn while beyond is RE296/QN-BW of No. 214, whose aircraft wore double aircraft letters. (via Gp Capt W. J. Taylor)

Code	Unit	Type	Dates	Example	Theatre	Remarks
JX	1	Harvard T.2B	8.47-6.48	FX411/JX-K	UK	
JX	1	Oxford T.2	8.47-6.48	LX132/JX-N	UK	
JX	1	Meteor F.4	6.48-9.50	VW270/JX-D	UK	
JX	1	Meteor T.7	49-51	VW487/JX-J	UK	
JX	1	Meteor F.8	9.50-51	VZ438/JX-E	UK	
K2	*7 GCF*		*45*		*UK*	*use not known*
K7	6 OTU	Oxford 1	45-7.47	N4737/K7-DC	UK	
K7	6 OTU	Warwick GR.5	45-7.47	HG115/K7-AH	UK	
K7	6 OTU	Mosquito B.6	45-7.47	RF890/K7-MX	UK	
K7	6 OTU	Mosquito T.3	45-7.47	TV956/K7-MC	UK	
K7	6 OTU	Lancaster B.3	45-7.47	RF271/K7-LF	UK	
K7	6 OTU	Beaufighter TT.10	45-7.47	RD709/K7-FG	UK	
K7	6 OTU	Wellington T.10	45-7.47	NA903/K7-AZ	UK	
K7	6 OTU	Spitfire LF.16	45-7.47	TE246/K7-SA	UK	to 236 OCU
K7	6 OTU	Note: 6 OTU used a 'type' letter after the unit code, followed by the individual letter, thus - Warwick A, Wellington A, Oxford D, Beaufighter F, Hurricane H, Lancaster L, Mosquito M, Spitfire S				
K7	236 OCU	Lancaster GR.3	7.47-5.51	SW338/K7-R	UK	ex 6 OTU
K7	236 OCU	Oxford T.1	7.47-5.51	N4737/K7-DL	UK	
K7	236 OCU	Tiger Moth T.2	*c* 49	EM905/K7-*	UK	
KC	617	Lancaster B.7(FE)	6.45-9.46	NX783/KC-G	UK	
KC	617	Lincoln B.2	8.46-1.52	SX936/KC-X	UK	
KC	617	Oxford C.2	6.49-51	NM331/KC-J	UK	
KD	226	OCU Meteor T.7	47-8.49	VW416/KD-F	UK	
KE	BLEU	Dominie C.1	10.45-11.49	NR687/KE-B	UK	
KE	BLEU	Proctor C.4	10.45-11.49	NP184/KE-C	UK	
KM	44	Lancaster B.3	12.41-6.47	PA256/KM-C	UK	
KM	44	Lancaster B.1(FE)	46-6.47	TW883/KM-Z	UK	
KM	44	Lincoln B.2	5.47-1.51	RF423/KM-K	UK	
KN	77	Dakota C.3, C.4	5.45-11.46	KP232/KN-K	FE	
KO	115	Lancaster B.1(FE)	46-1.50	ND720/KO-D	UK	
KO	115	Lincoln B.2	9.49-3.50	RE347/KO-G	UK	
KO	115	Washington B.1	6.50-11.51	WF447/KO-G	UK	
KR	61 OTU	Spitfire LF.16	10.45-7.47	TE382/KR-L	UK	to 203 AFS
KR	203 AFS	Spitfire LF.16e	7.47-9.49	RW390/KR-K	UK	
KR	226 OCU	Vampire FB.5	9.49-12.50	WA112/KR-F	UK	ex 203 AFS
KR	226 OCU	Meteor F.4	9.49-52	RA489/KR-C	UK	No 2 Tac Sqn
KR	226 OCU	Meteor T.7	9.49-6.55	WH250/KR-D	UK	No 2 Tac Sqn
KR	226 OCU	Meteor F.8	52-6.55	WK855/KR-L	UK	No 2 Tac Sqn
KY	242	Stirling C.5	2.45-1.46	PK152/KY-A	UK	
KY	242	York C.1	12.45-9.49	MW232/KY-M	UK	
L5	297	Halifax A.7	9.45-3.47	NA400/L5-L	UK	
LA	607	Spitfire F.22	50-6.51	PK523/LA-E	UK	
LA	607	Vampire FB.5	4.51-52	WA291/LA-K	UK	
LA	607	Harvard T.2B	*c* 50-51	FS921/LA-D	UK	
LE	40	York C.1	12.47-3.50	MW298/LE-G	UK	
LJ	600	Meteor T.7	7.49-51	WA665/LJ-S	UK	
LJ	600	Meteor F.4	3.50-51	RA379/LJ-V	UK	
LO	602	Spitfire F.21	50-5.51	LA227/LO-O	UK	
LO	602	Spitfire F.22	50-5.51	PK349/LO-D	UK	
LO	602	Harvard T.2B	50-51	KF584/LO-X	UK	
LO	602	Vampire FB.5	1.51-51	WA137/LO-D	UK	
LO	602	Meteor T.7	*c* 50-51	WF846/LO-V	UK	
LP	8 OTU	Mosquito PR.34	45-7.47	RG285/LP-94	UK	
LP	237 OCU	Mosquito PR.34	7.47-12.51	PF627/LP-62	UK	
LP	237 OCU	Spitfire PR.19	7.47-12.51	PM621/LP-81	UK	

As is readily apparent by the black and yellow identification stripes Valetta C.1 VW807/NU-T of No. 240 OCU had been involved in the Suez operation when seen in November 1956, but its retention of two-letter unit codes this late is noteworthy. (B. A. Forward)

The Brigand B.1 was used operationally overseas by three squadrons. The only one to wear a unit code was No. 45 in Singapore where VS864/OB-N is seen leading another over the naval base in the early 1950s. No. 45 used these same code letters from the beginning of the war until it relinquished Hornets in 1955. (via Wg Cdr C. G. Jefford)

Code	Unit	Type	Dates	Example	Theatre	Remarks
LP	237 OCU	Meteor T.7	c 48-12.51	WA667/LP-66	UK	
LP	237 OCU	Mosquito T.3	7.47-12.51	HK973/LP-73	UK	
LP	237 OCU	Oxford T.1	7.47-12.51	EB813/LP-73	UK	
LP	283	Warwick ASR.1	3.44-3.46	BV292/LP-Z	MedME	
LS	15	Lancaster B.7(FE)	12.43-3.47	HK619/LS-V	UK	
LS	15	Lincoln B.2	2.47-10.50	RF514/LS-B	UK	
LS	15	Washington B.1	1.51-4.53	WF498/LS-B	UK	
LX	228 OCU	Mosquito FB.6	5.47-2.49	TA503/LX-*	UK	ex 54 OTU
LZ	66	Spitfire LF.16e	9.46-3.47	SM355/LZ-W	UK	
LZ	66	Meteor F.4	5.48-1.51	VT122/LZ-B	UK	
LZ	66	Meteor T.7	50-51	VW485/LZ-A	UK	
MF	CFE (DFLS)	Tempest F.5	46-48	SN276/MF-J	UK	
MG	7	Lancaster B.1(FE)	7.43-1.50	SW265/MG-E	UK	
MG	7	Lincoln B.2	8.49-4.51	RE340/MG-D	UK	
MH	51	York C.1	1.50-10.50	MW277/MH-C	UK	
MP	76	Dakota C.4	5.45-9.46	KN664/MP-D	FE	
MR	245	Meteor F.3	8.45-3.48	EE286/MR-O	UK	
MR	245	Meteor F.4	11.47-6.50	VT125/MR-B	UK	
MR	245	Meteor F.8	6.50-51	WA836/MR-E	UK	
MS	SF Church Fenton	Hornet F.3	4.49-6.50	PX299/MS-G	UK	
MS	SF Church Fenton	Mosquito T.3	3.50-6.50	TW117/MS-A	UK	
NF	138	Lancaster B.1(FE)	12.46-9.47	PA415/NF-L	UK	
NF	138	Lincoln B.2	4.47-9.50	RF440/NF-X	UK	
NF	138	Oxford	46-c 49	V3537/NF-Y	UK	
NG	604	Spitfire LF.16e	48-5.50	TE436/NG-F	UK	
NG	604	Vampire F.3	11.49-50	VF329/NG-E	UK	
NR	605	Vampire F.1	50-5.51	TG381/NR-A	UK	
NR	605	Vampire FB.5	4.51-11.51	WA320/NR-F	UK	
NS	201	Sunderland GR.5	2.45-c 52	VB881/NS-A	UK	
NU	1382 (T)CU	Dakota C.4	8.45-1.48	KJ778/NU-Q	UK	to 240 OCU
NU	240 OCU	Dakota C.4	1.48-4.51	KK198/NU-N	UK	ex 1382 (T)CU
NU	240 OCU	Anson C.10	10.48-4.51	LT602/NU-D	UK	
NU	240 OCU	Valetta C.1	12.48-4.51	VW847/NU-H	UK	
NU	240 OCU	Devon C.1	12.48-4.51	VP974/NU-A	UK	
NV	BLEU		45		UK	use not known

Code	Unit	Type	Dates	Example	Theatre	Remarks
OB	45	Beaufighter TF.10	12.45-2.50	RD824/OB-K	FE	
OB	45	Brigand B.1	11.49-2.52	VS859/OB-V	FE	
OB	45	Buckmaster T.1	5.49-2.52	RP198/OB-Z	FE	
OB	45	Hornet F.3	1.52-5.55	WB898/OB-A	FE	
OF	97	Lincoln B.2	7.46-51	RE305/OF-N	UK	
OI	1665 HTCU	Halifax A.7	*c* 5.46-7.46	PN294/OG-B	UK	
OI	2	Spitfire F.14	11.44-1.51	TZ164/OI-A	Eur	
OI	2	Spitfire PR.19	1.46-4.51	PM549/OI-F	Eur	
OJ	149	Lancaster B.1(FE)	46-11.49	PA410/OJ-X	UK	
OJ	149	Lincoln B.2	10.49-3.50	RA709/OJ-V	UK	
OJ	149	Washington B.1	11.50-51	WF492/OJ-U	UK	
OL	83	Lancaster B.3	5.42-7.46	JA967/OL-S	UK	
OL	83	Lincoln B.2	5.46-*c* 51	RF369/OL-G	UK	
OM	107	Mosquito FB.6	2.44-9.48	RS816/OM-J	UK, Eur	to 11 Sqn
OM	11	Mosquito FB.6	10.48-*c* 49	TA489/OM-D	Eur	ex 107 Sqn
ON	56	Meteor F.3	4.46-9.48	EE365/ON-N	UK	ex 124 Sqn
OQ	5	Tempest F.2	3.46-7.47	PR559/OQ-R	FE	
OQ	1385 HTCU	Halifax A.7	4.46-7.46	PN294/OG-B	UK	
OT	58	Mosquito T.3	10.46-*c* 52	VT589/OT-Z	UK	
OT	58	Mosquito PR.34	10.46-*c* 51	RG178/OT-R	UK	
OT	58	Anson C.19	10.46-9.51	VL357/OT-P	UK	
OT	58	Lincoln B.2	10.50-10.51	SX991/OT-C	UK	
OY	13 OTU	Mosquito FB.6	3.45-5.47	HJ741/OY-G	UK	
OZ	179	Lancaster GR.3	2.46-9.46	RE115/OZ-T	UK	to 210 Sqn
OZ	210	Lancaster GR.3	6.46-51	SW370/OZ-L	UK	ex 179 Sqn
P9	ASWDU	Liberator VI	45-*c* 46	EV871/P9-Q	UK	
P9	ASWDU	Walrus 1	45-*c* 47	W3076/P9-G	UK	
P9	ASWDU	Wellington GR.14	45-*c* 48	NC799/P9-A	UK	
P9	ASWDU	Halifax B.3	45-*c* 48	NA168/P9-H	UK	
P9	ASWDU	Warwick GR.2	45-*c* 47	HG365/P9-B	UK	
P9	ASWDU	Anson I	45-*c* 49	NK327/P9-F	UK	
P9	ASWDU	Mosquito FB.6	45-*c* 48	RF760/P9-Y	UK	
P9	ASWDU	Proctor C.3	*c* 45-*c* 51	HM480/P9-A	UK	
P9	ASWDU	Sunderland GR.5	*c* 45-*c* 51	PP122/P9-Q	UK	
P9	ASWDU	Beaufighter TF.10	*c* 45-*c* 46	RD468/P9-L	UK	
P9	ASWDU	Lancaster GR.3	1.46-52	RE164/P9-B	UK	
P9	ASWDU	Sea Otter II	3.46-*c* 51	JM827/P9-Q	UK	
P9	ASWDU	Hoverfly II	46-48	KL104/P9-T	UK	
P9	ASWDU	Brigand TF.1	*c* 47-*c* 51	RH808/P9-B	UK	
P9	ASWDU	Warwick GR.5	*c* 11.48	LM798/P9-M	UK	
P9	ASWDU	Anson C.19	48-49	PH829/P9-D	UK	
PF	43 OTU	Auster AOP.4	5.44-5.47	MT162/PF-J	UK	
PF	43 OTU	Auster AOP.6	*c* 46-5.47	TW523/PF-U	UK	to 227 OCU
PF	227 OCU	Auster AOP.5	5.47-5.50	TW461/PF-D	UK	ex 43 OTU
PF	227 OCU	Auster AOP.6	5.47-5.50	TW575/PF-B	UK	
PF	227 OCU	Auster T.7	5.47-5.50	WE549/PF-G	UK	to LAS
PF	LAS	Oxford 1	5.50-4.53	PK284/PF-A	UK	ex 227 OCU
PF	LAS	Auster AOP.6	5.50-4.53	TW568/PF-X	UK	
PH	12	Lincoln B.2	8.46-5.52	RF390/PH-K	UK	
PH	12	Tiger Moth T.2	6.49-	DE898/PH-F	UK	
PR	609	Spitfire LF.16E	50-2.51	SL561/PR-H	UK	
PR	609	Harvard T.2B	50-2.51	KF374/PR-B	UK	
PR	609	Meteor F.4	12.50-6.51	VT262/PR-B	UK	
PS	264	Mosquito NF.36	5.47-8.51	RL195/PS-A	UK	
PS	264	Oxford	*c* 47-49	P8894/PS-I	UK	
PU	187	Dakota C.4	3.45-11.46	KN655/PU-H	UK	to 53 Sqn

Code	Unit	Type	Dates	Example	Theatre	Remarks
PU	53	Dakota C.4	11.46-7.49	KN343/PU-U	UK	ex 187 Sqn
Q3	613	Spitfire F.22	50-3.51	PK573/Q3-Y	UK	
Q3	613	Vampire F.1	9.49-4.50	TG336/Q3-D	UK	
Q3	613	Vampire F.3	9.49-4.50	VF329/Q3-G	UK	
Q3	613	Vampire FB.5	2.51-*c* 11.51	VV616/Q3-K	UK	
Q3	613	Harvard T.2B	49-*c* 11.51	KF476/Q3-2	UK	
Q3	613	Meteor T.7	4.51-11.51	WA637/Q3-4	UK	
QE	CFE	Mosquito NF.30	10.44-10.50	NT442/QE-18	Eur	
QE	CFE	Mosquito FB.6	2.45-1.49	TA554/QE-3	Eur	
QK	APS Sylt	Master 2	*c* 45-48	DK823/QK-C	Eur	
QK	APS Sylt	Martinet 1	*c* 45-48	MS558/QK-5	Eur	
QM	42	Beaufighter TF.10	10.46-10.47	SR914/QM-Y	UK	
QN	214	Lancaster B.3	11.45-4.46	PA386/QN-Y	MedME	
QN	214	Lancaster B.1(FE)	11.46-2.50	TW882/QN-V	UK	
QN	214	Lincoln B.2	2.50-51	RE423/QN-G	UK	
QO	167	Harvard T.2B	2.53-53	KF604/QO-N	UK	
QO	167	Meteor T.7	2.53-4.53	WL346/QO-G	UK	
QO	167	Vampire FB.5	2.53-54	WA183/QO-X	UK	
QO	167	Valetta C.1	2.53-9.58	VX484/QO-E	UK	
QR	61	Lincoln B.2	5.46-*c* 51	RF576/QR-O	UK	
QT	57	Lincoln B.2	8.45-*c* 46	SX941/QT-A	UK	C Flt
QT	57	Oxford T.1	*c* 45-46	MP343/Q7-B	UK	C Flt
QU	RAFNICF	Anson C.19	46-3.50	VM392/QU-L	UK	
QU	RAFNICF	Proctor C.3	46-3.50	DX187/QU-B	UK	
QU	RAFNICF	Oxford C.2	45-3.50	X7060/QU-P	UK	
QU	RAFNICF	Anson C.12	49-50	PH624/QU-D	UK	
QV	19	Spitfire LF.16E	3.46-10.46	TE470/QV-B	UK	
QV	19	Hornet F.1	10.46-5.48	PX246/QV-A	UK	
QV	19	MosquitoT.3	7.47-51	TW113/QV-Z	UK	
QV	19	Hornet F.3	3.48-1.51	PX332/QV-D	UK	
RE	CFE	Tempest F.5	46-48	SN262/RE-M	UK	
RF	1510 RATF	Anson I	8.45-9.48	NK291/RF-A	UK	
RF	1510 RATF	Oxford T.1	8.45-9.48	RR330/RF-V	UK	
RG	208	Spitfire F.9	3.44-6.47	PV117/RG-E	MedME	
RG	208	Spitfire FR.18	8.46-51	TP295/RG-M	MedME	
RL	38	Lancaster ASR.3	7.46-*c* 51	RF323/RL-C	MedME	
RO	29	Mosquito NF.30	2.45-8.51	NT609/RO-S	UK	
RO	29	Mosquito NF.36	8.46-10.50	RL175/RO-P	UK	
RO	29	Mosquito T.3	*c* 9.49	VA893/RO-Q	UK	
RS	30	Tempest II	3.46-12.46	PR583/RS-G	FE	
RS	229 OCU	Beaufighter TT.10	12.50-12.52	RD859/RS-17	UK	2 Sqn
RS	229 OCU	Oxford T.1	12.50-*c* 53	MP450/RS-U	UK	2 Sqn
RS	229 OCU	Tempest TT.5	3.51-4.55	NB699/RS-39	UK	2 Sqn
RS	229 OCU	Vampire FB.5	12.50-*c* 56	VX977/RS-P	UK	2 Sqn
RS	229 OCU	Vampire T.11	1.53-11.58	WZ467/RS-25	UK	2 Sqn
RS	229 OCU	Hunter F.1	2.55-*c* 56	WT640/RS-G	UK	2 Sqn
RS	229 OCU	Hunter F.4	7.55-4.58	XF361/RS-22	UK	2 Sqn
RT	114	Mosquito FB.6	11.45-9.46	TE659/RT-B	MedME	to 8 Sqn
RT	8	Mosquito FB.6	9.46-4.47	TE821/RT-F	MedME	ex 114 Sqn
RT	8	Mosquito T.3	9.46-4.47	RR296/RT-N	MedME	ex 114 Sqn
S6	41 GCF	Miles M 28 Mk II	*c* 46	HM583/S6-M	UK	ex 41 GCF
S6	Maint Cd CS	Miles M 28 Mk II	4.46-*c* 9.46	HM583/S6-M	UK	ex 41 GCF
S7	500	Meteor F.3	50-10.51	EE403/S7-E	UK	
S7	500	Meteor F.4	7.51-1.52	VT197/S7-N	UK	
S7	500	Meteor T.7	50-51	VZ938/S7-G	UK	
S7	500	Harvard T.2B	50-51	KF718/S7	UK	

Code	Unit	Type	Dates	Example	Theatre	Remarks
SD	501	Vampire F.1	50-6.51	VF282/SD-R	UK	
SD	501	Meteor T.7	50-6.51	WA594/SD-G	UK	
SD	501	Harvard T.2B	c 47-51	KF670/SD-A	UK	
SH	64	Mustang III	1.44-5.46	KH449/SH-D	UK	
SH	64	Mustang IV	8.45-6.46	KM256/SH-W	UK	
SH	64	Hornet F.1	3.46-5.48	PX284/SH-B	UK	
SH	64	Hornet F.3	5.48-4.51	PX391/SH-R	UK	
SH	64	Mosquito T.3	48-4.51	VT593/SH	UK	
SJ	21 OTU	Wellington T.10	8.43-3.47	LN893/SJ-W	UK	
SK	165	Spitfire F.9	6.45-9.46	PL317/SK-A	UK	
SL	13 OTU	Tempest F.2	c 45-5.47	MW759/SL-X	UK	
SL	13 OTU	Mosquito B.6	11.43-5.47	TA476/SL-A	UK	
SN	230 OCU	Lincoln B.2	2.49-9.53	RF562/SN-N	UK	
SN	230 OCU	Oxford T.1	2.49-c 51	PH299/SN-D	UK	
SR	101	Lincoln B.2	8.46-6.51	RF362/SR-D	UK	
SR	101	Oxford T.1	c 46-51	NM331/SR-J	UK	
ST	228 OCU	Martinet TT.1	5.47-12.51	EM444/ST-I	UK	ex 54 OTU
ST	228 OCU	Wellington GR.18	5.47-12.50	ND108/ST-D	UK	
SW	43	Meteor F.4	2.49-9.50	VT257/SW-T	UK	
SW	43	Meteor T.7	2.49-4.51	VW488/SW-V	UK	
SW	43	Meteor F.8	9.50-4.51	VZ513/SW-Y	UK	
SW	253	Spitfire F.9	11.44-5.47	PT462/SW-A	MedME, Eur	
TA	4 (C)OTU	Sunderland GR.5	c 10.44-7.47	RN302/TA-H	UK	to 235 OCU
TA	235 OCU	Sunderland GR.5	7.47-51	ML778/TA-P	UK	ex 4 (C)OTU
TB	51	Stirling C.5	8.45-12.46	PK115/TB-X	UK	
TB	51	York C.1	1.46-10.50	MW261/TB-Y	UK	
TH	20	Martinet TT.1	2.49-9.51	HN884/TH-K	UK	
TH	20	Harvard T.2B	2.49-9.51	KF561/TH-Z	UK	
TH	20	Vampire F.1	2.49-3.51	TG447/TH-M	UK	
TH	20	Spitfire LF.16E	2.49-9.51	TE448/TH-E	UK	
TH	20	Tiger Moth T.2	2.49-c 50	T8072/TH-E	UK	
TH	20	Vampire F.3	11.49-9.51	VT868/TH-O	UK	
TH	20	Beaufighter TT.10	2.50-9.51	RD758/TH-L	UK	
TL	35	Lancaster B.1(FE)	12.45-10.49	TW880/TL-F	UK	
TL	35	Lincoln B.2	8.49-2.50	SX983/TL-S	UK	
TM	504	Meteor F.4	50-51	VZ403/TM-A	UK	

The ubiquitous NAAFI van stops work on the Meteor F.3s of No. 124 Sqn at Bentwaters in early 1946 shortly before it was renumbered as No. 56 Sqn, which retained the same code letters; EE400/ON-H is the nearest example. (R. I. Clarke)

Although not generally worn on photo-reconnaissance Mosquitos during the Second World War, unit codes were applied after the war, though otherwise the wartime scheme remained in use, as seen on PR.34 RG300/OT-A of No. 58 Sqn when visiting St Eval in 1946. (R. E. Hilliard)

Code	Unit	Type	Dates	Example	Theatre	Remarks
TM	504	Meteor T.7	50-51	WA610/TM-M	UK	
TM	504	Harvard T.2B	50-51	KF156/TM-Z	UK	
TO	61 OTU	Master 2	6.41-7.47	DK881/TO-N	UK	
TO	203 AFS	Martinet TT.1	7.47-9.49	HP255/TO-W	UK	
TO	203 AFS	Harvard T.2B	7.47-9.49	FX360/TO-P	UK	
TO	203 AFS	Tiger Moth T.2	7.47-9.49	T5465/TO-A	UK	to 226 OCU
TO	226 OCU	Martinet TT.1	49-3.54	HN947/TO-Y	UK	ex 203 AFS
TO	226 OCU	Harvard T.2B	49-8.50	FS739/TO-Z	UK	
TO	226 OCU	Tiger Moth T.2	9.49-51	T5465/TO-A	UK	
TS	657	Auster AOP.5	12.44-12.46	TJ672/TS-D2	UK	
TS	657	Auster AOP.6	6.46-51	VF573/TS-E	UK	
TS	657	Hoverfly 2	4.47-4.51	KN840/TS-L	UK	
TW	141	Mosquito NF.36	6.46-12.51	RL154/TW-E	UK	
UB	63	Spitfire LF.16E	9.46-5.48	TE392/UB-P	UK	
UB	63	Meteor F.3	4.48-6.48	EE292/UB-F	UK	
UB	63	Meteor F.4	6.48-1.51	VT198/UB-B	UK	
UB	63	Meteor T.7	12.50-51	VW489/UB-Q	UK	
UH	21 OTU	Oxford T.1	45-3.47	PH177/UH-J	UK	
UH	21 OTU	Martinet 1	45-3.47	JN301/UH-X	UK	to 202 AFS
UH	202 AFS	Wellington T.10	3.47-12.47	LP156/UH-Z	UK	ex 21 OTU
UK	CFE	Proctor C.2	c 10.46	LZ791/UK-X	UK	
UM	152	Spitfire F.14	1.46-7.46	RM908/UM-G	FE	
UM	152	Tempest F.2	7.46-3.47	PR747/UM-L	FE	
UP	4	Mosquito FB.6	8.45-7.50	RS678/UP-T	Eur	ex 605 Sqn
UP	4	Vampire FB.5	7.50-51	WA120/UP-A	Eur	
US	56	Meteor F.3	4.46-9.48	EE271/US-H	UK	
US	56	Meteor F.4	8.48-12.50	RA434/US-Q	UK	
US	56	Meteor T.7	7.49-51	WA629/US-Z	UK	
UT	17	Spitfire LF.16E	2.49-3.51	SM406/UT-H	UK	
UT	17	Oxford T.2	2.49-4.51	NJ296/UT-Y	UK	
UT	17	Harvard T.2B	2.49-4.51	FX222/UT-M	UK	
UT	17	Beaufighter TT.10	5.49-3.51	RD771/UT-Z	UK	
UU	61 OTU	Spitfire F.14	10.45-7.47	SM896/UU-B	UK	to 203 AFS
UU	203 AFS	Spitfire LF.16E	7.47-9.49	TE479/UU-F	UK	ex 61 OTU
UU	203 AFS	Spitfire FR.18E	7.47-9.49	TP315/UU-Z	UK	

On becoming part of Fighter Command in 1949 the RAuxAF squadrons resumed the use of two-letter codes. Some, like No. 501 (County of Gloucester) Sqn, had their old wartime code reallocated. Vampire F.1 TG305/SD-F shows this while landing at Elmdon in 1949, the prominent number 2 being added for the Cooper Air Race. (F. G. Swanborough)

With the cliffs of Hong Kong behind, Hornet F.3 WB879/W2-B of No. 80 Sqn sits at dispersal at Kai Tak in 1952 shortly before the code was replaced by a handsome coloured squadron marking. (C. Lynch)

Code	Unit	Type	Dates	Example	Theatre	Remarks
UU	203 AFS	Spitfire PR.19	7.47-9.49	PM637/UU-H	UK	
UU	203 AFS	Spitfire F.22	48-9.49	PK402/UU-H	UK	to 226 OCU
UU	226 OCU	Spitfire LF.16	c 48	SM245/UU-A	UK	ex 203 AFS
UU	226 OCU	Spitfire F.14	9.49-51	TX984/UU-D	UK	
UU	226 OCU	Spitfire PR.19	9.49-8.50	TP315/UU-Z	UK	
UU	226 OCU	Spitfire F.22	9.49-51	PM579/UU-D	UK	
UU	226 OCU	Meteor T.7	9.49-51	WG943/UU-F	UK	
UU	226 OCU	Meteor FR.9	6.51-8.54	WB137/UU-C	UK	
UU	226 OCU	Meteor F.8	52-6.55	WH376/UU-M	UK	
UU	226 OCU	Vampire T.11	9.54-6.55	XE923/UU-T	UK	
UX	CFE/DFLS	Spitfire F.14	12.44-c 49	RM704/UX-A	UK	
UX	CFE/DFLS	Spitfire LF.16	12.44-c 49	RM704/UX-A	UK	
UX	CFE/DFLS	Meteor F.3	7.45-c 50	EE472/UX-P	UK	
V6	615	Spitfire F.22	50-9.50	PK519/V6-A	UK	
V6	615	Harvard T.2B	50-9.50	KF200/V6-X	UK	
V6	615	Meteor F.4	9.50-9.51	VT102/V6-S	UK	
V6	615	Meteor T.7	9.50-9.51	WA684/V6-W	UK	
V7	RWE	Lancaster B.3	7.45-9.46	ED906/V7-T	UK	
V7	RWE	Proctor C.3	7.45-9.46	DX197/V7-O2	UK	
V7	RWE	Anson C.19	7.45-9.46	TX223/V7-D	UK	to CSE
V7	CSE	Mosquito FB.16	9.46-	RG265/V7-X	UK	ex RWE
V7	CSE	Mosquito PR.34	9.46-	PF533/V7-V	UK	
V7	CSE	Mosquito B.35	9.46-51	TK629/V7-Z	UK	
V7	CSE	Lancaster B.1(FE)	9.46-47	TW659/V7-D	UK	
V7	CSE	Lancaster B.3	9.46-	ME371/V7-K	UK	
V7	CSE	Anson C.10	9.46-47	NK924/V7-J	UK	
V7	CSE	Anson C.11	9.46-48	NK996/V7-K	UK	
V7	CSE	Anson C.12	9.46-	MG134/V7-O	UK	
V7	CSE	Anson C.19	47-51	VM369/V7-J	UK	
V7	CSE	Lincoln B.2	50-51	SX956/V7-C	UK	
V7	CSE	Proctor C.3	9.46-48	DX197/V7-O	UK	
V7	CSE	Warwick V	9.46-	PN701/V7-J	UK	
V9	502	Spitfire F.22	50-1.51	PK316/V9-A	UK	
V9	502	Harvard T.2B	50-51	KF707/V9-Q	UK	
V9	502	Vampire FB.5	3.51-11.51	WA294/V9-C	UK	
V9	502	Meteor T.7	4.51-51	WF824/V9-N	UK	
VA	264	Mosquito NF.30	11.45-7.46	NT450/VA-B	UK	ex 125 Sqn
VA	264	Mosquito NF.36	11.45-46	RL146/VA-J	UK	
VF	SF Lindholme	Oxford I	c 5.45-c 1950	LP401/VF-A	UK	
VN	50	Lancaster I, III	5.42-11.46	RE133/VN-K	UK	
VN	50	Lincoln B.2	7.46-1.51	RF384/VN-H	UK	
VO	98	Mosquito B.16	11.45-8.48	PF596/VO-T	Eur	
VO	98	Mosquito B.35	8.48-2.51	TH995/VO-Y	Eur	
VS	MCS	Anson C.19	45-7.48	PH694/VS-AZ	UK	ex 510 Sqn
VS	MCS	Proctor C.3	45-7.48	HM308/VS-U	UK	
VS	MCS	Proctor C.4	45-7.48	NP163/VS-A	UK	to 31 Sqn
VS	31	Anson C.19	7.48-3.55	PH694/VS-Z	UK	ex MCS
VS	31	Proctor C.3	8.48-49	HM308/VS-U	UK	
VS	31	Proctor C.4	9.49-7.53	NP387/VS-B	UK	
VY	85	Mosquito NF.36	1.46-10.51	RL213/VY-F	UK	
W2	80	Tempest F.5	8.44-1.48	SN209/W2-E	Eur	
W2	80	Spitfire F.24	1.48-5.52	VN317/W2-P	Eur, FE	
W2	80	Hornet F.3	12.51-12.52	WB879/W2-B	FE	
W3	SF Hemswell	Oxford T.1	46-47	AB722/W3	UK	
WB	BCIS	Lancaster B.3	12.44-6.47	HK763/WB-G	UK	
WB	BCIS	Lincoln B.2	12.44-6.47	RE283/WB-D	UK	

Code	Unit	Type	Dates	Example	Theatre	Remarks
WF	238	Dakota C.3	12.46-10.48	KG391/WF-G	UK	ex 525 Sqn
WF	238	Dakota C.4	12.46-10.48	KN292/WF-N	UK	
WH	APS Acklington	Spitfire LF.16E	3.50-7.51	TE407/WH-H	UK	
WH	APS Acklington	Martinet TT.1	3.50-7.51	JN543/WH-5	UK	
WH	APS Acklington	Mosquito FB.6	3.50-52	RF875/WH-E	UK	
WH	APS Acklington	Oxford T.1	3.50-7.54	R6285/WH-D	UK	
WH	APS Acklington	Meteor F.4	3.50-7.51	VT195/WH-C	UK	
WH	APS Acklington	Tempest TT.5	3.50-7.52	NV923/WH-8	UK	
WH	APS Acklington	Vampire F.3	3.50	VT797/WH-P	UK	
WH	APS Acklington	Meteor T.7	6.50-c 54	WF819/WH-G	UK	
WH	APS Acklington	Vampire FB.5	9.50-7.51	VZ269/WH-J	UK	
WH	APS Acklington	Balliol T.2	7.51-c 54	VR596/WH-K	UK	
WH	APS Acklington	Meteor F.8	7.52-c 54	VZ522/WH-V	UK	
WH	APS Acklington	Vampire T.11	8.52-c 54	WZ619/WH-K	UK	
WI	69	Mosquito FB.6	8.45-3.46	RS611/WI-R	Eur	
WI	69	Mosquito B.16	4.46-11.47	PF544/WI-F	Eur	
WP	90	Lancaster B.3	5.44-12.47	NN783/WP-E	UK	
WP	90	Lancaster B.1(FE)	46-5.47	SW309/WP-X	UK	
WP	90	Lincoln B.2	4.47-9.50	RR451/WP-N	UK	
WP	90	Washington B.1	10.50-51	WF442/WP-P	UK	
WQ	209	Sunderland GR.5	50-51	RN298/WQ-R	UK	
WS	9	Lancaster B.7	11.45-4.46	NX768/WS-S	UK	
WS	9	Lincoln B.2	7.46-5.42	SX977/WS-F	UK	
WS	9	Oxford T.1	5.49-50	BG273/WS-Z	UK	
WV	18	Mosquito Met.6	3.47-11.47	RF822/WV-F	FE	
WY	541	Spitfire PR.19	11.47-4.51	PS934/WY-R	UK	
WY	541	Meteor PR.10	12.50-51	VS983/WY-G	UK	
WY	541	Harvard T.2B	47-51	KF464/WY	UK	
WY	541	Meteor T.7	50-51	WG963/WY-Z	UK	
XB	224	Liberator GR.5	9.44-10.46	FL960/XB-O	UK	
XB	224	Lancaster ASR.3	10.46-11.47	RF314/XB-Q	UK	
XB	224	Halifax Met.6	3.48-1.52	RG691/XB-A	UK	
XC	26	Spitfire F.14	6.45-1.47	NH925/XC-N	Eur	
XC	26	Tempest F.2	11.46-4.49	PR782/XC-Q	Eur	
XC	26	Tempest F.5	11.46-4.49	SN345/XC-K	Eur	
XC	26	Vampire FB.5	4.49-4.51	VV531/XC-N	Eur	
XD	139	Mosquito B.16	2.44-11.48	MM200/XD-E	UK	
XD	139	Mosquito T.3	48-49	VA928/XD-M	UK	
XD	139	Mosquito B.35	10.48-51	TK620/XD-L	UK	
XE	CBE	Anson C.12	46-12.49	NL231/XE-D	UK	
XE	CBE	Anson C.19	46-12.49	VP513/XE-C	UK	
XE	CBE	Auster AOP.5	46-12.49	TW442/XE-A	UK	
XE	CBE	Proctor C.3	46-12.49	LZ578/XE-E	UK	
XK	46	Stirling C.5	2.45-3.46	PJ952/XK-F	UK	
XK	46	Dakota C.4	2.46-2.50	KN241/XK-K	UK	
XL	1335 CU	Meteor F.1	3.45-9.45	EE228/XL-P	UK	
XL	1335 CU	Meteor F.3	3.45-8.46	EE357/XL-B	UK	
XL	1335 CU	Meteor F.4	3.45-8.46	RA422/XL-T	UK	
XL	1335 CU	Spitfire F.18	3.45-8.46	TP434/XL-V	UK	
XL	1335 CU	Hornet F.1	3.45-8.46	PX281/XL-E	UK	
XL	1335 CU	Martinet TT.1	3.45-12.45	*****/XL-5	UK	
XL	1335 CU	Oxford T.2	3.45-8.46	T1251/XL-2	UK	To 226 OCU
XL	226 OCU	Hornet F.1	8.46-8.49	PX238/XL-D	UK	ex 1335 CU
XL	226 OCU	Meteor F.3	8.46-8.49	EE367/XL-B	UK	
XL	226 OCU	Oxford 1	8.46-8.49	V4277/XL-4	UK	

Code	Unit	Type	Dates	Example	Theatre	Remarks
XL	226 OCU	Hornet F.3	10.46-8.49	PX252/XL-V	UK	
XL	226 OCU	Meteor F.4	3.48-8.49	VT110/XL-A	UK	
XL	226 OCU	Tempest F.2	8.46-8.49	PR555/XL-Y	UK	
XL	226 OCU	Spitfire F.18	8.46-10.46	TP434/XL-V	UK	
XL	226 OCU	Vampire F.1	1.47-5.47	TG***/XL-N	UK	
XM	652	Auster AOP.6	9.46-51	TW625/XM-H	Eur	
XT	603	Spitfire F.22	50-7.51	PK341/XT-G	UK	
XY	203 AFS	Anson C.1	9.47-12.47	MH159/XY-A	UK	
Y3	518	Halifax Met.6	9.45-10.46	RG843/Y3-O	UK	to 202 Sqn
Y3	202	Halifax Met.6	10.46-5.51	ST818/Y3-A	UK	ex 518 Sqn
Y3	202	Oxford T.1	45-	V3729/Y3-Q	UK	
Y3	202	Anson C.19	9.49-2.52	PH713/Y3-Y	UK	
Y3	202	Halifax A.9	8.49-12.50	RT786/Y3-B	UK	
Y3	202	Hastings Met.1	5.50-51	TG567/Y3-G	UK	
YF	SF Scampton	Tiger Moth T.2	10.49-5.52	BB790/YF-Z	UK	
YH	21	Mosquito FB.6	9.43-10.47	RS532/YH-E	UK, Eur	
YP	23	Mosquito NF.30	8.45-2.47	NT336/YP-	UK	
YP	23	Mosquito NF.36	10.46-6.52	RL141/YP-B	UK	
YQ	616	Meteor F.3	50-5.51	EE293/YQ-J	UK	
YQ	616	Meteor F.4	4.50-12.51	RA429/YQ-H	UK	
YQ	616	Meteor T.7	4.51-12.51	VZ640/YQ-D	UK	
YQ	616	Harvard T.2B	50-51	KF997/YQ-C	UK	
YS	77	Dakota C.4	12.46-6.49	KJ907/YS-S	UK	ex 271 Sqn
YT	65	Spitfire F.16	3.46-9.46	TD134/YT-W	UK	
YT	65	Hornet F.1	6.46-6.48	PX282/YT-B	UK	
YT	65	Hornet F.3	4.48-4.51	PX346/YT-E		UK
YT	65	Mosquito T.3	49-4.51	VT609/YT-Z	UK	
YW	230 OCU	Mosquito B.35	1.48-3.49	VP201/YW-C	UK	
YW	230 OCU	Mosquito NF.19	4.48-1.49	TA356/YW-J	UK	
YY	1332 HTCU	York C.1	11.45-1.48	MW266/YY-W	UK	to 241 OCU
YY	241 OCU	York C.1	1.48-4.57	MW128/YY-B	UK	ex 1332 HTCU
ZA	10	Dakota C.4	8.45-12.47	KN555/ZA-V	UK	
ZA	MCS	Proctor C.3	45-7.48	LZ803/ZA-G	UK	
ZA	MCS	Dominie C.1	45-7.48	NF874/ZA-W	UK	
ZA	MCS	Oxford T.1	45-7.48	NM735/ZA-K	UK	
ZA	MCS	Anson I	45-7.48	AX258/ZA	UK	
ZA	MCS	Wellington X	45-7.48	PG253/ZA-J	UK	
ZD	222	Meteor F.3	10.45-12.47	EE423/ZD-L	UK	
ZD	222	Meteor F.4	6.47-9.50	VT184/ZD-Q	UK	
ZD	222	Meteor T.7	48-51	WF861/ZD-M	UK	
ZD	222	Meteor F.8	9.50-51	VZ554/ZD-N	UK	
ZE	CFE; NFLS	Mosquito NF.17	10.44-48	HK327/ZE-K	UK	
ZE	CFE; NFLS	Mosquito NF.30	10.44-7.50	NT567/ZE-X	UK	
ZE	CFE; NFLS	Oxford I	2.45-7.50	PH487/ZE-A	UK	
ZE	CFE; NFLS	Mosquito FB.6	2.45-c 47	RF876/ZE-H	UK	
ZE	CFE; NFLS	Meteor F.3	7.45-1.49	EE348/ZQ-J	UK	
ZE	CFE; NFLS	Mosquito NF.30	c 46	MM695/ZQ-Z	UK	
ZE	CFE; NFLS	Mosquito NF.36	c 47-7.50	RL157/ZE-M	UK	
ZK	25	Mosquito NF.30	9.44-9.46	NT378/ZK-G	UK	
ZK	25	Mosquito NF.36	9.46-10.51	RL207/ZK-Z	UK	
ZQ	BCIS	Wellington T.10	45-6.47	NA978/ZQ-S	UK	
ZQ	BCIS	Mosquito T.3	45-6.47	RR311/ZQ-A	UK	to BBU
ZQ	BBU	Lincoln B.1	7.48-11.49	RE242/ZQ-A	UK	ex BCIS
ZY	247	Tempest F.2	8.45-5.46	MW396/ZY-T	UK	
ZY	247	Vampire F.1	3.46-2.49	VF280/ZY-Y	UK	
ZY	247	Vampire F.3	10.48-12.49	VF344/ZY-S	UK	

Code	Unit	Type	Dates	Example	Theatre	Remarks

The Avro York was a mainstay of Transport Command in the late 1940s and initially retained the use of unit codes, as demonstrated by WM295/YY-M of No. 241 OCU at its Dishforth base in 1948 at the height of the Berlin Airlift. (J. D. R. Rawlings)

The Hastings entered service just as unit codes were being withdrawn and they were only applied to the Met. 1s of No. 202 Sqn which was part of Coastal Command. TG567/Y3-G was still wearing a code on 21 February 1951, but it was soon replaced by the single letter A. (No. 202 Sqn Records)

Belgium, 1945–62

Both the wartime units, Nos 349 and 350 Squadrons, continued to use their wartime codes, and as the post-war air force expanded, the system was extended and applied to the new units and used for around thirteen years. The codes should not be confused with the two-letter aircraft type identifier forming the first part of the serial as noted in the examples. Those codes shown in bold are a continuation of the wartime codes.

Code	Unit	Type	Example
3R	1 Sqn	Spitfire FR XIV	SG-56/3R-D
3R	1 Sqn	T-6B Harvard	H-64/3R-I
3R	1 Sqn	F-84E	FS-7/3R-O
3R	1 Sqn	F-84G	FZ-15/3R-E
3R	1 Sqn	F-84F	FU-44/3R-B
7J	7 Sqn	Meteor F 8	EG-39/7J-A
7J	7 Sqn	Hunter F.4	ID8/7J-J
7J	7 Sqn	Hunter F 6	IF132/7J-S
8S	31 Sqn	Spitfire FR.14	SG 50/8S-R
8S	31 Sqn	F-84G	FZ-6/8S-C
8S	31 Sqn	F-84F	FU-159/8S-T
B2	TTF	Spitfire FR.14	SG 108/B2-K
B2	TTF	Mosquito TT.3	MA 1/B2-A
B2	TTF	Mosquito TT.6	MC 2/B2-H
B2	TTF	Meteor T.7	ED 3/B2-Z
B2	TTF	Meteor F 8	EG 208/B2-W
EB	30 Sqn	F-84G	FZ-167/EB-L
GE	**349 Sqn**	**Spitfire FR.14**	**SG 5/GE-O**
GE	**349 Sqn**	**Spitfire LF.16**	**TB991/GE-L**
GE	**349 Sqn**	**Meteor F.4**	**EF 6/GE-T**
GE	**349 Sqn**	**Meteor F.8**	**EG 234/GE-A**
GV	Auxiliary Sqn	Spitfire FR.14	SG 14/GV-R
GV	Auxiliary Sqn	Spitfire	LF.16
GV	Auxiliary Sqn	Meteor F.4	EF 41/GV-D
H8	42 Sqn	F-84G	FZ-204/H8-G
H8	42 Sqn	RF-84F	FR-21/H8-V
IQ	Fighter School	Spitfire F XIV	SG-127/IQ-Z
IS	22 Sqn	Meteor F.8	EG-212/IS-J
IS	22 Sqn	F-84G	FZ-175/IS-P

Code	Unit	Type	Example
IS	22 Sqn	Hunter F.4	ID13/IS-L
IS	22 Sqn	Hunter F.6	IF-139/IS-J
JE	26 Sqn	Meteor F.8	EG163/JE-N
JE	26 Sqn	F-84G	FZ-196/JE-D
JE	26 Sqn	Hunter F.4	ID-52/JE-V
JE	26 Sqn	Hunter F.6	IF-58/JE-S
K5	33 Sqn	Meteor F.8	EG-224/K5-K
KT	1 Wing	Meteor NF.11	EN3/KT-G
KT	11 Sqn	Mosquito NF.30	MB 13/KT-S
KT	11 Sqn	Meteor NF.11	EW-3/KT-G
MN	**350 Sqn**	**Spitfire FR.14**	**SG 94/MN-L**
MN	**350 Sqn**	**Spitfire LF.16**	**TD235/MN-M**
MN	**350 Sqn**	**Meteor F.4**	**EF 28/MN-M**
MN	**350 Sqn**	**Meteor F. 8**	**EG 201/MN-E**
MS	29 Sqn	Meteor F.8	EG 36/MS-N
ND	10 Sqn	Mosquito NF.30	MB-20/ND-E
ND	10 Sqn	Meteor NF.11	EN 3/ND-G
OV	8 Sqn	Meteor F.8	EG 23/OV-M
OV	8 Sqn	Hunter F.4	ID-26/OV-K
OV	8 Sqn	Hunter F.6	IF-61/OV-W
RA	27 Sqn	Spitfire FR.14	SG 57/RA-D
RA	27 Sqn	F-84G	FZ-14/RA-K
RA	27 Sqn	F-84F	FU-132/RA-M
S2	9 Sqn	Meteor F.8	EG-46/S2-L
S2	9 Sqn	Hunter F.4	ID-34/S2-M
SV	4 Sqn	Meteor F.4	EF 38/SV-P
SV	4 Sqn	Meteor F.8	EG 172/SV-G
UR	2 Sqn	Spitfire FR.14	SG-15/UR-B
UR	2 Sqn	F-84G	FZ-27/UR-M
UR	2 Sqn	F-84F	FU-94/UR-M
VT	25 Sqn	Meteor F.8	EG 99/VT-A
XO	24 Sqn	Meteor F.8	EG-206/XO-A
YL	3 Sqn	Spitfire FR.14	SG-120/YL-P
YL	3 Sqn	F-84G	FZ-77/YL-M
YL	3 Sqn	F-84F	FU-6/YL-A
Z6	23 Sqn	Spitfire FR.14	
Z6	23 Sqn	F-84G	FZ-125/Z6-A
Z6	23 Sqn	F-84F	FU-91/Z6-R
ZC	367 Sqn	Anson	NA 6/ZC-C
ZC	367 Sqn	Oxford	O 4/ZC-M

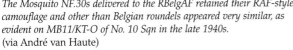

The Mosquito NF.30s delivered to the RBelgAF retained their RAF-style camouflage and other than Belgian roundels appeared very similar, as evident on MB11/KT-O of No. 10 Sqn in the late 1940s.
(via André van Haute)

Unit codes remained in use with the RBelgAF into the era of modern fighters, as may be seen on this neat formation of F-84F Thunderstreaks of No. 3 Sqn wearing the unit's YL code; FU-4 is YL-M.
(via André van Haute)

Canada 1947–59

RCAF Routine Order 250 dated 9 May 1947 promulgated a list of five-letter registrations for the RCAF in accordance with the International Civil Aviation Organisation (ICAO) system. RCAF aircraft would be prefixed VC, naval aircraft VG and civil aircraft CF. After the hyphen came the two-letter unit identifier (code) with the individual aircraft letter completing the registration that was meant to be worn in full above and below the wings.

The unit code and aircraft letter were worn on the fuselage in the conventional manner and these ran sequentially, from AA for No. 400 Squadron and so on. However, as no other military services adopted this civil system, it was discontinued by order promulgated on 19 November 1951. New two-letter unit codes were then assigned, though in practice some units were allocated the same letters, or continued to use the old codes. After this time too, the individual aircraft letter was replaced by the last three digits of the serial number. From early 1958 the RCAF ceased to use unit codes, replacing them with the letters 'RCAF', and they were out of use by 1961.

Code	Unit	Type	Dates	Example	Theatre	Remarks
AA	400	Harvard II	5.47-11.51	3125/AA-F	NA	
AA	400	Vampire F.3	3.48-11.51	17051/AA-P	NA	
AB	401	Harvard II	5.47-9.58	3288/AB-G	NA	
AB	401	Vampire F.3	3.48-2.56	17017/AB-A	NA	
AB	401	Silver Star Mk 3	12.54-58	31439/AB-349	NA	
AB	401	Sabre Mk 5	10.56-58	23315/AB-315	NA	
AB	401	Harvard IIb	c 55	20680/AB-680	NA	
AB	401	Otter	10.60-	3662/AB-662	NA	
AC	402	Harvard II	5.47-3.57	3316/AC-316	NA	
AC	402	Vampire F.3	4.48-11.50	17059/AC-P	NA	
AC	402	Mustang Mk 4	11.50-9.56	9564/AC-F	NA	
AC	402	Silver Star Mk 3	11.54-8.56		NA	
AC	402	Expeditor Mk 3	11.56-c 58	1435/AC-435	NA	
AD	403	Harvard II	8.49-11.51	3093/AD-D	NA	
AD	403	Mustang Mk 4	11.50-11.51	9288/AD-S	NA	
AF	404	Lancaster 10MR	4.51-11.51	FM220/AF-M	NA	
AG	405	Lancaster 10MR	3.50-11.55	KB857/AG-N	NA	
AH	406	Mitchell II	6.48-11.51		NA	
AJ	407	Lancaster 10MR	7.52-c 55	KB973/AJ-973	NA	
AK	408	Norseman IV	5.51-9.53	787/AK-F	NA	
AK	408	Canso A	1.49-9.59	****/AK-W	NA	
AK	408	Lancaster 10 P	1.49-c 51	FM217/AK-R	NA	
AM	410	Vampire F.3	12.48-5.51	17063/AM-P	NA	
AM	410	Sabre Mk 2	5.51-11.54	19144/AM-T	NA	
AM	410	Sabre Mk 5	11.54-9.56	23056/AM/056	Eur	
AN	411	Harvard II	2.51-9.58		NA	
AN	411	Vampire F.3	7.51-11.55	17042/AN-T	NA	
AN	411	CF 100 Mk 5	11.56-58	18483/AN-483	NA	
AO	412	Goose Mk 2	53	386/AO-Q	NA	

Code	Unit	Type	Dates	Example	Theatre	Remarks
AO	412	Expeditor Mk 2	4.47-c 55	1534/AO-N	NA	
AO	412	Dakota Mk 4	4.47-c 55	KJ936/AO-H	NA	
AO	412	North Star	4.49-11.51	17520/AO-R	NA	
AP	413	Norseman VI	4.47-11.50	371/AP-N	NA	
AP	413	Canso A	4.47-11.50	11018/AP-J	NA	
AP	413	Dakota Mk 4P	4.49-11.50	KN427/AP-R	NA	
AP	413	Lancaster 10P	5.47-11.50	FM212/AP-A	NA	
AP	413	Sabre Mk 2, 5, 6	11.51-4.57	23083/AP083	NA/Eur	
AP	413	CF 100 Mk 5	5.57-58	18651/AP-651	NA	
AQ	414	Dakota Mk 3P, 4P	5.47-11.50	KN256/AQ-J	NA	
AQ	414	Sabre Mk 4/5/6	11.52-7.57	23407/AQ-407	NA/Eur	
AQ	414	CF 100 Mk 5	8.57-58		NA	
AS	416	Mustang Mk 4	1.51-3.52	9247/AS-B	NA	
AS	416	Sabre Mk 2, 5, 6	3.52-1.57 1	9250/AS-250	NA/Eur	
AS	416	CF 100 Mk 5	2.57-58	18579/AS-579	NA	? use
AT	417	Harvard II	5.47-8.48	3063/AT-W	NA	
AT	417	Mustang Mk 4	5.47-8.48	9580/AT-B	NA	
AU	418	Harvard II	10.46-1.53	3100/AU-D	NA	
AU	418	Mitchell II	1.47-51	*****/AU-JY	NA	
AW	420	Harvard II	8.49-8.56	3337/AW-B	NA	
AW	420	Mustang Mk 4	8.49-8.56	9224/AW-N	NA	
AX	421	Vampire F.3	9.49-12.50	17030/AX-C	NA	
AX	421	Sabre Mk 2, 5, 6	12.51-58	23062/AX-062	NA/Eur	
BA	424	Harvard II	11.47-c 51	3766/BA-P	NA	
BA	424	Mustang Mk 4	11.47-c 51	9253/BA-S	NA	
BB	425	CF 100 Mk 4, 5	11.54-1958		NA ? use	
BB	427	Sabre Mk 2, 5, 6	9.52-58	19415/BB-415	NA/Eur	
BC	426	Dakota Mk 4	5.47-6.48	KN664/BC-B	NA	
BH	430	Sabre Mk 2, 5, 6	11.51-58	23733/BH-733	NA/Eur	
BN	435	Dakota Mk 3, 4	8.46-51	976/BN-A	NA	
BO	436	C-119G	4.53-c	57	NA	
BQ	438	Harvard II	11.46-	58 3213/BQ-213	NA	
BQ	438	Vampire F.3	4.48-9.53	17067/BQ-067	NA	
BQ	438	Silver Star Mk 3	11.54-58	21326/BQ-326	NA	
BQ	438	Sabre Mk 5	10.56-58	23356/BQ-356	NA	
BR	434	Sabre Mk 2, 5, 6	7.52-58	19434/BR-434	NA/Eur	
BS	Trenton SF	Harvard II	?		NA	
BT	441	Vampire F.3	3.51-6.51	17067/BT-O	NA	
BT	441	Sabre Mk 2	6.51-6.53	19152/BT-C	NA/UK	
BT	441	Sabre Mk 5, 6	6.53-58	2317/BT-017	Eur	
BU	442	Harvard II	5.47-c 56	3062/BU-C	NA	
BU	442	Vampire F.3	4.48-c 6.52	17075/BU-Y	NA	
BU	442	Mustang Mk 4	c 6.52-6.53	9579/BU-P	NA	
BV	444	Chipmunk Mk 1	5.48-3.49	18001/BV-Y	NA	
BV	JATC LAS	Bell 47D	c 52	9609/BV-W	NA	
BV	444	Sikorsky S-51	c 52	9604/BV-S	NA	
BX	JATC HS	Sikorsky S-51	c 61	****/BX-S	NA	
BZ	AAS	Mustang Mk 4	late 40s-52	9294/BZ-K	NA	
CA	Edmonton SF	Dakota Mk 4	c 49	KG634/CA-A	NA	
CA	112 (T) Flt	CG-4A Hadrian	c 52	9529/CA-X	NA	
CB	417	Mustang Mk 4	50s	9560/CB-560	NA	
CB	417	Harvard IV	50s	20279/CB-T	NA	
CB	CACCF	Dakota Mk 4 (TT)	c late 40s	KG580/CB-G	NA	
CB	CACCF	Norseman			NA	
CB	CACCF	Harvard II	c 55	20450/CB-450	NA	
CC	JATC HS	Sikorsky S-51	c 61	****/CC-X	NA	
CD	?	Expeditor	c late 40s	1341/CD-B	NA	
CF	?	Dakota Mk 4	c late 40s		NA	
CG	Sea Island SF?	Dakota Mk 4	c late 40s		NA	
CG	Sea Island SF?	Expeditor			NA	
CH	103 S&R Flt	Lancaster 10 ASR	40s-50s	KB997/CH-N	NA	
CJ	123 RF	Lancaster X	c late 40s	KB904/CJ-P	NA	
CJ	123 RF	Canso A		11093/CJ-	NA	
CJ	123 RF	Otter			NA	

Code	Unit	Type	Dates	Example	Theatre	Remarks
CK	CEPE	Sabre Mk 2	*c* mid 50s	19101/CK-R	NA	test or prototype a/c
CK	CEPE	Anson Mk 5	*c* late 40s	12518/CK-D	NA	
CL	?	Dakota Mk 4	*c* 55			
CP	1 FIS	Mitchell 3PT	50s	5204/CP-808	NA	
CQ	CNS	Dakota Mk 4	mid 50s	KG350/CQ-G	NA	
CQ	CNS	Lancaster 10 NT	mid 50s	FM208/CQ-208	NA	
CV	RAF test	CF 100 Mk 4	*c* mid 50s	18322/CV-322	NA	For RAF evaluation
CX	107 RU	Lancaster 10 ASR	52-58	FM213/CX-213	NA	
CZ	412 (Jet Flt)		mid 50s		NA	
DA	1 FTS	Harvard Mk 2	late 40s	****/DA-M	NA	
DA	*Trenton TT Flt?*	*Ventura GR 5 (TT)*	*early 50s*	*2254/DA-Q*	*NA*	
DB	1 FTS	Harvard II	late 40s	3337/DB-Q	NA	
DC	*1 AD ITF*	*Dakota*	*50s*		*NA*	
DC	*1 AD ITF?*	*Lancaster 10*			*NA*	
DC	*CFS?*	*Silver Star Mk 3*	*53-54*	*21005/DC-005*	*NA*	
DD	CEPE	Mustang Mk 4	*c* late 40s	9552/DD-P	NA	
DD	CEPE	Mitchell Mk II	*c* late 40s	KL154/DD-N	NA	
DF	*?*	*Expeditor*	*?*		*NA*	
DG	ARS	Dakota Mk 4	late 40s-50s	976/DG-A	NA	
DH	1 ANS	Dakota Mk 4	40s-50s	KG350/DH-W	NA	
DJ	2 (M) OTU	Lancaster 10MR	early-mid 50s		NA	
DJ	North Bay SF	Expeditor	mid 50s	1547/DJ-547	NA	ex 2 OTU ?
DK	AAS	Ventura Mk 5	47-52	2263/DK-R	NA	
DK	AAS	Dakota 3	*c* 52	KG563/DK-563	NA	
DL	432	CF 100 Mk 4/5	12.54-58	18741/DL-741	NA	
ET	435	C-119G	51-*c* 55	22101/ET-*	NA	
FB	CEPE	Mustang Mk 4	early 50s	9565/FB-N	NA	
FB	CEPE	CF 100 Mk 1	early 50s	18102/FB-K	NA	
FB	CEPE	CF 100 Mk 2	early 50s	18105/FB-H	NA	
FB	CEPE	CF 100 Mk 4	early 50s	18112/FB-S	NA	
FB	CEPE	Vampire F.3	52-53	17007/FB-R	NA	
FC	*CEPE?*	*Mustang Mk 4*	*51-53*		*NA*	
FC	*CEPE?*	*Vampire F.3*			*NA*	
FC	CEPE	Lancaster 10		FM148/FC-D	NA	
FC	CEPE	Dakota 3 53		FZ695/FC-A	NA	
FG	433	CF 100 Mk 4, 5	2.55-58	18433/FG-433	NA	
GA	*?*	*Norseman*	*?*		*NA*	
GB	*?*	*Expeditor*	*52*		*NA*	
GC	137 Tspt Flt	Freighter Mk 31	52-59	9850/GC-850	Eur	Part of 412 Sqn
GD	FIS	Harvard II	?	20247/HK-H	NA	
GG	1 FTS	Harvard II	early 50s	3034/GG-Q	NA	
GJ	1 (F) OTU	Vampire F 3	late 40s	1728/GJ-G	NA	
GM	1 FTS	Mustang Mk 4	*c* late 40s	9234/GM-X	NA	
GM	CFS	Mitchell Mk III	*c* 52	FW220/GM-M	NA	
GO	FIS	Harvard Mk 2	*c* 52-55	20414/GO-414	NA	
GO	FIS	Silver Star Mk 3	mid 50s	21026/GO-026	NA	
GO	FIS	Mitchell Mk II	*c* 52	KL139/GO-139	NA	
GP	1 FTS	Chipmunk Mk 1	late 40s	18019/GP-Y	NA	
GQ	1 (F) OTU	T-33A	mid-late 50s	14675/GQ-D	NA	
GS	CFS	Lancaster 10	*c* 51	FM211/GS-X	NA	
GS	1 ANS	Harvard	*c* 52	2713/GS-H	NA	
GS	1 ANS	Dakota 3, 4	*c* 52	KN281/GS-B	NA	
GU	2 FTS	Harvard II	early 50s	3085/GU-W	NA	
GV	AAS	?	mid 50s		NA	
GW	400	Silver Star Mk 3	4.55-10.58	21463/GW-463	NA	
GW	400	Sabre Mk 5	10.56-10.58	23204/GW-204	NA	
HG	428	CF 100 Mk 4, 5	6.54-58	18525/HG-525	NA	
HH	2 ANS	Expeditor Mk 3N	*c* late 40s	1434/HH-J	NA	
HH	CNS	Dakota 3N	50s	KG345/HH-B	NA	
HK	3 FTS	Harvard II	50s	20247/HK-H	NA	
HO	418	Mitchell Mk II	*c* 51-58	KL149/HO-149	NA	
HO	418	Expeditor Mk 3	*c* 51-58	1589/HO-589	NA	
HO	3 FTS	Harvard IIB	*c* 52-55	****/HO-G	NA	
HO	418	Silver Star Mk 3	8.56-58		NA	

Code	Unit	Type	Dates	Example	Theatre	Remarks
HO	3 FTS	Harvard II	50s		NA	
HQ	FIS	Dakota Mk 4	early 50s		NA	
HS	3 FTS	Harvard IIB	c 52-55	2708/HS-N	NA	
HT	3 FTS	Harvard IIB	c 52-55	****/HT-U		
HU	1 AGS	Harvard II	early 50s	2930/HU-G	NA	
HY	WPU	Silver Star Mk 3	c mid 50s	21098/HY-098	NA	
HY	WPU	CF 100 Mk 5	c mid 50s	18556/HY-556	NA	
HX	?	Harvard Mk II	early 50s	****/HX-Y	NA	
IG	439	Sabre Mk 2/5/6	11.51-58	23661/IG-661	NA/Eur	
JA	Saskatoon SF				NA	use not known
JB	4 FTS	Harvard 4	53	23079/JB-T	NA	
JC	1 AFS	Mitchell Mk III	52-c 54		NA	
JF	3 OTU	CF 100 Mk 3, 5	11.52-58	18132/JF-132	NA	
JL	Chatham S&R Flt			NA use not known		
JW	3 OTU	CF 100 Mk 5	c 52-58		NA	
JX	?	Mitchell III	?		NA	
KC	137 Tspt Flt	Freighter Mk 31C & 31M	c 52-8.63	9697/KC-697	Europe	
KE	440	CF100 Mk 3, 4, 5	10.53-58	18150/KE-150	NA/Eur	
KH	Trenton SF				NS	use not known
KH	411	Harvard II	c 51-9.58	2918/KH-918	NA	
KH	411	Silver Star Mk 3	10.55-58	21463/KH-463	NA	
KH	411	Sabre Mk 5	10.56-58	23312/KH-312	NA	
KH	411	Expeditor Mk 3	c late 50s	1473/KH-473	NA	
KL	Moose Jaw SF		c mid 50s		NA	use not known
KM	1 AFS	Expeditor 3	c 52	2295/KM-A	NA	
KQ	3 FTS	?	53-58		NA	
KR	?	Sikorsky H-5	c 52	9606/KR-606	NA	
KR	?	Canso A	c 52	048/KR-048	NA	Recce fitted a/c
KT	105 C&RF	Dakota Mk 4	c 54	KJ956/KT-956	NA	
KT	105 C&RF	Otter		3691/KT-691	NA	
LF	Comox SF	Expeditor Mk 3	c mid 50s	1679/LF-679	NA	
LK	AMCCF	Mitchell Mk III	c mid 50s	?	NA	
LP	409	CF 100 Mk 3/4/5	11.54-58	18402/LP-402	NA	
LV	Camp Bordon SF	Expeditor Mk 3	c 52	1424/LV-424	NA	
MH	?	Dakota Mk 4	c 52		NA	
MH	?	Silver Star Mk 3	58	21324/MH-324	NA	
ML	2 FTS	Silver Star Mk 3	c 55	21077/ML-077	NA	
ML	2FTS	Mitchell II (TT)	c 52	HD326/ML-G	NA	
MN	408	Lancaster 10 PR	c 51-58	FM122/MN-122	NA	
MN	408	Canso A	c 51-58	11056/MN-056	NA	
MN	408	Norseman VI	51-9.53		NA	
MN	408	Dakota Mk 4	1.55-58		NA	
MN	408	Otter	2.53-9.57	3663/MN-663	NA	
MZ	?	Expeditor Mk 3	c 52		NA	
MZ	?	Harvard IV	61	20293/MZ-293	NA	
NH	?	Expeditor Mk	3		NA	
NM	?	Dakota Mk 4	c 58	KP221/NM	NA	
NO	?	Harvard II			NA	
NQ	423	CF 100 Mk 3, 4	7.53-58	18389/NQ-389	NA/Eur	
OC	?	Silver Star Mk	3		NA	
OJ	4 FTS	Harvard IV	c 45	20426/OJ-426	NA	
OT	?	Canso A			NA	
ON	Downsview SF	Harvard IV 58		20212/ON-212	NA	
OU	JATC Rivers	Sikorsky S-51	c 51-56	9602/OU-602	NA	
OU	JATC Rivers	Mustang Mk 4	c 51-56	9594/OU-594	NA	
OU	JATC Rivers	Auster AOP.6	c 51-56	16673/OU-673	NA	
OZ	412	Comet I	c 53	5301/OZ-301	NA	
OZ	412	Canso A	c 53	9830/OZ-830	NA	
PF	443	Harvard II	12.51-9.58	3137/PF-137	NA	
PF	443	Mustang Mk 4	11.52-10.56	9268/PF268	NA	
PF	443	Sabre Mk 5	8.56-58	23310/PF-310	NA	
PN	164 or 426?	Dakota Mk 4	c 47	KG****/PN-A	NA	with No. 9 (T) Gp
PP	2 FTS	Expeditor Mk 3	c 54	1594/PP-594	NA	

Code	Unit	Type	Dates	Example	Theatre	Remarks
PP	2 FTS	Silver Star Mk 3	53-55	21272/PP-272	NA	
PR	403	Harvard Mk II	11.51-10.56		NA	
PR	403	Mustang Mk 4	*c* 51-58	9263/PR-263	NA	
PR	403	Silver Star Mk 3	11.55-2.57		NA	
PR	403	Expeditor Mk 3	8.56-58		NA	
PR	403	Otter	10.56-58		NA	
PV	424	Mustang Mk 4	*c* 52-55	9264/PV-264	NA	
PV	424	Silver Star Mk 3	*c* 56-58	21469/PV-469	NA	
PW	111 C&RF	Dakota Mk 3	*c* 55	KG568/PW-568	NA	
PX	CEPE	Lancaster 10	late 50s	KB848/PX-848	NA	
PX	CEPE	Mustang		9270/PX-270	NA	
PX	CEPE	Mitchell		HD326/PX-376	NA	
PX	CEPE	B-25 59		HD326/PX-326	NA	
PX	CEPE	Sabre Mk I		19101/PX-101	NA	
PX	CEPE	Sabre Mk 6	*c* 58	23559/PX-559	NA	
PX	CEPE	Dakota Mk 4		KN676/PX-676	NA	
PX	CEPE	C-119F		22120/PX-120	NA	
PX	CEPE	Otter		3668/PX-668	NA	
PX	CEPE	CF-100 Mk 3	*c* 54	18134/PX-134	NA	
PX	CEPE	Sabre 2	*c* 58	19410/PX-410	NA	
QJ	*?*	*Canso A*		*9830/QJ-830*	NA	
QJ	420	Mustang Mk 4	*c* 52	9599/QJ-599	NA	
QN	*?*	*Canso A*			NA	
QP	406	Mitchell Mk III	11.51-58	5244/QP-244	NA	
QT	*401*	*Otter*			NA	*use not known*
QT	121 KU	Lancaster 10 ASR	*c* 54-59	KB974/QT-974	NA	
QT	121 KU	Norseman Mk 4	*c* 54-59	787/QT-787	NA	
QT	121 KU	Sikorsky H-5	*c* 54-59	9606/QT-606	NA	
QT	121 KU	Canso A	*c* 54-59	11067/QT-067	NA	
QT	121 KU	Otter	*c* 54-59	3680/QT-680	NA	
QT	121 KU	Dakota Mk 3	*c* 54-59	FZ692/QT-692	NA	
QT	121 KU	Piaseki H-21A	*c* 54-59	9612/QT-612	NA	
QZ	103 RU	Otter	*c* 54-58	3673/QZ-673	NA	
QZ	103 RU	Canso A		9830/QZ-830	NA	
QZ	103 RU	PBY-5A		11047/QZ-047	NA	
QZ	103 RU	Vertol H 21	Late 1950's	9614/QZ-614	NA	
RG	*Moose Jaw SF*				NA	*use not known*
RL	Test Unit	CF-105 Arrow	late 50s	25201/RL-201	NA	
RO	*Chatham SF*				NA	*use not known*
RU	*Rockcliffe*				NA	*use not known*
RX	407	Lancaster 10 MR	7.52-58	KB894/RX-894	NA	
SA	445	CF 100 Mk 3, 4	4.53-58	18138/SA-138	NA/Eur	
SB	*?*	*Norseman*	*?*	*?*		*NA*
SL	442	Vampire F.3	53-56	17074/SL-074	NA	
SL	442	Harvard Mk 2	51-58	2904/SL-904	NA	
SL	442	Sabre Mk 5	56-58	23222/SL-222	NA	
SP	404	Lancaster 10 MR	11.51-55	FM172/SP-G	NA	
SP	404	P-2V5 Neptune	3.55-58	24110/SP-110	NA	
SP	404	Argus Mk I	*c* 58	20711/SP-711	NA	
ST	*?*	*Silver Star Mk 3*			NA	
SU	CFS	Mitchell 50s		5203/SU-203	NA	
SU	*Summerside SF ?*	*Sabre Mk 5*	*mid 50s*	*23350/SU-350*	NA	
SU	*Summerside SF ?*	*Harvard IV*			NA	
SV	2 AOS	B-25J Mitchell	*c* 52	5258/SV-258	NA	
SV	2 AOS	Dakota Mk 3	*c* 52-*c* 58	658/SV-658	NA	
SV	2 AOS	Expeditor Mk 3	*c* 52-*c* 58		NA	
SV	402	Expeditor Mk 3	8.56-58	1457/SV-457	NA	Continued use in error of 2 AOS code
TF	422	Sabre Mk 2, 4, 5, 6	1.53-58	23068/TF-068	NA/Eur	
TQ	104 KU Flt	Harvard IV	*c* 55-57	20214/TQ-214	NA	
TZ	*AMC*	*Dakota Mk 4*			NA	*? unit*
UD	419	CF 100 Mk 4	3.54-58	18204/UD-204	NA/Eur	
UM	1 FTS	Chipmunk Mk 1	55-60	18079/UM-079	NA	
UN	*?*	*Harvard IV*			NA	
VC	1 FTS	S-51	*c* 53	9607/VC-GBC	NA	

Code	Unit	Type	Dates	Example	Theatre	Remarks
VC	1 FTS	Chipmunk	c 53	179/VC-GPD	NA	
VC	1 FTS	Bell 47D	c 53	9609/VC-BVW	NA	
VH	444	Sabre Mk 5, 6	c 55-58	23670/VH-670	Eur	
VN	405	P-2V5 Neptune	11.55-58	24121/VN-121	NA	
VN	405	Argus Mk 1	5.58	20710/VN-710	NA	
VR	102	KU Flt Otter			NA	
VT	*?*	*Harvard IV*		*20437/VT-437*	*NA*	
XK	406	B-25J Mitchell	11.51-56	5267/XK-267	NA	
XK	406	Silver Star Mk 3	9.56-6.58	21159/XK-159	NA	
XK	406	Expeditor Mk 3	c 1958	2362/XK-362	NA	
XS	2 FTS	Harvard IV		20435/XS-435	NA	
XV	2 OTU	Lancaster Mk 10 MR	c 51-58	KB960/XV-960	NA	
XV	2 OTU	P-2V5 Neptune	c 55-58		NA	
XV	2 OTU	Argus Mk 1	c 58-61	20719/XV-719	NA	
YT	*?*	*Harvard IV*			*NA*	
ZE	*JATC Flt?*	*Auster AOP 6*			*NA*	*? use*
ZX	103 Flt	Otter	c 57		NA	

The Canadian-designed Chipmunk Mk 1 served the RCAF well as a primary trainer and in contrast to the RAF's T.10 had a 'bubble' type canopy. This all-yellow example is 18022/UM-022 of No. 1 FTS at Centralia.(J. McNulty)

For communications and light transport throughout the Canadian wilderness, the RCAF employed a variety of small flying boats and floatplanes. Among the former was this Grumman Goose Mk II, 386/AO-Q of No. 412 Sqn taxiing on the Ottawa River on 14 May 1953. (Canadian Forces)

The licence-built T-33 was the standard jet trainer for many years and as the T-33A-N Silver Star was procured in large numbers. Among the major users was No. 2 FTS at Gimli, which was the owner of 21568/PP- 568. (Larry Milberry)

The standard maritime patrol type for the RCAF during the mid 1950s was the P-2E Neptune which was used by several units, including the Greenwood-based No. 404 Sqn, the owner of 24110/SP-110 in 1955. (Canadian Forces)

For some years after the Second World War the RCAF employed large numbers of B-25 Mitchells on a wide variety of tasks, including target towing, for which this Mk II HD326/ML-G wore the customary black and yellow colours. The ML code is believed to relate to No. 2 FTS. (J. McNulty)

For transport support within its various bases in Europe, during the 1950s the RCAF employed a small number of Bristol B 170 Freighters which wore tactical camouflage, but with prominent service and unit legends; 9699/GC-699 belonged to No. 137 Transport Flight as seen in 1956. (J. D. R. Rawlings)

Wearing a prominent badge proclaiming the ownership of No. 413 Sqn, Norseman floatplane 2495/AP-P lies moored on a lake in northern Ontario during the summer of 1948, by which time the RCAF had dopted its distinctive maple-leaf roundel. (Canadian Forces)

The Canadair CF.100 Mk 4B was evaluated by the RAF in the 1950s, for which 18322 was given the code CV, which appears to relate to no specific unit but which was only worn for the period of evaluation. (via J. D. Oughton)

The unit of C-45 Expeditor 2379/DJ-379 is the Station Flight at RCAF North Bay, as is apparent from the fuselage titles. From the early 1950s individual aircraft letters were replaced by the last three digits of the aserial number and flanked the roundel with the unit code. (J. McNulty)

The RCAF's first post-war maritime aircraft was the Lancaster 10MR modified for the role and used by several re-formed units which had served with Coastal Command. These included No. 407 Sqn based on the west coast at Comox, which used FM219/RX-219 in 1955; note the APS-33 radar radome. (No. 407 Sqn)

As aircraft became available, numbers of Sabre Mk 5s were issued to reserve units including two based on the west coast. Here 23222/SL-222 of No. 442 Sqn leads 23071/SL-071 and No. 443's 23115/PF-115 over the snow-capped Rocky Mountains near Sea Island in March 1957. (No. 442 Sqn Records)

From time to time aircraft of Canadian Forces Air Command squadrons were authorised to be finished in a special commemorative colour scheme, usually relating to the squadron's badge. However, during the fiftieth anniversary commemorations of the 1944 D-Day landings, several CF aircraft sent to Europe were painted to represent the markings of Second Word War aircraft of the unit; one indeed even replicated the serial. The practice has been repeated occasionally since then. Known examples are shown below:

Code	Unit	Type	Dates	Example	Remarks
9G	441	CF-188 Hornet	6.94	188781/9G-A	Port side
G9	430	CH-136 Kiowa	6.94	136251/G9-M	Wore Mustang I serial AG664
GX	415	CP-140 Aurora	7.99	1401114/GX-N	
JE	441	CF-188 Hornet	6.94	188781/JE-J	Personal code of Wg Ldr, Wg Cdr J. E. Johnson
KH	403	CH-135 Huey	6.94	135140/KH-T	
KH	403	CH-136 Kiowa	6.94	136210/KH-E	
LQ	405	CP-140 Aurora	7.99	140105/LQ-Y	

The Royal Canadian Navy used codes in the period 1947–52 which were applied in much the same way as RCAF codes. Those applied are set out below.

Code	Unit	Type	Dates	Example
AA	883	Seafire F.15	5.47-9.48	SW869/AA-H
AA	883	Sea Fury FB.11	9.48-5.51	VR918/AA-Y
AA	871	Sea Fury FB.11	5.51-8.56	TG118/AA-B
AB	826	Firefly FR.1	5.47-10.50	PP412/AB-K
AB	826	TBM-3E	10.50-5.51	53545/AB-Z
AB	881	TBM-3E	5.51-3.57	53503/AB-S
BC	803	Sea Fury FB.11	2.48-5.51	TG113/BC-K
BD	825	Firefly FR.4	8.47-2.49	VG966/BD-G
BD	825	Firefly AS.5	2.49-5.51	VH139/BD-F
BD	880	Firefly AS.5	51-52	
BD	880	TBM-3E	51-52	53437/BD-B
BG	AG Cdr	Sea Fury FB.11	48-51	TG120/BG-C
TF	743	Swordfish II	9.46-11.48	
TF	743	Harvard II	47-5.54	3233/TF-Y
TF	743	Avenger AS.3	48-52	8628/TF-Z
TG	1 TAG	Seafire F.15		PR435/TG-C
TG	1 TAG	Firefly T.1	48-49	DT975/TG-Y
TG	1 TAG	Firefly T.2	49-	MB941/TG-W

Czechoslovakia, 1946–7

After the end of the Second World War, the RAF's Czechoslovak squadrons remained under British control, but adopted Czech markings, while retaining their unit codes. On 30 August 1945 the Czech squadrons were incorporated into the reconstituted Czech Air Force. On 15 February 1946 the three fighter squadrons were formally disbanded by the RAF and became fighter regiments, the codes changing at the same time, and these were carried with an individual aircraft number; the RAF serial numbers were retained. For completeness, these codes are also noted below.

Code	Type	RAF Sqn	Example	Czech Unit	Code	Example
DU	Spitfire IX	312	MH474/DU-F	10th Ftr Regt	KR	TE510/KR-2
				12th Ftr Regt	DZ	TE560/DZ-7
NN	Spitfire IX	310	MH999/NN-G	4th Ftr Regt	JT	SL633/JT-10
				5th Ftr Regt	MP	SL650/MP-10
PP	Liberator VI	311	EV943/PP-F	-	-	-
RY	Spitfire IX	313	NH422/RY-Y	7th Ftr Regt	IV	TE517/IV-2
			8th Ftr Regt	LS		TE564/LS-7

When they were transferred to the re-formed Czechoslovak Air Force the RAF's Czech squadrons initially retained their well-known unit codes, as may be seen in this line-up of the Spitfire IXs of No. 312 Sqn at Prague in February 1946. No. 312 formed the 10th and 12th Fighter Regiments, whose aircraft were then recoded. (P. H. T. Green Collection)

The 4th Fighter Regiment, which used the JT code, was formed from No. 310 Sqn, Spitfire IX TE524/JT-5, when seen here in 1947, still carried the badge of No. 312 Sqn! (P. H. T. Green Collection)

Denmark

Denmark, which did not man any exile squadrons within the RAF, did use a similiar code system from 1951 to 1960. It is beyond the scope of the present volume.

France, 1944–53

The use of unit codes post-war by the French Air Force (l'Armée de l'Air) is complicated and is best explained by including late wartime usage. It might also be helpful if the broad structure of units is described.

During the period in question the approximate equivalent of the RAF wing or USAAF group was the groupement, in turn comprising several groupes (squadrons). The groupes comprised escadrilles (flights). The groupes were of three types: GB – groupe de bombardement (bomber); GC – groupe de chasse (fighter); and GR – groupe de reconnaissance. Generally units were shown by the wing type followed by the squadron (groupe) number then the wing (groupement) number in the form GC 1/3 (1st Squadron of the 3rd Fighter Wing). (The groupe number is often shown in Roman numerals but for simplicity they are given in Arabic form in the table below.) Finally, groupes were accorded names with some territorial or historical significance and these names help to define lineage of units. Thus GB 1/19 was Gascogne in 1945; these names were, however, frequently transferred to new groupes over time.

The Free French Air Force (FFAF) units, although allocated a French unit designation also had an RAF squadron number, for example No. 342 Squadron was also GB 1/20 Lorraine. These units, and those formed under the RAF in the Mediterranean during 1943, were all allocated RAF unit codes.

The French Air Force was reformed on 3 July 1943 by merging the FFAF and the former Vichy French units. The latter, mainly based in the Mediterranean, took part in the Tunisian campaign and later began receiving better equipment for service in the Italian campaign and that in southern France. In September 1944 the 4th Fighter Wing and the B-26 Groupes were integrated into the US XII Tactical Air Command for the Italian campaign. However, when the wings were incorporated into the new 1st Tactical Air Force from 1 December 1944, RAF/USAAF-type alphanumerical codes were allocated, though these were generally not applied until 1945.

In practice, the French units operating in southern France and indeed those forming during the invasion in France itself, operated with a high degree of independence. The units under RAF control were formally disbanded into French control and renumbered in November 1945. Many retained their original equipment for several years.

After the war some units kept their wartime code letters, particularly the original FFAF units, until a general reorganisation of unit codes in the late 1940s. In about 1949 a new system superficially similar to the wartime system was introduced whereby a two-character code described the groupement and by initial letter of the name of the groupe followed by the individual aircraft letter. For example, GC 1/4 Dauphine had aircraft coded 4D-* where * was the individual aircraft letter. This later system is beyond the scope of this book, but has been described briefly to avoid confusion.

Code	RAF Sqn Number	French Destination	Type	Dates	Example
2Y	345 RAF	GC 2/2 Berry	Spitfire IX	9.44-4.45	PT913/2Y-Y
3U		GC 1/4 Navarre	P-47D	44-46	44-20037/3U-A
5A	329 RAF	GC 1/2 Cigognes	Spitfire XVI	2.45-3.45	TB388/5A-H
5A	329 RAF	GC 1/2 Cigognes	P-47D	46-49	44-20009/5A-T
5A	329 RAF	GC 1/2 Cigognes	Vampire FB.5 4	9-50	VZ166/5A-G
7E	327 RAF	GC 1/3 Corse	Spitfire IX	12.43-11.45	
8J	326 RAF	GC 2/7 Nice	Spitfire IX	12.43-11.45	ML301/8J-L
8X	31 BG USAAF	GB 1/22 Maroc	B-26B	44-11.45	44-6817/8X-02
8X	31 BG USAAF	GB 1/22 Maroc	B-26G	c 3.45-46	44-67856/8X-18
9V		GC 2/5 Lafayette	P-47D	44-46	44-33390/9V-J
AF		GC 3/6 Rousillon	P-47D	44-46	44-33434/AF-Y
C9		GC 1/5 Champagne	P-47D	44-46	44-33389/C9-B
DU		EC 2/2 Cote d'Or	Vampire FB 5	49-50	VZ221/DU-D
GW	340 RAF	GC 4/2 Ile de France	Spitfire XVI	2.45-11.45	SM292/GW-Z
H7	346 RAF	GB 2/23 Guyenne	Halifax VI	3.45-49	RG607/H7-X
I3		GC 2/3 Dauphine	P-47D	44-46	42-26157/I3-Y
L8	347 RAF	GB 1/25 Tunisie	Halifax VI	3.45-49	PP165/L8-P
NL	341 RAF	GC 3/2 Alsace	Spitfire XVIe	3.45-11.45	TD133/NL-C
NL	341 RAF	GC 3/2 Alsace	P-47D	46-47	44-89823/NL-R
NL	341 RAF	GC 3/2 Alsace	Vampire FB.5	49-50	VX965/NL-A
OA	342 RAF	GB 1/20 Lorraine	Mitchell III	5.45-12.45	KJ729/OA-S
Q5	31 BG USAAF	GB 1/19 Gascogne	B-26B		
S8	328 RAF	GC 1/7 Provence	Spitfire IX	12.43-11.45	
R7		GR 2/33 Savoie	F-6	45-48	441417/R7-L
R7		GR 2/33 Savoie	P-51	45-48	4410889/R7-N
TG		GC 3/3 Ardennes	P-47D	44-45	44-33379/TG-F
U6	327 RAF	GC 1/3 Corse	Spitfire IX	12.43-11.45	MJ415/U6-S
W4		GR 1/33 Belfort	F-5B, G	44-46	4268233/W4-B

During the Second World War the French Air Force units serving with the RAF were numbered in the RAF's 300 series and allocated unit codes, though these were not always applied. No. 327 Sqn, also known as GC 1/3 Corse, flew Spitfire IXs like MJ415/U6-S seen in Germany just after the war. Behind it is a P-47D coded 3U of GC1/4 Navarre. (S. Joanne)

During the Second World War the Free French No. 341 Sqn wore the code NL. After transfer to the post-war French Air Force it became EC 2/2 Alsace and used the letters again, including on Vampire FB.5 VX965/NL-A at Metz in 1949. (via D. Watkins)

Netherlands, 1945–c 1960

After the war, the Royal Netherlands Air Force based the numbers of the squadrons of its reformed air force around those of the wartime RAF Dutch units. Only one, No. 322 Squadron, was, however, an air force unit; the other two, Nos 320 and 321, had been manned by Royal Netherlands Navy personnel who continued to use these numbers. The air force, however, then formed most of its squadrons with the same numbers as a number of RAF wartime squadrons in the 300 series which during the war had been formed from personnel from other Allied nations. Remarkably, in the cases of Nos 311 and 312 Squadrons both the number and the wartime codes were assumed, though there was no link between the units. Those numbers resurrected were 311, 312 and 313 (Czech) and 326, 327 and No. 328 (French). Note that the S8 code of No. 328 Squadron was reversed in Dutch use. Others, like Nos 323, 324, 325, 700, 701 and 702 Squadrons had never previously existed in the RAF. As in other tables wartime codes continued into use after the war are shown bold, including where the units had not been Dutch.

Code	Unit	Type	Example
3P	324 Sqn	Meteor F.4	****/3P-10
3P	324 Sqn	Meteor F.8	I-108/3P-8
3P	324 Sqn	Hunter F.4	N-101/3P-23
3P	324 Sqn	Hunter F.6	N202/3P-R
3W	**322 Sqn**	**Spitfire LF.9**	**MK732/3W-17**
3W	**322 Sqn**	**Spitfire T.9**	**BS147/3W-22**
3W	**322 Sqn**	**Meteor F.4**	****/3W-33
3W	**322 Sqn**	**Meteor F.8**	****/3W-10
3W	**322 Sqn**	**Hunter F.4**	**N-124/3W-27**
3W	**322 Sqn**	**Hunter F.6**	**N-227/3W-16**
4R	325 Sqn	Meteor F.4	****/4R-8
4R	325 Sqn	Meteor F.8	I-115/4R-S
4R	325 Sqn	Hunter F.4	N-106/4R-16
4R	325 Sqn	Hunter F.6	N-251/4R-2
5G	299 Sqn	L-18 Super Cub	****/5G-71
6A	700 Sqn	F-86K	541269/6A-7
7E	327 Sqn	Meteor F.4	
7E	327 Sqn	Meteor F.8	****/7E-5
7E	**327 Sqn**	**Hunter F.4**	**N-168/7E-12**
8A	298 Sqn	Auster III	R-11/8A-13
8A	298 Sqn	L-18 Super Cub	****/8A-72

Code	Unit	Type	Example
8A	298 Sqn	OH-23 Raven	****/8A-206
8S	328 Sqn	Meteor F.4	****/8S-6
8S	328 Sqn	Meteor F.8	****/8S-11
8T	314 Sqn	F-84G	****/8T-23
8T	314 Sqn	F-84F	P-105/8T-25
9I	326 Sqn	Meteor F.8	****/9I-Z
9I	326 Sqn	Hunter F.4	N-121/9I-5
DU	**312 Sqn**	**F-84G**	**K-64/DU-19**
DU	**312 Sqn**	**F-84F**	**P-126/DU-18**
PP	**311 Sqn**	**F-84E**	**K-2/PP-3**
PP	**311 Sqn**	**F-84G**	**K-74/PP-20**
PP	**311 Sqn**	**F-84F**	**P-***/PP-22**
TA	313 Sqn	F-84G	****/TA-19
TA	313 Sqn	T-33A	
TB	315 Sqn	F-84G	K-***/TB-19
TB	315 Sqn	F-84F	P-163/TB-9
TC	316 Sqn	F-84G	K-***/TC-5
TC	316 Sqn	F-84F	P-255/TC-12
TP	306 Sqn	F-84E	K-8/TP-23
TP	306 Sqn	F-84G	P-***/TP-6
TP	306 Sqn	RF-84F	P-7/TP-7
TP	306 Sqn	RT-33A	****/TP-20
Y7	701 Sqn	F-86K	Q-337/Y7-15
Y9	323 Sqn	Meteor F.4	I-35/Y9-5
Y9	323 Sqn	Meteor F.8	****/Y9-30
Y9	323 Sqn	Hunter F-4	N-128/Y9-8
ZU	334 Sqn	C-47 Dakota	X-9/ZU-9
ZX	702 Sqn	F-86K	541340/ZX-14

Like other European air forces, after the war the RNethAF used a similar coding system to the RAF, though they used individual numerals instead of a letter, as seen on Meteor F.4 3P-5 of No. 324 Sqn when visiting Thorney Island in June 1949. (RAF Thorney Is Records)

The sole Dutch fighter squadron with the RAF during the war was No. 322 Sqn which, when re-formed in the post-war RNethAF, revived the use of its wartime combination on several types, including the Spitfire F.9, like MK732/3W-17. (P. R. Arnold Collection)

Norway, 1945–70

As with the Netherlands, the Royal Norwegian Air Force also used the numbers of RAF units manned by other Allies, in this case Nos 335 and 336 (Greek) Squadrons, although there was no historical connection. Numbers 337, 338 and 339 had not previously been used within the RAF.

Soon after the war, from 1946 to 1951, a three-letter aircraft identification was used, with the first letter defining the type and the second and third the actual aircraft. These identifications were applied in much the same way as codes and thus cause some confusion. The type letters were as follows:

A Spitfire
B Vampire
F Mosquito; Super Cub
K Catalina
L Cornell
M Harvard
N Storch
O Otter
R Norseman
S Northrop N-3PB
T Lodestar, Dakota
U Safir
V Oxford
W Anson
Y Ju-52

In 1951 front-line aircraft were re-marked with the previous RAF codes, or where the squadron had no RAF history a new two-character code was introduced. Second-line units continued with the aircraft identification system until 1958 when the latter system was abandoned; some units adapted their aircraft identification letters into unit codes. For example, Safir trainers marked U-AB to U-AZ, became UA-B to UA-Z. Two types which acquired two-letter unit codes after 1958 were the L-19A (CE) and the H-19D (HA). In some instances where all individual letter codes had been used, units resorted to using numbers.

Finally, there was one interesting anomaly. F-86K 541245 of No. 337 Squadron was inadvertently coded 2X-E, rather than ZK-E. The codes had been applied in the UK with one character being wrongly described on the specification and one being painted in error!

Code	Unit	Type	Example
AH	332 Sqn	Vampire F.3	*****/AH-B
AH	332 Sqn	F-84G	528296/AH-L
AH	332 Sqn	F-86F	531082/AH-A
AH	332 Sqn	F-86K	541236/AH-H
AH	332 Sqn	F-5A	669210/AH-P
AH	332 Sqn	F-5B	669241/AH-Y
AK	? 334 Sqn	Mosquito FB.6	*****/AK-F
AU	PTS	Safir	7345/AU-Z
AZ	717 Sqn	RF-84F	527319/AZ-C
AZ	717 Sqn	RF-5A	689108/AZ-P
BE	720 Sqn	Bell 47J	1039/BE-G
BW	335 Sqn	C-47	315652/BW-N
BW	335 Sqn	C-119F	12699/BW-D
BW	335 Sqn	C-130H	6810952/BW-A
CE	Army Field Artillery	L-19A	
DP	718 Sqn	T-33A	******/DP-H
DP	718 Sqn	F-5A	6714903/DP-J
DP	718 Sqn	F-5B	14907/DP-X
FA	Observer Service	L-18C	
FN	**331 Sqn**	**F-84G**	**522956/FN-L**
FN	**331 Sqn**	**F-86F**	**531151/FN-A**
FN	**331 Sqn**	**F-104G**	**12626/FN-T**
JT	720 Sqn	Bell 47G	698/JT-P
JT	720 Sqn	UH-1B	14079/JT-D
KK	**333 Sqn**	**PBY-5A Catalina**	**466213/KK-G**
KK	**333 Sqn**	**Bell 47G**	**641/KK-S**
KK	**333 Sqn**	**HU-16B Albatross**	**515281/KK-E**
KK	**333 Sqn**	**P-3B Orion**	**156603/KK-P**
MU	338 Sqn	F-84G	573132/MU-B
MU	338 Sqn	F-86F	525219/MU-T
MU	338 Sqn	F-5A	6510562/MU-A
PX	336 Sqn	Vampire F.3	42232/PX-U
PX	336 Sqn	F-84G	
PX	336 Sqn	F-86F	525167/PX-N
PX	336 Sqn	F-5A	6413375/PX-F
RI	334 Sqn	Mosquito FB.6	TE920/RI-O
RI	334 Sqn	F-84G	519833/RI-C

Code	Unit	Type	Example
RI	334 Sqn	F-86F	525192/RI-E
RI	334 Sqn	F-86K	41319/RI-P
RI	334 Sqn	F-5A	669217/RI-E
SI	339 Sqn	Vampire F.3	42234/SI-K
SI	339 Sqn	Vampire FB.52	V0445/SI-G
SI	339 Sqn	F-86K	41232/SI-X
SI	339 Sqn	UH-1B	6512853/SI-I
T3	717 Sqn	RF-84F	58745/T3-S
WH	**330 Sqn**	**Arado Ar 196A**	***/WH-N**
WH	**330 Sqn**	**F-84G 5**	**28402/WH-A**
WH	**330 Sqn**	**HU-16B Albatross**	**517203/WH-C**
XJ	719 Sqn	DHC-6 Twin Otter	67056/XJ-K
XJ	719 Sqn	UH-1B	12853/XJ-A
ZK	337 Sqn	Vampire FB.52	V0404/ZK-T
ZK	337 Sqn	Vampire T.11	*****/ZK-Y
ZK	337 Sqn	F-86K	541284/ZK-V

First seen on Spitfires in 1941, No. 332 Sqn's code continued in use with the unit after the war, including the F-86K Sabres, like 541236/AH-H, an all-weather fighter, seen in the mid-1960s. (RNorAF)

For units which had no wartime existence, the post-war RNorAF allocated them new code combinations. One such unit was No. 718 Sqn which by 1970 was flying the Freedom Fighter for advanced and operational conversion duties. The two-seat F-5B 14907/DP-X was visiting Lossiemouth in 1970. (R. C. B. Ashworth)

The RAF's code system was finally abandoned by the RNorAF in 1972 by which time the Bodo-based F-104G Starfighters of No. 331 Sqn had added colourful distinctive fin markings. The letters had been in continuous use since the squadron was formed with Hurricanes in 1941; F-104G 12232/FN-T is nearest with FN-H and FN-F behind. (RNorAF via Lt Col H. Sandnes)

South Africa 1946–58

The Air Staff Instruction issued by South Africa Defence Headquarters under signature of the SASO, Brigadier J. Durrant and dated 12 November 1946 laid down the specifications for the markings of the post-war SAAF. These included '… the allocation of Squadron Identification Letters to Service Squadrons'.

Not all codes were actually worn, but most replicated those used by the squadrons during the Second World War. Some units, such as Nos 17 and 22 Squadrons which had not used unit codes during the war, were allocated 'new' combinations. They gradually fell out of use as the SAAF re-equipped, the last recorded use being on No. 22's PV-1 Venturas around 1960.

Code	Unit	Type	Dates	Example	Remarks
AX	1	**Spitfire LF 9**	*c* 46-49	5539/AX-G	
AX	1	**Vampire FB.5**	49-51	206/AX-D	
DB	2	**Spitfire LF.9**	46-48		
JS	60	Dakota III/IV	46-50	6837/JS-X	
JS	60	Spitfire LF 9 (PR)	46-50	5536/JS-B	
JS	60	Ventura II (B-34)	46-50	5110/JS-J	
JS	60	Mosquito PR 16	46-50	4802/JS-Q	
LB	21	Ventura II (B-34)	49-51	6023/LB-C	
MS	17	Ventura V (PV-1)	47-58	6478/MS-K	

Code	Unit	Type	Dates	Example	Remarks
MT	22	Ventura V (PV-1)	54-*c* 60	6515/MT-L	
OD	28	Dakota III, IV	9.46-55	6843/OD-A	
OP	42	Flt/Sqn Auster AOP.5	*c* 53-57	5402/OP-B	
OZ	**24**	**Ventura II (B-34)**	*c* **48**	**6118/OZ-B**	
PH	27				*Allocated not used*
RB	35	Sunderland GR.5	5.45-57	RN296/RB-M	
RB	35	Anson floatplane	*c* 46	3158/RB-Z	
ST	25				*Allocated not used*
VL	**12**	**Anson**	**10.46-c 50 4566/VL-G**		

The Ventura remained in service in some numbers with the SAAF after the war. This B-34, 6079/LB-G, belonged to No. 21 Sqn which was part of No. 3 Bomber Wing and is seen flying from Zwartkop in May 1948. (SAAF)

An unusual user of unit code letters was No. 42 (AOP) Flight, which was later transferred to the Army. Its six Auster AOP.5s, like 5402/OPB, wore the code forward of the springbok roundels. (SAAF)

No. 35 Sqn SAAF developed this unique Anson floatplane seen at Durban in 1946. It wore the unit's code, as did No. 35's Sunderlands, though the Anson, 3158/RB-Z, was used only as a water skills trainer for new flying-boat pilots and did not fly in this configuration! (A. W. Hall)

CHAPTER 13

Post-war Transport Command Call-signs

On 8 September 1945 RAF Transport Command issued a listing of what were apparently four-letter unit codes. These were in fact the wireless/telegraphy (W/T) radio call-signs for the individual aircraft, allowing the RAF's transport organisation to track the location of its aircraft, particularly on the long-range trooping runs to the Middle East and India. The first letter, O, denoted Transport Command. The second letter denoted the aircraft type as listed below (those marked in italics were allocated and used as call-signs but with no evidence of their application as painted codes):

A	Anson	B	*Britannia*
D	Dakota	F	Dakota, *Argosy*
G	Hastings	H	Halifax
J	Hudson	K	Lancastrian, *Argosy*
L	Liberator, *Heron*	N	Devon, *Valetta*
P	*Pembroke*	Q	Sunderland, Sandringham
R	Stirling, Valetta	S	Skymaster, *Valetta*
T	*Comet*	V	Valetta, *Viking*
W	York	X	Warwick
Y	York	Z	Seaford, miscellaneous types

The third letter identified the squadron or unit and the fourth the individual aircraft within that unit, thus ODFA identifies RAF Transport Command Dakota of No. 30 Squadron, aircraft A. The squadron at this time used the unit code letters JN, so this Dakota would wear the codes JN-A on its fuselage.

It was the original intention that the system should be applied to the aircraft in the manner of unit codes, flanking the fuselage, but in practice this did not happen and they were usually carried on the nose cone, or on either side of the nose in small letters. Additionally, as some units had more than twenty-six aircraft on strength they began adding the suffix W, so the twenty-seventh aircraft on strength was AW, the twenty-eighth BW and so on. Interestingly, because its aircraft operated under Transport Command control on some charters, British Overseas Airways Corporation (BOAC) was allocated the unit designator Z in its call-sign.

The system changed slightly in 1947 when the prefix M was added. Although the call-signs continued in use into the 1950s, their marking on aircraft was dropped by about 1955. Another form of apparent coding was also an element of the call-sign painted in large letters on the fuselage sides of some Hastings of Nos 53, 99 and 511 Squadrons in the late 1950s. This was in the form GA* or JA* where * is the individual aircraft letter.

In the tables below the call-signs are shown, together with the contemporary two-character code where this was allocated. It does not follow that all units actually applied the latter; for confirmation and examples refer to chapter 11. OAA 24 NQ Anson

Sunderland III ML788 was transferred to BOAC in 1944 as G-AGKX and thus wore the Company's speedbird motif; it became the prototype Sandringham as seen here. The letters relate to its Transport Command W/T call-sign. **(British Airways)**

Four-letter Codes

Call-sign	Unit	Two-letter code	Type(s)	Call-sign	Unit	Two-letter code	Type(s)
OAA	24	NQ	Anson	ODW	52		Dakota
OAA	437	Z2	Anson	ODX	1680 Flt		Dakota
OAF	147		Anson	ODY	1333(T)CU	CM	Dakota
OAG	1359 Flt		Anson	ODZ	BOAC		Dakota
OAP	ADLS		Anson	OFA	10	ZA	Dakota
ODA	24	NQ	Dakota	OFA	437	Z2	Dakota
ODB	187	PU	Dakota	OFB	206		Dakota
ODC	238	WF	Dakota	OFB	271	YS	Dakota
ODC	436		Dakota	OFB	62		Dakota
ODD	437	Z2	Dakota	OFC	435		Dakota
ODD	62		Dakota	OFD	575	I9	Dakota
ODD	525	WF	Dakota	OFG	46	XK	Dakota
ODE	62		Dakota	OFH	216	GH	Dakota
ODF	147		Dakota	OFM	435	8J?	Dakota
ODG	1359 Flt		Dakota	OFN	575	I9	Dakota
ODJ	78	EY	Dakota	OFR	238	WF	Dakota
ODK	241	OCUYY	Dakota	OFT	187	PU	Dakota
ODK	512	HC	Dakota	OFU	233	5T	Dakota
ODK	575	I9	Dakota	OFV	271	EY	Dakota
ODM	436		Dakota	OFV	78	EY	Dakota
ODN	271	YS	Dakota	OFZ	BOAC		Dakota
ODO	437	Z2	Dakota	OHA	297	L5	Halifax
ODP	525	WF	Dakota	OHB	304	QD	Halifax
ODR	48	I2	Dakota	OHC	1665 HCU	OI	Halifax
ODS	1330	CU	Dakota	OHD	301	GR	Halifax
ODT	53	PU	Dakota	OHF	620	D4	Halifax
ODU	31	CB	Dakota	OHH	644	9U	Halifax
ODU	77	YS	Dakota	OHL	113		Halifax
ODV	10	ZA	Dakota	OJG	1359 Flt	ZW	Hudson

Warwick C.III HG280 of No. 167 Sqn, seen just after the war, had the letters OX-GX flanking the roundel, which were not a unit code, but as explained in the text, the type, unit and aircraft letter can be ascertained. (**M. P. Marsh**)

Call-sign	Unit	Two-letter code	Type(s)
OKD	1359 Flt	ZW	Lancastrian
OKD	24		Lancastrian
OKZ	BOAC		Lancastrian
OLA	53	FH	Liberator
OLB	59	BY	Liberator
OLB	246		Liberator
OLC	86	XQ	Liberator
OLD	206	PQ	Liberator
OLF	220	8D	Liberator
OLL	111 OTU	X3	Liberator
OLM	206	PQ	Liberator
OLN	102	EF	Liberator
OLP	426	OW	Liberator
OLT	59	BY	Liberator
OLW	86	XQ	Liberator
OLW	426	OW	Liberator
OLY	53	FH	Liberator
OLX	220	8D	Liberator
OLZ	BOAC		Liberator
OOG	1359 Flt	ZW	Dominie
OOJ	MCS	CB	Dominie
OQZ	BOAC		Sunderland, Sandringham
ORA	51	TB	Stirling
ORJ	51	TB	Stirling
ORK	242	KY	Stirling
ORL	46	XK	Stirling

Call-sign	Unit	Two-letter code	Type(s)
ORO	158	NP	Stirling
ORP	196	7T, ZO	Stirling
ORS	299	5G	Stirling
ORS	570	E7	Stirling
ORT	1588 HD Flt		Stirling
OSD	232		Skymaster
OSK	233		Skymaster
OXB	304	QD	Warwick
OXG	167		Warwick
OYA	51	MH, TB	York
OYB	246	VU	York
OYC	511		York
OYD	1359 Flt	ZW	York
OYD	24		York
OYF	242	KY	York
OYR	59	BY	York
OYZ	BOAC		York
OZZ	BOAC		Seaford

Hastings C.1a TG532 seen wearing the three-letter identification GPK when serving in the Far East with No. 48 Sqn in the late 1950s. The letters related to the last three letters of the aircraft's W/T call-sign. (**Author's Collection**)

Five-letter Codes

Call-sign	Unit	Two-letter code	Type(s)	Call-sign	Unit	Two-letter code	Type(s)
MOAL	TCCF		Anson	MOHA	297	L5	Halifax
MOAY	31	CB	Anson	MOHC	113		Halifax
MOAZ	Colerne CF		Anson	MOHC	295	8E	Halifax
MOBC	242	OCU	Beverley	MOHD	47		Halifax
MOBM	84		Beverley	MOJZ	36		Hastings
MOBX	Abingdon		Beverley	MOKD	24		Lancastrian
MOCA	99, 511		Britannia	MOKG	114		Argosy
MOCE	99		Britannia	MOLG	QF		Heron
MOCF	99, 511		Britannia	MOND	Benson	5I	Valetta
MOCP	99, 511		Britannia	MONL	TCCF		Devon C.1
MODA	1	P&GTS	Dakota	MONT	2 TAF CS		Devon C.1
MODA	24	NQ	Dakota	MONX	RAF Benson		Devon C.1
MODB	53	PU	Dakota	MONY	31, MCS	CB	Devon C.1
MODC	24	NQ	Dakota	MOPT	2 TAF CS		Pembroke
MODC	27		Dakota	MOPY	MCS		Pembroke
MODC	62		Dakota	MORC	240 OCU	NU	Valetta
MODD	238	5T	Dakota	MORG	30	JN	Valetta C.1
MODF	30	JN	Dakota	MORG	70		Valetta C.1
MODG	QF		Dakota	MORM	84		Valetta C.1
MODH	216		Dakota	MORT	2 TAF	CS	Valetta C.1
MODL	MedME	CS	Dakota	MORV	Malta	CTTS	Valetta C.1
MODP	1325 Flt		Dakota	MOSC	30	JN	Valetta C.1
MODU	?		Dakota	MOTA	216		Comet C.1
MODW	Silver City		Dakota	MOTF	216		Comet C.1
			(trooping)	MOTP	216		Comet C.1
MODX	?		Dakota	MOVF	622		Valetta
MOFA	18		Dakota	MOWA	40	LE	York C.1
MOFB	77	KN,YS	Dakota	MOWB	59	BY	York C.1
MOFC	62		Dakota	MOYA	51	TB	York C.1
MOFG	46	XK	Dakota	MOYB	99		York C.1
MOFG	114		Argosy	MOYC	511		York C.1
MOFM	114		Dakota	MOYD	24		York C.1
MOGB	47		Hastings	MOYD	59	BY	York C.1
MOGC	242	OCU	Hastings	MOYF	242	KY	York C.1
MOGF	?		Valetta	MOYG	206		York C.1
MOGH	70		Hastings	MOYU	HQ India	CF	York C.1
MOGP	48		Hastings	MOZF	Airwork		Hermes
MOGX	?		Hastings				(trooping)
MOGZ	24		Hastings				

The W/T call-sign had been worn across the nose cone of several transport types, including the Hastings. One of the last recorded uses was MOGCF on C.1a TG581 of No. 242 OCU at Coltishall in 1963. (V. Flintham)

CHAPTER 14

Post-war Training and Reserve Codes

In 1946 a new system of coding for aircraft in Flying Training, Technical Training and Reserve Commands was introduced. It comprised a four-letter code, the first letter F, R or T denoting the Command, the second and third letters the unit and the fourth the individual aircraft. Because some training units had many aircraft on the inventory they were given several consecutive codes.

The university air squadrons were originally re-formed within Flying Training Command, switching to Reserve Command in 1947, at which time the auxiliary squadrons were also reformed within Reserve Command, where they were given the new style of codes.

The four-letter codes were intended to be displayed across the roundel in the form FAA⊙A but in practice they were applied in a number of ways as illustrated in the tables.

Flying Training Command

Three-letter unit codes were allocated first in order of seniority to the service flying training schools (SFTS) which retained them in their renaming as simple flying training schools (FTS). The training units used a wide variety of aircraft and only representative serials are given.

Code	Unit	Type(s)	Example	Presentation
FAA	19 SFTS, 19 FTS, RAFC	Harvard T.2B	KF448/FAA-A	
FAB	19 SFTS, 19 FTS, RAFC	Harvard T.2B	KF191/FAB-H	
FAC	19 SFTS, 19 FTS, RAFC	Harvard T.2B	FS815/FAC-Z	
FAD	19 SFTS, 19 FTS, RAFC	Harvard T.2B	FX441/FAD-Z	F⊙ADZ
FAE	19 SFTS, 19 FTS, RAFC	Tiger Moth T.2, Prentice T.1	Tiger Moth T5822/FAE-J	
FAF	19 SFTS, 19 FTS, RAFC	Tiger Moth T.2, Prentice T.1	Prentice VR227/FAF-B	
FAG	19 SFTS, 19 FTS, RAFC	Anson T.1, Anson T.21, Vampire F.1, Meteor T.7	Anson I NK563/FAG-A	FA⊙GA F⊙AGH
FAI	20 SFTS, 2 FTS	Harvard T.2B, Prentice T.1	Harvard T.2B KF435/FAI-R	F⊙AIR
FAJ	20 SFTS, 2 FTS	Harvard T.2B KF270/FAJ-E		
FAK	20 SFTS, 2 FTS	Tiger Moth T.2, Harvard T.2B, Prentice T.1	Harvard T.2B KF250/FAK-J	F⊙AKJ
FAL	20 SFTS, 2 FTS	Anson T.1, Tiger Moth T.2, Prentice T.1	Prentice T.1 VS630/FAL-X	FA⊙LI
FAM	20 SFTS, 2 FTS	Tiger Moth T.2	DE720/FAM-K	⊙FAMK
FAN	21 SFTS	Harvard T.2B	FT383/FAN-G	
FAO	21 SFTS	Harvard T.2B	FT346/FAO-G	FA⊙OG
FAP	21 SFTS	Harvard T.2B	KF469/FAP-E	
FAP	21 SFTS	Harvard T.2B	FT224/FAQ-J	
FAS	16(P)FTS	Oxford T.2, Anson T.1, Magister T.1	Oxford PG999/FAS-M	
FAT	16(P)FTS	Tiger Moth T.2, Magister T.1	Magister R1918/FAT-M	
F	BA 7 SFTS, 7 FTS	Wellington T.10, Harvard T.2B, Oxford T.2	Harvard KF481/FBA-D	
FBB	7 SFTS, 7 FTS	Oxford T.2, Wellington T.10, Harvard T.2B	Oxford NM796/FBB-O	
FBC	7 SFTS, 7 FTS	Tiger Moth T.2, Harvard T.2B	Tiger Moth EM905/FBC-N	
FBD	7 SFTS, 7 FTS	Prentice T.1, Harvard T.2B	Harvard FX428/FBD-D	
FBE	7 SFTS, 7 FTS	Prentice T.1, Anson T.1	Prentice VR291/FBE-A	
FBG	6 SFTS, 6 FTS	Prentice T.1, Harvard T.2B	Harvard FE910/FBG-I	
FBH	6 SFTS, 6 FTS	Prentice T.1, Harvard T.2B	Harvard KF275/FBH-A	
FBI	6 SFTS, 6 FTS	Prentice T.1, Harvard T.2B, Tiger Moth T.2, Balliol T.2	Tiger Moth R4785/FBI-F	
FBJ	6 SFTS, 6 FTS	Harvard T.2B, Magister T.1, Anson T.1, Prentice T.1	Harvard T.2B KF268/FBJ-C	FB⊙JC

Code	Unit	Type(s)	Example	Presentation
FBK	6 SFTS, 6 FTS	Harvard T.2B	KF691/FBK-L	
FBP	3 SFTS, 3 FTS	Prentice T.1, Harvard T.2B, Tiger Moth T.2	Prentice T.1 VS243/FBP-N	FBP◉N
FBQ	3 SFTS, 3 FTS	Tiger Moth T.2, Anson T.1, Magister T.1	Magister L5925/FBQ-K	
FBR	3 SFTS, 3 FTS	Prentice T.1, Harvard T.2B	Prentice VR230/FBR-E	
FBS	3 SFTS, 3 FTS	Harvard T.2B	FX265/FBS-F	
FBT	3 SFTS, 3 FTS	Harvard T.2B	KF513/FBT-H	F◉BTA (stbd)
FBU	3 SFTS, 3 FTS	Harvard T.2B	KF156/FBU-O F	B◉UC
				F◉BUJ
FBV	3 SFTS, 3 FTS	Tiger Moth T.2	T7995/FBU-V	
FCA	17 SFTS, 17 FTS, 1 FTS	Harvard T.2B, Oxford T.2	Oxford DF409/FCA-Z	
FCB	17 SFTS, 17 FTS, 1 FTS	Oxford T.2, Harvard T.2B	Harvard FX256/FCB-B	
FCC	17 SFTS, 17 FTS, 1 FTS	Oxford T.2, Harvard T.2B, Magister T.1	Magister L8262/FCC-Z	
FCD	17 SFTS, 17 FTS, 1 FTS	Harvard T.2B	FX331/FCD-X	
FCE	17 SFTS, 17 FTS, 1 FTS	Harvard T.2B, Tiger Moth T.2	Harvard FX402/FCE-I	
FCF	17 SFTS, 17 FTS, 1 FTS	Spitfire 5B, 16, Harvard T.2B	Spitfire 16 SM350/FCF-X	
FCG	17 SFTS, 17 FTS, 1 FTS	Spitfire 16, Prentice T.1	Prentice VS689/FCG-O	
FCI	22 SFTS, 22 FTS	Harvard T.2B, Tiger Moth T.2	Harvard FT258/FCI-R	
FCJ	22 SFTS, 22 FTS	Harvard T.2B, Anson T.1	Anson NK956/FCJ-F	
FCK	22 SFTS, 22 FTS	Harvard T.2B, Tiger Moth T.2	Tiger Moth DE175/FCK-X	
FCL	22 SFTS, 22 FTS	Tiger Moth T.2, Prentice T.1	Prentice VS616/FCL-T	
FCM	22 SFTS, 22 FTS	Prentice T.1	VS653/FCM-D	
FCT	ECFS, EFS, RAFFC	Harvard T.2B	FT330/FCT-D	
FCU	ECFS, EFS, RAFFC	Oxford T.2, Athena T.1	Oxford EB863/FCU-J	
FCV	ECFS, EFS, RAFFC	Buckmaster T.1, Anson T.12, Magister T.1, Master GT.2, Hotspur T.2	Anson T.12 PH843/FCV-S	FCVS◉ FC◉VE
FCW	ECFS, EFS, RAFFC	Spitfire LF.9, Meteor F.3, F.4 Spitfire LF.9	BS348/FCW-C	FC◉WC
FCX	ECFS, EFS, RAFFC	Mosquito T.3, Lancaster B.1FE, B.3, B.7FE, Anson C.19, Lancastrian C.2 Lancaster B.3	Lancastrian VL976/FCX-Y JA845/FCX-T	
FDA	21(P)AFU, 21(P)RFS, 1(P)RFU	Oxford T.2, Harvard T.2B, Spitfire 16, Meteor T.7	Oxford NM796/FDA-D Spitfire LF.16 TE203/FDA-A	
FDB	21(P)AFU, 21(P)RFS, 1(P)RFU	Oxford T.2, Wellington T.10	Wellington RP505/FDB-E	FD◉BE
FDC	21(P)AFU, 21(P)RFS, 1(P)RFU	Tiger Moth T.2, Oxford T.2, Harvard T.2B, Wellington T.10	Oxford T.2 PH517/FDC-H	FD◉CH
FDD	21(P)AFU, 21(P)RFS, 1(P)RFU	Oxford T.2, Spitfire 16, Harvard T.2B	Oxford PH355/FDD-J	
FDE	21(P)AFU, 21(P)RFS, 1(P)RFU	Oxford T.2	EB720/FDE-W	
FDF	21(P)AFU, 21(P)RFS, 1(P)RFU	Oxford T.2	R5952/FDF-U	
FDG	21(P)AFU, 21(P)RFS, 1(P)RFU	Anson T.1, Oxford T.2	Anson N9571/FDG-P	
FDI	CFS	Lancaster B.7FE, Prentice T.1, Oxford T.2, Anson T.12	Lancaster B.7 NX735/FDI-D	
FDJ	CFS	Meteor T.7, F.4, Vampire F.3, Oxford T.2, Spitfire 16, Magister T.1	Vampire VT856/FDJ-L	
FDK	CFS	Oxford T.2, Magister T.1	Magister L8262/FDK-H	
FDL	CFS	Tiger Moth T.2, Oxford T.2, Chipmunk T.10, Auster AOP.5	Auster TW440/FDL-A	
FDM	CFS	Harvard T.2B, Auster AOP.5	Harvard FT246/FDM-X	
FDN	CFS	Harvard T.2B, Oxford T.2	Harvard FS742/FDN-J	
FDO	CFS	Buckmaster T.1, Anson T.1, Mosquito T.3, FB.6, Harvard T.2B	Harvard T.2B FS744/FDO-U	FD◉OY
FDQ	10 FIS, 8 EFTS	Tiger Moth T.2 N6539/FDQ-E		
FDR	10 FIS, 8 EFTS	Tiger Moth T.2 DE678/FDR-B		
FDS	10 FIS, 8 EFTS	Tiger Moth T.2 DE718/FDS-B		

The Prentice T.1 was the RAF's first trainer with side-by-side seating and served for a relatively short time. It was finished in the contemporary colour scheme. VR225/FBE-H of No. 7 FTS is seen visiting Tangmere in 1950 and shows one presentation of the code. (J. D. R. Rawlings)

The Buckmaster T.1 was a trainer which saw limited service with a variety of training units and as a conversion trainer to the Brigand. This example, RP246/FCV-E, belonged to the Empire Flying School and shows an even code presentation. (MoD)

The Empire Air Navigation School at Shawbury was the operator of this Mosquito B.16, RV-9 318/FGF-H in 1947. The presentation of the code as F-GFH is yet another of the great variety of ways these four-letter codes were applied. (via Air Cdre G. R. Pitchfork)

The Meteors of No. 203 Advanced Flying School at Driffield had their codes presented in a more conventional style as shown by T.7 VW440/FMK-H and F.4 VT110/FMJ-N. (via J. D. Oughton)

When the RAuxAF was re-formed after the war it was part of Reserve Command and so wore its sequential codes, with the R and A being constant. The third letter denoted the unit, starting with A. Thus O represented No. 608 (North Riding) Sqn, whose Spitfire F.22 PK340/RAO-C is seen at Ouston in 1948. (R. Lindsay)

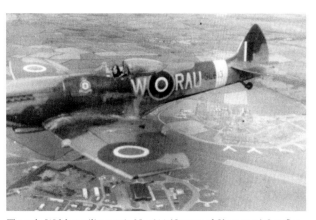

The only Welsh auxiliary unit, No. 614 (County of Glamorgan) Sqn flew RAU-coded Spitfire LF.16s when it was re-formed. Caught flying over its base at Llandow in 1947, SL813/RAU-W also carries the squadron badge adjacent to the cockpit. (No. 614 Sqn Association)

Code	Unit	Type(s)	Example	Presentation
FDT	10 FIS, 8 EFTS	Magister T.1, Anson T.1	Magister N3954/FDT-G	
FDU	Beam Approach School	Oxford T.2	HM479/FDU-B	
FDV	Beam Approach School	Oxford T.2	V4270/FDV-R	
FDW	Beam Approach School	Harvard T.2B	KF541/FDW-D	
FDW	CFS	Spitfire 9C, Harvard T.2B	Spitfire BS848/FDW-O	
FDY	SFC, SATC	Hawk Major, Anson T.1, T.20, T.21	Hawk Major HL538/FDY-Z	
FEA	1 GTS	Master GT.2	EM323/FEA-V	
FEB	1 GTS	Master GT.2	DM269/FEB-B	
FEC	1 GTS	Master GT.2, Anson T.1	Anson NK371/FEC-V	
FEE	1 GTS	Tiger Moth T.2	NM129/FEE-A	
FEG	3 GTS	Master GT.2	DL464/FEG-A	
FEH	3 GTS	Master GT.2	EM264/FEH-A	
FEI	3 GTS	Tiger Moth T.2	NL971/FEI-D	
FEJ	3 GTS	Hotspur I, II	BT598/FEJ-D	
FEK	3 GTS	Master GT.2	EM380/FEK-Y	
FEO	21 HGCU	Oxford	PG974/FEO-H	
FEP	21 HGCU	Halifax A.7	PP374/FEP-D	
FER	21 HGCU	Horsa II	TL413/FER-U	FE⊙RZ
FFA	10 AGS	Wellington T.10	HE742/FFA-L	
FFB	10 AGS	Spitfire Vb	AR323/FFB-D	
FFD	10 AGS	Wellington T.10, Horsa 2	Horsa TL555/FFD-O	
FFF	11 AGS	Wellington T.10, Halifax	Wellington LP914/FFF-A	
FFG	11 AGS	Master GT.2	DM325/FFG-O	
FFI	5 ANS, 1 ANS	Tiger Moth T.2, Anson T.1, T.21, C.19, Oxford T.2	Oxford LX274/FFI-F	
FFJ	5 ANS, 1 ANS	Anson T.1, T.21, Wellington T.10, Tiger Moth T.2	Anson T.1 EF871/FFJ-C	
FFK	5 ANS, 1 ANS	Wellington T.10, Tiger Moth T.2	Wellington RP312/FFK-G	
FFM	7 ANS, 2 ANS	Anson T.1, Oxford T.2, Tiger Moth T.2, Wellington T.10	Anson NK670/FFM-N	
FFN	7 ANS, 2 ANS	Anson T.1	NK401/FFN-E	
FFO	7 ANS, 2 ANS	Wellington T.10	HE214/FFO-L	
FFP	7 ANS, 2 ANS	Anson T.20, T.21	VS588/FFP-Z	F⊙FPZ
FFS	10 ANS	Wellington T.10	RP504/FFS-J	
FFT	10 ANS	Anson T.1	MG595/FFT-G	
FGA	EAAS, RAFFC	Spitfire F.16, Lancaster B.3, B.7FE, Wellington T.10, GR.13, Valetta C.1, C.2, Hastings C.1, Anson C.19, Martinet TT.1, Lincoln B.2 Lancastrian C 2	Spitfire TB295/FGA-T Lancaster B.7 NX779/FGA-B Lancastrian VM730/FGA-C	
FGB	EAAS, RAFFC	Wellington T.10, GR.14	NC198/FGB-O	
FGC	EAAS, RAFFC	Anson T.1, T.12, C.19, T.21, Mosquito FB.6, Master T.2, Wellington T.10, Magister T.1, Spitfire 16, Martinet TT.1, Athena T.2, Vampire FB.5, Meteor T.7, Lancaster B.3, Harvard T.2B	Mosquito RF853/FGC-R Spitfire LF.16 SL574/FGC-U Anson C.19 PH843/FGC-F	
FGE	EANS, CNS, CNCS	Wellington T.10, GR.13	NC606/FGE-A	FGE⊙A
FGF	EANS, CNS, CNCS	Lancaster B.1FE, Anson T.1, T.21, Oxford T.2, Spitfire F.16, Halifax B.6	Lancaster B.1 PD328/FGF-A Halifax B.6 ST814/FGF-B	FGF⊙A
FGG	EANS, CNS, CNCS	Lancaster B.1FE, B.7FE, Anson T.21, Halifax B.6, Mosquito B.35, Tiger Moth T.2, Meteor F.3	Meteor EE413/FGG-I Lancaster B.7 NX720/FGG-M	
FHA	1 EFTS	Tiger Moth T.2	T-7862/FHA-B	⊙FHAB
FHB	1 EFTS	Tiger Moth T.2	N-5470/FHB-G	⊙FHBG
FHE	2 EFTS	Tiger Moth T.2	NM133/FHE-U	
FHF	2 EFTS	Tiger Moth T.2	N9456/FHF-B	

Code	Unit	Type(s)	Example	Presentation
FHG	2 EFTS	Anson T.1	MG519/FHG-B	
FHI	3 EFTS	Tiger Moth T.2	N5445/FHI-V	
FHJ	3 EFTS	Tiger Moth T.2	L6944/FHJ-S	
FHK	3 EFTS	Tiger Moth T.2	T6774/FHK-H	
FHM	4 EFTS	Tiger Moth T.2	R4975/FHM-I	
FHN	4 EFTS	Tiger Moth T.2	N6580/FHN-H	
FHO	4 EFTS	Tiger Moth T.2	R4763/FHO-D	
FHQ	6 EFTS	Tiger Moth T.2	N9116/FHQ-S	
FHR	6 EFTS	Tiger Moth T.2	T7998/FHR-A	
FHS	6 EFTS	Tiger Moth T.2	N6977/FHS-P	
FHV	7 EFTS	Tiger Moth T.2	N6478/FHV-O	
FHW	7 EFTS	Tiger Moth T.2	T6918/FHW-Z	
FHX	7 EFTS	Tiger Moth T.2	T7089/FHX-A	
FIC	11 EFTS	Tiger Moth T.2	T7115/FIC-J	
FIJ	15 EFTS	Tiger Moth T.2	N6865/FIJ-H	
FIK	15 EFTS	Tiger Moth T.2	R4904/FIK-B	
FIN	16 EFTS	Tiger Moth T.2	T7048/FIN-O	
FIO	16 EFTS	Tiger Moth T.2	N9394/FIO-J	
FIP	16 EFTS	Tiger Moth T.2	T6907/FIP-O	
FIR	18 EFTS	Tiger Moth T.2	T6182/FIR-M	
FIS	18 EFTS	Tiger Moth T.2	R4845/FIS-E	
FIV	21 EFTS	Tiger Moth T.2, Auster AOP.5	Tiger Moth DE153/FIV-E	
FIW	21 EFTS	Tiger Moth T.2, Auster AOP.5	Auster RT489/FIW-B	
FIX	21 EFTS	Tiger Moth T.2, Harvard T.2B	Tiger Moth T6801/FIX-Y	
FJA	22 EFTS	Tiger Moth T.2, Auster AOP.5	Auster TW500/FJA-Y	
FJB	22 EFTS	Tiger Moth T.2, Auster AOP.5	Tiger Moth DE269/FJB-B	
FJC	22 EFTS	Tiger Moth T.2, Auster AOP.5	Tiger Moth R5216/FJC-K	
FJD	22 EFTS	Tiger Moth T.2	DE241/FJD-G	
FJF	24 EFTS	Tiger Moth T.2	R5109/FJF-A	
FJG	24 EFTS	Tiger Moth T.2, Magister T.1	Magister P2493/FJG-W	
FJJ	28 EFTS	Tiger Moth T.2	T6400/FJJ-F	
FJK	28 EFTS	Tiger Moth T.2	L6938/FJK-G	
FJN	29 EFTS	Tiger Moth T.2	T6861/FJN-A	
FJO	29 EFTS	Tiger Moth T.2	DE450/FJO-I	
FJP	29 EFTS	Tiger Moth T.2	T5963/FJP-L	
FJR	CGS	Tiger Moth T.2	N9278/FJR-K	
FJS	CGS	Lancaster B.1FE, Lincoln B.2, Wellington T.2, T.10	Lancaster NX645/FJS-C	
FJT	CGS	Mosquito FB.6, Spitfire LF.16E, Meteor F.3	Mosquito HP989/FJT-A	
FJU	CGS	Martinet TT.1, Tempest TT.5, Proctor C.4, Harvard T.2B, Balliol T.2	Tempest SN321/FJU-D	
FJV	CGS	Spitfire LF.16E, Meteor F.3, F.4, T.7	Spitfire TE259/FJV-A	
FJW	CGS	Spitfire LF.16E, Vampire FB.5, T.11	Vampire VV559/FJW-A	
FJX	CGS	Master T.2, Harvard T.2B, Meteor T.7, F.8	Meteor T.7 WE917/FJX-J	
FKA	1511 BAT Flt	Oxford T.2		
FKB	JSSC	Oxford T.2, Proctor C.3	Oxford NM753/FKB-A	
FKD	1537 BAT Flt	Oxford T.2		
FKF	1547 BAT Flt	Oxford T.2 DF426/FKF-X		
FKN	FTC Comms Flt	Proctor C.3, Oxford C.1, Harvard T.2B, Magister T.1, Anson C.10, C.19	Harvard FS752/FKN-C	
FKO	21 Gp Comms Flt	Dominie C.2, Anson C.10, C.19, Proctor C.3, C.4, Oxford C.2, Harvard T.2B	Dominie NR697/FKO-A	
FKP	23 Gp Comms Flt	Anson C.19, Proctor C.2, Harvard T.2B	Anson VM314/FKP-T	
FKQ	25 Gp Comms Flt	Tiger Moth T.2, Anson C.10, C.19, Magister T.1, Proctor C.3	Proctor C.3 LZ710/FKQ-C	F⊙KQC
FKR	54 Gp Comms Flt	Proctor C.3	LZ636/FKR-C	

Code	Unit	Type(s)	Example	Presentation
FKS	SF Cranwell	Proctor C.3, Oxford C.2, Tiger Moth T.2	Oxford HN839/FKS-A	
FLA	Cambridge UAS	Tiger Moth T.2	W7950/FLA-A	
FLB	Aberdeen UAS	Tiger Moth T.2		
FLC	Edinburgh UAS	Tiger Moth T.2		
FLD	Glasgow UAS	Tiger Moth T.2		
FLE	Queens (Belfast) UAS	Tiger Moth T.2		
FLF	St Andrews UAS	Tiger Moth T.2		
FLG	Liverpool UAS	Tiger Moth T.2		
FLH	Manchester UAS	Tiger Moth T.2		
FLI	Leeds UAS	Tiger Moth T.2	T5616/FLI-A	
FLJ	Durham UAS	Tiger Moth T.2	DE953/FLJ-B	
FLK	Birmingham UAS	Tiger Moth T.2	T6101/FLK-B	
FLL	Nottingham UAS	Tiger Moth T.2	DE978/FLL-B	
FLM	Bristol UAS	Tiger Moth T.2		
FLN	Swansea UAS	Tiger Moth T.2		
FLO	London UAS	Tiger Moth T.2	T7449/FLO-A	
FLP	Southampton UAS	Tiger Moth T.2, Oxford T.2	Oxford HN938/FLP-C	
FLQ	Oxford UAS	Tiger Moth T.2		
FLR	Perth UAS	?		proposed
FLS	Wolverhampton UAS	Tiger Moth T.2		
FLT	Derby UAS	?		proposed
FLU	Yatesbury UAS	?		proposed
FLV	Cambridge UAS	Tiger Moth T.2	T7487/FLV-A	
FMA	201 AFS	Wellington T.10, Tiger Moth T.2	Wellington NC426/FMA-F	FM⊙AF
FMB	201 AFS	Wellington T.10	NR502/FMB-U	
FME	202 AFS	Wellington T.10	NA791/FME-J	
FMI	203 AFS	Vampire F.1, FB.5	VX979/FMI-K	
FMJ	203 AFS	Meteor F.4, T.7	VT332/FMJ-U	V⊙FMJ
FMK	203 AFS	Meteor T.7, Tiger Moth T.2	Tiger Moth DF129/FMK-W	FMK⊙M
FMO	204 AFS	Mosquito FB.6, T.3, Tiger Moth T.2	Mosquito FB.6 SZ974/FMO-R	FMO⊙R
			Mosquito T.3 LR581/FMO-J	

Mosquito NF.30 RK936/RAW-H of No. 616 (South Yorkshire) Sqn at Finningley in 1949 also wears a squadron badge, but this time on the fin within a white disc. The colour scheme is generally similar to the wartime night-fighter scheme. (Air Cdre G. R. Pitchfork)

Reserve Command

Reserve Command was formed in May 1945 and assumed responsibility for the re-created Auxiliary Air Force squadrons, the refresher flying schools (RFS), various communications flights and the university air squadrons. Codes were allocated logically with the RA series going to the operational squadrons of the AAF, the RC series to refresher schools and communications flights and the RU series to the university air squadrons, this time with the third letter being the initial letter of the university except for Leeds (RUY) and Southampton (RUZ), which clashed with London and St Andrews. Finally, when the air observation post squadrons formed reserve flights in the 1900 series in 1949 they were added in the RO series in squadron order. All very tidy!

Code	Unit	Type(s)	Example	Presentation
RAA	500 Sqn	Mosquito T.3	TV963/RAA-Q	
RAA	500 Sqn	Mosquito NF.19	TA352/RAA-D	
RAA	500 Sqn	Mosquito NF.30	NT606/RAA-H	
RAA	500 Sqn	Oxford T.1	RR329/RAA-R	
RAA	500 Sqn	Harvard T.2B	KF423/RAA-B	
RAA (port)	500 Sqn	Meteor F.3	EE420/RAA-B	BO• RAA
RAA	500 Sqn	Meteor T.7	VZ638/RAA-C	
RAB	501 Sqn	Spitfire LF.16E	TE288/RAB-D	
RAB	501 Sqn	Harvard T.2B	KF670/RAB-A	
RAB	501 Sqn	Vampire F.1	TG373/RAB-E	
RAC	502 Sqn	Mosquito B.25	KB565/RAC-*	
RAC	502 Sqn	Mosquito NF.30	MV524/RAC-*	
RAC	502 Sqn	Oxford I	V3398/RAC-Z	
RAC	502 Sqn	Harvard T.2B	FX249/RAC-R	
RAC	502 Sqn	Spitfire F.22	PK316/RAC-D	
RAD	504 Sqn	Mosquito T.3	HJ997/RAD-M	
RAD	504 Sqn	Mosquito NF.30	NT562/RAD-M	
RAD	504 Sqn	Spitfire F.14E	NH779/RAD-U	
RAD	504 Sqn	Spitfire F.22	PK328/RAD-D	
RAD	504 Sqn	Oxford I	NM421/RAD-X	
RAD	504 Sqn	Harvard T.2B	KF579/RAD-X	
RAD	504 Sqn	Meteor F.4	VT321/RAD-G	
RAG	600 Sqn	Spitfire F.14	TZ175/RAG-D	
RAG	600 Sqn	Spitfire F.21	LA330/RAG-F	
RAG	600 Sqn	Spitfire F.22	PK389/RAG-W	
RAG	600 Sqn	Harvard T.2B	FT414/RAG-B	
RAH	601 Sqn	Spitfire LF.16E	RW394/RAH-W	
RAH	601 Sqn	Harvard T.2B	FX399/RAH-V	
RAI	602 Sqn	Spitfire FR.14E	TX985/RAI-B	
RAI	602 Sqn	Spitfire F.21	LA198/RAI-G	
RAI	602 Sqn	Spitfire F.22	PK369/RAI-B	
RAI	602 Sqn	Harvard T.2B	KF374/RAI-Y	
RAJ	603 Sqn	Spitfire LF.16E	SL719/RAJ-N	
RAJ	603 Sqn	Spitfire F.22	PK362/RAJ-N	
RAJ	603 Sqn	Harvard T.2B	KF449/RAJ-B	
RAK	604 Sqn	Spitfire LF.16E	SL615/RAK-Y	
RAK	604 Sqn	Harvard T.2B	KF709/RAK-Y	RAK◉Y
RAL	605 Sqn	Mosquito T.3	VT593/RAL-*	
RAL	605 Sqn	Mosquito NF.30	MM790/RAL-F	
RAL	605 Sqn	Harvard T.2B	KF145/RAL-M	
RAL	605 Sqn	Vampire F.1	TG348/RAL-A	RAL-P (port nose)
RAN	607 Sqn	Spitfire FR.14E	RM740/RAN-G	
RAN	607 Sqn	Spitfire F.22	PK384/RAN-F	
RAN	607 Sqn	Harvard T.2B	FX280/RAN-B	
RAO	608 Sqn	Spitfire F.22	PK325/RAO-F	
RAO	608 Sqn	Mosquito T.3	VT588/RAO-L	

Code	Unit	Type(s)	Example	Presentation
RAO	608 Sqn	Mosquito NF.30	NT471/RAO-9	
RAO	608 Sqn	Oxford I	NM409/RAO-M	
RAO	608 Sqn	Harvard T.2B	FT457/RAO-N	
RAP	609 Sqn	Mosquito T.3	VA883/RAP-U	
RAP	609 Sqn	Mosquito NF.30	NT422/RAP-D	
RAP	609 Sqn	Oxford I	MP448/RAP-Y	
RAP	609 Sqn	Spitfire LF.16E	SL561/RAP-H	
RAP	609 Sqn	Harvard T.2B	KF645/RAP-X	RAP⦿X
RAQ	610 Sqn	Spitfire FR.14E	MV350/RAQ-J	
RAQ	610 Sqn	Spitfire F.22	PK430/RAQ-G	
RAQ	610 Sqn	Harvard T.2B	FT282/RAQ-Y	
RAR	611 Sqn	Spitfire FR.14E	NH707/RAR-H	
RAR	611 Sqn	Spitfire F.22	PK381/RAR-E	
RAR	611 Sqn	Harvard T.2B	KF223/RAR-Y	
RAS	612 Sqn	Spitfire FR.14E	NH800/RAS-K	
RAS	612 Sqn	Spitfire LF.16E	TE385/RAS-N	
RAS	612 Sqn	Harvard T.2B	FX283/RAS-S	
RAT	613 Sqn	Spitfire FR.14E	MV247/RAT-A	
RAT	613 Sqn	Spitfire F.22	PK353/RAT-H	
RAT	613 Sqn	Harvard T.2B	KF470/RAT-3	
RAT	613 Sqn	Vampire F.1	TG336/RAT-D	
RAU	614 Sqn	Spitfire LF.16E	TE120/RAU-A	
RAU	614 Sqn	Spitfire F.22	PK501/RAU-D	
RAU	614 Sqn	Harvard T.2B	KF470/RAU-B	
RAV	615 Sqn	Spitfire FR.14E	NH792/RAV-W	
RAV	615 Sqn	Spitfire F.21	LA208/RAV-F	
RAV	615 Sqn	Spitfire F.22	PK372/RAV-M	
RAV	615 Sqn	Harvard T.2B	KF639/RAV-Z	
RAW	616 Sqn	Meteor F.3	EE307/RAW-O	RAW⦿O (port)
RAW	616 Sqn	Mosquito T.3	VA923/RAW-B	
RAW	616 Sqn	Mosquito NF.30	NT508/RAW-F	
RAW	616 Sqn	Oxford T.2	NM749/RAW-3	
RAW	616 Sqn	Harvard T.2B	KF733/RAW-B	
RCA	RCCF	Proctor C.3	HM294/RCA-E	
RCA	RCCF	Proctor C.4	NP342/RCA-K	
RCA	RCCF	Spitfire LF.16E	TE335/RCA-N	
RCA	RCCF	Harvard T.2B	FS921/RCA-L	
RCA	RCCF	Anson C.12	PH643/RCA-P	
RCA	RCCF	Anson C.19	VM357/RCA-M	
RCB	12 RFS	Tiger Moth T.2	DE715/RCB-F	
RCB	12 RFS	Anson T.21	VV323/RCB-3	
RCD	15 RFS	Tiger Moth T.2	PG640/RCD-W	
RCD	15 RFS	Anson I	NK327/RCD-Y	
RCD	15 RFS	Anson T.21	VS572/RCD-1	R⦿CD1
RCE	61 Gp CF	Auster AOP.5	TW452/RCE-D	RCE⦿D
RCE	61 Gp CF	Anson I	W1731/RCE-F	
RCE	61 Gp CF	Anson C.12	PH840/RCE-L	
RCE	61 Gp CF	Dominie C.2	NR744/RCE-A	
RCE	61 Gp CF	Proctor C.3	HM362/RCE-G	
RCF	62 Gp CF	Proctor C.3	LZ759/RCF-A	
RCF	62 Gp CF	Anson C.12	PH707/RCF-B	
RCG	63 Gp CF	Tiger Moth T.2	T6159/RCG-O	
RCG	63 Gp CF	Anson I	AX501/RCG-C	
RCG	63 Gp CF	Auster AOP.5	TW453/RCG-G	
RCH	64 Gp CF	Anson I	MG969/RCH-C	
RCH	64 Gp CF	Anson C.12	PH644/RCH-C	
RCH	64 Gp CF	Proctor C.4	NP234/RCH-B	
RCH	64 Gp CF	Dominie C.4	X7351/RCH-F	
RCH	64 Gp CF	Oxford C.2	LX634/RCH-J	

Reserve Command also controlled various Reserve Flying Schools, including No. 18 RFS at Fairoaks, which used this Anson T.21, VV300/RCT-4 which shows a non-standard code presentation.

Code	Unit	Type(s)	Example	Presentation
RCH	64 Gp CF	Auster AOP.5	TW460/RCH-A	
RCI	66 Gp CF	Auster AOP.5	TJ348/RCI-J	
RCI	66 Gp CF	Anson I	MG237/RCI-B	
RCI	66 Gp CF	Anson C.12	PH700/RCI-C	
RCI	66 Gp CF	Anson C.19	VM364/RCI-E	
RCI	66 Gp CF	Dominie C.2	HG728/RCI-K	
RCI	66 Gp CF	Proctor C.3	Z7212/RCI-G	
RCJ	17 RFS	Anson T.21	VV908/RCJ-3	
RCJ	17 RFS	Spitfire LF.16E	TD344/RCJ-7	
RCJ	17 RFS	Tiger Moth	T.2 N9402/RCJ-A	
RCJ	17 RFS	Beaufighter TT.10	RD781/RCJ-11	
RCK	3 RFS	Tiger Moth T.2	T7021/RCK-B	
RCK	3 RFS	Anson T.21	VV324/RCK-2	
RCL	14 RFS	Tiger Moth T.2	R5137/RCL-C	
RCL	14 RFS	Anson T.1	MG564/RCL-1	
RCL	14 RFS	Anson T.21	VV311/RCL-2	
RCL	14 RFS	Chipmunk T.10	WB751/RCL-3	
RCM	1 RFS	Anson T.21	WB462/RCM-7	RCM●7
RCM	1 RFS	Tiger Moth	T.2 DE432/RCM-C	
RCM	1 RFS	Chipmunk T.10	WB647/RCM-C	
RCN	4 RFS	Tiger Moth T.2	T7272/RCN-L	
RCO	6 RFS	Tiger Moth T.2	N6840/RCO-V	
RCP	7 RFS	Tiger Moth T.2	T7213/RCP-D	
RCQ	8 RFS	Tiger Moth T.2	R5120/RCQ-F	
RCQ	8 RFS	Anson T.21	VV882/RCQ-T	
RCR	11 RFS	Tiger Moth T.2	R4851/RCR-W	
RCR	11 RFS	Anson I	N9785/RCR-C	
RCR	11 RFS	Anson T.21	VV250/RCR-W	R●CRW
RCR	11 RFS	Chipmunk T.10	WB696/RCR-C	

Code	Unit	Type(s)	Example	Presentation
RCS	16 RFS	Tiger Moth T.2	DE268/RCS-A	
RCT	18 RFS	Anson I	LT283/RCT-1	
RCT	18 RFS	Anson T.21	VV255/RCT-3	R●CT3; RCT●3
RCT	18 RFS	Tiger Moth T.2	NL827/RCT-Y	
RCT	18 RFS	Chipmunk T.10	WB628/RCT-T	RCT●T
RCU	22 RFS	Tiger Moth T.2	DE673/RCU-B	
RCU	22 RFS	Anson I	MG446/RCU-2	
RCU	22 RFS	Chipmunk T.10	WB575/RCU-L	RCU●L
RCV	24 RFS	Tiger Moth T.2	R5251/RCV-L	
RCV	24 RFS	Anson T.21	VS562/RCV-2	
RCW	25 RFS	Tiger Moth T.2	DE568/RCW-J	
RCX	2 RFS	Tiger Moth T.2	T7404/RCX-B	
RCY	5 RFS	Tiger Moth T.2	N9255/RCY-B	
RCY	5 RFS	Anson T.21	WB454/RCY-W	
RCY	5 RFS	Chipmunk T.10	WB676/RCY-L	
RCZ	9 RFS	Tiger Moth T.2	T6194/RCZ-E	
RCZ	9 RFS	Anson T.21	WB453/RCZ-AF	
ROA	661/1960 Flt	Auster AOP.5	TW449/ROA-A	
ROA	661/1960 Flt	Auster AOP.6	VX112/ROA-S	ROA●S
ROB	662	Auster AOP.5	TJ380/ROB-C	
ROB	662	Auster AOP.6	VX113/ROB-V	
ROC	663	Tiger Moth T.2	N6616/ROC-Z	
ROC	663	Auster AOP.5	TJ340/ROC-C	
ROC	663	Auster AOP.6	VW993/ROC-B	
ROD	664	Tiger Moth T.2	EM915/ROD-P	
ROD	664	Auster AOP.5		
ROD	664	Auster AOP.6	VX122/ROD-Q	
ROG	665	Tiger Moth T.2	T7909/ROG-Z	
ROG	665	Auster AOP.5	TW454/ROG-K	
ROG	665	Auster AOP.6	VX124/ROG-G	
RSA	23 RFS	Tiger Moth T.2	DE410/RSA-G	

Flying near Exeter in 1946, Dominie I NR750 of the Halton Station Flight wears its THA code, identifying its base as belonging to Technical Training Command. (via M. W. Payne)

Code	Unit	Type(s)	Example	Presentation
RSA	23 RFS	Anson T.21	VV307/RSA-X	
RSB	10 RFS	Tiger Moth T.2	T7467/RSB-B	
RUA	Aberdeen UAS	Tiger Moth T.2	EM907/RUA-O	
RUB	Birmingham UAS	Tiger Moth T.2	NL910/RUB-A	
RUC	Cambridge UAS	Tiger Moth T.2	T5639/RUC-B	
RUC	Cambridge UAS	Chipmunk T.10	WB566/RUC-E	
RUD	Durham UAS	Tiger Moth T.2	T5616/RUD-E	
RUE	Edinburgh UAS	Tiger Moth T.2	N6720/RUE-B	
RUE	Edinburgh UAS	Chipmunk T.10	WB620/RUE-C	
RUG	Glasgow UAS	Tiger Moth T.2	DE-864/RUG-D	RUG◉D
RUL	London UAS	Tiger Moth T.2	T7449/RUL-A	RUL◉A
RUL	London UAS	Chipmunk T.10	WB604/RUL-A	
RUM	Manchester UAS	Tiger Moth T.2	N6851/RUM-A	
RUM	Manchester UAS	Chipmunk T.10	WD326/RUM-A	
RUM	Manchester UAS	Dominie I	X7452/RUM-A	
RUN	Nottingham UAS	Tiger Moth T.2	DE978/RUN-B	
RUO	Oxford UAS	Tiger Moth T.2	T6026/RUO-D	◉RUOD
RUO	Oxford UAS	Tiger Moth T.2	T7793/RUO-B	
RUO	Oxford UAS	Chipmunk T.10	WB624/RUO-D	
RUQ	Queens (Belfast) UAS	Tiger Moth T.2	T7605/RUQ-Z	
RUS	St Andrews UAS	Tiger Moth T.2	N9205/RUS-C	
RUY	Leeds UAS	Tiger Moth T.2	NM118/RUY-A	
RUY	Leeds UAS	Chipmunk T.10	WB661/RUY-C	
RUZ	Southampton UAS	Tiger Moth T.2	NM140/RUZ-A	

Technical Training Command

The codes developed by Technical Training Command were different from those for Flying Training and Reserve Commands in that the second and third letters generally related to the unit base. Entries noted in italics are where there is no evidence of use.

Code	Unit	Type(s)	Example	Presentation
TAL	*Aldermaston Comms Flt*	?		
TBR	Staff College Flt Andover	Oxford C.2, Dominie C.2, Proctor C.3, Magister T.1, Spitfire 8, Auster AOP.3	Proctor HM293/TBR-E	
TCA	1 RS	Halifax T.6, Proctor C.4	Halifax RG874/TCA-B	
TCE	*Carew Cheriton SF*	?		
TCN	Cranwell SF	Proctor C.3	HM302/TCN-B	
TCO	Cosford SF	Tiger Moth T.2, Anson I	Tiger Moth NL760/TCO-B	
TCR	1 RS	Proctor C.4, Anson T.21, Tiger Moth T.2, Dominie T.2, Oxford T.2	Anson T.21 VV366/TCR-B	TC◉RB (port)
TCW	*Carew Cheriton SF*	?		
TDE	EARS Debden	Oxford T.2, Anson T.1, T.21, T.22, Proctor C.4, Tiger Moth T.2	Oxford T.2 NM356/TDE-G	TDE◉G H◉TDE
TFA	1 SP	Anson 1	NK340/TFA-A	TFA◉A
THA	Halton SF	Anson C.10, C.12, C.19, Proctor C.3, C.4, Dominie C.1, C.2, Tiger Moth T.2	Anson C.10 NL171/THA-A	A◉THA (stbd)
THE	Parachute Test Flt Henlow	Dakota C.3, Halifax T.6, Tiger Moth	Halifax RG871/THE	
THI	A&AEE	Dominie C.2		
THL	24 GCF	Proctor C.1	P6242/THL-B	
THO	*Hornchurch SF*	?		
TIH	1 FPU	Proctor C.3	LZ759/TIH	

The Meteor NF.11s of the Alhorn-based No. 125 Wing carried single-letter codes for a time before they were replaced by squadron markings. No. 96 Sqn's aircraft were coded L, like WD696/L-B seen here; aircraft of its sister unit, No. 256 Sqn, may have been uncoded. (Official)

Code	Unit	Type(s)	Example	Presentation
TLO	Locking SF	Proctor C.1, C.3	LZ804/TLO-A	
TMA	4 RS	Proctor C.4, Anson T.22	Proctor NP239/TMA-B	
TMD	4 RS	Proctor C.4	NP356/TMD-D	
TME	4 RS	Tiger Moth T.2	T6167/TME-D	
TML	4 RS	Dominie T.2	NF673/TML-A	
TOC	1 OATS	Oxford T.2, Proctor C.4, Spitfire 11	Proctor RM225/TOC-C	
TSA	St Athan SF	Proctor C.3	HM351/TSA-A	
TSI	*RAF (Belgian) Training School*	?		
TSM	4 RS	Dominie T.1, Anson T.22, Proctor C.4	Proctor NP309/TSM-C	
TSN	*RAF (Belgian) Training School*	?		
TSO	27 GCF	Anson C.19, Dominie C.1, C.2, Proctor C.4, Master 2	Proctor NP161/TSO-B	
TTE	22 GCF	Anson C.19, Proctor C.4, Vega Gull	Vega Gull X9340/TTE-C	
TWM	1 SP	Anson 1	NK340/TWM-A	
TWY	TTCCF	Proctor C3, C.4, Auster AOP.5, Messenger 1, Anson C.10, C.12, C.19, Dominie C.1, C.2	Dominie RL961/TWY-G	

CHAPTER 15

2nd Tactical Air Force, Germany 1952–4

With the general abandonment of two-letter unit codes in 1951, single-letter codes were introduced for RAF 2nd Tactical Air Force units in Germany. Each station was usually allocated the letters A, B and L for each of the three squadrons in the based wing. In addition the letters C, T and W were used less frequently. Generally the day-fighter aircraft involved were finished in plain silver, although later they were camouflaged.

The scheme was only intended to differentiate between aircraft on a given base, hence there was considerable duplication within the theatre. The dates shown are those for the type in service with the unit, rather than the dates within which the given codes were used. Where an entry is in italics either the unit allocated code is not known, or it is known but without evidence of application. The scheme was abandoned in 1954 and replaced by coloured insignia.

Code	Unit	Type	Dates	Example	Station/wing
A ?	*256*	*Meteor NF.11*	*11.52-1.59*		*Ahlhorn 125 Wing*
L	96	Meteor NF.11	11.52-*c* 56	WD696/L-B	Ahlhorn 125 Wing
T	256	Meteor NF.11	11.52-1.c56	WD632/T-Y	Ahlhorn 125 Wing
A	112	Vampire FB.5	5.51-2.54	WA372/A-H	Bruggen 135 Wing
B	130	Vampire FB.5	8.53-4.54	WE844/B-A	Bruggen 135 Wing
T	112	Vampire FB.5	5.51-2.54	VV687/T-O	Bruggen 135 Wing
A	541	Meteor PR.10	12.50-9.57	WB156/A-B	Buckeburg 34 Wing
A	541	Meteor T.7	6.51-54	WG963/A-Z	Buckeburg 34 Wing
B	2	Meteor FR.9	12.50-5.56	VZ611/B-Z	Buckeburg 34 Wing
B	2	Meteor PR.10	3.51-7.51	WB155/B-A	Buckeburg 34 Wing
T	79	Meteor FR.9	11.51-8.56	WB121/T-H	Buckeburg 34 Wing
T	79	Meteor T.7	11.51-8.56	WG973/T-Z	Buckeburg 34 Wing
A	94	Vampire FB.5	12.50-6.54	VV700/A-C	Celle 139 Wing
A	94	Venom FB.1	1.54-9.57	WR284/A-G	Celle 139 Wing
B	145	Vampire FB.5	3.52-8.54	VV666/B-G	Celle 139 Wing
B	145	Venom FB.1	5.54-6.57	WE371/B-T	Celle 139 Wing
L	16	Vampire FB.5	12.48-7.54	WA190/L-M	Celle 139 Wing
L	16	Venom FB.1	1.54-6.57	WE431/L-P	Celle 139 Wing
T	93	Vampire FB.5	11.50-3.54	VV221/T-P	Celle 139 Wing
A	118	Vampire FB.5	5.51-9.54	WA317/A-T	Fassberg 121 Wing
A	118	Vampire T.11	5.51-9.54	WZ517/A-Z	Fassberg 121 Wing
A	118	Venom FB.1	9.53-5.55	WE388/A-M	Fassberg 121 Wing
A	266	Venom FB.1	4.51-5.56	WE457/A-N	Fassberg 121 Wing
B	14	Vampire FB.5	50-5.53	WG845/B-B	Fassberg 121 Wing
B	14	Venom FB.1	5.53-6.55	WE363/B-A	Fassberg 121 Wing
L	98	Vampire FB.5	2.51-8.53	WE841/L-D	Fassberg 121 Wing
T	98	Vampire FB.5	5.51-3.52	WA235/T-D	Fassberg 121 Wing
L	98	Venom FB.1	8.53-7.57	WK413/L-Z	Fassberg 121 Wing
A ?	*93*	*Vampire FB.5*	*11.50-4.54*		*Jever 122 Wing*
B	4	Vampire FB.5	7.50-12.53		Jever 122 Wing
B	4	Sabre F.4	3.54-8.55	XB775/B-M	Jever 122 Wing
T	93	Vampire FB.5	11.50-4.54	WA191/T-G	Jever 122 Wing
T	93	Sabre F.4	3.54-1.56		Jever 122 Wing
T	112	Vampire FB.5	3.52-7.53	WA283/T-F	Jever 122 Wing

Code	Unit	Type	Dates	Example	Station/wing
A	234	Vampire FB.5	8.52-1.54	WA256/A-H	Oldenburg 124 Wing
L	20	Vampire FB.9	7.52-1.54	WR139/L-E	Oldenburg 124 Wing
L	20	Vampire FB.5	11.52-1.56	VZ229/L-N	Oldenburg 124 Wing
T	26	Vampire FB.5	4.49-9.52	WA178/T-J	Oldenburg 124 Wing
T	26	Vampire FB.9	6.52-11.53	WR153/T-J	Oldenburg 124 Wing
W	234	Vampire FB.5	8.52-1.54	WA260/W-D	Oldenburg 124 Wing
W	234	Vampire FB.9	8.52-1.54	WR242/W-B	Oldenburg 124 Wing
A ?	*68*	*Meteor NF.11*	*3.52-1.59*		*Wahn 148 Wing*
B	87	Meteor NF.11	3.52-11.57	WD734/B-G	Wahn 148 Wing
A	3	Vampire FB.5	5.49-6.53	VV445/A-T	Wildenrath 137 Wing
B	67	Vampire FB.5	9.50-5.53	VZ354/B-Z	Wildenrath 137 Wing
L	71	Vampire FB.5	10.50-10.53	WA223/L-J	Wildenrath 137 Wing
C	2 TAF CS	Anson C.12	51-52	PH588/C-E	Wildenrath
C	2 TAF CS	Tiger Moth T.2	51-52	T6909/C-X	Wildenrath
C	2 TAF CS	Proctor C.4	51-52	RM223/C-H	Wildenrath
C	2 TAF CS	Valetta C.1	51-52	VX573/C-A	Wildenrath
A	266	Vampire FB.5	7.52-11.52	VZ301/A-M	Wunstorf 123 Wing
A	266	Venom FB.1	4.51-5.56	WE457/A-N	Wunstorf 123 Wing
B	5	Vampire FB.5	3.52-6.54	WG843/B-C	Wunstorf 123 Wing
B	5	Venom FB.1	12.52-8.55	WE329/B-X	Wunstorf 123 Wing
L	11	Vampire FB.5	8.50-12.52	VX474/L-A	Wunstorf 123 Wing
L	11	Venom FB.1	8.52-8.53	WE309/L-P	Wunstorf 123 Wing
L	266	Vampire FB.5	7.52-6.54	VV444/L-J	Wunstorf 123 Wing

Seen being refuelled at Celle on 5 May 1954, Vampire FB.5 WA123/AR of No. 94 Sqn illustrates the code well; the other squadrons of No. 139 Wing were identified by B and L. (No. 94 Sqn Records)

No. 118 Sqn (No. 121 Wing) at Fassburg also used the squadron code A as worn on Venom FB.1 WE388/A-M in 1955, though the black flashes were also a squadron insignia. The other units of the wing, Nos 14 and 98 Sqns again used B and L. (B. G. Faulkes)

Meteor FR.9 VZ603/B-A of No. 2 Sqn illustrates the simple natural metal colour scheme and markings worn before the reintroduction of camouflage and unit insignia. It was part of No. 34 Wing at Buckeburg.

Taken at Stansted on a foggy day, this photograph of Sabre F.4 XB774/ B-M of No. 4 Sqn is the only one to have come to light showing the 2 TAF single-letter code on this type. The only other Sabre unit thought to have worn codes was its sister unit in No. 122 Wing at Jever, No. 93 Sqn. (R. Lindsay)

CHAPTER 16

RAF Coastal Command

Like the 2nd Tactical Air Force in Germany, Coastal Command also adopted single-letter codes. From March 1951 each station was usually allocated the letters A, B, L and T for each of up to four squadrons on the airfield. In addition the letters C, D, F, G and H were used for second-line units. Presentation varied, with the unit code usually on the rear fuselage and the aircraft letter on the nose. No. 240 Squadron applied the unit letter aft of the fuselage roundel and the aircraft letter forward of it, while Nos 204 and 269 Squadrons used the unit code only. Unit letters were allocated on a station basis to avoid duplication, just as Coastal Command had used single-number codes on a station basis for a period during the war.

The codes were applied in grey initially against white fuselage sides, but when the colour scheme changed to dark sea grey overall the codes were painted in white. The dates shown are those for the type in service with the unit, rather than the dates within which the given codes were used. The scheme was itself abandoned in 1955 and replaced by coloured squadron numbers.

Code	Unit	Type	Dates	Example	Base
	18 Group				
A	202	Halifax Met 6	10.46-5.51	ST809/A-V	Aldergrove
A	202	Hastings Met.1	10.50-7.54	TG623/A-D	Aldergrove
B	269	Shackleton MR.1A	1.52-12.58	VP284/B-E	Ballykelly
B	269	Shackleton MR.2	4.53-9.54	WL738/B-K	Ballykelly
G	JASS Flt	Shackleton MR.1	c 52-56	WB850/G-X	Ballykelly
G	JASS	Shackleton MR.2	c 52-56	WR967/G-B	Ballykelly
L	240	Shackleton MR.1A	5.52-56	WB858/L-A	Ballykelly
T	204	Shackleton MR.2	1.54-4.56	WR956/T-Q	Ballykelly
A	120	Shackleton MR.1	3.51-3.53	WB844/A-F	Kinloss
A	120	Shackleton MR.2	4.53-8.54	WL758/A-F	Kinloss
A	217	Neptune MR.1	1.52-3.56	WX504/A-H	Kinloss
C	236 OCU	Shackleton MR.1	4.51-58	VP268/C-Y	Kinloss
C	236 OCU	Neptune MR.1	52-56	WX551/C-O	Kinloss
B	203	Neptune MR.1	3.53-9.56	WX521/B-L	Topcliffe
L	210	Neptune MR.1	12.52-1.57	WX528/L-Y	Topcliffe
T	36	Neptune MR.1	7.53-2.57	WX545/T-C	Topcliffe
	19 Group				
A	42	Shackleton MR.1	6.52-7.54	WG510/A-F	St Eval
A	42	Shackleton MR.2	6.52-4.66	WG556/A-J	St Eval
B	203	Lancaster GR.3	8.46-3.53	RE206/B-B	St Eval
B	203	Lancaster ASR.3	8.46-3.53	RF210/B-D	St Eval
B	206	Shackleton MR.1A	9.52-5.58	WG508/B-X	St Eval
B	206	Shackleton MR.2	2.53-6.54	WL742/B-Z1	St Eval
L	228	Shackleton MR.2	7.54-3.59	WR959/L-O	St Eval
L	210	Lancaster GR.3	6.46-2.53	RE115/L-T	St Eval
T	220	Shackleton MR.1A	9.51-10.56	WB821/T-L	St Eval
T	220	Shackleton MR.2	3.53-7.54	WL737/T-K	St Eval
A	201	Sunderland GR.5	2.45-2.57	VB889/A-D	Pembroke Dock
B	230	Sunderland GR.5	1.45-2.57	SZ563/B-R	Pembroke Dock
D	235 OCU	Sunderland GR.5	7.47-10.53	RN304/D-M	Pembroke Dock
F	ASWDU	Shackleton MR.1	1.53-	WG532/F-F	St Mawgan
F	ASWDU	Shackleton MR.2	c 55-	WL789/F-D	St Mawgan
F	ASWDU	Lancaster GR.3	c 48-c 53	SW370/F-C	St Mawgan

Code	Unit	Type	Dates	Example	Base
F	ASWDU	Sycamore HC.12	2.52-3.53	WV982/F-Y	St Mawgan
F	ASWDU	Anson C.19	c 50-c 57	PH565/F-G	St Mawgan
H	1 MRS/SMR	Lancaster GR.3	1.51-9.56	RE159/H-U	St Mawgan
RAF Gibraltar					
B	224	Halifax Met.6	5.48-3.52	RG851/B-O	Gibraltar
B	224	Shackleton MR.1A	8.51-10.54	WB819/B-H	Gibraltar
B	224	Shackleton MR.2	5.53-10.66	WG558/B-R	Gibraltar

By the time the RAF introduced the Neptune MR.1 to service in early 1952, single-letter codes were also in vogue within Coastal Command. No. 217 Sqn was the first to receive them and one of its aircraft, WX505/A-J, shows the marking scheme to advantage. **(Gp Capt P. H. Stembridge)**

The unit code on the Shackleton was usually worn on the rear fuselage just forward of the tail, with the aircraft letter on the nose. MR.2 WL742/B-Z of No. 206 Sqn is seen during a visit to Gibraltar in mid-1953 and shows the fitting of the mid-upper turret, which was later removed. (R. C. B. Ashworth)

Still with its beaching gear attached, but with outboard engines running, Sunderland GR.5 ML817/D-P of No. 235 OCU eases forward to its mooring at Calshot in 1953. The Pembroke Dock-based operational units, Nos 201 and 230 Sqns used A and B respectively. (HQ Coastal Command)

Flying Training Command and Reserve Command Single-letter Codes

From about 1952 a new system of identifying individual training aircraft was introduced in the UK. It was similar to the system used in Rhodesia with the Rhodesian Air Training Group, shown in the first table below. Since training aircraft rarely ventured far afield the need was simply to identify individual aircraft, typically in the circuit or on the ground. In the new scheme units applied one of several letters as unit identifiers with a second, individual, aircraft letter or number.

There will have been some general instruction, since the format was applied consistently, albeit with confusion since where letters were used they were reversed on each side of the aircraft fuselage. Thus a unit like 215 AFS using M and N might easily have had two similar aircraft coded MO• N and NⓈ M with the presentation reversed on the starboard fuselage side! It must have been a nightmare for busy air traffic controllers. The most commonly used unit letters were M, N, O and P. The system was also used by Reserve Command as shown in the third table.

Rhodesian Air Training Group

Code	Unit	Type(s)	Example	Presentation
4 FTS	D	Anson I, C.19, T.20	MG358/DB	
4 FTS	A, W	Tiger Moth T.2	DE370/AA	
4 FTS	B, D, F, G, H	Harvard T.2B	EX253/D-C	
4 FTS	H	Chipmunk T.10	WD354/H-10	
5 FTS	W	Tiger Moth T.2	N6902/WG	
5 FTS	G, X	Harvard T.2A	EX753/X-J	
5 FTS	G, Z	Anson T.20	VS503/Z-Y	⊙ZY
5 FTS	G	Chipmunk T.10	WG413/G-37	

Flying Training Command

Code	Unit	Type(s)	Example	Presentation
202 AFS	N, O	Vampire FB.5	WA194/N-18	
202 AFS	N, O	Vampire T.11	WZ448/O-47	
202 AFS	N	Meteor T.7	WF794/N-46	
203 AFS	O, X	Meteor T.7	WF776/O-G	
203 AFS	O, X	Meteor F.4	VT129/X-J	
205 AFS	M, O, R, W, X, Y, Z	Meteor T.7	WG965/O-U	
205 AFS	M, O, R, W, X, Y, Z	Meteor F.4	RA493/T-Z	T⊙Z
206 AFS	M, Y	Meteor F.4	VT182/Y-34	
206 AFS	M, W, Y	Meteor T.7	WH192/M-75	
207 AFS	P, S	Meteor F.4	VW256/P-11	
207 AFS	P, S	Meteor T.7	WH200/S-20	
215 AFS	M, N	Meteor F.4	VT319/M-X	
215 AFS	M, N	Meteor T.7	WH114/N-A	N⊙A
1 FTS	K, N, P	Harvard T.2B	FT360/K-B	B⊙K (stbd)
1 FTS	K, M	Prentice T.1	VS641/M-F	
1 FTS	M, N, O, P, Y	Provost T.1	XF903/P-R	P⊙R
2 FTS	F, L, M, N, T, X	Prentice T.1	VS689/M-L	
2 FTS	N, O, P, R	Harvard T.2B	KF977/N-N	N⊙N

Code	Unit	Type(s)	Example	Presentation
2 FTS	O, P, Q, R	Provost T.1	XF885/O-A	O●A
2 FTS	U	Anson T.21	WJ517/U-P	
2 FTS	Q	Jet Provost T.1	XD677/Q-M	
3 FTS	M, N, O	Prentice T.1	VS259/M-E	
3 FTS	M, N, P, Q, S, T	Provost T.1	WW382/M-A	
3 FTS	O, P, R	Harvard T.2B	KF237/O-P	
6 FTS	F, M, N, X	Prentice T.1	VS263/M-J	
6 FTS	D, M, N, O, P	Provost T.1	WV429/N-Z	Z●N
6 FTS	N, O, P, Q	Harvard T.2B	KF165/O-E	O●E
7 FTS	D, E, Q	Balliol T.2	WG126/D-U	D●U (port) U●D (stbd)
7 FTS	M, P	Prentice T.1		
7 FTS	N, O, P	Harvard T.2B	KF924/N-K	
8 AFTS	S, U	Oxford T.2	X6871/S-P	S●P (port)
8 AFTS	O, X	Meteor T.7	VT308/O-16	
9 AFTS	M, O, P	Oxford T.2	LX349/M-C	
9 AFTS	M	Harvard T.2B	KF290/M-E	
9 AFTS	M	Chipmunk T.10	WP974/M-P	
10 AFTS	M, P	Oxford T.2	DF418/M-X	
10 AFTS	P	Chipmunk T.10	WP853/P-H	
22 FTS	L, M, O, P, X, Y	Prentice T.1	VS364/Y-Z	
22 FTS	R, U, Y	Harvard T.2B	FX279/R-G	
22 FTS	M, N, P, Y	Provost T.1	FX279/R-G	
CFS	I	Vampire FB.5	WA359/I-V	

These Provost T.1s of Ternhill-based No. 6 FTS, with WV448/N-S leading WV444/N-W and WV427/N-J, carry one of the unit identification letters allocated to the school, though with several letters allocated and often worn in a variety of positions, the system was confusing! (MoD)

Tucked in close in a vertical climb, Balliol T.2 WG126/D-U of No. 7 FTS at Cottesmore wears the standard trainer colour scheme of the 1950s, including the yellow training bands. (MoD)

Code	Unit	Type(s)	Example	Presentation
CFS	K, L, M, N, X	Prentice T.1	VS610/K-L	
CFS	K, M, N, O, P, Q, X	Provost T.1	XF609/K-X	K⊙X (stbd)
CFS	M, N, O	Harvard T.2B	FX350/N-Z	N⊙Z (port)
CFS	I, M	Anson C.12, C.19	PH810/M-A	A⊙M (stbd)
CFS	M	Chipmunk T.10	WK590/M-B	
CFS	O	Meteor T.7	WL403/O-K	O⊙K
CFS	I, N, V	Vampire T.11	WZ585/VX	
CFS	R, S	Jet Provost T.3	XN549/R-Y	
CFS	M	Valetta C.1	WJ496/MF	
CFS	M	Varsity T.1	WL686/MA	
CFS	C	Canberra T.4	WT480/CC	
CFS	S	Sycamore HR.14	XG547/S-T	S⊙T (port)
CFS	W	Whirlwind HAR.10	XR485/W-Q	
RAFC	A	Harvard T.2B	FS840/A-D	
RAFC	A, B, C	Balliol T.2	WG117/C-P	
RAFC	D, J	Chipmunk T.10	WK558/DH	
RAFC	J	Provost T.1	WW393/JD	JD⊙
RAFC	F, S	Prentice T.1	VR257/F-D	
RAFC	G	Anson T.21	VV257/G-C	
RAFC	E, J	Anson C.19	TX229/EK	
RAFC	N	Valetta T.3	WJ484/N-B	
RAFC	N	Varsity T.1	WF392/N-A	
RAFTC	S	Anson T.22	VV367/S-O	O⊙S (stbd)
RAFTC	S	Chipmunk T.10	WB706/S-M	
RAFTC	S	Varsity T.1		

Reserve Command

Code	Unit	Type(s)	Example	Presentation
2 BANS	N	Anson T.21	VV951/N-G	G⊙N
3 CAACU	A	Mosquito TT.35	TA642/A-R	
22 RFS	D	Oxford	NM357/DA	
22 RFS	C	Anson T.21	VV312/CA	
22 RFS	A	Chipmunk T.10	WK617/AK	

The coding system used by Flying Training Command during the 1950s was confusing, but Harvard T.2b FS899 of the Central Flying School repeats its individual letter on the nose, which helps identify the unit code as O. (via J. J. Halley)

CHAPTER 18
RAF Single-letter Codes Since 1970

In early 1970 the RAF started using single-letter unit codes again, initially with the Support Helicopter Force and then in RAF Germany. Over the years there appears to have been little logic in the system in that the letters are duplicated, although not within a specific type. Further, not all units used the system, even those with similar types on the same base at the same time. Thus at one stage Harriers of No. 3 Squadron were letter coded while No. 4 Squadron used just a single individual letter and No. 1 Squadron applied numerals. The Buccaneer units (including their Hunter trainers) used the unit code letter as the *second* letter. One unit – 229 OCU (65(R)), later 56 (R), Squadron – had to resort to individual aircraft numbers as well as letters at the peak of the Tornado training effort in the early 1990s.

Photo-reconnaissance units have tended to use their own single- character systems, apart from the Canberras of No. 39 Squadron/1 PRU. Omitted from this list are the FAA Sea King HC.4 of 846 NAS (V*), 848 NAS (W*) and 707 NAS (Z*). Also omitted are the Vigilant T.1 gliders coded S*, T* and U* and the Viking T.1 gliders coded V*, W*, X* and Y* which from 1996 were allocated randomly to the volunteer gliding schools.

Great care has to be taken in attributing codes to units since in many cases aircraft are loaned or transferred from one unit to another with a change of squadron markings but no change in code! Further, some letters are used on the same type with different units over time: for example F was used on Tornado GR.1s of No. 16 Squadron in Germany and later on aircraft of No. 12 Squadron in the UK. Exceptionally, No. 617 Squadron was allowed to revert to the wartime Lancaster code AJ worn during the famous dambuster raids of 1943. The apparent code B on Tornado GR.1s of the TTTE (example ZA321/B-58) was not a code but a nationality indicator (B – Britain, G – Germany, I – Italy)

Two codes which do not relate to units are J and W, which are used on the Tornado GR.1 and Harrier GR.7 respectively. They are believed to identify aircraft specially equipped for deployment on Operations *Jural* and *Warden*. For a time in the early 1990s the Harrier OCU (20R) applied the digit 3 then 5 with an individual aircraft letter on Harrier GR.3s and GR.5s respectively.

The selection of letters is not always arbitrary. Some units used the initial letter of the main feature of their badge and those identified are noted below, though as some were renumbered, the previous code remained.

C	237 OCU Buccaneer, Hunter (Cutlass)
D	234 (R) Sqn Hawk (Dragon)
F	12 Sqn Buccaneer, Hunter (Fox)
P	CFS Hawk (Pelican)
S	208 Sqn Buccaneer, Hunter (Sphinx)
T	74 (R) Sqn Hawk (Tiger)

Code	Unit	Type	Dates	Example	Theatre	Remarks
Buccaneer Force Lossiemouth						
F	12	Buccaneer S.2B	84-86	XW530/HF	UK	code reversed
F	12	Hunter T.7	84-86	XL609/YF	UK	code reversed
F	12	Hunter T.7B	84-86	XL568/ZF	UK	code reversed
S	208	Buccaneer S.2B	84-86	XX900/MS	UK	code reversed
S	208	Buccaneer S.2C	84-86	XV359/VS	UK	code reversed
S	208	Hunter T.7	84-86	XL616/YS	UK	code reversed
C	237 OCU	Buccaneer S.2A	84-85	XV355/AC	UK	code reversed
C	237 OCU	Hunter T.7	84-86	XL613/UC	UK	code reversed
C	237 OCU	Hunter T.7B	84-86	XL614/YC	UK	code reversed
C	237 OCU	Hunter T.8C	84-86	XF967/XC	UK	code reversed
Canberra Force Wyton, Marham						
A	39/1 PRU	Canberra PR.9	84-date	XH175/AP	UK	
A	39/1 PRU	Canberra T.4	94-date	WJ480/AT	UK	
B	231 OCU	Canberra B.2	83-92	WE113/BJ	UK	
B	231 OCU	Canberra T.4	83-92	WJ879/BH	UK	
B	CTSF	Canberra B.2T	92-93	WJ731/BK	UK	
B	CTSF	Canberra T.4	92-93	WT480/BC	UK	

Code	Unit	Type	Dates	Example	Theatre	Remarks
B	CTSF/39	Canberra PR.7	92-97	WH779/BP	UK	
C	100	Canberra B.2	82-91	WP515/CD	UK	
C	100	Canberra E.15	84-91	WJ756/CL	UK	
C	100	Canberra PR.7	84-91	WT519/CH	UK	
C	100	Canberra TT.18	83-91	WJ682/CU	UK	
D	207	Devon C.2	83-84	WB534/DB	UK	Wyton det only
E	360	Canberra T.17	82-10.94	WJ986/EP	UK	

Support Helicopter Force

Code	Unit	Type	Dates	Example	Theatre	Remarks
A	72	Wessex HC.2	69-84	XS674/AH	UK	
A	72	Puma HC.1	97-date	XW214/AB	UK	
B	WCF	Wessex HC.2	83-84	XR509/BM	UK	
B	18	Wessex HC.2	70-82	XR504/BF	Ger	
B	18	Chinook HC.1	82-93	ZA672/BX	UK, Ger	
B	18	Chinook HC.2, 2A	93-date	ZA671/BB	Ger, UK	
B	18	Puma HC.1	92-97	XW218/BW	Ger, UK	
C	33	Puma HC.1	71-date	XW214/CK	UK	
D	230	Puma HC.1	71-96	XW226/DK	Ger, UK	
E	7	Chinook HC.1	83-95	ZA718/EQ	UK	
E	7	Chinook HC.2	94-date	ZA713/EM	UK	
F	240 OCU	Chinook HC.1	81-91	ZA704/FJ	UK	
F	240 OCU	Puma HC.1	81-93	XW225/FE	UK	
N	27	Chinook HC.2, 2A	95-date	ZH777/NY	UK	
N	27(R)	Puma HC.1	95-98	XW217/NK	UK	
W	2 FTS	Wessex HC.2	83-97	XS679/WG	UK	

Harrier Force

Code	Unit	Type	Dates	Example	Theatre	Remarks
3	233 OCU	Harrier GR.3	89-92	XV748/3D	UK	
3	20 (R)	Harrier GR.3	92	XV748/3D	UK	
5	20 (R)	Harrier GR.5	93-94	ZD354/5C	UK	
A	233 OCU	Harrier GR.5	90-91	ZD401/AA	UK	
A	3	Harrier T.4A	84-85	ZB603/AZ	Ger	
A	3	Harrier GR.3	82-88	XZ965/AM	Ger	
A	3	Harrier GR.5	89-91	ZD327/AJ	Ger	
A	3	Harrier GR.7	91-94	ZD471/AB	Ger	
B	SAOEU	Harrier T.4	92	XW269/BD	UK	
C	4	Harrier GR.3	81-88	XV740/CA	Ger	
C	4	Harrier GR.7	90-94	ZG533/CF	Ger	
W	Op Warden	Harrier GR.7	93-94	ZD467/WA		

The current form of unit codes began appearing in 1969 on tactical helicopters and the system has continued to this day. The first aircraft to adopt them were the Wessex HC.2 helicopters of No. 72 Sqn at Odiham where XR523/AE was photographed in August 1970. (Author)

Lightning F.6 XR763/AP of No. 5 Sqn climbs out from Akrotiri, Cyprus, for another practice shoot in June 1987. The senior unit at its home at Binbrook it used the letter A, while No. 11 had B and the LTF D. C had been reserved for a planned, but never formed, third squadron. (RAF Lossiemouth)

Code	Unit	Type	Dates	Example	Theatre	Remarks
Hawk Trainers Leeming and Valley						
C	100	Hawk T.1	92-99	XX312/CF	UK	
C	100	Hawk T.1A	91-date	XX290/CI	UK	
D	4 FTS (234(R))	Hawk T.1A	93-94	XX286/DK	UK	
D	4 FTS (208(R))	Hawk T.1	94-date	XX317/DL	UK	
P	4 FTS (19(R))	Hawk T.1	94-date	XX236/PK	UK	
P	CFS	Hawk T.1A	93	XX187/PB	UK	
T	4 FTS (74(R))	Hawk T.1A	92-00	XX350/TC	UK	
Jaguar Force Bruggen, Coltishall						
A	14	Jaguar GR.1	77-85	XX960/GP	Ger	
A	14	Jaguar T.2	84-85	XX150/AZ	Ger	
B	17	Jaguar GR.1	77-85	XX768/BA	Ger	
B	SAOEU	Jaguar GR.1B	97	XX725/BG	UK	
C	20	Jaguar GR.1	77-84	XZ374/CA	Ger	
D	31	Jaguar GR.1	77-85	XZ381/DP	Ger	
E	6	Jaguar GR.1	82-90	XX741/EJ	UK	
E	6	Jaguar GR.1A	89-99	XX970/EH	UK	
E	6	Jaguar GR.1B	96-99	XZ369/EF	UK	
E	6	Jaguar T.2	84-00	XX144/ET	UK	
E	6	Jaguar T.4	00-date	XX845/ET	UK	
E	6	Jaguar GR.3	97-date	XX737/EE	UK	
F	41	Jaguar GR.1A	91-99	XZ360/FN	UK	
F	41	Jaguar T.2A	95-00	XX847/FX	UK	
F	41	Jaguar T.4	00-date	XX835/FY	UK	
F	41	Jaguar GR.3	97-date	XZ104/FM	UK	
G	54	Jaguar GR.1	81-89	XV738/GJ	UK	
G	54	Jaguar GR.1A	85-96	XX720/GQ	UK	
G	54	Jaguar GR.1B	96-99	XX748/GK	UK	
G	54	Jaguar GR.3	97-date	XZ367/GP	UK	
G	54	Jaguar T.2B	85-00	XX146/GT	UK	
G	54	Jaguar T.4	00-date	XX146/GT	UK	
P	16	Jaguar GR.3	01-date	XX974/PB	UK	
P	16	Jaguar T.4	01-date	XX840/PS	UK	

This impressive line-up of Phantom FGR.2s of No. 64 (R) Sqn at Leuchars on 22 April 1987 was to announce their arrival there from Coningsby. The nearest aircraft, XT900/CO had a blue fin and was also the aircraft of the commanding officer! (RAF Leuchars)

Code	Unit	Type	Dates	Example	Theatre	Remarks
Lightnings Binbrook						
A	5	Lightning F.3	80-6.88	XR718/AS	UK	
A	5	Lightning F.6	80-6.88	XR770/AA	UK	
A	5	Lightning T.5	80-6.88	XS416/AT	UK	
B	11	Lightning F.3	80-6.88	XR718/BK1	UK	
B	11	Lightning F.6	80-6.88	XR773/BR	UK	
B	11	Lightning T.5	80-6.88	XS452/BT	UK	
D	LTF	Lightning F.3	80-6.88	XP771/DD	UK	
D	LTF	Lightning F.6	80-6.88	XR726/DF	UK	
D	LTF	Lightning T.5	80-6.88	XS420/DV	UK	
Phantoms Leuchars and Wildenrath						
A	43	Phantom FG.1	7.86-7.89	XT863/AS	UK	
A	43	Phantom FGR.2	88-7.89	XV406/AV	UK	
A	19	Phantom FGR.2	89-91	XV487/AA	Ger	
B	92	Phantom FGR.2	89-91	XV464/BN	Ger	
B	111	Phantom FG.1	7.86-10.89	XV592/BL	UK	
C	228 OCU (64(R))	Phantom	FGR.2	2.87-1.91	XT900/CO	UK
Air Defence Tornados						
A	229 OCU (65(R))	Tornado F.2	84-88	ZD901/AA	UK	
A	229 OCU (65(R))	Tornado F.3	86-92	ZE159/AW	UK	
A	56(R)	Tornado F.3	92-02	ZG770/AP	UK	
B	29	Tornado F.3	87-10.98	ZE207/BJ	UK	
C	5	Tornado F.3	88-02	ZE941/CI	UK	
D	11	Tornado F.3	88-02	ZE764/DH	UK	
E	23	Tornado F.3	88-93	ZE810/EN	UK	
F	25	Tornado F.3	89-02	ZE290/FE	UK	
G	43	Tornado F.3	89-02	ZE961/GA	UK	
H	111	Tornado F.3	90-02	ZE251/HB	UK	
S	F.3 OEU	Tornado F.3	94 only	ZE889/SB	UK	
T	56	Tornado F3	03-date	ZE786/TF	UK	
Strike Tornados (excluding recce units 2 and 13 Sqns)						
A	9	Tornado GR.1	86-99	ZA602/AZ	Ger	

When No. 240 OCU took delivery of its Chinook HC.1 helicopters it was eventually allocated the unit code F sequentially within the Support Helicopter Force. ZA672, seen over its Odiham base, is coded FF. (MoD)

Code	Unit	Type	Dates	Example	Theatre	Remarks
A	9	Tornado GR.4	98-date	ZD811/AB	Ger, UK	
B	14	Tornado GR.1	87-99	ZD718/BH	Ger	
B	14	Tornado GR.4	99-date	ZD712/BX	Ger, UK	
C	17	Tornado GR.1	84-4.99	ZD742/CZ	Ger	
D	31	Tornado GR.1	84-99	ZA461/DK	Ger	
D	31	Tornado GR.4	99-date	ZA541/DZ	Ger, UK	
E	15	Tornado GR.1	84-91	ZA453/EG	Ger	
F	16	Tornado GR.1	84-91	ZA740/FL	Ger	
F	12	Tornado GR.1B	93-date	ZA453/FD	UK	
G	20	Tornado GR.1	84-92	ZA401/GJ	Ger	
J	27	Tornado GR.1	89-92	ZA562/JT	UK	
L	45(R)	Tornado GR.1	91 only	ZA***/LA	UK	Gulf service only
M	617	Tornado GR.1	88-92	ZA548/ML	UK	
AJ	617	Tornado GR.1	92-date	ZA462/AJ-M	UK	
AJ	617	Tornado GR.4	00-date	ZD880/AJ-T	UK	
T	15(R)	Tornado GR.1	92-date	ZA563/TC	UK	
T	15(R)	Tornado GR.4	99-date	ZA548/TQ	UK	
TA	15(R)	Tornado GR.1	99-date	ZA324/TA-Y	UK	overrun codes
J	Op Jural	Tornado GR.1	97-99	ZD790/JF		

Typhoon Force

Code	Unit	Type	Dates	Example	Theatre	Remarks
A	17	Typhoon T1, F2	c 9.03-date	ZJ802/AB	UK	
B	29	Typhoon T1, F2	c 5.04-date	ZJ915/BY	UK	
C	3	Typhoon F2	-	-	UK	Allocated not used
D	11	Typhoon F2	10.06-date	ZJ931/D	UK	
QO	3	Typhoon F2	4.06-date	ZJ918/QO-L	UK	

Typhoon F2 ZJ917/QO-G of No3 SQN wears the wartime code letters that the unit has re-introduced.
HQ Air Command

CHAPTER 19

Personal or Title Codes

From time to time, and with no apparent rules, officers have applied their initials in some form or another to aircraft, often in the same style as unit codes. The practice seems to have started in late 1941 and the privilege seems to have been accorded to officers of wing commander rank or above but there were exceptions. Certainly the Hunters of 1417 Flt in Aden carried the initials of pilots of flight lieutenant rank.

The application of personal initials was almost totally confined to fighters, exceptions being communications types and the occasional Mosquito. The most commonly marked types were the Spitfire, Typhoon and Tempest and post-war the Meteor and Hunter.

It will be noted that there are occasions where over time the rank of aircrew suggests demotion. This is simply a reflection of a change from wartime ranks to substantive peacetime ranks for officers who remained in the RAF as regulars after the war had ended.

In general the presentation of initials was similar to that of

unit codes, sometimes spanning the fuselage roundel as CR C or apart from it as DRS or JMR. Less common was application in conjunction with unit codes, for example in the form YT JAS or WR RR. Occasionally officers used some form of letters other than their initials; Wing Commander Denys E Gillam, for example, used double letters including RR and ZZ.

Another form of letter codes was the use of unit or function initial letters. Examples include SW (strike wing) and FCCS (Fighter Command Communications Squadron). Such 'codes', usually of post-war application, are also listed below. In the table below identified personal 'codes' are listed. The first comprehensive lists were published in Aviation News in 1981 and repeated in Air-Britain's Aeromilitaria in 1999. This current chapter draws heavily from these series of articles. For completeness, and to avoid possible confusion, where known, initials of USAAF, French and RN pilots have been included as these too were often worn on British aircraft types.

Code	Name	Role/Unit	Type	Serial	Theatre	Years
AA	S/L A J R Adam	AHQ Burma	Mustang IV	KM557	FE	46-47
AAC	S/L A A Case	FCCS	Mosquito VI	HR343	UK	45
AAY	?	RWE	Spitfire Vb	AA915	UK	45
ACB	A C Bartley		Spitfire		UK	?
ACS	W/C A C Smith	125 Wing	Spitfire IX	MK614	UK	44
AD	W/C A H Donaldson	OC Luqa Wing	Spitfire Vc	BR529	MedME	42
ADJL	W/C A D J Lovell	OC Safi Wing	Spitfire V		MedME	43
ADS	G/C A D Selway	SC Aston Down	Hurricane IIa	Z2515	UK	44-45
AF	Lt Cdr A J B Forde	WL 21st TBR Wg (HMS Illustrious)	Barracuda II	P9970	FE	44
AF	W/C A Ferguson	OC 9 Sqn	Tornado GR.1	ZD892	Eur	86
AFO	S/L A F Osborne	OC 66 Sqn	Sabre F.4	XD753	UK	54-57
AG	?	FLS	Spitfire IX		UK	44
AGC	?	WC Flying Horsham St Faith	Meteor F.8	WL173	UK	
AGM	W/C A G Malan	WL Biggin Hill	Spitfire Vb		UK	41-44
AGP	W/C A G Page	OC 125 Wing	Spitfire IX		UK	44
AHD	W/C A H Donaldson	WC Flying Colerne	Whirlwind I	P7007	UK	42
AHD	W/C A H Donaldson	?	Meteor F.8	WE932	UK	
AJ	Brig Jesse Auton	OC 65th FW	P-47D	42-26059	UK	45
AJW	?	904 Wing	Thunderbolt	KL187	FE	45
AI16	W/C A Ingle	WC Flying 16 Wing	Typhoon Ib	JP436	UK	43
AKG	G/C A K Gatward	SC Odiham	Meteor F.8	WK672	UK	55-56
AL	?	SF Biggin Hill	Spitfire IX	EN568	UK	
AMT	L/C A M Tritton	WL 15th Ftr Wg(HMS Illustrious)	Corsair II	JT***	FE	44-45
AV	W/C Alois Vasatlo	WL Exeter Wing	Spitfire Vb	BM592	UK	42
ALW	W/C A L Winskill	WL Turnhouse	Vampire FB.5	WA430	UK	51-52
AR	W/C A Riegels	336 Sqn	F-86F	52-4734	Norway	62
AVH	?	41 Sqn	Spitfire F.21	LA299	UK	46-47
AVRJ	W/C A V R Johnstone	WL Krendi Wing	Spitfire V	?	MedME	43
AVRJ	G/C A V R Johnstone	SC Fairwood Common	Spitfire Vb	BL450	UK	43-44
AW	?	12 GCF	Anson T.20	VS494	UK	52

Code	Name	Role/Unit	Type	Serial	Theatre	Year(s)
AW	W/C A R Wright	WC Flying Waterbeach	Hunter F.5	WP186	UK	58
B	W/C R E P Booker	OC 122 Wing	Tempest V	NV641	UK	45
BA	?	?	Spitfire Vc	LZ949	Italy	45
BAE	G/C B A Eaton	OC 239 Wing	Kittyhawk		MedME	44
BAE	G/C B A Eaton	OC 239 Wing	Mustang III	FB260	MedME	44-45
BD	W/C B Drake	WL Krendi	Spitfire V	JK228	MedME	43
BD	W/C B Drake	WC Flying Linton on Ouse	Meteor F.8	WA921	UK	51
BD	W/C B Doggett	OC 56 Sqn	Phantom FGR.2	XV470	UK	91
BEFH	W/C B E F Hermansen	331 Sqn	F-86F	52-5256	Norway	59-62
BF	W/C B E Finucane	WC Flying Hornchurch	Spitfire Vb	BM308	UK	42
BF	?	?	Spitfire IX	EN632	MedME	45
BFR	?	121 Wing	Typhoon Ib	MN753	UK	44
BH	W/C B Heath	OC 324 Wing	Spitfire IX	MJ628	Eur	44
BH	W/C B E F Hermansen	331 Sqn	F-86F	52-5256	Norway	59-62
B-H	S/L B Hamnes	338 Sqn	F-86F	52-5245	Norway	63-64
BK	W/C C B F Kingcome	OC 244 Wing	Spitfire V	?	UK	44
BK	W/C C B F Kingcome	OC 324 Wing	Spitfire IX	TB539	Eur	46
BM	S/L B Meyer	332 Sqn	F-86F	53-1227	Norway	57-59
BOG	W/C E Haabjoern	OC 124 Wing	Typhoon Ib	?	UK	44
BT	W/C B Titchen	OC 56 Sqn	Phantom FGR.2	XV420	UK	89
BWR	?	FLS	Spitfire Vb	?	UK	43
CAG	Maj C A Golding	3 Sqn SAAF	Spitfire IX	?	MedME	44-45
CEM	? W/C C E Malfroy	HQ 10 Group	Spitfire I	?	UK	
CEO	?	2 TAF CS	Spitfire Vc	EE745	Eur	45
CFA	W/C C F Ambrose	WC Flying Wildenrath	Sabre F.4	?	Germany	54
CFB	W/C C F Bradley	WC Flying 132 Wing	Spitfire XVI	PT959	Eur	45
CFC	W/C C F Currant	CO 122 AFHQ	Spitfire Vb	?R7262	UK	43-44
CFC	W/C C F Currant	WL 122 Wing	Typhoon Ib	R7262	UK	44
CFG	W/C C F Gray	WL Malta	Spitfire	?	Malta	43-45
CG	W/C C L Green	WC Flying 121 Wing	Typhoon Ib	MN666	UK	44
CG	G/C C L Green	OC 124 Wing	Typhoon Ib	MP156	Eur	44
CG	W/C C F Gray	WC Flying 322 Wing	Spitfire V	EN350	UK	43
CG	W/C C F Gray	WC Flying Lympne	Spitfire XIV	RM787	UK	44
CGL	AC C G Lott	OC Caledonian Sector	Meteor F.8	WK787	UK	52-56
CGP	Lt Col C G Peterson	Ops Off 4 FG USAAF	Spitfire V	BL449?	UK	43
CI	?	?	Spitfire IX	?MJ847	MedME	
CJ	?	?	Hurricane I	?	UK	39
CM	W/C D Crowley-Milling	WC Flying Odiham	Meteor F.8	WH444	UK	53
CM	Cdt C Martell	CO 80 OTU	Spitfire IX	MH368	UK	45
CMM	Col C M McCorkle	OC 31 FG, USAAF	Spitfire VIII	JF452?	MedME	44
CMM	Col C M McCorkle	OC 31 FG, USAAF	P-51B Mustang	42-106511	MedME	44
CR	G/C Charles Riley	SC Changi	Spitfire VIII	?	FE	46-47
CRC	W/C C R Caldwell	1 Wing RAAF	Spitfire V	BR295	FE	44
CRC	W/C C R Caldwell	1 Wing RAAF	Spitfire IX	JL394	FE	44
CSV	S/L C Scott-Vos	CO 247 Sqn	Harvard T.2B	KF691	UK	46
CWL	S/L C W Lockhart	OC 101 R&SU	Spitfire VIII	?	FE	45
CWL	? W/C C W Lovatt	Cranwell	Vampire T.11	WZ570	UK	60
DAB	AVM D A Boyle	AOC 11 Gp	Mosquito VI	PZ193	UK	45
DAM	?	84 GCF	Anson	NK727	UK	46
DB	W/C D Bader	WL Tangmere	Spitfire IIa	P7966	UK	41
DB	W/C D Bader	WL Tangmere	Spitfire Va	W3185	UK	41
DB	G/C D Bader	CFE	Spitfire IX	RK917	UK	45-46
DB	AC D A Boyle	AOC Fighter Command	Meteor F.8	WK979	UK	53
DBH	Maj D B Hauptfleisch	OC 2 Sqn SAAF	Kittyhawk	?	MedME	42-43
DC	G/C Coburn	OC Weston-super-Mare	Hurricane	286 Sqn aircraft	UK	42
DEK	S/L D E Kingaby	OC 72 Sqn	Vampire FB.5	VZ841	UK	51-52
DFS	W/C D F Sheen	WC Flying Leuchars	Hunter F.1	WW641	UK	55-56
DFS	W/C D F Sheen	WC Flying Leuchars	Hunter F.4	XF993	UK	c56
DFS	G/C D F Spottiswood	SC Linton on Ouse	Sabre F.4	XD736	UK	54-56
DGA	W/C D G Andrews	WL Matlaske	Spitfire IX	?	UK	45
DGH	W/C D G Honor	17 Sec Benghazi?	Hurricane	?	MedME	42-43
DGM	G/C D G Morris	OC 132 Wing	Auster V	RT514	UK	44-45
DGM	G/C D G Morris	OC 132 Wing	Spitfire IX	PL463	UK	44-45
DGS	W/C D G Smallwood	OC 286 Sqn	Spitfire	?	UK	42

One of the most famous pilots to use a personal 'code' was Wg Cdr Douglas Bader, the indomitable legless fighter ace who applied his initials to Spitfire II P7966/D-B when he was the Tangmere wing leader in the summer of 1941. (T. R. Allonby)

The use of personal codes by the USAAF was rare, but an exception was Lt Col Fred M. Dean, whose initials appeared on his Spitfire Vc when he was commander of the 31st FG from Gozo in July 1943. (via B. Cull)

Code	Name	Role/Unit	Type	Serial	Theatre	Year(s)
DGS	W/C D G Smallwood	OC 286 Sqn	Hurricane II	?	UK	43
DGS	W/C D G Smallwood	OC Predannack Wing	Spitfire IX	MH333	UK	44
DGS	G/C D G Smallwood	SC Biggin Hill	Meteor F.8	WH480	UK	53-55
DGS	G/C D G Smallwood	SC Biggin Hill	Hunter F.5	?	UK	55
DH	W/C D L Hughes	OC 33 Sqn	Javelin FAW.7	XH835	UK	60
DH	W/C D L Hughes	OC 33 Sqn	Javelin FAW.9	XH773	UK	60-62
DH	W/C D Hamilton	OC 11 Sqn	Tornado F.3	ZE765	UK	88
DHL	Col D H Loftus	WL 7 SAAF Wing	Kittyhawk	?	MedME	43-44
DHL	Col D H Loftus	WL 7 SAAF Wing	Spitfire VIII	5501	S Africa	46
DJF	S/L D J Fowler	OC 19 Sqn	Hunter F.6	XG159	UK	57
DJS	G/C D J Scott	OC 123 Wing	Typhoon Ib	R8843	UK	45
DJS	G/C D J Scott	OC 123 Wing	Auster III	?	UK	45
DJS	G/C D J Scott	OC 84 Gp SU	Typhoon Ib	PD605	Eur	45
DJW	?	Cranwell	Jet Provost T.4	XR643	UK	68
DMA	?	Culmhead	Spitfire	?	UK	44
DNF	S/L D N Ford	72 Sqn	Spitfire IX	?	MedME	44
DO	W/C W A Douglas	WC Flying 134 (Czech) Wing	Spitfire IX	LZ920	Eur	44-44
DPA	Directorate of Accident Prevention		Att'd 617 Sqn	P-38J		
UK	44			44-223517		
DPA	DoAP	Att'd FCCS	Mosquito PR.34	VL625	UK	45-46
DPA	DoAP	Bovingdon	Proctor III	LZ683	UK	45-46
DPA	DoAP	Att'd FCCS	Spitfire XVI	MH731	UK	46
DRS	G/C D R Shore	OC 239 Wing	Mustang IV	KM182	Italy	45
DRW	W/C D R Walker	Lincs Sector HQ	Mustang IV	KM232	UK	46
DS	W/C W G G Duncan-Smith		OC 324 Wing	Saiman 202	MedME	43
DS	W/C W G G D Smith	W/L Krendi Wing	Spitfire V	AR560	MedME	44
DS	W/C W G G D Smith	W/L Safi Wing	Spitfire IX	JK650	MedME	44
DS	W/C W G G D Smith	SC Turnhouse	Vampire FB.5	WG833	UK	53-54
DT	S/L D M Taylor	OC 195 Sqn	Typhoon Ib	JP438, EK273	UK	43
DT	Maj S F du Toit	7 Wing SAAF	Spitfire VIII	?	MedME	43-44
DT	Lt Col S F du Toit	8 Wing SAAF	Spitfire	?	MedME	45
DUT	Maj S F du Toit	OC 2 Sqn SAAF	Spitfire V	MA853	MedME	44
DUT	Col S F du Toit	OC 8 Wing SAAF	Spitfire IX	MA853	MedME	44-45
DW	? W/C R M B Duke-Woolley		Spitfire IX	?		45
DW	F/L ?	1417 Flt	Hunter FR.10	XE599	Aden	67
EC	?	CFS	Meteor NF.14	WS745	UK	55-58
ED	?	OC 72 OTU	Tomahawk IIb	EK431	MedME	42-43
EDM	W/C E D Mackie		Tempest V	SN228		45
EE	S/L E Erla	334 Sqn	F-84G	51-10219	Norway	52-53
EH	W/C E Haabjoern	W/C Flying 124 Wing	Typhoon Ib	MN358	UK	44
EHT	W/C E H Thomas	W/C Flying Biggin Hill	Spitfire IX	BR369	UK	42
EJ	?	? 138 Wing	Mosquito VI	RF645	UK	45-46
EJC	W/C E J Cassidy	OC 324 Wing	Spitfire		Italy	

Code	Name	Role/Unit	Type	Serial	Theatre	Year(s)
EJC	W/C E F Charles	?	Spitfire IX	PT396	UK	
ELM	W/C E L McMillan	W/L Bruggen	Hunter F 4	XE714	Eur	57
EMD	G/C E M Donaldson	WL Fassberg	Vampire FB.5	WA396	Germany	52
ENW	W/C E N Woods	OC 249 Sqn	Spitfire	**311	MedME	43
EOS	E O Stigset	?	F-84G	5111113	Norway	
EP	?	FLS	Spitfire IX	?	UK	44-45
EPA	Col E P Allen	9th TAC AF	Spitfire IX	?	UK	44
EPW	W/C E P Wells	W/C Detling	Spitfire IX	?	UK	44
ERB	W/C E R Baker	OC 146 Wing	Typhoon Ib	MN291	UK	44
ES	G/C F S S Stapleton	SC Linton-on-Ouse	Meteor F.4	VT266	UK	50
ES	G/C F S S Stapleton	SC Linton-on-Ouse	Auster AOP.6	TW575	UK	50
ES	A/C F S S Stapleton	OC Northern Sector	Meteor F.8	WK991	UK	56
ES	A/C F S S Stapleton	OC Northern Sector	Hunter F.6	XE618	UK	57-58
ES	?		Meteor F.8	WK991	UK	
ET	?	CFS	Meteor F.8	WK942	UK	54
EW-?	G/C E W Whitley	Commandant FLS	Spitfire Vb	EP770	UK	44
EWW	W/C E W Wright	WC Flying Linton-on-Ouse	Sabre F.4	XD763	UK	55
FA	?	73 OTU	Spitfire Vb	ER934	MedME	
FA	?	ADLS	Anson X	NK589	UK	c45
FAH	Maj/Lt Col F A Hill	31 FG USAAF	Spitfire IX	EN329	MedME	43
FB	G/C F Boyd	SC Baigachi	Spitfire VIII	MD371	FE	44
FB	?	131 Sqn	Spitfire II		UK	41
FC	possibly station initials	11 APC Fairwood Common	Spitfire IX	RK901	UK	45
FCCS	unit initials	FCCS	Meteor F.8	WK672	UK	57-58
FCCS	unit initials	FCCS	Meteor T.7	WL436	UK	59
FCCS	unit initials	FCCS	Meteor NF.14	WS848	UK	61
FCT	?	SF Northolt	Hurricane IIa	Z2487	UK	41-42
FD	W/C F Dolezal	OC Exeter Wg/134 Wing	Spitfire LFVb	EP461	UK	43
FD	W/C F Dolezal	OC Exeter Wg/134 Wing	Spitfire LFVb	EE625	UK	43
FDH	?	CFE	Meteor NF.11	WD648	UK	52
FG	W/C F D Hughes	1417 Flt	Hunter FR.10	XF441	MedME	65
FGB	Maj F D G Bird RM	OC 759 NAS	Spitfire I	P9397	UK	43-44
FGB	Maj F D G Bird RM	OC RNAS Lee-on-Solent	Seafire III	NF500	UK	44-45
FGG	W/C F G Grant	WC Flying 143 Wing	Typhoon Ib	RB205	UK	44-45
FH	W/C F W Hillock	OC 143 Wing	Auster V	MT367	UK	44
FHP	?	? 748B NAS	Wildcat		UK	
FMD	Lt Col F M Dean	31st FG USAAF	Spitfire V	?	UK	43
FMD	Lt Col F M Dean	31st FG USAAF	Spitfire Vc	ER259	MedME	43
FMD	Lt Col F M Dean	31st FG	Spitfire IX	EN329	MedME	43
FMT	W/C F M Thomas	WCF 233 OCU	Vampire FB.5	WA245	UK	56
FN	S/L C N Foxley-Norris	FCCS	Spitfire IX	MH374	UK	45
FOG	?	? 19 Sqn	Spitfire LF.16	TE396	UK	47
FRC	W/C F R Carey		Hurricane IIc	?	Burma	44
FRC	W/C F R Carey	OC 135 Wing	Tempest F.2	PR674	Germany	47
FSC		? PRDU	Mosquito PR.34	RG190	UK	

Personal 'codes' continued in use into the jet era, though the CO of No 64 Sqn, Wg Cdr P.D. Wright, merely added a small 'PD'to Javelin FAW.9 XH834/W in the early 1960s. (Author's Collection)

The Wing Commander Operations of Fighter Command's Yorkshire Sector was W.A. Nel whose nickname was 'Tiny'. This accounts for the initials WA-TN on his Hornet F.1 PX216 when it was seen at its Linton on Ouse base in the late 1940s. (Sqn Ldr D. Hyman)

Code	Name	Role/Unit	Type	Serial	Theatre	Year(s)
GAM	W/C G A Mason	W/C Flying Leuchars	Hunter F.4	XF993	UK	57
GBJ	W/C G B Johns	W/C Flying Bruggen	Vampire FB.5	VZ847	Germany	53-54
GC	?	? 601 Sqn	Spitfire Vb	AB328	Egypt	42
GC	F/L G T Coles	1417 Flt	Hunter FR.10	XE614	Aden	65
GCA	G C Atherton	Attached BAF	Meteor F.8	EG222	Belgium	52-54
GCK	W/C G C Keefer	W/C Flying 126 Wing	Spitfire IX	MK826	UK,Europe	44
GCK	W/C G C Keefer	W/C Flying 125 Wing	Spitfire XIV	RM809	Europe	45
GCK	W/C G C Keefer	W/C Flying 127 Wing	Spitfire XIV	MV263	Europe	45
GD	? G/C G Denholm	?	Mustang IV	?KH734		45
GDE	?		Spitfire Vc			
GFA	? W/C G F Anderson	? 56 OTU	Tempest V	EJ811	UK	45
GG	Cne G Gauthier	GC II/7	D.520	347	Vichy Fr	41
GG	Cne G Gauthier	326 Sqn/ GC 1/7	Spitfire IX	8J-GG	MedME	45
GG	Cdt G Garde	CFI FS Mekenes	D.520	?	Eur	44
GHB	S/L G H Beaton	OC 228 OCU	Javelin FAW.9	XH898	UK	66
GJ	G/C E G Jones	OC 121 Wing	Typhoon Ib	RB375	Europe	45
GKG	G/C G K Gilroy	OC 324 Wing	Spitfire V	JK143	MedME	43
GKG	G/C G K Gilroy	SC Wittering?	Spitfire IX	?	UK	44-45
GL	S/L G N Lewis	OC 208 Sqn	Hunter FGA.9	XE530	Arabia	64
GM	W/C E G L Millington	W/L Scottish sector	Vampire FB.5	WA430	UK	52-55
GM	W/C E G L Millington	W/L Scottish sector	Vampire FB.5	WG833	UK	52-55
GP	?	? 181 Sqn	Typhoon Ib		UK	43
GR	?	81 Sqn	Spitfire IX	EN455	MedME	43
GRC	? W/C G R Cook	Tangmere	Hunter F.5	WP141	UK	55
GT	F/L G W Timms	1417 Flt	Hunter FR.10	XF460	Arabia	64
GVW	Maj G V Williams	OC 2nd FS USAAF	Spitfire Vc	?	MedME	43-43
GW	S/L J H Granville-Jones	OC Nicosia	Hunter F.6	XG168	Cyprus	58-59
HB	AVM H Broadhurst		Hurricane		MedME	42
HB	AVM H Broadhurst		Spitfire VIII	JF330	Italy	43
HB	AVM H Broadhurst	BAFO CS	Storch	VX154	Italy	43
HBW	W/C H A C Bird-Wilson	OC Perranport	Mustang III	KH447	UK	44
HBW	W/C H A C Bird-Wilson	WL Bentwaters	Spitfire IX	MK782 & MJ845	UK	44
HBW	W/C H A C Bird-Wilson	OC Bentwaters	Mustang III	KH500	UK	44-45
HBW	W/C H A C Bird-Wilson	OC 226 OCU	Meteor F.3	EE357	UK	45-46
HCG	W/C H C Godefroy	W/C Flying 127 Wing	Spitfire IX		UK	43
HCG	W/C H C Godefroy	83 Group	Spitfire IX	?PL201	UK	44
HCR	Col H C Rau	CO 20th FG	P-51D	?	UK	44-45
HD	W/C H S L Dundas	W/L 324 Wing	Spitfire V	JL122	UK	44
HD	W/C H S L Dundas	W/C Flying 244 Wing	Spitfire VIII, IX	?	UK	44-45
HEW	?	Tangmere	Hunter F.5	WP123	UK	58
HFB	? W/C H F Burton	W/C Flying 239 Wing	Kittyhawk	FR347	MedME	43
HFO'N	? W/C H F O'Neill	W/C Flying Horsham St Faith	Spitfire XVI	TE457	UK	46
HFO'N	W/C H F O'Neill	W/C Flying Horsham St Faith	Meteor III	EE357	UK	47
HFO'N	W/C H F O'Neill	W/C Flying Middleton St George	Hunter F.6	XG165	UK	57
HGG	G/C H G Goddard	OC 170 Wing	Hurricane IIc	LE294	FE	44
HGG	G/C H G Goddard	OC 170 Wing	Spitfire VIII	JG253	FE	45
HH	AC H A V Hogan	OC Northern sector	Meteor F.8	WK724	UK	52-53
HH	AC H A V Hogan	OC Northern sector	Oxford I	NJ310	UK	52-53
HJW	G/C H J Wilson	HSF Tangmere	Meteor I	EE221	UK	46
HK	?	? 268 Sqn	Typhoon Ib	EK991	Eur	44
HK	W/C H C Kenward	OC 74 Sqn	Meteor III	EE401	UK	45
HL	W/C J Hlado	OC Czech Wing?	Spitfire IX	SL628	Cz	45-46
HM	Maj H Mehre	OC 331 Sqn	Spitfire IX	BS458	UK	43-44
HM	G/C H Mehre	OC 132 Wing	Spitfire IX	PT884?	Norway	45
HM	G/C H Mehre	132 Wing	Bf.108		Norway	45
HMH-J	AVM H M H Jørgensen	AC Eastern Norway	F-84G	5110899	Norway	56-59
HMS	W/ H M Smith?	W/C Flying APS Lubeck	Spitfire XIV	TZ198	Germany	47
HMT	S/L H M H Tudor	OC 264 Sqn	Meteor NF.11	WM186	UK	53-54
HMT	W/C H M H Tudor	OC 238 OCU	Meteor NF.14	WS847	UK	57
HNT	Maj H N Tanner USAF	OC 257 Sqn	Meteor F.8	WL141	UK	53
HPB	W/C H P Blatchford	W/C Flying Digby	Spitfire Vb	EP126		
HR	?	263 Sqn	Meteor III	EE404	UK	46
HW	S/L H Wergeland	330 Sqn	F-84G	522900	Norway	56
HW	W/C H Wergeland	WL Ørland Wing	F-86F	525192	Norway	58

Lt Col Werner Christie of the RNorAF was one of a number of senior orwegian officers to wear his initials on his aircraft. One of these was - 84G Thunderjet 511113 at Gardermoen in the mid 1950s. In this instance, the presence of No. 330 Sqn identifier on the nose helped as its code was WH! (Luftforsvaret via Nils Mathisrud)

One of the first personal 'codes' to appear in India was on Mohawk IV BS790 at Agartala in late 1942. It was flown by the wing leader of No. 169 Wing, Sqn Ldr W.H. Pitt-Brown, who later commanded No. 121 Wing with Typhoons, one of which was marked WP.B. (Wg Cdr W. H. Pitt-Brown)

Code	Name	Role/Unit	Type	Serial	Theatre	Year(s)
HWA	?	?	Spitfire II	P7287	UK	42
HWB	W/C H F Burton	W/C Flying 239 Wing	Kittyhawk		MedME	42
IRC	W/C I R Campbell	WL Oldenburg	Hunter F 4	WV260	Eur	c56-57
IRG	W/C I R Gleed	WL Ibsley Wing	Spitfire Vb	AA742, AB934, AB380	UK	41-42
IRG	W/C I R Gleed	OC 244 Wing	Spitfire Vc	AR274?	UK	42
IRG	W/C I R Gleed	OC 244 Wing	Spitfire Vb	ER170, AB502	MedME	43
JAK	W/C J A Kent	OC Polish Wing, Northolt	Spitfire Vb	AB790	UK	41
JAK	W/C J A Kent	WCF 123 Wing	Typhoon Ib	RN431	Eur	45
JAK	W/C J A Kent	WCF 123 Wing	Tempest V	NV708	Eur	46
JAK	W/C J A Kent	Biggin Hill	Meteor F.8	WH480, WK731	UK	54
JAM	W/C J A Mackie	FCHQ	Mosquito XVI	NS877	UK	45
JAS	S/L J A Storrar	OC 65 Sqn	Spitfire IX	MH358	UK	43
JAS	W/C J A Storrar	WL Hunnsdon	Mustang IV	KM232	UK	45
JAS	W/C J A Storrar	239 Wing	Yak 9	72/7087	MedME	46
JAS	W/C J A Storrar	239 Wing	Mustang	KM264	MedME	46
JAS	S/L J A Storrar	OC 610 Sqn	Meteor F.8	WH506	UK	52-53
JAS	W/C J A Storrar	OC 610 Sqn	Meteor F.8	WK988	UK	53-
JB	W/C J R Baldwin	WCF 146 Wing	Typhoon Ib	MN935	UK	44
JB	G/C J R Baldwin	OC 123 Wing	Typhoon Ib	SW470, SW496	UK	44
JBII	W/C J R Baldwin	WCF 146 Wing	Typhoon Ib	PD521	UK	44
JBW	W/C J B Wray	WCF 122 Wing	Tempest V	EJ750	UK	44
JBW	W/C J B Wray	WCT 56 OTU	Tempest V	NV729, EJ520	UK	45
JC	S/L J Castagnola	OC 41 Sqn	Hunter F.5	WP186	UK	57
JCB	W/C J C Button	WCF 123 Wing	Typhoon Ib	RN431	UK	45
JCB	W/C J C Button	WCF Wunstorf	Tempest V	NV708	Eur	46-47
JCB	W/C J C Button	SF Biggin Hill	Meteor F.8	WH480	UK	54
JCBE	S/L J C B Ebbesen	332 Sqn	F-84G	52-8302	Norway	53-54
JCBE	S/L J C B Ebbesen	331 Sqn	F-86F	?	Norway	
JCF	?	249 Sqn	Spitfire Vc		Italy	44
JCF	W/C J C Forbes	OC 264 Sqn	Meteor NF.14	WS841, WS844	UK	56-57
JCW	W/C J C Wells	WCF 146 Wing	Typhoon Ib		Eur	44-45
JD	G/C J Darwen	OC 239Wing	Kittyhawk III	FR868	MedME	43
JDW	W/C J D Warne	OC Surabaya	Thunderbolt II	KL339	FE	46
JE	AC J Embling	OC Eastern Sector	Meteor F.8	WK795	UK	57
JE	W/C J Ellis	W/L Krendi	Spitfire V	JK533	MedME	43
JEFF	W/C G W Northcott	WL 126 Wing	Spitfire IX	PV229	Eur	45
JEFF	W/C G W Northcott	WCF 127 Wing	Spitfire XIV	MV263	Eur	45-46
JEJ	W/C J E Johnson	WCF Kenley Wing	Spitfire IX	EN398	UK	43
JEJ	W/C J E Johnson	WL 125 Wing	Spitfire XIV	MV263 & MV257	UK	45-45
JEJ	GC J E Johnson	34 Wing	Spitfire XI	PM147	UK	45
JEJ	GC J E Johnson	WC 125 Wg	Storch	1256	UK	45
JEJ	W/C J E Johnson	W/L Wildenrath	Vampire FB.5	WG834	Germany	53
JEJ	GC J E Johnson	SC Wildenrath	Sabre F.4		Germany	54
JEP	Maj J E Pearson	8 Wing SAAF	Spitfire IX		MedME	45
JF	W/C J Fraser	OC 60 Sqn	Javelin FAW.9	XH846	FE	64-65
JFE	W/C J F Edwards	WCF 127 Wing	FW 190		Germany	45

Code	Name	Role/Unit	Type	Serial	Theatre	Year(s)
JG	W/C J Grandy	SC Duxford	Typhoon Ib	R7684	UK	42
JG	W/C J Grandy	WCF Northern Sector	Meteor F.8	WA909	UK	51-52
JGH	AVM J G Hautry	AOC 4 Gp	Spitfire Vb	BL415	UK	45
JGH	W/C J G Hudson	FCCS	Oxford	V3571	UK	45
JGT	G/C J G Topham	SC Waterbeach	Meteor F.8	WH404	UK	59
JH	? W/C J W E Holmes	? 84 GCF	Tempest V		Germany	45
JH	Lt Col J Human	OC 7 Wing SAAF	Spitfire IX	MH***	MedME	45-46
JH	W/C J A Hemingway	WCF Duxford	Meteor F.8	WK887	UK	56-57
JH	W/C J E S Hill	WCF Horsham St Faith	Meteor F.8	WL173	UK	56
JH	W/C J E S Hill	WCF Horsham St Faith	Hunter F.4	WV314	UK	57
JHD	W/C J H Deall	WCF 146 Wing	Typhoon Ib	? SW449	UK	45
JHW	W/C J H Walton	OC 25 Sqn	Javelin FAW.9	XH880, XH883	UK	60-62
JK	W/C J Kent	WC Training AHQ East Med	Hurricane	P2623	MedME	43
JK	W/C J G Keep	WCF 121 Wing	Typhoon Ib	?	Eur	45
JK	W/C J Kowalski	W/L 131 Wing	Spitfire IX	MK370	Eur	44
JM	F/L ?	1417 Flt	Hunter FR.10	XE589	Aden	
JM	J Mørtvedt		F-84G	5110142	Norway	-59
J-M	W/C J Mørtvedt	Ørland Wing	F-86F	52-5218	Norway	61-62
JMC	W/C J M Checketts		Spitfire	*B509		
JMR	AM Sir James Robb	AOC Fighter Command	Mosquito XVI	NS561	UK	45
JMR	AM Sir James Robb	AOC Fighter Command	Mosquito XVI	NS561	UK	45
JMR	AM Sir James Robb	AOC Fighter Command	Spitfire IX	MJ843	UK	45
JMR	ACM Sir James Robb	CinC AFWE	Spitfire XVI	SL721	UK	46-48
JMR	ACM Sir James Robb	CinC AFWE	Spitfire PR.19	PM659	UK	48
JMR	ACM Sir James Robb	CinC AFWE	Meteor F.4	EE549	UK	47-48
JMT	W/C J M Thompson	OC Luqa Wing	Spitfire V	AR560 & EP122	MedME	43
JOC	?		Spitfire			42
JP	W/C J R A Peel	Kenley	Spitfire	?	UK	40
JP	W/C J R A Peel	SC Debden	Spitfire	?	UK	42
JR	G/C J Rankin OR W/C J A Read SF Duxford		Meteor F.8	WE927	UK	54
JR	W/C J Ryg		Spitfire LF IX	PT536	Norway	45
JRG	? W/C J R Gibbons	Tangmere	Hunter F.5	WP144	UK	57
JS	G/C J Spencer	SC Binbrook	Lightning F.3A	XR728	UK	87-88
JSC	Lt Col J S Coward	OC 52nd FG, USAAF	Spitfire Vc	JK550	MedME	43
JW	G/C P R Walker	OC 135 Wing	Spitfire IX	?	Eur	44
JW	A/C J Worrall	SC Eastern Sector	Meteor F.8	WK795	UK	55
JWB	AVM J W Baker	AOC 12 Group	Spitfire F.21	LA232	UK	45-46
JZ	W/C J Zumbach	W/L 133 Wing	Mustang III	HB868	UK	44
KB	Lt Col K Birksted	WCF 132 Wing	Spitfire IX	MH830, MJ462	UK	43 44
KB	W/C K Birksted	OC Bentwaters Wing	Mustang III or IV	*****/KB	MedME	45
KB	? W/C K R Bowhill	616 Sqn	Meteor F.8	WL166	UK	56
KBBC	W/C K B B Cross	242 Wing	Spitfire IX	EN270	MedME	
KBBC	G/C K B B Cross	SC Eastern Sector	Meteor F.8	WA773	UK	51-52
KC	?		Spitfire Vb	?	MedME	
KE	?	MCCS	Spitfire XVI	TE388	UK	48-49
KEC	?		Proctor C.4	HM184	UK	50-51
KK	?		Spitfire Vb	?	MedME	
KL	?	FLS	Hurricane	?	UK	44
KM	W/C K Mrazek	WL Exeter Wing	Spitfire Vb	AR 502 & EN765	UK	42-43
KNL	W/C C D North-Lewis	WCF 124 Wing	Typhoon Ib	MN922, MP189, RB208	Eur	44 44 44-45
KR	F/L K R M Remfrey	SF Linton-on-Ouse	Meteor T.7	WH209	UK	52-53
KS	F/L K A Simpson	1417 Flt	Hunter FR.10	XF429	Aden	
KSY	?		Spitfire	?		45
KW	?	CFE	Spitfire IX	?	UK	45
LBP	?	SF North Weald	Vampire FB.5	VZ841	UK	51-52
LG	?	FCCS	Anson C.12	PH626	UK	46
LG	?	1417 Flt	Hunter FGA.9	XE530	Aden	?
LHB	W/C L H Bartlett	WCF Wattisham	Meteor F.8	WA764	UK	53
LJ	S/L L A Jones	OC 8 Sqn	Hunter FGA.9	XE654	Aden	63
LJ	Cdt L Jaquenet	345 Sqn	Spitfire XVI	?	Eur	45
LL	?	233 OCU	Hunter F.1	WT625	UK	56
LM	W/C L A Malins	WCF Linton-on-Ouse	Meteor F.8	WH401	UK	53

Code	Name	Role/Unit	Type	Serial	Theatre	Year(s)
LM	W/C L A Malins	WCF Linton-on-Ouse	Sabre F.4	XD763	UK	54
LOB	AVM L O Brown	AOC 84 Gp	Spitfire IX	MK910	UK	44
LOL	?	337 Wing	Spitfire IX	MA507	MedME	45
LV	?	30 Sqn	Tempest II	PR566	FE	46
LVC	W/C L V Chadburn	WCF Digby	Spitfire Vb	EP548	UK	43
LVC	W/C L V Chadburn	WCF 127 Wing	Spitfire IX	MJ824	UK	44
LW	Lt Col L A Wilmot	WL 322 Wing	Kittyhawk		Italy	43
LW	Lt Col L A Wilmot	WL 322 Wing	Spitfire IX	MA408	MedME	44
LW	Lt Col L A Wilmot	OC 239 Wing	Mustang III	FB260	MedME	43-44
M	Cdt Jules Morlat	CO GC II/3	Dewotine D520	343	MedME	41
M	Cdt Jules Morlat	CO GCDA 550	Hurricane IIc	HW750	MedME	44
M	Lt Col Jules Morlat	CO GCDA 550	P-47D	4226513/M-X	MedME	c 47
MA	W/C Max Aitken	Banff Wing	Mosquito		UK	44-45
MB	W/C M V Blake	W/L Portreath	Spitfire Vb	W3561	UK	42
MD	?	263 Sqn	Meteor III	EE243	UK	45
MG	M Gran	RNoAF	F-84G	528302	Norway	53-
MH	S/L M E Hobson	OC 92 Sqn	Hunter F.6	XG239; XF521	UK	57-58
MHD	G/C M H Dwyer	SC Lubeck	Mosquito FB.6	RS639	Eur	47-49
MHM	W/C M H Miller	OC 60 Sqn	Javelin FAW.9	XH839; XH721; XH872 FE		65-68
MID	Cdt M I Dorance	345 Sqn	Spitfire IX	?	Eur	
MJ	W/C M T Judd	WCF 143 Wing	Typhoon Ib	MN518	UK	44
MJ	J Mørtvedt	338 Sqn	F-86F	531226	Norway	
MJL	?	?	Spitfire Vc	JL122	MedME	43-44
MK	W/C M Kellett	WCF Middle Wallop	Meteor F 3	EE401	UK	47
MLB	W/C M Le Bas	WCF Gutersloh	Vampire FB 5	WE842	Eur	c 51-52
MLB	W/C M Le Bas	WCF Wildenrath	Sabre F.4	?	Eur	54
MLD	W/C M G L Donnet	WCF Hawkinge	Spitfire IX	NH476	UK	44
MLD	W/C M G L Donnet	WCF Bentwaters	Mustang III	KH500; KM121 UK		45
MLD	Col M L Donnet	CO 1 Wg BAF	Spitfire F 14	SG34	Belg	c 50
MLD	Col M L Donnet	SASO 83 Gp BAF	Meteor F 4	EF24	Belg	c 51
MLR	W/C M L Robinson	WL Tangmere	Spitfire Vb	W3770	UK	42
MMS	W/C M M Stephens	WC Hal Far	Spitfire V	?	MedME	43
MP	G/C M G F Pedley	SC Linton-on-Ouse	Meteor F.8	WK741	UK	53-54
MP	G/C M G F Pedley	SC Linton-on-Ouse	Sabre F.4	XD736	UK	54
MR	A/C M W S Robinson	SC Caledonian	Hunter F.4	XF304	UK	57
MRA	?	HQ 10 Group	Hurricane IIc	?	UK	42
MRIF	W/C M R Ingle-Finch	WCF 124 Wing	Typhoon Ib	?	UK	45
MRIF	W/C M R Ingle-Finch	WCF 124 Wing	Tempest V	?	UK	45
MRIF	W/C M R Ingle-Finch	WCF 124 Wing	Spitfire XIV	?	UK	46
MS	W/C M J A Shaw	WCF Church Fenton	Meteor F.8	WF677	UK	57
MS	W/C M J A Shaw	WCF Church Fenton	Meteor NF.14	WS833	UK	58
MWSR	A/C M W S Robinson	SC Caledonian	Meteor F.8	WK787	UK	56
MWSR	A/C M W S Robinson	SC Caledonian	Hunter F.4	XF304	UK	57
NKJ	W/C N K Jørstad	WL Gardermoen Wing	Vampire FB.52	?	Norway	
NLA	S/L G Aalpoel	118 Sqn	Spitfire	?N3044	UK	41
NP	W/C N Poole	OC 33 Sqn	Meteor NF.14	WS844	UK	57-58
NP	W/C N Poole	OC 33 Sqn	Javelin FAW.9	XH853	UK	58-59
NW	?	poss North Weald	Meteor F.8	WK689	UK	52
NW	?	HCCS	Anson C.19	VM313	UK	56
OGW	?	12 GCF	Anson C.12	?	UK	46-47
OH	Maj O Harby	336 Sqn	F-86F	?	Norway	
OHV	?		Spitfire 16	TE339	UK	48
OK-1	ACM Sir Keith Park	AOC Malta	Hurricane I	?	MedME	40
OK-2	ACM Sir Keith Park	AOC Malta	Hurricane IIc	?	MedME	42-43
OL	W/C ?	258 Wing	Hurricane I		UK	42
OO	W/C D R Walter	WCF 124 Wing	Typhoon Ib	JP730	UK	43-44
OTMA	O T Mehn-Andersen		F-84G	528394	Norway	-58
OTMA	G/C O T Mehn-Andersen Ørland AB		F-86F	52-5203	Norway	62-63
PB	S/L P M Brothers	OC 61 OTU	Spitfire I/II	?	UK	43
PB	W/C P M Brothers	WCF Culmhead	Spitfire VII	MB882	UK	44
PB	W/C P M Brothers	WCF Predannack	Spitfire XIV	?	UK	44
PB	W/C W Pitt-Brown	WCF Horsham St Faith	Meteor F.8	VZ559	UK	51
PB	W/C P P C Barthrop	WCF Waterbeach	Meteor F.8	WH415	UK	53-56
PB1	HRH Prince Bernhardt 24 Sqn; MCS		Beech D.17S	DR628	UK	41-45

Code	Name	Role/Unit	Type	Serial	Theatre	Year(s)
PDQ	F/L B O'Shaugnessy	93 FSP	Spitfire	?	France	45
PDW	W/C P D Wright	OC 64 Sqn	Javelin FAW.9	XH834	FE	65-66
PFS	W/C P F Steib	WCF Church Fenton	Meteor F.8	WF677	UK	54-56
PG	?		Spitfire V	?	Italy	45
PGJ	G/C P G Jameson	OC 122 Wing	Auster	?	Europe	45
PH	W/C P H Hugo	WCF Hornchurch	Spitfire	?	UK	42
PH	G/C P H Hugo	OC 322 Wing	Spitfire IX	EN240	MedME	43
PHB	S/L P H Beake	CFE	Tempest V	NV961	UK	45
PHW	W/C P H Woodruff	WCF 337 Wing	Spitfire IX	MA507	MedME	44-45
PJS	W/C P J Simpson		Spitfire Vb	BM273	UK	42
PJS	W/C P J Simpson	WCF 145 Wing	Spitfire IX	?	UK	43-44
PJS	W/C P J Simpson	WCF 135 Wing	Spitfire IX	ML357	UK	44
PJS	W/C P J Simpson	WCF Tangmere	Hunter F.5		UK	55
PLB	S/L P L Bateson-Jones	Church Fenton	Spitfire F.21	LA253	UK	46
PLB	S/L P L Bateson-Jones	Church Fenton	Meteor II	EE403	UK	46
PLN	S/L P L Nissen	337 Sqn	F-86K	54-1268	Norway	
PM	W/C P G H Mathews	WCF Leuchars	Meteor F.8	WK814	UK	53
PM	W/C P G H Mathews	WCF Leuchars	Hunter F.1	WT649	UK	55
PMB	W/C P M L Bond	WCF Horsham St Faith	Mustang, Spitfire		UK	45-46
PMcLB	W/C P M L Bond	WCF Eastern Sector	Hornet F.1	PX273	UK	46
PMO	?	84 Gp	Spitfire XVI	TD376	UK	45
PN	?	SF Bassingbourn	Anson T.20	VS509	UK	52
PN	F/L R Neal	1417 Flt	Hunter FR.10	XF429	Aden	67
PO	W/C P Olver	OC 244 Wing	Spitfire IX	EN448	MedME	43
PO-B	W/C P G O'Brien	WCF Portreath	Spitfire V	EE615	UK	43
PP	G/C R P R Powell	OC 121 Wing	Typhoon Ib	RB380	UK	45
PPH	W/C P P Hanks	WCF Luqa	Spitfire Vc	BR498	MedME	42
PPH	W/C P P Hanks	WCF 123 Wing	Tempest V	NV708	Eur	48
PS	W/C P Smith	OC 60 Sqn	Javelin FAW.9	XH722	FE	61-62
PST	W/C P S Turner	WL 127 Wing	Spitfire IX	TB300	Eur	45
PST	G/C P S Turner	OC 127 Wing	Bf 108		Eur	45
PT	S/L P D Thompson	OCF Biggin Hill	Meteor F.8	WL134	UK	55
PT	S/L P D Thompson	OCF Biggin Hill	Hunter F.5	WP186	UK	56-57
PW	W/C H de C A Woodhouse	OC 16 Wing	Typhoon Ib	JP671, JR219, MN141	UK	43-44
PW	W/C P R W Wickham	SF Peterhead	Mustang IV	KM237	UK	45
PW	W/C P R W Wickham	Turnhouse	Spitfire F.21	LA284	UK	47
PW	W/C P R W Wickham	Duxford	Meteor F.8	WK887	UK	c55
PWB	W/C P G W Barnes	57 OTU	Spitfire V	?	UK	45
PWB	W/C P G W Barnes	SC North Weald	Vampire FB.5	VZ841	UK	51
RA	A/C R L R Atcherley	OC CFE	Meteor III	EE235	UK	45
RA	A/C R L R Atcherley	OC CFE	Spitfire IX	MK868	UK	45
RA	AVM R L R Atcherley	AOC 12 Gp	Meteor F.8	WF707, WK680, WK927	UK	51-56
RA	S/L R Aytoun	OC 263 Sqn	Hunter F.5	WP108	UK	55-56
RAB	Lt Cmdr R A Berg	WCF 132 Wing	Spitfire IX	MJ462	UK	44
RAB	Lt Col R A Berg	WCF 132 Wing	Spitfire IXe	PV181	Europe	44-45
RB	W/C R Berry	WCF 322 Wing	Spitfire IX	EN199	MedME	44
RB	?	FLS	Spitfire IX	?	UK	45
RB	W/C R P Beamont	WCF 150 Wing	Tempest V	JN749	UK	44
RB	W/C R P Beamont	WCF 122 Wing	Tempest V	JN751	Eur	44
RB	W/C R P Beamont	Chilbolton	Tempest II	MW***	UK	45
RB	F/L ?	1417 Flt	Hunter FR.10	XR460	Aden	66-67
RBH	?	CFE	Meteor III	EE241	UK	45
RBL	W/C R B Lees	244 Wing	Spitfire IX	?	UK	45
RC	W/C R W Cox	WCF Wahn	Mosquito B.35	VP178	Eur	50
RC	S/L R C Chambers	OC 1417 Flt	Hunter FR.10	XE589	Aden	66
RCH	W/C R C Haines	SC Turnhouse	Meteor F.8	WL116	UK	57-58
RCW	W/C R C A Waddell	WCF 39 Wing	Spitfire XIV	RN114	UK	45
RD	W/C R T P Davidson	WCF 121 Wing	Typhoon Ib	JP496	UK	43-44
RD	W/C R T P Davidson	WCF 143 Wing	Typhoon Ib	MN518	UK	44
RD	S/L R H Dixon	OC 92 Sqn	Hunter F.6	XG239, XF521	UK	57-58
RDE	W/C R D Elliot	WCF 84 GSU	Spitfire IX	PV159	Eur	45
RDE	W/C R D Elliot	WCF 84 GSU	Tempest V	?	Eur	45
RDF	?	Debden	Spitfire IX	?	UK	45
RduV	W/C D le R du Vivier	WCF 324 Wing	Spitfire IX	MJ628	UK	44

Code	Name	Role/Unit	Type	Serial	Theatre	Year(s)
RduV	W/C R du Vivier	OC 239 Wing	Spitfire IX	MJ625	Italy	44
RDY	W/V R D Yule	WCF 125 Wing	Spitfire IX	?	UK	44
RDY	W/V R D Yule	WCF Horsham St Faith	Meteor F.8	WF695	UK	44
REB	W/C R E Bary	WCF 239 Wing	Kittyhawk III	FR507	MedME	43
REB	W/C R E Bary	OC 244 Wing	Spitfire IX	ML404	MedME	45
RF	S/L R H G Freer	OC 92 Sqn	Hunter F.6	XE621	UK	56
RFB	W/C R F Boyd	WC Kenley Wing	Spitfire V	?	UK	46
RGD	G/C R G Dutton	SC Waterbeach	Meteor F.8	WH404	UK	56-57
RGD	S/L R G Dixon	12 GCF	Meteor F.8	WK969	UK	57
RH	W/C R Harries		Spitfire II	P7933	UK	
RH	AM Sir Roderic Hill	AOC ADGB	Spitfire Vb	AA916	UK	44
RH	AM Sir Roderic Hill	AOC ADGB	Spitfire IX	MJ843	UK	44-45
RH	AM Sir Roderic Hill	AOC ADGB	Tempest V	JN876	UK	45
RH	AM Sir Roderic Hill	AOC ADGB	Mosquito VI	HR343	UK	45
RH	F/L R Hulbert	3 APS	Spitfire IX	ML242	UK	45
RHC	W/C R N H Courtney	WCF 906 Wing	Spitfire VIII	MV432	FE	45
RHG	W/C R H M Gibbes	WL 80 Wing RAAF	Spitfire VIII	A58-307, A58-497 A58-602		
	Australia, New Guinea	44-45				
RHH	W/C R H Harries	WCF 134 Wing	Spitfire IX	?	UK	44
RHR	W/C R H Riggall	OC 907 Wing	Spitfire VIII	JF902	FE	45
RJC	Lt Cdr R J Cork	CFI No 2 NAFS; OC 761 NAS	Seafire Ib	NX957	UK	43
RC	Lt Cdr R J Cork	WL 15th Ftr Wg (HMS Illustrious)	Corsair II	JT269	FE	43-44
RH	Capt R C Hay RM	DAWT Lee on Solent	Seafire IIc	MB349	UK	43
RIKE	G/C R I K Edwards	SC Tangmere	Meteor F.8	WL176	UK	54
RIKE	G/C R I K Edwards	SC Tangmere	Hunter F.5	WP123	UK	58
RJ	F/L R Johns	1417 Flt	Hunter FR.10	XE549	Aden	64-67
RJ(?G)	? G/C R J Gosnell	SC Wildenrath	Sabre F.4	?XB669	Eur	54
RLS	W/C R L Smith	SC Ouston	Vampire FB.5	VZ305	UK	54-55
RM	W/C R Marples	WCF 124 Wing	Spitfire Vb	EP245	UK	44
RM	?	FLS	Spitfire	?	UK	45
RMG	S/L E M Goodale	OC 26 Sqn	Mustang I	AM148	UK	42
RMH	AM Sir Roderic Hill	AOC FC	Tempest V	JN876	UK	45
RPB	W/C R P Beamont	WCF 122 Wing	Tempest V	JN751	UK	44
RR	W/C D E Gillam	WCF Duxford	Typhoon Ib	?	UK	42
RR	Lt Col R H Rogers	OC 40 Sqn SAAF	Spitfire IX	PT672	MedME	43
RST	W/C R S Tuck	WL Biggin Hill	Spitfire Vb	BL336	UK	41-42
RT	?	203 AFS	Spitfire LF.16	SL551	UK	47
RWM	W/C R W McNair	W/C 126 Wing	Spitfire IX	?	UK	43-44
RWO	W/C R W Oxspring	WL West Malling Wing	Spitfire XIV	?	UK	44
RWO	W/C R W Oxspring	WL 124 Wing	Spitfire XIV	NH714	Eur	45
RWO	W/C R W Oxspring	WCF Met Sector	Meteor III	EE482	UK	46
RWO	W/C R W Oxspring	WCF Met Sector	Meteor III	EE482	UK	46
SB	?	DFLS	Typhoon Ib	?	UK	45
SBG	W/C S B Grant	WL Krendi	Spitfire V	?	MedME	43
SC	?	Caledonian Sector	Hunter F.4	XF304	UK	54
SCW	G/C S C Widdows	SC Eastern Sector	Meteor F.8	WA773, WK795	UK	52-54
SD	?	145 Wing	Spitfire Vc	EF541	UK	44
SEP	?	AOC Gibraltar	Hurricane I	?	MedME	43
SF	?	SF Linton-on-Ouse	Meteor T.7	WH209	UK	53
SFS	W/C S F Skalski	WCF 133 Wing	Mustang III	FZ152	UK	44
SM	W/C F D S Scott-Malden	WCF North Weald	Spitfire Vb	AB202	UK	42
SS	W/C S F Skalski	WCF 131Airfield	Spitfire IX	BS556	Eur	c 43-44
SS	W/C S F Skalski	WL 133 Wing	Mustang III	FZ152	UK	44
SS	W/C S F Skalski	WCF 133 Wing	Spitfire IX	RK853	UK	45
SS	W/C R W F Sampson	WCF ? Wing	Spitfire IX	RK853	Eur	44
SW	Strike Wing Aden	8/43 Sqns	Hunter FGA.9	XE645	Aden	66-67
TA	T Andersen	332 Sqn	F-84G	519945	Norway	-57
TA	W/C T Andersen	WL Rygge Wing	F-86F	53-1117	Norway	58
TB	?	OC 256 Sqn	Meteor NF.11	WD645	Eur	c 55
TBB	G/C T B del La P Beresford OC 324 Wing		Spitfire VIII;	MB973	MedME	45
TBB	G/C T B del La P Beresford OC 324 Wing		Spitfire IX	TB539	MedME	45
TC	Maj T Cooke	OC 40 Sqn SAAF	Spitfire IX	PL458	MedME	44
TE	? S/L Edwards	OC 587 Sqn	Hurricane IIb	KZ675	UK	44
TH	Lt Cdr T W Harrington	WL 5th Ftr Wing (HMS Indomitable)	Hellcat II	JW860	FE	44-45

Code	Name	Role/Unit	Type	Serial	Theatre	Year(s)
TJJ	?	?	Spitfire IX	MH530	MedME	45
TM	? G/C C S Morice	OC 121 Wing	Tempest V	SN212	UK	45
TN	W/C T Nowierski	WL 133 Wing	Mustang III	HB886, KH865	UK	44
TN	S/L W A 'Tiny' Nel	AHQ Hong Kong	Spitfire F 24	VN496	FE	50
TP	?	23 Sqn	Venom NF.2	WL858	UK	54
TP	?	234 Sqn	Sabre F.4	XB589	Eur	55-56
TR	G/C T H Rolski	OC 133 Wing	Mustang III	HB822	UK	45
TRB	? G/C T R Burne	FRU	Spitfire LF.16	TE455	UK	47-49
T-RH	Maj R C Hay RM	WL 47th Ftr Wing (HMS Victorious)	Corsair II	JT427	FE	44-45
TSW	? W/C T S Wilkinson	Northern Sector	Proctor III	LZ707	UK	52
TT	AVM T C Traill	AOC 12 Group	Spitfire F.21	LA232	UK	46-48
TT	AVM T Traill	12 Group CF	Spitfire F.21	LA232	UK	48
TUL	?	RAF Halton	Spitfire	?	UK	42
TV	S/L T Vybiral	OC 312 Sqn	Spitfire Vb	? AR511	UK	c 43
TW	?	? 148 Wing	Tempest V	?	UK	44
V	S Lt Georges Valentin	GC II/7	Dewotine D520	136	MedME	c 42
V	Cne Georges Valentin	GC II/7	Spitfire Vb	EP813	MedME	c 43
VA	?	323 Wing	Spitfire IX	?	MedME	44
VL	?	39 Sqn	Mosquito NF.36	RL151	MedME	49-53
VSB	A/C V S Bowling	SC Northern Sector	Meteor F.8	WK991	UK	53-55
VSB	A/C V S Bowling	AOC 11 Group	Meteor F.8	WK943	UK	56
VSB	?		Meteor F.8	WK991	UK	
VY	W/C T Vybiral	WL 134 Wing	Spitfire IX	MK483; ML171 Eur		44- 45
WAD	?	?	Spitfire F 21	LA253	UK	c 46
WATN	W/C W A 'Tiny' Nel	WC Ops Linton-on-Ouse	Hornet F.1	PX216	UK	48-49
WAS	W/C W A Smith	WCF Fassberg	Vampire FB.5	WA340	UK	51-53
WAS	W/C W A Smith	SC Ouston	Vampire FB.5	WA419	UK	56
WC	?	43 Sqn	Hunter F.6	XG237	UK	60-61
WCW	W/C W C West	WL 122 Wg	Hunter F 4	XF315	Eur	56-57
WD	W/C W Dring	WCF 123 Wing	Typhoon Ib	PD466	UK	44
WES	G/C W E Surplice	SC Rivenhall	Stirling IV	LK171	UK	44
WFD	AVM Sir William F Dickson AOC Desert AF		Spitfire VIII	JF814	MedME	44
WHC	Lt Col W H Christie	WCF Hunsdon Wing	Mustang	KH790	UK	45
WHC	W/C W H Christie	WL Gardemoen Wing	Vampire FB.52	VO445	Norway	
WHC	W/C W H Christie	WL Sola Wing	F-84G	5111113	Norway	
WL	? Wing Leader	WL Celle	Vampire FB.5	WA195	Eur	50-51
WL	? Wing Leader	WL Oldenburg	Sabre F.4	XB886	Eur	55
WL	? Wing Leader	WL Wahn	Meteor NF.11	WM156	Eur	54-57
WPB	W/C W Pitt-Brown	WCF 121 Wing	Typhoon Ib	? MP155	UK	44
WPB	S/L W Pitt-Brown	169 Wing	Mohawk IV	BS790	FE	42-43
WRM	W/C W R McBrien	OC 126 Wing	Spitfire Vb		UK	43
WT	?	322 Wing	Spitfire XI	EN408	MedME	?
WTC	Capt W T Couchman	FONAS	Seafire III	NF500	UK	44
WV	W/L W Vale	59 OTU	Hurricane	?	UK	42-43
WVC	W/C W V Crawford-Compton		WCF 345 Wing	Spitfire IX	NH590	UK 44
WVC	G/C W V Crawford-Compton		FCCS	Spitfire IX	MK128	UK 45
XX	various	OC 20 Sqn	Hunter FGA.9	XJ673	FE	62-70
XX	W/C R H B le Brocq	OC 20 Sqn	Harrier GR.1	XV702	Eur	71-72
XX	W/C R H B le Brocq	OC 20 Sqn	Harrier GR.3	XV810	Eur	73-74
YE	Lt Col Yves Ezamo	Insp of Ftrs, AdlA	Mosquito PR 16	TA615	France	1949
ZW	W/C Walerian Zak	WL 133 Wing	Spitfire IX	?	Eur	c 44
ZW	W/C Walerian Zak	WCF Coltishall	Mustang III	FB217	UK	c 45-46
ZZ	W/C D E Gillam	WL Duxford	Typhoon Ib	R7655, R7698	UK	42
ZZ4	G/C D E Gillam	84 GSU	Tempest V	SN102	UK	45
ZZII	W/C D E Gillam	OC 146 Wing	Typhoon Ib	MN587	Eur	44
ZZIII	W/C D E Gillam	84 GSU	Tempest	?	UK	45

APPENDIX A

USAAF

When the USAAF deployed the first units of the 8th Air Force to the United Kingdom in July 1942 they were brought into the RAF two-character system. At this time the number of permutations available was increased by including the letters C and I and numbers – the latter always in combination with a letter. The system extended to aircraft of the 9th Air Force and to a limited extent the Mediterranean-based units of the 12th and 15th Air Forces.

The 8th Air Force controlled the strategic bombing force based in the east of England with its associated escort fighters and little in the way of support units. The 9th Air Force was established as a tactical air force to support the invasion of Europe, hence there was a predominance of troop carrier units, light bombers and P-47 fighter escorts. The 12th Air Force controlled most US fighter and bomber units in the Mediterranean, with just the B-24s in that theatre operated within the 15th Air Force.

In the table below, all known codes are shown in numerical sequence by squadron within air force in the order fighter, bomber, reconnaissance, transport and other. Where a code is known but not the unit the reader is advised to go first to the main index at chapter 3. An asterisk following a letter or number indicates a single-character unit code where * is the individual aircraft identification. This device was used by several units in the Mediterranean theatre.

The USAAF also used colours and symbols to indicate squadrons, groups, wings and divisions, with individual letters or numbers as aircraft identifiers, such letters or numbers sometimes repeated within the group. These identifiers have been well documented elsewhere and are outside the scope of the present volume.

8th Air Force

Unit	Code	Type(s)
65 Fighter Wing HQ	JA	P-47C, D, M; P-51B, D
27 FS, 1 FG	HV	P-38J
38 FS, 55 FG	CG	P-38H, J; P-51
48 FS, 14 FG	ES	P-38J
49 FS, 14 FG	QU	P-38F, G, J
55 FS, 20 FG	KI	P-38H, J; P-51C, D, K
61 FS, 56 FG	HV	P-47C, D, M
62 FS, 56 FG	LM	P-47C, D, M
63 FS, 56 FG	UN	P-47C, D, M
71 FS, 1 FG	LM	P-38J
77 FS, 20 FG	LC	P-38H, J; P-51C, D, K
79 FS, 20 FG	MC	P-38H, J; P-51C, D, K
82 FS, 78 FG	MX	P-38G; P-47C, D; P-51D

Unit	Code	Type(s)
83 FS, 78 FG	HL	P-38G; P-47C, D; P-51D
84 FS, 78 FG	WZ	P-38G; P-47C, D; P-51D, K
94 FS, 1 FG	UN	P-38J
307 FS, 31 FG	MX	Spitfire V, IX
308 FS, 31 FG	HL	Spitfire V
309 FS, 31 FG	WZ	Spitfire V
328 FS, 352 FG	PE	P-47D; P-51B, C, D
334 FS, 4 FG	QP	P-47C, D; P-51B, D, K
334 FS, 4 FG	XR	Spitfire V
335 FS, 4 FG	WD	P-47C, D; P-51B, D, K
335 FS, 4 FG	AV	Spitfire V
336 FS, 4 FG	VF	P-47C, D; P-51B, D, K; Spitfire V
336 FS, 4 FG	MD	Spitfire V
338 FS, 55 FG	CL	P-38H, J; P-51
343 FS, 55 FG	CY	P-38H, J, P-51D
350 FS, 353 FG	LH	P-47D; P-51D, K
351 FS, 353 FG	YJ	P-47D; P-51D, K
352 FS, 353 FG	SX	P-47D; P-51D, K
354 FS, 355 FG	WR	P-47D, P-51B, D, K
357 FS, 355 FG	OS	P-47D, P-51
358 FS, 355 FG	YF	P-47D, P-51
359 FS, 356 FG	OC	P-47D, P-51D
360 FS, 356 FG	PI	P-47D; P-51D
361 FS, 356 FG	QI	P-47D; P-51D
362 FS, 357 FG	G4	P-51B, C, D
363 FS, 357 FG	B6	P-51B, C, D
364 FS, 357 FG	C5	P-51B, C, D
368 FS, 359 FG	CV	P-47D; P-51B, C, D
369 FS, 359 FG	IV	P-47D; P-51B, C, D
370 FS, 359 FG	CR	P-47D; P-51B, C, D
374 FS, 361 FG	B7	P-47D; P-51
375 FS, 361 FG	E2	P-47D, P-51D
376 FS, 361 FG	E9	P-47D, P-51D
383 FS, 364 FG	N2	P-38J; P-51D
384 FS, 364 FG	5Y	P-38J; P-51D
385 FS, 364 FG	5E	P-38J; P-51D
434 FS, 479 FG	L2	P-38J; P-51D
435 FS, 479 FG	J2	P-38J; P-51D
436 FS, 479 FG	9B	P-38J; P-51D
486 FS, 352 FG	PZ	P-47D; P-51B, C, D
487 FS, 352 FG	HO	P-47D; P-51B, C, D
503 FS, 339 FG	D7	P-51B, C, D
504 FS, 339 FG	5Q	P-51B, C, D

Unit	Code	Type(s)	Unit	Code	Type(s)
505 FS, 339 FG	6N	P-51B, C, D	506 BS, 44 BG	QK	B-24D, E, H, J, L, M
551 FS, 495 FTG	DQ	P-47C, D; P-38	508 BS, 351 BG	YB	B-17F, G
552 FS, 495 FTG	VM	P-47D	509 BS, 351 BG	RQ	B-17F, G
554 FS, 357 FTG	B9	P-38	510 BS, 351 BG	TU	B-17F, G
555 FS, 496 FTG	C7	P-51; Spitfire XI	511 BS, 351 BG	DS	B-17F, G
4 BS, 34 BG	Q6	B-24H, J; B-17G	524 BS, 379 BG	WA	B-17F, G
7 BS, 34 BG	R2	B-24H, J; B-17G	525 BS, 379 BG	FR	B-17F, G
15 BS, 27 BG	MQ	Boston III (of 226 Sqn RAF)	526 BS, 379 BG	LF	B-17F, G
18 BS, 34 BG	8I	B-24H, J; B-17G	527 BS, 379 BG	FO	B-17F, G
36 BS, 801 BG	R4	B-17F, G, B-24D	532 BS, 381 BG	VE	B-17F, G
66 BS, 44 BG	QK	B-24D, E, H, J, L, M	533 BS, 381 BG	OQ	B-17F, G
67 BS, 44 BG	NB	B-24D, E, H, J, L, M	534 BS, 381 BG	JZ	B-17F, G
68 BS, 44 BG	WQ	B-24D, E, H, J, L, M	535 BS, 381 BG	PL	B-17F, G
322 BS, 91 BG	LG	B-17F, G	544 BS, 384 BG	SU	B-17F, G
323 BS, 91 BG	OR	B-17F, G	545 BS, 384 BG	JD	B-17F, G
324 BS, 91 BG	DF	B-17F, G	546 BS, 384 BG	BK	B-17F, G
325 BS, 92 BG	NV	B-17E, F, G; YB-40	547 BS, 384 BG	SO	B-17F, G
326 BS, 92 BG	JW	B-17E, F, G; YB-40	548 BS, 385 BG	GX	B-17F, G
327 BS, 92 BG	UX	B-17E, F, G; YB-40	549 BS, 385 BG	XA	B-17F, G
328 BS, 93 BG	GO	B-24D, E, H, J, L, M	550 BS, 385 BG	SG	B-17F, G
329 BS, 93 BG	RE	B-24D, E, H, J, L, M	551 BS, 385 BG	HR	B-17F, G
330 BS, 93 BG	AG	B-24D, E, H, J, L, M	564 BS, 389 BG	YO	B-24D, E, H, J, L, M
331 BS, 94 BG	QE	B-17F, G	565 BS, 389 BG	EE	B-24D, E, H, J, L, M
332 BS, 94 BG	XM	B-17F, G	566 BS, 389 BG	RR	B-24D, E, H, J, L, M
333 BS, 94 BG	TS	B-17F, G	567 BS, 389 BG	HP	B-24D, E, H, J, L, M
334 BS, 95 BG	BG	B-17E, F, G	568 BS, 390 BG	BI	B-17F, G
335 BS, 95 BG	OE	B-17E, F, G	569 BS, 390 BG	CC	B-17F, G
336 BS, 95 BG	ET	B-17F, G	570 BS, 390 BG	DI	B-17F, G
337 BS, 96 BG	QJ	B-17F, G	571 BS, 390 BG	FC	B-17F, G
338 BS, 96 BG	BX	B-17F, G	576 BS, 392 BG	CI	B-24H, J, L, M
339 BS, 96 BG	AW	B-17F, G	577 BS, 392 BG	DC	B-24H, J, L, M
349 BS, 100 BG	XR	B-17F, G	578 BS, 392 BG	EC	B-24H, J, L, M
350 BS, 100 BG	LN	B-17F, G	579 BS, 392 BG	GC	B-24H, J, L, M
351 BS, 100 BG	EP	B-17F, G	600 BS, 398 BG	N8	B-17G
358 BS, 303 BG	VK	B-17E, F, G	601 BS, 398 BG	3O	B-17G
359 BS, 303 BG	BN	B-17F, G	602 BS, 398 BG	K8	B-17G
360 BS, 303 BG	PU	B-17E, F, G	603 BS, 398 BG	N7	B-17G
364 BS, 305 BG	WF	B-17F, G	612 BS, 401 BG	SC	B-17G
365 BS, 305 BG	XK	B-17F, G	613 BS, 401 BG	IN	B-17G
366 BS, 305 BG	KY	B-17F, G	614 BS, 401 BG	IW	B-17G
367 BS, 306 BG	GY	B-17F, G	615 BS, 401 BG	IY	B-17G
368 BS, 306 BG	BO	B-17F, G	652 BS, 25 BG	YN	B-24; B-17; Mosquito XVI
369 BS, 306 BG	WW	B-17F, G	653 BS, 25 BG	WX	Mosquito XVI
391 BS, 34 BG	3L	B-24H, J; B-17G	654 BS, 25 BG	BA	B-26; Mosquito XVI
401 BS, 91 BG	LL	B-17F, G	700 BS, 445 BG	IS	B-24H, J, L, M
406 BS, 482 BG	J6	B-24	701 BS, 445 BG	MK	B-24H, J, L, M
406 BS, 801 BG	L7	L-5	702 BS, 445 BG	WV	B-24H, J, L, M
407 BS, 92 BG	PY	B-17E, F, G; YB-40	703 BS, 445 BG	RN	B-24H, J, L, M
409 BS, 93 BG	YM	B-24D, E, H, J, L, M	704 BS, 446 BG	FL	B-24H, J, L, M
410 BS, 94 BG	GL	B-17F, G	705 BS, 446 BG	HN	B-24H, J, L, M
412 BS, 95 BG	QW	B-17E, F, G	706 BS, 446 BG	RT	B-24H, J, L, M
413 BS, 96 BG	MZ	B-17F, G	707 BS, 446 BG	JU	B-24H, J, L, M
418 BS, 100 BG	LD	B-17F, G	708 BS, 447 BG	CQ	B-17G
422 BS, 305 BG	JJ	B-17F, G	709 BS, 447 BG	IE	B-17G
423 BS, 306 BG	RD	B-17E, F, G	710 BS, 447 BG	IJ	B-17G
427 BS, 303 BG	GN	B-17F, G	711 BS, 447 BG	IR	B-17G

Unit	Code	Type(s)	Unit	Code	Type(s)
712 BS, 448 BG	CT	B-24H, J, L, M	832 BS, 486 BG	3R	B-24H, J; B-17G
713 BS, 448 BG	IG	B-24H, J, L, M	833 BS, 486 BG	4N	B-24H, J; B-17G
714 BS, 448 BG	EI	B-24H, J, L, M	834 BS, 486 BG	2S	B-24H, J; B-17G
715 BS, 448 BG	IO	B-24H, J, L, M	835 BS, 486 BG	H8	B-24H, J; B-17G
728 BS, 452 BG	9Z	B-17G	836 BS, 487 BG	2G	B-24H, J; B-17G
729 BS, 452 BG	M3	B-17G	837 BS, 487 BG	4F	B-24H, J; B-17G
730 BS, 452 BG	6K	B-17G	838 BS, 487 BG	2C	B-24H, J; B-17G
731 BS, 452 BG	7D	B-17G	839 BS, 487 BG	R5	B-24H, J; B-17G
732 BS, 453 BG	E3	B-24H, J, L, M	844 BS, 489 BG	4R	B-24H, J
733 BS, 453 BG	E8	B-24H, J, L, M	845 BS, 489 BG	T4	B-24H, J
734 BS, 453 BG	F8	B-24H, J, L, M	846 BS, 489 BG	8R	B-24H, J
735 BS, 453 BG	H6	B-24H, J, L, M	847 BS, 489 BG	S4	B-24H, J
752 BS, 458 BG	7V	B-24H, J, L, M	848 BS, 490 BG	7W	B-17G; B-24
753 BS, 458 BG	J4	B-24H, J, L, M	849 BS, 490 BG	W8	B-17G; B-24
754 BS, 458 BG	Z5	B-24H, J, L, M	850 BS, 490 BG	7Q	B-17G; B-24
755 BS, 458 BG	J3	B-24H, J, L, M	851 BS, 490 BG	S3	B-17G; B-24
784 BS, 466 BG	T9	B-24H, J, L, M	852 BS, 491 BG	3Q	B-24H, J, L, M
785 BS, 466 BG	2U	B-24H, J, L, M	853 BS, 491 BG	T8	B-24H, J, L, M
786 BS, 466 BG	U8	B-24H, J, L, M	854 BS, 491 BG	6X	B-24H, J, L, M
787 BS, 466 BG	6L	B-24H, J, L, M	855 BS, 491 BG	V2	B-24H, J, L, M
788 BS, 467 BG	X7	B-24H, J, L, M	856 BS, 492 BG	5Z	B-24H, J
789 BS, 467 BG	6A	B-24H, J, L, M	857 BS, 492 BG	9H	B-24H, J
790 BS, 467 BG	Q2	B-24H, J, L, M	858 BS, 492 BG	9A	B-24H, J
791 BS, 467 BG	4Z	B-24H, J, L, M	859 BS, 492 BG	X4	B-24H, J
803 BS, RCM	R4	B-24, B-17	860 BS, 493 BG	N6	B-17G; B-24
812 BS, 482 BG	MI	B-24, B-17	861 BS, 493 BG	Q6	B-17G; B-24
813 BS, 482 BG	PC	B-24, B-17	862 BS, 493 BG	8M	B-17G; B-24
814 BS, 482 BG	SI	B-24, B-17	863 BS, 493 BG	Q4	B-17G; B-24

B-26C Marauder 4296246/TQ-H belonged to the 559th BS/387th BG of the 9th AF. The code letters had previously been used by the London flying boats of the RAF's No. 202 Sqn earlier in the war. (US National Archives)

Unit	Code	Type(s)
13 PS, 7 PG	ES	Spitfire, F-5A, B, C
22 PS, 7 PG	G2	Spitfire, F-5A, B, C
BAD 1	BU	various
3 GTTF	LJ	P-47B
4 GTTF	AZ	Lysander; Havoc I, II; Vengeance

P-47D Thunderbolt 4275587/B8-V belonged to the USAAF's 379th FS of the 362nd FG. Here it wears a typical mid-war scheme including white unit codes which were within the British system, though a joint document has not come to light. (US National Archives)

Escort fighters of several 8th AF groups may be seen in this view. The nearest P-51D Gentle Annie is from the 20th FG's 79th FS while beyond is 4414111/PE-X of the 328th FS/352nd FG next to which is an LM coded P-47D of the 62nd FS/56th FG. (via Harry Holmes)

Unit	Code	Type(s)
4 GTTF	ZS	AT-23B
5 ERS, 496 FG	5F	P-47D; B-17; OA-10A; P-51
2906 OTG	LA	P-47C, D; P-38H, J
8th AF Tech Ops	Q3	Various

9th Air Force

Unit	Code	Type(s)
3 CCRS	W9	B-26
9th AF Recon Sqn	8O	F-6A
10 FS, 50 FG	T5	P-47D
22 FS, 36 FG	3T	P-47D
23 FS, 36 FG	7U	P-47D
53 FS, 36 FG	6V	P-47D
81 FS, 50 FG	2N	P-47D
313 FS, 50 FG	W3	P-47D
353 FS, 354 FG	FT	P-47D; P-51B, D
355 FS, 354 FG	GQ	P-47D; P-51B, D
356 FS, 354 FG	AJ	P-47D; P-51B, D
362 FS, 357 FG	G4	P-51B, C, D
364 FS, 357 FG	C5	P-51B, C, D
365 FS, 358 FG	CH	P-47D
366 FS, 358 FG	IA	P-47D
367 FS, 358 FG	CP	P-47D
377 FS, 362 FG	E4	P-47D
378 FS, 362 FG	G8	P-47D
379 FS, 362 FG	B8	P-47D
380 FS, 363 FG	A9	P-51D
381 FS, 363 FG	B3	P-51D
382 FS, 363 FG	C3	P-51D
386 FS, 365 FG	D5	P-47D
387 FS, 365 FG	B4	P-47D
388 FS, 365 FG	C4	P-47D
389 FS, 366 FG	A6	P-47D
390 FS, 366 FG	B2	P-47D
391 FS, 366 FG	A8	P-47D
392 FS, 367 FG	H5	P-38; P-47D
393 FS, 367 FG	8L	P-38; P-47
394 FS, 367 FG	4N	P-38; P-47
395 FS, 368 FG	A7	P-47D
396 FS, 368 FG	C2	P-47D
397 FS, 368 FG	D3	P-47D
401 FS, 370 FG	9D	P-38; P-51; F-5
402 FS, 370 FG	E6	P-38; P-51
404 FS, 371 FG	9Q	P-47D
405 FS, 371 FG	8N	P-47D
406 FS, 371 FG	4W	P-47D
410 FS, 373 FG	R3	P-47D
411 FS, 373 FG	U9	P-47D
412 FS, 373 FG	V5	P-47D
428 FS, 474 FG	F5	P-38
429 FS, 474 FG	7Y	P-38
430 FS, 474 FG	K6	P-38
485 FS, 370 FG	7F	P-38; P-47; P-51
492 FS, 48 FG	F4	P-47D
493 FS, 48 FG	I7	P-47D

The B-17G Fortress was one of the most famous types of the war. This example is 4338626/TS-A of the 8th AF's 333rd BS/94th BG and was filmed from a sister ship while letting down to land in 1944. (via Harry Holmes)

Unit	Code	Type(s)
494 FS, 48 FG	6M	P-47D
506 FS, 404 FG	4K	P-39; P-47D
507 FS, 404 FG	Y8	P-39; P-47D
508 FS, 404 FG	7J	P-39; P-47D
509 FS, 405 FG	G9	P-47D
510 FS, 405 FG	2Z	P-47D
511 FS, 405 FG	K4	P-47D
512 FS, 406 FG	L3	P-47D
513 FS, 406 FG	4P	P-47D
514 FS, 406 FG	O7	P-47D
449 BS, 322 BG	PN	B-26B
450 BS, 322 BG	ER	B-26B
451 BS, 322 BG	SS	B-26B
452 BS, 322 BG	DR	B-26B
453 BS, 323 BG	VT	B-26B
454 BS, 323 BG	RJ	B-26B
455 BS, 323 BG	YU	B-26B
456 BS, 323 BG	WT	B-26B
494 BS, 344 BG	K9	B-26B
495 BS, 344 BG	Y5	B-26B
496 BS, 344 BG	N3	B-26B
497 BS, 344 BG	7I	B-26B
552 BS, 386 BG	RG	B-26B
553 BS, 386 BG	AN	B-26B; A-26
554 BS, 386 BG	RU	B-26B
555 BS, 386 BG	YA	B-26B
556 BS, 387 BG	FW	B-26B
557 BS, 387 BG	KS	B-26B
558 BS, 387 BG	KX	B-26B
559 BS, 387 BG	TQ	B-26B
572 BS, 391 BG	P2	B-26B
573 BS, 391 BG	T6	B-26B
574 BS, 391 BG	4L	B-26B
575 BS, 391 BG	O8	B-26B
584 BS, 394 BG	K5	B-26B
585 BS, 394 BG	4T	B-26B
586 BS, 394 BG	H9	B-26B, C

Unit	Code	Type(s)
587 BS, 394 BG	5W	B-26B
596 BS, 397 BG	X2	B-26B
597 BS, 397 BG	9F	B-26B
598 BS, 397 BG	U2	B-26B
599 BS, 397 BG	6B	B-26B
640 BS, 409 BG	W5	A-20G; A-26A
641 BS, 409 BG	7G	A-20G; A-26A
642 BS, 409 BG	D6	A-20G; A-26A
643 BS, 409 BG	5I	A-20G; A-26A
644 BS, 410 BG	5D	A-20G; A-26B
645 BS, 410 BG	7X	A-20G; A-26B
646 BS, 410 BG	8U	A-20G; A-26B
647 BS, 410 BG	6Q	A-20G; A-26B
668 BS, 416 BG	5H	A-20G
669 BS, 416 BG	2A	A-20G
670 BS, 416 BG	F6	A-20G
671 BS, 416 BG	5C	A-20G; A-26A
10 RS, 69 RG	YC	A-24; B-25; F-6; L-5; P-40; P-51
12 RS, 67 RG	ZM	Spitfire V; L-4; A-20; P-51D
15 RS, 10 PG	5M	F-6; L-4; L-5; P-51D
15 RS, 67 RG	5M	F-6; L-4; Spitfire
22 RS, 69 RG	QL	F-6; P-40;, P-51D
30 PS, 10 PG	I6	F-5; P-38
31 PS, 10 PG	8V	F-5; F-6; P-38; P-51D
33 PS, 363 RG	2W	F-5; P-38
33 RS, 67 RG	SW	F-5; P-38J; P-51
34 PS, 10 PG	S9	A-20; F-5; P-38
34 RS, 69 RG	XX	A-20; F-5; P-38
107 RS, 67 RG	AX	Spitfire Vb; L-4; A-20; P-51D; F-6B
109 RS, 67 RG	VX	Spitfire V; L-4; A-20; P-51D
111 RS, 69 RG	N5	F-6; L-5; P-51
153 RS, 67 RG	DA	Spitfire V; L-4; A-20; P-51D
160 RS, 363 RG	A9	F-6; P-51D
161 RS, 363 RG	B3	F-6; P-51D
162 RS, 363 RG	C3	F-6; P-51D

Unit	Code	Type(s)
? TCS, ? TCG	AP	C-47
14 TCS, 61 TCG	3I	C-47; C-53
15 TCS, 61 TCG	Y9	C-47; C-109
23 TCS, 349 TCG	Q8	C-47
29 TCS, 313 TCG	Z7	C-47; C-53
32 TCS, 314 TCG	S2	C-47; C-53; C-109
34 TCS, 315 TCG	NM	C-47; C-46
36 TCS, 316 TCG	4C	C-47; C-53
37 TCS, 316 TCG	W7	C-47; C-53
43 TCS, 315 TCG	UA	C-47; C-46
44 TCS, 316 TCG	6E	C-47; C-53
45 TCS, 316 TCG	T3	C-47; C-53
47 TCS, 313 TCG	N3	C-47; C-53
48 TCS, 313 TCG	5X	C-47; C-53
49 TCS, 313 TCG	H2	C-47; C-53
50 TCS, 314 TCG	2R	C-47; C-53
53 TCS, 61 TCG	3A	C-47; C-53
59 TCS, 61 TCG	X5	C-47; C-109
61 TCS, 314 TCG	Q9	C-47; C-53
62 TCS, 314 TCG	E5	C-47; C-53
71 TCS, 434 TCG	CJ	C-47
72 TCS, 434 TCG	CU	C-47
73 TCS, 434 TCG	CN	C-47
74 TCS, 434 TCG	ID	C-47
75 TCS, 435 TCG	SH	C-47; C-53
76 TCS, 435 TCG	CW	C-47; C-53
77 TCS, 435 TCG	IB	C-47; C-53
78 TCS, 435 TCG	CM	C-47; C-53
79 TCS, 436 TCG	S6	C-47
80 TCS, 436 TCG	7D	C-47
81 TCS, 436 TCG	U5	C-47
82 TCS, 436 TCG	3D	C-47
83 TCS, 437 TCG	T2	C-47
84 TCS, 437 TCG	Z8	C-47
85 TCS, 437 TCG	9O	C-47
86 TCS, 437 TCG	5K	C-47
87 TCS, 438 TCG	3X	C-47
88 TCS, 438 TCG	M2	C-47
89 TCS, 438 TCG	4U	C-47
90 TCS, 438 TCG	Q7	C-47
91 TCS, 439 TCG	L4	C-47
92 TCS, 439 TCG	J8	C-47
93 TCS, 439 TCG	3B	C-47
94 TCS, 439 TCG	D8	C-47
95 TCS, 440 TCG	9X	C-47; C-53
96 TCS, 440 TCG	6Z	C-47; C-53
97 TCS, 440 TCG	W6	C-47; C-53
98 TCS, 440 TCG	8Y	C-47
99 TCS, 441 TCG	3J	C-47; C-53
100 TCS, 441 TCG	8C	C-47; C-53
301 TCS, 441 TCG	Z4	C-47; C-53
302 TCS, 441 TCG	2L	C-47; C-53
303 TCS, 442 TCG	J7	C-47; C-53
304 TCS, 442 TCG	V4	C-47; C-53
305 TCS, 442 TCG	4J	C-47; C-53
306 TCS, 442 TCG	7H	C-47; C-53

Unit	Code	Type(s)
309 TCS, 315 TCG	M6	C-47; C-53; C-109
310 TCS, 315 TCG	4A	C-47; C-53; C-109
312 TCS, 349 TCG	9E	C-46; C-109
313 TCS, 349 TCG	3F	C-46; C-47
314 TCS, 349 TCG	LY	C-46; C-47
1 PFS	IH	B-26
14 LS	6C	L-5; UC-78
14 LS	9S	L-5; UC-78
153 LS, 67 RG	ZS	A-20, L-4
153 LS	8R	A-20; Oxford; L-4
155 LS, 10 PG	O9	A-20; F-3

12th Air Force

Unit	Code	Type(s)
2 FS, 52 FG	QP	Spitfire V
4 FS, 52 FG	WD	Spitfire V
5 FS, 52 FG	VF	Spitfire V
27 FS, 1 FG	HV	P-38J
48 FS, 14 FG	ES	P-38J
49 FS, 14 FG	QU	P-38J
71 FS, 1 FG	LM	P-38J
93 FS	Q	P-39M
94 FS, 1 FG	UN	P-38J
95 FS, 82 FG	A*	P-38J
96 FS, 82 FG	B*	P-38J
97 FS, 82 FG	C*	P-38J
307 FS, 31 FG	MX	Spitfire V
308 FS, 31 FG	HL	Spitfire V
309 FS, 31 FG	WZ	Spitfire V
162 RS, 1- PG	1X	P-5; F-6
32 BS, 301 BG	A	B-17F, G
340 BS, 97 BG	0*	B-17F, G
341 BS, 97 BG	1*	B-17F, G
342 BS, 97 BG	2*	B-17F, G
346 BS, 99 BG	I	B-17F, G
347 BS, 99 BG	II	B-17F, G
348 BS, 99 BG	III	B-17F, G
352 BS, 301 BG	B	B-17F, G
353 BS, 301 BG	C	B-17F, G
414 BS, 97 BG	4*	B-17F, G
416 BS, 99 BG	IV	B-17F, G
419 BS, 301 BG	D	B-17F, G

15th Air Force

Unit	Code	Type(s)
756 BS, 459 BG	6*	B-24H
757 BS, 459 BG	7*	B-24H
758 BS, 459 BG	8*	B-24H
759 BS, 459 BG	9*	B-24H

APPENDIX B

US Army

The US Army used a very large number of light aircraft (estimated at 3,000) in Europe between 1942 and 1945. They were mainly used for liaison and artillery spotting purposes and most had unit codes applied in a similar way to the system shared by the RAF and USAAF.

In northern Europe the army units were allocated two-digit codes, while in the Mediterranean theatre two-letter codes were applied. The system in Italy and southern Europe extended to British, French and Canadian units. In many cases there were no individual aircraft letters while some aircraft had twocharacter individual identifiers. In general the letters I and O were not used to avoid confusion with 1 and 0.

In the table below the identified codes are shown by unit. This list is based on the work of Ken Wakefield, who first described the system in an article in Aviation News in October 1991 and then in greater detail in his books The Fighting Grasshoppers and Lightplanes at War. The allocation of units is believed to be correct for around June 1944, although some units transferred between armies at this time. Where the deployment of units to Armies is uncertain they have been shown at the end of the section.

EUROPEAN THEATRE Twelfth Army Group

Unit	Code	Type(s)
1st US Army		
153rd Liaison Sqn	8R	L-5
Arty HQ, 1st Army	23	L-4; L-5
82nd AB Div	57	L-5B
101st AB Div	58	L-4; L-5
18th FA Gp	59	L-4
V Corps Arty	39	L-4H
1st Inf Div	34	L-4
VII Corps Arty	26	L-4H
4th Inf Div	36	L-4, L-5
9th Inf Div	33	L-4; L-5
79th Inf Div	46	L-4, L-5
XIX Corps Arty	?	L-5
2nd Arm Div	49	L-4H
3rd Arm Div	52	L-
30th Inf Div	44	L-4
119/228 FA Gps	32	L-4
8th Arm Div	21	L-
35th Inf Div	45	L-4H
69th Inf Div	51	L-4

Unit	Code	Type(s)
76th Inf Div	37	L-4
84th Inf Div	87	L-4
3rd US Army		
14 LS	6C	L-5, UC-78
Arty HQ, 3rd Army	24	L-4; L5
VIII Corps Arty	62	L-4; L-5
4th Arm Div	53	L-4H; L-5
6th Arm Div	55	L-4; L-5
8th Inf Div	38	L-4
79th Inf Div	?	L-4
XV Corps Arty	29	L-4H
5th Inf Div	?	L-4; L-5
83rd Inf Div	47	L-4; L-5
90th Inf Div	48	L-4; L-5
XII Corps Arty	28	L-5E
XII Corps Arty	69	L-4; L-5
XX Corps Arty	?	L-4, L-5
2nd French Arm Div	72	L-4
103rd Inf Div	93	L-4B
106th Inf Div	94	L-4
9th US Army		
125 LS	?	L-5
Arty HQ, 9th Army	63	L-4H
III Corps Arty	62	L-4; L-5
10th Arm Div	? 78	L-L-4; L-5
26th Inf Div	74	L-4H; L-5C
44th Inf Div	?	L-4; L-5
95th Inf Div	?	L-4; L-5
102nd Inf Div	?	L-4; L-5
104th Inf Div	?	L-4; L-5
VIII Corps Arty	?	L-4; L-5
5th Arm Div	54	L-4J
2nd Inf Div	25	L-4
29th Inf Div	43	L-4; L-5
XIII Corps Arty	68	L-4H
9th Arm Div	67	L-4
94th Inf Div	65	L-4; L-5
Deployment not known		
173rd Liaison Sqn	L1	L-5
7th Arm Div	56	L-4
14th Arm Div	97	L-4
?16th Arm Div	40	L-4
17th AB Div	73	L-4

Unit	Code	Type(s)
? 42nd Inf Div	70	L-4
78th Inf Div	86	L-4
86th Inf Div	13	L-4
99th Inf Div	89	L-4
?	76	L-4
280th FA Bn	79	L-4
100th Inf Div	92	L-4B

MEDITERRANEAN THEATRE

Unit	Code	Type(s)
5th US Army Italy, Central Europe		
121 LS	?	L-4; L-5
5th Army Arty HQ	A	L-4
II Corps Arty HQ	B	L-4; L-5
1st Arm Div Arty HQ	AA	L-4
1st Arm Div, 27th Arm FA Bn	AB	L-4
1st Arm Div, 68th Arm FA Bn	AC	L-4
1st Arm Div, 91st Arm FA Bn	AD	L-4
18th FA Bgde HQ	GA	L-4
932nd FA Bn	GD	L-4
936th FA Bn	GF	L-4
937th FA Bn	GG	L-4
985th FA Bn	GI	L-4
71st FA Bgde HQ	HA	L-4
194th FA Bn	HB	L-4
935th FA Bn	HC	L-4
995th FA Bn	HG	L-4
77th FA Gp	G	L-4
34th Inf Div Arty HQ	CA	L-4
34th Inf Div, 125th FA Bn	CB	L-4
34th Inf Div, 151st FA Bn	CC	L-4
34th Inf Div, 175th FA Bn	CD	L-4
34th Inf Div, 185th FA Bn	CE	L-4
13th FA Bgde	FA	L-4
1st Bn 17th Regt and 17th FA Bn	FB	L-4
2nd Bn 17th Regt and 630th FA Bn	FC	L-4
1st Bn 36th Regt and 36th FA Bn	FD	L-4
2nd Bn 36th Regt and 633rd FA Bn	FE	L-4
1st Bn 178th Regt and 178th FA Bn	FF	L-4
2nd Bn 178th Regt and 194th FA Bn	FG	L-4
173rd FA Bn	FI	L-4
141st FA Bn	GB	L-4
173rd FA Bn	GC	L-4
933rd FA Bn	GE	L-4
938th FA Bn	GH	L-4
88th Inf Div, Arty HQ	SA	L-4
88th Inf Div, 337th FA Bn	SB	L-4
88th Inf Div, 338th FA Bn	SC	L-4
88th Inf Div, 339th FA Bn	SD	L-4
88th Inf Div, 913th FA Bn	SE	L-4
91st Inf Div Arty HQ	NA	L-4, L-5
91st Inf Div, 346th FA Bn	NB	L-4
91st Inf Div, 347th FA Bn	NC	L-4

Unit	Code	Type(s)
91st Inf Div, 348th FA Bn	ND	L-4
91st Inf Div, 916th FA Bn	NE	L-4
85th Inf Div, Arty HQ	TA	L-4
85th Inf Div, 328th FA Bn	TB	L-4
85th Inf Div, 329th FA Bn	TC	L-4
85th Inf Div, 403rd FA Bn	TD	L-4
85th Inf Div, 910th FA Bn	TE	L-4
IV Corps Arty HQ	M	L-4, L-5
HQ First DMI Arty Regt (French)	KA	L-4
1st Bn (French)	KB	L-4
2nd Bn (French)	KC	L-4
3rd Bn (French)	KD	L-4
4th Bn (French)	KE	L-4
HQ RACL (French)	WA	L-4
1st Bn (French)	WB	L-4
2nd Bn (French)	WC	L-4
HQ 63rd RAA (French)	ZA	L-4
1st Bn (French)	ZB	L-4
2nd Bn (French)	ZC	L-4
3rd Bn (French)	ZD	L-4
HQ 64th RAA (French)	YA	L-4
1st Bn (French)	YB	L-4
2nd Bn (French)	YC	L-4
3rd Bn (French)	YD	L-4
HQ 67th RAA (French)	XA	L-4
1st Bn (French)	XB	L-4
2nd Bn (French)	XC	L-4
3rd Bn (French)	XD	L-4
4th Bn (French)	XE	L-4
HQ 69th RAA (French)	IA	L-4
1st Bn (French)	IB	L-4
2nd Bn (French)	IC	L-4
3rd Bn (French)	ID	L-4

7th US Army Southern France

Unit	Code	Type(s)
72 LS	?	L-5
7th Army Arty HQ	?	L-4, L-5
VI Corps Arty HQ	C	L-4; L-5
17th FA Gp, 7th Army	E	L-4
3rd Inf Div Arty HQ	BA	L-4B
3rd Inf Div, 9th FA Bn	BB	L-4
3rd Inf Div, 10th FA Bn	BC	L-4
3rd Inf Div, 39th FA Bn	BD	L-4
3rd Inf Div, 41st FA Bn	BE	L-4
36th Inf Div, Arty HQ	DA	L-4
36th Inf Div, 131st FA Bn	DB	L-4
36th Inf Div, 132nd FA Bn	DC	L-4
36th Inf Div, 133rd FA Bn	DD	L-4
36th Inf Div, 155th FA Bn	DE	L-4
45th Inf Div Arty HQ	EA	L-4
45th Inf Div, 158th FA Bn	EB	L-4
45th Inf Div, 160th FA Bn	EC	L-4
45th Inf Div, 171st FA Bn	ED	L-4
45th Inf Div, 189th FA Bn	EE	L-4

Unit	Code	Type(s)	Unit	Code	Type(s)
6th FA Gp HQ	JA	L-4	601st FA Bn	UB	L-4
59th Arm FA Bn	JB	L-4	602nd Glider FA Bn	UC	L-4
69th Arm FA Bn	JC	L-4	French Corps	J	L-4
93rd Arm FA Bn	JD	L-4	**Deployment not known**		
35th FA Gp	K	L-4	178th FA Gp	H	L-4
35th FA Gp HQ	LA	L-4	194th FA Gp HQ	N	L-4
1st Bn 77th FA Regt	LB	L-4	248th FA Bn	FJ	L-4
2nd Bn 77th FA Regt	LC	L-4	631st FA Bn	FK	L-4
36th FA Gp	F	L-4	932nd FA Bn	FN	L-4
141st FA Bn	FH	L-4	933rd FA Bn	FO	L-4
634th FA Bn	FL	L-4	935th FA Bn	FP	L-4
937th FA Bn	FS	L-4	936th FA Bn	FR	L-4
938th FA Bn	FT	L-4	939th FA Bn	FU	L-4
939th FA Bn	HD	L-4	976th FA Bn	FV	L-4
976th FA Bn	HE	L-4	977th FA Bn	FX	L-4
977th FA Bn	HF	L-4	985th FA Bn	FY	L-4
460th Para FA Bn	UD	L-4	995th FA Bn	FZ	L-4
463rd Para FA Bn	UE	L-4	697th FA Bn	OB	L-4
522nd FA Bn	UF	L-4	698th FA Bn	OC	L-4

Above: The code R-8 either side of the US national marking indicates that this Stinson L-5 Sentinel, 42-98989, belongs to B Flight of the 153rd Liaison6Sqn which was part of the US 1st Army in France. (L. Shrum via K. G. Wakefield)

Left: Seen during the drive across the Volturno River toward Cassino, on 14 December 1943, Piper L-4B 43-671 belongs to the 3rd Infantry Division6Artillery HQ, and is thus coded BA. The FA serial prefix indicates Field Artillery. (USAF via K. G. Wakefield)

APPENDIX C

Fleet Air Arm

The coding system in use by the Fleet Air Arm (FAA) during the war dated from May 1939 and included catapult squadrons and training units. The unit code was a letter/number combination which, unlike the RAF system, was based on logic. The second element – a number – denoted the class of aircraft (for example 6 was fighter) while the letter which preceded it denoted the parent carrier or shore base. For catapult aircraft, typically carried on capital ships, the prefix letter would denote the vessel or formation. The individual aircraft letter was carried after the unit code.

There were variations on the scheme. From about 1942 a number of embarked units took to using just the carrier and individual aircraft letters (no type numbers). Then from 1944 embarked units used the carrier letter to denote the embarked air wing rather than the host carrier. Further, the codes could be repeated but usually only between, not within, theatres. Where the number of aircraft in the unit exceeded the number of letters available (usually in training units),various ways were found of duplicating individual aircraft letters. Finally, to add to the confusion, aircraft used in the United States for training usually had a further letter between the base and function characters. Full details are given at the end of the table.

The details shown below are only those necessary to identify the unit. They are taken in full from The Squadrons of the Fleet Air Arm by Ray Sturtivant (see Bibliography), which is the standard reference on the subject. Great care needs to be taken when researching FAA codes since the presentation could come in many forms, most of which are illustrated in the aforementioned reference.

Unit	Code	Type(s)	Carrier/base
700	Y2	Firefly, Seafire XV, Oxford, Harvard III	Yeovilton
701	B8	not used	1st Battle Sqn
701	C8	Swordfish I	1st Battle Sqn
701	L0	Oxford I, Traveller I, Heston, Harvard III, Dominie I, Seafire XV, Expeditor I, Anson X	
702	E8	Swordfish	2nd Battle Sqn
704	FD3	Mosquito III, VI	Ford, Thorney Island
705	AR1	Swordfish II	Ronaldsway
705	B8	Swordfish I	Battle Cruiser Sqn
705	C8	not used	Battle Cruiser Sqn

Unit	Code	Type(s)	Carrier/base
707	AH8	Avenger III	Burscough
707	O7	Swordfish II, III	Burscough
707	O8	Barracuda III	Burscough
708	O	Firebrand II	Gosport
709	S3	Harvard IIb, III	St Merryn
709	S5	Hellcat I, II, Seafire III,	F.45 St Merryn
709	S6	Hellcat I	St Merryn
710	A9	Walrus I	HMS Albatross
710	AR6	Barracuda II	Ronaldsway
710	AR7	Barracuda II	Ronaldsway
710	AR2	Barracuda II, Anson I	Ronaldsway
710	AR3	Barracuda II	Ronaldsway
710	AR4	Barracuda II	Ronaldsway
710	AR5	Barracuda II	Ronaldsway
710	R2	Barracuda II, III	Ronaldsway
710	R3	Barracuda II, III	Ronaldsway
710	R4	Barracuda II	Ronaldsway
710	R5	Barracuda II	Ronaldsway
710	R6	Barracuda II	Ronaldsway
710	R7	Barracuda III	Ronaldsway
711	C6	Barracuda II, Reliant, Avenger	Crail
711	F9	Walrus	1st Cruiser Sqn
711	C1	Swordfish I, II, Albacore I, Barracuda II, Avenger I	Crail
711	C2	Swordfish I, Albacore I, Anson I, Barracuda II, Avenger I	Crail
711	C3	Anson I, Barracuda I	Crail
711	C4	Barracuda II, Avenger, Swordfish I	Crail
711	C5	Albacore I, Barracuda II, Avenger	Crail
711	C6	Barracuda II	Crail
712	G9	Walrus I	2nd Cruiser Sqn
712	H9	Reliant, Sea Otter	Hatston
713	AR2	Barracuda II, Anson I	Ronaldsway
713	AR3	Barracuda II	Ronaldsway
713	AR4	Barracuda II	Ronaldsway
713	AR5	Barracuda II	Ronaldsway
713	R2	Barracuda II, III	Ronaldsway
713	R3	Barracuda II, III	Ronaldsway
713	R4	Barracuda II	Ronaldsway
713	R5	Barracuda II	Ronaldsway

Unit	Code	Type(s)	Carrier/base	Unit	Code	Type(s)	Carrier/base
713	R6	Barracuda II	Ronaldsway			Corsair III	
713	R7	Barracuda III	Ronaldsway	736	S3	Firefly FRI	St Merryn
713	H9	Seafox I	3rd Cruiser Sqn	736B	Y-	Seafire LIII	Speke, Woodvale
714	AT1	Barracuda II	Rattray				Farm
714	AT2	Barracuda II	Rattray	737	A1	Barracuda II, III	Arbroath
714	I1	Barracuda II	Rattray	737	A2	Swordfish I, Anson I	Arbroath
714	I2	Barracuda II	Rattray	737	D1	Walrus I	Dunino
714	J9	Walrus I	4th Cruiser Sqn	737	K4	Anson, Swordfish II	Inskip
714	I3	Barracuda II	Rattray	738	V7	Avenger I, II, III	Brunswick
714	F1	Barracuda II	Fearn	738	?V8	Corsair II	Bar Harbour
714	F2	Barracuda II	Fearn	740	A4	Albacore	Arbroath
715	K9	Walrus I	5th Cruiser Sqn	740	A5	Walrus	Arbroath
715	S4	Seafire III, XVII, Corsair III	St Merryn	740	AA5	Walrus	Arbroath
716	I0	Sea Otter I	Eastleigh	740	M9	Walrus I, Reliant I, Oxford	Machrihanish
716	L9	Seafox	6th Cruiser Sqn	741	S3	Firefly FRI	St Merryn
717	I3	Barracuda II	Rattray	741	A2	Swordfish	Arbroath
717	F1	Barracuda II	Fearn	741	A3	Swordfish I, II	Arbroath
717	F2	Barracuda II	Fearn	741	S2	Firefly FRI	St Merryn
717	AT3	Barracuda II	Rattray	741	S5	Firefly FRI, Seafire III, XVII	St Merryn
717	AT4	Barracuda II	Rattray	744	K7	Swordfish II	Machrihanish
717	I4	Barracuda II	Rattray	744	N4	Barracuda II	Maydown
718	BH1	Seafire III	Ballyhalbert	744	N6	Barracuda II, III, Avenger II	Maydown
718	BH2	Corsair III, IV	Ballyhalbert	744	N7	Swordfish II, III	Maydown
718	BH6	Seafire III	Ballyhalbert	746	L0	Fulmar II	Wittering
718	C9	Seafox	8th Cruiser Sqn	747	AR2	Barracuda II, Anson I	Ronaldsway
718	G3	Spitfire PR XIII	Henstridge	747	AR3	Barracuda II	Ronaldsway
718	G1	Spitfire Vb, Seafire Ib, III	Henstridge	747	AR4	Barracuda II	Ronaldsway
718	G3	Seafire III	Henstridge	747	AR5	Barracuda II	Ronaldsway
719	S1	Spitfire Vb, Wildcat IV	St Merryn	747	R2	Barracuda II, III	Ronaldsway
719	A4	Firefly FR.1	HMS Implacable	747	R3	Barracuda II, III	Ronaldsway
720	FD8	Anson I, Oxford	Ford	747	R4	Barracuda II	Ronaldsway
720	P9	Walrus I	NZ Sqn	747	R5	Barracuda II	Ronaldsway
722	T8	Reliant	Tambaram	747	R6	Barracuda II	Ronaldsway
722	T9	Martinet TTI	Tambaram	747	R7	Barracuda III	Ronaldsway
723	N8	Corsair, Martinet I	Nowra	747	F1	Barracuda II	Fearn
727	GP2	Tiger Moth II, Harvard III, Seafire XV	Gosport	747	F2	Barracuda II	Fearn
				747	K2	Barracuda II	Inskip
728	M8	Martinet I, Seafire IIc, III, Mosquito XXV, Beaufort I	Ta Kali	747	? F4	Barracuda II	Fearn
				748	P7	Corsair III, Hellcat I	Dale
729	K7	Oxford, Harvard	Katukurunda	748	S7	Wildcat I, V, Corsair III, IV, Spitfire Va, Seafire Ib, III, Harvard III	St Merryn
730	AR0	Firefly I Ayr					
731	E3	Swordfish, Seafire Ib, Barracuda II, Firefly I, Fulmar II, Corsair III	East Haven	749	W2	Walrus, Goose	Piarco
				750	B	Barracuda II	Piarco
731 ?	E4	Firefly I	East Haven	750	W0	Shark II Ford,	Piarco
731 ?	E6	Firefly I	East Haven	750	W1	Shark II Ford,	Piarco
732	D2	Anson I, Hellcat II	NF Drem	751	A4	Walrus	Arbroath
733	C8	Barracuda II, Avenger I, II	China Bay	751	AA4	Walrus	Dundee
733	C9	Wildcat V	China Bay	751	AA5	Walrus	Dundee
734	W0	Whitley VII	Worthy Down	751	W9	Walrus	Ford, Arbroath
735	AH4	Barracuda II, Hellcat I	Burscough	752	W0	Proctor Ia	Ford
735	AH7	Anson I	Burscough	752	W3	Proctor I, II, IIa	Ford, Piarco
735	O1	Barracuda II, III	Burscough	753	A3	Swordfish I	Arbroath
735	O4	Barracuda II	Burscough	753	A4	Swordfish, Albacore, Barracuda II	Arbroath
736	AC	Barracuda II, Seafire Ib, Avenger II, Wellington XI,	St Merryn	753	A5	Albacore, Barracuda II,	Arbroath

Unit	Code	Type(s)	Carrier/base	Unit	Code	Type(s)	Carrier/base
		Reliant		761	G4	Seafire III	Henstridge
753	A6	Barracuda II	Arbroath	761	G5	Seafire III, Defiant TT III	Henstridge
753	A7	Barracuda II	Arbroath	761	G6	Seafire III	Henstridge
753	W4	Shark II, Swordfish I,	Lee-on-Solent,	762	FD5	Oxford I	Ford
		Albacore I	Arbroath	762	FD6	Beaufort II, Mosquito III, VI	Ford
754	A1	Lysander, Albacore	Arbroath	762	HA3	Beaufort II, Mosquito XXV	Halesworth
754	A5	Lysander, Albacore	Arbroath	762	L9	Beaufighter I	Lee-on-Solent
754	W5	Seafox I, Walrus	Lee-on-Solent,	762	P1	Beaufort II, Wellington XI	Dale
			Arbroath	762	P2	Oxford	Dale
755	W6	Lysander III, IIIa,		763	K5	Avenger I, II	Inskip
		Proctor IIa, Seamew I	Worthy Down	763	P5	Swordfish I	Lee-on-Solent
755	X3	Shark II	Worthy Down	763	Y4	Swordfish	Worthy Down
756	K	Swordfish II	Katukurunda	764	Y9	Swordfish I	Lee-on-Solent
756	K1	Avenger I, II	Katukurunda	765	BL3	Kingfisher I, Walrus	Sandbanks
757	P	Reliant I, Harvard IIb,	Puttalam	765	L3	Walrus I	Lee-on-Solent,
		Seafire III					Sandbanks
757	T	Corsair IV	Tambaram	765	L8	Wellington X, XI	Lee-on-Solent
757	X6	Osprey III	Worthy Down	765	Y8	Swordfish I, Seafox I	Lee-on-Solent
758	U1	Oxford	Hinstock	766	I1	Firefly FRI	Rattray
758	U2	Oxford, Harvard III,	Hinstock	766	I2	Firefly FR I	Rattray
		Tiger Moth II		766	I3	Firefly FR I	Rattray
758	U3	Oxford, Anson I,	Hinstock	766	I6	Firefly FR I	Rattray
		Tiger Moth, Harvard IIb, III		766	I7	Firefly FR I	Rattray
758	X5	Skua II, Osprey III, Shark	Worthy Down,	766	K1	Swordfish II, III, Firefly I,	Inskip
			Eastleigh			Sea Hurricane IIc	
758 ?	T3	Anson I		766	K2	Swordfish II, III, Firefly I	Inskip
758X	J4	Oxford	Eglinton	766	K3	Swordfish II, III,	Inskip
759	Y1	Sea Hurricane Ib,	Yeovilton			Master GT.II	
		Wildcat IV, V, Spitfire I, Vb,		766	K5	Firefly I	Inskip
		Seafire Ib, Corsair III		767	IT1	Firefly I	Milltown
759	Y2	Oxford, Master I,	Yeovilton	767	IT2	Firefly I	Milltown
		Spitfire Va, Vb, Seafire III,		767	IT3	Firefly I, Seafire III	Milltown
		Sea Hurricane Ib,		767	IT4	Firefly I	Milltown
		Corsair III, Harvard III,		767	IT5	Firefly I	Milltown
		Wildcat IV, V		767	IT6	Firefly I	Milltown
759	Y3	Spitfire I, Vb, Seafire IIc, III,	Yeovilton	767	IT7	Firefly I	Milltown
		Tiger Moth, Corsair III,		767	T0	Albacore I	Arbroath
		Harvard III, Wildcat IV, V		767	T4	Swordfish I, Albacore I	Donibristle,
759	Y4	Seafire III, Wildcat V,	Yeovilton				Hyeres,
		Corsair III					Arbroath
759	Y5	Seafire III, Harvard III,	Yeovilton	767	T-	Swordfish	Donibristle,
		Corsair III					Hyeres
759	Y6	Seafire III, Harvard III,	Yeovilton	767	A1	Swordfish	Arbroath
		Wildcat V, Corsair III		767	E1	Firefly I, Barracuda II	East Haven
759	Y7	Seafire, Corsair III	Yeovilton	767	E2	Swordfish, Albacore I	East Haven
760	K1	Sea Hurricane IIc	Inskip	768	B2	Spitfire Vb, Swordfish,	East Haven,
760	L2	Seafire III	Lee-on-Solent			Barracuda, Traveller,	Donibristle
760	P7	Skua II, Roc I? Eastleigh,	Yeovilton			Firefly I	
760	W7	Sea Hurricane Ib	Yeovilton	768	E2	Seafire III, Corsair IV,	East Haven
760	W8	Sea Hurricane Ib	Yeovilton			Barracuda II	
760	W9	Sea Hurricane Ib	Yeovilton	768	M2	Wildcat I, Swordfish II,	Machrihanish
760	Y7	Skua II, Roc	Eastleigh			Sea Hurricane Ib,	
760 ?	W4	Sea Hurricane	Yeovilton			Spitfire Vb, Seafire IIc	
761	G1	Spitfire Vb, Seafire Ib, III	Henstridge	769	A1	Swordfish	Arbroath
761	G3	Seafire III	Henstridge	769	E1	Firefly I, Barracuda II	East Haven
761	G2	Seafire III	Henstridge	769	E2	Swordfish, Albacore I	East Haven

Unit	Code	Type(s)	Carrier/base
769	E4	Barracuda II	East Haven
769	I5	Barracuda II	Rattray
769	I6	Barracuda II	Rattray
769	T6	Sea Gladiator	Donibristle
770	B8	Blenheim IV	Donibristle
770	C8	Skua II	Crail
770	D8	Seafire IIc, Blenheim IV	Drem
771	GP0	Oxford I	Gosport
771	GP8	Mosquito XXV, Martinet TTI	Gosport
771	GP9	Seafire III, XV	Gosport
771	R5	Swordfish I, Henley III, Skua II, Defiant TTI, Chesapeake, Roc I,	Hatston, Twatt
771	T8	Blenheim IV, Martinet I, Boston II, III, Corsair II, Roc I, Skua II, Swordfish I, Gladiator, Hurricane IIc, Havoc I	Twatt
771	Z8	Wildcat IV	Zeals
772	AR8	Martinet TTI, Mosquito XVI, XXV	Ayr
772	AR9	Boston III, Corsair III	Ayr
772	BR8	Blenheim IV, Firefly NFII, Beaufighter X	Ayr
772	K9	Fulmar II	Machrihanish
772	M8	Chesapeake I, Fulmar I, Skua II, Walrus, Blenheim IV	Machrihanish
772	O8	Martinet TTI	Burscough
772	O9	Seafire III	Burscough
772	R3	Swordfish I	Portland, Lee-on-Solent
772 ?	AR	Defiant TTIII	Ayr
772 ?	BR8	Corsair III	Ayr
772 ?	BR9	Corsair III	Ayr
772 ?	O0	Martinet TTI	Burscough
773	R4	Swordfish I, Walrus I	Bermuda
774	O4	Shark II, Swordfish I	Aldergrove
774	S6	Swordfish I, Albacore I, Barracuda II	St Merryn
776	R7	Hurricane IIc	Woodvale
776	R8	Martinet TTI, Swordfish II, Traveller, Hurricane IIc	Woodvale
776 ?	V9	Martinet I	Woodvale ?
778	C0	Swordfish I, Barracuda II, Martlet IV, Firefly I, Corsair	Crail
778	FD9	Seafire III, XV, Barracuda II	Ford
778	X0	?	Lee-on-Solent, Arbroath
780	BY1	Swordfish I, II	Charlton Horethorne
780	L1	Barracuda II, Blenheim I, Tiger Moth II, Swordfish I, Proctor Ia	Lee-on-Solent
780	U1	Seafire XV, Oxford, Firefly I	Hinstock

Unit	Code	Type(s)	Carrier/base
780	U2	Harvard IIb, III, Lancaster	Hinstock, Peplow
780	U3	Oxford Hinstock	
781	L0	Swordfish I Lee-on-Solent	
781	L0	Hudson IV Heath Row	
781	L8	Oxford II Lee-on-Solent	
781	L9	Oxford I, Dominie, Vega Gull, Walrus, Proctor Ia, Swordfish I	Lee-on-Solent
781	Q1	?	Lee-on-Solent
782	B8	Dominie I	Donibristle
783	A0	Anson I, Wellington I, Firefly FR.I, Avenger I, Barracuda II, Walrus, DH.86, Swordfish II	Arbroath
783	A6	Anson I, Swordfish	Arbroath
784	D2	Anson I, Hellcat II NF	Drem
784	B0	Fulmar I, II, Anson I, Reliant	Drem
784	D1	Firefly I NF	Drem
784	D3	Anson I	Drem
784	D5	Hellcat IINF	Drem
784	P3	Anson I	Dale
784	P8	Firefly I	Dale
785	C1	Swordfish I, II, Albacore I, Barracuda II, Avenger I	Crail
785	C2	Swordfish I, Albacore I, Anson I, Barracuda II, Avenger I	Crail
785	C3	Anson I, Barracuda I	Crail
785	C4	Barracuda II, Avenger, Swordfish I	Crail
785	C5	Albacore I, Barracuda II, Avenger	Crail
786	C1	Swordfish I, II, Albacore I, Barracuda II, Avenger I	Crail
786	C2	Swordfish I, Albacore I, Anson I, Barracuda II, Avenger I	Crail
786	C3	Anson I, Barracuda I	Crail
786	C4	Barracuda II, Avenger, Swordfish I	Crail
786	C5	Albacore I, Barracuda II, Avenger	Crail
786	C7	Anson I, Swordfish, Reliant	Crail
786	C8	Anson I, Reliant	Crail
787	YO-	Fulmar I, Sea Hurricane IIc, Swordfish	Wittering, Tangmere
789	W8	Martinet TTI, Beaufighter II	Wingfield
789	W9	Beaufighter II	Wingfield
790	BY0	Oxford Charlton	Horethorne
790	Y0	Oxford Charlton	Horethorne
790	Z0	Firefly I	Zeals
790	Z1	Mosquito XXV	Zeals
790	Z8	Firefly I	Zeals
790	P0	Mosquito XXV	Dale
790 ?	P2	Firefly I	Dale
790 ?	P3	Oxford, Seafire III	Dale

Unit	Code	Type(s)	Carrier/base	Unit	Code	Type(s)	Carrier/base
790	P7	Mosquito IV	Dale	803	A8	Skua II	HMS Ark Royal
790B	D1	Firefly I NF	Drem	803	S6	Skua II Wick,	Hatston
790B	P8	Firefly I	Dale	804	C6	not used	HMS Courageous
791	A8	Swordfish I, II, Skua II,	Arbroath	804	C6	Hellcat II	29th Naval
		Roc I, Defiant TT.I,					Fighter Wing
		Sea Hurricane Ib,		804	C8	Hellcat II	29th Naval
		Blenheim IV					Fighter Wing
791	A9	Albacore	Arbroath	804	K6	Hellcat II	3rd Naval
792	S8	Martinet TTI, Defiant TTIII	St Merryn				Fighter Wing
793	W5	Reliant I	Piarco	804	O8	Hellcat II	29th Naval
793	W6	Roc I, Albacore	Piarco				Fighter Wing
793	W7	Fulmar I, II	Piarco	804	S7	Sea Hurricane Ia, Ib	Hatston, Belfast
793	W8	Martinet TTI	Piarco	805	C7	not used	HMS Courageous
794	A4	Firefly FR.1	HMS Implacable	805	O5	Seafire XV, Firefly FR.1	HMS Ocean
794	A5	Seafire III	HMS Implacable	806	L6	Skua II, Roc I	HMS Illustrious
794	BY8	Defiant TTIII	Charlton	806B	O	Fulmar II	HMS Illustrious
			Horethorne	807	D5	Seafire III	4th Naval
794	J1	Corsair III	Eglinton				Fighter Wing
794	J2	Seafire III	Eglinton	807	H	Seafire IIc, III	HMS Hunter
794	J3	Wildcat VI	Eglinton	808	C7	Hellcat II	29th Naval
794	J4	Martinet TT.1	Eglinton				Fighter Wing
794	P1	Sea Hurricane Ib	Dale	808	K6	Hellcat I, II	3rd Naval
794	P2	Master II	Dale				Fighter Wing
794	P8	Defiant TTI, Martinet TTI	Dale	809	D6	Seafire III	3rd Naval
794	S1	Seafire IIc	St Merryn				Fighter Wing
794	Y8	Defiant TTI Charlton	Horethorne	809	S	Seafire IIc, III	HMS Stalker
795	A4	Firefly FR.1	HMS Implacable	810	A2	Swordfish I	HMS Ark Royal
797	L9	Beaufighter II	Colombo	810	N6	Barracuda III	HMS Queen
797	R8	Defiant TT	Colombo	811	FD4	Mosquito VI, TR.33	Ford
798	L1	Barracuda II, Blenheim I,	Lee-on-Solent	811	U4	Swordfish I	HMSs Furious,
		Beaufort I, Beaufighter II,					Courageous
		Seafire IIc		812	A2	Swordfish I	HMS Argus
798	L2	Master II, Barracuda II,	Lee-on-Solent	812	G3	Swordfish I	HMS Glorious
		Firefly I, Harvard III		812	N1	Barracuda II	HMS Vengeance
798	L3	Spitfire Vb, Seafire IIc,	Lee-on-Solent	812	R2	Swordfish I	HMS Argus
		Tiger Moth II,		812	V4	Firefly I	HMS Vengeance
		Harvard IIb, III, Avenger II		813	E4	Swordfish I	HMS Eagle
798	L4	Seafire IIc	Lee-on-Solent	813	FD1	Firebrand IV	Ford
798	U2	Harvard III Hinstock,	Peplow	813	G	Swordfish II	HMS Campania
798?	L1	Oxford	Lee-on-Solent	814	A3	Swordfish I	HMS Ark Royal
800	A6	Skua II, Roc I	HMS Ark Royal	814	B1	Barracuda II	HMS Venerable
800	C3	Hellcat IINF	29th Naval	814	H3	Swordfish I	HMS Ark Royal
			Fighter Wing	814	R1	Barracuda	HMS Venerable
800	E	Hellcat I, II	HMS Emperor	815	C3	not used	HMS Courageous
800	K3	Hellcat II	3rd Naval	815	I7	Barracuda III	Rattray
			Fighter Wing	815	L3	Swordfish I	HMS Illustrious
801	A7	Skua II	HMS Ark Royal	815	L4	Swordfish I	HMS Illustrious
801	P6	Seafire III	30th Naval	815	S6	Swordfish II	Mersa Matruh
			Fighter Wing	815	S7	Albacore I	Mersa Matruh
801	P8	Seafire III	30th Naval	815	U3	Swordfish I	HMS Furious
			Fighter Wing	816	C4	not used	HMS Courageous
801	U6	Skua II	HMS Furious	816	O6	Firefly FR.I	HMS Ocean
801	P7	Seafire III	30th Naval	816	U4	Swordfish I	HMS Furious
			Fighter Wing	817	C5	not used	HMS Courageous
802	G6	Sea Gladiator	HMS Glorious	818	A3	Swordfish I	HMS Ark Royal
803	A7	Skua II	HMS Ark Royal	818	A5	Swordfish I	HMS Ark Royal

Unit	Code	Type(s)	Carrier/base	Unit	Code	Type(s)	Carrier/base
818	U3	Swordfish I	HMS Furious	892	O5	Hellcat IINF	HMS Ocean
819	L5	Swordfish I	HMS Illustrious	893	Ø9	Wildcat IV	HMS Formidable
820	A4	Swordfish I	HMS Ark Royal	894	H6	Seafire III	24th Wing
821	A5	Swordfish I	HMS Ark Royal	894	P6	Seafire III	24th Naval
821	I8	Barracuda III	Rattray				Fighter Wing
821	N	Barracuda II, III	HMS Puncher	896	B7	Hellcat II	HMS Empress
821	S5	Albacore I	Hal Far	896	B8	Hellcat II	HMS Empress
822	U5	Swordfish I	HMSs Furious,	898	B0	Hellcat II	HMS Pursuer
			Courageous	898	B9	Hellcat II	HMS Pursuer
824	E5	Swordfish I	HMS Eagle	899	C	Seafire III	HMS Chaser
825	G5	Swordfish I	HMS Glorious	899	K	Seafire III	HMS Khedive
826	F4	Albacore I	HMS Formidable	1701?	P3	Sea Otter	Ponam
826	L4	Albacore I	HMS Illustrious	1702	O2	Sea Otter I	HMS Ocean
826	S4	Albacore I	Dekheila	1792	O4	Firefly INF	HMS Ocean
827	A1	Barracuda II	HMS Colossus	1830	A7	Corsair II	15th Naval
827	U1	Barracuda II	HMS Colossus				Fighter Wing
828	A1	Barracuda II	HMS Implacable	1831	Y8	Corsair IV	HMS Glory
828	S5	Albacore I	Hal Far	1833	A6	Corsair II	15th Naval
829	F5	Abacore I	HMS Formidable				Fighter Wing
831	K1	Avenger II	HMS Begum	1834	T7	Corsair II	47th Naval
835	Y	Swordfish III	HMS Nairana				Fighter Wing
835	Z	Swordfish III	HMS Nairana	1835	V11	Corsair IV	Brunswick
836	M1	Swordfish II	Macships Wing	1836	T8	Corsair II	47th Naval
836	M2	Swordfish II	Macships Wing				Fighter Wing
836	M3	Swordfish III	Macships Wing	1839	R5	Hellcat I, II	5th Naval Fighter
836	M4	Swordfish III	Macships Wing				Wing
837	Y1	Barracuda II	HMS Glory	1840	K7	Hellcat II	3rd Naval Fighter
842	F	Wildcat V, Swordfish II	HMS Fencer				Wing
845	H1	Avenger I	HMS Empress	1844	R6	Hellcat I, II	5th Naval Fighter
846	J	Avenger I, II, Wildcat VI	HMS Trumpeter				Wing
849	P1	Avenger I, II	HMS Victorious	1845	V7	Corsair III	Brunswick
851	S	Avenger I	HMS Shah	1846	U5	Corsair IV	HMS Colossus
853	Q	Avenger II, Wildcat VI	HMS Queen	1846	U6	Corsair IV	HMS Colossus
853	T	Avenger II, Wildcat VI	HMS Tracker	1846	U7	Corsair IV	HMS Colossus
854	J4	Avenger I	HMS Illustrious	1846	V4	Corsair III	Brunswick
854	Q4	Avenger I	HMS Illustrious	1848	V9	Corsair I, II	Brunswick
856	P	Avenger II, Wildcat VI	HMS Premier	1849	V11	Corsair III	Brunswick
857	W1	Avenger II	HMS Indomitable	1850	N5	Corsair IV	HMS Vengeance
857	W7	Avenger II	HMS Indomitable	1850	V16	Corsair	Brunswick
879	A	Seafire IIc, III	HMS Attacker	1850	V8	Corsair IV	HMS Vengeance
879	D4	Seafire IIc, III	4th Naval	1851	R6	Corsair IV	HMS Venerable
			Fighter Wing	1851	V7	Corsair IV	Brunswick
880	P7	Seafire III	30th Naval	1852	V10	Corsair IV	Brunswick
			Fighter Wing	1853	V11	Corsair IV	Brunswick
881	B	Wildcat II	HMS Illustrious	FP ?	R1	Proctor	Stretton
881	U	Wildcat VI	HMS Purser	HQ Flt	G8	Walrus?	Hatston
882	S	Wildcat VI	HMS Searcher	SF	A9	Reliant	Arbroath
885	D6	Seafire IIc, III	3rd Naval Fighter	SF	AH8	Reliant I	Burscough
			Wing	SF	AR8	Oxford, Anson I	Ronaldsway
885	K8	Hellcat II	3rd Naval	SF	BR9	Sea Otter	Ayr
			Fighter Wing	SF	C9	Anson I	Crail
885	Ø6	Seafire IIc	HMS Formidable	SF	E8	Barracuda II, Reliant,	East Haven
887	H5	Seafire III	24th Wing			Tiger Moth T.2	
887	P5	Seafire III	24th Naval	SF	EL0	Reliant I, Dauntless I,	Eastleigh
			Fighter Wing			Sea Otter I, Tiger Moth II,	
888	Ø7	Wildcat II	HMS Formidable			Wellington Ic	

Unit	Code	Type(s)	Carrier/base
SF	F9	Reliant	Fearn
SF	G9	Reliant I, Tiger Moth T.2	Henstridge
SF	I9	Oxford I, Monospar ST25, Sea Otter I	Eastleigh
SF	J9	Traveller, Reliant I	Eglinton
SF	K8	Barracuda II, Reliant, Hellcat II	Katukurunda
SF	K9	Firefly FR.I	Inskip
SF	M9	Traveller	Machrihanish
SF	O9	Reliant I, Anson I	Burscough
SF	P0	Mosquito XXV	Dale
SF	P9	Reliant I, Oxford I, Anson I	Dale
SF	Q9	Oxford I, Reliant I	Belfast
SF	R0	Reliant I, Expeditor	Ronaldsway
SF	R9	Reliant I, Wellington	Stretton
SF	S9	Reliant I	St Merryn
SF	ST9	Dominie I, Oxford I	Stretton
SF	T9	Reliant	Twatt
SF	Y0	Oxford	Yeovilton
SF	Y9	Reliant I, Beaufort TII, Anson I, Wellington XI	Yeovilton
?	B9	Wildcat	?
?	D4	Albacore I	Donibristle
?	E1	Anson I	East Haven
?	G1	Swordfish III	Henstridge
?	I6	Seafire III	Rattray
?	KM2	Wildcat	
?	Q2	Firefly FR.1	?
VCS 7*	4	Seafire III, Spitfire Vb	Lee-on-Solent

* USN unit usually flying SOC Seagulls and attached to the Air Spotting Pool (808, 885 (coded 2), 886 (coded 3) and 897 NAS and 26 and 63 Sqns RAF) at D-Day using borrowed aircraft from FAA and RAF.

System

The system dated from May 1939 and included catapult squadrons and training units. The unit code was a letter number combination which could be repeated but usually only between, not within, theatres. The central number denoted class:

- 1–5 Spotter reconnaissance
- 6–7 Fighter
- 8 Catapult (wheeled with floats)
- 9 Catapult (floatplanes)
- 0 Experimental

The prefix letter denoted the parent carrier:

- A HMS *Ark Royal*
- B HMS *Indefatigable* (from 1940)
- C HMS *Courageous* (vacant from 1940)
- E HMS *Eagle*
- F HMS *Formidable*
- G HMS *Glorious*
- H HMS *Hermes*
- L HMS *Illustrious*

- M Under construction
- N HMS *Indomitable*
- O Observer training aircraft (1940 armament training)
- Ø HMS *Formidable* (Operation *Torch* 1942 only)
- P Converted liner carrier (1940 pools)
- Q Converted liner carrier (1940 comms and misc)
- R HMS *Argus* (1940 fleet requirements)
- S Shore-based operational squadrons (from 1940)
- T Flying training aircraft
- U HM *Furious*
- V HMS *Victorious*
- W Shore station aircraft
- X Experimental
- Y Shore station aircraft (1940 torpedo and fighter schools)
- Z Shore station aircraft

In practice O was used by operational pools, R by fleet requirements units, T by deck landing training squadrons, W for observer training squadrons, X by TAG squadrons except X8 (service trials unit), Y by fighter, seaplane and torpedo schools. When some schools became too large to maintain the numbers they were allowed to use the number element 0.

In the cases of catapult aircraft (numbers 8 and 9) the prefix letter denoted the parent ship or formation:

- A HMS *Albatross*
- B Battle cruiser squadron
- C 1st Battle Squadron
- D Battleships in reserve
- E 2nd Battle Squadron
- F 1st Cruiser Squadron
- G 2nd Cruiser Squadron
- H 3rd Cruiser Squadron
- J 4th Cruiser Squadron
- K 5th Cruiser Squadron
- L 6th Cruiser Squadron
- M Cruisers in reserve
- N 8th Cruiser Squadron
- P Armed merchant cruiser
- Q Armed merchant cruiser
- U Spare
- V Spare

By May 1941 some stations were using 1 and 2 for multi-seat aircraft. From May 1942 the letter element extended to cover the parent station for non-operational units; such was the growth that there were additions to this system in early 1943 to include two letters in some instances. Then from 1944 overseas bases were added with duplication; these are shown in italics in the list. The eventual list was:

- A Arbroath
- A *Addu Atoll (Gan, Indian Ocean), later Brisbane (Australia)*
- B Easthaven (Donibristle from 1943)
- B Bankstown (*Australia*)
- C Crail (from 1943)
- C *China Bay (Trincomalee) (Ceylon)*
- D Donibristle (Dunino 1943 then Drem)
- D *Dekheila (Egypt)*
- E Eastleigh (Easthaven from 1943)

F	Lawrenny Ferry (Fearn from 1943)		DO	Dunino
G	Henstridge (from 1943)		EL	Eastleigh
G	*Gibraltar*		EV	Evanton
H	Hatston		FD	Ford
H	*Hastings (Sierra Leone) later Cochin (India)*		GM	Grimsetter
I	Eastleigh (from 1943 then Crimond)		GP	Gosport
J	Eglinton		HA	Halesworth
J	*Jervis Bay (Australia)*		IT	Milltown
K	Machrihanish (Inskip from 1943)		ST	Stretton
K	*Katukurunda (Ceylon)*			
L	Lee-on-Solent			
L	*Colombo (Ceylon)*			
M	St Merryn (Machrihanish from 1943)			
M	*Ta Kali (Malta)*			
N	Henstridge (Maydown from 1943)			
N	*Kantali (Ceylon) later Nowra (Australia)*			
O	Burscough from 1943			
P	Campeltown (Dale from 1943)			
P	*Puttalam (Ceylon) later Ponam (Admiralty Is)*			
Q	Sydenham (from 1943)			
Q	Coimbatore (India)			
R	Stretton (Ronaldsway from 1943)			
R	*Port Reiz (Kenya) later Sulur (India)*			
S	Sandbanks (St Merryn from 1943)			
T	Twatt			
T	*Tambaram (India)*			
U	Hinstock (from 1943)			
V	Evanton (Woodvale from 1943)			
W	Worthy Down			
W	*Wingfield (South Africa)*			
X	Abbotsinch (from 1943)			
Y	Yeovilton			
Z	Grimsetter from 1943 (later Zeals)			
AA	Dundee			
AH	Burscough			
AN	Campbeltown; Anthorn			
AR	Ronaldsway; Ayr			
AT	Crimond (renamed Rattray)			
AY	Haldon			
BH	Ballyhalbert			
BY	Charlton Horethorne			
CM	Culham			

From October 1943 some embarked squadrons had taken to using just a letter denoting the carrier combined with an individual aircraft letter. In August 1944 a refined system for embarked units was devised, based on wings. This comprised a letter for the wing followed by a number for the squadron and then an individual aircraft letter. The wing letters were:

A	15
B	26
C	29
D	4
E	16
F	35
G	28
H	24
I	11
J	44
K	3
L	6
M	18 (Macships)
N	40
O	10
P	30
Q	43
R	5
S	49
T	47
U	22
V	42
W	7
X	33
Y	37
Z	13

The RN use of similar types to the RAF can lead to confusion with unit codes, as is illustrated by Seafire III coded S5-G which at first glance could easily be a Spitfire, especially as the European-style markings are so similar in monochrome photographs. (via R. C. Sturtivant)

In 1939 the Fleet Air Arm introduced unit codes on its aircraft, though they were often presented without a gap, as can be seen on Walrus I L2253/J9-G of No. 714 Sqn from HMS Manchester. (via R. C. Sturtivant)

At the same time the squadron type numbers changed:

1–3	TBR
4	Two-seat fighter and dive bomber
5–9 and 0	Fighters

The third character was the aircraft letter. As numbers grew, instead of using the 0 code for 'extra' aircraft, letters were duplicated but with a horizontal bar over the individual letter. From January 1943 this changed to the use of black individual letters for any duplications. However, some units adopted a two-letter individual identifier, whereas other units used a letter prefix to the unit code for the second series.

Squadrons working up in the United States used a central letter B (British), in the form 2BA while others, especially those operating Corsairs, incorporated a V in the code in the form 2V10.

Towards the end of the war in the Pacific, FAA embarked aircraft applied the US Navy practice of putting the two-letter carrier code on the fin with three digits on the nose, these being both the individual and squadron identifiers. This system was to be applied after the war across the FAA to the present day, although the shore bases were to use two-letter codes while carriers used a single letter.

Corsair III JS853/E3-S of No. 731 Sqn at East Haven in 1945 is finished in a very similar manner to contemporary RAF fighters other than the 'Royal Navy' legend. The common RN practice of splitting codes, as here with the code apparently 3S, is a ready form of confusion. (via R. C. Sturtivant)

RAF Codes by Unit

Below are the codes worn by major RAF units. For the sake of convenience they are in three separate lists covering squadrons, flights (including conversion units) and OTUs and their post-war successors, the AFSs and OCUs. Codes noted in italics are unconfirmed while codes in bold are those used between September 1939 and the autumn of 1946. Codes are shown in order of application and include the three-letter Reserve Command codes and the various single-digit or single-letter codes used up to the time of writing. *Not* included are the Transport Command call-sign codes.

Where a code was not worn during the war the notation **nwc** (no wartime code) is used to clarify whether any code shown in normal type is pre-war or post-war. The notation **nf** (not formed) is used to indicate those squadrons which were included in the AMO A154/39 code list but which did not form.

Readers coming straight to this appendix may wish to be reminded that not all squadrons carried codes, even when allocated them.

Squadrons

Sqn	AMO A1545/39	1938-51 codes
1	NA	NA, **JX**, JX
2	KO	KO, **KO, XV, OI**, OI, B
3	OP	OP, **QO, JF**, J5, A
4	FY	TV, FY, **TV**, NC, UP, B, C
5	QN	**OQ**, OQ, 7B, B, A, C
6	XE	ZD, *XE*, **JV**, JV, E
7	LT	LT, **MG, XU**, MG, E
8	YO	**HV, A**, RT
9	KA	KA, **WS**, WS, A
10	PB	PB, **ZA**, ZA
11	OY	YH, **YH**, EX, OM, L, B, D
12	QE	QE, **PH, GZ**, PH, F
13	AN	AN, **OO**
14	BF	BF, **LY, CX**, CX, B, A, B
15	EF	EF, **LS, DJ**, LS, E, T
16	KJ	KJ, EE, UG, **EE**, EG, L, F
17	UV	UV, **YB**, UT, B, C
18	GU	GU, **WV**, WV, B
19	WZ	WZ, **QV**, QV, A
20	PM	**HN**, HN, 6D, TH, L, C, 3, 5, G
21	JP	JP, **YH**, YH
22	VR	*VR*, **OA**
23	MS	MS, **YP**, YP, E
24	ZK	*ZK, 2D*, **ZK**, NQ
25	RX	RX, **ZK**, ZK, F

Sqn	AMO A1545/39	1938-51 codes
26	HL	HL, **RM, XC**, XC, T
27	MY	**PT**, N, J
28	US	**BF**
29	YB	YB, **RO**, RO, B
30	DP	DP, **VT, RS**, RS, JN
31	ZA	ZA, **EE**, 5D, CB, VS, D
32	KT	KT, **GZ**, GZ
33	TN	SO, TN, **NW, RS, 5R**, 5R, C
34	LB	LB, **EG**, 4M, 6J, 8Q
35	WT	WT, **TL**, TL, FB
36	VU	VU, **OE, RW**, DM, T
37	FJ	FJ, **LF**
38	NH	NH, **HD**, RL
39	SF	**XZ, A**
40	OX	OX, **BL**, BL, LE
41	PN	PN, **EB**, EB, F
42	*QD*	*QD*, **AW**, QM, A
43	NQ	NQ, **FT**, SW, A, G
44	JW	JW, **KM**, KM
45	DD	DD, **OB**, OB, L
46	RJ	RJ, **PO**, *FH*, **XK**, XK
47	EW	EW, **KU**
48	*ZW*	*ZW*, **OY**, I2
49	XU	XU, **EA**, EA
50	QX	QX, **VN**, VN
51	UT	UT, **MH, C6**, MH, TB
52	MB	MB, *ZE, AL*
53	TE	TE, **PZ, 1**, *FH*, PU
54	DL	DL, **KL, DL**, HF, G
55	GM	**KQ**
56	LR	LR, **US**, ON, US, B, A
57	EQ	EQ, **DX**, DX, QT
58	BW	BW, **GE, 1, BY**, OT
59	PJ	PJ, **TR, AE, 1, BY, WE**, BY
60	AD	AD, **MU**
61	LS	LS, **QR**, QR
62	JO	JO, **FX**
63	NE	NE, ON, nwc, FJ, UB
64	XQ	XQ, **SH**, SH
65	FZ	FZ, **YT**, YT
66	RB	RB, **LZ**, HI, LZ
67	QT	**RD**, B
68	YA	**WM**, *A*
69	MJ	nwc, WI
70	DU	DU, **SJ**

Sqn	AMO A154/39	1938-51 codes	Sqn	AMO A154/39	1938-51 codes
71	EL	XR, L	127	HF	*BZ*, 9N, EJ
72	SD	RN, SD, **RN**, AP, FG, A	128	DQ	WG, M5
73	HV	HV, **TP**	129	SS	DV
74	JH	JH, **ZP, 4D**, 4D	130	TX	PJ, **AP**, AP, B
75	FO	FO, **AA, JN**, AA	131	RK	NX
76	NM	NM, **MP**, MP	132	TD	FF
77	ZL	ZL, **KN**, *TB*, KN, DV, YS	133	YR	MD
78	YY	YY, ED, **EY**, EY	134	AA	G, GQ
79	AL	AL, **NV**, T	135	GO	WK
80	GK	OD, GK, **YK, AP, EY, W2**, W2	136	XY	HM
81	WK	F, **FL**, A	137	TS	SF
82	OZ	OZ, **UX**, ES	138	WO	NF, AC, NF
83	QQ	*QQ*, **OL**, OL	139	SY	SY, XD, XD
84	UR	VA, **PY**	140	RM	DP, ZW
85	NO	NO, **VY**, VY	141	UD	TW, TW
86	DE	*BX*, 2, XQ	142	KB	KB, **QT, 4H**
87	PD	PD, **LK, G**, B	143	TK	HO, 1, NE
88	HY	HY, **RH**	144	NV	NV, PL, 1
89	LG	**WP**	145	SO	SO, ZX, B
90	TW	TW, **WP, XY**, WP	146	YZ	NA
91	HQ	DL, DL	147	RT	*5F*
92	GR	GR, QJ, 8L, DL, B	148	BS	BS, **FS**, AU
93	RN	HN, J, DV, DV, A, T	149	LY	LY, OJ, **TK**, OJ
94	ZG	FZ, **GO**, A	150	DG	DG, **JN, IQ**
95	PX	**SE**	151	GG	TV, GG, DZ
96	SJ	ZJ, **6H**, L	152	YJ	UM, L, UM, UM
97	MR	*MR*, **OF**, OF	153	XZ	TB, P4
98	OE	*OE*, *QF*, **VO**, VO, L	154	KD	HT, *F*, HT, HG
99	VF	VF, **LN**	155	FL	DG
100	RA	RA, **NK, HW, FZ, JA**, HW, C	156	TB	GT, *YG*
101	LU	LU, **SR**, *MW*, SR	157	VW	RS
102	TQ	TQ, **DY**, EF	158	HT	NP, DK
103	GV	GV, **PM**	159	NS	nwc
104	PO	PO, **EP**, EP	160	JJ	**BS**, BS
105	MT	MT, **GB**	161	AX	JR, MA
106	XS	XS, **ZN**	162	KY	CR, CR
107	BZ	BZ, **OM**, OM	163	NK	Z1
108	MF	MF, **LD**	164	OO	FJ, UB
109	EH	HS, HS	165	YP	SK, SK
110	AY	AY	166	GB	AS, *GB*, AS
111	TM	TM, **JU**, JU, B, H	167	WJ	VL, QO
112	XO	XO, **RT, GA**, A, T	168	XF	OE, EK, QC
113	BT	BT, **AD**	169	JQ	VI
114	FD	FD, **RT**, RT	170	HS	BN, TC
115	BK	BK, **KO, BK, A4, IL**, KO	171	RS	6Y
116	ZD	II	172	LF	OG, 1, WN
117	EX	LD	173	TV	nwc
118	RE	NK, A	174	RO	JJ, XP
119	OM	NH	175	GL	HH
120	MX	OH, BS, A	176	AS	nwc
121	JY	AV	177	QF	nwc
122	WM	**MT**	178	UL	nwc
123	ZE	XE	179	RH	OZ, OZ
124	PK	ON	180	DR	EV
125	FN	VA	181	WB	EL
126	UN	HA, *A*, TD, MK, 5J	182	JT	XM

Sqn	AMO A154/39	1938-51 codes	Sqn	AMO A154/39	1938-51 codes
183	LN	HF	238	TR	VK, KC, WF, FM
184	JM	BR	239	XB	HB
185	ZM	ZM, GL, *F*, GL	240	SH	SH, BN, L
186	MK	XY, AP	241	EZ	RZ
187	GP	PU, PU	242	YD	KY, LE, B, LE, KY
188	XD	nf	243	NX	SN, WP
189	LM	CA	244	VM	nwc
190	JB	G5, 6S, L9	245	DX	DX, MR, TM, MR
191	EV	nwc	246	MP	VU
192	QS	DT, HS	247	HP	HP, ZY, ZY
193	RQ	DP	248	QK	WR, 3, DM, VV
194	FW	nwc	249	VY	GN, T, GN, GN
195	NP	JE, A4	250	YE	LD
196	KG	ZO, 7T	251	FF	AD
197	AG	OV	252	GW	PN, BT
198	PU	TP	253	TL	SW
199	DO	EX	254	HJ	QY, QM, 3
200	UE	TF	255	BY	YD
201	VQ	VQ, **ZM**, **1**, **NS**, NS, A	256	SZ	JT, *A*
202	JU	*JU*, **TQ**, **AX**, **TJ**, Y3, A	257	DT	DT, FM, A6
203	PP	PP, **NT**, **CJ**, CJ, B	258	FH	ZT
204	RF	RF, **KG**, T	259	VP	nwc
205	KM	FV	260	OB	MF, HS
206	WD	*WD*, **VX**, **1**, **4**, *PQ*, B	261	WY	X, FJ
207	NJ	NJ, **EM**, EM, D	262	QY	nwc
208	GA	GA, **YR**, **RG**, RG, S	263	SK	HE, HE
209	FK	*FK*, **WQ**, WQ	264	WA	PS, PS, VA
210	VG	VG, **DA**, OZ, L	265	KU	nwc
211	LJ	*LJ*, **UQ**	266	UO	UO, **ZH**, FX, A, L
212	QB	nwc	267	AO	KW
213	AK	AK, **AK**, AK	268	JN	KL, **OE**, **NM**, EG
214	UX	UX, **BU**, *PX*, QN	269	KL	KL, **UA**, **HK**, B
215	BH	BH, **LG**	270	WP	nwc
216	VT	VT, **SH**, **LO**, GH, H	271	ZJ	BJ, YS, DV, L7
217	YQ	YQ, **MW**, A	272	SM	XK, TJ
218	SV	SV, **HA**, **XH**	273	HH	HH, **HH**, MS
219	AM	FK	274	MU	YK, JJ, NH
220	HU	HU, *PK*, **NR**, **2**, **WP**, **MB**, **ZZ**, 8D, T	275	WS	PV
			276	QM	AQ
221	VB	DF	277	TP	9J, BA
222	UP	ZD, ZD	278	RY	MY
223	QR	AO, 6G	279	AU	OS, RL
224	PW	*PW*, **QX**, **2**, **XB**, XB, B	280	FX	MF, 2, YF
225	LX	LX, **WU**	281	SR	FA
226	KP	KP, **MQ**	282	VA	B4
227	BU	9J	283	JV	FG, LP, LP
228	TO	TO, BH, **DQ**, **1**, UE, L	284	BE	nwc
229	DB	RE, HB, X, 9R	285	GH	VG
230	FV	NM, **DX**, **4X**, 4X, B, C, D	286	QL	NW
231	KR	VL	287	YV	KZ
232	XN	EF	288	VV	RP
233	EY	EY, **ZS**, 5T	289	TT	YE
234	AZ	AZ, FX, A, W	290	FT	X6
235	SU	LA, 1, 2	291	MM	8Q
236	FA	ND, *1*, 2, **FA**, MB	292	UZ	nwc
237	MH	DV	293	XJ	ZE

Sqn	AMO A154/39	1938-51 codes	Sqn	AMO A154/39	1938-51 codes
294	AF	FD	350	YM	MN
295	HX	PX , 8E, 8Z	360		nwc, E
296	KZ	XH, 7C, 9W	400		SP
297	GS	QA, L5, P5, L5	401		YO
298	QH	O6 , 8A, 8T	402		AE
299	AT	X9, 5G	403		KH
300	ZN	BH	404		EE, 2, EO
301	MW	GR, GR	405		LQ
302	EG	QH, WX	406		HU
303	NN	RF, PD	407		C1, 1, 2, RR
304	UB	NZ, 2, QD	408		EQ
305	BV	SM	409		KP
306	HK	UZ	410		RA
307	VK	EW	411		DB
308	BM	ZF	412		VZ
309	XV	AR, WC	413		QL
310	UG	NN	414		RU
311	HD	KX, PP	415		GX, 2, 6U, NH
312	KW	DU	416		DN
313	LH	RY	417		AN
314	UY	nf	418		TH
315	OG	PK	419		VR
316	NL	SZ	420		PT
317	WU	JH	421		AU
318	XP	LW	422		DG, 2
319	VE	nf	423		AB, 3, YI
320	SP	*TD*, NO	424		QB
321	JS	nwc	425		KW
322	ZQ	3W, VL	426		OW
323	GN	nf	427		ZL
324	PQ	nf	428		NA
325	EA	nf	429		AL
326	QU	8J, *9I*	430		G9
327	LP	7E, U6	431		SE
328	MN	S8	432		QO
329	OA	5A	433		BM
330	KE	GS, WH	434		WL
331	LD	FN	435		*8J*
332	WW	*HG*, AH	436		U6
333	VN	3, KK	437		Z2
334	BJ	AG, *VB*	438		F3
335	XT	FG	439		5V
336	ZP	nwc	440		I8
337	OK	nf	441		9G
338	ML	nf	442		Y2
339	KN	nf	443		2I
340	YK	GW	450		OK, DJ
341	PL	NL	451		BQ, NI
342	LK	OA	452		UD
343	ND	nwc	453		FN, FU
343	GT	nwc	454		TD
345	AQ	2Y	455		UB, 2
346	XL	H7	456		*PZ*, SA, RX
347	BB	L8	457		BP, XB
348	FR	nf	458		MD, FU
349	OS	GE	459		GK

Sqn	AMO A154/39	1938-51 codes	Sqn	AMO A154/39	1938-51 codes
460		UV, AR	587		M4
461		UT, 2	595		**7B**, 7B
462		Z5	600	MV	MV, **BQ, 6**, RAG, LJ
463		JO	601	YN	YN, **UF**, HT, RAH
464		SB	602	ZT	LO, ZT, **LO**, RAI, LO
466		HD	603	RL	*RL*, **XT**, RAJ, XT
467		PO	604	WQ	WQ, **NG**, NG, RAK
485		OU	605	HE	HE, **UP**, *ML*, RAL, NR
486		SA	606	BG	nf
487		EG	607	LW	LW, **AF**, RAN, LA
488		NF, ME	608	PG	PG, **UL, 6T**, 6T, RAO
489		XA, *3*, **P6**	609	BL	BL, **PR**, RAP, PR
500	SQ	SQ, **MK**, S7, RAA	610	JE	DW, RAQ, DW
501	ZH	*ZH*, **SD**, SD, RAB	611	GZ	*GZ*, **FY**, FY, RAR
502	KQ	KQ, **YG, 2, V9**, RAC	612	DJ	**3**, **WL**, RAS, 8W
503	VJ	nwc	613	ZR	*ZR*, **ZR, SY**, Q3, RAT, QJ
504	AW	AW, **SD, TM**, TM, RAD	614	YX	**YX**, LJ, RAU, 7A
505	YF	nf	615	RR	RR, **KW**, RAV, V6
506	FS	nf	616	QJ	QJ, **QJ, YQ**, RAW, YQ
507	GX	nf	617	MZ	**AJ, KC, YZ**, KC, M, AJ
508	DY	nf	618	BN	nwc
509	BQ	nf	619	KV	PG
510	RG	RG, *VS*	620	TF	D4, QS
511	SN	nwc	621	ER	nwc
512	UQ	HC	622	UF	GI
513	RZ	*CS*	623	ON	IC
514	OV	JI, A2	624	KK	nwc
515	YW	3P	625	NU	CF
516	PF	nwc	626	SG	UM
517	SW	X9	627	WX	AZ
518	FM	Y3, Y3	628	ES	nwc
519	BP	Z9	629	LQ	nf
520	JL	2M	630	BO	LE
521		TE, 5O	631	XX	6D, 6D
524		7R	632	LO	nf
525		*8P*, WF	633	AE	nf
526		MD	634	DS	nf
527		WN	635	NB	F2
528		OS	636	VZ	nf
529		KX	637	UK	nf
530		*NH*	638	PZ	nf
532		QM	639	KX	R9
540		nwc, DH	640	XA	C8
541		ES, WY, A	641	EU	nf
547		3, 2V	642	MQ	nf
548		TS	643	QZ	nf
549		ZF	644	FE	2P, 9U
550		BQ	645	KF	nf
567		I4	646	YG	nf
570		E7, V8	647	ZS	nf
571		8K	648	YT	nf
575		I9	649	HA	nf
576		UL	650	MA	T7
577		3Y	651		MA-MD
578		LK	652		nwc, XM
582		6O	654		QA-QD

Sqn	AMO A154/39	1938-51 codes
655		PA-PD
657		VA-VD, TS
660		BG
661		OE
662		ET
666		*BX*
667		U4
679		3M
691		5S, 5S
692		P3
695		4M, 4M, 8Q
1435		V

Flights/Conversion Units

These units include a range of support flights – mostly uncoded – and conversion units, some of which were very large. These latter were in the 1300 and 1600 series and their role and size to some extent explains the number of codes in use.

421	DL
1316	*WK*
1322	*DA*
1323	QF
1332	YY, YY
1333	ZR, CM
1335	nwc, XL
1336	ZS
1359	*ZW*
1380	EZ, JB, KG
1381	7Z, I5, 7Z
1382	NU, NU
1383	GY
1384	Q6
1385	OQ
1401	BN, TE
1402	nwc, DO
1409	AE
1417	AG
1429	KV
1430	KU
1472	RG
1473	ZB
1476	*UX*
1477	KK
1508	*UQ*
1510	RF
1513	LL
1516	QW
1521	J6
1527	PY
1528	*YM*
1529	GL
1552	PN, SS, ER
1555	DR
1556	*VT*
1557	AB

1561	*VM*
1562	B9
1586	GR
1606	D2
1651	BS, QQ, YZ
1652	GV, JA
1653	A3, H4, MX, *M9*
1654	JF, UG
1656	EK, BL
1657	AK, XT
1658	TT, ZB
1659	FD, RV
1660	*KT*, TV, YW
1661	GP, KB
1662	KF, PE
1662	OO
1663	SV
1664	DH, ZU
1665	*FO*, NY, OG, OI
1666	ND, QY
1667	GG, *KR*, LR
1668	2K, CE, J9
1669	6F, L6
1677	HM
1678	SW
1680	MJ
1681	LT
1682	UH
1683	PB
1684	FP
1685	KA
1686	BT
1687	4E
1688	6H
1689	9X, 9X
1690	9M
1692	4X
1695	3K
1697	DR
1699	4Z

Only a few Vampire T.11 trainers wore unit codes, as the aircraft were delivered just as the system was falling into disuse. One that did carry codes in 1956 was XE923/UU-T of No. 226 OCU.

OTUs/AFSs/OCUs

During the war the OTUs prepared aircrew for squadron service and were the final posting before operational service. They were numbered between 1 and 152 with some gaps. The OTUs continued to operate for some years after the war and were directly followed by AFSs in the range 201–215 or OCUs in the range 226–242.

Codes shown in bold type are those used in wartime while codes in plain type are those applied after the war.

2	ZR
3	*HR*, **KG**, **SG**
4	**QZ**, **TA**, TA
5	*WA*
6	**FE**, *LP*, **OD**, K7
8	*BE*, BE
10	*EL*, **JL**, **RK**, **UY**, **ZG**
11	**KH**, **KJ**, **LG**, **OP**, **TX**
12	**FQ**, *GJ*, **JP**, **ML**
13	**EV**, **FV**, **KQ**, **OY**, **SL**, **UR**, **WO**, D, XJ, FV, OY, SL
14	**AM**, **GL**, **VB**
15	**EO**, **FH**, **KK**
16	**GA**, **JS**, **XG**
17	**AY**, **JG**, **WJ**
18	**EN**, **VQ**, **XW**
19	**UO**, **XF**, **ZV**
20	**AI**, **HJ**, **JM**, **MK**, **XL**, **YR**, **ZT**
21	**ED**, **SJ**, **UH**, SJ, UH
22	**DD**, **LT**, **OX**, **XN**
23	**BY**, **FZ**, **WE**
24	**FB**, **TY**, **UF**
25	PP
26	**EU**, **PB**, **WG**
27	**BB**, **UJ**, **YC**, **YL**
28	**LB**, **QN**, **WY**
29	TF
30	**BT**, **KD**, **TN**
41	*6R*, *IO*
42	**GM**, *GO*
43	**BD**, **PF**, PF
51	**BD**, **PF**
52	*CT*, **GK**, **NS**, **OQ**, **TJ**
53	**KU**, **MV**, **OB**, **QG**
54	**BF**, **LX**, **ST**, **YX**, ST
55	**EH**, **PA**, **UW**, **ZX**
56	**FE**, **GF**, **HQ**, *HO*
57	**JZ**, **LV**, **PW**, **XO**
58	**P9**, **PQ**, **XB**, **ZZ**
59	**4Q**, **7L**, **II**, **MF**
60	AT
61	*BV*, **DE**, **HX**, **KR**, **TO**, **UU**, DE, KR, TO, UU
63	*GJ*
73	F
73	E
77	*AX*
80	**3H**, **JB**
81	**EZ**, **KG**
82	**9C**, **BZ**, **KA**, **TD**
83	**FI**, **GS**, **MZ**
84	**CO**, **CZ**, **IF**
85	**9P**
86	**Y7**
105	**7Z**, **8F**, I5
107	**CM**, **ZR**
109	**GY**
111	**3G**, *H3*, **X3**
131	A, B, C, D
132	**9Y**
202	UH
203	**JH**, *KR*, TO, UU
226	**BB**, **HX**, **KD**, **KR**, **TO**, UU, XL
227	**BD**, **PF**
228	C, LX
229	**ES**, **RS**, A
230	**A3**, **SN**
231	B
233	3, A
235	**TA**, D
236	**K7**, C
237	**BE**, **LP**, C
240	**NU**, F
241	YY

Most operational training units during the Second World War had a number of support aircraft on strength additional to their main equipment. No. 228 OCU, which trained night fighter crews, used Martinet EM444/ST-1 as a utility type.

APPENDIX E

Captured Enemy Aircraft

Numerous enemy aircraft were captured and used for a variety of purposes by Allied units. Most were uncoded or retained their original (German, Italian or Japanese) codes. Those noted either had applied just the unit letters of the parent squadron or were fully coded, sometimes with '?' as the individual character. A few used personal codes, being the initial letters of the pilot.

Details in this section are mainly drawn from War Prizes by Phil Butler, published in 1993 and the definitive work on the subject.

Code	Unit	Type	Dates	Example	Theatre	Remarks
AK	213	Ju 87B	42	/AK-?	N Africa	Ex S7+LL of 3/StG 3
AN	417	MC202	2.43	/AN		
AX	1 SAAF	Bf 109F or G?	c mid-43	/AX-?	Tunisia	
AX	1435	Bf 109G-2	9.43	/AX	Malta	ex I/JG27
CV	3 RAAF	Ba 25	c 41	/CV	N Africa	
CV	3 RAAF	Bf 109F	c 10.42	/CV-V	N Africa	
CV	3 RAAF	Ca 164	c 1.43	/CV	N Africa	
CV	3 RAAF	Bf 109G	c 43	/CV-V	N Africa	
CV	3 RAAF	Ca 309	1.43-9.43	/CV-V	N Africa	
CV	3 RAAF	Cant Z501	8.43-9.43	/CV	Sicily	
CV	3 RAAF	MC 205V	8.43-9.43	MM9377/CV-V	Italy	
DAB	?	Fi 156C	45	/DAB	Germany	personal code
DB	411	Ju 88H-1	6.45	/DB	Germany	
DN	416	Bf 108	c.45	DN-X	Eur	
DS	?	Saiman 202/I	11.43	/DS	Italy	
DV	93	Ju W34	c 45	/DV	Austria	
EA	CFE, EAF	Bf 109G	4.45	VD358/EA-2	UK	
EA	CFE, EAF	Fw 190A-4	5.45	PN999/EA-4	UK	
EA	CFE, EAF	Bf 110C-5	44	AX772/EA-7	UK	
EA	CFE, EAF	Ju 88A-4	1.45	EE205/EA-9	UK	
EB	41	FW 190F-8	5.45	/EB-?	Denmark	
EP	84 GCS	SM 82	1.46-7.46	VN158/EP	Germany	
EY	80	Bf 109F	c 11.42-5.43	/EY	N Africa	2 captured & used
FS	450	Fiat CR.42	c 42	MedME		
GA	112	Ca 100	8.43-	/GA-1	Italy	ex Catania Aero Club
GA	112	Ca 100	8.43?	/GA-2	Malta	
GA	112	Ju 87D	42	/GA-S	N Africa	
GA	112	SM 81	1943	/GA	Tunisia	
GA	112	MC 202	mid 1943	/GA	N Africa	ex 90 Squadriglia
GL	185	Bf 109G		/GL-?		
GN	249	Fiat Cr 42	1942-3	/GN-I	N Africa	
HB	AVM Harry Broadhurst	Fi 156	47	/HB	UK	later VX154
HS	260 Sqn	He 111H	12.42-	*****/HS-?	N Africa	ex III/KG4
HS	260 Sqn	Fiat G50	8-10.41	*****/HS-?	Palestine	
HS	260 Sqn	Bf 109F	c 42	/HS-!	N Africa	
HS	260	MC 200	1943	MM****/HS	MedME	
HV	61FS/56FG	He 111H-20	c.45	701152/HV-A	UK/Eur	
JFE	W/C J F Edwards	FW 190F	5.45	/JFE	Germany	127 Wing

Code	Unit	Type	Dates	Example	Theatre	Remarks
KJ	4 SAAF	Bf 109F	1.43-	/KJ-?	N Africa	
KW	267	Bf 110D	9.41-3.42	4035/KW	Heliopolis	ex II/ZG76
LW	318	Bf 109G	46	/LW	Italy	
MB	?	Ju 88G	46		Germany	
OK	450	Ca 100	8.43	/OK-?	Italy	ex Catania Aero Club
OK	450	Hs 126	11.42	/OK	N Africa	
PGJ	?	Ju W34	6.45	/PGJ	Germany	personal code
QJ	92 Sqn	Arado Ar 96	8.43	/QJ	Sicily	
RN	72 Sqn	Saiman 200	9.43	/RN-I	Sicily	
S6	41 GCF	Bf 108B-1	5.44-4.46	AW167/S6-K	UK	
SA	486	Bu 181	5.45	/SA	Germany	
UF	601	Ju 87D	11.42-2.43	/UF	N Africa	
UF	601	Fiat Cr 42	1942-3	/UF	N Africa	
VZ	412	Ju 87D-5	4.45	/VZ-?	Germany	
WD	4 FS/52 FG	Breda 15S	c late 43	/WD-4F	MedME	
WH	330	Arado Ar196A	c 11.45	/WH-N	Eur	
WJC	83 GCS	Fi 156C	9.45-4.46	VM296/WJC	N Europe	
X8	87 FS, 79 FG	Bf 109G-2	43	/X8-7	N Africa	ex 2(H)/14
XM	182	FW 190A	45	/XM-?	Germany	
ZX	145	SM 79	2.43-6.43	MM22174/ZX	N Africa	Named 'Gremlin HQ'

The Australians of No. 3 Sqn RAAF used quite a number of captured enemy aircraft, which were invariably painted in their markings. One of the most elegant was this Macchi MC 205V MM9977 which, after its capture in Italy, became CV-V. (Author's Collection)

Among the enemy aircraft used by No. 260 Sqn in North Africa was this Messerschmitt Bf 109F which in keeping with practice had full RAF markings and unit code. In place of an aircraft letter many had a question mark, but unusually this aircraft has an exclamation mark. (Wg Cdr J. F. Edwards)

Captured twin-engined aircraft were often pressed into service as 'hacks' for transport support. The Heliopolis-based communications squadron, No. 267, for example, refurbished and used this captured Bf 110C as a high-speed personnel transport. It is believed to have been repainted, but certainly wore properly applied markings and codes and was usually flown by the CO. (H. Dennis)

Fictitious Codes

For film or publicity purposes aircraft are sometimes marked with codes which were either not allocated at all or which were worn by aircraft of another type or unit. Many still photographs exist of these aircraft, which results in confusion. Among those identified are:

Code	Unit	Type	Dates	Example	Film/Remarks
TU	TTU	Beaufort I	40-41	W6494/TU-Z	Wartime documentary
FG		Curtiss Hawk 75A	1941	*****/FG-K	Nazi propaganda film *Kampfgeschwader Lutzow*
SD	118	Spitfire II	1943		First of the Few
SD	501	Hurricane	1953	'V5276'/SD-Y	Reach for the Sky
HT	'633'	Mosquito T.3	1965	HJ682/HT-B	633 Squadron
AI		Spitfire IX	1968	'N3924'/AI-P	Battle of Britain
DO		Spitfire	1968	'N3313'/DO-D	Battle of Britain
EQ		Spitfire V	1968	'N*321'/EQ-M	Battle of Britain
CD		Spitfire	1968	'N2211'/CD-A	Battle of Britain
KV		Hurricane II	1968	'H3423'/KV-H	Battle of Britain
MI		Hurricane	1968	'H3423'/MI-C	Battle of Britain
PR		Spitfire	1968	5718M/PR-O	Battle of Britain
HB	-	Sea Fury FB.10	1971	WH589/HB-O	Owned by Ormond Haydon-Baillie
HF	183	Harvard (Typhoon)	1976	4312721/HF-L	Bridge Too Far
NE		S-51	1981	*****/NE-X	Eye of the Needle
NS		Spitfire IX	1988	NH238/NS-T	Piece of Cake
RF		Spitfire Vb	2000	'AR3185'/RF-M	Pearl Harbor

The use of genuine aircraft for the making of films often saw them painted in fictitious codes, or sometimes in quite accurate markings. This latemodel Hurricane, posing as P2619 is in the markings of No. 56 Sqn for the making of the film Angels 15 during the 1950s. (Author's Collection)

Other Wartime Unit Identifiers and Markings

At various times during the war some units used forms of marking other than codes to identify their aircraft. In the case of No. 73 Squadron, for example, for much of the war its aircraft wore a form of its colourful pre-war marking and this in place of unit codes!

However, in most cases where some form of individual marking was worn, it was restricted to the squadron badge, often worn on the fin, and usually for quite short periods or on specific types. In any event these markings were unofficial and were relatively rare and of course compromised the *raison d'être* of the squadron codes. Examples are shown; those marked * were used without, or in place of, squadron codes.

Sqn	Type	Period	Theatre	Marking
17	Spitfire XIV	45-46	FE	Mailed fist on nose
26	Tomahawk	41-42	UK	Springbok head on white of fin flash
30	Thunderbolt II	45	FE	Palm tree on white fin i/d band
39*	Marauder III	44-45	MedME	Winged bomb on nose
43	Spitfire IX	45-46	MedME	Black/white check on fin top
73*	Hurricane I, II	41-43	MedME	Pre-war spearhead marking across roundel (colours varied)
	Spitfire V, IX	43-44		
80	Tempest V	45-46	Eur	Bell on fin top
85	Hurricane I	39-41	UK/France	Hexagon on fin or under cockpit
87	Hurricane I	39-40	France	Pre-war spearhead & sqn badge on fin retained
112	Tomahawk IIb	41	MedME	Shark mouth marking
	Kittyhawk I, II, IV	41-44		
	Mustang III, IV	44-46		
141	Beaufighter VIf	42-43	UK	Pre-war spearhead & sqn badge across nose
145	Spitfire VIII	44-45	MedME	Sqn badge in disc above fin flash or on nose
152	Spitfire VIII, XIV	44-45	FE	Leaping panther across roundel
208*	Hurricane I	41	MedME	White lightning flash through roundel
213	Hurricane I	42	MedME	Hornet in roundel in place of red centre
234	Mustang III, IV	45-46	MedME	Red eagle on forward fuselage
238	Spitfire VIII	44	MedME	Black Hydra on nose
253	Spitfire VIII	45-46	MedME	Sqn badge in disc above fin flash
274*	Hurricane I, II	42-43	MedMe	Blue or black lightning flash through roundel or under cockpit
	Spitfire V, IX	43-44		
421	Spitfire IX	43-45	UK/Eur	Sqn badge on nose
443	Spitfire XVI	45	Eur	Sqn badge in shield on nose
601	Hurricane I	40-41	UK	Sqn badge on centre stripe of fin flash
	Airacobra	41-42	UK	Sqn badge in disc above fin flash
	Spitfire VIII	44-45	MedME	
605	Hurricane I	40	UK	Sqn badge on white of fin flash
607	Hurricane I	40	UK	Sqn badge on white of fin flash
	Spitfire VIII	45	FE	Sqn badge above fin flash or on nose
609	Typhoon Ib	42-43	UK	Sqn badge below cockpit
3 SAAF	Hurricane I	41-42	E Africa	Sqn badge on nose
12 SAAF	Ju 86K	40	E Africa	Winged springbok on nose
	Maryland	41		
24 SAAF	Boston III	42-43	MedME	Sqn badge on nose

In addition, aircraft of the 'Free European' squadrons usually wore a representation of their national flag or roundel, generally around the cockpit area. Aircraft of the Free French squadrons carried the Cross of Lorraine and markings of the French Air Force flights or *escadrille's* whose traditions they carried

In addition to unit codes several squadrons wore some other distinctive form of marking. The auxiliaries of No. 601 (County of London) Sqn carried their 'winged sword' badge on their aircraft for almost the entire war! In the Mediterranean it was worn on the fin within a white disc as on Spitfire Vc EP689/UF-X in 1943. (P. R. Arnold Collection)

One of the more striking unit markings was this leaping panther which adorned No. 152 Sqn's Spitfires toward the end of the war in Burma. As modelled here on Mk VIII UM-R it straddled the SEAC-style roundel on both sides of the fuselage and was also carried on the replacement Mk XIVs. (R. Johnson)

A typical post-war adornment was the squadron badge in its full form, worn in a variety of locations on the fuselage. On the Spitfire F.21s of No. 615 (County of Surrey) Sqn like LA195/RAV-E it was carried well forward on the nose, just aft of the spinner. (D. J. Coxhead)

The Junkers Ju 86Z airliners modified for bombing duties with No. 12 Sqn SAAF were identified for a time by the unit's winged springbok badge worn in white on the dark green camouflage. The extended ventral dustbin turret is of note. (SAAF)

RAF Code Colours

The issue of colour schemes of wartime aircraft remains controversial and great care is needed in asserting markings. What follow are not intended to be definitive or comprehensive notes on the topic but rather a general guide. The illustrations throughout the book give a good idea of the variation in markings.

Early instructions for code marking required them to be painted in mid-grey, stores ref. 33B/157; in practice the tone varied considerably from station to station. Codes were to be applied in 48 in (122 cm) characters, with 6 in (15 cm) strokes, although on fighters they were usually applied in 30 in (76 cm) characters. The alphabet used was a very plain sans-serif type the proportions of which were: height 8; width 5; thickness 1; space between letters 1. In style the letters were square, but with rounded corners. This style caused some confusion in that there was little difference between D and O, and in due course much rounder characters were used.

Fighters

From the outset codes on fighters were painted in mid-grey as described above. The colour was later standardised as medium sea grey and applied to all fighters, day and night, until at least the end of 1941.

1 July 1942 the colour for codes was changed to sky type S for day fighters and red for black and dark green/medium seagrey night fighters, including Hurricanes, Beaufighters, Havocs and Mosquitoes. Day fighter variations included red unit code with a white or yellow individual aircraft letter on Typhoons of No. 198 Squadron.

In the Middle East the fighter units were less disciplined in the application of unit codes and markings. White (for example No. 250 Squadron), light grey, cerulean blue and red were all applied and several units used red codes outlined in white including No. 43 Squadron. At least one aircraft of No. 145 Squadron had blue codes outlined in white. By 1944 No. 152 Squadron Spitfires in Italy had black codes on desert camouflage. Yellow codes were reported to have been applied to Spitfires of No. 185 Squadron on Malta.

In the Far East fighters wore light grey codes initially, but these changed to white in 1943 and were marked in only 12 in (30 cm) or 18 in (46 cm) high letters. Towards the end of the war some Thunderbolts were flown in bare metal finish with small black codes.

In the immediate post-war period codes tended to be white on camouflaged aircraft and black on those in natural metal finish.

Bombers

Initially, unlike fighters, the bomber types applied white codes, typically 48 in (122 cm) high where possible but only 24 in (61 cm) high on the fuselage boom of the Hampden. Soon into the war codes were changed to light grey in some units, but white persisted as well. However from the end of April 1942 ident dull red was used on night bombers and sky on Mosquitoes. The latter type also sported red codes outlined in white (No. 162 Squadron and dark blue (No. 105 Squadron). Some Halifax units applied yellow codes including Nos 10 and 78 Squadrons while aircraft of No. 102 Squadron had red unit codes with grey individual letters. Lancasters of 5 Group squadrons had red codes outlined in yellow.

In the Middle East codes were used rather less than in the UK, but from the start of the war, where applied they were in medium grey or white. The situation in the Far East was similar and as with fighters in that theatre, some bombers in silver finish wore black codes (Mosquitoes of No. 84 Squadron). In the immediate post-war period code colours reverted to pre-war white.

Coastal Command

At the start of the war Coastal Command strike fighters had the standard medium grey codes. In June 1942 code letter colours were formally changed to red or grey. On Beaufighters these included red (for example No. 236 Squadron) and red outlined in medium grey (No. 404 Squadron). Later again there was some further variation with Mosquitoes of No. 143 Squadron sporting black codes outlined in yellow.

For the patrol types codes were white changing to medium grey with the onset of war. From 1942 code colours, where applied, were medium sea grey on the colour scheme of temperate sea/sky and dark slate grey on the temperate sea/white painted aircraft. As the white scheme took hold dark slate grey or red codes became the norm. Towards the end of the war some aircraft carried black codes.

Transport Command

At the beginning of the war there was a handful of transports within the RAF, confined to Bombays, finished in dark green and dark earth with grey codes. The Albemarles and Liberators which followed from 1942 were in a temperate sea scheme but generally, at this stage, uncoded. From 1943 red codes were applied to Albemarles, which were then finished dark green and dark earth. Dull (ident) red remained the norm on successive types including on the olive drab finished Dakotas.

On the Dakotas there were exceptions, including full codes or individual letters in grey, white, sky and yellow. As with other types, transports began to apply black codes on bare metal finish at the end of the war.

Miscellaneous

Aircraft operating in various other functions applied codes including air-sea rescue, photo-reconnaissance, army co-operation and artillery spotting. In general the marking of codes followed the general pattern described above. Thus most codes to mid-1942 were in various shades of grey, while those on types intended for use at night – typically the Lysanders used for agent drops – often painted them in red.

APPENDIX I

Abbreviations

AACF	Anti-aircraft Co-operation Flight
AACU	Anti-aircraft Co-operation Unit
AAS	Air Armament School
AC	Air Commodore
a/c	Aircraft
ACM	Air Chief Marshal
ADC	Aide de Camp
ADGB	Air Defence Great Britain
ADLS	Air Delivery Letter Service
ADLSS	Air Despatch Letter Service Squadron
AEAF	Allied Expeditionary Air Forces
AFDU	Air Fighting Development Unit
AFS/U	Advanced Flying School/Unit
AFWE	Air Forces Western Europe
AGS	Air Gunnery School
AM	Air Marshal
AMC	Air Material Command
AMCCF	Air Material Command Communications Flight; Air Mobility Command Communications Flight (RCAF)
ANS	Air Navigation School
AOC	Air Officer Commanding
AOPS	Air Observation Post School
AOS	Air Observers School
APC/S	Armament Practice Camp/Station
AROS	Air Radio Officer's School (RCAF)
ASRTU	Air-Sea Rescue Training Unit
ASWDU	Air-Sea Warfare Development Unit
AVM	Air Vice-Marshal
BAFO	British Air Forces of Occupation
BANS	Basic Air Navigation School
BATF	Beam Approach Training Flight
BBU	Bomb Ballistics Unit
B	CCF Bomber Command Communications Flight
BCDU	Bomber Command Development Unit
BCFU	Bomber Command Film Unit
BCIS	Bomber Command Instructors' School
BDTF	Bomber Defence Training Flight
BG	Bomb Group
BLEU	Blind Landing Experimental Unit
BS	Bomb Squadron
BSDU	Bomber Support Development Unit
BTTF	Bomber Target Towing Flight
C&RF	Communications and Rescue Flight
CAC	Coastal Artillery Co-operation (RCAF)
CACCF	Central Air Command Communications Flight (RCAF)
CACU	Coastal Artillery Co-operation Unit
CBE	Central Bomber Establishment

CCFATU	Coastal Command Fighter Affiliation Training Unit
CCFIS	Coastal Command Flying Instructors' School
CCRC	Combat Crew Replacement Centre (US)
Cdt	Commandant (French)
CEPE	Central Experimental and Proving Establishment (RCAF)
CF	Communications Flight
CFE	Central Fighter Establishment
CFS	Central Flying School
CGS	Central Gunnery School
CinC	Commander-in-Chief
CNCS	Central Navigation and Control School
Cne	Capitaine (French)
CNS	Central Navigation School
Col	Colonel
CSE	Central Signals Establishment
CTSF	Canberra Training and Standards Flight
CU	Conversion Unit
CW	Communications Wing
DFLS	Day Fighter Leaders' School
EAAS	Empire Air Armament School
EANS	Empire Air Navigation School
EARS	Empire Air Radio School
EFS	Empire Flying School
EFTS	Elementary Flying Training School
ERS	Emergency Rescue Squadron (US)
FCCRS	Fighter Command Control and Reporting School
FCCS	Fighter Command Communications Squadron
FE	Far East
FG	Fighter Group (US)
FGS	Fighter Gunnery School (RNZAF)
FIDU	Fighter Interception Development Unit
FIS	Flying Instructors' School
FIU	Fighter Interception Unit
F/L	Flight Lieutenant
FLS	Fighter Leaders' School
Flt	Flight
FONAC	Flag Officer Naval Air Command
FS	Fighter Sector; Fighter Squadron
FTC	Flying Training Command
FTG	Fighter Training Group
FTS	Flying Training School
FU	Film Unit
GB	Groupe de Bombardement (French)
G/C	Group Captain
GC	Groupe de Chasse (French)
GCF	Group Communications Flight
Gp	Group

GPTF	Glider Pick-up Training Flight	RF	Rescue Flight (RCAF)
GPU	Glider Pick-up Unit	RG	Reconnaissance Group
GR	Groupe de Reconnaissance (French)	RIAF	Royal Indian Air Force
GRS	General Reconnaissance School	RNethAF	Royal Netherlands Air Force
GRU	Gunnery Research Unit	RNFS	Royal Navy Fighter Squadron (Western Desert
GSU	Group Support Unit		under RAF control)
GTS	Gunnery Training Squadron (RNZAF)	RNorAF	Royal Norwegian Air Force
GTTF	Gunnery Tow Target Flight	RNZAF	Royal New Zealand Air Force
HCCS	Home Command Communications Squadron	RS	Radio School; Reconnaissance Squadron
HCF	Hornet Conversion Flight	RU	Rescue Unit (RCAF)
HCU	Heavy Conversion Unit	RWE	Radio Warfare Establishment
HRH	His/Her Royal Highness	S&R	Search and Rescue
HSF	High-speed Flight	S&R	Flt Search and Rescue Flight
HTCU	Heavy Transport Conversion Unit	SAAF	South African Air Force
IAF	Indian Air Force	SAC	School of Army Cooperation
ITS/W	Initial Training School/Wing	SAOEU	Strike Attack Operational Evaluation Unit
JATC	Joint Air Training Centre (RCAF)		Satt Satellite
KU	Composite Unit (RCAF)	SC	Station Commander
LFS	Lancaster Finishing School	SDF	Special Duties Flight
LS	Liaison Squadron	SEAC	South-East Asia Command
Lt	Col Lieutenant Colonel	SF	Station Flight
MAEE	Marine Aircraft Experimental Establishment	SFTS	Service Flying Training School
Maj	Major	SFU	Signals Flying Unit
MCCS	Maintenance Command Communications	SGCF	Southern Group Communications Flight
	Squadron	SGR	School of General Reconnaissance
MCS	Metropolitan Communications Squadron	SGSF	Southern Group Communications Flt
MedME	Mediterranean and Middle East	S/L	Squadron Leader
Met Flt	Meteorological Flight	SMR	School of Maritime Reconnaissance
MOTU	Maritime Operational Training Unit	SofAC/SAC	School of Army Co-operation
MRS	Maritime Reconnaissance School	SRAF	Southern Rhodesian Air Force
MSFU	Merchant Ship Fighter Unit	SSCF	Southern Sector Communications Flight
MU	Maintenance Unit	SU	Support Unit (RNZAF)
NA	North America	SW	Signals Wing
NAS	Naval Air Station	SWPA	South West Pacific Area
NEFSF	North East Fighter Sector Flight	TCG	Troop Carrier Group
NEI	Netherlands East Indies	TCMF	Transport Command Meteorological Flight
NFLS	Night Fighter Leaders' School	TCS	Troop Carrier Squadron
OCU	Operational Conversion Unit	TEU	Tactical Exercise Unit
OEU	Operational Evaluation Unit	TSCU	Transport Support Conversion Unit
OTG	Operational Training Group (US); Observation	Tspt Flt	Transport Flight
	Training Group	TTC	Technical Training Command
OTU	Operational Training Unit	TTCCF	Technical Training Command Communications
PAU	Pilotless Aircraft Unit		Flight
PFNTU	Pathfinder Force Navigation Training Unit	TTF	Tactical Training Flight (Belgium)
PFS	Pathfinder Squadron (US)	TTF	Target Towing Flight
PG	Photo Group	TTU	Torpedo Training Unit
PRDU	Photographic Reconnaissance Development	UAS	University Air Squadron
	Unit	USAAF	United States Army Air Forces
PS/G	Photographic Squadron/Group	USN	United States Navy
PTS	Parachute Training School	W/C	Wing Commander
RAAF	Royal Australian Air Force	WCF	Wessex Conversion Flight
RAF	Royal Air Force	WCF	Wing Commander Flying
RAFC	Royal Air Force College	WCT	Wing Commander Training
RAFFC	Royal Air Force Flying College	WCU	Washington Conversion Unit
RAFNICF	RAF Northern Ireland Communications Flight	Wg	Wing
RATF	Radio Aids Training Flight	WL	Wing Leader
RAuxAF	Royal Auxiliary Air Force	WPU	Weapons Practice Unit
RBelgAF	Royal Belgian Air Force	WPU	Weapons Proving Unit (RCAF)
RCAF	Royal Canadian Air Force	WTU	Warwick Training Unit
RCCF	Reserve Command Communications Flight		

Biblography

Becker, D. (1995) *On Wings of Eagles*. Durban: South African Air Force.

Bowyer, M. J. F. (1973) *Bombing Colours 1937–73*. Cambridge: Patrick Stevens.

Bowyer, M. J. F. (1969) *Fighting Colours 1937–1969*. London: Patrick Stevens.

Bowyer, M. J. F. and Rawlings, J. D. R. (1979) *Squadron Codes 1937–56*. Cambridge: Patrick Stevens.

Darby, C. (1978) *RNZAF The First Decade 1937–46*. Melbourne: Kookaburra Technical Publications Pty.

Ehrengardt, C-J. (2000) *Camouflage and Markings No 1 – French Air Force 1938–1945*. Fleurance: AeroEditions.

Flintham, V. (1998) *Aircraft in British Military Service*. Shrewsbury: Airlife.

Freeman, R. (1991) *The Mighty Eighth*. London: Arms and Armour Press.

Freeman, R. (1993) *Royal Air Force of World War Two in Colour*. London: Arms and Armour Press.

Halley, J. J. (1988) *Squadrons of the Royal Air Force and Commonwealth 1918–1988*. Tonbridge: Air-Britain.

Jefford, C. G. (1988) *RAF Squadrons*. Shrewsbury: Airlife.

Lumsden, A. and Thetford, O. (1993) *On Silver Wings: RAF Biplane Fighters Between the Wars*. London: Osprey.

Kostenuk, S. and Griffin, J. (1977) *RCAF Squadrons and Aircraft*. Ottawa: Canadian War Museum.

Milberry, L. (1985) *Sixty Years, The RCAF & CF Air Command 1924–1984*. Toronto: CANAV Books.

Moyes, P. (1964) *Bomber Squadrons of the RAF and Their Aircraft*. London: Macdonald.

Rawlings, J. D. R. (1969) *Fighter Squadrons of the RAF and Their Aircraft*. London: Macdonald.

Rawlings, J. D. R. (1982) *Coastal, Support and Special Squadrons of the RAF and Their Aircraft*. London: Jane's.

Robertson, B. (1955) *Aircraft Markings of the World 1912–1967*. Letchworth: Harleyford.

Robertson, B. (1955) *Aircraft Camouflage and Markings 1907–1954*. Letchworth: Harleyford.

Rogers, L. (2001) *British Aviation Squadran Markings of World War I*. Altglen: Schiffer.

Sturtivant, R and Balance, T. (1994) *The Squadrons of the Fleet Air Arm*. Tonbridge: Air-Britain.

Sturtivant, R. Hamlin, J. and Halley, J. J. (1997) *Royal Air Force Flying Training and Support Units*. Tonbridge: Air-Britain.

Wakefield, K. (2000) *Lightplanes at War*. New York: Tempus. (1995) *Units of the Royal Australian Air Force*, Vols 1, 2, 3 & 4. Canberra: Australian Government Publishing Service.

(1946) *Royal Indian Air Force at War*. New Delhi: General HQ.

In addition readers are advised to refer to the Air-Britain Royal Air Force Aircraft series of monographs by serial blocks, the Putnam series of individual aircraft manufacturers and the Air-Britain type and unit monographs which expand on the details contained in the serial series.